Amsterdamer Beiträge
zur neueren Germanistik

herausgegeben von

Gerd Labroisse
Gerhard P. Knapp
Anthonya Visser

Amsterdamer Beiträge
zur neueren Germanistik
Band 55 — 2003

Body Dialectics in the Age of Goethe

edited by

Marianne Henn and Holger A. Pausch

Amsterdam — New York, NY 2003

Die 1972 gegründete Reihe erscheint seit 1977 in zwangloser Folge in der Form von Thema-Bänden mit jeweils verantwortlichem Herausgeber.

Reihen-Herausgeber:

Prof. Dr. Gerd Labroisse, Sylter Str. 13A, D – 14199 Berlin
Tel./Fax: (49)30 89724235
E-Mail: Gerd.Labroisse@t-online.de

Prof. Dr. Gerhard P. Knapp, University of Utah, Dept. of Languages and Literature, 255 S. Central Campus Dr. Rm. 1400, USA – Salt Lake City, UT 84112
Tel.: (1)801 581 7561, Fax (1)801 581 7581 (dienstl.)
bzw. Tel./Fax: (1)801 474 0869 (privat)
E-Mail: gerhard.knapp@m.cc.utah.edu

Prof. Dr. Anthonya Visser, Universiteit Leiden, Duitse taal en cultuur, Postbus 9515, NL – 2300 RA Leiden
Tel.: (31)71 5272071, Fax: (31)71 5273309 (dienstl.)
bzw. Tel.: (31)71 565 2156 (privat)
E-Mail: a.visser@let.leidenuniv.nl

Redaktion: Prof. Dr. Anthonya Visser

All titles in the Amsterdamer Beiträge zur neueren Germanistik (from 1999 onwards) are available online: See www.rodopi.nl

Electronic access is included in print subscriptions.

The paper on which this book is printed meets the requirements of 'ISO 9706: 1994, Information and documentation - Paper for documents - Requirements for permanence'.

ISBN: 90-420-1076-2
©Editions Rodopi B.V., Amsterdam - New York, NY 2003
Printed in The Netherlands

Anschriften der Autorinnen und Autoren/List of Contributors:

Dr. Karin Barton
129 Iroquois Place
CA - Waterloo, Ontario, N2L 2S6

Heather Benbow
University of Melbourne, Dept. of German and Swedish Studies
AUS - Melbourne VIC 3010

Dr. Sophie Boyer, Assistant Professor of German
Bishop's University, Dept. of Modern Languages
CA - Lennoxville (Quebec) J1M 1Z7

Dr. Jane V. Curran, Associate Professor
Dalhousie University, Dept. of German
6135 University Avenue
CA - Halifax, NS B3H 4P9

Dr. Stefani Engelstein, Assistant Professor of German
University of Missouri, Dept. German and Russian Studies
454 GCB
USA -, Columbia, MO 65211

Dr. Marjanne E. Goozé
201 Joseph E. Brown Hall
The University of Georgia, Dept. of Germanic and Slavic Languages
USA - Athens, GA 30602

Dr. Marianne Henn, Professor of German
University of Alberta, Modern Languages and Cultural Studies
200 Arts Building
CA - Edmonton, AB T6G 2E6

Andrea Heitmann
Ohio State University, Dept. of Germanic Languages and Literatures
314 Cunz Hall
1841 Millikin Road
USA - Columbus, OH 43210

Dr K. F. Hilliard
University of Oxford, St. Peter's College
UK – Oxford, OX1 2DL

Daniel Kramer
Harvard University, Dept. of Germanic Languages and Literatures
365 Barker Center
12 Quincy Street
USA - Cambridge, MA 02138

Dr. Elisabeth Krimmer
Mount Holyoke College, Dept. of German Studies
USA - South Hadley, MA 01075

Dr. Alexander Mathäs, Associate Professor of German
University of Oregon, Dept. of Germ. Languages and Literatures
USA - Eugene, OR 97403-1250

Dr. Gaby Pailer, Associate Professor of German
The University of British Columbia, Dept. of European Studies
1873 East Mall
CA - Vancouver BC V6T 1Z1

Dr. Holger A. Pausch, Professor of German
University of Alberta, Modern Languages and Cultural Studies
CA - Edmonton AB T6G 2E6

Dr. Matthew Pollard
University of Victoria, Dept. of Germanic and Russian Studies
P.O. Box 3045 STN CSC
CA - Victoria, BC V8W 3P4

Dr. Daniel Purdy, Associate Professor of German
Pennsylvania State University
311 Burrowes Building,
USA - University Park, PA 16802

Dr. William C. Reeve, Professor
Queen's University, Dept. of German
CA - Kingston, ON K7L 3N6

Dr. Hans-Günther Schwarz, Professor
Dalhousie University, Dept. of German
6135 University Avenue
CA - Halifax, NS B3H 4P9

Dr. Karin A. Wurst, Professor
Michigan State University, German Studies Program
644 Wells Hall
USA - East Lansing, MI 48824-1027 USA

Inhalt

Marianne Henn and Holger A. Pausch

Introduction: Genealogy and Construction of Body Identity in the Age of Goethe

It seems at first glance that throughout the ages human beings always complied with and never resisted a curiously irrational desire to change the appearance of the body. The body adjusts constantly to cultural transformations of its visual presentation and inner needs ranging from subtle and refined statements to outrageous and, at times, self-destructive demonstrations of new standards and norms. The history of fashion and changes of the body type are replete with noteworthy examples: from the embellishments and panniers of the eighteenth century to the hourglass corset and bustle of the nineteenth[1] to cosmetics and beauty surgery of today or, from a different point of view, to physical mutilation, dietetics, mating games, and so forth.

These adaptations of the body to new cultural standards and norms are set in motion by two factors: social forces causing profitable changes and thus attempting to shape the body according to novel expectations, and persons willingly submitting to a re-shaping procedure. However, the two factors are not in opposition since there is no enforced subjugation. In fact, a conspiracy seems to exist between social forces shaping the body and persons being shaped so that it can be difficult to decide which of the two dominates, as Philippe Comar observes in his illuminating book *Images of the Body*.[2]

Michel Foucault attempted to answer this question with his analysis of microphysics and flows of power by referring to two conditions in a triangular relation that depends on the production of truth and right.[3] Central to his investigation is the observation that what makes power generally accepted, "is the simple fact that it doesn't only weigh on us as a force that says no, but that it traverses and produces things, it induces pleasure, forms

[1] Walter Benjamin, before his untimely death, had planned the "metaphysics of fashion" for his *Arcades Project*. Transl. by Howard Eiland and Kevin McLaughlin. Cambridge, Mass. and London, England 1999. He regarded fashion not only as the modern measure of time but it also "embodies the changed relationship between subject and object that results from the 'new' nature of commodity production". See Susan Buck-Morss: *The Dialectics of Seeing. Walter Benjamin and the Arcades Project*. Cambridge, Mass. and London, England 1997. Pp. 96-101, here p. 97.

[2] Philippe Comar: *Images of the Body*. New York 1999. P. 122.

[3] See esp. the following sections: Body/Power; Lecture Two: 14 January 1976; Truth and Power. In: *Power/Knowledge. Selected Interviews and Other Writings 1972-1977*. Ed. by Colin Gordon. New York 1980. Pp. 55-62, 92-108, 109-133. For an excellent introduction to power theory see Barry Hindess: *Discourses of Power. From Hobbes to Foucault*. Cambridge, Mass. 1996.

of knowledge, produces discourse".[4] Consequently, this form and mechanism of power depends on the adaptability of bodies.[5] And given the fact that the "human body had become essentially a force of production from the time of the seventeenth and eighteenth century, all forms of its expenditure which did not lend themselves to the constitution of the productive forces [...] were banned, excluded and repressed".[6] Thus, in the eyes of Foucault, an interdependent relationship developed between power and body, as it became the vehicle of power and not its point of application.[7] By virtue of this parasitic dependency of power on the body, it seems the individual, in a peculiarly complex and non-transparent way, became, for lack of a better word, addicted to the demands of power.[8] Hence Foucault speaks of the "fascism in us all, in our heads and in our everyday behavior, the fascism that causes us to love power, to desire the very thing that dominates and exploits us".[9] This craving, to expand Foucault's argument, motivates the body to adapt to new cultural standards and norms which are continuously produced by the flows of power because the individual not only discovers personal justification and social acceptance through his/her participation in the power production of truth and right and its dissemination but also gratification by means of the inducement of pleasure.

A particularly intriguing part of cultural programming in the realm of human imagination[10] in fact caused and made possible the existential-intellectual condition outlined above and all its far–reaching consequences: the mind-body problem, perhaps the best known and oldest problem in philosophy dating back at least to Plato.[11] However, by looking this far into history, it is interesting to note that the first leading dualist, Plato, strangely enough did not differentiate between mind and soul.[12] In most cases the two

---

[4] Truth and Power: Ibid. P. 119.

[5] Two Lectures: Ibid. P. 104.

[6] Ibid. P. 100.

[7] Ibid. P. 98. Even though Foucault mentioned the problem of resistance toward power in different works briefly, he does not explore this possibility in detail.

[8] See e.g. Gilles Deleuze and Félix Guattari's fascinating study of the body and capitalism: *Anti-Oedipus. Capitalism and Schizophrenia*. Minneapolis, Minn. 1994.

[9] Foucault: Preface. In: Deleuze and Guattari: *Anti-Oedipus*. P. xiii.

[10] For a fascinating introduction into philosophy and history of imagination see Richard Kearney: *The Wake of Imagination. Toward a Postmodern Culture*. New York 1998.

[11] For an introduction see especially *Psyche and Soma. Physicians and Metaphysicians on the Mind-body Problem from Antiquity to Enlightenment*. Ed. by John P. Wright and Paul Potter. Oxford 2000.

[12] In German philosophy the body-mind problem is still called the "Leib-Seele-Problem". The literature on this is vast. For an extensive introduction and bibliography see Hans Jörg Sandkühler: Erkenntnis / Erkenntnistheorie. In: *Europäische En-*

terms are used synonymously which presented to later religious belief systems the possibility to posit their principles in terms of a philosophical
methodology. This is highly problematic because Plato theorized that not
only are soul or mind and body two separate entities he also put forward the
very momentous notion that the soul is capable of a separate existence after
the body's death. Thus he connected a seemingly tangible corporeal condition (mind/soul) in this life with a brighter world beyond.[13]

In general terms, the mind-body problem raises the following questions:
How is a relationship between two fundamentally different conditions possible, that is, an entity located in space, the body, and an entity that is not
spatial, the mind/soul? Where are the points of contact and how are commands from the non-spatial spiritual realm communicated to the corporeal
space continuum? Some kind of material form or substance had to function
as translator to make the contact possible. Approximately two thousand
years later, Descartes came up with a slightly new but not original answer:
he maintained the pineal gland, which is actually not part of the brain, establishes the interface between the mind and the rest of the brain. For a long
time, the pineal gland, an enigmatic endocrine organ, had been of interest to
anatomists. While Plato and his contemporaries thought it was a valve that
controlled the flow of memories into consciousness, Descartes declared it
the seat of the soul. But he still did not answer the question how the interface between the spatial corporeality of the pineal gland and the non-spatial
soul works. Thus he did not present a radical new insight. The pineal gland
is still understood as a two-way valve. This control device channels the flow
of images of the physical world – as perceived by the brain via the senses of
the body – to the soul and in reverse channels the commands from the soul
to the brain which coordinates physical activities that influence the world.

Yet Descartes' pineal gland theory, which presents a metaphorical or,
from a different perspective, an allegorical answer to the mind-body prob-

zyklopädie zu Philosophie und Wissenschaften. Ed. by Hans Jörg Sandkühler. Vol. I.
Hamburg 1990. Pp. 772-904.

[13] The *Phaedo* – the starting point of a wide-ranging discourse throughout the ages
culminating in the "Unsterblichkeitsdebatte" in Enlightenment – is well known for
Plato's argument for the immortality of the soul (70c-80c) and doctrines concerning
body and soul (80c-84b). For a discussion on various aspects of the mind/soul-body
relationship see T. M. Robinson: The Defining Features of Mind-Body Dualism in
the Writings of Plato. In: *Psyche and Soma.* Pp. 37-55. Aristotle's psycho-
physiological account of the soul-body relationship, in contrast to Plato, did not
separate the mind/soul from the body. He contended that body and soul constitute
nothing more than two different viewpoints of the same foundational phenomena,
form and matter, an idea that unfortunately soon after joined, as Foucault would
have it, the category of "suppressed knowledges".

lem, is more than a somewhat forced curiosity.[14] By appearing to have discovered the physical coordinates of the soul, this ancient mythological construct, the immaterial feature or essence of a human being which existed in the body during life and separated after death, suddenly no longer represented an unknown quantity in the equation of worldly existence but in fact a seemingly tangible quality with an actual location within the "machine" of the body. Thus, in the pursuit of his ideas, Descartes' "rational" brand of dualism[15] developed into an apparently scientific methodology with intriguing practical applicability. Its impact on the development of modern sciences from mathematics to psychology is a case in point.[16] Yet Descartes' rational dualism and subsequent far-reaching impact on the evolution of modern sciences came at a considerable price, as history has proven again and again: anthropocentrism and, connected with its inherent anti-humanism, devaluation of the body which, in the context of Descartes' concept of the body-machine of humans, was a unique and original innovation.[17]

In classical antiquity and the Middle Ages the body, as an element in the chain of being or the book of nature, was understood as part of the cosmos or, of a larger whole to which a sacred relationship existed. This relationship could have considerable consequences if its fundamental rules of operation were ignored.[18] Comar describes its significance in antiquity with the following episode:

> The ancient Greeks, always so attentive to the significance of the body, developed funerary rites that reflected its importance. Whereas *kouroi*, permanent and idealized stone effigies, were erected on the tombs of heroes, the cadaver of an enemy was subjected to a morbid ritual of annihilation called *aikia*, outrage to the body. It was dismembered and its parts scattered, so that it forever lost its formal integrity. The body of a defeated adversary was thus symbolically denied the

---

[14] Regarding Descartes' concept of the soul in a broader context see Nicholas Jolley: *The Light of the Soul: Theories of Ideas in Leibniz, Malebranche, and Descartes*. New York 1990.

[15] In contrast to traditional forms of dualistic thought (e.g. god and the world, nature and spirit, subject and object, believing and knowing, soul and body, etc.), Descartes theorized that reality is based on two different "substances": one is thought, or the "mind", the other is extension, or matter.

[16] See e.g. Peter Robert Dear's study: *Revolutionizing the Sciences. European Knowledge and Its Ambitions, 1500 – 1700*. Princeton, N.J. 2001.

[17] Almost a century after Vesalius' first public dissection of a human body in 1540, Descartes describes the body as a machine in *Discourse on Method*, published in 1637.

[18] For an extensive discussion of historical and general aspects of this theme see *Der kosmische Mensch*. Ed. by Andreas Resch. München, Paderborn, Wien 1973.

right to incarnate the values of unity and beauty. The ultimate degradation, for the Classical mind, was the eradication of all traces of the body's existence.[19]

Since the ancient Greeks considered the body to be in harmony with the universe, beauty was understood as evidence of this harmony. The annihilation of an enemy's body destroyed this accord. The essential being was isolated, negated, and dissolved during the violent act of dismemberment resulting in a non-entity in this world and the next. Without the body, the essence and identity of the dead person evaporated and she/he became a mere shadow in the Orcus, the underworld. In antiquity, the importance of the body as the object of strict protocols was defined by its social position.[20] Since the body reflected the social identity of the individual, specific body protocols and social standing were amalgamated; the one could not exist without the other.[21] This ancient concept of a synthesis of being, an interdependent merger or union of body and identity which post-modern theories of identity construction seem to favour again,[22] was dismantled by Descartes at the dawn of modern man and woman. He turned the body into an object of knowledge and the subject into a knowing self that is separated from the objective body-machine. Thus, after undergoing the fundamental Cartesian paradigm shift, this physical automaton was now ready for a new cultural inscription.

In Descartes' view, both human beings and animals are bound in terms of functions to a comparable body-machine. However, as Luc Ferry in his groundbreaking work observes, the difference is that animals have been reduced to "simple mechanistic states" and "denied intelligence, affectivity, and even sensitivity", incapable of suffering and feeling.[23] Thus "Cartesian humanism is without doubt the doctrine that went the farthest in devaloriz-

---

[19] Comar: *Images of the Body*. P. 62.

[20] The study of the body in antiquity is a relatively new area of research. At least two foundational studies should be mentioned: Michel Foucault: *The History of Sexuality*. Transl. by Robert Hurley. 3 vols. New York 1990; Aline Rousselle: *Porneia. On Desire and the Body in Antiquity*. Transl. by Felicia Pheasant. New York and Oxford 1988.

[21] For a detailed investigation see Jonathan Walters: Invading the Roman Body. Manliness and Impenetrability in Roman Thought. In: *Roman Sexualities*. Ed. by Judith P. Hallett and Marilyn B. Skinner. Princeton, N.J. 1997. Pp. 29-43.

[22] The idea is to understand that human identity may be an illusion, easily dispelled and even replaced by factors such as states of the body, stress, injury, or technology, medical science, etc., the subject an image producing entity endlessly weaving commodity entangled tales of different identities.

[23] For example, Cartesian thought was used widely to justify such things as experimentation on animals, without anesthesia.

ing nature in general and animals in particular".[24] For this reason, modern ecocentrism finds in Cartesianism its absolute enemy, "the perfect model of anthropocentrism which accords *all* rights to men and *none* to nature, including animals"[25] because, in order to define the subject, the "sole and unique pole of meaning", nature had to be "divested of all moral value".[26]

Anthropocentrism or, polemically phrased, "human chauvinism", is deeply embedded in the consciousness of western societies since Aristotle, who believed animals were a product of nature for man's benefit, a sentiment that was also advocated by the Christian faith a few centuries later. However, as a consequence of Descartes' form of anthropocentrism, the early modern human being, looking back at the medieval conditions of his origin, found himself in a rather unique situation that was characterized by a profound isolation from and disdain for nature and body. In this environment of seclusion, Cartesian-Christian spiritualism was born with its excessive separation of the world of spirit and matter as compared to Platonic dualism and the Judeo-Christian tradition, which also place the spirit and its law above nature. This form of spiritualism, together with idealism, characterizes a large part of modern philosophy.[27] Thus the modern individual lost touch with her/his body and nature, that is, the modern subject became the "antinatural being par excellence",[28] and was ready to be re-inscribed with a new culture, modified moral standards, or an ethical significance regarding her/his own unique sense of self. In Germany, this far-reaching complex

---

[24] Luc Ferry: *the new ecological order*. Transl. by Carol Volk. Chicago 1995. P. xxix.

[25] Ibid. P. 21.

[26] Ibid.

[27] Cartesian thought, of course, was also challenged. It inspired the anti-Cartesian tradition. Descartes infuriated Voltaire who saw in animals a kinship with humans. Jeremy Bentham went even further and argued animals are objects of moral consideration. Rousseau is entirely anti-Cartesian and to some extent are also Kant and Fichte. Nietzsche condemned all Platonic-Christian dualism as it merely conceals reality. Today, a mechanistic explanation of the mind and consciousness described as highly organized brain chemistry is dominant. All decisions one imagines being made by the ego's free will are really performed by bits of brain tissue that are not conscious but whose activity adds up to what we believe consciousness is. Recently a version of this view was published by Daniel M. Wegner: *The Illusion of Conscious Will*. Cambridge, Mass. 2002. Terrence Deacon, the author of *The Symbolic Species. The Co-evolution of Language and the Brain* (New York and London 1997), disagrees with mechanistic explanations such as Wegner's. He theorizes that consciousness is information coming out of chaos; it is a fundamental property of the universe, like space, time or gravity, and therefore not reducible. See also the highly illuminating study by John D. Caputo: *More Radical Hermeneutics. On Not Knowing Who We Are*. Bloomington and Indianapolis 2000.

[28] Ferry: *the new ecological* order. Pp. xxviii and 54.

process or universal alphabetisation, which included the entire social sphere, took place in the Age of Goethe.[29]

As a product of the "antinatural" condition of anthropocentric Cartesian humanism, identity features of the modern mind are constructed exclusively in terms of the mind's discursive cultural environment without acknowledging that its natural body is indeed locked into an interdependent and highly influential relationship with nature. As Nigel Thrift points out: "[p]robably 95 percent of embodied thought is non-cognitive, yet probably 95 percent of academic thought has concentrated on the cognitive dimension of the conscious 'I'".[30]

Gottfried Wilhelm Leibniz reflected upon this bio-intellectual condition. He defended the notion that organic bodies (of which man considers himself the highest form) are never the product of chaos. They are always the result of seeds in which there was some preformation or, in technical terms, the result of a kind of a blue-print according to which the body was constructed, as Deleuze and Guattari maintain in their *Anti-Oedipus*, along the lines of discursive manifestations of energy, particle flows, and possibilities. Thus, bodies are subject to intricate and conflicting opportunities, which are organized and managed by different categories of time and space, that is, by dissimilar environments in contrast to the abstraction of a singular nature. Such bodies are produced through different social practices which derived from – as Judith Butler would have it – a multitude of unrelated "performative acts" disrupting the "material flow between body and the environment"[31] at a time when the cardinal humours of medical wisdom were replaced by a pathology of the neuro-muscular body. From the perspective of literary anthropology, in the second part of the 18th century body, soul, concepts of reality, and intellect "treten in einen Zusammenhang, der die bis dahin gültigen metaphysischen und wissenspragmatischen Aufteilungen durchkreuzt und an diesem Kreuzungspunkt einer besonderen Vorstellung vom *Menschen* Raum gibt".[32] The medium of this new interrelationship between metaphysical,

---

[29] See especially Friedrich A. Kittler: *Discourse Networks 1800/1900*. Transl. by Michael Metteer, with Chris Cullens. Foreword by David E. Wellbery. Stanford, CA. 1990. Here part I: "1800", pp. 3-173.

[30] Nigel Thrift: Still Life in Nearly Present Time. The Object of Nature. In: *Bodies of Nature*. Ed. by Phil Macnaghten and John Urry. London, Thousand Oaks, New Dehli 2001. Pp. 34-57, here p. 36.

[31] Phil Macnaghten and John Urry: Bodies of Nature. Introduction. In: *Bodies of Nature*. Pp. 1-11, here p. 9. The description and analysis of such mechanisms and strategies of body construction caused by unintended "ruptures" (Foucault) and scientific paradigm changes in the flow of history is the topic of Albrecht Koschorke's important book *Körperströme und Schriftverkehr. Mediologie des 18. Jahrhunderts*. München 1999. This book is the source of the following observations and references.

[32] Koschorke. P. 9.

social, and scientific ideas, that is, the carrier of the changing matrix of social energies is the body, the irreducible upon which, according to Foucault,
discourses "inscribe" meaning in accordance with prevailing disciplinary
powers in a specific historical time frame.

Probably the most important location for observing, analysing, and describing social energies and strategies that reconstruct the body is literature.
This applies especially to the area of emotions and the meaning of marriage[33] insofar as the literary discourse – along the lines of power relations –
in the act of describing these new social conditions produces them at the
same time: fiction invents reality. Thus, in the 18th century, perception and
dissemination of literature had a fundamental function in constructing and
establishing the emotional life and well-being of its readers to an extent that
was practically unheard-of. In a way, social behaviour, numerous decency
demands, and civility were influenced by the discourse of modern emotions
produced in literature.[34]

"One of the features of this new 'civility' was the physical withdrawal of
the individual body and its waste products from contact to others",[35] a process that enhanced the isolation of the body in order to prepare it for new
inscriptions such as the view that only the weak and frail male body is lascivious and not the physically powerful. For example, Ernst Jünger's much
maligned and ridiculed concept of "iron eroticism" has its roots in this cultural environment, the separation of sexual pleasure from procreation, the
devaluation of the female orgasm or many mythologies regarding sexuality
of children.[36] At the same time, psychology was slowly established as a science and thus ancient humoural-pathological explanations of physiological
functions were overcome step by step with medicine. Around 1800, medicine still believed that all illnesses have their point of origin in the abdomen,
leading the evolutionary path and replacing the humoural-pathological concept of the body with the system of nerves,[37] the medium for a new code of

---

[33] Now it was the task of marriage to cultivate medieval animalism of unrestrained
sexuality and change it into a socially productive form of existence as expressed in
numerous morality pamphlets and preparatory literature for marriage.

[34] See esp. chapter II.10 in Korschorke: *Körperströme*.

[35] Lawrence Stone: *The Family, Sex and Marriage in England, 1500-1800*. London
1977. P. 256.

[36] For example G. S. Roetger: *Ueber Kinderunzucht und Selbstbeflekkung. Ein Buch
bloß für Aeltern, Erzieher und Jugendfreunde, von einem Schulmanne*. Hg. und mit
einer Vorrede und Anmerkungen begleitet von Schl. Züllichau. Freystadt 1787.

[37] Even though the concept of nerves has its roots in antiquity, in neurology Galen is
thought to be the author of the view that the brain is the origin of the nerves of sensation, and the spinal cord of those of motion. See e.g. T. V. N. Persaud: *A History
of Anatomy: The Post-Vesalian Era*. Springfield, Ill. 1997 and esp. Mary A. B. Bra-
zier: *A History of Neurophysiology in the 17th and 18th Centuries. From Concept to
Experiment*. New York 1984.

sensibilities, deep feeling, and emotional receptivity as it was constructed, with incredible success, in the literary discourse. "Autrefoi", Diderot writes, "mademoiselle avait des vapeurs; ce sont aujourd'hui des nerfs".[38]

The neurological body assimilates and deals with social conflicts, demands or crises in a fundamentally different way than the humoural body because it now perceives by way of sensitive nerve receptors all positive and negative phenomena it encounters, a medium that connects the brain (intellect) with reality outside its inner space. As a consequence, the most important task of literature was to re-describe and thereby reconstruct along the line of new narratives the image of the world, which it did with astounding efficiency and effect. While in the Anglo-Saxon world Shakespeare is accredited with the invention of the modern human,[39] in Germany this process occurred almost a century later.

It was understood that the image of the world was in fact based on the neurological or "nervous" perception of reality, a mechanism that produced all information necessary to construct reality in an intricate process of interpretation and imagination. Accordingly the body of man and woman was no longer considered a receptive organ inscribed by reality but was re-defined as a medium that actually composes reality by imagining it: when we think about a phenomenon we help to create it.[40] This practice, however, is ultimately dependent on writing because imagination cannot flourish without a narrative space and appropriate rhetorical means, thus marking the beginning of the golden age of belles-lettres in which literature, for the first time, became an important part of life for a larger section of society: literature invented all existential stage directions as it described how people were supposed to feel and think about themselves, others, and the world; thus literature was vigorously consumed and discussed in many households and gatherings.

This change of attitude toward reading reflects the origin and formation of a personal and private sphere, an uninterrupted solitude in which individuals were able to occupy themselves with all the imagination had to offer, to build, along the trajectory of finding the "truth", imaginary worlds.[41]

---

[38] Diderot: *Le Neveu de Rameau*. In: *Œuvres Complètes*. Ed. by Henri Coulet et al. Paris 1989. Vol. XII. Pp. 31-196, here p. 145.

[39] Harold Bloom: *Shakespeare: The Invention of the Human*. New York 1998.

[40] This is not the place to discuss the epistemological discourse of reality perception. For an excellent introduction see Richard Kearney's *The Wake of Imagination* mentioned in footnote 10.

[41] This process of imagination or the mind creating the "truth" was superbly described by Marcel Proust: *Remembrance of Things Past*. 3 vols. New York 1981, here vol. 1, p. 49: "It alone [my own mind] can discover the truth. But how? What an abyss of uncertainty, whenever the mind feels overtaken by itself; when it, the seeker, is at the same time the dark region through which it must go seeking and

Imagination and reading caused a change in behaviour, feeling, and way of thinking which, in the eyes of Enlightenment critics, endangered traditional social structures as the person, being consumed by literature, is engulfed by her/his own inner world. From this point of view, literature intensifies the division of the individual between body and mind and causes the transference from the physical realm into the realm of the imaginary. "Der Umgang mit Büchern," says Koschorke, "etabliert eine Art Selbsterfahrung, die die Unzusammengehörigkeit und das Auseinanderstreben von Leib und Seele manifest werden läßt".[42]

Yet the annulment of the body through literature does promote its devaluation, the devaluation of female sexuality (the entire female body being a sexual organ), and individual self-observation. Distance to the body that was caused by reading also opens the door to an imaginary realm in which that which was taken, the body, can be recreated in all manner of conceivable ways.[43] Simply through the act of imagination, it was possible to "realize", at least in one intangible aspect, Enlightenment's best-known utopia, that is, its program to recreate man in his entirety, a complete human being. Imagination surpassing the borders of the actual and "de-realizing" reality as reflected in the literary discourse turned into a highly effective tool with intriguing consequences. The imagined body alone became the target of countless models of identity formation and image production with a controlling efficiency powerful enough to subvert social demands and expectations. As a result, the membranes of body identity became permeable, opening, first a faint murmur, to the countless possibilities of an imagined more desirable otherness. One example may suffice to describe one of the many literary, social, economic, emotional, and intellectual consequences of this culture of the imagined body in the realm of a bourgeois subject who had deduced her/his existence from the fictitious sphere of an imagined universal narrative.

In his book *Eingebildete Körper. Phantasierte Sexualität in der Goethezeit*, Stephan Schindler describes and analyses the entanglement of the bourgeois subject in the realm of the imaginary in the discourse on sex; he observes that desire turns away from the physical body in favour of an

---

where all its equipment will avail nothing. Seek? More than that: create. It is face to face with something which does not yet exist, to which it alone can give reality and substance, which it alone can bring into the light of day".

[42] Koschorke: Körperströme. P. 198.

[43] One of the most important and amusing examples is Johann Caspar Lavater's four volume opus *Aussichten in die Ewigkeit* (1768-1778) which describes life after death.

imagined one.[44] He maintains that this transfer of desire to the imaginary, the "ungeheuerliche Fleischwerdung der Phantasie",[45] reflects a structural characteristic of the modern conception of sexuality. The famous love scene in chapter eleven, part one, of Goethe's novel *Die Wahlverwandtschaften* (1809) is the starting point of Schindler's investigation. Eduard and Charlotte, a married couple, had lost their libidinous interest in each other. After the arrival of their guests, Ottilie and the Captain, they develop a deep affection for them. One night, Eduard and Charlotte, in a fortuitous moment, embrace and during sexual intercourse the two imagine Ottilie and the Captain in their respective arms. They neglect each other while committing a form of imaginary adultery:

> In der Lampendämmerung sogleich behauptete die innre Neigung, behauptete die Einbildungskraft ihre Rechte über das Wirkliche: Eduard hielt nur Ottilien in seinen Armen, Charlotten schwebte der Hauptmann näher oder ferner vor der Seele, und so verwebten, wundersam genug, sich Abwesendes und Gegenwärtiges reizend und wonnevoll durcheinander.[46]

Imagination, Schindler comments, bypasses commands, duties, and expectations of the love-marriage, a concept that began to take hold in society after 1770. A love-match was not only supposed to satisfy physical desire but ideally the partners were meant to observe monogamy and the precepts of religious and political procreation which enabled them to communicate in a sphere of moral and intellectual friendship. Yet imagination was able to circumvent these commands. It allowed partners, in contrast to many marriage realities, to find physical fulfilment in a kind of sexual "virtual reality".[47]

Foucault in his *History of Sexuality* points out that western man has been engaged for over three centuries in the discourse on sex, which was not just a "collective curiosity or sensibility" but the result of a "power mechanism that functioned in such a way that discourse on sex [...] became essential" because "[t]oward the beginning of the eighteenth century, there emerged a political, economic, and technical incitement to talk about sex", not from the perspective of "morality alone but from rationality as well".[48] Foucault examines the connection between the discourse on sex and power with its tri-

---

[44] Stephan Schindler: *Eingebildete Körper. Phantasierte Sexualität in der Goethezeit*. Tübingen 2001. See also Marlene Lohner: *Goethes Caravanen. Verkörperung der Phantasie im Spätwerk*. Frankfurt/M. 2001.

[45] Schindler: Eingebildete Körper. P. 10.

[46] Johann Wolfgang Goethe: *Werke*. Vol. 6: *Romane und Novellen* I. Hamburger Ausgabe. München 1981. P. 321.

[47] Schindler: Eingebildete Körper. Pp. 10-11, 12.

[48] Michel Foucault: *The History of Sexuality*. New York 1990. Vol. 1. Pp. 23, 24.

angular correlation to right and truth in detail. Yet, in addition to this web of correspondences, the discourse on sex also revived and significantly intensified the medical discourse and, above all, the enigmatic human faculty of imagination. It is not possible to overestimate the central role that sexuality and imagination played in the early modern period.[49] This new anthropological discourse on sex was the driving force behind imaginative power and motivated the social construction of its pathologies.

Yet the most important and revolutionary consequence of the nexus between sex and imagination was a new capability of the subject. That is, imagination triggered the process of self-reflexivity and thus enabled the subject to project self-referential meaning into areas of culture and nature which were incomprehensible or inaccessible until then. The many forms of self-referential meaning that were projected along the trajectories of imagination into the space of the unknown were based – because other epistemological options are closed – on concepts of the body, namely the way the early modern body was perceived, thought of, and understood. The literary discourse in the Age of Goethe is intimately linked to the examination, exploration, and invention of creative strategies which re-inscribe the body in order to re-describe the world. The medieval subject was occupied with "reading" the book of nature for which she/he represented a minute but nevertheless integrated part of text, that is, she/he was occupied with the hermeutics of existence. As a representational medium, she/he saw the body as allegory of the world.[50] In contrast, the subject of the 18th century discovered the body and its parameters as a heuristic cognitive tool providing the capability to construct, lead and influence imagination, a new narrative or new connections of understanding regarding the inner and outer world, thought and matter, in other words, insights, carried by discourse networks, of which no one had been aware before.

Literature was the common denominator that provided the body with a narrative space necessary to establish these discourse networks.[51] Or seen from a different point of view, literature was of primary importance for the construction of the modern body without which the wealth of artistic and scientific knowledge could not have been created. Thus, in a peculiar way which is still not fully understood, body parameters, narrative space, and imagination merge in a strangely interdependent fusion, as one cannot exist

---

[49] See e.g. the not yet published proceedings of the DFG-Forschergruppe "Imagination und Kultur" at the Ruhr-Universität Bochum of the conference "Sexualität und Imagination. Pathologien der Einbildungskraft im medizinischen Diskurs der frühen Neuzeit (1500-1800)" held from May 23-24, 2002, at the Institut für Geschichte der Medizin, Markstrasse 258A, 44799 Bochum, Germany.

[50] See Michel Foucault: *The Order of Things. An Archaeology of the Human Sciences*. New York 1973, esp. chapter 2: "The Prose of the World", pp. 17-45.

[51] See Kittler's seminal work *Discourse Networks 1800-1900*.

without the other, and as a result a mechanism was set up that produces the flows of cultural knowledge. The contributions to this volume examine a wide range of construction strategies of the body and its significance in reference to such discourse networks of cultural knowledge with surprising results. The essays unfold a detailed, varied, and differentiated insight into the productive interrelated dynamics of body parameters, narrative space, and imagination pointing to their inherent fragile equilibrium, a balance that not only implies seemingly endless possible permutations of cultural conditions but also potential dangers and limitations if cultural memory is tempted to neglect one part of the triad over the other.

Daniel Purdy

Sculptured Soldiers and the Beauty of Discipline: Herder, Foucault and Masculinity

This paper analyses how eighteenth-century Prussian disciplinary interests differed from the tasteful judgments of civil society. Two modes of visibility, the tactical and the fashionable are contrasted. Both are shown to be distinct from disinterested aesthetic contemplation. Michel Foucault's discussion of Jeremy Bentham's panopticon serves to theorize the mechanisms of control deployed within the army. This paper argues that the fashionable and erotic appearance of the eighteenth-century Prussian soldier provides an account of how male dressers generally appear within the visible field of modern fashionable society. In order to understand how male bodies could be both tactically controlled by the military and erotic, I turn to neo-classical aesthetics of the eighteenth-century. Johann Gottfried Herder's description of how sculptures are perceived combines a neo-classical sensibity with a keen appreciation of how bodies appear within a field of vision. Herder's essay Plastik *provides a cultural anthropology of eighteenth-century taste as it converges with tactical regimes of the newly organized Prussian army.*

Die Zeitung für die elegante Welt, Berlin's most fashionable magazine reported that on December 31, 1800 at the first New Year's Eve Ball of the new century a young officer came to a sudden fatal end. As witnesses recounted, the young man had spent the entire evening dancing with the many attractive young ladies attending the regimental ball. Taking a short break from waltzing, the officer, a certain Herr von D., walked over to the buffet to drink a glass of lemonade. Having consumed this refreshment, he returned to the dance floor where he collapsed dead. Later medical investigators determined that the dashing young man was strangled by his own uniform, which was, according to the latest style, closely tailored to match the contours of his athletic physique. According to the fashion journal, the pressure from his skin-tight uniform and elaborately constrictive cravat was so great that a single glass of punch was enough to choke him.

Readers of society novels such as Thackery's *Vanity Fair* will recall scenes in which soldiers, particularly officers, paraded around ladies in tight uniforms which showed their musculature. Caroline de la Motte-Fouqué describes these early dandies as follows:

So nach Büsten zugestutzt, legten sie eine dicke, mit Fischbein gesteifte, mit Watte gefütterte Cravate um den Hals, setzten einen unförmlich großen, dreieckigen Hut hinten nach dem Genicke zu, so daß die eine Spitze vorn über der Stirn auf dem antik frisirten Kopf in die Höhe stand, trugen Pantalons von weißem oder leichtgeröthetem Seidentrikot, welche mit den Strümpfen zusammengewoben, den Schein völligen Unbekleidetseyns gewährten, und hingen nun den kurzen, engen, abgeschnittenen Uniformsrock oder den Civilfrack darüber. Man wird versucht, hierbei an Wilde zu denken, denen die europäische Soldatenjacke über das allzunatürliche Volkskostüme gezogen ward.[1]

She continues a little later: "Ja man ging hierin bald noch weiter. Das Knappe konnte nicht knapp, das Natürliche nicht natürlich genug ausfallen. Deßhalb wurden jene Trikotpantalons *feucht* angezogen, damit sie sich gewissermaßen mit der Haut des Körpers amalgamirten".[2] Baron de Frénilly was amusingly direct about the situation in his memoirs:

> men were going around naked; their shape was no longer hidden. [...] an army of tight-fitting yellow kerseymere breeches, round hats, and dress coats swarmed like Huns to the heart of the Empire. To be fashionable, these breeches had to be so tight that you needed assistance to put them on. Art and prudence, too, had to be observed when walking, and still more when dancing; whilst talent was a *sine qua non* when sitting down or stooping, for the least thoughtless movement rendered them liable to some catastrophe or other.[3]

As one can imagine the story of the fashionable officer published in Berlin was not the only version of this cautionary tale. Tales of gallant officers strangled by their own tight-fitting uniforms circulated widely in Prussian high society. Instead of lemonade sometimes it was a single grape that dealt the death-blow. But the problem could not have existed just in the fevered minds of fashion devotees. Army regulations specifically stipulated that uniforms not be cut so tightly that they constrained movement. The 1790 ordinances instructing the crown prince's infantry regiment stated explicitly: "Der Rock muß überall am Leibe anschließen, doch nicht zu eng, damit der Kerl sich zu regen im Stande ist".[4] For most of the eighteenth century, Prussia had been famous for its well-drilled, uniformed troops. The sight of an elite unit marching mechanically across an open field with bayonnets drawn was meant to terrify Prussia's potential enemies. Frederick William I and his son Frederick II were well aware of how the appearance of a soldier could affect military tactics. However, for all

---

[1] Caroline de la Motte-Fouqué: Geschichte der Moden, vom Jahre 1785-1829: Als Beytrag zur Geschichte der Zeit. Reprinted in: *Jahrbuch der Jean-Paul-Gesellschaft* 12 (1977). P. 35.

[2] Ibid.

[3] *Recollections of Baron de Frénilly*. Ed. by Arthur Chuquet. Trans. by Frederic Lees. New York 1909. P. 48.

[4] Instruktion, die der Kronprinz seiner Infanterie und Regiment gegeben (1790). In: *Urkunden und Kommentare zur Entwicklung der Altpreussischen Uniform*. Ed. by Hans Bleckwenn. Osnabrück 1971. P. 227.

their attention to military dress and drill, they were adament that their soldiers not become dandies and fencing masters in the French manner.[5] The Prussian military was a success because it operated as a machine. Standardized uniforms were part of the disciplinary regime that turned every soldier into an instrument. Uniforms were not meant to appeal; they were supposed to increase the army's control over the soldier's body.[6]

In the following paper, I will examine how the military's interests differed from the tasteful judgments of civil society. In particular, I will contrast two modes of visibility: the first, tactical, the second, fashionable. Both are distinct from yet a third mode, disinterested aesthetic contemplation. Michel Foucault's discussion of Jeremy Bentham's panopticon still serves as an apt theorization of the mechanisms of control deployed within the army.[7] The operation of fashionable viewing on the body of men has, on the other hand, been inadequately theorized. The predominate psychoanalytic, Lacanian tradition places women at the center of fashionable vision.[8] My argument regarding the fashionable, and erotically compelling, appearance of the soldier, or any modern man in civil society, will first require an account of how male dressers appear within the visible field of fashionable society. Men are so rarely the object of fashionable commentary that little has been written about what it means for a modern man to be the object of heterosexual fashion judgment. Foucault's disciplinary model is an obvious starting place for thinking about the appearance of male bodies in a visible field, however, his model denies the operation of erotic desire of any sort. This refusal needs to be understood dialectically as the sign of an anxiety about the interference erotic desire produces within a disciplinary regime, as well as a means of introducing a new functionalized eroticism, the athletic body of our Prussian officer.[9] In order to understand how male bodies could be both tactically controlled by the military and erotic, we need to turn to

---

[5] Curt Jany: *Geschichte der peußischen Armee vom 15. Jahrhundert bis 1914.* Osnabrück 1964. P. 766.

[6] For a more detailed description of Frederick II's views on uniforms, see my *The Tyranny of Elegance: Consumer Cosmopolitanism in the Era of Goethe*. Baltimore 1998. Pp. 195-216.

[7] Michel Foucault: *Discipline and Punish: The Birth of the Prison.* Trans. by Alan Sheridan. New York 1979. Pp. 195-228.

[8] Some important examples are Shari Benstock and Suzanne Ferriss (eds.): *On Fashion.* New Brunswick, N.J. 1994; Jane Gaines and Charlotte Herzog (eds.): *Fabrications: Costume and the Female Body.* New York 1990; Elizabeth Wilson: *Adorned in Dreams: Fashion and Modernity.* Berkeley 1985. The single most influential essay on the costumed female in the field of vision, "Visual Pleasure and Narrative Cinema", can be found in Laura Mulvey: *Visual and Other Pleasures.* Bloomington, Indiana 1989. Pp. 14-28.

[9] My thesis need not contradict Steve Neale's reading of the disavowal of male eroticism in cinema as a sign of repressed homosexual desire in: Masculinity as Spectacle. In: *The Sexual Subject: A Screen Reader in Sexuality.* London 1992. Pp. 277-287.

neo-classical aesthetics of the eighteenth-century.[10] Johann Gottfried Herder's phenomenological account of how sculptures are perceived combines a neo-classical sensibity with a keen appreciation of how bodies appear within a field of vision.[11] Herder's writing on sculpture will provide a cultural anthropology of eighteenth-century taste as it converges with tactical regimes of the newly organized Prussian army.

With the tremendous success of France's revolutionary armies, the Prussian military recognized the failings of Frederick the Great's rigid system of military training.[12] Rather than employ discipline through direct supervision and physical coercion, the Prussian military tried increasingly to inspire its troops. Already under Frederick, the aesthetic appeal of well-groomed uniforms arrayed in formation had served as a means of unifying the army and terrifying outsiders. Between 1797 and 1806, the former crown prince, now King Frederick William III, made many fashionable changes to the Prussian uniform, letting it be known that he preferred his officers to maintain a certain stylish appearance. The once strict boundary between the army and the civilian population had become blurred. Fashion was now mobilized to bind the officer corp to the king. Discipline and the effects that it had on the hard-working body became new ideals of beauty. A relay chain of observation developed within the army which was very similar to the hierarchical flow of imitation in society. But because the uniform was already codified by law and tradition, the only feature which could be adjusted so as to draw the special attention of an observer was the tailoring. This attention to detail then formed the basis for a male-male circle of observation and admiration centered on the king as the model and primary observer. *Die Zeitug für die elegante Welt* reported in 1801: "Der preußische Offizier trägt sich jetzt überhaupt äußerst jung, nett und knapp. Der König liebt dies, und ist Selbst äußerst knapp und nett in seiner Uniform, die zwar äußerst einfach, aber sehr schön sitzt".[13] As system of observation, the "aesthetic appreciation" of military dress was organized differently than the panopticon model Foucault describes. The central position of authority functions both as object and observer, allowing thereby a not completely asymmetrical flow of power. Officers, in admiring the king's uniform, were thereby encouraged to imitate his dress on a level of detail that exceeded the regulations. This extra degree of conformity arose outside the established routine of military training, and it points to the

---

[10] Two illuminating art historical studies of the neo-classical representation of the idealized male body are Abigail Solomon-Godeau: *Male Trouble. A Crisis in Representation*. London 1997 and Alex Potts: *Flesh and the Ideal. Winckelmann and the Origins of Art History*. New Haven 1994.

[11] Johann Gottfried Herder: *Plastik* (1770). In: *Werke* (Hanser). Ed. by Wolfgang Pross. Vol. 2. Munich 1987. Pp. 401-464.

[12] Gordon Craig: *The Politics of the Prussian Army, 1640-1945*. London 1964. Pp. 26-53; Max Jahn: *Geschichte der Kriegswissenschaft, vornehmlich in Deutschland*. Reprint of 1891 edition. Vol. 3. Hildesheim 1966. Pp. 2122-2164.

[13] *Zeitung für die elegante Welt*. January 15, 1801. P. 55.

peculiarity of modern synthesis of discipline and beauty.[14]

Inevitably, Frederick William III's fashionable innovations in the Prussian uniform were not well received by the old guard.[15] To bring uniforms into line with civilian menswear implied a subordination of military tradition and regimen to the tastes and opinions of the public at large. Frederick William's reforms did not respect the distinction between fashion, aesthetics, and disciplinary interests. The army's need to control the soldier down to the smallest detail was, despite appearances, fundamentally different from the judgments rendered by a journal reader. Fashionable aesthetics and military discipline shared an attention to detail, yet when understood as a network of relations between the observed and the observer, they constituted two very different modes of visuality.

***

The classical style of the Prussian soldier should not be understood solely as a fashionable aberration, rather it is an extreme manifestation, an allegorical embodiment, of the Enlightenment's synthesis of critical reason with neo-classical aesthetics. The simple dress of the soldier manifests the Enlightenment principle that all bodies are equally subject to reason, which in post-revolutionary Prussia was all too often understood to be the administrative apparatus of the state. One of the first texts to conjoin ancient Greek art with an explicit critique of feudal society was Rousseau's 1750 *Discourse on the Arts and Sciences*. Rousseau uses the example of dress in order to posit a radically new economy of political power; one in which the body of the worker or peasant signified true virtue and strength. In the first section of the *Discourse* he states unequivocally: "Richness of apparel may proclaim the man of fortune, and elegance the man of taste; but true health and manliness are known by different signs. It is under the homespun of the laborer, and not beneath the gilt and tinsel of the courtier, that we should look for strength and vigor of body".[16] Rousseau's argument reverses the prevailing assumptions of the feudal dress code, while at the same time stating a preference for the body over clothing. The ultimate intentions of Rousseau's argument are made clear in the next paragraph, where he writes:

External ornaments are no less foreign to virtue, which is the strength and activ-

---

[14] For a subtle analysis of militarist conformity to the Prussian monarch's appearance, see Jeffrey Schneider: The Pleasure of the Uniform: Masculinity, Transvestism, and Militarism in Heinrich Mann's *Der Untertan* and Magnus Hirschfeld's *Die Transvestiten*. In: *Germanic Review* 72.3 (1997). Pp. 183-200.
[15] Erhart Berckenhagen and Gretel Wagner (eds.): *Der bunte Rock in Preußen: Militär und Ziviluniform, 17. bis 20. Jahrhundert*. Berlin 1981. P. 140.
[16] Jean Jacques Rousseau: *The Social Contract and Discourses*. Trans. by G. D. H. Cole. New York 1950. P. 148.

ity of the mind. The honest man is an athlete, who loves to wrestle stark naked; he scorns all those vile trappings, which prevent the exertion of his strength, and were, for the most part, invented only to conceal some deformity.[17]

Here Rousseau is harkening back explicitly to ancient Sparta when he celebrates the naked athletic body as the embodiment of strength in a moral and political sense, as well as physical.

Rousseau's arguments were intended as means of escaping the world of luxurious fashion, and as it happens so often, they became a means of reinventing elite styles. Within the terms of courtly society, as Rousseau understood it when he wrote his *Discourse*, nakedness and the accompanying virtues of a laboring body pointed to a utopian existence outside the conventions of class distinction and public display. Yet by the time the young cavalry officer began dressing for the New Year's Eve ball, Rousseau's idealized vision of clothes and the body had lost its oppositional character. By 1800 in such military capitals as Berlin and Paris, the classical body had come to signify the progressive aspirations of the centralized state. The feudal, representational character of clothes had been replaced by a modern aesthetic of understated simplicity that relied on uniformity in design and color to keep sartorial extravagances in check. If clothes did have a semiotic purpose, then it was to reveal the individual traits of the person, his or her personality, education, morality, and sensibility. Class distinctions never disappeared, of course, but they were definitively not the first concern of fashion. To the extent that it was possible, clothes were meant to mediate between a new modern concept of universal humanity and the particular condition of the individual dresser. Oddly enough, nakedness spanned the almost unbridgeable distance between these two ideals. The nude simultaneously revealed the general condition of humanity without suppressing the particular. A naked body is both generic and intimate, and for this reason, it seemingly embodied the standards of the Enlightenment without denying the specifics of the individual person. Within fashionable society at the end of the eighteenth century, nakedness was an ideal that meant that the body should be covered without seeming to be so. The cultural historian Eduard Fuchs described this tendency as "in den Kleidern nackt zu erscheinen".[18]

The toga-like gowns worn by women of the Napoleonic era are unquestionably the most famous examples of garments that induced the impression of "nakedness". With a clear sense of the political connotations clothes had after the French Revolution, Caroline de la Motte-Fouqué described the advent of this new Greek nudity as a stunning transformation:

Kein schnellerer Wechsel läßt sich in dem Herkömmlichen denken, als der war, da

[17] Rousseau. P. 148.
[18] Eduard Fuchs: *Illustrierte Sittengeschichte. Das bürgerliche Zeitalter*. Vol. 3. Munich 1912. P. 189.

man vom Abend zum Morgen die gefeierte Dame des Tages im griechischen Gewande, dicht unter der Brust gegürtet, dessen anschmiegender Faltenwurf weich
herabfloß, die Arme bis über die Hälfte des Oberarmes entblößt, das Haar nach
dem Nacken herab in einen Knoten geschlungen, einer antiken Statue ähnlich,
über den unklassischen Boden schreiten sah. [...] In plastischer Harmonie fügte
sich das Einzelne zum Ganzen, und ehe man es geträumt, sahe sich ein lebendes
Geschlecht in bewegliche Bilder antiker Museen umgeschaffen.[19]

La Motte Fouqué understood neo-classicism as the liberation of the body which
shared in the fervor of the Bastille's storming as well as the cosiness of English
country living. Rome, revolutionary France, and the English gentry were but
some of the connotations this new preference for transparency invoked. With so
many connotations, the style was quick to take over salons and middle class
homes. The *Mode Journal* reported in 1797: "In der That ist jetzt die Nuditäten-
Mode bey unsrer Schönen des Tages soweit gediehen, daß sie von obenherab
einer schönen Wilden fast ganz gleichen [...]".[20] Then again it noted in 1807:
"Denn es giebt nach jetzigem Modesystem nichts eleganteres, als so elegant wie
möglich zu seyn, und dennoch so gut als nackt zu erscheinen".[21]

Histories of fashion record the feminine variety of the "nakedness" style –
women wearing diaphanous toga-like gowns. Yet they often pass over the masculine version of this mode – the wrapping of the torso and legs in skin-tight,
white breeches and undergarments.[22] Cultural critics have long presumed the
existence of a gendered division wherein women display their bodies for male
spectators. As useful as this framework has been for feminist and psychoanalytic
interpretations, it does have the unfortunate effect of discounting masculine
erotic performances as perversions. What remains unexplained is how masculine nudity was legitimized within the strict guidelines of respectable society
and military discipline.[23] What were the circumstances that allowed young men
to show off their physical features aggressively, particularly their genitals, in
public without suffering censure? What complicated justifications were required
to allow masculine erotic display.

---

[19] La Motte-Fouqué. P. 28

[20] Christina Kröll and Jörn Göres: *Heimliche Verführung*. Düsseldorf 1978. P. 87.

[21] Ibid. P. 89.

[22] The most important work on the history of dress and the nude is Anne Hollander:
Seeing through Clothes. New York 1978. P. 228; Diana de Marley: *Fashion for Men.
An Illustrated History*. New York 1985; François Boucher: *20,000 Years of Fashion.
The History of Costume and Personal Adornment*. New York 1987; Katell le Bourhis
(ed.): *The Age of Napoleon. Costume from Revolution to Empire: 1789-1815*. New
York 1989; Farid Chenoune: *A History of Men's Fashion*. Trans. by Deke Dusinberre.
Paris 1993.

[23] Hollander considers dress primarily in terms of art historical traditions. She connects neo-classical male dress with Rennaissance fashions and the work of painters
such as Andrea Mantega (1431-1506). Pp. 225-235.

The masculine variety of the naked style has had a troubled reception because costume historians have held to the modern orthodoxy that true masculine elegance avoids drawing attention to itself. The sexual attractiveness of the feminine neo-classical dress has assured its continued place in fashion history because the same orthodoxy presumes that women alone are permitted to flaunt their features. Hence, the late eighteenth-century eroticization of the male body through suggestively tailored uniforms has been passed over as an embarrassing aberration. Tight and erotic uniforms contradict the principled masculine refusal to become an object of desire. Bourgeois masculine displays required considerable institutional reassurances that the integrity of the individual subject, his newly discovered autonomy and will, would not be dissolved within the multifarious interpretations to which his appearance would be subjected. To elude the imperious and potential desiring glances of the public, the handsome soldier constituted himself as subject to a unidirectional, rational, and unerotic disciplinary gaze. His own dress invoked a power regime that laid claim to his physical movements by turning his entire body into an object of disciplinary control. By wearing the military markings, by parading his own readiness for action and obedience, this new erotic soldier casts aside the spectacular desires of the court. The tight clothes of soldiers and civilians alike declare openly that the body underneath has willingly submitted itself to a command structure that had no avowed interest in erotic desire. Yet the appeal of muscular young men in skin-tight clothes was undeniable. The more the young men insisted that they were dressing solely for the sake of some higher principle, the more dashing they were in the eyes of desirous spectators. As *Die Zeitung für die elegante Welt* reported: "Der Anblick des preußischen Militärs, wenn es in Reih und Glied steht, gewährte schon immer einen eben so reinen, als glänzenden Anblick. Viele Tausende rein, weiß und fleckenlos, dicht und knapp angezogen zu sehen, macht einen angenehmen Eindruck".[24] This pleasant impression, I would argue, is very important. It raises the problem of how important aesthetics are within the operation of disciplinary institutions. Michel Foucault has argued that modern disciplinary power has the ability to produce identities even as it coerces the body to obey a set of commands. That disciplinary institutions force bodies to behave in very specific ways is obvious to anyone who has read Foucault's *Discipline and Punish*.[25] The argument that gives most readers trouble is Foucault's claim that disciplinary power also has a positive, creative character, one that generates new identities as opposed to just pushing already existing subjects into new molds. The pleasant impression that the Berlin fashion correspondent experiences while observing a military review is precisely one of those positive creations of disciplinary power. Foucault scrupulously avoids discuss-

[24] *Zeitung für die elegante Welt*. January 15, 1801. P. 54.
[25] Foucault cares more about prisoners than soldiers, though he does treat the soldier as an ideal figure, see *Discipline and Punish. The Birth of the Prison*. Trans. by Alan Sheridan. New York 1979. P. 135.

ing the relationship between aesthetic and erotic pleasure to institutional power regimes, yet I would argue this relation is one of the avenues by which individual identity is created.[26] By taking satisfaction in his own appearance as he operates within a strict command structure, the individual soldier is able to create a subjectivity that is not at odds with the institution. Indeed, the pleasure that he as well as any other spectator derive from his appearance becomes both a sign and an instrument of personal volition. The eighteenth-century nudity style is one example of how modern masculinity employs aesthetic pleasure within a power structure that insists on the functional deployment of the body. The soldier eroticizes his body not by resisting coercive discipline, but by becoming hyper-disciplined. He goes too far in carrying out military commands and thereby proves to himself and others that he is doing so voluntarily and for his own reasons. The apparent nakedness of the soldier is not a humiliating, forced stripping of the insignias that define identity. On the contrary, the tight leggings functioned as personal assertions of the same naturalized body that Rousseau celebrated in his *Discourse*.

The willingness of fashionable individuals to display themselves as if they were nude underscores the importance of volition within bourgeois society, as well as within the reformed armies of Prussia. Generals who led armies against the French quickly realized that soldiers fought much more effectively when they were emotionally invested in their cause. By moving away from a system of purely coercive discipline, the Prussian military in the 1790s tried to find ways to allow individual soldiers to invest themselves while operating within a command structure. The steady eroticization of the uniformed body introduced aesthetics into an institution that had up until then prided itself on not paying attention to such niceties. Frederick the Great, like his father before him, was proud that his soldiers did not dress and behave like French fencing masters. The Prussian reputation for machine-like efficiency was deliberately intended to counter the tendency for eighteenth-century officers to behave like courtiers. In its earliest history, the modern uniformed army was supposed to dispel all thoughts of beauty, grace, and the giving of pleasure to others. Such self-serving gestures were eliminated by a tactical regime that handled soldiers as interchangeable parts in a giant factory. Modern armies have, of course, never given up tactical control of soldier's bodies, but the nudity fashion shows that soldiers, as well as the general public, can develop a fascination with the regimented body. At no point though does the pleasure of wearing or watching uniforms overrule the practical requirements of military service, just as the business suit for all its restrained elegance is never meant to become an end in itself. The suit like the uniform acquires an aesthetic quality because it assiduously insists

---

[26] Daniel Roche also points out other positive effects: "[The uniform] creates through education, realises a personage and affirms a political project by demonstrating omnipotence". In: *The Culture of Clothes: Dress and Fashion in the Ancien Regime*. Trans. by Jean Birrell. Cambridge 1994. P. 229.

that it is concerned only with functional performance. So long as the male dresser purports not to know the beauty of his own rigorous behavior, so long as the purpose of his clothes is clearly defined and practical, the visual impression can be disavowed as accidental or, better still, an effect produced only within the consciousness of the observer, over whom the uniformed male has, of course, no control.

While gender studies has not concentrated on the history of masculinity before the twentieth century, a few theories do dominate the discussion, most notably J. C. Flügel's characterization of the late eighteenth century as "The Great Masculine Renunciation".[27] The term appears in Flügel's early psychoanalytical study, The Psychology of Clothes, first published in 1930. For Flügel it means that, at the end of the eighteenth century, men "suffered a great defeat" because they "gave up their right to all the brighter, gayer, more elaborate, and more varied forms of ornamentation, leaving these entirely to the use of women, and thereby making their own tailoring the most austere and ascetic of the arts".[28] Whereas under the courtly fashion system, men competed openly with women to draw the greatest attention to their attire through the use of expensive fabrics, gold and silver trim, precious jewels, expansive wigs and ostentatious footwear, the new regime insisted that men cease to make a spectacle of themselves.[29] Instead of catching the eye through the latest fashion, men were now obliged to dress "correctly", according to a uniform standard of simplified dress. Without a doubt, Flügel was correct in calling attention to the rather sudden shift in attire and its accompanying redefinition of gender.[30] His term continues to be used as a kind of theoretical shorthand. Kaja Silverman has adapted Flügel's thesis along Lacanian lines by arguing that male dressers are not actually outside the

---

[27] The scholarship on German soldierly masculinity in the twentieth century focuses on the First World War and the proto-fascist responses to the trauma mechanized warfare created. The most important studies are Klaus Theweleit's two volume Male Fantasies. Trans. by Stephen Conway, Erica Carter, and Chris Turner. Minneapolis 1987 and 1989 and the considerable work of George Mosse. For a last glance over a long career, see Mosse's Fallen Soldiers. Reshaping the Memory of the World Wars. New York 1990. Further important works include Bernd Widdig: Männerbünde und Massen. Zur Krise männlicher Identität in der Literatur der Moderne. Opladen 1992 and Jay Baird: To Die for Germany. Heroes in the Nazi Pantheon. Bloomington 1990. The classic portrayal of the First World War and English literature is Paul Fussell: The Great War and Modern Memory. New York 1975. Parallels between the Vietnam War and the First World War can be drawn from Susan Jeffords: The Remasculinization of America: Gender and the Vietnam War. Bloomington 1989.

[28] J. C. Flügel: The Psychology of Clothes. London 1971. P. 111.

[29] The classical study on courtly self-presentation continues to be Norbert Elias: The Court Society. Trans. by Edmund Jephcott. Oxford 1983.

[30] Two recent historical studies of dress reiterate Flügel's thesis, Phillippe Perrot: Fashioning the Burgeoisie: A History of Clothing in the Nineteenth Century. Trans. by Richard Bienvenu. Princeton 1994 and John Harvey: Men in Black. Chicago 1995.

realm of visibility (the gaze) even though they define themselves according to the seeing–being seen dyad Flügel proposes.[31] Male subjects, Silvermann demonstrates, see themselves as seeing. In other words, the realm of all visibility includes women at the center as subjects of male looks and male observers who watch each other watching women. Masculine looking moves between women on display and other men who display that they are looking at women. For Silvermann, the "Great Masculine Renunciation" operates both as an ideological account of masculinity and as an accurate description of costume history. Modern masculinity depends upon being seen as an observer, and not as body on display.[32]

Even as she complicates Flügel's gendered distinction between those who look and those who are seen, Silvermann explains the male-male looking as a triad in which male observers need a female figure to serve as the shared object. Only by looking at a woman can men look at each other, goes the argument. In a sense, Silvermann's position correlates to the homosocial triangles described by Eve Sedgwick.[33] Indeed the "Great Masculine Renunciation", the masculine abandonment of finery and the increased insistence on a correct asceticism, matches very closely the emergence of a paranoid concern over homosexuality in male society. Women in the triangulated looks, described by Silvermann, become the anchor that secures male-male observation as respectably heterosexual. The more heightened the anxiety between men becomes, the more value is placed on the presence of the shared female image.

Underlying Flügel's notion of renunciation is an aesthetic that gives preference to brilliant decoration. Flügel assumes that beauty and pleasure come in rococo and baroque forms, and like many fashion commentators, he presumes that women's high fashion preserved this style well into the twentieth century. Male attire, when it "renounced" brightness, also gave up all claim to beauty and pleasure. By implication then, Flügel treats the functionalized shapes of modernity as devoid of aesthetic pleasure, hardly a surprising position given that, as Mark Wigley and Mary McLeod have shown, early twentieth-century Modernists often defined their own projects in opposition to the gaudy baubles of consumer culture.[34] Nevertheless, it would be a tremendous mistake to assume that functionalized bodies lacked all aesthetic sensibility. To presume that

---

[31] Kaja Silverman: Fragments of a Fashionable Discourse. In: *Studies in Entertainment. Critical Approaches to Mass Culture*. Ed. by Tania Modleski. Bloomington 1986. Pp. 139-152.

[32] Silverman. P. 143.

[33] Eve Kosofsky Sedgwick: *Between Men: English Literature and Male Homosocial Desire*. New York 1985. Pp. 21-27.

[34] Mark Wigley: *White Walls, Designer Dresses. The Fashioning of Modern Architecture*. Cambridge 1995; Mary McLeod: Undressing Architecture. Fashion, Gender and Modernity. In: *Architecture in Fashion*. Ed. by Deborah Fausch, Paulette Singley, Rodolph El-Khoury, and Zvi Efrat. New York 1994. Pp. 38-123.

only bright clothes conveyed eroticism and beauty overlooks the attractions of modern design and dress.

The neo-classical restraint of the Prussian soldier, the exercise and grooming required to achieve the look of ancient sculpture, and the clear intent to draw the attention of onlookers suggest the existence of an unspoken, masculine beauty of understatement. Embedded within the supposed functionalism of military garb lies an aesthetic appreciation that goes unannounced. This aesthetic quality arises out of the functionalization of the body and yet is at odds with it, for to admit that the military uniform looks attractive to others, threatens to turn it into just another form of finery. The well-toned soldier maneuvers between two modes of visibility: one judges the body in terms of its integration into the machinery of military discipline, the other looks at the body with desire and art. Neo-classical aesthetics allows these two modes to overlap: the drilled body is also the beautiful Greek sculpture.

The thesis of masculine renunciation is made more complicated by the development of a soldierly aesthetic. The dark functional dress of soldiers and respectable bourgeois men lacks an aesthetic quality only if we accept a Kantian notion of aesthetics that separates beauty from the self-interested logic of practical reason. If one follows the neo-classicical thread that equates beauty with athleticism, then it is possible to posit a masculine mode of beauty that incorporates functionalism, a beauty that relies upon or is sustained by the capacity to act practically. The athletic Greek body provides a model of functional masculine beauty while also rejecting the courtly model of men and women competing for attention. Thus Flügel is not wrong for noting that the courtly model of ornamental fashion was rejected as unmasculine in the 18th century, however, he overlooks the subtler forms of masculine display that pervade modern culture. Indeed, the classicist body is but one such mode; another is represented by the principle that understatement can serve as a means of gaining attention, i.e., the dandy's attraction through renunciation.

Kaja Silvermann's adjustment of Flügel's argument is valuable but it does not consider how men look directly at each other, for it overrates the gendered divide between observer and observed. Men are very often aware of each other's appearance, they evaluate each other with the presumption that they in turn are being seen by others outside the circuit of homosocial observation. The example of the Prussian soldiers shows how the army functions first as a circuit of male-male observation which then becomes integrated into a second circuit of viewing when it comes into contact with fashionable society. Military traditionalist were very interested in preserving the boundaries between the army's disciplinary regime and fashionable society. The possibility that soldiers would beome objects of aesthetic or erotic attention threatened to undermine the functional logic of military discipline. Indeed the introduction of the standardized military uniform at the end of the seventeeth century could readily be understood as a first step towards Flügel's "Great Masculine Renunciation". Standardized military dress in Prussia or any other European army had only just been introduced. The boundaries between military and civilian had previously been loosely defined, and they continued to be far more fluid than in the twentieth century. Soldiers often sold their worn uniforms to clothing traders. In certain regions of Prussia, farmers could be seen wearing cast-off military jackets. Thus, the diffusion of military uniforms into civilian society – through imitation or the reselling of old uniforms – would have been an important means of popularizing a restrained attire for men. To wear simple, dark clothes was to invoke military order and readiness. The dark blue uniform of the Prussian army with its lack of ensignias would have been an ideal model for stoically reserved masculine appearance. However, as much as military dress can be said to have influenced male fashion, the example of the tight-dressed Prussian officer shows that fashionable tastes, in this case neo-classical, also exercise an influence on military manners. In other words, the boundary between the military and civilian society was permeable enough for movement in both directions.

Foucault's *Discipline and Punish* provides a compelling account of subjectivity in the eighteenth century, yet rarely is the work read as a genealogy of masculinity. Given that his work has been challenged on occasion for not considering the particular conditions of female subjects, it might not be far-fetched to posit that the implicit gender analysis of *Discipline and Punish* concerns the formation of masculinity during the eighteenth century.[35] Many of the institutions Foucault describes – prisons, barracks, boarding schools – were populated largely by men. As Foucault himself notes, the disciplinary regimes constructed in these sites proliferated to other institutions, thus to argue that *Discipline and Punish* can be read narrowly as a history of masculinity, does not deny the work's continuing relevance to feminism.

By understanding the disciplinary regimes of the prison and the army as specialized means of constituting masculine subjects, we do not need to follow Flügel's claim that male subjects receded from visibility by changing their style of dress. By using *Discipline and Punish* to describe male subjectivity, we can discuss masculinity as it operates within institutions that exclude women, i.e., realms that are deliberately non-fashionable. Military disciplinarity becomes a mode of masculinity, a pressure that hovers around Prussian men without relying immediately on a polar opposition between masculine and feminine. By reading disciplinary subjects as at least initially masculinized, we can explain Flügel's "Great Masculine Renunciation" as a transition between different modes of visibility, rather than along the axis of visible/invisible. "Renunciation" may describe how disciplinary regimes rejected courtly spectacle, but it fails to identify the subtler and more pervasive forms of surveillance that surround Enlightenment males. By using Foucault's account of the transition from courtly spectacle to disciplinary supervision, we can explain how men can be subject to heightened visual control while adopting an understated, self-effacing,

---

[35] Caroline Ramazanoglu and Janet Holland: Women's sexuality and men's appropriation of desire. In: *Up Against Foucault: Explorations of Some Tensions Between Foucault and Feminism*. Ed. by Caroline Ramazanoglu. London 1993. P. 250.

non-ornamental eroticism.

The case of the beautiful Prussian requires an analysis of how divergent visual regimes overlapped. The soldier passed from the strict all male environment of the military into the fashionable world with its many divergent opinions and aesthetic judgments. In order to explain how the young officer was seen, we need to refer to eighteenth-century theories of how bodies, and perhaps also sculptures, were perceived by the general public. We need to consider what it meant for a disciplined body to become visual in the understated terms of neoclassical fashion culture. Ideally we could compare the mechanisms of disciplinary power with the judgments of tasteful opinion, in order to outline the shifting pressures the male body undergoes as it moves from the military to the fashionable world, or in other words, from a homosocial to a heterosexual regime of visuality. The difference between disciplinary, that is to say functionalized, modes of visuality and aesthetic contemplation expressed itself in the discourse of eighteenth-century aesthetics as the need for artistic judgment to distinguish itself from all utilitarian appropriations of art. The established tradition of aesthetic theory asserted the autonomy of art from the state's utilitarian control of people and things, as well as from the fashion-driven public's whimsical desires. German aesthetic theories of the eighteenth century are usually evaluated in terms how they define artistic autonomy. Seen as a major innovation for modern philosophies of art, the principle that works of art should be evaluated in terms of their internal, formal composition rather than of their capacity to be instrumentalized by institutions or individual admirers, has been reaffirmed by German critics up through Theodor Adorno. Scholars trained in the Frankfurt School tradition have furthered the claim that aesthetic autonomy was first formulated as a reaction against a "rising tide" of consumer culture and popular reading.[36]

Rather than retrace the successful formulation of a tradition, I would like to examine aesthetic theory that failed to make the canonical cut because it described aesthetic contemplation in terms antithetical to the Kantian standard of disinterestedness. Johann Gottfried Herder's celebration of classical Greek sculpture in *Plastik: Einige Wahrnehmungen über Form und Gestalt aus Pygmalions bildendem Traume* (1770 and 1778) has the fate of describing quite accurately how popular opinions about three dimensional art were formulated. Unwittingly, for this was certainly not his intention, Herder's essay described how stylish opinions were formulated. What started as a radical critique of rococo mannerism, ended up as a portrayal of how the average well-read bourgeois perceived sculptures, as well as people dressed up in imitation of them. Herder wrote a philosophical anthropology which was ultimately criticized by his peers precisely because it all too accurately represented ordinary taste. If anything,

---

[36] Jochen, Schulte Sasse: *Die Kritik an der Trivialliteratur seit der Aufklärung. Studien zur Geschichte des modernen Kitschbegriffs.* Munich 1972.

Herder erred on the side of phenomenological experience, for he explained how humans perceive art, without providing a formal account of the artwork's distinctive features. Understood historically, Herder's theory sheds light on how eighteenth-century observers felt about bodies displayed in the classical Greek mode.[37] His work is particularly suited for understanding popular perceptions because he insists that true art should create an illusion that suspends the distinction between reality and fantasy. Herder's aesthetics of sculpture does not have a long resonance within the German tradition precisely because it did not acknowledge the autonomy of art from the particular interests of the desiring observer – all the more reason why it helps explain fashionable judgments. Within a Kantian schema, fashion exists somewhere between art and practical thought, thus the fad for a classically sculptured appearance is a popular correlate to Herder's aesthetic enthusiasm for Greek statues.[38]

In Herder's essay we find an aesthetic that refuses to maintain a distinterested distance, and thereby threatens the autonomy of the work of art. Rather than evaluate Herder's *Plastik* on the delicate matter of whether it respected the autonomy of art, I would like to treat it as an anthropological model that describes how classically educated, eighteenth-century subjects constituted themselves in relation to objects of desire that fell just short of being autonomous works of art. If we accept the criticism that Herder's theory fails to sufficiently explain the nature of artistic perception, because it posits a subject who sensually incorporates the art object, then we can re-deploy Herder's theory, against his own intentions, as a theory that describes how members of the aristocracy and *Bürgertum* perceived such non-autonomous things, as commodities and fashionable people. Herder's theory of classical sculpture is particularly appropriate for understanding fashionable perception, given the late eighteenth century's modish enthusiasm for Greek and Roman designs in everything from clothes, hairstyles, and cosmetics to furniture, decorations, and architecture. While Herder's sensualism overlooked the need for detachment in artistic contemplation, it did go a long way toward explaining consumer desire, where restraint is less common.

Following the Enlightenment's philosophical concern to differentiate the various artistic genres from one another, Herder argues that humans perceive sculptures very differently than paintings. Our apprehension of three dimensional objects does not occur through sight alone, rather we comprehend solidity and depth through the touching. Even if we stand politely at a distance from

---

[37] August Langen draws a connection between Herder's *Plastik* the popular game of performing attitudes. Langen's study continues to be the richest source on eighteenth-century visual performances, see: Attitüde und Tableau in der Goethezeit. In: *Jahrbuch der deutschen Schillergesellschaft* 12 (1968). Pp. 206-207

[38] For a more detailed discussion of Garve's application of Kantian categories to fashion, see Daniel Purdy: *Consumer Cosmopolitanism in the Era of Goethe*. Baltimore 1998. Pp. 54-55.

a marble statue, our visual contemplation presumes an imaginary movement of our hands over and around the surface of the figure, for otherwise we could not intuit the fundamental form of sculpture, namely its existence as a three-dimensional solid. Eyesight is the supremely philosophical sense, according to Herder. It is capable of making the sharpest and subtlest distinctions. For the sake of his argument, however, Herder explains that if vision were our only sense then we would understand the world as a flat surface, with shades of colors and shapes arranged across a range but not into a depth. In order to make sense of three dimensional figures, eyesight needs to borrow knowledge from the experience of touching objects, holding them in our hands, running our fingers across them. Herder cites the tendency of children to grasp objects as they are first learning about them as proof that our visual understanding of the material world is at first founded upon the coordination of feeling and sight. Children touch what they can see. Because the hand is guided by the eyes, children touch only what they can first see. We grow to believe that vision is the primary sense when in fact children rely heavily on their tactile feeling of objects. We think we are seeing something when in fact we are feeling it. The experience of holding an object is subsumed into our looking at it. Herder's essay presents both a theory of child development and a genealogy of sensual perception. At times his argument moves backward seeking to deduce the sensual experiences that must inevitably be presumed within visual perception of objects. At other moments, he begins with the *tabula rasa* of an infant, or following Diderot's famous example, a blind man whose sight is restored, to explain how the coordination of sight and touch are required for a normal perception of the world.

Herder's model of childhood development has reminded several contemporary scholars of Lacan's theory of the mirror stage.[39] It might be useful to compare the two accounts of sensual perception in the formation of the subject, in order to understand their dissimilarity. Lacan argues that the sight of its own mirror image allows the infant to create an imaginary identity that anticipates the bodily mastery it will attain only later.[40] The identification that the infant forms at this early stage, when it projects itself onto the mirror image, becomes the primary template for later relationships wherein the subject identifies himself with others as if they were mirror images. Lacan presumes that the mirror image appeals so strongly to the infant because he is "still sunk in his motor

---

[39] Two cogent Lacanian readings of Herder's *Plastik* are Dorothea von Mücke: *Virtue and the Veil of Illusion: Generic Innovation and the Pedagogical Project in Eighteenth-Century Literature.* Stanford 1991. Pp. 174-179 and Catriona MacLeod: Floating Heads: Weimar Portrait Busts. In: *Unwrapping Goethe's Weimar: Essays in Cultural Studies and Local Knowledge.* Ed. by Burkhard Henke, Susanne Kord, and Simon Richter. Rochester, NY 2000. Pp. 65-66.

[40] Jacques Lacan: The Mirror Stage as Formative of the Function of the I. In: *Ecrits: A Selection.* Trans. by Alan Sheridan. New York 1977.

incapacity".[41] The mirror image gives the infant a fictional sense of agency and bodily wholeness that he in fact does not yet possess. Under Lacan's scheme vision provides the first sense of physical cohesiveness. The coherence of the mirror image is taken as an accurate representation of the infant, when in fact the formal coherence of the image does not really correspond to the physical motor skills of the infant. The baby cannot control himself nearly as much as the structure of the image implies. Its legs, arms, head, etc. are not all arranged into the single entity that the sight of itself in the mirror would seem to imply.

Herder goes even further in detailing how an infant literally grasps an image and incorporates it. However, unlike Lacan, Herder maintains that eyesight is actually a secondary development. According to Herder's theory, vision, and in particular the (mis)identification with an image, requires that the infant first has a physical sense of its own body before it can identify an image as a representation of itself. Images make sense, according to Herder, because we first have acquired a feeling for bodies; their weight, solidity, and shape are then transposed onto images. Lacan presumes that vision is primary in the formation of narcissistic self; Herder argues that a physical intuition precedes visual recognition.[42] "Da steht der kleine Experient und tastet und wägt und mißt mit Händen und Füßen sehend und fühlend, um sich die ersten Begriffe von Gestalt, Größe, Raum, Entfernung, Beschaffenheit der Körper um ihn zu sichern. Seine erste Känntnis ist eigentlicher Begriff, Ideen durchs Gefühl: seine kleinen tastenden Hände sind ihm die ersten Organe der Weltwissenschaft und Naturkunde".[43] While Lacan describes the mirror stage as so formative that later relationships repeat the child's initial identification with his mirror image, Herder insists that the infant's physical contact with his environment guides his later relationship to the outside world. "Lasset ihn tasten, lasset ihn versuchen! lasset ihn durch Fehlgriffe zur Wahrheit kommen: je mehr er da versucht hat, desto solider wird er denken: je mehr er da gefehlt hat, desto weniger wird er sein ganzes Leben durch fehlen dürfen".[44] According to Herder's theory, the sight of itself in a mirror would not make sense to an infant had it not already developed a sensual intuition of its own body. Further, the concept of physical coherence cannot be learned from an image. Herder argues that to the eyes alone the image appears as a fragmented collection of colors and shapes; only when sight has been coordinated with the physical sensations of touch can a child perceive that an image

---

[41] Ibid. P. 2.

[42] "Die ersten Begriffe von Farbe, Figur, Weite der Körper lernten sich bloß durch ein langes Gegeneinanderhalten einzelner Empfindungen; allein eben durch das lange Gegeneinanderhalten, wurden sie uns geläufig: die Mittelglieder zwischen ihnen verdunkeln sich: sie bleiben als simple unmittelbare Empfindung, und so nehmen wir sie in Gebrauch, im Übersehen der Anwendung, in der fertigen, schnellen, unbemerkenden Gewohnheit?" In: Herder: *Werke* (Hanser). Vol 2. P. 63.

[43] Herder: *Plastik*. P. 408.

[44] Ibid. P. 408.

represents a bodily whole. Not only does the physical intuition of the body precede knowledge of its appearance, but Herder goes so far as to imply that the child's feeling of its own body grounds his subjectivity. In a draft for the *Plastik* essay, Herder makes this point with Cartesian rhetoric "Ich fühle mich! Ich bin!"[45]

Both Herder and Lacan present models of childhood development that ultimately describe the subject as narcissistic. Lacan, of course, uses the term. Herder's model of perception claims that seeing is predicated upon the experience of grasping. To see something three-dimensionally, to perceive its reality as a solid, requires the observer to recreate through vision the sensual experience of holding an object. Built into Herder's model of visuality is the notion that looking really amounts to drawing an object to one's own body, feeling and holding it. The synesthesia of vision and touch is not merely metaphorical. Herder does not merely claim that looking at a sculpture is like touching it. He insists that we could not make sense of a thing's spatial existence except for the fact that visual perception is based upon the memory of physical contact with an object. Lacan and Herder both describe a formative childhood experience in which the perception of image results in a narcissistic misrecognition, an illusion that one tends to mistake as truth and as oneself. The key distinction in their scepticism vis-à-vis the image is that Herder insists that the illusion is built upon the erasure of earlier childhood perceptions through the sense of touch, whereas Lacan does not consider the mirror image of the self to be predicated upon earlier stages of perceptual development.

As much as the sight and feeling are integrated in our perception of the world, they are activated to different degrees by different art forms. Painting, colors, and lines arranged on a canvas address vision more purely than sculpture, which requires an intuition of touch even if one is looking only at the marble figure. Anticipating Cubism, Herder argues that if sight were forced to rely solely upon its own capabilities, it would distort and flatten sculptures into corners and angles because it is unable to represent to itself the fullness, roundness, and depth of the form.[46] The person standing before a statue intuitively

---

[45] Herder: *Sämtliche Werke*. Ed. by Bernhard Suphan. Vol. 8. Berlin 1892. P. 96. Hans Dietrich Irmscher draws the strongest anti-cartesian conclusions from Herder's formulation: "Dies ist zweifellos als Kontrafaktur zu der cartesianischen Formel 'cogito, ergo sum' gemeint, mit der der Philosoph die Quelle aller Gewißheit glaubte angegeben zu haben. Herder aber setzt an die Stelle des Denkens [...] die Erfahrung der eignen Leiblichkeit als einzig verläßlichen Ursprung der Selbst- und Welterkenntnis". Irmscher: Grundzüge der Hermeneutik Herders. In: *Bückeburger Gespräche über Johann Gottfried Herder – 1971*. Ed. by Johann Gottfried Maltusch. Bückeburg 1973. P. 33.

[46] "Das Gesicht zerstört die schöne Bildsäule, statt daß es sie schaffe, es verwandelt sie in Ecken und Flächen, bei denen es viel ist, wenn sich nicht das schönste Wesen ihrer Innigkeit, Fülle und Runde in lauter Spiegelecken verwandle; unmöglich kanns also Mutter dieser Kunst sein". In: Herder: *Werke* (Hanser). Vol. 2. P. 474.

relies upon a mixture of senses in order to "grasp" the sensuous figure. Herder takes the Pygmalion myth as a prescription for the proper artistic contemplation of sculpture. The observer moves his eye across the sculpture as if it were a hand. "[S]ein Auge ward Hand, der Lichtstrahl Finger".[47] The ordinary museum goer would, according to Herder, assume the position of the creative artist when viewing a sculpture. Like Pygmalion, he must hold the sculpture in his arms, at least figuratively, although the artist must literally grasp the human figure of marble if he is to succeed. "Wehe dem Apollo-, dem Herkulesbildner, der nie einen Wuchs Apollos umschlang, der eine Brust, einen Rücken Herkules' auch nie im Traume fühlte!"[48]

The artistic effect of sculpture depends upon its creating the impression of an actual existing being appearing before the observer. Whereas painting represents through an image that stands in for the reality it represents, successful sculpture recreates the physical existence of what it represents, so that the distinction between the two is suspended in the moment of aesthetic apprehension. The shape and weight of a sculpture give it a presence in the material world that an image lacks. Painting, according to Herder, shows an illusion that looks like what it represents whereas the plastic arts create a material object. Herder gives preference to sculpture because of this materiality. "Endlich, die Bildnerei ist Wahrheit, die Malerei Traum; jene ganz Darstellung, diese erzählender Zauber".[49]

As Inka Mülder-Bach has shown, the Pygmalion myth was central to the eighteenth-century's understanding of sculpture.[50] The myth not only teaches Herder that the viewer must approach the sculpture as someone who wishes to hold it sensuously, it also sets a standard for aesthetic accomplishment, namely that the sculpture must create the illusion of being alive. "Eine Statue muß *leben*: ihr Fleisch muß sich beleben: ihr Gesicht und Mine sprechen. Wir müssen sie anzutasten glauben und fühlen, daß sie sich unter unsern Händen erwärmt. Wir müssen sie vor uns stehen sehen, und fühlen, daß sie zu uns spricht. Siehe da zwei Hauptstücke der Sculptur *Fleisch und Geist*".[51]

If Herder's ideal sculpture is one that gives the illusion of having life, what does he make of living beings who try to look like statues? Once artworks step into ordinary life, how is one to preserve any distinction between the two? Herder's reflections in *Plastik* did not address the concerns for artistic autonomy that was to weigh so heavily on the minds of Weimar thinkers in the 1790s. In the 1770s Herder contrasts the semi-clad beauty of Greek sculpture with the restrictive courtly clothes of rococo fashion. The eternal verities of sculpture stood in sharp contrast to the broad dresses and tight bodices women wore for

---

[47] Herder: *Werke* (Hanser). Vol. 2. P. 474.
[48] Ibid. P. 475.
[49] Herder: *Werke* (Hanser). Vol. 2. P. 478.
[50] Inka Mülder-Bach: *Im Zeichen Pygmalions: Das Modell der Statue und die Entdeckung der "Darstellung" im 18. Jahrhundert.* Munich 1998. Pp. 49-93.
[51] Herder: *Sämtliche Werke* (Suphan). Vol. 8. P. 88.

the first three-quarters of the eighteenth century. Herder's celebration of unrestrictive Greek styles had distinct political and social ramifications which he refrained from spelling out, but could not be missed.

> Hier ist ein Weg über das Falsche unsrer Kleider Physisch, Moralisch und Politisch zu reden: ich bleibe aber blos bei dem Künstlichen. Geben sie was mehr, und Bessres in Form, als das Fühlbare des Körpers? Nein! Sie verbergen, sie verhehlen, sie betrügen, sie erkälten, sie sagen nichts: weg mit ihnen so viel als möglich.[52]

The Pygmalion myth was a fantasy of social transformation in which ancient art remolded the social condition of the body. By liberating the body through Greek artistic style, Herder implied that the individual would also be lifted out of his conformity to feudal tradition. Just as Rousseau draws on the naked Spartan wrestler as his ideal image of liberation, Herder imagines that his aesthetic theory takes aim at restrictive political hierarchies in Germany. Bodices for Herder are part of a "Chinesisch-Gothisch-Christliche Zucht der Kleider" that contains sensuality and the body's natural expressiveness.[53] The "gothic" strictures of courtly costume are, of course, aligned with a political order that similarly contains critical intellectual discourse. The corsetted body in Herder's mind becomes an allegory, or in eighteenth-century terms, a physiognomic sign of social repression. By implication, a society that dresses in the manner of Greek antiquity would implicitly embody Enlightenment values. The naiveté of this unspoken equation became obvious once the Greek nude style became widespread.

Herder's contemporaries understood that the Pygmalion myth was better suited for explaining fashion-driven erotic desires, than it was for describing aesthetic judgments of autonomous art works.[54] Hegel in his lectures on aesthetics warned that by dismantling the boundary between art and life the Pygmalion myth allowed for the appropriation of artistic style for political and social needs. August Wilhelm Schlegel reworked Ovid's version when he published his "Pygmalion" in Schiller's *Musen-Almanach* in 1797. Schlegel's Pygmalion is an inwardly-oriented soul, filled with melancholy dreams, hardly the sensualist that Herder imagines. When he prays to the gods for his fantasy's fulfillment, he addresses Urania, not Venus, thereby further removing the taint of sexual desire from his artistic admiration. Finally, in seeking approval from Zeus before transforming the sculpture, Urania states explicitly that Pygmalion honors only the highest spiritual form of beauty and that he is free from burning sensual desire. "Sieh! allein von allen Erdensöhnen / Hat Pygmalion, dem

---

[52] Ibid. P. 89.

[53] Ibid. P. 91.

[54] Helmuth Pfotenhauer: *Um 1800. Konfigurationen der Literatur, Kunstliteratur und Ästhetik*. Tübingen 1991. Pp. 31-35.

höchsten Schönen / Huldigend, und frei vom Sinnenbrand, / Sich zu meinem Dienst gewandt".[55] Despite Schlegel's didactic separation of sexual desire from the aesthetic appreciation of beauty, Hegel reads the myth as the antithesis of an artist elevating himself spiritually through the contemplation of beauty.

> Es findet hier das Umgekehrte dessen statt, was Herr von Schlegel z. B. in der Geschichte des Pygmalion so ganz prosaisch als die Rückkehr des vollendeten Kunstwerks zum gemeinen Leben, zum Verhältnis der subjektiven Neigung und des realen Genusses ausspricht, eine Rückkehr, die das Gegenteil derjenigcn Entfernung ist, in welche das Kunstwerk die Gegenstände zu unserem Bedürfnisse setzt und ebendamit deren eigenes selbständiges Leben und Erscheinen vor uns hinstellt.[56]

Goethe is not at all impressed by the Pygmalion myth as a paradigm for artistic creation. The story implies that beautiful art arises from personal desire, and not from a spiritual principle above the particular individual. Goethe cuts to the quick, noting that ancient treatises on sculpture are peppered with allusions to young men who spend the night with sculptures, seeking and finding sexual gratification.[57] These stories have nothing to do with the creation of true art, he insists. "Die Tradition sagt: daß brutale Menschen gegen plastische Meisterwerke von sinnlichen Begierden entzündet wurden".[58] Instead of permitting the erotic fusion of art and observer, Goethe imposes a taboo on just such relations: "Die Liebe eines hohen Künstlers aber zu seinem trefflichen Werk ist ganz anderer Art; sie gleicht der frommen heiligen Liebe unter Blutsverwandten und Freunden".[59] The principle of artistic autonomy functions like the ban on incest, sublimating desire in the name of spiritually motivated artistic form. Were the myth taken at face value then Pygmalion was nothing more than an artistic poseur, just the sort of accusation levelled at fashion. "Hätte Pygmalion seiner Statue begehren können, so wäre er ein Pfuscher gewesen, unfähig eine Gestalt hervorzubringen, die verdient hätte, als Kunstwerk oder als Naturwerk geschätzt zu werden".[60] Herder's claim that the contemplator holds or fondles the statue through looking clearly allows the work of art to become integrated within personal desire. His repeated references to looking that feels the shape of a statue

[55] August Wilhelm Schlegel: *Sämtliche Werke*. Ed. by Eduard Böcking. Vol. 1. Leipzig 1846. P. 46.
[56] Georg Wilhelm Friedrich Hegel: *Ästhetik*. Vol. 2. Berlin 1976. P. 210.
[57] Foucault uses such an anecdote when discussing the difference between Greek ideas of sleeping with boys or women. See Michel Foucault: *The History of Sexuality: The Care of the Self*. Trans. by Robert Hurley. New York 1986. P. 211.
[58] Johann Wolfgang von Goethe: *Diderot's Versuch über die Mahlerei*. In: *Werke*. Weimarer Ausgabe. Ed. on the behest of the grand duchess Sophie von Sachsen. Weimar 1900. I 45 P. 263.
[59] Ibid.
[60] Ibid.

has a clearly grasping, erotic tone. The myth suspends the difference between a beloved person and art. Both are incorporated into the will of the observer. Fashionable emulation of Greek sculpture further vitiates the boundary between art and ordinary life, and thus the visual touching that Herder describes when viewing a beautiful piece of marble, would have become even more intense when faced with a person dressed as a sculpture. The neo-classical fashions of 1800 enact the Pygmalion myth on a social scale. When young men and women began dressing as sculptures sprung to life, they readily invoked the erotic appreciation Herder had outlined a quarter century before.

Plastik provides a starting point for showing how late eighteenth-century fashionable perception overlapped, sometimes aligning itself with, other times contradicting, the interests of military tactics. The central thesis of Herder's essay, that seeing a three-dimensional figure presumes the imaginative act of grasping or holding it, conspicuously employs metaphors that also describe the body within disciplinary and fashionable fields of vision. Both Herder's haptic sight and Foucault's panopticon describe vision that grasps or holds the body. Yet in most of their operations, these two modes of visuality are distinguished from each other by the manner in which they direct power. For Herder, aesthetic contemplation is a narcissistic process in which the act of looking reflects back on the observer, exciting him. Herder's claim that the contemplator holds or fondles the statue through vision clearly allows the work of art to become integrated within personal desire. His repeated references to looking that feels the shape of a statue have a grasping erotic tone. In the panoptical prison, with its central tower and its exposed cells on the perimeter, power flows away from the point of observation onto the incarcerated bodies. Within aesthetics the subject is constituted by looking upon beauty, whereas within the panopticon, the subject is produced by being seen. The prisoner, if anything, might be aligned with the statue – both are viewed, however, they each have a very different status. The sculpture may be evaluated critically in terms of its successful representation (*Darstellung*) of beauty, however, its legitimacy is secured by an artistic tradition that honors Greek antiquity. The subject within a disciplinary regime is purely an instrument, completely exposed to the manipulations of the central observing authority. The disciplinary observer has a one-sided relationship to the observed. The machinery of disciplinary power does not even require the presence of real individiuals at the central point of observation, for the surveillance tower sees without being exposed to the effects of vision. The point of a disciplinary field of vision is to direct and control the bodies within it. Aesthetic vision has no real purpose other than to elevate the spiritual state of the observer. In the erotically charged, social interaction of fashionable society, this heightened subjective state, brought on by observation, might more honestly be described as the desire to hold, caress, press up against and probe another's body. By theorizing the link between sight and sexual contact, Herder's analysis of vision that grasps the beautiful body comes closest to describing the look of fashion with its distinctly "untactical" interest.

The young officer who choked to death represents the point at which the two modes of visually holding the body converge. If the corset represented the ornamental constrictions of courtly ceremony, then the soldier squeezed lifeless by a uniform molded to him becomes an allegory of the natural, functional body under the double grip of fashion and discipline. His tight uniform combines the screen-effect of drapery with the personalized hold of military discipline. The uniform grips the body so closely that it can scarcely breath or move, and yet the visual effect is one of nakedness. The clothes cover the body with such intensity that they become almost a second skin, a natural part of the body, and thereby are almost no covering at all. The tight uniform of the Prussian soldier enacts a naturalization of power, an external force that bears down to such an extent that it almost presses itself into the body, giving on-lookers the impression that they can see through the uniform. The uniform was both invisible and visible, depending on how one looked, with desire, with control, or both.

Karin A. Wurst

Designing the Self: Fashion and the Body

The modern (embodied) self was produced by an internalization of the disciplining force of civilization. Fashion around 1800 constructs a complicated celebration of "naturalness" revealing the "natural" body while, at the same time, pointing to the cultural "constructedness" of the seemingly natural. Unlike high culture, the fashion discourse does not seek to hide, veil, and internalize its "constructedness" but instead draws attention to the "natural" as the culturally constructed product of modern self-discipline.

> [...] die schöne Gestalt des reizenden Weibes, sittsam umkleidet, ohne verstellt zu seyn, ist doch gewiß der freundlichste Anblick in der Natur. ("Neue Moden aus Paris", III, 70)[1]

The Enlightenment with its concept of progress began to regard conditions and people as changeable and individualistic. In the dynamic modern world, the self was no longer firmly grounded in a fixed order of things with its predetermined hierarchies but was called on to take an active role in shaping the self. As Norbert Elias argued, the modern (embodied) self was produced by an internalization of the disciplining force of civilization. In the process of directing the disciplining force on itself, the self became self-reflexive and began to function as both subject and object. As the target of the disciplining force, the body plays a complex role. As we will see, this cultural production of the body (embodiment) has to be seen as a process of continually creating new kinds of bodies. Fashion renders this tension between the myth of the body as a "natural" phenomenon and its cultural "constructedness" visible. Fashion around 1800 constructs a complicated celebration of "naturalness" revealing the "natural" body while, at the same time, pointing to the cultural "constructedness" of the seemingly natural, as the motto suggests. Like classicist philosophy and aesthetics, the fashion discourse – under which I subsume the material objects themselves and the discussion of fashion – is concerned with the status of the aesthetic experience in the formation of the self. Unlike its pendant in high culture – in particular, Friedrich Schiller's aesthetic treatises and his followers in the idealist tradition and in *Geschichtsphilosophie,* which argued

---

[1] As the complete original of the monthly, *Journal des Luxus und der Moden,* has become rare, I will use the modern (abridged) reprint to make the references more accessible. Friedrich Justin Bertuch and Georg Melchior Kraus (eds.): *Journal des Luxus und der Moden.* Ed. by Werner Schmidt. 4. vols. Rpt. Hanau 1967-70. As the *Journal* includes many anonymous articles and contributions identified by initials, only their titles will be provided unless the contributor is well known. The Roman numerals refer to the volume number and the Arabic numbers to the page numbers.

that the evils of civilization depriving man could also bring an paradisiacal state back on a higher level of self-conscious perfection in the work of art – the fashion discourse does not seek to hide, veil, and internalize its "constructedness" but instead draws attention to it.[2]

After a brief discussion on the relationship between body and fashion, this article discusses the role of the classical vision of the body in the construction of middle-class (autonomous and individualistic) identity. In particular, this study explores the historical moment in fashion that was influenced by the classicist celebration of a seemingly "natural" concept of the beautiful (clothed) body, which was in effect created by fashion. With this constellation we are reminded of the underlying telos of Schiller's aesthetic education, in which he sees culture, on the path of reason, leading back to nature by offering an integrated image of (wo)man in the work of art. "Art's sensual fullness allows the subject to find a reflection of himself in an imaginary whole that provides him with a sense of completion and wholeness".[3]

The source for this discussion is the first and foremost fashion journal of its day, Johann Friedrich Justin Bertuch's *Journal des Luxus und der Moden* (1786-1827). By its very nature as a fashion primer (i.e., as a manual teaching the art of fashion), it draws attention to the disciplining force – the integration of the rational and the sensual – that was required for the creation of the seemingly natural beautiful body. The didactic moment raised doubts as to whether the civilizational discipline could be successfully naturalized, as aestheticians like Schiller hoped. After all, classicist aesthetics anchored the graceful natural body – and with it bourgeois autonomy and individuality – "on a level where it was not conscious of itself".[4] Paul de Man has pointed to both the seductive and deluded aspects of this construct:

> The idea of innocence recovered at the far side and by the way of experience, of para-
> dise consciously regained after the fall into consciousness, the idea, in other words,

---

[2] See also Schneider who picks up on de Man's reading of Kleist's *Marionettentheater* which focused on the rhetorical fragmentation of the text critical of the idealist tradition. Paul de Man: Aesthetic Formalizations. Kleist's *Über das Marionettentheater.* In: *The Rhetoric of Romanticism.* Ed. by Paul de Man. New York 1984. Pp. 263-290. Helmut Schneider: Deconstruction of the Hermeneutic Body. Kleist and the Discourse of Classical Aesthetics. In: *Body and Text in the Eighteenth Century.* Ed. by Veronica Kelly and Dorothea von Mücke. Stanford 1994. Pp. 209-226.

[3] Friedrich Schiller: Ueber die ästhetische Erziehung des Menschen in einer Reihe von Briefen. In: *Schillers Werke.* Nationalausgabe. Vol. 20: Philosophische Schriften. In coll. with Helmut Koopmann ed. by Benno von Wiese. Weimar 1962. Pp. 309-412, here 6. Brief, p. 328. Andreas Gailus: Of Beautiful and Dismembered Bodies. Art as Social Discipline in Schiller's *On Aesthetic Education of Man.* In: *Impure Reason. Dialectic of Enlightenment in Germany.* Ed. by W. Daniel Wilson and Robert C. Holub. Detroit 1993. Pp. 146-165, here p. 149. I tend to agree with Gailus that Schiller predominantly refers to a male subject, however, the issue of gender in Schiller's theoretical writings would benefit from a more careful analysis; thus my reference to "(wo)man".

[4] Schneider. P. 211.

of a teleological and apocalyptic history of consciousness is, of course, one of the most seductive, powerful, and deluded topoi of the idealist and romantic period.[5]

In Kleist's *Marionettentheater*-Essay, de Man detects a suspicion that Schiller's idealist model "is itself flawed, or worse, if it covers up this lesion [i.e., the potentially violent streak in Schiller's own aesthetic theory, K. W.] by a self-serving idealization, then the classical concept of aesthetic education is open to suspicion".[6] Not unlike Kleist's essay, the fashion discourse also raises doubts about the possibility of a return to "natural beauty" after the highly sculpted body of the ancien régime. Yet the ever-changing flow of fashion and the fashion journal as teacher and disciplinarian continually remind the self of the conscious effort and cultural work required to achieve the ideal.

The body is intricately associated with dress; one could not fully exist without the other. Eicher and Roach-Higgins define the dressed person as "a gestalt that includes body, all direct modifications of the body itself, all three-dimensional supplements added to it".[7] Body modifications include skin colorings, hair-dress, and perfume, among others; supplements are three-dimensional objects such as purses, gloves, shoes, fans and other items completing the outfit. The *Journal des Luxus und der Moden* describes both – the total ensemble and details making the body culturally visible and thus "draws the body so that it can be culturally seen, and articulates it in a meaningful form".[8] Clothing is the cultural metaphor of the body and the material with which we write a representation of the body into our cultural context.[9] Dress helps to produce men and women as social beings as it fuses aesthetic, moral, and medical arguments in the construction of bourgeois identity.

For the context of the late eighteenth-century, the term "fashion" (instead of clothing) is more appropriate because it points to the fact that dress (and with it the body) began to be regarded as ever changing. Fashion inscribes the body as caught in the historical process of modernization, in the shift from a stratificational differentiation to the functional differentiation of society. The concept of fashion

---

[5] de Man. P. 267.

[6] de Man. P. 280. For a discussion of the violence underlying Schiller's social discipline see also Andreas Gailus: Of Beautiful and Dismembered Bodies. Art as Social Discipline in Schiller's *On Aesthetic Education of Man*. In: *Impure Reason. Dialectic of Enlightenment in Germany*. Ed. by W. Daniel Wilson and Robert C. Holub. Detroit 1993. Pp. 146-165 in passim.

[7] Joan Eicher and Mary Ellen Roach-Higgins: Definition and Classification of Dress. In: *Dress and Gender. Making and Meaning*. Ed. by Ruth Barnes and Joanne B. Eicher. New York 1991. Pp. 8-28, here p. 13.

[8] Kaja Silverman: Fragments of a Fashionable Discourse. In: *Studies in Entertainment. Critical Approaches to Mass Culture*. Ed. by Tanja Modleski. Bloomington 1986. Pp. 139-152, here p. 145.

[9] Elizabeth Wilson: Fashion and the Postmodern Body. In: *Chic Thrills. A Fashion Reader*. Ed. by Juliet Ash and Elizabeth Wilson. Berkeley, Los Angeles 1993. Pp. 3-16, here p. 6.

adds the dimension of temporality (and functional suitability, i.e., clothing designed for different occasions and specific activities) to clothing as modern dress is no longer fixed and stable, and prescribed by sumptuary laws and traditions. On the contrary, modern dress is characterized by the desire for change and novelty: "Genie, Caprice und Zufall sind meistens ihre Schöpfer; Durst nach Neuheit und Abwechslung [...] machen sie unbeständig und schnell wechselnd".[10] Thus the term fashion will be used in this article because it denotes the specificity of dress in modern society.

The study of fashion has a central function in a consideration of the body in cultural studies,[11] especially during the eighteenth century, as personal appearance becomes a type of oeuvre, which was carefully constructed by the individual. My study is informed by the Foucauldian premise that fashion can be used to study the process "by which the individual constitutes and recognizes himself *qua* subject".[12] It is therefore yet another area where we can catch a glimpse at the conditions "in which human beings 'problematize' what they are, what they do, and the world in which they live".[13] Fashion is one of the "arts of existence", those "intentional and voluntary actions by which men not only set themselves rules of conduct, but also seek to transform themselves, to change themselves in their singular being, and to make their life into an oeuvre that carries certain aesthetic values and meets certain stylistic criteria".[14] This implied negotiation of at least momentarily fixed identities allows Foucault to make room for a moment of agency and resistance when compared to his earlier portrayal of human bodies as passive and constituted by power and discipline (*Discipline and Punish*). Individuals are not only the passive object of the fashion discourse (and later the fashion industry) but display moments of agency, when they act as subjects designing themselves.

As the self was confronted with the task to think about, and act on, its own design, to be self-reflexive, the fashionably clothed body begins to function as a medium for self-creation and self-display. This moment of choice in designing the fashionable body, as an important part of the unique self, required taste and cultural knowledge. For the formation of taste in fashion, the audience relied predominantly on the *Journal des Luxus und der Moden*.

The *Journal* attributes the interest in self-adornment to the desire to appear pleasant and attractive, and legitimizes the occupation with the self by postulating that members of the human race consider social differentiation and distinction desirable:

[Der] Wunsch zu gefallen, und sich auszuzeichnen, ist der Geist, der mit dem Grundstoffe der menschlichen Natur bey allen Völkern der Erde innigst verwebt ist.

[10] Bertuch and Kraus: Einleitung. In: *Journal*. I. P. 29.

[11] Elizabeth Wilson. P. 15.

[12] Michel Foucault: . *The History of Sexuality*. Vol. 2: *The Use of Pleasure*. New York 1986. P. 6.

[13] Ibid. P. 10.

[14] Ibid Pp. 10-11.

Nur Materie und Zeichen sind verschieden. Je reicher und verfeinerter eine aufgeklärte Nation ist, desto bequemer, schöner, geschmackvoller und mannigfältiger sind auch ihre Moden.[15]

According to the *Journal*, the human desire for beautification of the body and for social distinction, i.e., the cultural construction of the self, defines human nature throughout all cultures of the world. Fashion appeals to the playful creation of the appearance of the self by planning, designing, and then "trying on" the latest designs. The self as aesthetic object and work of art required continuous work to select from all the possibilities affecting body and mind to shape it into a desired whole. Within the framework of what was considered fashionable at any given time and what was available for purchase within the person's financial means, the self had to select and assemble an outfit that suggested his/her individuality. The subject uses its cultural knowledge to transform itself into the object of its own design.

The *Journal* is not only influenced by the popular philosophy of its day but also by classicist thought. This, of course, is hardly surprising as its editors, Bertuch and Kraus, were highly educated members of the Weimar society.[16] The underlying assumption of classicist thought is that the "aesthetic experience was fundamental to what it is to be human".[17] Of course, classicist aesthetics with its foremost theoretician, Schiller, refers to high art, not the popular decorative arts (such as fashion) in the discussion of the aesthetic education of the self. Yet, on a most abstract level, both Schiller and the popular philosophy of his day grappled with similar issues, such as the role of culture in the integration of the rational and sensual side of human beings. Overall, popular philosophy sought to design and disseminate a comprehensive way of life that enhances the mental, spiritual and physical health and well-being of the bourgeoisie, in which the equilibrium between the sensual and rational forces played an important role. With its functional and aesthetic qualities (the emphasis in this article is on the latter), fashion brings many of these issues in focus.

The aesthetic contemplation and deliberate design of the self advocated in the *Journal* reads like a popularization of Schiller's description of the aesthetic education of man, in which man's aesthetic contemplation requires mastery over his environment and his own senses:

Erst, wenn er in seinem ästhetischen Stande, sie [die Sinnenwelt] außer sich stellt oder *betrachtet*, sondert sich seine Persönlichkeit von ihr ab, und es erscheint ihm eine Welt, weil er aufgehört hat, mit derselben Eins auszumachen. [...] Die ihn vor-

---

[15] Bertuch and Kraus: Einleitung. I. P. 29.

[16] Gerhard R. Kaiser and Siegfried Seifert (eds.): *Friedrich Justin Bertuch (1747-1822): Verleger, Schriftsteller und Unternehmer im klassischen Weimar*. Tübingen 2000. In passim.

[17] Lesley Sharpe: *Schiller's Aesthetic Essays. Two Centuries of Criticism*. Columbia, S. C. 1995. P. 2.

dem nur als *Macht* beherrschte, steht jetzt als *Objekt* vor seinem richtenden Blick.[18]

Schiller considers the agency of the subject in its own design, including his/her appearance, a central task for the individual:

> Der Mensch aber ist zugleich eine *Person*, ein Wesen also, welches *selbst* Ursache, und zwar absolut letzte Ursache seiner Zustände seyn, welches sich nach den Gründen, die es aus sich selbst nimmt, verändern kann. Die Art seines Erscheinens ist abhängig von der Art seines Empfindens und Wollens, also von Zuständen, die er selbst in seiner Freyheit, und nicht die Natur nach ihrer Nothwendigkeit bestimmt.[19]

Individual appearance is not determined by "nature" but by conditions that s/he can control, by the individual's feelings and desires, and by his/her cultural knowledge. Fashion problematizes the issue of agency in the construction of the self because it makes apparent that, in a given culture and historical moment, there is never complete freedom (full autonomy) for individual life choices but merely a range of available options.[20] While classicist philosophy is primarily concerned with shaping the mind and intellect with the ultimate goal of creating moral beings, its concept of agency also envisions a similar control over the appearance of the body.

In *Ueber Anmuth und Würde*, Schiller extends the moment of agency to the control over the body in the pursuit of beauty. He separates beauty into two entities: beauty (*Schönheit*) and grace (*Anmuth*). The beautiful body belongs to both the sphere of nature and reason because it contains a fixed or static element (nature) and a man-made dimension created by human reason and culture: "Die Schönheit ist daher als die Bürgerin zwoer Welten anzusehen, deren einer sie durch *Geburt*, der anderen durch *Adoption* angehört; sie empfängt ihre Existenz der sinnlichen Natur, und *erlangt* in der Vernunftwelt das Bürgerrecht".[21] Schiller uses the concept of grace (*Anmuth*) to account for the man-made, cultural quality of beauty that completes the given natural beauty: "Anmuth ist eine Schönheit, die nicht von der Natur gegeben, sondern von dem Subjekte selbst hervorgebracht wird".[22] Consequently, the self plays an important role in shaping his/her appearance.[23]

---

[18] Schiller: Ueber die ästhetische Erziehung. 25. Brief. Pp. 394-395.

[19] Friedrich Schiller: Ueber Anmuth und Würde. In: *Schillers Werke.* Nationalausgabe. Vol. 20: Philosophische Schriften. Pp. 251-308, here p. 262.

[20] See also the discussions in Adelson and Wilke, which, however, refer to a twentieth-century context. Leslie Adelson: *Making Bodies, Making History. Feminsim and German Identity.* Lincoln 1993. P. 19. Sabine Wilke: *Ambiguous Embodiment. Construction and Destruction of Bodies in Modern German Literature.* Heidelberg 2000. Pp. 8-9.

[21] Schiller: Ueber Anmuth und Würde. P. 260.

[22] Ibid. P. 255.

[23] It is self-evident that we have to assume gender-specific forms of self-determination

Overall, the project of the Schillerian aesthetic socialization seeks to transform human beings from within by reorganizing their affective structures.[24] Rather than forcing the rational side of man to combat the sensual side, Schiller envisions a harmonious relationship between the two, a balance. In the act of aesthetic contemplation, the balanced harmony between rationality and sensuality, the coercion of one over the other, is sublated ("hebt [...] auf").[25] Yet this equilibrium is only a veiling of the coercive force of self-discipline that is made to seem effortless and quasi natural: "Die Anmuth läßt der Natur da, wo sie die Befehle des Geistes ausrichtet, einen Schein von Freywilligkeit".[26] While classicist aesthetics argues for veiling the disciplinary forces of reason shaping the body and its image – the "idealist notion of nature on the invisible leash, or the hidden strings, of her master, reason"[27] – fashion draws attention to the cultural work on the (beautiful) body. Even when showcasing the "natural" body as in the classicist-inspired fashion around 1800, fashion discourse shows that the "natural" is achieved with artifice and a self-conscious effort.

The contours of the new body-conscious fashion emerge through the contrast with the fashion of the previous decades (Ill. 1; Ill. 2). The comparison reveals the ideal of (relatively) body revealing clothes.[28] Evoking the image of revealing the "natural" beauty of the body in fashion around 1800 is a discursive effect rather than an actual phenomenon, as the illustrations depict images that are considerably less revealing than the descriptions suggest (Ill. 3; Ill. 4). After all, the discursive context of these descriptions is the classicist aesthetic ideal as it was developed in art (history) by Winckelmann and Herder, which was primarily based on examples from statuary and consequently emphasized corporeality and sensuousness. Although these ideas were developed with the model of sculpture in mind, they found their way into popular culture not only in the immense interest in plaster copies by the Weimar sculptor Gottlieb Martin Klauer[29] but also into fashion. Art criticism foregrounds the fluid unbroken lines of the body of the white marble statues (Winckelmann) and, in the case of clothed statues, the body-hugging quality of clothing modeled after wet cloths covering the body (Herder). Comparing the fashions of 1786, the first issue of the *Journal*, and the present issue (1803), the editor applies this sculptural gaze to fashion in his devaluation of artifice in dress distorting the overt sensuality of flowing graceful contours of the

---

within the given gender roles of Schiller's historical context, but the issue of gender would go beyond the scope of the present study.

[24] Schiller: Ueber die ästhetische Erziehung. 3. Brief. Pp. 314-315. See also Gailus. P. 152.

[25] Ibid. P. 314.

[26] Schiller: Ueber Anmuth und Würde. P. 297.

[27] Schneider. P. 211.

[28] The fact that to our contemporary sensibilities they are hardly revealing reminds us of the historical specificity of expectation and viewing conventions.

[29] Catriona MacLeod: Floating Heads. Weimar Portrait Busts. In: *Unwrapping Goethe's Weimar. Essays in Cultural Studies and Local Knowledge.* Ed. by Burkhard Henke, Susanne Kord, and Simon Richter. Rochester 2000. Pp. 65-96, here p. 68.

54

(beautiful) body:

> Anfangs sieht man noch jene geschnürten Taillen der Damen, jene Forteressen auf ihren Häuptern, jene Wolkenfrisuren [...] allmälig simplificirt sich alles; [...] eine Revolution in der Mode entwickelt sich auch während jener großen Volksrevolution [...]. Wir sehen fast alles was den Körper zwängt und beengt ist verschwunden [...]. Natürlich gelockt, oder leicht verschlungen, höchstens mit einigen Blumen oder einem simplen Schmucke durchzogen ist das Haar der Dame, zwanglos schließt sich das Gewand an die Form des Körpers, das einfache Weiß ist die Lieblingsfarbe, denn Simplicität, nicht grelle, überladene Zusammensetzungen liebt die jetzige Mode.[30]

The cultural climate of classicism around 1800 devalued the earlier artifice and the elaborate body-shaping, exaggerating the hour-glass shape of the body, its highly stylized ornamentation and elaborate coloring, and its particular attention to the head that was achieved with elaborate and expansive hairstyles. The highly manipulated body required not only skill, imagination, and creativity to produce its artifice (not to mention the financial means for an appropriate staff) but also a significant amount of discipline to wear. If the new fashion is "zwang- los", by implication, the old fashion exerted a significant amount of force in shaping and molding the body and thus represented a significant disciplining effort. It constrained its wearers to deliberate and moderate movements. It slowed the gait and halted spontaneous unmeasured movements. It elicited certain forms of conduct and social conventions (for example, women not only needed assistance with putting the dress on but also with performing certain activities such as retrieving a dropped item).

The new fashion eliminates some of these external restrictions. I would contend that this does not imply that less discipline is directed at the body but that the graceful body has to internalize and naturalize discipline. The disciplining force is refocused on the body itself and its transformation to approximate the ideal, as we will see. The terminology "simplifiziert", "simple", "Simplicität", "natürlich", "zwanglos", "einfache", and the multiple use of "leicht" suggests a return to a beauty that is closer to nature. Yet the contributor also makes clear that this is not a naive revealing of the "natural" body but a highly artificial presentation of an aestheticized body modeled after the cultural ideal, the revival of Greek antiquity ("die erneuerte Griechin").[31] Not unlike Schiller's paradoxical axiom in his philosophy of history, his concept of aesthetic education (or socialization) according to which the lost unity of the self through civilization and consciousness can be recovered on a higher level of self-conscious perfection,[32] the natural beauty of the body of the original Greek that culture and civilization had destroyed can be recreated on a higher level with the help of cultural achievements and knowledge.

---

[30] Anonymous: Ueber die Veränderung der Mode und das Resultat derselben für den gegenwärtigen Zeitpunkt. In: *Journal*. II. Pp. 26-31, here pp. 27-29.
[31] Ibid. II. P. 29.
[32] Schiller: *Ueber die ästhetische Erziehung*. 6. Brief. P. 328. Schneider. P. 210.

Hair and dress have to envelop the head and body in graceful waves and fluid uninterrupted lines, as in the paintings by Angelika Kauffmann and Elisabeth Louise Vigée Le Brun (Ill. 5). Earlier more elaborate and artificial ornamentation is replaced with ornamentation that suggests natural qualities (flowers, leaves, seashells, etc.), not with a complete lack of ornamentation.

In other texts more detail is added that provides information on how the ideal is achieved. These descriptions (and occasional illustrations) were intended to serve as models to be imitated, as the *Journal* saw itself not only as a creator of good taste for the middle class but also as an economic facilitator, namely, as a more economical and speedier replacement of the earlier fashion dolls, which had modeled the latest styles. While the fashion dolls were largely a phenomenon of the nobility and the European courts, the visual representation and descriptions in the periodical press were a more suitable means of information for the emerging middle class as fashion consumers. As a monthly, the *Journal* could react quickly to new trends from within the German States or abroad. In a contribution reporting on the latest fashion from Paris (1807), the task and effort of creating the seemingly natural becomes reinforced. In this contribution, all the main issues that dominate the discussion of the ideal of naturalness in dress are assembled, the construction of the ideal, the precondition of a beautiful body to achieve this ideal, and the warning of excesses:

> Bei alle dem muß ich bekennen, daß ich nie und nirgends noch so schöne Toiletten sah, als diesen Frühling. Der Schnitt der Kleider ist dem Körper angemessen, die Gürtel bezeichnen sanft unter dem Busen die Rundung und das Ebenmaß der Taille, und das faltenlose Kleid, dessen schräge Blätter nur im Rücken einige Falten haben, schmiegt sich gehorsam um die körperliche Fom und huldigt den Naturschönheiten, indem es keine Ansprüche darauf macht, sie zu verhüllen oder zu ersetzen. [...] Sobald nicht transparente Stoffe, tiefe Ausschnitte u. dergl. eine Frau halbnackt, oder so gut als ganz nackt erscheinen lassen, wüßte ich nicht zu tadeln, daß man das Werk der Natur nicht durch affektirte Verstellung verhunzen und beschimpfen will. Wann hat je die Schaamhaftigkeit verlangt, daß die Frauen sich in ein Futteral stecken? Solche Ziererei kommt wohl der Häßlichkeit zu statten, die einen gesunden Vorwand zum Verbergen eines ungesunden Körperbaues sucht; aber die schöne schlanke Gestalt des reizenden Weibes, sittsam umkleidet, ohne verstellt zu seyn, ist doch gewiß der freundlichste Anblick der Natur.[33]

This kind of dress claims to envelop the body without binding or altering its "natural" shape and neither covers flaws nor replaces less desirable features with more desirable ones, for example, through body shaping or the assistance of undergarments adding or taking away volume. Instead it flatteringly and modestly veils and heightens the beauty of the slender body of the virtuous woman, representing the most favorable image in nature. Especially in its last sentence this

---

[33] Anonymous: Neue Moden aus Paris. In: *Journal.* III. Pp. 69-70, here p. 70.

contribution creates a complex yet not logically stringent and not causally conclusive discursive intermingling of artifice and nature. This rhetorical strategy of argumentation by association is quite typical for the *Journal* and is to be expected as the *Journal* offers a wide range of viewpoints in its contributions and presents itself as a discussion forum by offering conflicting opinions on especially controversial topics, such as the desirability of tight-lacing (discussed below) or the advisability of introducing a national costume to strengthen national pride. Despite its claim of the "naturalness" of these body-enhancing fashions, the contribution reveals the features of the dress that create it. The description reveals the elements that create the "look"– the position of the belt, the choice of fabric, its color, cut, and ability to drape and flow well – and initiates the readership in the art of achieving the seemingly natural. It draws further attention to the cultural "constructedness" of the seemingly natural.

The classical ideal as it is interpreted in fashion criticism is not a return to a naive revealing of a seemingly natural body but a highly artificial re-creation of a *semblance* of the natural that heightens the beauty of the material body. It is culture and its achievements, like the soft fabrics and careful discipline, that produce the seeming naturalness of the body.

Critics of classical fashion point to its excesses that no longer suggest graceful "cultured nature" but a falling back to uncivilized nakedness:

> Die junge Dame [...] schwebt so zephyrlich in rothen geschnürten griechischen *Sandalen* einher. Den ganzen Contour ihres schönen, oder nicht schönen Körpers, umhüllet *so wenig Stoff*, daß man glauben sollte, sie sey nur in gewebte Nebel und Farben der Morgenröthe gekleidet, und kenne wenigstens das Bedürfniß eines Hemdes, worauf unsre Mütter und Großmütter noch etwas hielten, ganz und gar nicht. Ihr ganzer Anzug, die *Straußenfeder* und *Bandeaux* auf dem Kopfe mitgerechnet, wiegt nicht mehr als 18 Loth [...]. Sie ist so ganz von allem Irdischen befreyt, da sie durchaus die schöne *Contoure des Halbnackten* durch keine angehängte *Tasche* unterbrechen will.[34]

To this critic, the form-revealing flowing fabrics are so light and sheer, mere hints of fabric, that they appear as transparent clouds veiling the body. Here simplicity is interpreted as an unpleasant reduction of the amount of fabric used and its opaqueness and its consequent lack of the ability to cover the body adequately. Here the beautiful silhouette created by the naturally draped gown ("schmiegt sich gehorsam um die körperliche Form"[35]) praised in the first contribution is not read as an allusion to the classical nudes but instead suggests a lack of civilizational discipline.

Another critic condemns this semi-nakedness as immoral by connecting the extremes of naturalness – nakedness – with prostitution as the ultimate marker of uncivilized behavior:

[34] Anonymous: Moden von 1801. In: *Journal.* II. Pp. 67-68.
[35] Anonymous: Neue Moden aus Paris. In: *Journal.* III. P. 70.

Die bisherige Griechische, eigentliche *Pariserinnen*‑Tracht aber, mit dem offenen Busen, dem entblößten Nacken und Rücken, dem *ganz* kurzen, durchsichtigen Aermel, den wenigen, jede Form bezeichnenden Falten, sey nicht bloß zur Auszeichnung der öffentlichen Mädchen denselben *verstattet*, sondern diesen sogar ganz ausdrücklich von der Polizei, als der ihren Neigungen und ihrer Lebensweise so angemessenen Tracht, *anbefohlen.*[36]

Here, the natural is labeled as immoral semi-naked exhibitionism, which reveals those body parts (the bosom, neck, back, and arms) that should remain covered for the sake of modesty and morality. While the allusion to the beautiful body and its erotic attraction was considered desirable to some (as represented in the image of the lightly veiled nude in the tradition of antique statuary) to others its exaggeration suggested uncivilized sexuality (the sexualized nakedness of the prostitute). In modern German body criticism distinguishing between "Leib" and "Körper", "Leib" represents "das Fremde, Ausgegrenzte und nicht vom Diskurs erfaßte".[37] Art historians traditionally make a similar distinction between the naked body and the nude; the latter represents the highly conventionalized and idealized body based on the cultural ideal of natural beauty ushered in by the Enlightenment and perfected by neo-classicism: "The nude remains the most complete example of the transformation of matter into form [...]. The category of the naked describes the body outside of cultural representation".[38] This distinction echoes Schiller's aesthetic education, where he discusses that in art, matter is dissolved into form[39] in the beautiful body. The contributions in the *Journal* make it clear that exaggeration of the body-revealing fashion resists the body's transformation into an aesthetic form, which pushed naturalness beyond the limits of the beautiful.

These contributions also imply that only the beautiful body can be enhanced by this body-revealing fashion with its celebration of naturalness. Bodies that do not measure up might as well be hidden in vestimentary encasements ("in ein Futteral stecken").[40] The other voices merely hint at the fact that a less-than-perfect body in body-revealing fashions is not a desirable sight.[41] This argument places new pressure on the shaping and designing, the "construction", of the material body. The self is not only called upon to design a "natural" body with clothing, but also to alter the shape of the material body itself to approximate the ideal. If the garments no longer play a significant role in shaping the body, the body proper needs to be transformed.

---

[36] W. v. Ch.: Was Sitte, was Mode sey, oder Teutscher Frauen Volkstracht. In: *Journal*. III. Pp. 47-54, here p. 52.

[37] Gabriele Genge: Einleitung. In: *Sprachformen des Körpers in Kunst und Wissenschaft*. Ed. by Gabriele Genge. Tübingen 2000. Pp. 9-15, here p. 15.

[38] Kenneth Clarke: *The Nude. A Study of Ideal Art*. London 1956. P. 23.

[39] Schiller: *Ueber die ästhetische Erziehung*. 22. Brief.

[40] Anonymous: Neue Moden aus Paris. In: *Journal*. III. P. 70.

[41] Anonymous: Moden von 1801. In: *Journal*. II. Pp. 67-69, here p. 67.

The discussions on the corset or tight-lacing highlight this change. The *Journal* reports on the debates on tight-lacing that occupied the medical establishments, moralists and the wearers of the body-shaping corset.[42] In the name of health and reason, which was equated with allowing the body to remain in its "natural" state, the (male) medical establishment argued for abolishing the corset. The *Journal* engages in the debate because of what it calls female protests against the abolishment of the corset. One of the contributions argues that women do not wish to be set free against their will[43] and cites the following reasons for keeping the corset: "Die Schnürbrust hält den Leib ohne Anstrengung in einer geraden Stellung, sie schützt ihn im Winter gegen Erkältung, und ohne sie wird der schlanke Wuchs nicht gebildet, der doch nach dem Urtheile der Männer ein wesentliches Stück der Schönheit ausmacht".[44] For the female advocate of the corset, it has practical functions like other garments providing warmth and thus aiding in keeping the body healthy. Furthermore, its rigid structure assists in maintaining good posture, which, according to the medical knowledge of the time, is an important prerequisite for the unimpeded flow of bodily fluids necessary for good health. The third, aesthetic, argument is most interesting for our context.

The (female) advocate considers the corset necessary to achieve the desired ideal of beauty for women, the slender mid-section and well-defined waist. She suggests that the body does not naturally display this shape but that it is a culturally constructed ideal, which consequently also requires artificial means to achieve it: "Warum erheben die Dichter den schlanken Erlenwuchs, und die leichte Grazien-Gestallt, wenn sie eine vollkommene Schönheit singen? Gebt der Eitelkeit unsres Geschlechts weniger Nahrung! und wer weiß, ob nicht der Mißbrauch des Schnürens von selbst aufhört".[45] She attributes the celebration of ideal – not natural – beauty that masquerades as natural (the metaphor "schlanker Erlenwuchs" associates this ideal of feminine beauty with nature) in culture with the need for artificial means to create it. This argument resists the veiling of the disciplining forces that are required to create seemingly natural beauty.

Another female correspondent argues for the abolishment of the corset also in the name of health. She foregrounds the pain associated with the disciplining force of the corset on the body, molding it into a shape that it does not naturally possess. The discomfort is so severe that it makes its wearer look forward to the short respites at night when the tormentor can be put aside:

> Nie hat wohl ein armer Gefangner in seinem Kerker und Fesseln mehr geseufzt, als ich in dieser unglücklichen Schnürbrust, die mich so preßte, engte und peinigte, daß ich jeden Abend dem Himmel recht herzlich dankte, wenigstens bis den andern

---

[42] Anonymous: Die Schnürbrust vor einem weiblichen Tribunale. In: *Journal*. I. Pp. 107-109, here p. 108.

[43] Anonymous: Vertheidigung der Schnürbrüste. In: *Journal*. I. Pp. 110-113, here p. 110.

[44] Ibid. P. 112.

[45] Ibid. P. 113.

59

Morgen davon befreyet zu seyn, damit alle die Schwielen und rothen Flecken die sie mir den Tag über gedrückt, die Nacht hindurch Zeit hatten sich zu erhohlen [...].[46]

For strategic reasons, I would contend, so that she does not have to question the celebration of the natural as beautiful, she argues that the corset forces its wearer into an artificial puppet- or automaton-like appearance ("hölzerne[..] Puppen ohne Grazie und Reiz").[47] According to this argument, artifice can only create artifice. It can only hinder or hurt a healthy body and thus should only be used to strengthen an infirm body.[48] Juxtapositioning the healthy and the unhealthy (or infirm) body paves the way for direct intervention on the site of the body itself. By associating the healthy body with the body in its "natural" state and equating both with beauty, the stage is set for a direct manipulation of the body so that it takes on a certain shape "naturally" (i.e., without artificial contraptions like the corset or tight-lacing). However, if the transformation of the body itself was unsuccessful or impossible, late eighteenth-century fashion – despite its emphasis on naturalness – nevertheless relied on prostheses to make the body conform to the classical ideal, for example by adding inserts for men's white stockings so that they would emulate the muscular calves of marble statuary.[49] Although our contributors do not mention this particular body-shaping practice, it renders the cultural "constructed-ness" of the "natural" even more obvious.

The dominant popular discourse of the time favored self-modification through practices such as diet, exercise, and cosmetics to replace external body shaping techniques. This interest in self-modification finds its expression especially in the debates on health, which we associate, for example, with the dietetic health reforms of Christoph Wilhelm Hufeland (1762-1836), the most famous physician of the neo-classical period[50]. His state-of-the-art knowledge found entry into the popular discourse with his influential medical treatise, *Makrobiotik, oder die Kunst das Leben zu verlängern* (1794; 2nd ed.) which was a comprehensive primer for reasonable living, and with his many contributions to the periodical press of his time, for example to the *Journal des Luxus und der Moden*. Hufeland's contribution was enlisted to advocate personal hygiene, frequent bathing, laundering, and outdoor exercise as a means to achieve optimum health[51] and, by implication, beauty. As the *Journal* makes clear repeatedly, a healthy body is the prerequisite for beauty: "Gesundheit [... ist] das einzige und unfehlbarste Schönheitsmittel".[52]

---

[46] C. S.: Responsium über die Schnürbrüste. In: *Journal*. I. Pp. 114-17, here p. 115.
[47] Ibid. P. 116.
[48] Ibid. P. 117.
[49] Erika Thiel: *Geschichte des Kostüms. Die historische Mode von den Anfängen bis zur Gegenwart*. Wilhelmshafen 1980. P. 291 and MacLeod: Klauer. Pp. 80-81 endnote 1.
[50] Klaus Pfeifer: *Medizin der Goethezeit: Christoph Wilhelm Hufeland und die Heilkunst des 18. Jahrhunderts*. Köln 2000. In passim.
[51] Erinnerung an die Bäder und ihre Wiedereinführung in Teutschland nebst einer Anweisung zu ihrem Gebrauch und bequemer Einrichtung derselben in den Wohnhäusern vom Hrn. G. Rth. Hufeland und L. Rth. Bertuch. In: *Journal*. II. Pp. 139-175.
[52] Bertuch: Empfehlung eines Universal-Schönheitsmittels. In: *Journal*. I. Pp. 244-246,

To facilitate these healthful activities, such as bathing, the *Journal* offers a comprehensive approach to lifestyle changes, which discusses the latest technical inventions and provides suggestions as to the integration of the appropriate facilities and furnishings into the household.

Another contributor advocates exercise in the form of the proper use of the spas encouraging as much physical activity as possible (dancing instead of card games, and walks instead of spending excessive time on elaborate dress). The contributor suggests that the *Journal* design a "Baad-Uniform", which would facilitate these activities and was simple and naturally attractive.[53] The comfort and ease of the "Baad-Uniform" eliminates the need for the frequent change of dress to suit the decorum of the various activities that take place at the spa ranging from taking walks and the waters to dinners and evening entertainment. The time saved could, instead, be spent on the healthful activities offered at the spas.

Exercise is recognized as a key to shaping the body that conforms to the ideal of "natural" beauty. Modern science and technology is enlisted to facilitate physical exercise. To make this endeavor more convenient, the *Journal* showcases the "Gymnastikon", an English invention allowing its users to get exercise at home.[54] The contribution alludes to the role that vigorous physical activity played in the creation of natural beauty in Antiquity. Since this ideal is no longer possible in the modern world with its more fragmented sedentary lifestyle, especially in the cold northern climate, a sophisticated technological invention of modern culture, such as the "exercise machine" ("Gymnastikon")[55] for indoor use, has to assist in the creation of the modern healthy and beautiful body.[56]

Furthermore, natural beauty becomes conceptually linked with the new medical knowledge, which focused more on a comprehensive description of healthy living as a form of long term prevention than on quick cures. The beautification of the natural body in fashion in the vein of neo-classicist art criticism overlapped with, and was supported by, the modern medical discourse which devised a strict regimen for a "natural", healthy way of life, creating the scientific underpinning for the bourgeois way of life. Publications such as the *Journal* played a significant role in the dissemination and popularization of this state of the art knowledge of both

---

here p. 244.

[53] Dr. Z** in Br**: Vorschlag zu einer allgemeinen Baad-Uniform für Damen. In: *Journal*. I. Pp. 104-107.

[54] Anonymous: Das neue Gymnastikon. In: *Journal*. II. Pp. 132-137.

[55] "Diese Maschine [...] besteht aus einem aufrechtstehenden Gerüste, gerade groß genug, um einen Menschen zu fassen. Die Bewegung der untern Extremitäten wird durch zwey Tretschemel hervorgebracht, so wie die an den obern Gliedern durch zwey Kurben [cranks] in jeder erforderlichen Tiefe. Diese Kurben werden durch ein Rad bewegt, welches durch ein Band mit einem ähnlichen Rade unten an den Trittschemeln zusammenhängt. Wer also an Händen und Füßen zugleich Bewegung zu haben wünscht, darf nur durch das Auftreten die Trittschemel in Bewegung setzen. [...] man erhält im Ganzen hierdurch ebendie Bewegung, die man durch einen Spaziergang von 2 bis 10 englischen Meilen in *einer* Stunde erhalten könnte". Ibid. Pp. 134-135.

[56] Ibid. P. 133.

the aesthetic and the medical discourses.

The foundation of a beautiful or attractive body is health, and health is no longer seen as a divine gift or fate but can to some degree be manipulated by the subject. The self is called on to make use of most up-to-date (medical) knowledge to actively intervene in assuring optimal health: "Die Mittel, diesen natürlichen und nothwendigen Zustand [der Schönheit] zu erhalten, müssen der Natur gemäß seyn".[57] The ideal, the beautiful "natural" body, is not a fixed pre-existing one but is seen as a cultural task to be achieved. The body can be improved by a healthy lifestyle. Consequently, suggestions are made for the proper use of clothing. The *Journal* includes information on the latest scientific findings regarding the effect of certain materials (linen, silk, wool, cotton, fur, etc.), the most suitable use of particular items of clothing (hats, cravats, stocking, shoes, etc.), and forms of body-shaping (like powder and pomade) on the health and well-being of the body.[58] These deliberate measures of improvement suggest a degree of agency and power that the individual has at his/her disposal to alter his/her own body. At the same time, the body is subjected to a rigorous disciplining regimen that included the prescription for moderation in sleeping, food, drink, and stimulants. This was coupled with the advocacy of regular physical exercise in the fresh air, adequate living conditions, and varied activities. This system of moderation disciplining the body was also extended to the psyche and the emotional stability of the individual.[59] Nature is subjected to reason as the materiality of the self is subjected to reasoned life choices. Not unlike the fashion discourse, the medical discourse made the steps of the regiment for a healthy disciplined lifestyle explicit. In the name of achieving the ideal of "natural" health and beauty, the body had to be subjected to a significant disciplining effort.

To sum up: The discourse of fashion surrounding the neo-classicist ideal of "natural" beauty makes apparent that the "natural" is a semblance of naturalness, a naturalness that merely hides its own artifice. Not unlike the Schillerian grace this represents the staging of nature by a self-empowering human subject yearning to perfect itself precisely in that "which is beyond its controlling the very uncontrollable, manipulating the body's contingency".[60] However, as the fashion discourse (with the assistance of the medical discourse) discusses the strategies and techniques to achieve "natural" beauty, it resists the classicist veiling of the civilizing forces designing the self and its body. Fashion and the fashion discourse dismantle the "natural" as the culturally constructed product of modern self-discipline.

---

[57] Anonymous: Mittel, die weibliche Schönheit zu erhalten. In: *Journal.* I. Pp. 228-233, here p. 232.

[58] Ueber die Kleider in medicinischer Rücksicht. In: *Journal.* I. Pp. 162-182 and Hufeland: Medicinisches Gutachten über die Benutzung der Wolle zur unmittelbaren Bekleidung der Haut. In: *Journal.* II. Pp. 139-175.

[59] Robert Tobin: *Doctor's Orders: Goethe and Enlightenment Thought.* Lewisburg 2001. P. 118.

[60] Schneider. P. 212.

Ill. 1:

Journal des Luxus und der Moden 1787

Ill. 2:

Journal des Luxus und der Moden 1789

Ill. 3:

Journal des Luxus und der Moden 1801

Ill. 4:

Journal des Luxus und der Moden 1802

Illustrations 1 to 4 are courtesy of the Bertuch Collection in the library of the
Friedrich Schiller Universität Jena.

Ill. 5:

Varvara Ivanovna Narishkin, née Ladomirsky (1800).
Columbus Museum of Art, Ohio

Elisabeth Louise Vigée Le Brun "Varvara Ivanovna Narishkin" 1800.
With the permission of the Columbus Museum of Art, Ohio.

Marjanne E. Goozé

Posing for Posterity: The Representations and Portrayals of Henriette Herz as "Beautiful Jewess"

This essay examines the topos of the "beautiful Jewess" through an analysis of the portraits of the salonnière Henriette Herz as gendered performance. Investigated is Herz's own complicity in these representations and their relation to her own memoirs as a process of self-fashioning. Two poems and two satires that refer to Herz are also treated in this context, the satires standing in contradistinction to the iconography of the "beautiful Jewess".

In the eyes of all her contemporaries, Henriette Herz, née de Lemos (1764-1847), was extraordinarily beautiful. Even as a child, her beauty placed her in a public position as a representative of the enlightened Jewish community in Berlin.[1] In her first memoir, set down in the 1820s and narrated in the form of a pietist autobiography, Herz attributes her vanity to the flattery and attention she received at the young age of eight and nine.[2] She had fully blossomed by age twelve: "man sah als schönes Kind, das für sein Alter ungemein gross war, mit Wohlgefallen auf mich".[3] As she matured, her body became an object of admiration, an object for both female and male artists from which they projected an image of Jewish female beauty.

This chronological consideration of the portrayals of Henriette Herz has a two-fold aim. The first is to offer a historical survey of the artistic representations of her as a "beautiful Jewess". The examination of the portraits highlights both the representation of Herz in terms of the topos and explores how such representations disclose certain historical and biographical truths about Henriette Herz as an individual. Also addressed are two poems and two satires that refer to her. They counterbalance the idealized aesthetic of Jewish female beauty found in the portraits. Herz's fame as a renowned beauty and

---

[1] Henriette Herz: Jugenderinnerungen von Henriette Herz. Ed. by Heinrich Hahn. In: *Mittheilungen aus dem Litteraturarchive* in Berlin 1 (1896). Pp. 139-184, here pp. 145, 148-50. Herz's two memoirs, as well as two collections of her memoirs and letters, all bear remarkably similar titles. Therefore they will be cited here under the names of the editors. The two most significant are Heinrich Hahn and J. Fürst. Hahn published her handwritten memoir in 1896. Fürst posthumously published her memoir based on her manuscript, letters, other documents, and her conversations with him. The first edition appeared in 1850; a second, expanded edition was published in 1858.

[2] Hahn. Pp. 145, 150.

[3] Hahn. P. 159.

salonnière[4] spurred satirical drawings and texts; they demonstrate how the public role she played in Berlin society incited negative responses. Both the portraits and satires contribute to the understanding of the motif of the "beautiful Jewess" as it manifested itself during the salon era.

The second aim of this survey bases itself on the supposition that Herz was more than just a passive object of the artist's gaze. As the subject of the portraits, she exerted some influence over her own depiction. Each important painting, drawing, and sculpture of Herz initiates questions such as how she and the artist represent the beautiful Jewess, and to what extent Herz's image serves as a reflection of her own personality or as a cultural and gendered performance. Assessing how Herz viewed these works is difficult, because she did not provide us with her own evaluation of these works of art in either of her two memoirs or in her extant letters. Instead, the contemporary observer must herself "read" the portraits and the written record for evidence of self-fashioning – for traces of her participation in the creation of her image.

Therefore, in this essay, the analysis is undertaken by employing a kind of double vision. The initial gaze at these representations takes place from the standpoint of the outside observer. Secondly, I venture, not without some risk, to attribute to Herz herself some of the responsibility for the resulting portraits. Through this practice of double vision it should be possible both to avoid a one-sided reading of Herz as an exploited object of Christian bias and to eschew an equation of her image with an essentialized self – that is, to perceive Herz as an embodied self, but not fully to equate self and body. Due to the absence of textual evidence, it remains impossible precisely to determine to what extent Herz herself was conscious of the symbol of the "beautiful Jewess" and of the gendered representation of Jews in German culture. However, as a tolerated Jew in Prussia, as the wife of Markus Herz who had studied with Kant, as a voracious reader, as a student of many languages, and in her role as salonnière, it would have been practically impossible for Henriette Herz to have avoided being confronted with the stereotypes and imagery pertaining to Jews at that time. For this reason, it is important to consider these portrayals of Henriette Herz cognizant of how Christians conceptualized Jewish difference in gendered terms.

Gendered Jews

In studying the symbol of the beautiful Jewess, it is first essential briefly to

---

[4] I have chosen to use the French spelling for the term 'salonnière' as there is no agreement in German or English critical texts. Within quotations, it will appear as printed. The terms 'salon' and 'salonnière' were not used by Herz, Rahel Levin Varnhagen or their guests to characterize themselves or their social activities. Social and literary historians have invoked these terms and, for better or worse, they have taken root.

articulate how Christian Europe has not only a tradition of racializing the (male) Jewish body, but also of sexualizing cultural or racial difference.[5] Sander Gilman, in his books *The Jew's Body* and *Jewish Self-Hatred*, concentrates on the prevalent "image of the Jewish male as female", linking the Jew "with the corrupt nature of woman", with the sin of Eve.[6] The European philosophical mind-body dualism that marks the disembodied mind as masculine and inscribes the body as feminine, clashes with the Jewish tradition's "very insistence on embodiedness", as Daniel Boyarin points out in *Unheroic Conduct*, his examination of Jewish masculinity.[7] While Boyarin privileges this differently gendered performance by Jewish males, he never ignores its consequences for Jewish women. Anti-Semitic feminization of the Jewish male leaves little or no room for women. Ann Pellegrini points out how Gilman's correction of this stereotype leads him to ally masculinity and race, and femininity and gender: "One consequence of this separation of masculinity and race, on the one side, and femininity and gender, on the other, is that the Jewish woman cannot appear in Gilman's analysis except in drag: as a Jewish man *or* as a 'whitened' and presumptively Gentile woman. *All Jews are womanly, but no women are Jews*".[8] "[Y]et," as Pellegrini astutely observes, "the Jewish female, no less than the Jewish male, is articulated through discourses of race and gender. [...] Jewishness – as performatively constituted and publically performed – clearly needs to be thought through the female Jewish body, no less than through the male".[9] The gendered performance of the beautiful Jewess is a locus for analyzing such intersections of "race and gender". As shall be shown, Henriette Herz's gendered performance demonstrates both her awareness of this topos and perhaps her own manipulation of it.

The Beautiful Jewess

The topos of the beautiful Jewess has received surprisingly little general critical attention. Florian Krobb's work, *Die schöne Jüdin*, investigates this figure in German prose texts. The beautiful Jewess, who converts out of love

---

[5] Ann Pellegrini: Whiteface Performances. "Race", Gender, and Jewish Bodies. In: *Jews and Other Differences. The New Jewish Cultural Studies*. Ed. by Jonathan Boyarin and Daniel Boyarin. Minneapolis 1997. Pp. 108-149, here p. 108.

[6] Sander L. Gilman: *Jewish Self-Hatred. Anti-Semitism and the Hidden Language of the Jews*. Baltimore 1986. P. 75.

[7] Daniel Boyarin: *Unheroic Conduct. The Rise of Heterosexuality and the Invention of the Jewish Man*. Berkeley 1997. P. 8. This essay relies on both Gilman's and Boyarin's analyses of how Christian Europe sexualizes Jewish male identity as feminine. A thorough exploration of the differences between them lies beyond the scope of this study. I do, however, concur with Pellegrini's critique of Gilman.

[8] Pellegrini. P. 118.

[9] Pellegrini. Pp. 109-110.

for a Christian man, conforms to the character ideals of her time.[10] She reconfirms, especially during the age of Enlightenment, the presumption that physical beauty reflects inner goodness. But in spite of this presumption, the beauty of the Jewess still signifies difference. In his 1946 essay on anti-Semitism Jean-Paul Sartre remarked: "There is in the words 'a beautiful Jewess' a very special sexual signification, one quite different from that contained in the words 'beautiful Rumanian', 'beautiful Greek', or 'beautiful American', for example. This phrase carries an aura of rape and massacre".[11] Moreover, other European women considered beautiful, such as Poles and Italians, are identified by nationality; only Jews and Gypsies are linked to a "people".[12]

Jewish beauty is subject to violation because it is depicted as different than European beauty. The Jewish woman, like Rebecca in Walter Scott's *Ivanhoe*, has dark hair and eyes; her coloring may be described as "oriental" and her build as classically Greek.[13] She may be seen as a "natural" creature, existing outside of her purportedly denatured community,[14] leading to an essentialized or even a racialized view of the Jewish female. This topos objectifies because it arises outside of Jewish culture.[15] Remarkably, none of the portraits of Herz link sexuality with the threat of violence. The beautiful Jewess can represent the exceptional Jew – the willing convert to Christian beliefs and mores. She also poses a challenge to the prevailing aesthetic ideal through her differently signified beauty. 18th-century aestheticians believed, however, that Jews were themselves incapable of appreciating this ideal.[16]

Henriette de Lemos as Hebe

> Dies ist die holde, muntre Hebe!
> Wer sah der Götter Abbild je,
> So ganz im feinsten Reizgewebe
> Und schöner noch als Pasithe?[17]

[10] Florian Krobb: *Die schöne Jüdin. Jüdische Frauengestalten in der deutschsprachigen Erzählliteratur vom 17. Jahrhundert bis zum Ersten Weltkrieg.* Tübingen 1993. P. 41.

[11] Jean-Paul Sartre: *Anti-Semite and Jew.* Trans. by George J. Becker. New York 1948. *Réflexions sur la Question Juive.* Paris 1946. P. 48.

[12] Krobb. P. 19.

[13] Krobb. P. 51.

[14] Krobb. P. 94.

[15] It is not within the scope of this study to address this topos or Jewish female beauty in terms of a historically Jewish aesthetic. Suffice it to say that the Jewish elite of Herz's era were not unaware of these characterizations.

[16] Gilman: *Jewish Self-Hatred.* P. 119.

[17] Qtd. in Henriette Herz: *Henriette Herz. Ihr Leben und ihre Zeit.* Ed. by Hans Landsberg. Weimar 1913. P. 155.

Thus begins the first stanza of a song attributed to Markus Herz's colleague Aaron Gomperz[18] and written in honor of his wedding to Henriette de Lemos on December 1, 1779. The song, which also goes on to compare her to Juno,[19] was clearly composed in reference to the 1778 portrait of her painted by the renowned portraitist Anna Dorothea Lisiewski Therbusch (1721-1782) (see Ill. 1). She was a member of the French Académie Royale who had been commissioned to paint portraits of the Prussian royal family and was known as a portraitist and painter of mythological scenes. She also painted portraits of those in the Lessing-Ramler circle.[20] In this painting, the 14-year-old Henriette poses as Hebe. The daughter of Hera and Zeus, she is the goddess of youth. Also known as Ganymeda, Hebe was cupbearer to the gods until she was dismissed, because she fell down while pouring nectar and exposed herself. Ensconced in colorful flowers, Henriette de Lemos, who had been engaged to Markus Herz since she was twelve and a half years old, seems to be exhibiting herself to the desirous male gaze. Rather than representing Hebe as beautifully chaste, the portrait appears to catch her on the verge of indecent exposure. The off-the-shoulder décolleté hints at the revelation of the areola of one breast. This is a mature body, depicted in flowing, rounded lines: the hips are full; the curved arm and shoulder plump; the slightly parted legs between which the flower garland and the drapery fall suggest sexual availability; the long, flowing dark hair frames the face and the body. The head appears to be proportionally rather small.[21] Looking straight at the viewer, the dark eyes return the viewer's gaze. There is no trace of shyness or modesty. This teenager appears self-conscious of her own beauty.

Is the painting merely a stylized portrait typical of 18th-century classicism? Many women in England and France also had their portraits painted as Hebe.[22] Or does the painting also serve as a representation of the beautiful Jewess? As has been previously noted, the allusion to classical antiquity in describing Jewish female beauty is a common aspect in the iconography of the topos. Although the painting employs a motif popular with many women of the time, this portrait was not commissioned by the young girl herself. In

[18] Martin L. Davies: *Identity or History? Marcus Herz and the End of the Enlightenment*. Detroit 1995. P. 272.

[19] Qtd. in Landsberg. P. 155.

[20] Ludwig Geiger: *Berlin 1688-1840. Geschichte des geistigen Lebens der preussischen Hauptstadt*. 2 vols. 1893-95. Aalen 1987. Vol. 1. Pp. 691-693.

[21] J. Fürst (ed.): *Henriette Herz. Ihr Leben und ihre Erinnerungen*. 2nd ed. Berlin: 1858. P. 31. This observation is made by Herz's editor in his introduction to her memoir. See also: Fanny Lewald: *Meine Lebensgeschichte*. Ed. by Gisela Brinker-Gabler. Frankfurt/M. 1980. P. 232.

[22] Liliane Weissberg: Weibliche Körperschaften: Bild und Wort bei Henriette Herz. In: *Von einer Welt in die andere. Jüdinnen im 19. und 20. Jahrhundert*. Ed. by Jutta Dick and Barbara Hahn. Vienna 1993. Pp. 71-92, here p. 75.

posing, the as yet unmarried Henriette becomes an eroticized symbol of Jewish female sexuality couched within the familiar iconography of Greek mythology. The painting, which was later displayed in her marital home, the site of her salon, had both a private and a semi-public function.[23] As a portrait of his young wife, it offered itself to the loving gaze of Markus Herz. In this way, its eroticism falls within the sanctioned bounds of marital sexuality. The mythological subject also represents Markus Herz's and the Berlin Jewish Enlightenment's (*Haskala*)[24] ties to the ideals of the Enlightenment: he was a student of Kant and an author of philosophical works. Within the context of the semi-public sphere of the salon, other admirers of Henriette Herz viewed the painting. For these mostly Christian and male viewers, the Jewish body on display both "in person" and in this work of art performs socially and artistically: as a salonnière she facilitated social and intellectual interaction; as a beautiful woman, she provided aesthetic pleasure. These performances at the same time confirm and undermine sexual and cultural stereotypes. As a "classical" beauty, Herz conforms to aesthetic ideals, thereby encouraging men, such as Count Alexander von Dohna, to fall in love with her and to even propose marriage after Markus's death. But for most viewers and salon guests, the classical imagery cannot completely cover up her difference as a Jew, and indeed serves as an iconographic reference to the topos of the beautiful Jewess. Moreover, the erotic pose reinforces the impression of the female Jewish body as an object of sexual availability. The elderly Herz reflected back in her memoirs on how, at even this young age, she was flattered by the frequent male advances instigated by her renowned beauty. Her discussion of these male attentions is framed by the confessional mode of repenting of her sin of vanity. Even though she was only fourteen at the time she sat for the painting, she had to have been aware of the revealing nature of her attire and of her pose. She was certainly conscious of the effect she had on men. In her first confessional memoir, she blamed herself for attracting these men, because she did not know how to behave properly so as to keep them at a distance.[25] The painting's classical reference permitted this exhibition of her physical charms. It may be surmised that the repentance expressed in the memoir accurately reflects her youthful enjoyment of her own beauty.

Later observers disagree in their interpretations of the Therbusch painting. Peter Seibert concludes that Herz, both in her portraits and in the eyes of contemporary observers, simultaneously is seen as representing a "klassisches Schönheitsideal" and the topos of the beautiful Jewess.[26] For Angelika Wesenberg, Herz sits "in konventioneller, erlernter Haltung da, ein

---

[23] Lewald. P. 233.

[24] David Sorkin: *The Transformation of German Jewry 1780-1840*. Oxford. 1987.

[25] Hahn. P. 183.

[26] Peter Seibert: *Der literarische Salon. Literatur und Geselligkeit zwischen Aufklärung und Vormärz*. Stuttgart 1993. Pp. 124-125.

braves junges Mädchen".[27] Martin Davies, who writes about her in his biography of Markus Herz and in an article devoted to the portraits, sees a contrast in the symbolism: the "naïve expression" contrasts with the sensuality of the bare shoulder and hair that are a reminder of her future role as Herz's wife.[28] In addition, he claims the portrait also symbolizes Eve and the Earth mother, pointing to an "anticipation of fecundity".[29] Although he provides no justification for this reading, the flowers and the fullness of the body may have prompted this interpretation. Davies helpfully situates the Therbusch work within the context of Kant's and Schiller's aesthetics, elucidating how through beautiful appearance women "exert moral influence".[30]

Liliane Weissberg has written extensively about some of the portraits. Her readings are valuable for the emphasis she places on them as indices of aspiring Jewish acculturation and emancipation. Weissberg asserts that Herz's social position as a Jew without civil rights could not justify such a portrait: only "Schönheit adelt sie zur mythologischen Figur".[31] In this reading, however, Weissberg overlooks a tradition of contemporary portraits of fashion-conscious Jewish women who, bolstered by emancipatory hopes, had themselves depicted as classical nymphs and Roman ladies.[32] For this reason, Weissberg also contends that Herz's beauty is not represented as specifically Jewish: "Herz's beauty is that of Greece".[33] Yet, her reading of the painting emphasizes the particularly Jewish elements. In traditional renditions Hebe offers the cup to an eagle symbolizing Jupiter, but in Christian iconography the eagle symbolizes rebirth through baptism. Therbusch omits the eagle, also the symbol of Prussia. So rather than offering the wine to Jupiter or to a male symbol, she is perhaps offering it to her husband, as the sharing of wine is part of the Jewish marriage ceremony.[34] The omission indicates Herz's Judaism and lack of civil rights. I would also add that she holds the cup not as an offering, but as if she is about to drink from it herself.

In this way, the portrait appears self-contained: the lines of the body and

---

[27] Angelika Wesenberg: Anton Graff. Bildnis Henriette Herz, 1792. *Museumspädagogik/Besucherdienst*. Berlin 1992. P. 1.

[28] Davies: *Identity or History?* P. 148.

[29] Martin L. Davies: Portraits of a Lady: Variations on Henriette Herz (1764-1847). In: *Women Writers of the Age of Goethe* 5 (1992). Pp. 45-74, here pp. 46-47.

[30] Davies: Portraits. P. 52.

[31] Weissberg: Weibliche Körperschaften. P. 74.

[32] Pauline Paucker: Bildnisse jüdischer Frauen 1789-1991: Klischee und Wandel. In: *Von einer Welt in die andere. Jüdinnen im 19. und 20. Jahrhundert*. Ed. by Jutta Dick and Barbara Hahn. Vienna 1993. Pp. 29-46, here p. 30.

[33] Liliane Weissberg: Henriette Herz Remembers. A Jewish Woman's Memoirs. In: *Studies on Voltaire and the Eighteenth Century* 304 (1992). Pp. 844-847, here p. 847.

[34] Weissberg: Weibliche Körperschaften. Pp. 76-77.

the objects form a circle. Although revealing and outward looking, Herz appears, in the final analysis, to be in charge of her body and her world, grasping the flower garland and the cup. Perhaps this is attributable to the female artist, but it is also indicative of the mature Herz's reputed physical and sexual restraint. The body is offered up for the viewer's appreciative gaze, but only one viewer will be granted its sensual and sexual pleasures, and that is her husband, Markus Herz.

The wedding poem also compares Henriette to Juno and to Pasithea.[35] Also called Aglaia, Pasithea is said to be one of the three Charities who personify beauty and grace; love flowed from their gaze. Gomperz's poem, which also compares the physician and philosopher Markus Herz to Socrates and Hippocrates, reflects the classical models of the Enlightenment.[36] Although they were still religiously observant Jews, the acculturated couple also embody Enlightenment ideals. As the wedding poem phrases it, Henriette's beauty and "Ihr aufgeklärter Verstand" complimented her husband, "den Verehrer / Erhabener Philosophie / Ihn den Gefühlsquellenlehrer / In der Empfindungstheorie!"[37]

At this moment, the ideals of the Berlin Jewish elite converged with those of the broader German and European culture. As a classical beauty, Herz epitomized biblical Jewish beauty for her coreligionists and for an educated Christian public that was open to the idea of civil emancipation for Jews, although the latter usually held the conviction that emancipation would lead to conversion.

"Junoische Gestalt": Johann Gottfried Schadow

The young Johann Gottfried Schadow (1764-1850) frequented the salon of Markus and Henriette Herz, who in the 1780s received guests two evenings a week.[38] A clay bust of Henriette, which broke during firing, was his first known sculpture.[39] Two years later, he completed both a drawing and a bust of her. He also later did an etching of Markus.[40] Schadow's future wife Marianne Devidels was also Jewish and a friend of Henriette's.[41] The 1783 drawing and bust each portray Henriette Herz differently. In the drawing, she appears as an exotic beauty, while the bust evinces what Schadow de-

[35] Davies erroneously reads "Pasithe" as "Pasiphae". Davies: Portraits. P. 48.

[36] Qtd. in Landsberg. P. 155.

[37] Qtd. in Landsberg. P. 154-155.

[38] Qtd. in Henriette Herz: *Henriette Herz in Erinnerungen, Briefen und Zeugnissen.* Ed. by Rainer Schmitz. Frankfurt/M. 1984. P. 411.

[39] Angelika Wesenberg: Zwischen Aufklärung und Frühromantik. Jugendjahre in Berlin. In: *Johann Gottfried Schadow und die Kunst seiner Zeit.* Ed. by Bernhard Maaz. Cologne 1994. Pp. 41-47, here p. 41.

[40] Wesenberg: Zwischen Aufklärung. P. 41.

[41] Hahn. P. 175.

scribed as classical beauty. He praises Herz, "die mit dem fünfzehnten Jahre eine junoische Gestalt erreicht hatte und hierin die weibliche Anmut über-schritt".[42] Schadow's is the first recorded observation describing Herz's form and size as exceeding the accepted aesthetics for female grace and beauty.

The chalk and pencil drawing shows Herz in a modified version of the head covering required of married Jewish women (see Ill. 2). Indeed Herz complains in her memoirs about the uncomfortable "Kopfzeug",[43] which she later exchanged for a wig and soon abandoned altogether.[44] The very long, flowing locks of the Therbusch painting have been shortened and peek out of the turban-like scarf. Her later editor, Hans Landsberg, refers to this por-trayal as "stark antikisierend".[45] Not only revealing her hair, but also her shoulders, Herz seems to be challenging the clothing requirements for Jew-ish matrons: hair, shoulders, elbows, and knees must remain covered. Her face appears in half profile, but again she gazes directly at the viewer. The darkly shaded background highlights her luminescent skin. Even though the over-the-shoulder gaze could be interpreted as a conventional "come hither" pose, here Herz appears less to invite the observer's desire than to be turning her own gaze upon the artist or viewer. In this way, her self-awareness is reflected through Schadow's artistry. He portrays her as an active participant in the creative process.

By virtue of its form alone, the sculpted bust of Herz that Schadow com-pleted in 1783 exhibits classical influence (see Ill. 3). Schadow sold at least six castings of the bust. Purchasers were Markus Herz, Dorothea Mendels-sohn Veit, the painter Johann Friedrich Darbes, Leopold von Göckingk, Graf von Burghoff, and Graf Dohna, all members of her circle.[46] Herz sym-bolizes the goddess Juno, with whom she was often compared. The simple drapery hints at the large body and small head. The 19-year-old posed for him at the home of Schadow's parents and Marianne Devidels was also pre-sent at some of the sittings.[47] In classical style, Herz's luxuriant hair is un-covered. However, unlike the Therbusch painting, and, as we shall see, the famous portrait by Anton Graff, she does not look directly at the viewer. Of course, the three-dimensionality of the object permits the viewer to place himself in her line of sight. Rather than meeting the observer's gaze directly, Herz turns her attention elsewhere. As a depiction of Herz during the initial popularity of her salon, the sculpture is revealing in that it seems to portray her as a listener and observer. There can be no doubt that she was conscious

---

[42] Qtd. In Wesenberg: Graff. P. 2.

[43] Hahn. P. 164.

[44] Hahn. P. 173.

[45] Landsberg. P. 99.

[46] Bernhard Maaz (ed.): *Johann Gottfried Schadow und die Kunst seiner Zeit.* Co-logne 1994. P. 202.

[47] Maaz. P. 202.

of her beauty, but the pose and the concealing drapery show a self-controlled young woman. Here, for the first time, her intelligence as well as her beauty are exhibited.

There is one other known drawing of Herz by Schadow, sketched some years later at a musical salon.[48] In the sketch she appears regally, and the drawing provides a good indication of her statuesque figure. Whether portrayed classically or exotically, Henriette Herz's image represents for her contemporaries and for posterity the ideal of the beautiful Jewess.

Herz's statuesque figure led others to identify her with Juno. She was full-figured and extraordinarily tall. Statues render Juno "as a standing matron of statuesque proportions and severe beauty".[49] First compared to Juno in Gomperz's wedding song, Schadow also refers to her "junoische Gestalt" at age 15. In the 1790s Karl August Böttiger wrote in his diary: "Sie gehört durch ihre kolossalischen Vollkommenheiten zu den stolzen junoischen Schönheiten".[50] Her imposing height and presence, as well as her facial beauty, inspired such remarks. Her personality also contributed to these comparisons. With the Humboldt brothers and others, she founded a *Tugendbund* that had its own statutes and goals of mutual *Bildung*.[51]

The most well-known textual description of her is an acrostic poem by Ludwig Robert, Rahel Levin Varnhagen's brother:

> Junonische Riesin,
> Egypt'sche Marquisin,
> Tugendverübend,
> Treuer, als liebend,
> Entzückt mit Gewalt.
> Hundertfach herzlos,
> Edel und schmerzlos,
> Rüstig und kalt,
> Zu jung für so alt.[52]

Written in 1803 and spelling her name (Jette Herz), she is both Junoesque and "Egyptian". Robert's description highlights the way in which the topos of the beautiful Jewess relies on the imagery of both classical antiquity and the "exotic" east, emphasizing an ancient nobility. For the Romantics, the

---

[48] A photograph of this sketch may be found in Nachum T. Gildal: *Die Juden in Deutschland von der Römerzeit bis zur Weimarer Republik.* Cologne 1997. P. 140.

[49] Juno. www.britannica.com.

[50] Qtd. in Seibert. P. 124.

[51] Fürst. P. 157. See also Marjanne E. Goozé: Introduction and Bibliography: Henriette Herz (1764-1847). In: *Bitter Healing. German Women Writers from 1700 to 1830. An Anthology.* Ed. by Jeannine Blackwell and Susanne Zantop. Lincoln 1990. Pp. 299-300.

[52] Qtd. in Landsberg. P. 65.

Middle East was considered exotic and as the "east". Moreover, Robert offers an amusing, if not uncritical assessment of her character: he alludes to
her *Tugendbund*, plays on her name ("herzlos"), conveys her reputation for
being a good friend but lacking in passion ("Treuer, als liebend"), and reprimands her for not aging gracefully ("Zu jung für so alt") – something
noted by others as well. There is a poignancy to this poem, written when she
was 39. On January 19, 1803, Markus Herz died, leaving her virtually des-
titute. It is possible that "herzlos" refers to his death, but it seems highly
unlikely that Robert would have been so callous as to describe the grieving
widow as "schmerzlos".

Emancipatory Aspirations: Anton Graff's Portrait

The most well-known portrait was completed in 1792 by Anton Graff
(1736-1813) (see Ill. 4). He attained a reputation for painting the academics
and artists of the Enlightenment (Mendelssohn, Spalding, Ramler, Sulzer,
Corona Schröter, Herder, Elisa von der Recke), as well as noblemen and -
women.[53] Markus Herz commissioned the picture of his then 27-year-old
wife. In a letter to Graff (May 5, 1792), Markus thanks him for the work,
referring to it as "Ihr schönes Meisterstück", and noting that it has been
hanging for eight days in his room. He refrains from criticizing the painting,
but mentions how others have commented on how various features resemble
Henriette. He does suggest that Graff might make a few improvements when
he next comes to Berlin – a matter that "mit einem Pinselzuge abzuhelfen
ist".[54] There is no indication that any corrections were ever made. That Markus paid for so many artistic renditions of his wife demonstrates both his
appreciation of her beauty and his love for her. An observer may also ad-
duce from this that she consciously posed, that she participated in her own
portrayal. In these later portraits, it is even more likely that she exercised
some influence on both the pose and her attire.

   Henriette Herz sits angled slightly away from the viewer in this painting
but turns her head so that she looks directly at the observer. Graff's portrait
clearly references Leonardo da Vinci's painting of the *Mona Lisa* (*La Gio-
conda*). The angled position of the body and turn of the head, the placement
of the hands, and even the slight smile are the same as in Leonardo's work.
Yet, the portrait is typical of Graff's work in that he illustrates the individuality of the subject, concentrating on the face. Beate Becker describes his
portraiture technique:

> Nun wird ihm der Körper unwichtig, und er wählt in den meisten Bildnissen den
> ruhig geschlossenen Umriß des Brustbildes.[...] Mit der gleichen eindringlichen
> Charakteristik wie die Augen, die weniger durch ihre Größe, als durch die Le-

---

[53] Wesenberg: Graff. P. 2.
[54] Qtd. in Landsberg. P. 157.

bendigkeit und Intensität des Schauens wirken, wird die Umgebung der Augen gestaltet, die Zeichnung der Brauen, die Wölbung des Lides. Der sprechende Blick sucht Kontakt mit dem Beschauer.[55]

The subject's environment is also omitted;[56] so is the use of strong coloring.[57] As a follower of the Enlightenment, Graff emphasized facial physiognomy as indicative of the subject's character and mind. The rest of the body, even the body of a beautiful woman, is given little importance. Sulzer describes Graff's method, emphasizing the importance Graff placed on capturing the subject's eyes and gaze:

'Ich habe mehr als einmal bemerkt, daß verschiedene Personen, die sich von unserem Graf [sic], der vorzüglich die Gabe hat, die ganze Physiognomie in der Wahrheit darzustellen, haben mahlen [sic] lassen, die scharfen und empfindungsvollen Blicke, die er auf sie wirft, kaum vertragen können, weil jeder bis in das Innere der Seele zu dringen scheinet'.[58]

Ironically, Schadow, who acquired the painting after Herz's death,[59] criticized Graff precisely for his failure to adequately capture her eyes.[60]

The 27-year-old Henriette Herz presided over the most famous salon in Berlin. As depicted here, she is still lovely, but no longer girlish. Fashionably attired, she wears no head covering. She appears comfortable with herself. Herz gazes confidently at the viewer, returning the observer's own gaze with interest and intelligence. The scarf crossed over her bosom conceals rather than reveals her charms. One hand holds her forearm, forming a self-wrapping in the opposite direction as the scarf. This gesture is indicative of Herz's restraint, perhaps confirming Robert's characterization of her as "Treuer, als liebend". The scarf and hand gesture wrap and constrain the body. Only the free flowing curly hair, topped only by a headband, and the smiling lips signify her lively social activities. Not posing as a mythological figure, she represents herself. Herz's self-fashioning, however, speaks to her desire fully to assimilate into the surrounding culture. In his "Bemerkungen eines Reisenden durch die königlich preußischen Staaten", a contemporary observer wrote of the Jewish women in Berlin: "Sehr viele tragen ihre Haare jetzt ebenso wie die Christen und unterscheiden sich auch in der Kleidung nicht von uns. [...] Das schöne Geschlecht der Israeliten spielt in Berlin eine

---

[55] Beate Becker: Einführung. In: *Anton Graff 1736-1812. Ausstellung, Berlin 1963*. Berlin 1963. Pp. 5-16, here p. 11.

[56] Becker. P. 11.

[57] Wesenberg: Graff. P. 2.

[58] Qtd. in Wesenberg: Graff. P. 2.

[59] Maaz. P. 203.

[60] Wesenberg: Graff. P. 2.

große Rolle".[61] However, the pursuits of these women also prompted criticism of "Schöngeisterei".[62]

This emphasis on the emancipatory aspirations of Jewish women reflects the realities of the lives of the Jewish elite of Berlin – the men received religious education and went into business, while the women took up secular pursuits, in particular devoting themselves to modern literature and philosophy, which led to the salons of Herz, Rahel Levin, Sara Levy, and others.[63] Schleiermacher responded in a letter written on August 4, 1798 to his sister Charlotte's concerns that the young theologian was spending too much time among Jews with the following characterization:

Daß junge Gelehrte und Elegants die hiesigen großen jüdischen Häuser fleißig besuchen, ist sehr natürlich, denn es sind bei weitem die reichsten bürgerlichen Familien hier, fast die einzigen, die ein ofenes Haus halten und bei denen man wegen ihrer ausgebreiteten Verbindungen in allen Ländern Fremde von allen Ständen antrift. Wer also auf eine recht ungenirte Art gute Gesellschaft sehn will läßt sich in solchen Häusern einführen, wo natürlich jeder Mensch von Talenten, wenn es auch nur gesellige Talente sind, gern gesehn wird und sich auch gewiß amüsirt, weil die jüdischen Frauen – die Männer werden zu früh in den Handel gestürzt – sehr gebildet sind, vor allem zu sprechen wißen und gewöhnlich eine oder die andere schöne Kunst in einem hohen Grade besizen.[64]

Herz also left a written record of her life in her second memoir, which she narrated to J. Fürst. He published it posthumously, first serially in a newspaper and then in two book editions (1850, 1858). An etching made of the Graff portrait serves as the frontispiece. Fürst repeatedly describes Herz's physical appearance as corresponding to the aesthetic ideals of classical antiquity,[65] going even further to note: "Ja sie wurde eine Art von Probirstein für weibliche Schönheit".[66] He bases this on a kind of contest, clearly modeled on the Judgment of Paris, that Markus Herz initiated, comparing her with the beautiful wife of a Russian general.[67]

The question must be addressed, however, as to what extent, as Davies claims, here and in the memoir, "Henriette is again offered to the public as

[61] Qtd. in Ruth Glatzer (ed.): *Berliner Leben 1848-1805*. Berlin 1956. P. 227. Cf. Krobb. P. 81.

[62] Qtd. in Glatzer. P. 227.

[63] Cf. Fürst. Pp. 121-22, 125.

[64] Friedrich Schleiermacher: *Kritische Gesamtausgabe*. V. Abteilung (Briefe). Ed. by Andreas Arndt and Wolfgang Virmond. 5 vols. Berlin, New York 1985-2000. Vol. 2. P. 370.

[65] Fürst. Pp. 30-31.

[66] Fürst. P. 31.

[67] Hahn. Pp. 171-72.

an aesthetic object of admiration".[68] He perceives her as merely a passive object exhibited for male admiration. However, this thesis conflicts with the very nature of portraiture, which is to reveal something of the individuality and personality of the subject. Further, I contend that a more complex process of deliberate self-fashioning and display is occurring here. Fürst saw this as well, when he decided to include this picture in the memoir. In Fürst's book, the picture compliments her own verbal portrait gallery in which she speaks of the important people with whom she associated. This type of memoir, organized into various "portraits", was not unusual for the time. Karl August Varnhagen published his own *Galerie von Bildnissen*. Narrated in Herz's voice, the memoir presents her version of her life refracted through an account of her relationships with others. Although she shared with Fürst her correspondence and the first, unpublished memoir, Herz burned a good deal of her correspondence before her death. This was a woman who was highly motivated to control her own image and reputation. The Graff portrait provides initial evidence of her wish to control her own image.

Lastly, does this portrait represent the ideal of the beautiful Jewess? Concurring with Fürst, later critics emphasize its classical beauty. Gustav Kühne combines biblical and classical references, speaking of the "Prophetenernst der Stirn" and of her as a "Hebräerin" with "marmorschönen und marmortugendhaften" attributes.[69] Yet, her Romanesque qualities are not entirely feminine. Just as her size indicates that she transgressed the boundaries of feminine grace, the portrayal of the line of her jaw here, in the later Schadow drawing, and in the Schöner portrait conveys the sternness of a Roman general rather than of a Roman matron.[70] Herz's facial features have been slightly masculinized, diverging here a bit from the aesthetic ideal, yet not to the extent that the image breaks out of the frame of the topos. Jewish difference remains represented here through gendered difference. In Herz's case, the eroticized and exoticized feminine beauty of the Jewess allures because it simultaneously both reinforces a conventional European aesthetic for female beauty and contests the underlying assumptions of cultural and gender difference.

"Mad. Moses" and "Judenweiber": Salon Satires

In these portraits, Herz represents simultaneously the beautiful Jewess as biblical or classical beauty and, in her dress and gaze, the emancipatory aspirations of modern German Jewry. But not everyone responded positively to these aspirations or to the salonnières. There was contempt "for the Jews'

---

[68] Davies: Portraits. P. 50.

[69] Gustav F. Kühne: Henriette Herz. In: *Deutsche Männer und Frauen. Eine Galerie von Charakteren.* Leipzig 1851. Pp. 214-244, here p. 225.

[70] My thanks to Susan Cocalis for making this observation.

desire to become part of the system, to abandon their difference".[71] Blatantly anti-Semitic tracts, such as those by Grattenauer, warned against the alluring accomplishments of salon women when combined with "einer schönen Weiblichkeit".[72] As both a female and a Jewish dominated space, the salon feminized the locus of social interaction. The Jewish salonnières trespass into what should be male-dominated semi-public space. As Jews and women they caused a "'Verweiblichung der Kultur'".[73] Later, more critical poems such as 'Blumen und Kerzen' by Ludwig Robert[74] and Heine's well-known, 'Sie saßen und tranken am Teetisch',[75] as well as Eichendorff's critical salon depiction in *Ahnung und Gegenwart*[76] and his 1847 essay criticizing women writers, "Die deutsche Salon-Poesie der Frauen",[77] substantiate the later or post salon-era perception of a salon sociability dominated by frivolous women. The idealized *Geselligkeit* of the salon of 1800 had devolved into the much derided "ästhetischen Thee".[78] Although the cultural background of the salonnières does not play a role in these later depictions, there can be no doubt that during the heyday of the Berlin Jewish salon in the last decade of the 18th and the first of the 19th century, the salon, as embodied by its Jewish hostess, was both a Jewish and a female dominated space. The founding by Achim von Arnim and Clemens Brentano of the *christlich-deutsche Tischgesellschaft*, whose statutes specifically barred women, Jews, and "Philister",[79] further testifies to the resistence to this perceived feminine and Jewish influence on "German" culture.

Two satires exemplify early negative responses to the salon at the height of its activity. The first, "Sechs Stunden aus Fink's Leben" by Bernhardi, depicts an entire salon evening. It contains two Jewish characters. A young man, educated, exhibiting popular taste, fashion, and social skills is only

---

[71] Gilman: *Jewish Self-Hatred*. P. 148.

[72] Qtd. in Pia Schmid: *Zeit des Lesens – Zeit des Fühlens: Anfänge des deutschen Bildungsbürgertums. Ein Lesebuch*. Berlin 1985. P. 209.

[73] Sabine Gürtler and Gisa Hanusch: Tischgesellschaften und Tischszenen in der Romantik. In: *Athenäum. Jahrbuch für Romantik* 2 (1992). Pp. 223-241, here p. 225. They only point this out in reference to women and do not specifically refer to Jews in this way.

[74] Qtd. in Peter Gradenwitz: *Literatur und Musik im geselligem Kreise. Geschmacksbildung, Gesprächsstoff und musikalische Unterhaltung in der bügerlichen Salongesellschaft*. Stuttgart 1991. P. 100.

[75] Heinrich Heine: Sie saßen und tranken am Teetisch. *Werke*. Ed. by Christoph Siegrist. 4 vols. Frankfurt/M. 1968. Vol.1. P. 46.

[76] Joseph von Eichendorff: *Ahnung und Gegenwart*. Stuttgart 1984. Pp. 132-140.

[77] Joseph von Eichendorff: Die deutsche Salon-Poesie der Frauen. In: *Sämtliche Werk. Historisch-kritische Ausgabe*. Ed. by Wilhelm Kosch et al. Vol. 8, Part 1. Regensburg 1962. Pp. 63-80.

[78] Bernd Wegener: Über den ästhetischen Thee. In: *Neue Deutsche Hefte* 30.2 (1983). Pp. 284-97, here p. 295 and Seibert. P. 281.

[79] Qtd. in Reinhold Steig: *Kleist's Berliner Kämpfe*.1901. Bern 1971. P. 22.

lightly satirized.[80] The second character parodies Henriette Herz, even though Bernhardi did not know her:

> Jene – Madame Moses ist eine Jüdin, und von ihr werden Sie wohl schon bemerkt haben, daß sie sich mit Mühe so viel Grazie erworben hat, daß sie dadurch ungemein mißfällt. – Sie ist in dieser Gesellschaft die eigentliche schöne Seele, sie hat von Jugend auf viel Umgang mit guten Köpfen gehabt, – welche ihr eine runde Summe von allgemeinen durchgreifenden ästhetischen Ideen hinterließen, die sie jetzt jedem neuen Bekannten groschenweise zuzählt.[81]

Bernhardi continues, noting how "Madame Moses" masquerades as a character from Goethe's *Torquato Tasso*, as a "Prinzessin im Tasso",[82] thereby highlighting the famed Goethe fanaticism among the salonnières. Friedrich Schlegel identified "Madame Moses" as Herz in a letter to his brother August Wilhelm. He impugned Bernhardi's own class background and literary talents:

> Wie seyd Ihr denn dazu gekommen, grade den lampoon auf die Herz zu excerpiren? – Es ist leicht die manquirteste Stelle im Buch. Er kennt die Herz gar nicht, wie er denn überall nicht von der besten Gesellschaft ist. Ein lampoon der fehl trift und ohne genaue Kentniß der Indivi[dualität] gemacht wird, ist doch auch gar nichts.[83]

The second satire had broad repercussions, leading Schleiermacher's superior, Friedrich Sack, to question his association with Herz and the Schlegel brothers,[84] his "Verbindungen mit Personen von verdächtigen Grundsätzen und Sitten [...]".[85] Schleiermacher realized that Sack was referring to Herz, Dorothea Veit, and Friedrich Schlegel, writing his sister Charlotte in 1801 and telling her that Sack "wahrscheinlich die Herz und Schlegel meinte jedoch ohne sie zu nennen [...]".[86] Johannes Falk's satire, structured in imitation of Goethe's *Das Jahrmarkts-Fest zu Plundersweilern*, parodies the current book market and especially Schlegel's *Lucinde*

---

[80] A. F. Bernhardi and Sophie Bernhardi: Sechs Stunden aus Fink's Leben. In: *Reliquien. Erzählungen und Dichtungen*. Ed. by Wilhelm Bernhardi. 3 vols. Altenburg 1847. Vol. 2. Pp. 125-194, here pp. 156-57.

[81] Bernhardi. P. 170.

[82] Bernhardi. P. 170.

[83] Friedrich Schlegel: *Kritische Friedrich Schlegel Ausgabe*. Ed. by Ernst Behler et al. Munich 1958-. Vol. 24. P. 41.

[84] Ruth Drucilla Richardson: *The Role of Women in the Life and Thought of the Early Schleiermacher (1768-1806). An Historical Overview*. Lewiston 1991. (Schleiermacher: Studies-and-Translations 7). P. 111.

[85] Schleiermacher. V. Abt. Vol. 5. P. 3.

[86] Schleiermacher. V. Abt. Vol. 5. P. 152.

and Schleiermacher's *Vertraute Briefe*.[87] Immediately preceding the satire, Falk's volume also includes a parodistic review of the *Vertraute Briefe*. Both Goethe's and Falk's works present Jewish themes in the plays performed at the fairs (Falk also includes them in the fair itself). Goethe recounts, in part, the story of the beautiful queen Esther (although the play breaks off before she reaches the decision to save her people). Falk, in satirizing *Lucinde* and the *Vertraute Briefe,* includes "Judenweiber" and "Eine Berliner Jüdinn".[88] In the satire and the book review, he also warns against the perceived blurring of gender roles in these texts.[89] Ironically, Bernhardi is also lampooned in this satire.[90]

A caricature accompanies the satire (see Ill. 5). In the lefthand corner, Herz is depicted with Schleiermacher, who is carrying a copy of his own "Reden über die Religion". Behind them walk the Schlegel brothers. Herz is by far the largest figure in the entire scene. Falk renders her height accurately, but also depicts her as fat, an attribute never ascribed to her by her contemporaries. The drastic size and height differential between Herz and Schleiermacher was, however, something even they found ridiculous. Schleiermacher, who more than once rebutted suggestions that he would like to marry Herz, wrote that "ihre kolossale königliche Figur" was so much the opposite of his, that even if they had wished to marry, they would have made a ridiculous couple.[91] Responding in part to Falk's satire, Schleiermacher assessed Herz's beauty as excessive and so imposing as to be unappealing to men, as he wrote her in his letter of November 12, 1802.[92] Schleiermacher continued his characterization of his friend somewhat jokingly by comparing the unattractiveness of her overly beautiful body with the shortcomings of her personality ("Geist").[93] He forges the crucial link between her physicality, which is both "imponierend" and "passiv", and the attractiveness of her mind: "Ebenso kläglich steht es nun um Deinen Geist [...] die asthenische geistliche Sinnlichkeit kommt auch zu kurz [...]".[94] His frankness in this statement testifies to the closeness of their friendship. Herz was proud of her ability to maintain a close, but platonic friendship with

---

[87] Albert L. Blackwell: *Schleiermacher's Early Philosophy of Life. Determinism, Freedom, and Phantasy.* Chico, CA 1982. P. 262.

[88] J[ohannes] D[aniel] Falk: Der Jahrmarkt zu Plundersweilern. Parodie des Göthischen. In: *Taschenbuch für die Freunde des Scherzes und der Satire.* Vol. 5. Weimar 1801. Pp. 307-390, here p. 324.

[89] J[ohannes] D[aniel] Falk: Vertraute Briefe über Friedrich Schlegels Lucinde. In: *Taschenbuch für die Freunde des Scherzes und der Satire.* Vol. 5. Weimar 1801. Pp. 273-306, here pp. 296-97, 300-03. Der Jahrmarkt. P. 327.

[90] Falk: Der Jahrmarkt. P. 324.

[91] Schleiermacher. V. Abt. Vol. 5. P. 52.

[92] Qtd. in Schmitz. P. 357.

[93] Qtd. in Schmitz. Pp. 357-58.

[94] Qtd. in Schmitz. Pp. 357-58.

Schleiermacher. In 1815 she wrote August Twesten of her feelings for Schleiermacher, whom "ich [...] so lange kenne und liebe, mit der reinsten *völlig leidenschaftslosen* Liebe immer geliebt habe".[95]

As Rahel Levin noted, Herz was indeed aware of how her friends described her.[96] In June 1809, Rahel Levin also did not mince words when she conveyed to Wilhelm von Humboldt a quite negative impression of Herz, speaking of "der kolossalen Gestalt, der kolossalen Jahre und der kolossalen Erfahrung".[97] As she matured, Herz was not only aware of her beauty and its effect on others, but also of her reputation and her own shortcomings. Yet, the less than flattering observations of her friends and acquaintances should not be equated with the contemptuous portrayals in the satires. Falk's and Bernhardi's characterizations display the exaggeratedly sized or fancifully attired female Jewish body as an object of derision and ridicule. This oversized and socially influential gendered body – the body of the salons – threatened to alter the dominant German culture.

Herz at 38

The final painting of Henriette Herz by Georg Schöner (1774-1841) was completed in 1802 when she was 38 (see Ill. 6). Schöner had been a student of Anton Graff. Created at the height of her fame, the Herz of this painting exhibits signs of age. Her simple, yet fashionable clothing drapes the full figure. Rather than looking directly at the viewer, she turns her attention to the side. As in the Schadow sculpture, she appears to be listening intently to someone else. Unlike all of the other depictions, we not only see her long nose, but also its profile. Although by no means a stereotypical "Jewish" nose, its prominence discloses what might be considered a more typically Jewish physiognomy.[98] The beautiful Jewess is clothed as a Roman matron, in part keeping with contemporary fashion. The entire outfit is darkly colored, as well as the background, oddly presaging her impending widowhood in January 1803 and the demise of the salon. Interestingly, neither Davies nor Weissberg discuss this painting and Wilhelmy omits it from her list of works of art portraying Herz.[99]

---

[95] Henriette Herz: Briefe von Henriette Herz an August Twesten (1814-1827). Ed. by Georg Heinrici. In: *Zeitschrift für Bücherfreunde* N.S. 5.2. (1914). Pp. 301-316, 333-347, here p. 334.

[96] Rahel Varnhagen: *Gesammelte Werke*. Ed. by Konrad Feilchenfeldt, Uwe Schweikert and Rahel E. Steiner. 10 vols. Munich 1983. Vol. 1. P. 507.

[97] Rahel Varnhagen: *Gesammelte Werke*. Vol. 9. P. 40.

[98] Cf. Gilman: *The Jew's Body*. Pp. 169-193.

[99] Petra Wilhelmy: *Der Berliner Salon im 19. Jahrhundert (1780-1914)*. Berlin, New York 1989 (Veröffentlichungen der historischen Kommission zu Berlin 73).

The Aging Beauty

The final two pencil drawings to be discussed were made within days of each other by Wilhelm Hensel (1764-1861) in 1823 when Herz was 59 (see Ill. 7 and 8). Wearing the turbans she regularly sported in her later years, perhaps to cover her graying hair, the drawings reveal a still quite handsome woman.[100] Yet critics disagree as to how the Hensel drawings characterize her. Paucker describes the profile as "das einer lebensnahen, stattlichen jüdischen Matrone";[101] whereas Davies ignores the substantiveness of the body depicted in the drawings and observes: "Significant here is their plainness, – of medium: she no longer warrants a portrait in oils, but in pencil; – and of image: the absence of the body, the concealment of her hair. This is not the *salonière*. But to say that this is Henriette herself would be an unwarranted assertion".[102] The woman portrayed is, according to Davies, no longer Jewish at all, but the sketches are simple and illustrate "the ascetic ideals of the pietism, which under Schleiermacher's influence, Henriette adopted when she converted to Protestantism early in June 1817".[103] However, it seems to me that Davies countermands his own reticence to assert that "this is Henriette herself". If she represents a Christian pietist, then Hensel's sketches must to a certain degree reflect a deliberate posing. As is the case with the earlier portraits, these drawings are products of an artistic endeavor in which there is some collaboration between sitter and artist.

In these two conflicting views expressed by Davies and Paucker the entire problematic of the topos of the beautiful Jewess and of the essentialized and gendered Jewish body present themselves. The image serves as a positive representation of Judaism, or, more commonly, it functions as a Christian icon where the beautiful Jewess (and by extension the entire Jewish people) can be deemed beautiful because she converted to Christianity. Her outer beauty becomes a reflection of her inner Christian faith. Long a friend of Schleiermacher, Herz converted after her mother's death. In 1823, the same year as these sketches, she began writing her spiritual autobiography, thematizing her beauty as the main source of her vanity, insisting that it had long since faded. This gave her permission in 1829 "von meiner damaligen, anerkanndten Schönheit zu sprechen, von der auch keine Spur mehr sichtbar ist".[104] Some observations by Dorothea Schlegel and Caroline von Humboldt would seem to document the loss of her beauty. During her trip to Italy in 1817-19, Herz spent a great deal of time with both of them. Dorothea

---

[100] Wilhelm von Humboldt and Caroline von Humboldt: *Wilhelm und Caroline von Humboldt in ihren Briefen*. Ed by Anna von Sydow. 7 vols. Berlin 1906-1916. Vol. 6. Pp. 550-51.

[101] Paucker. P. 32.

[102] Davies: Portraits. P. 59.

[103] Davies: Portraits. P. 64.

[104] Hahn. P. 180.

Schlegel wrote to Rahel Varnhagen about how shocked she was, seeing Herz after such a long time: "Die arme Herz hat aber hier so verlohren an Schönheit, und ist dermaßen mager geworden, daß ich erschrocken war wie ich sie zuerst wieder sah".[105] Caroline Humboldt wrote her husband about "[d]as eigentliche Verschwinden der Schönheit".[106] However, these drawings, as well as other contemporary reports, indicate that Herz may have exaggerated in her memoir.[107] Indeed, as late as 1819, Herz received a marriage proposal from the much younger Immanuel Bekker.[108] Ludwig Börne, who was so madly in love with her in 1803 that he had to leave the Herz home in Berlin where he was staying and return to his parents, also referred to her as "eine Juno", in 1828 when she was 64. He noted as well: "die Spuren ihrer Schönheit erkennt man noch".[109]

Can these drawings, and indeed all of the artistic works discussed here, merely represent an individual — someone who lived as both a Jew and a Christian — or must her image always be colored by the later observer's projection of what she ought to represent? What is clear, is that all of these interpretations of the portraits, including my own, to a greater or lesser extent "read" Herz's life and character through the artistic work of others. She embodies in them both a willing and an unwilling symbol of the beautiful Jewess, of classical and "oriental" beauty, of the aesthetics of the Enlightenment, of acculturated Jews, and of the Christian convert. Only in her two memoirs and extant letters does Herz speak for herself.

Therefore, I would like to let Herz have the last word and close with a quotation from Herz's letter to August Twesten, written in 1817 at the time of her conversion. She elucidates her own awareness of the false dichotomy between mind and body, especially as it is applied to women:

> Sehen Sie, lieber Freund, wenn die Frauen jung und hübsch sind, dann giebt es gar zu viele Männer, die ihnen einbilden, daß es ihr Geist, ihr Gemüth ist, das sie anzieht, gar nicht das Aeussere. Die besseren Männer mögen sich selbst darüber täuschen, ich will nicht richten; die besseren Frauen glauben ihnen das aufs Wort und freuen sich, daß sie außer dem hübschen Gesicht Eigenschaften des Geistes und des Herzens haben, die ihnen die Freundschaft und Achtung vorzüglicher edler Männer zuziehen und *fürs Leben* sichern; denn sie sind nicht vergänglich wie jenes. So lebt und drusellt so eine arme Frau fort bis die weiße glatte Haut gelblich und welk wird, die glänzenden Augen matt, der Mund eingefallen, die

---

[105] Friedrich Schlegel: *Kritische Friedrich Schlegel Ausgabe*. Vol. 30. P. 175.

[106] Wilhelm and Caroline von Humboldt. Vol. 6. P. 550.

[107] Caroline Bauer's 1824 observation. Qtd. in Landsberg. P. 94.

[108] Wilhelm and Caroline von Humboldt. Vol. 6. P. 572. See also Herz's correspondence with Bekker. Henriette Herz: *Letters to Immanuel Bekker from Henriette Herz, S. Pobeheim and Anna Horkel*. Ed. by Max J. Putzel. Bern 1972. (German Studies in America 6).

[109] Qtd. in Schmitz. P. 423.

Nase spitz u.s.w. Da sieht sie dann, was die meisten jener *vorigen* Freundschafts-Versicherer gehalten hat, die sie in ihrem Herzen aufgenommen hatte. Die haben dann längst schon wieder ein griechisches Profil mit *vorzüglichen Geist- und Herzensgaben* gefunden. So leicht und fast scherzend ich Ihnen dies gesagt habe, lieber Twesten, so hat es doch seine sehr ernsthafte und gründlich wahre Seite, die sie auch wohl herausfinden und als wahr erkennen werden; und deshalb will ich nicht weitläufiger darüber sein und Ihnen langweilig werden.[110]

Henriette Herz was aware of how her beauty and intellect impacted others. Herz was conscious of the fact that almost all her life she had put herself and her body on display. At the same time, she tried to exert some control over how she was perceived by burning much of her correspondence and narrating only selected portions of her life story. Her relation to her own image and story was one of both active engagement and restraint. Herz both posed for posterity and tried to control her posthumous reputation. Whether in her own writings or rendered in works of art, her gendered performance, her "posing" is merely a matter of degree. On a personal level, she was rather successful in controlling her image. But as a model of the beautiful Jewess, her image encouraged the persistence of a stereotype. In the end, the dichotomies of body and mind, of tradition and assimilation, and of Judaism and Christianity remain unresolved. The story of love and infatuation – of appearance and reality – that she relates in this letter can now also be interpreted metaphorically as a reflection of the way in which the relationship between German Christians and Jews became gendered, where the Jews perform the role of the "Frauen" and the Christians of the "Männer".

---

[110] Herz: Briefe von Henriette Herz an August Twesten. P. 337.

Illustration 1

Anna Dorothea Therbusch: Portrait of Henriette Herz (1778).
Photo: Jörg P. Anders.
Permission of Bildarchiv Preußischer Kulturbesitz.

Illustration 2

Johann Gottfried Schadow: Drawing of Henriette Herz (ca. 1783).
Black chalk and pencil.
Bildarchiv der Akademie der Künste, Berlin.

Illustration 3

Johann Gottfried Schadow: Bust of Henriette Herz (1783)
Photo: Klaus Göken
Permission of Bildarchiv Preußischer Kulturbesitz

Illustration 4

Anton Graff: Portrait of Henriette Herz (1792)
Permission of Bildarchiv Preußischer Kulturbesitz

Illustration 5

Excerpt from a
caricature from *Taschenbuch für die Freunde des Scherzes und der Satire*.
Ed. by J. D. Falk. Vol. 5. Weimar 1801.

Illustration 6

Georg Adolf Schöner: Portrait of Henriette Herz (1802)
Photo: Christel Lehmann
Published with the permission of Stadtmuseum Berlin
Photography: Stadtmuseum Berlin

Illustration 7

Wilhelm Hensel: Henriette Herz. Pencil drawing. Inv. 5/4
Permission of Bildarchiv Preußischer Kulturbesitz

Illustration 8

Wilhelm Hensel: Henriette Herz. Pencil drawing. Inv. 5/5
Permission of Bildarchiv Preußischer Kulturbesitz

Holger A. Pausch

Beobachtungen zur Genealogie der Körperfeindlichkeit als Erbmangel und Notwendigkeit im kulturellen Gedächtnis der Aufklärung

Resentment of the body image, a well known and highly influential phenomenon of the modern world, led to a multitude of serious social consequences. Rooted in Cartesian humanism and its tradition to devaluate nature and the physical reality of the human body, "for man is the antinatural being par excellence" (Luc Ferry), this essay, after a brief discussion of historical and theoretical suppositions, investigates three exemplary procedures of humanistic culture in the Enlightenment which caused this resentment in the form of identity deficits: the alphabetisation of society, immortality debate, and physiognomy.

I.

Die Auffassung des Körpers als Schlachtfeld, auf dem rücksichtslos ein komplexes Kräftespiel politischer, ästhetischer und moralischer Ideologien, medizinischer Hoffnungen, erotischer Wunschvorstellungen und vor allem des Konsums mit seinen Fiktionen des Begehrens und Genießens plakativ ausgetragen wird, spielt in der gegenwärtigen Kulturtheorie eine zentrale Rolle.[1] In diesem Kontext wird der Körper als Medium kultureller Inskriptionen durch performative Vorgänge erfasst, die zwar gesellschaftliche Kohärenz erzeugen, doch dabei auch versuchen, das Zufällige, Konstruierte, Herbeigeholte der jeweils produzierten Gestaltung des Körpers zu verdecken, um den Eindruck seines universalen, natürlichen Ursprungs zu vermitteln.[2] Besonders in den letzten zehn Jahren wurden Fragen der Körperproblematik, die im oben angesprochenen Rahmen der Kulturtheorie davon ausgehen, dass das Zusammenspiel der kulturellen Phänomene, umfassend miteinander verbunden im gesellschaftlichen Universum von Zeichenbeziehungen, als ein integrierter und vor allem sinnvoller Text zu lesen ist, in einem Umfeld intensiver Forschung unter dem Begriff literarische Anthropologie behandelt.[3] Die verhältnismäßig junge Disziplin analysiert und beschreibt die

---

[1] Zur Einführung s. Gabriele Genge (Hg.): *Sprachformen des Körpers in Kunst und Wissenschaft*. Tübingen 2000.

[2] Als eine der ersten bahnbrechenden Arbeiten dieser Themenstellung s. Judith Butler: *Gender Trouble*. New York 1990.

[3] Interessant in diesem Zusammenhang ist die Tatsache, dass der Begriff "Körper" in Wörterbüchern der Psychologie (abgesehen von "Körperbautypen") und Philosophie (abgesehen von "Körperkultur") nicht auftaucht. Sogar der *Brockhaus* verzichtet bis auf den Hinweis auf "Körpermaße" in der biologischen Anthropologie auf

von Kultur und Wissenschaft betriebenen Inskriptionsstrategien des menschlichen Körpers und Bewusstseins im Wirkungsbereich kognitiver Systeme, die in der Geschichte auf der Grundlage neuer Medien entwickelt wurden.[4] In diesem reich differenzierten und, bezüglich seiner konkreten Bedeutung, aufschlussreichen Forschungsbereich bleibt jedoch eine Frage, die hier gestellt wird, sonderbar unberücksichtigt, das Problem der Körperfeindlichkeit und ihre Entwicklung in der Aufklärung.

Grundsätzlich bezeichnet das angesprochene Phänomen die geistige, emotionale oder auch unbewusste Feindlichkeit gegenüber der Zeichenqualität des eigenen Körpers, eine Feindlichkeit, die immer dann ausgelöst werden kann, wenn das dem Blick der Öffentlichkeit ausgelieferte eigene Körperbild, der sogenannte "öffentliche" Körper, mit den makellosen Gestalten und ihren reinen identitätsbegründeten Handlungsformen in den Medien verglichen und als mangelhaft oder unzureichend empfunden wird, also mit dem Maßstab attraktiver Körperutopien und perfekter Zielbilder, die in der medial-fiktiven Industrie als erstrebenswert, erreichbar und vorteilhaft vorgezaubert werden.[5] Körperfeindlichkeit bezeichnet demnach eine gegen den eigenen Körper gerichtete, durch Unzufriedenheit, Unlust, Widerwillen oder Missfallen motivierte und nicht selten mit katastrophalen Konsequenzen verbundene Abneigung, und zwar als Reaktion auf ideale und daher nicht erreichbare Standards und Normen, die in den Bereichen der Gesellschaft, Medien und Werbung verbreitet, propagiert oder impliziert werden. Infolgedessen steht, vereinfacht gesehen, im Zentrum der Körperfeindlichkeit das Motiv des Begehrens.

Dabei geht es um den kuriosen Versuch, den eigenen Körper, der im Vergleich mit ästhetischen Normen und mustergültigen Dimensionen des makellosen Körpers in der Werbung, im Konsum, der Unterhaltungsindustrie und in den fiktiven Bildsphären der Comic Books und phantasierten Erotik als minderwertig eingestuft wird, gegen den allgemein begehrten umzutauschen. Gegen einen Körper folglich, der dem ästhetischen Leistungs-

eine Definition des Begriffs. Der Sachverhalt, dass der Körper als Inskriptionsmedium der Kultur zu verstehen und zu beschreiben ist, wird in diesen Bereichen lexikalischen Wissens noch nicht reflektiert.

[4] Zur Einführung in die Problematik s. bes. die bahnbrechende Arbeit von Albrecht Koschorke: *Körperströme und Schriftverkehr. Mediologie des 18. Jahrhunderts.* München 1999; Claudia Öhlschläger und Birgit Wiens (Hg.): *Körper – Gedächtnis – Schrift. Der Körper als Medium kultureller Erinnerung.* Berlin 1997; José Luis Bermúdez, Anthony Marcel und Naomi Eilan (Hg.): *The Body and the Self.* Cambridge, Mass. 1995; Geil Weiss: *body images. embodiment as intercorporeality.* New York und London 1999.

[5] Zu Funktion und Bildqualität der Reklamephotographie s. Holger Pausch: "Der neue Blick": Physiognomie und Sprachbildlichkeit im Wirkungsbereich der Photographie im Werk Else Lasker-Schülers. In: *Else Lasker-Schüler-Jahrbuch zur Klassischen Moderne.* Hg. von Lothar Bluhm und Andreas Meier. Trier 2000. S. 144-166.

soll bzw. den Auflagen und Direktiven der Bildwelt des gesellschaftlichen Wunschdenkens entspricht. Diese mit zielgerichteten Handlungsenergien verbundene Metamorphose, gemeint ist der Umtausch des negativ gesehenen konkreten eigenen Körpers gegen den begehrten medial-fiktiven, gelingt aber nur dann, wenn der eigene Körper nach dem Muster des im Bewusstsein der Gesellschaft vagabundierenden idealen Körperkonzepts umgestaltet bzw. im Vorgang einer Simulation reproduziert wird, damit er die Normen der allgemeinen Begehrlichkeit und damit die des Erfolgs repräsentiert. Misslingt der Versuch, was bekanntlich fast immer der Fall ist, so kann dies zur Bestrafung des eigenen Körpers führen, zur Körperfeindlichkeit, für die sich ohne Schwierigkeiten eine ganze Palette von Beispielen finden lassen. So etwa gestörtes Essverhalten wie Bulimie und Anorexie bzw. Ess- und Pubertätsmagersucht.[6] Weiter: Hungerkuren, Diäten, kosmetische Chirurgie, Formen des Selbsthasses, Sucht nach Strafe, Depression, Minderwertigkeit, Schizophrenie als Körperflucht, antisoziales Verhalten und zwanghaftes Body Building,[7] das Suizid als endgültige Form der Körperbestrafung usw., kurz alle Formen und Folgen der Unzufriedenheit und des Unbehagens mit sich selbst im Rahmen eines gestörten Verhaltens gegenüber dem eigenen Körper.[8]

[6] S. dazu die aufschlussreichen Informationen der Web Seite www.britannica.com s. v. "Bulimia". Über zwei Millionen Amerikaner leiden unter diesen Eßstörungen. S. auch *International Journal of Eating Disorder*.

[7] Dazu heißt es das Phänomen der Körperfeindlichkeit erhellend in dem kürzlich erschienen Aufsatz "When brawn takes over the brain": "Picture someone who can't stand to look in the mirror because it makes them feel too inadequate, unattractive and plain. A person who hates their body, and tries to radically transform it by changing their diet, their exercise regimen and the whole focus of their life. Someone who sacrifices their career, their relationship and even their health to try to conform to unattainable body ideals that have been foisted on them through movies, advertising and other media. [...] 'The number of men in the United States and Canada who have an actual psychiatric disorder involving body image is well over the million mark', said Harrison Pope. The Harvard University psychology professor calls this widespread but little known problem a 'health crisis', adding that many millions more men suffer significant distress and feelings of dissatisfaction about their bodies, though not strongly enough to be diagnosed officially with a disorder". In: *National Post* (22. August 2000). S. A15. S. auch Yvonne Wiegers: Male Bodybuilding. The Social Construction of a Masculine Identity. In: *Journal of Popular Culture* 32 (1998). H. 2. S. 147-161.

[8] Seit einigen Jahren ist die Psychiatrie im Blickwinkel des Konzepts "body image disorders" und der diagnostischen Begriffe "muscle dysmorphia", "bigorexia" oder "reverse anorexia" auf Körperfeindlichkeit aufmerksam geworden, weil über drei Millionen amerikanische Männer Steroide missbrauchen. Einleitende Informationen s. Harrison G. Pope, Katherine A. Philipps und Roberto Olivardia: *The Adonis Complex. Secret Crisis of Male Body Obsession*. o. O. 2000; Brian Pronger: *The Arena of Masculinity: Sports, Homosexuality and the Meaning of Sex*. Toronto 1992; Harrison G. Pope, Amanda J. Gruber et al.: Body Image Perception Among

Auch das historisch weit zurückzuverfolgende Interesse an anorganischen Seinszuständen auf Kosten organischer Formen, das beispielsweise in der Kulturgeschichte im Bereich der Maschinen, Modelle oder Moden, der Gliederpuppen, Marionetten, Roboter, Cyborgs, Androiden, Automaten usw. immer wieder faszinierte, also anorganische Umbildungen des menschlichen Körpers, reflektiert Körperfeindlichkeit. Oder in der Gegenwart die Unzulänglichkeit des organischen Körpers signalisierenden Anwendungsgebiete der Microchipinplants und Bionik,[9] der Handelektronik wie Handys und mobile Palmcomputer mit Internetanschluss, die den Körper global vernetzen, der virtuellen Realitätsspiele usw. Angesprochen sind jene Fälle, deren Ziel es ist, Grenzen des Organischen zu überwinden.[10] Nicht zu vergessen die vielen pathologischen Erscheinungen der Körperfeindlichkeit, beispielsweise Selbstverstümmelung, das Phänomen der psychosomatischen Erkrankungen, Drogenmissbrauch, Sex Change oder Kindesmord aus sozialen und Schwangerschaftsunterbrechung aus kosmetischen Gründen. Die grauenhafteste Form der Körperfeindlichkeit aber ist das Konzept des mechanischen Tötens, besonders im Kontext der sogenannten "Volksbereinigung", der "Reinigung des Volkskörpers" von "Fremdelementen", wie die Rechtfertigung für das einstige Morden von Zigeunern, Homosexuellen, nord- und südamerikanischen Ureinwohnern, Juden, Andersdenkenden u. v. a. m. lautete.

Es geht hier nicht darum, einen Katalog der Folgen der Körperfeindlichkeit aufzustellen, sondern um den Hinweis ihres erstaunlichen Formenreichtums, ihrer Verbreitung und Verschiedenartigkeit in fast allen Bereichen der Gesellschaft und Kultur, ein Hinweis, der zu der Frage führt, wie sich diese höchst sonderbaren, auf den ersten Blick wenig sinnvoll erscheinenden und dennoch weit verbreiteten körperfeindlichen Verhaltensformen entwickeln konnten? Wie kann die Genealogie dieser tief in der menschlichen Psyche verankerten Verhaltensweisen erfasst werden? Dass Körperfeindlichkeit kein "natürliches" menschliches Phänomen ist wie Essen, Trinken und Schlafen, von dieser Auffassung darf ohne Bedenken ausgegangen

Men in Three Countries. In: *American Journal of Psychiatry* 157 (2000). S. 1297-1301 und Roberto Olivardia, Harrison G. Pope: Muscle Dysmorphia in Male Weightlifters. A Case-Control Study. In: *American Journal of Psychiatry* 157 (2000). S. 1291-1296.

[9] Angesprochen sind normale Körperleistungen verstärkende Inplants oder Zusätze, womit sich das neuste Gebiet der "bionic technology" beschäftigt. Das Science Fiction Genre benutzt die Begriffe "bionic man" oder "bionic woman". Dieser Thematik liegt das Problem zugrunde, unter welchen Voraussetzungen der Körper als künstliche Konstruktion kopiert und nachgestaltet werden kann.

[10] Zum Arsenal der Körperelektronik s. Terry Retter (Hg.): *PriceWaterhouse-Cooper's Technology Forecast 2003*. Es handelt sich um eine jährlich erscheinende Veröffentlichung im Format eines Telephonbuchs, in dem Entwicklungen und Trends in der elektronischen Industrie in den nächsten beiden Jahren vorausgesagt und diskutiert werden.

werden. Doch in welchem Umfeld der Kultur hatte Körperfeindlichkeit eine Funktion und konnte sich aus diesem Grund entwickeln? Um den Zugang zu diesem komplexen Phänomen, bei dem es sich vor allem um eine alltägliche Erscheinung der Moderne handelt, zu erleichtern, ist es sinnvoll die Aufmerksamkeit auf jene Vorgänge der Identitätsbildung zu richten, die das Fundament des modernen Bewusstseins bilden, also auf die in der Aufklärung.[11] Und in diesem Kontext werde ich mich vor allem auf die Probleme der Erzeugung von Identitätsdefiziten konzentrieren, weil in dem Umfeld die angesprochene Fragestellung deutlich herausgearbeitet werden kann.

II.

Der methodische Ansatz der modernen literarischen Anthropologie ist ein effektiver Ausgangspunkt. In ihr geht es im wesentlichen darum, den Körper als das inskriptionsfähige Medium kultureller Repräsentationen zu erfassen, als eine Art, so die Postmoderne, von Anfang an beschriebene Wachstafel oder, so die Aufklärung, Tabula rasa, die immer wieder im Reaktionsreflex auf veränderte kognitive Bedingungen inskribiert werden kann. Mittels des auf sie erneut Eingeschriebenen greift sie dann ihrerseits wiederum rückwirkend und neue Maßstäbe setzend auf die Gestaltungsvorgänge und das Verständnis des als Wirklichkeit erfassten Kulturraums produktiv ein, d. h. mittels des neu geprägten Körperkonzepts, das den neuen Maßstab setzt, um die Welt neu zu beschreiben.[12] In diesem Licht gesehen signalisiert das Konzept des Körpers eine in sich ruhende passive Materialität, deren Kontur durch Kräfte bestimmt und gestaltet wird, die auf sie von außen Oberflä-

---

[11] Die komplexen Probleme klassisch philosophischer, mittelalterlicher und frühneuzeitlicher Formen der Körperfeindlichkeit werden im folgenden Argumentationszusammenhang nicht berücksichtigt, da sie sich in einem grundlegend verschiedenen kognitiven Umfeld befinden. Brent Holland hat mich darauf hingewiesen, dass der Ursprung der Körperfeindlichkeit, wie sie sich bereits in den Körpervorstellungen mittelalterlich-christlicher Denker wie Albertus Magnus und Thomas von Aquino bemerkbar macht, in den idealistischen und materialistischen Darstellungen des Körper-Seele-Dualismus bei Platon und Aristoteles erfasst werden kann. Das ist besonders bei Platon der Fall, der im Körper das verwesende Grab der Seele sah, weil er die Seele, dem göttlichen Bereich entfernt, gefangen hielt.

[12] Ausführliche Studien und Beispiele s. Katie Conboy, Nadia Medina und Sarah Stanbury (Hg.): *Writing on the Body. Female Embodiment and Feminist Theory.* New York 1997; Steve Pile: *The Body and the City: Psychoanalysis, Space, and Subjectivity.* London, New York 1996; Margaret J. M. Ezell und Katherin O'Brien O'Keeffe (Hg.): *Cultural Artifacts and the Production of Meaning. The Page, the Image, and the Body.* Ann Arbor 1994; Mike Featherstone, Mike Hepworth und Bryan S. Turner (Hg.): *The Body. Social Process and Cultural* Theory. London 1991; Elisabeth Bronfen: *Over Her Dead Body. Death, Femininity and the Aesthetic.* Manchester 1992; Barbara Duden: *Der Frauenleib als öffentlicher Ort. Vom Mißbrauch des Begriffs Leben.* Hamburg 1991.

chen, Grenzen und Formen verändernd einwirken. Oder anders gesehen, der Körper wird als eine Art Urmasse in den Händen kultureller Kräfte konzipiert, und zwar zum Zweck der Konstruktion, der Realisation und Repräsentation eben dieser kulturellen Kräfte, solange bis das Spiel, dessen Regeln sich in der Geschichte immerfort und ziellos verändern, von neuem beginnt.

Dieses literaranthropologische, in sich kreisende Körperkonzept stummer Faktizität, das modernen Kulturanalysen als theoretische Voraussetzung zugrunde liegt, hat seine Brauchbarkeit in vielen Fällen erwiesen. So steht beispielsweise in der Geschlechteranalyse *Gender Trouble* von Judith Butler, in der die These vertreten wird, dass die alltägliche Vorstellung der natürlichen Geschlechtsidentität ein Fabrikat bzw. ein performatives Konstrukt einer im Machtdiskurs produzierten Fiktion ist, die oben angesprochene Funktion des Körperbegriffs an zentraler Stelle, und zwar im kritischen Bezug auf die bisherige Diskussion zum Thema im Kontext der Namen Descartes, Freud, Sartre, Beauvoir, Foucault, Wittig, Irigaray u. a. Butler gelingt es, die Frage der Konstruktion der Körperidentität zu beantworten, indem sie den neutralen geschlechtsfreien Körper, der am Ausgangspunkt der philosophischen Analyse hätte stehen müssen, mit dem geschlechtsspezifischen vertauscht. Auf diesem Weg entwickelt sie hinsichtlich der Konstruktion des Körpers das bemerkenswerte Ergebnis, dass nicht biologische Bedingungen, sondern performative Akte den Vorgang beherrschen.

> [...] acts, gestures, and desire produce the effect of an internal core or substance, but produce this *on the surface* of the body, through the play of signifying absences that suggest, but never reveal, the organizing principle of identity as a cause. Such acts, gestures, enactments, generally construed, are *performative* in the sense that the essence or identity that they otherwise purport to express are *fabrications* manufactured and sustained through corporeal signs and other discursive means. That the gendered body is performative suggests that it has no ontological status apart from the various acts which constitute its reality. This also suggests that if that reality is fabricated as an interior essence, that very interiority is an effect and function of a decidedly public and social discourse, the public regulation of fantasy through the surface politics of the body, the gender border control that differentiates inner from outer, and so institutes the "integrity" of the subject.[13]

In Butlers Argument ist besonders wichtig, dass der geschlechtsspezifische Körper, der durch innere und äußere performative Akte gebildet wird, über diese Sachlage hinaus keinen ontologischen Status als autonomes Objekt besitzt.[14] Infolgedessen entsteht der geschlechtsspezifische Körper gleich-

---

[13] Butler. S. 136.

[14] Butlers Standpunkt führt bekanntlich in epistemologische Schwierigkeiten. Darauf geht sie aber nicht ein, weil in diesem Fall die Grundpfeiler des Arguments zusammenbrächen, woran sie verständlicherweise nicht interessiert ist. Im Grunde geht es um die Frage, ob der Körper, bevor er als Begriff erfasst wurde, als Objekt

zeitig und in einem Handlungszug mit den ihn bezeichnenden Gesten seiner Selbstdarstellung. Ohne Sequenzen der Entwicklung und des Ursprungs gelangt er somit wie Sprache als funktionierendes Konzept auf einmal und in einem Zug ins Sein. Mit wenigen Worten, der Körper ist die Summe seiner Verhaltensweisen im Zeitpunkt seiner begrifflichen Entstehung.

In dieser Perspektive ist auch Körperfeindlichkeit als konkreter performativer Akt zu beschreiben, durch den sich der Körper, methodisch wie oben im Rahmen seiner geschlechtsspezifischen Handlungsweisen, realisiert, hier allerdings in den Formen eines bestimmten, sich selbst feindlich gesinnten Zustands, und zwar als Reaktion auf Reize, denen er ausgesetzt wurde. Doch worin bestehen die performativen Akte der Körperfeindlichkeit und unter welchen historischen Bedingungen konnten sie sich entwickeln? Um diese Frage zu beantworten, zunächst ein kurzer Exkurs in die sich in der Aufklärung entwickelnde Konsumindustrie und ihre Entstehungsgründe. Um 1750 nämlich beginnt im Umfeld des wirtschaftlichen Wachstums, des Frühkapitalismus und der sich recht schnell entwickelnden Konsumansprüche eine Phase der Körperkonsolidierung, und zwar im Blickwinkel einer die Ansprüche der Zeit reflektierenden, erstaunlich effektiven Inskriptionsstrategie, für die ich im folgenden den Begriff Erzeugung eines Identitätsdefizits benutzen werde.

III.

In seiner klassischen Arbeit[15] berichtet Werner Sombart, dass der gewaltige Bedarf an Luxusgütern absolutistischer Höfe in Frankreich, Russland, Österreich und Preußen, einschließlich der Monarchie in England, eine noch

---

existiert oder nicht, ein nicht zu lösendes Problem, das zu zwei Körperkonzepten führte, die besonders im Rahmen feministischer Theorien des Essentialismus (der geschlechtliche Körper hat an sich eine Wesenheit und Identität) und Konstruktivismus (der geschlechtliche Körper entsteht durch performative Akte) diskutiert werden. Der Essentialismus gilt allerdings als überholt, und zwar im Kontext der Auffassung, dass Sprache nicht graduell sondern auf einmal als Konsequenz einer kognitiven Entdeckung als funktionierendes Signifikationssystem entstanden ist (Derrida, Kristeva u. a.). In dieser Hinsicht entsteht zusammen mit der Sprache der Begriff des Körpers als ein von Anfang schon kulturell eingeschriebenes Medium, weswegen die Frage nach dem Status des Körpers vor der Sprachfindung als nicht mehr sinnvoll erscheint. Zur Kontroverse zwischen Essentialismus und Konstruktivismus s. Franziska Meier: *Emanzipation als Herausforderung. Rechtsrevolutionäre Schriftsteller zwischen Bisexualität und Androgynie.* Wien, Köln, Weimar 1998. S. 9-15. In letzter Zeit sind in der Debatte außerdem noch die Argumente der Evolutionspsychologie und der Soziobiologie zu berücksichtigen. S. z. B. Hilary Rose und Steven Rose (Hg.): *Alas, Poor Darwin. Arguments Against Evolutionary Psychology.* New York 2000.

[15] Werner Sombart: *Liebe, Luxus und Kapitalismus. Über die Entstehung der Modernen Welt aus dem Geist der Verwendung.* Berlin o. J.

in der Renaissance unvorstellbare Konsumindustrie mit allen erforderlichen Marktmechanismen entwickelte. In seiner in der Tradition Sombarts stehenden Untersuchung entscheidet sich Daniel Purdy, den Weg Sombarts hinsichtlich quantitativ-soziologischer Fragen der Konsumkultur in der Aufklärung in Deutschland – "from the first stirrings of desire to the first formulations of capitalist industries" – zu verlassen.[16] Er erhellt das Problem der Bedeutung des begehrten Konsums von Luxus- und Modeartikeln in der frühen Bildungsphase der modernen Gesellschaft am Beispiel der nachvollziehenden Beziehung des Lesers zu Texten, die Konsumwünsche erzeugen. Sie motivieren die Leser, sich mit den Helden, Ideen oder Empfehlungen der Texte zu identifizieren, um mit diesen über den entsprechenden erworbenen Gegenstand – beispielsweise mit einer Nachschneiderei des blaugelben Outfits von Werther – medial und imaginativ in Kontakt zu treten bzw. sie zu vertreten.[17] Gegen dieses Leseverhalten hatten sich bekanntlich viele pädagogische Schriften der Aufklärung mit verärgerten und sogar hysterischen Kritiken gewendet, weil imaginatives sich mit dem Helden identifizierendes Lesen nicht nur verderbe, sondern zusätzlich ein abartiges, unheilbringendes Wünschen und Sehnen wecke, was bis in den Horror zwanghaften Onanierens verkommen könnte. „Imagination was dangerous because it epitomized self-centered desire, immoderation, unreality, passion, and greed".[18] Dennoch wird trotz dieser Warnung die seit dem Mittelalter wirksame feudal-mechanistische Verwaltung des Körpers aufgegeben und durch einen von der bürgerlichen Gesellschaft installierten neuen Kontrollmechanismus des Beobachtens und Befragens ersetzt, oder mit den Worten Michel Foucaults, durch „those formidable disciplinary régimes in the schools, hospitals, barracks, factories, cities, lodgings, families".[19]

Der erstaunliche Verbrauch von Luxusgütern im Bereich absolutistischer Höfe, so noch Purdy, motivierte das Bürgertum, dem Konsum der Aristokratie nachzueifern. Die junge Konsumindustrie versuchte das neue Bedürfnis, das besonders durch Modejournale und Literatur gefördert wurde, zu befriedigen. Mit diesen imitierten modischen Ausstattungen und luxuriösen Requisiten konnte das den aristokratischen Höfen fern stehende Bildungsbürgertum die eigenen Rituale des Wohlstands und Symbole des Prestiges, der Disziplin und des Wettbewerbs in Cafés, Wohnungen, Büros, Familiensalons, öffentlichen Parks und auf dem Lande zur Schau stellen. Kurz, Purdy vermutet im Imitationsprinzip das Identität bildende Inskriptionspro-

[16] Daniel Purdy: *The Tyranny of Elegance. Consumer Cosmopolitanism in the Era of Goethe*. Baltimore, London 1998. S. xiii.

[17] Ibid.

[18] Isabel V. Hull: *Sexuality, State, and Civil Society in Germany, 1700-1815*. Ithaca 1996. S. 272. Zitiert nach Purdy. S. 36.

[19] Michel Foucault: Body/Power. In: *Power/Knowledge. Selected Interviews & Other Writings, 1972-1977*. Hg. von V. Colin Gordon. New York 1980. S. 58.

gramm des modernen modisch gekleideten Körpers, wobei allerdings, wie es scheint, ein wichtiges Problem übersehen wird.

Zunächst wäre grundsätzlich darauf hinzuweisen, dass wir nur jene Dinge imitieren, die erreichbar sind, worauf Roland Barthes in seinen Analysen der Mythen des Alltags wiederholt aufmerksam gemacht hat.[20] Den Lebensstil der englischen Königin, des Sultans von Brunei oder des Microsoftmanagers Bill Gates nachzuahmen, fällt demzufolge keinem ein. Und in dieser Perspektive gesehen hat mit großer Wahrscheinlichkeit auch das gehobene aufgeklärte Bürgertum nicht daran gedacht, die Lebensart von Versailles, des Schlosses Fontainebleau oder die des heimischen Landesfürsten zu kopieren. Ein Beispiel aus der frühen Neuzeit ist die schwäbische Familie der Fugger, die sich dies hätte finanziell leisten können, es aber nicht tat. Die Gründe also, warum sich mit der Aufklärung Mode und Konsumbedarf von Luxusgütern lebhaft entwickelten, werden durch das Motiv, Aristokratie, Modejournale und Literatur zu imitieren, sicherlich ansatzweise erklärt, aber nicht ausreichend.

In Diskursen, die sich mit den Erfolgen der Aufklärung in Wissenschaften, Künsten und Philosophie beschäftigen, wird oft eine ihrer Entdeckungen übersehen, die im vorliegenden Zusammenhang wichtig und folgenreich ist, und zwar die Einsicht in die Tatsache, dass der Körper nicht nur mittels seiner Arbeitskraft und seines Know-how Vermögen produziert, sondern dies vor allem auch durch seine Veranlagung zu konsumieren, nach Neuem zu verlangen und nach Wohlstand zu streben bewirkt.[21] Weigerte sich der Körper über die existentiellen Grunderfordernisse hinaus zu konsumieren, bräche die Welt wie wir sie kennen zusammen. Die Bedeutung dieser folgenschweren Tatsache war der Aufklärung nicht unbekannt geblieben. Und aus dem Grund war die Konsumbegabung des Körpers, diese These liegt der vorliegenden Arbeit zugrunde, als zentrales Identitätsmerkmal zu sichern und, ideologisch und mythologisch maskiert, in den Diskursen der Gesellschaft zu verankern. Vor allem aber waren hinsichtlich der Konsumkapazität des Körpers jene Identitätsaspekte unbrauchbar, die Selbstzufriedenheit und Selbstgenügsamkeit signalisierten. Mit anderen Worten, die Lösung der Aufgabe, einen hohen Konsumbedarf zu motivieren, bestand weniger in der Förderung begrenzter Imitationsbedürfnisse aristokratischer Kreise, der Modejournale und Literatur, sondern vielmehr darin, den modernen Körper gezielt und dosiert mit Motiven eines nie zu befriedigenden Unbehagens und

---

[20] Roland Barthes: *Mythologies*. London 1973. Bes. Myth Today. S. 117-174.

[21] So werden beispielsweise Machtverhältnisse und Ideologie in der Aufklärung in vielen Fällen in der Perspektive der herrschenden Gesellschaftsklasse analysiert und beschrieben, die seit dem 17. Jahrhundert den Körper als das grundlegende Produktionsmedium betrachtet und sich dementsprechend bemüht, jede Tätigkeit des Körpers, die nicht dem Vorgang der Vermögensproduktion dient, zu unterbinden. Die zentrale ökonomische Rolle der Vermögen bildenden Konsumkapazität des Körpers wird dabei nicht berücksichtigt.

Unzufriedenseins sich selbst gegenüber zu inskribieren, was allerdings ohne René Descartes' Axiom von der Souveränität der Vernunft, die Grundlage des modernen Subjektivismus und des arithmetisch-logischen Rationalismus, nicht möglich gewesen wäre.

Die Schrift-Spuren von Subjektivität führen zwar bis ins späte Mittelalter zurück, dennoch war es zuerst Descartes, der das subjektive Individuum bekanntlich in den Mittelpunkt eines philosophischen Systems stellt, den Dualismus von Körper und Bewusstsein identifiziert, formuliert und beide Sphären mit den größten und keineswegs immer positiven Konsequenzen isoliert. Für ihn ist der Mensch in den Bereichen des Denkens und der Ausdehnung angesiedelt, d. h. er ist nunmehr gespalten. Auf der einen Seite ist er "denkende Substanz", auf der anderen ist er seinem Körper nach, wie sämtliche Lebewesen, eine Maschine.[22] Aus diesem Grunde konnte das in ihren Anfängen zuerst von der Aufklärung begeistert und lebhaft entwickelte moderne Maschinenwesen entstehen, eben weil Descartes den ontologischen Status des Menschen in Opposition zur Natur platziert und ihm eine analytische Methode der Weltbetrachtung vermittelt, ohne die er nicht daran hätte denken können, die Techniken zu erschaffen, die die Bewältigung und Beherrschung der Natur vorstellbar und die Alphabetisierung des Körpers und seiner Kultur möglich machten. An dieser Stelle historischer Entwicklungslinien ist der Ursprung des sinnenfeindlichen Rationalismus der Aufklärung zu lokalisieren. Dieser stellt den ideologischen Rahmen, in dem für die komplexe Aufgabe ökonomisch sinnvolle Identitätsdefizite zu erzeugen eine ganze Reihe von Lösungen entwickelt wurden, aus der im folgenden drei konkrete Beispiele behandelt werden, und zwar aus dem Umfeld der Alphabetisierung der aufgeklärten Gesellschaft, der Unsterblichkeitsdebatte und der Physiognomie. Die Gründe dieser vermeintlich sonderbaren Auswahl werden weiter unten deutlich werden.

IV.

Der Begriff der Alphabetisierung der aufgeklärten Gesellschaft bezeichnet im wesentlichen das Vermögen, individuelle Selbstbeobachtungen im Rahmen der literarischen Kultur zu versprachlichen und damit als Mechanismus der Identitätsbildung zu erfassen. Die Alphabetisierungskampagne der Aufklärung, beobachtet Albrecht Koschorke, setzt zunächst damit ein, "die Idee einer im Spiegel sichtbar werdenden körperlichen Ganzheit[23] zu destruie-

---

[22] Der Körperbegriff Descartes' beeinflusste besonders die Überwindung des mittelalterlichen humuralpathologischen zugunsten des neuzeitlichen neurobiologischen oder organologischen Körperkonzepts.

[23] Im Gegensatz zur frühneuzeitlichen Auffassung des aus Teilen bestehenden Körpers vgl. z. B. David Hillman und Carla Mazzio: *The Body in Parts: Fantasies of Corporeality in Early Modern Europe*. New York 1997.

ren",[24] weil die Identitätsbildungsprogramme nur insofern durchführbar sind, "insoweit sie die gewissermaßen voralphabetischen Identitäten, mit denen sie es anfangs zu tun haben, zerstören". Hinsichtlich dieser vormaligen Identitäten statuieren sie "einen Mangel, dessen Behebung sie dann in einer Arbeit unendlicher Perfektibilisierung in Aussicht stellen".[25] Angesprochen ist der auf die ehemalige Zusammengehörigkeit von Leib und Seele bezügliche Makel, der für die Ideologie der Aufklärung, die in der Entkörperung der Seele die wichtigste Tugend sieht, nicht tragbar ist, geht es ihr doch, so noch einmal Koschorke, um die das "gesamte lebensweltliche Empfinden durchdringende Entsemiotisierung der Vorgänge des unteren leiblichen Stratums".[26] Der von diesem Programm der Entsexualisierung betroffene Körper unterliegt einer Strategie der Identitätsbildung, die den symbolischen Tod des ehedem geschlechtlichen Körpers anstrebt, weil er nicht Männlichkeit und Stärke beherbergt, sondern allein Schwäche und Lüsternheit. Parallel der Absicht, auch den weiblichen Körper im Rahmen seiner Personalisierung zu entsexualisieren, propagiert der pädagogische Diskurs eine Abkühlung der animalischen Wärme des Körpers mit kalten Bädern, dünnen Bettdecken, leichter Winterbekleidung, frugalen Diäten usw.[27]

Der Versuch und das Bemühen, die sexuellen Bedürfnisse des aufgeklärten Körpers zu neutralisieren, ging mit der Installation der Körperfeindlichkeit als identitätsbildendem Programm Hand in Hand. Doch das allerdings nur mit begrenztem Erfolg, zumal der Widerstand des sexuellen Körpers gegen seine Unterdrückung unter dem Mantel der öffentlichen Ideologie ununterbrochen weiterschwelte. Dieser Mangel an Erfolg aber war für den herrschenden Machtdiskurs nicht weiter problematisch, denn der Zweifel, dass der eigene Körper unzureichend gestaltet ist und ihm Fehler, Untugenden und Laster anhaften, die mit angebotenen, käuflich zu erwerbenden Therapien, Mitteln und Waren behoben werden können, war gesät und saß nun fest in der Psyche des aufgeklärten Menschen. Oder anders gesehen, das Identitätsmerkmal der Feindlichkeit gegenüber Bedingungen des eigenen Körpers, das die Konsumindustrie ohne Unterbrechung zu stimulieren vermag, konnte als Strategie der Identitätsdefizitbildung als erfolgreich abgeschlossen gelten.

---

[24] "Sei es", heißt es weiter, "daß unter Rückgriff auf barocke Drastik die Spiegelbetrachterin die Pocken bekommt [...], sei es, daß man sie mit Anschluß an das weite Feld der Marmorfrauen-Motivik 'einem leblosen Venus-Bilde' gleichstellt oder mit den Metaphern der Marionette und der Puppe in Verbindung bringt, wie sie im Zeitalter des ausgehenden Cartesianismus für das nur Körperliche und Mechanische geläufig sind". Koschorke. S. 244.
[25] Koschorke S. 242.
[26] Ibid. S. 268.
[27] Ibid. S. 209.

Es war aber nicht nur die durch die Alphabetisierungskampagne hervorgerufene Einsicht in die Identitätsdefizite bildende Unzulänglichkeit des eigenen Körpers, die Bedürfnisse nach Konsum- und Luxusgütern weckte, von denen man hoffte und glaubte, dass sie die angesprochenen Körpermängel beheben oder zumindest maskieren konnten. Es standen vielmehr eine ganze Reihe von Strategien zur Verfügung, die Identitätsmerkmale Unbehagen und Feindlichkeit gegenüber dem eigenen Körper in der Form eines Identitätsdefizits zu inskribieren, damit Bedürfnisse entstehen, die zur Nachfrage des Angebots von Konsum- und Luxusgütern führen. Dabei bildet weniger der sinnenfeindliche Rationalismus der Aufklärung, wie im oben beschriebenen Fall, den Ausgangspunkt, sondern eine eigentümlich faszinierte Hinwendung zu anorganischen Zustandsformen des Seins und Denkens, wie sie im Kontext der Unsterblichkeitsdebatte und der physiognomischen Rhetorik Lavaters, um nur zwei weitere Beispiele zu nennen, besonders deutlich werden.

V.

Ein günstiger Einstieg in die Unsterblichkeitsdebatte ist der vor wenigen Jahren von Gisela Luginbühl-Weber herausgegebene deutsch-französische Briefwechsel zwischen Johann Kaspar Lavater (1741-1801), dem Naturforscher Charles Bonnet (1720-1794) und dem zwischen beiden vermittelnden Genfer Pfarrer Jacob Benelle (1717-1794),[28] denn die Edition beschäftigt sich unter anderem auch mit den metaphysisch-theologischen Fragen der Unsterblichkeit, und zwar im Kontext der sich in der Aufklärung etablierenden geschlossenen Glaubenssysteme und der Emanzipation des anthropologischen Denkens aus metaphysischen Traditionen im Umfeld der Namen Breitinger, Bodmer, Klopstock, Gellert, Haller, Iselin, Sulzer, Kant, Spalding, Ernesti, Jerusalem, Cramer, Resewitz, Basedow, Herder, Mendelssohn u. a. Vor allem aber wird im Licht dieser Korrespondenz das Streben der Aufklärung nach einer Form des anorganischen Denkens deutlich, das die Inskriptionsstrategien der durch wirtschaftliche Erwägungen als wünschenswert erklärten Körperfeindlichkeit mit Auswirkungen und Konsequenzen überhaupt erst ermöglichte, die, wie eingangs kurz skizziert, uns heute besonders belasten.

Angeregt wurde die Korrespondenz mit Bonnet von Lavater. In seinem ersten Brief vom 18. Dezember 1768 macht er Bonnet auf den großen Einfluß aufmerksam, den seine Werke auf ihn ausgeübt hätten, besonders auf die vierbändigen *Aussichten in die Ewigkeit* (1768-1778).[29] In dieser "gigantischen Schrulle" (Harald Landry) wird der Versuch unternommen, in

---

[28] Gisela Luginbühl-Weber (Hg.): *Johann Kaspar Lavater – Charles Bonnet – Jacob Benelle. Briefe 1768-1790. Ein Forschungsbeitrag zur Aufklärung in der Schweiz.* Halbbd. 1 Briefe. Halbbd. 2 Kommentar. Bern 1997.

[29] Luginbühl-Weber. S. 5.

prosaischem Ernst das Leben in Wohnungen und Palästen des Jenseits zu schildern, in denen sich, nach ihrem irdischen Tod, glänzend entwickelte Menschen aus unsterblicher Substanz aufhalten. Interessant an diesen oft verspotteten Traktaten Lavaters ist allerdings der Versuch, das Leben nach dem Tod wissenschaftlich zu begründen, wozu ihn, in der Form von Analogieschlüssen, die erstaunlichen Metamorphosen in der Biologie anregten, Metamorphosen vom Samen zum fertigen Organismus, oder von der Raupe zum Schmetterling.

Diese seltsame Schrift wurde besonders von der *Contemplation de la Nature* (1764) und der *Palingénésie philosophique* des damals viel beachteten Bonnet inspiriert,[30] die Lavater noch im Erscheinungsjahr 1769 übersetzt und kommentiert hat. Er war wie Lessing, Goethe und viele ihrer Zeitgenossen davon fasziniert, dass der Naturforscher und Naturphilosoph Bonnet alle psychischen Erscheinungen auf Nervenprozesse zurückführt und die Seele als ein Organ im Sinn einer einfachen immateriellen Substanz, die sich auch nach dem Tod erhält, veröbjektivierte.[31] Um deren konkrete Beschreibung im Zustand der personifizierten Unsterblichkeit bemühte sich Lavater in seinen *Aussichten*, die er später in der Form eines Gedichtes zu verarbeiten gedachte, und zwar im Licht der "progressiven Vervollkommnung der menschlichen Natur und Geisteskräfte".[32] In dieser Hinsicht glaubte er philosophisches, theologisches und literarisches Neuland zu betreten.[33]

Lavater, dem nach Luginbühl-Weber die umfassende Bonnet-Rezeption in Deutschland zu verdanken ist,[34] versteht Bonnets *Palingénésie philosophique* als "Gedanken über vergangenen und künftigen Zustand lebender Wesen",[35] und zwar in einer Schöpfungsgeschichte, die sich zu einer "Wiederherstellungsgeschichte" verändert.[36] Bonnet geht von einer "Katastrophentheorie" aus, die besagt, "daß es im Lauf der Erdgeschichte [...] mehrmals [...] zu großen Revolutionen komme, zu weltweiten Flut- und Erdbenkatastrophen, nach denen alles Leben scheinbar verschwinde, in Wirklichkeit aber in unvergänglichen 'Reparaturkeimen' weiterlebe und zur vorbestimmten Zeit in anderer Form wieder erscheine".[37]

Somit gibt es nach Bonnet keinen Tod, "sondern Wiederherstellung des irdischen Körpers aus unverweslicher, licht- oder ätherähnlicher Materie zu ewigem Leben", in dem die Entwicklung vom gedankenlosen bis zum den-

[30] Ibid. S. 275.
[31] Ibid. S. 283.
[32] Ibid. S. 281.
[33] Ibid. S. 277.
[34] Ibid. S. 284.
[35] Ibid. S. 289.
[36] Ibid. S. 291.
[37] Ibid. S. 290.

kenden Menschen stattfindet.[38] Lavaters *Aussichten*, erklärt Luginbühl-Weber, "gründen auf den gleichen Vorstellungen; gehen aber, auf Anregung Zimmermanns [...], in der detaillierten Darstellung weit über Bonnet hinaus", hinsichtlich seiner Darstellung eines unvergänglichen "pneumatischen Leibs", dem die Eigenschaften der "aktiven und passiven Durchdringlichkeit, Schnelligkeit, Unkränkbarkeit, Unverwundbarkeit und Schmerzlosigkeit, Feinstofflichkeit, Selbstausbreitungskraft, Zusammendrängbarkeit, Elastizität [und] Anpassungsfähigkeit des christusgleichen Körpers" gegeben sind. Diese Begriffe waren den zeitgenössischen naturwissenschaftlichen Schriften der theoretischen Medizin entlehnt. Der künftige, sich im Jenseits befindende vollkommene Körper war für Lavater und Bonnet "Voraussetzung für vollkommenes, d. h. allumfassendes und fehlerfreies Denken, Fühlen und Erkennen, zu dem nach damaliger Ansicht das menschliche Geschlecht sich hinentwickeln werde".[39]

Mittels der Kombination religiöser Thesen und naturwissenschaftlicher Grundsätze, die heut als kurios und verstiegen befremdet, war für die Aufklärung um Lavater und Bonnet die Dimension des Jenseitigen, in die der unsterbliche Mensch nach seinem diesseitigen Tod hinübergerettet wird, dem Licht der rationalen Vernunft zugänglich und damit beschreibbar, womit sich diese Vorstellungen deutlich vom tradierten religiösen Denken absetzten. Mit anderen Worten, das menschliche Dasein, in dem organisches Leben nur noch als ein unbedeutender Durchgangszustand vor seiner jenseitigen konkreten ätherischen Existenz angesehen wurde,[40] hatte den letzten Grad seiner Mathematisierbarkeit erreicht. Und damit wurde es als das ausgesprochene Ziel des organischen Lebens angesehen, dem eigentlichen wertvollen Sein in dem ins Jenseits verlegten Existenzraum des unsterblich Anorganischen zuzustreben. D. h. das Ziel der Überwindung der organischen Phase des Lebens bestand in der eigenen Auslöschung, im Tod. So sehr war die religiöse Aufklärung von den Möglichkeiten, Folgen und Aussichten ihres abstrakt-anorganischen Denkens fasziniert, dass sie das Schicksal des organischen Lebens im politischen Dasein, wie dies schon einmal Luther beispielhaft formuliert hatte, nicht bekümmerte, denn für sie war die Welt weitgehend enträtselt. Die vorliegenden Briefe verdeutlichen, zusammen mit dem ausführlichen Kommentar, wie sehr Bonnet und Lavater von den Konsequenzen des eigenen Denkens beeindruckt waren. Besonders

---

[38] Ibid. S. 301.

[39] Ibid. S. 302.

[40] Der kulturgeschichtliche Ursprung der Feindlichkeit gegenüber dem eigenen organischen Körper geht auf das den Lutherischen Protestantismus beeinflussende Werk *De civitate Dei* des Kirchenvaters Augustinus (354-430) zurück. Hier wird der Körper des Menschen, der mit seiner Seele auf eine unreine Art vereinigt ist, dem teuflischen Bereich (*civitas diaboli*) zugerechnet. Es ist die Aufgabe der Kirche, der unrein mit dem Körper verbundenen Seele die Rückkehr in das Reich Gottes (*civitas Dei*) zu ermöglichen.

die Sprache Lavaters[41] signalisiert mit ihrer feierlich-ehrfürchtigen Stilhaltung die Bedeutungstiefe göttlicher Schöpfungsgedanken, die er erfasst zu haben glaubte, denn er war davon überzeugt, in sinnlich wahrnehmbaren Verkehr mit Gott treten und übernatürliche Offenbarungen erhalten zu können.

Die Vorstellung und Hinwendung zu einer mechanistisch-anorganischen Existenz unsterblicher Körper im Jenseits aber gestaltet im Reflex rückwirkend Existenzbedingungen im Diesseits. D. h. ein Identitätsdefizit entsteht, das nun ein Wünschen und Verlangen auslöst, die als mangelhaft empfundene Erscheinung, Gestalt und Ausstrahlung des eigenen Körpers zu veredeln, was aber nur noch mittels einer sekundären Fiktion vom eigenen Ich gelingen kann, und zwar mit Hilfe der immer wieder frisch ausgetüftelten und bereitgestellten Waren, Therapien, Diäten und Luxusgüter der Konsumindustrie. Für diese Dinge ist nun ein endloser Bedarf geweckt, weil das in der Aufklärung entwickelte und konstruierte Identitätsdefizit des organischen Körpers unterbrochen nach Mitteln der eigenen Vervollkommnung, Ausstattung, Maskierung oder zumindest kosmetischer Veränderung verlangt, die käuflich zu erwerben sind. Das Verlangen diese Wünsche zu erfüllen war so stark, dass der gegen die Konsumindustrie ankämpfende aufgeklärte pädagogische Diskurs wirkungslos blieb.

In diesem Blickwinkel ist es dann auch konsequent, wenn die Aufklärung, motiviert durch die anorganischen Tendenzen ihres Denkens, mit der Mechanisierung der Welt beginnt, was zu einer Erfolgsexplosion in den Wissenschaften führt.[42] Sie entdeckt Elektrizität und erfindet die Infinitesimalrechnung, das Thermometer, die Dampfmaschine und den Ballonflug. Weiter: die Gliederpuppe, den mechanischen Menschen, Prothesen, Androiden und den Cyborg, die Automatisierung, das Maschinenwesen und die Rechenmaschine, aber auch die Guillotine, das mechanisierte Töten. Marionettenspiele gehörten in der Aufklärung zu den beliebtesten Unterhaltungen in Städten und Dörfern. Modelle, Standards und Normen des Menschen werden im ästhetischen Diskurs entwickelt. Zusammen mit Uniformen tritt das Modewesen in Erscheinung und mit ihm das Mannequin, beziehungsweise die Pandora, eine vor dem Aufkommen des Modejournals im 17. und 18. Jahrhundert aus Paris an Fürstenhöfe versandte Modepuppe, der später die sterilen, anorganisch deformierten Modepuppen der Schaufenster und Laufstege folgen. Die Standardisierung des Körpers, dem jedes Ausschreiten in die Vielfalt organischer Formen Schritt um Schritt abgerungen wird, beginnt und führt zu einer mechanistisch-modischen Normierung der

---

[41] S. Kamal Radwan: *Die Sprache Lavaters im Spiegel der Geistesgeschichte*. Göppingen 1972.
[42] S. z. B. Thomas L. Hankins: *Science and the Enlightenment*. New York 1985; Margaret C. Jacob: *Scientific Culture and the Making of the Industrial West*. New York 1997.

menschlichen Gestalt und Bekleidung, die sich als Diktat und Diktatur des Zeitgeistes jeden Widerstand überwindend unaufhaltbar etabliert. Um die dem Organischen entzogenen mechanistischen Normierungstendenzen des menschlichen Körpers in der Aufklärung zu verdeutlichen, bieten sich als besonders markantes Beispiel die überaus erfolgreichen psychologisch-mechanistischen *Physiognomischen Fragmente* (4 Bde., 1775-1778) Lavaters an.[43] Physiognomie beschreibt für Lavater die nicht zu leugnende "Wahrheit des menschlichen Gesichts", und zwar als göttliche Wahrheit, die sich dem Betrachter als "in der Natur gegründete Wissenschaft" stellt.[44] Lavater war überzeugt, die körperliche Ausprägung der Seele in Merkmalen des Gesichts und Schädels feststellen zu können. In der Perspektive der modernen Kulturtheorie gelingt also Lavater auf diesem Weg die Konstruktion und Programmierung des menschlichen Gesichts als Ausdruck einer verfestigten Moral und Ideologie, dessen geistige Konzeption als Sprachbild im Rahmen des mit der Umgestaltung kognitiver Methoden verbundenen Umbruchs von Wissensstrukturen im 15. und 16. Jahrhundert auftaucht.[45] Lavaters *Physiognomische Fragmente* haben die Beschreibung und Gestaltung des Gesichts in der Literatur und bildenden Kunst grundlegend beeinflusst, weil er vor allem daran glaubte, das "Alphabet der Offenbarung"[46] als Vernunft in der Schöpfung des menschlichen Gesichts entziffert zu haben. Auf diesem von ihm erfundenen Schöpfungsalphabet beruht demgemäß die wiederum Identitätsdefizite erzeugende Normierung der moralisch verfestigten Ausdrucksweise des menschlichen Gesichts, was Lavater schließlich weltlichen Ruhm einbrachte und sozusagen eine Position als Weichensteller in der Kulturgeschichte Europas, die kaum zu überschätzen ist. Ohne seine analytische Anthropologie und physiognomische Rhetorik sähe heute die Beschreibung und metaphorische Gestaltung des menschlichen Gesichts anders aus.

[43] S. in dem Zusammenhang bes. Lavaters *Hundert Physiognomische Regeln*, die ein Jahr nach seinem Tod im fünften Band *Nachgelassene Schriften* (1802) von Georg Geßner herausgegeben wurden. Nachdruck Hildesheim 1993.
[44] Johann Caspar Lavater: *Physiognomische Fragmente zur Beförderung der Menschenkenntnis und Menschenliebe*. Eine Auswahl mit 101 Abbildungen. Hg. von Christoph Siegrist. Stuttgart 1984. S. 5 und 7. S. auch Hans-Georg von Arburg: Johann Caspar Lavaters Physiognomik. Geschichte – Methodik – Wirkung. In: *Das Kunstkabinett des Johann Caspar Lavater*. Hg. von Gerda Mraz und Uwe Schögl. Wien 1999. S. 40-59.
[45] S. Holger Pausch: Dialektik des Sehens. Beobachtungen zur Genealogie des Gesichts in der Literatur. In: *Das Sprach-Bild als textuelle Interaktion*. Hg. von Gerd Labroisse und Dick van Stekelenburg. Amsterdam und Atlanta, GA. 1999. S. 15-44.
[46] Lavater benutzt den Begriff in dem Gedicht 'Der Menschenschädel'. In: *Deutsche Dichtung im 18. Jahrhundert*. Hg. von Adalbert Elschenbroich. München 1960. S. 433.

Aufbau und Struktur der *Physiognomischen Fragmente* erinnern an My-
sterienspiele, in denen die Kräfte des Guten und Bösen in Konflikt geraten,
um den Zuschauer zu motivieren, sich mit den ersten zu identifizieren und
die zweiten zu verabscheuen. Die physiognomische Rhetorik Lavaters basiert auf diesen Gegensätzen des Guten und Bösen. Wie im Mysterienspiel
wird auch hier das Böse bzw. die Kategorie negativer Physiognomien als
abschreckendes Beispiel dargestellt. In diesem Sinn beschreibt Lavater das
Gesicht einer "Dirne" als Zeichen des "tiefsten Grads der menschlichen La-
sterhaftigkeit" (58).[47] Zur Physiognomie des Bauernfängers heißt es: "Was
macht dieses Gesicht häßlich? Disharmonie! Schiefheit – Vielfachheit – und
was bewirkt dieses? – Falschheit und Niederträchtigkeit" (58). In der Zeichnung Judas' sieht Lavater "eine abgehärtete, verjährte Bosheit, die sich von
Abgrund zu Abgrund fortgewälzt hat: Ein Geiz, der jedes Menschen Empfindung gelassen Hohn spricht, das ist's, was uns vornehmlich in diesem
Gesicht aufstößt" (52).

Demgegenüber stehen die Anmerkungen zu zwei Karikaturen von Voltaire: "In beiden ist Genius wetterleuchtender Schalkheit" (74). Das Bild
Herders wird mit den Worten kommentiert: "Ein äußerst feinsichtiger,
durchdringender, vielfassender mächtigdenkender Kopf, der besonders alles
Schwache, Lächerliche, Fehlerhafte der Menschheit durch und durch
schaut" (50). Und über einen Kupferstich des jungen Goethe gerät Lavater
sogar ins Schwärmen: "Hier ist Lebendigkeit, Adel, Feinheit! Wie schmilzt
da Jüngling und Mann in Eins! Wie sanft, wie ohn' alle Härte, Steifheit,
Gespanntheit, Lockerheit; wie unangestrengt und harmonisch" (32). Die
pädagogische Absicht der polarisierten Bildkommentare Lavaters besteht
darin den Leser zu veranlassen, dem Vorbild "edler" Menschen nachzueifern, Vorbildern demnach, mit denen sich der durchschnittliche Bürger des
Alltags, wenn er sich nicht aberwitzig überschätzt, niemals vergleichen
kann. Die auf diesem Weg entstandene Differenz zwischen Wunschvorstel-
lung und Wirklichkeit erzeugt aber wieder Identitätsdefizite, die der Ideologie des Konsumierens entsprechend die individuelle Befindlichkeit und das
Verhältnis dem eigenen Körper gegenüber belasten. Die Folge ist ein
Handlungsbedarf, der mittels des Verbrauchs von Produkten vorübergehend
neutralisiert wird, bis der nächste durch ein Identitätsdefizit ausgelöste Im-
puls den gleichen psychologischen Mechanismus erneut in Gang setzt.

Abschließend ließe sich an dieser Stelle noch einwenden, dass das Erzeugen von Identitätsdefiziten, kulturhistorisch gesehen, im Grunde doch dem
Alter der menschlichen Zivilisation entspricht. Antike Werke der plasti-
schen Kunst Ägyptens, Kretas, Mesopotamiens, besonders die der klassischen Antike, denen mathematische Proportionen des Körpers zugrunde liegen, sind alle Idealisierungen der menschlichen Gestalt. Und aus dem Grund
dienen sie auch als Mittel, Identitätsdefizite zu erzeugen, vorausgesetzt na-

---

[47] Die folgenden Zitate stammen aus der Ausgabe *Physiognomische Fragmente*.
Ausgewählt und kommentiert von Friedrich Märker. Oldenburg 1949.

türlich, dass der Identitätsbegriff der Aufklärung in die Frühgeschichte übertragen werden kann, was zu bezweifeln ist. Doch wie steht es mit jüngeren Geschichtsabschnitten, beispielsweise dem Mittelalter? War es nicht die erklärte Absicht, mit der Darstellung idealistisch überhöhter Gestalten in der epischen Literatur und der rücksichtslosen Kritik sündiger Menschen in Predigten Identitätsdefizite zu erzeugen? Zweifellos. Doch es darf dabei nicht vergessen werden, dass die Formen mittelalterlicher Identitätsdefizite nicht auf Individuen zugeschnitten waren, sondern auf Gruppen. Dabei handelte es sich im Sinne der scholastischen Psychologie um typologische Diskurse, die dem einzelnen Menschen den Ausweg offen hielten, sich als nicht angesprochen zu betrachten. Erst die Alphabetisierung des aufgeklärten Körpers, die den individuellen Zustand des einzelnen Körpers, also persönliche Eigenheiten und Eigenschaften versprachlicht, verstellt den Rückzug in die Gruppenidentität, ins Unpersönliche. Dementsprechend beziehen sich beispielsweise Lavaters negative Indizien der Nase, Stirn und Augen nicht mehr auf universal-typologische Merkmale wie in der mittelalterlichen Physiognomie. Jetzt handelt es sich um individuelle Seelenzeichen eines bestimmten Charakters, die nicht mehr ins Ungefähre zu reflektieren sind.[48] Identitätsdefizite, die auf Lavaters physiognomischen Regeln basieren, sind konkret, individuell und auf eine bestimmte Person bezogen. Mit anderen Worten, die Inskription des aufgeklärten Körpers mit Identitätsdefiziten produziert die Gestaltungsmerkmale seiner Individualität.

Das ist das Neue an den aufgeklärten Formen der Bildung von Identitätsdefiziten. Sie beruhen im wesentlichen darauf, dass das Bild der Aufklärung, das sie sich von Mensch und Gesellschaft machte, die sie neu gestalten wollte, trotz der einseitigen Propagierung mechanistischer Körpernormen ambivalent und zwiespältig, im Grunde gespalten ist.[49] Im Blickwinkel dieser Ideologie verweist beispielsweise ihr berühmtes Schlagwort "Zurück zur Natur"[50] im Kontext der faszinierten Hinwendung der Aufklärung zur Sphäre des Todes, des Anorganischen, körperlich Unsterblichen, eben nicht nur auf die grünen Vorstellungsmuster unverbrauchter Wiesen und Wälder, sondern, in seiner dialektischen Inversion, auch auf die vorangestellten anorganischen Dimensionen der Natur, ohne die die Existenz im organischen Sein undenkbar ist, weil sie auf ihnen beruhen. Das pädagogische Bekämpfen und Verweigern des sexuellen Begehrens, der Imagination und der

---

[48] Die Literatur zu diesem Problem der Lavaterschen Physiognomie ist zu umfangreich, um zitiert zu werden. Einen Überblick vermittelt die systematische Bibliographie zum Thema "Physiognomie und Charakter" in Kirstin Breitenfellner: *Lavaters Schatten. Physiognomie und Charakter bei Ganghofer, Fontane und Döblin.* Dresden, München 1999. S. 219-271.

[49] S. bes. Max Horkheimer und Theodor Adorno: *Dialektik der Aufklärung. Philosophische Fragmente.* Frankfurt/M. 1984.

[50] S. dazu auch Thomas Koebner: *Zurück zur Natur: Ideen der Aufklärung und ihre Nachwirkung.* Heidelberg 1993.

Freude an modischen Luxusgütern (eben die verbotenen Kirschen in Nachbars Garten), die Standardisierung und Normierung des "natürlichen" Körpers als mechanistische Konstruktion und die Reduktion des endlos variablen Gesichtsbilds auf eine Serie physiognomischer Identitätsmerkmale sind nicht nur ideologische Reflexe. Sie produzieren vielmehr, was zu beschreiben gewesen war, ökonomisch und politisch sehr effektive Identitätsdefizite, die in einer Vielzahl von Aufmachungen, neben ihrer Funktion als Medien der gesellschaftlichen Kontrolle, den Konsum ununterbrochen beleben. Es ist somit besonders der die organisch-biologische Begrenzung überwindende Aspekt des Anorganischen in der Vernunft der Aufklärung, dessen Nachwirkung in den weit verbreiteten Erscheinungen der Körperfeindlichkeit heute wieder zu erkennen ist.

In dieser Hinsicht eine letzte Anmerkung. Die vorliegende Darstellung möchte nicht, obgleich der Anschein diesen Punkt beinahe zu bestätigen scheint, als gegenaufklärerisches Argument verstanden werden. Im Gegenteil, zumal sich der Standpunkt ohne große Schwierigkeiten vertreten ließe, dass es zur Aufklärung bisher keine Alternative gibt, zu einer Aufklärung also, die sich nicht davor scheut, in der Tradition Nietzsches oder Wittgensteins die eigenen Fundamente zu hinterfragen.[51] In diesem Umfeld aber ist Körperfeindlichkeit ein Phänomen im kulturellen Gedächtnis, dessen negative Eigenschaft als Erbmangel erkannt wird. Doch dieser Erbmangel hat sich zu einer Notwendigkeit entwickelt,[52] zu einem grundlegenden Instrument gesellschaftlicher Kontrolle, ohne das die vertrauten Funktionsweisen des menschlichen Zusammenlebens nicht zu sichern sind.

---

[51] S. beispielsweise Peter Sloterdijk: *Kritik der zynischen Vernunft*. Frankfurt/M. 1983. Auch geht es in der postmodernen Kulturtheorie überhaupt um das Sezieren aufklärerischer Grundlagen, also bei Foucault, Bourdieu, Deleuze, Derrida, Kristeva, Althusser u. v. a.

[52] Im Militärbereich, auf den hier nicht eingegangen werden konnte, und in der Industrie verweisen Paul Baran und Paul Sweezy auf Körperfeindlichkeit in der Aufmachung anti-humaner Produktionsprogramme: "But it is not only those who man and supply the military machine who are engaged in an anti-human enterprise. The same can be said in varying degrees of many millions of other workers who produce, and create wants for, goods and services which no one needs. And so interdependent are the various sectors and branches of the economy that nearly everyone is involved in one way or another in these anti-human activities: the farmer supplying food for troops fighting in Vietnam, the tool and die makers turning out the intricate machinery needed for a new automobile model, the manufacturers of paper and ink and TV sets whose products are used to control the minds of people, and so on and so on". In: *Monopoly Capital*. New York 1966. S. 344.

Karin Barton

Apum Rex/Regina: Goethes Bienenlehre als Schlüssel zu *Wilhelm Meisters Wanderjahren*

In the Wanderjahre, *Goethe draws attention to bees by introducing a name-shifting female character as a "wild humble-bee", obscuring the biological sex of a gender-shifting "terrestrial being", and describing the illustrated key of/to the novel in terms strikingly similar to contemporary entomological concepts of the bee sting. The paper discusses such comparisons derived from the morphological and behavioral attributes of social insects in connection with concurrent debates regarding the social and sexual organization of Hymenoptera, and the unsettling discovery of the femaleness of the alleged King of the bees. Read as a fable of swarming bees, Goethe's most enigmatic novel emerges as a summary of discourses during the Enlightenment on the issue of how gender tends to be "naturally" constructed in response to major changes in economic and demographic conditions.*

"Cet aiguillon est semblable à un petit dard, qui, quoique très-délié, est cependant creux d'un bout à l'autre".[1] Gibt es eine lockere, poetische Verbindung zwischen der nüchtern-anatomischen Schilderung des Bienenstachels im Aufklärungszeitalter und dem als Pfeil beschriebenen und als Schlüssel abgebildeten zentralen Symbol von Goethes geheimnistuerischem Altersroman? Eine halbwegs repräsentative Anthologie der Vergleiche von Biene, Mensch und Dichter würde zahlreiche Bände füllen, kaum jedoch einen Hinweis auf diesen Roman der Sammler und Wanderer, der kinder- und ehelosen Amazonen, Jungfraumütter, arbeitsteiligen Handwerkerutopien und Kolonialisierungsprojekte enthalten, in dessen Zentrum eine kränkelnde, tendenziell körperlose alte Jungfer als "Stimme einer unsichtbar gewordenen Ursibylle rein göttliche Worte über die menschlichen Dinge ganz einfach aus[spricht]" (WJ 65).[2] Im antiken Mythos sind Bienen göttlichen Ursprungs, Reminiszensen des goldenen Zeitalters. Wird in den *Wanderjahren* ein am Bienenstaat orientiertes arbeitsteiliges Modell der Reproduktion und

---

[1] *Encyclopédie, ou dictionnaire raisonné des sciences des arts et des metiers.* Faksimiledruck der Ausgabe von 1751-1780. Stuttgart 1966. Bd. I. S. 19.
[2] *Wilhelm Meisters Lehrjahre* (LJ) und *Wanderjahre* (WJ) werden zitiert nach *Goethes Werke.* Hamburger Ausgabe in 14 Bänden. Hg. von Erich Trunz. München 1988 (HA). Andere zitierte Werkausgaben und Siglen: *Sämtliche Werke, Briefe, Tagebücher und Gespräche.* Hg. von Hendrik Birus et al. Frankfurt/M. 1985ff. (FA). *Sämtliche Werke nach Epochen seines Schaffens.* Hg. von Karl Richter. München 1985ff. (MA). *Goethes Werke.* Weimarer Ausgabe. Hg. im Auftrage der Großherzogin Sophie von Sachsen. Weimar 1887-1919 (WA).

Produktion vorgelegt? "To talk as bees would talk", schreibt Goethes bie-
nenkritischer Zeitgenosse James Leigh Hunt, "we must divest ourselves of
flesh and blood, and develop ideas modified by an untried mode of being,
and by unhuman organs".[3] Der vorliegende Beitrag versucht, anhand der
von Anthropomorphismen stark geprägten Kulturgeschichte der Bienen, den
Zusammenhang der Geschlechterverwirrung der *Lehrjahre* mit der allegori-
schen Anthropologie der *Wanderjahre* zu verdeutlichen.[4]

Wanderjahre und Bienenkönig: Goethes Gespräch mit Eckermann

Die *Lehrjahre* beginnen mit einer für beide Meister-Romane typischen und
in diesem Fall tragisch verlaufenden Überschreitung traditioneller Ge-
schlechterrollen. Mariane verweigert die durch Norberg übersandten Ingre-
dienzen des weiblichen Putzes samt dem beigelegten "Röllchen Geld" und
empfängt ihren Liebhaber, den "unbefiederten Kaufmannssohn" Wilhelm,
in jenem Männerkostüm, in dem Friedrich später von Wilhelm mit Mariane
verwechselt wird (LJ 9-11, vgl. 337). Die Eröffnung der *Wanderjahre* zeigt
Wilhelm und Marianes Sohn, Felix, an "grauser, bedeutender Stelle", der
Dialog zwischen Vater und Sohn konstatiert Analogien und Verwandtschaf-
ten entlang der *scala naturae*: Mineral, Pflanze, Tier und Mensch, der die
Naturphänomene identifiziert, ohne sich der ursprünglichen Benennungs-
motive noch genau zu erinnern. Die Vermischung von Tier und Mineral im
Begriff "Katzengold" kann der Vater dem fragenden Sohn nur durch Mut-
maßungen erklären: "Wahrscheinlich weil es falsch ist und man die Katzen
auch für falsch hält" (WJ 7).

An Vorurteilen und unbegründeten Verdächtigungen hinsichtlich Marianes scheinbarer Untreue scheitert nicht nur Wilhelms erste Liebe. Dass die
Natur immer wahr sei und nur der Mensch sich irre, ist ein oft wiederholter
Leitsatz Goethes. Er findet sich, vertreten durch Montan, nicht nur mehrfach
in den *Wanderjahren*, sondern auch in einem Gespräch mit Eckermann, in
dem anstatt der als "falsch" verschrienen (oft mit Frauen verglichenen) Katzen ein Insekt erwähnt wird, dessen ungewöhnliche geschlechtliche Organisation trotz intensiver, jahrtausendealter Bienenzucht und den seit der Antike sehr umfangreichen naturwissenschaftlichen, philosophischen und literarischen Diskursen über die Biene erst in der Neuzeit aufgeklärt wurde. Die

---

[3] Zitiert im Zusammenhang mit Hunts Kritik an der Auffassung menschlicher Gesellschaft als wohlgeordneter Bienenstaat bei Andrew Cooper: The Apian Way:
Virgil's Bees and Keat's Honeyed Verse. In: *Texas Studies in Literature and Language* 33 (1991). H. 2. S. 160-181, hier S. 164.
[4] Die umfassendste Studie zur Geschlechterthematik in den *Wanderjahren* stammt
von Henriette Herwig: *Das ewig Männliche zieht uns hinab: "Wilhelm Meisters
Wanderjahre". Geschlechterdifferenz, sozialer Wandel, historische Anthropologie.*
Tübingen und Basel 1997.

Berechtigung, aus vereinzelten und verstreuten Erwähnungen von Bienen und Hummeln (explizit an jeweils nur einer Stelle beider Romane) Aufschlüsse über den verdeckten Klassizismus der *Lehr-* und *Wanderjahre* zu erhalten, leitet sich aus den "Betrachtungen im Sinne der Wanderer" ab:

> Es steht manches Schöne isoliert in der Welt, doch der Geist ist es, der Verknüpfungen zu entdecken und dadurch Kunstwerke hervorzubringen hat. – Die Blume gewinnt erst ihren Reiz durch das Insekt, das ihr anhängt [...]. So ist es mit menschlichen Figuren und so mit Tieren aller Art beschaffen.
>
> Der Vorteil, den sich der junge Künstler hiedurch verschafft, ist gar mannigfaltig. Er lernt denken, das Passende gehörig zusammenbinden, und wenn er auf diese Weise geistreich komponiert, wird es ihm zuletzt auch an dem, was man Erfindung nennt, an dem Entwickeln des Mannigfaltigen aus dem Einzelnen, keinesfalls fehlen können (WJ 284-85).

Ganz ähnliche Verknüpfungen von Insekt und Poesie, Mensch und Tier, Einheit und Mannigfaltigkeit kennzeichnen auch das Gespräch mit Eckermann am 13. Februar 1829. Dort teilt Goethe mit, er werde sich nach Abschluss der *Wanderjahre* wieder den "große[n] Geheimnisse[n]" der Botanik widmen. Er wisse "manches", habe "von vielem [...] eine Ahndung", wolle sich diesbezüglich allerdings "wunderlich ausdrücken".[5] Bemerkenswert ist die Nähe dieser Ausführungen zur Charakterisierung des Altersromans als "Aggregat",[6] "Geschlinge",[7] als "Verband der disparatesten Einzelnheiten",[8] oder zu Goethes mehrfacher Versicherung, sein Roman sei zwar "nicht aus Einem Stücke", aber doch "in Einem Sinne"[9] verfasst. Angesichts der Hauptbeschäftigung der Bienen kann man sich in diesem Zusammenhang auch an die Romanfigur des Sammlers erinnert fühlen, der im Hinblick auf die Vergänglichkeit kultureller Artefakte die Leistung desjenigen rühmt, das bzw. "der am längsten sich erhält" (WJ 145):

> Die Pflanze geht von Knoten zu Knoten und schließt zuletzt ab mit der Blüte und dem Samen. In der Tierwelt ist es nicht anders [...]; bei den höher stehenden Tieren und Menschen sind es die Wirbelknochen, die sich anfügen und mit dem Kopf abschließen, in welchem sich die Kräfte konzentrieren. Was so bei Einzelnen geschieht, geschieht auch bei ganzen Korporationen.

---

[5] Johann Peter Eckermann: *Gespräche mit Goethe.* 13. Februar 1829. Die meist kurzen Gespräche werden unter dem betreffenden Datum zitiert und sind in den diversen Werkausgaben leicht auffindbar.

[6] Gepräch mit Kanzler von Müller, 18. Februar 1830. Vgl. die Diskussion bei Herwig: *Das ewig Männliche.* S. 5ff.

[7] Brief an Zelter, 5. Juni 1829. In: WA IV 45. S. 284.

[8] Brief an Rochlitz, 28. Juli 1829. In: WA IV 46. S. 27.

[9] Briefe an Boisserée, 23. Juli 1821 und Zauper, 7. September 1821; *Tag- und Jahreshefte* 1821. In: FA I 10. S. 852f.

Die Bienen, auch eine Reihe von Einzelheiten, die sich aneinander schließen, bringen als Gesamtheit etwas hervor, das auch den Schluß macht und als Kopf des Ganzen anzusehen ist, den Bienen-König. Wie dieses geschieht, ist geheimnisvoll, schwer auszusprechen, aber ich könnte sagen, daß ich darüber meine Gedanken habe.

So bringt ein Volk seine Helden hervor, die gleich Halbgöttern zu Schutz und Heil an der Spitze stehen; und so vereinigten sich die poetischen Kräfte der Franzosen in Voltaire. Solche Häuptlinge eines Volkes sind groß in der Generation, in der sie wirken; manche dauern später hinaus, die meisten werden durch andere ersetzt und von der Folgezeit vergessen.[10]

Die "Häuptlinge" werden als vom Volk (und der Nachwelt) abhängige "Halbgötter[..]" herausgestellt, die kulturelle und politische Dominanz des Mannes wird am Beispiel eines für den Menschen oft als vorbildlich gepriesenen staatenbildenden Insekts illustriert. Erstaunlicherweise beruht die Analogie auf der bis in die Goethezeit kursierenden, zu diesem Zeitpunkt jedoch auffallend anachronistischen Irrlehre vom *Rex Apum*. Die seit der Antike vorherrschende Auffassung wurde spätestens durch Jan Swammerdams (1637-1680) mikroskopischen Nachweis der Eierstöcke der Königin widerlegt:[11]

Als ich den 22. August 1673 einen Korb mit Bienen, die geschwärmt hatten, öffnete, fand ich in demselben einige tausend gemeine Bienen, einige hundert Hummeln oder Brutbienen, und einen König. Ich rede nach den gemeinen Begriffen und Ausdrücken. Denn in der That sind von Anfang der Welt her weder Bienenkönige noch Hummeln in Bienenkörben gewest. Es ist ein großer und unverantwortlicher Irrthum, daß man den Thieren dergleichen Namen beigeleget hat.[12]

Das androzentrische Weltbild der bienenzüchtenden Agrargesellschaften stand der nüchternen Erkenntnis der Vorgänge im Bienenstock lange im Wege. Der als Urvater der Entomologie apostrophierte Aristoteles verwarf die alte These von der Männlichkeit der (stachellosen) Drohnen ausgerechnet mit dem besonders aus entomologischer Sicht unhaltbaren Argument,

---

[10] Gespräch mit Eckermann, 13. Februar 1829.

[11] Dazu Friedrich S. Bodenheimer: *Materialien zur Geschichte der Entomologie bis Linné*. Bd. 1. Berlin 1928. S. 76-82 und S. 342-365.

[12] Übersetzung nach Bodenheimer, I, S. 354. Vgl. Jan Swammerdam: *Book of Nature; or, the History of Insects [...] with the Original Discovery of the Milk Vessels of the Cuttle-Fish, and many other curious Particulars. With the Life of the Author, by Hermann Boerhave*. Übers. aus dem holländischen und lateinischen Original von Thomas Flloyd. Überarb. und durch Anmerkungen von Reaumur und anderen ergänzt von John Hill. London 1758. S. 160.

die Natur bewaffne ausnahmslos Männer.[13] Die von Plinius verbreitete Erklärung der überragenden Größe des Bienenkönigs – er stehe als einziges Männchen im Stock einem stattlichen Harem von Weibchen gegenüber und sei so gegen Ermüdung geschützt[14] – erregte weit weniger moralische Entrüstung als der umgekehrte Fall. Die Bienenkönigin werde dadurch zu einer "base, notorious, impudent Strumpet" herabgewürdigt, "the most hateful and abominable Whore, with Gallants by Hundreds".[15] Die These vom Bienenkönig kann spätestens seit Mitte des 18. Jahrhunderts als wissenschaftlich erledigt gelten. *Apum Regina* beherrscht nicht nur das naturwissenschaftliche, sondern auch das populäre Bienenschrifttum von der *Encyclopédie* bis zur *Real-Enzyklopädie für die gebildeten Stände*.[16]

Ein Brief Goethes vom 28. Juni 1807 an Charlotte von Stein erwähnt beiläufig die amüsante poetische Vermenschlichung der Bienen. Das Tage-

---

[13] *De Generatione Animalium* III 10:759. In: *Aristotelis. Opera Omnia*. Griechisch-lateinischer Paralleldruck. Hg. von Cats Bussemaker. Nachdruck der Ausgabe von 1854. Hildesheim 1973. Bd. 3. S. 386.

[14] *Naturalis Historia* XI 16:46: "hunc esse solum marem, praecipua magnitudine, ne fatiscat". In: *C. Plini secundi. Naturalis Historia*. Hg. von Carolus Mayhoff. Stuttgart 1967. Bd. 2. S. 298.

[15] John Thorley: *Melisselogia or, the Female Monarchy. Being an Enquiry into the Nature, Order, and Government of Bees, Those Admirable, Instructive, and Useful Insects [...] now Published for the Benefit of Mankind*. London 1744. S. 93.

[16] Repräsentativ für das Bienenwissen der gesamten Goethezeit sind die Angaben in: *Allgemeine deutsche Real-Enzyklopädie für die gebildeten Stände*. Conversations-Lexikon. Leipzig 9. Originalauflage 1843. Bd. 2. S. 349f.: "Der Haushalt der Bienen ist bewunderungswürdig, jedoch nicht genau genug beobachtet, um alle ihre Eigenthümlichkeiten, über die noch viele Widersprüche herrschen, genau angeben zu können. Sie leben in zahlreichen Gesellschaften (Stöcken oder Schwärmen) zusammen, von denen jede aus ungefähr 20000 Arbeitsbienen, 1600 Drohnen und einem Weibchen, der Königin oder dem Weisel, besteht. Erstere [...] bilden den Staat und verrichten die zu dessen Erhaltung nothwendigen Arbeiten, sammeln Wachs und Honig und erbauen aus jenem mit wunderbarer Geschicklichkeit Zellen zur Aufbewahrung des Honigs und zur Ausbildung der Brut, die sie ernähren und pflegen. Die Drohnen [...] begatten sich mit der Königin und werden darauf von den Arbeitsbienen getödtet und aus dem Stocke geworfen. Die Königin ist größer als die übrigen Bienen [...], ihre Bestimmung ist es, das Geschlecht fortzupflanzen. Sie legt des Jahres wol 30-40 000 Eier, [...] ist die Seele des ganzen Stockes; ihr huldigen alle andern; neben ihr wird keine zweite geduldet; entstehen bei einer Brut mehre, so bilden sie entweder mit ihrem Anhange neue Schwärme und wandern mit diesen aus, oder sie werden umgebracht. [...] Das Ei aus einer Arbeitszelle in eine Königinzelle gelegt, gibt eine Königin, und so umgekehrt ein Ei aus einer Königinzelle in einer Arbeitszelle eine Arbeitsbiene. Sonach wären die letztern nichts Anderes als Weibchen mit verkümmerten Geschlechtsorganen".

buch verzeichnet Bemerkungen über "zwar anthropomorphistische aber artige Bemerkungen über das gesellige Leben der Thiere, [...] der Bienen, Ameisen usw." in Pierre Samuel Dupont De Nemours' (1739-1817) *Philosophie de l'univers* als Anregung zum Nachdenken über den "Zusammenhang aller Erscheinungen und über die Hauptmaximen der Natur".[17] Eine von Goethe 1804 lobend erwähnte Schrift von Johann Gottfried Lucas *Über den wissenschaftlichen Gang der Bienenzucht*, die später in Jena veröffentlicht wurde, illustriert und kritisiert die mit "Glaubensaugen"[18] gemachten Beobachtungen der neueren Bienenforscher (darunter Swammerdam, der noch an die nicht-genitale Befruchtung der Königin durch männliche Ausdünstungen der Drohnen glaubte). Lucas' Rezension der neuesten Bienenliteratur verdeutlicht, dass zu diesem Zeitpunkt längst nicht mehr das Geschlecht der Königin Gegenstand der erhitzten Debatten zwischen den sächsischen und fränkischen Bienenzüchtern und ihrer diversen Anhänger war. Die Schlichtung des Streites zugunsten des sächsischen Systems wird u. a. dem schweizer Bienenforscher François Huber zugeschrieben.[19] Sein Briefwechsel mit Charles Bonnet gilt als Klassiker der Bienenkunde.[20] Huber bestätigte die seit der Jahrhundertmitte kursierende, sich in der ersten Hälfte des 19. Jahrhunderts endgültig durchsetzende These von der Befruchtung der Königin durch die Drohnen, deren Kopulation 'hoch in der Luft' (also nicht im Bienenstock, sondern während des sog. Hochzeitsflugs) stattfindet und deshalb nie direkt beobachtet werden konnte. Er zeigte, dass die Kopulation zwar nicht für die Produktion unbefruchteter (Drohneneier), aber für die Produktion befruchteter Eier (Arbeiterinnen und Königinnen) unverzichtbar sei. Anhand dieser Differenzierung konnte erklärt werden, warum auch eindeutig unbefruchtete, von Geburt an isolierte Königinnen und, in seltenen Fällen, sogar Arbeiterinnen die Fähigkeit zur Eiablage besitzen. Hubers Beobachtungen ermöglichten zwar die Berichtigung bzw. Verabschiedung uralter Mythen über die Reproduktion der Bienen (Jungfrauengeburt, Spontangeneration, nicht-genitale Befruchtung), brachten jedoch zugleich die gängigen Auffassungen von der Ordnung der Natur und der Geschlechter in erhebliche Kalamitäten:

---

[17] WA III 3. S. 222.

[18] Johann Gottfried Lucas: Über den wissenschaftlichen Gang der Bienenzucht. In: *Jenaische Allgemeine Literatur-Zeitung* (JALZ). Nr. 69/70. 22./23. März 1805. S. 556. Vgl. S. 548: "[...] dass Maraldi seine Leser erst musste um Verzeihung bitten, wenn er, dem allgemeinen Naturgesetz zuwider, eine von Natur unterwürfige Kreatur, wie die Drohne zu den Arbeitsbienen ist, als männlichen Geschlechts darstellte. Spricht denn das für eine bestimmte Überzeugung dieser Männer?"

[19] Ibid. S. 547.

[20] François Huber: *Nouvelles observations sur les abeilles*. Genf 1792. Dazu S. L. Tuxen: Entomology systematizes and describes: 1700-1815. In: *History of Entomology*. Hg. von Ray F. Smith et al. Palo Alto 1973. S. 95-118. Zu Huber S. 105.

Die Arbeitsbienen sollen theils fruchtbar, theils unfruchtbar seyn. Wer begreift, wie die Natur unfruchtbare Geschöpfe anders, als zufällig hervorbringen könne? Vielweniger, wie fruchtbare und unfruchtbare ohne Zufall nach einerley Naturgesetzen auf derselben Bildungsstufe ihre gesetzmäßige Ausbildung erhalten haben? Dieser Verschiedenheit ungeachtet sollen sie, doch ohne Unterschied – Arbeitsbienen seyn und producieren können; und nicht sie – die Arbeitsbienen – sind von der Natur zur Fruchtbarkeit oder Unfruchtbarkeit bestimmt, sondern man sagt ausdrücklich, dass es von ihnen abhange, ob sie sich zu dem einen oder dem andern bestimmen wollen: folglich macht man sie gar zu Intelligenzen. Das ist ungereimt.[...] Welcher Verstand begreift es, dass sie gleichwohl unter sich ein Product Nr. 4 die Drohnen zeugen sollen?[21]

Goethes knappem Kommentar zu Lucas' Abhandlung ist nicht zu entnehmen, worauf sich die Zustimmung bezieht:

Den philosophierenden Bienenfreund könnte man wohl passieren lassen. Er hat nach meiner Überzeugung in der Sache recht, nur das Barocke seiner Konstruktionen macht die Leute stutzen. Vielleicht sagte man einmal unterm Strich ein paar Worte über die Sache und brächte sie auf menschlichen Grund und Boden.[22]

Goethes Tagebuch erwähnt am 25./26. Februar 1797 die Lektüre von Swammerdams *Historia generalis insectorum*.[23] In den Paralipomena finden sich Hinweise auf detaillierte anatomische Studien der Hymenoptera ("secierte eine Hummel"[24]). Die biologische Definition von Weiblichkeit ("Der Hauptpunkt der ganzen weiblichen Existenz ist die Gebärmutter"[25]) ist unvereinbar mit der einigermaßen fachgerechten Sektion von Hummeln einerseits, dem Postulat eines Bienenkönigs gegenüber Eckermann andererseits. Goethe, so ein Werkkommentar, "hatte sich in seinem Gartenhaus auch als Imker betätigt und weiß natürlich, daß es nur eine Bienenkönigin gibt".[26] Doch wurden von der Antike bis zur Moderne unter völlig schiefen Vorstellungen über Geschlecht und Reproduktionsmodus der Bienen erfolgreich Honig und Wachs produziert. Im Gespräch mit Eckermann geht es neben den Geheimnissen der Natur und Erkenntnisproblemen der Naturwissen-

---

[21] Lucas: Über den wissenschaftlichen Gang der Bienenzucht. S. 548f.

[22] Brief an Eichstädt, 12. Dezember 1804. FA II 5. S. 532

[23] FA II 4. S. 300.

[24] WA II 6. S. 406. Vgl. auch S. 444.

[25] HA 13. S. 179 (Erster Entwurf einer allgemeinen Einleitung in die vergleichende Anatomie, ausgehend von der Osteologie).

[26] Fritz Bergemann (Hg.): *Johann Peter Eckermann. Gespräche mit Goethe in den letzten Jahren seines Lebens*. Frankfurt/M. 1981. S. 797. Vgl. Goethes Tagebucheintrag zur Einwinterung seiner Bienen im November 1776. In: WA III 1. S. 26.

schaften auch um Analogiebildungen zwischen Bienenstaat, menschlicher Sozietät und Dichtung. Im Sinne der platonischen Analogie von Vaterschaft und Autorschaft, aber deutlich feminisiert, berichten die Gespräche mit Ekkermann auch von Goethes Erleichterung über die schwere Geburt der *Wanderjahre* und die unmittelbare Inangriffnahme neuer bzw. alter Projekte: "'Es geht uns wie den Weibern, [...] wenn sie gebären, verreden sie es, wieder beim Manne zu schlafen, und ehe man sich's versieht, sind sie wieder schwanger'".[27] Die im Werkkontext einmalige Behauptung eines Bienenkönigs im Gespräch mit Eckermann wird beim folgenden Versuch einer Entschlüsselung der *Wanderjahre* – als Archiv des Wissens wie auch des Irrens – im Sinne von Hartmut Böhmes Bemerkungen zu Goethes allegorischer Hermetik verstanden:

> Die historische Marginalität seiner Position ist Goethe völlig durchsichtig. So sehr, daß man den Hermetismus seines Altersstils verstehen könnte als eine Schreibweise, die die innersten Überzeugungen seines Naturdenkens aufgrund der Einsicht in ihre historisch exzentrische Positionalität ins Verborgene rückt. Der Goethesche Hermetismus wäre dann eine Form von Erinnerungsarbeit, der Archivierung von Gedächtnisspuren und verlorenen Wissensbeständen, die gegenüber dem ratiozentrischen Bewußtsein der zeitgenössischen Wissenschaften nahezu notwendig den Status eines "Subtextes", ja des "Verdrängten" und "Unbewußten" haben. [...] Diese Erinnerungsarbeit Goethes ist angelegt auf zukünftige Entzifferung [...]: die Aufarbeitung des historisch Verdrängten von Naturkonzepten, um deren Verdrängung Goethe bereits wußte. Er empfand diese als ebenso notwendig wie verlustreich.[28]

Verschlüsselte Offenbarungen: Pfeile mit Widerhaken

Die deutlichste Aufforderung zu dieser Erinnerungsarbeit und zukünftigen Entzifferung findet sich in Wilhelms Begegnung mit dem Sammler, der in den "Enkel[n]", in einer "neue[n] Generation" jenen Gehilfen findet, der "womöglich noch mehr auf hergebrachten Besitz hält" als der Alte, und "eine heftige Neigung zu wunderlichen Dingen empfindet" (WJ 146). Es ist dieser Gehilfe, der dem Oheim das von Felix gefundene, von Wilhelm beim Sammler verwahrte und schließlich samt des Schlüssels bei Hersilie landende geheimnisvolle Kästchen – "ein kleiner Oktavband" (WJ 43) und "Prachtbüchlein" (WJ 44) – überbringt. Der Sammler rät von einer Öffnung des Kästchens ohne Original-Schlüssel ab. Er empfiehlt die Glücksprobe und vermutet einen unerwarteten Fundort des Schlüssels: "'wenn Sie glück-

---

[27] Gespräch mit Eckermann, 20. Februar 1829.
[28] Hartmut Böhme: Lebendige Natur – Wissenschaftskritik, Naturforschung und allegorische Hermetik bei Goethe. In: DVjS 60 (1986). S. 249-72, hier S. 251.

lich geboren sind und wenn dieses Kästchen etwas bedeutet, so muß sich gelegentlich der Schlüssel dazu finden, und gerade da, wo Sie ihn am wenigsten erwarten'" (WJ 146). Hersilie findet den Schlüssel unerwartet in der Brusttasche des auf abenteuerlichen Wegen in ihre Hände geratenen Jäckchens des kleinen Fitz, der bereits beim Fund des Kästchens durch Felix eine undurchsichtige Rolle spielte. Ungewöhnlich und im Werkkontext einmalig ist auch Goethes Abbildung des hermeneutischen Schlüssels zum Buch/Kästchen im Text, deren Bedeutung für die Romaninterpretation in der Forschung umstritten ist (Abb. 1). Ergiebiger hat sich die erotisch überzeichnete Beschreibung des Schlüssels durch Hersilie erwiesen: "Hier aber, mein Freund, nun schließlich zu dieser Abbildung des Rätsels was sagen Sie? Erinnert es nicht an Pfeile mit Widerhaken? Gott sei uns gnädig!" (WJ 321). Die in der Forschung vielfach vermerkte Suggestion von Amors Pfeilen wird vom Kontext bestätigt. Doch die der Abbildung vorausgehende, sozusagen blinde Beschreibung des Schlüssels durch die das Fundobjekt ertastende Hersilie erinnert ebenso deutlich an ein stachliges Insekt:

> Mich treibt ein guter oder böser Geist, in die Brusttasche zu greifen; ein winzig kleines, stachlichtes Etwas kommt mir in die Hand; ich, die ich sonst so apprehensiv, kitzlich und schreckhaft bin, schließe die Hand, schließe sie, schweige, und das Kleid wird fortgeschickt. Sogleich ergreift mich von allen Empfindungen die wunderlichste. Beim ersten verstohlenen Blick seh' ich, errat' ich, zu Ihrem Kästchen sei es der Schlüssel (WJ 320).

Die Auffassung des Schlüssels als Bienenstachel schließt dessen Deutung als Pfeil Amors keineswegs aus. Verbindungen von Wurm (Insekt) und Cherub, Biene und Liebesgott bilden einen vielfach variierten Topos der Liebesdichtung. Bienen tauchen auch in Goethes dichterischer Produktion am häufigsten in erotisch-anakreontischen Gedichten auf. Seine *Kunst die Spröden zu fangen, Zwote Erzählung* schildert Amors Pfeil explizit als Bienenstachel.[29] Die Entomologie des 18. und 19. Jahrhunderts beschreibt den Stachel durchgängig im Sinne der eingangs zitierten *Encyclopédie* sowie im Sinne von Hersilies Formulierungen als "Pfeile mit Widerhaken" (WJ 321) bzw. Bart: "bearded darts",[30] "barbed darts".[31] In Anlehnung an Buffons

---

[29] WA I 1. S. 37.

[30] *Encyclopaedia Britannica, or, a Dictionary of Arts, Sciences, and Miscellaneous Literature [...] furnished by an Extensive Correspondence.* 3. erw. Ausgabe in 18 Bänden. Edinburg 1797. Bd. III. S. 121.

[31] Abraham Rees et al.: *The Cyclopedia; or, Universal Dictionary of Arts, Sciences, and Literature.* London 1819. Bd. IV, Stichwort "Bee" (ohne Seitenzahlen). Eine ausführliche Beschreibung findet sich bei einem der bekanntesten Kompilatoren der zeitgenössischen Naturkunde, dem von Goethe vor allem als Romanautor geschätzten Oliver Goldsmith: "The sting [...] is composed of three parts; the sheath, and two

Histoire Naturelle wird der Bienenstachel als Kuriosum, als kunstvoll ge-
schmiedetes – "like an iron bar from a smith's forge"– Meisterwerk der
Natur beschrieben, "which has received the finest polish that human art can
give it".[32] Dadurch ergibt sich eine metaphorische Brücke zwischen Natur-
und Kunstprodukt, Stachel und Schlüssel, die erklären mag, warum sich
Hersilies Beschreibung des Schlüssels zwar mit zeitgenössischen Beschreibungen des Bienenstachels mühelos in Verbindung bringen lässt, nicht aber
mit der Abbildung des Schlüssels im Text. Auf den Bruch zwischen Bild
und Kommentierung hat besonders Alfred Steer hingewiesen. Der Schlüssel
gleiche mitnichten einem Pfeil mit Widerhaken, sondern jenem Phallus, den
Goethe 1790 als antikisierend-kindliche Pornographie samt lateinischer
Glossierung seinem Herzog schickte.[33] Nach Goethes "Bemerkungen zur
Sammlung Priapeia" entsteht aus den Anweisungen der Carmina – Verbindung der Buchstaben E und D durch einen Querstrich – das Bild des Phallus
("pictus erit phallus").[34] Auf der Basis von Goethes Phallus-Zeichnungen
(Abb. 2) und der von Wilhelm Emrich und Friedrich Ohly vorgelegten
Deutungen von Kästchen und Schlüssel deutet Steer den Schlüssel als Stilisierung und Synthese des weiblichen (Schlüsselgriff als stilisierte *cista mystica*) und männlichen (Halm und Bart als Phallus) Geschlechtsorgans:

> […] by telling his readers that the key looks like arrows with barbs he has gua-
> ranteed that everyone will dutifully look for, and of course find, that resem-
> blance. If he had omitted such a misleading hint, it is much more likely that many
> would have hit on the actual symbolic content. […] Male and female, if united
> sexually, will produce offspring […]. Human sexuality, properly used and under-

darts, which are extremely small and penetrating. Both the darts have several small
points or barbs, like those of a fish-hook, which renders the sting more painful, and
makes the darts rankle in the wound". In: Oliver Goldsmith: *An History of the Earth
and Animated Nature*. 2. Aufl. London 1774. Bd. 3. S. 68. Vgl. August Baron von
Berlepsch: *Die Biene und die Bienenzucht in honigarmen Gegenden nach dem gegenwärtigen Standpunct der Theorie und Praxis*. Mühlhausen/Thüringen 1860. S.
20: "hornige[r] Stachelapparat" und S. 22: "Der Stachel der Königin ist nach unten
gekrümmt, […] um dem austretenden Ei eine bestimmte Richtung zu geben, bei den
Arbeitsbienen, die ihren Stachel fast ausschließlich als Waffe gebrauchen, ist der-
selbe gerade und dadurch, wie durch größere Anzahl der Widerhaken weit mehr ge-
schickt, in diesem Sinne zu agiren".

[32] John Wright (Hg.): *A Natural History of the Globe, of Man, of Beasts, Birds, Fis-
hes, Reptiles, Insects and Plants. From the Writings of Buffon, Cuvier and Other
Eminent Naturalists. A New Edition, With Modern Improvements and Five Hundred
Engravings*. Boston 1831. S. 124f.

[33] Alfred G. Steer Jr.: *Goethe's Science in the Structure of the "Wanderjahre"*.
Athens 1979. S. 133f.

[34] WA I 35. S. 198.

stood, results in a family, and thus makes accessible the treasures locked in the little casket. [...] This is the sense of the tale about "Saint" Joseph and his Maria, this is what Lucidor and Lucinde learned [...]. Lenardo and his *nußbraunes Mädchen* learn slowly how to achieve the proper relationship. The reader is left to assume that Wilhelm and his Natalie [...] are now looking forward to consummation of their desires.[35]

Doch von sehr wenigen Ausnahmen (z. B. Joseph und Marie) und vagen Vermutungen abgesehen, ist der Nachweis von kinderzeugenden Kopulationen in den *Wanderjahren* so schwierig wie im Bienenstock. Lucidor erreicht zwar die gewünschte Verbindung mit der idealen *mulier domestica* (Lucinde). Doch außer persönlichen, individualgeschichtlich geprägten Vorlieben steht der Ehe mit der vom Vater zugedachten reiselustigen und eigensinnigen Julie nichts im Wege. Die im Roman vielfach thematisierte und in dieser Erzähleinlage überdeutlich ausgesprochene Warnung vor der bienenstockhaften Tendenz der Menschheit, "die Welt erst bewohnbar zu machen, dann zu bevölkern und endlich überzubevölkern" (WJ 95), spricht gegen Speers Deutung dieser und anderer Liebesgeschichten. Denn auch die von Speer zitierte, in die Rahmenhandlung hineinreichende und mit großem Entsagungsaufwand gelungene Durchsetzung des väterlichen Plans (die Verbindung Hilaries mit Flavio) erfüllt nicht das ursprüngliche genealogische und inzestuös-ökonomische Kalkül des Majors, das Erbe der Familie für zukünftige Generationen zu sichern. Durch die Intervention der exogamen jungen Witwe und Makaries Vermittlung entstehen zwei noch nach mehrjähriger Pause kinderlose, reiselustige Paare, deren gegenseitige (geistig-künstlerische) Befruchtung nur in den oberen Regionen stattfindet.

Im Gegensatz zum Statusgefälle im Bienenstaat steht Mutterschaft in den *Wanderjahren* nicht hoch im Kurs. Viele zeittypische Kontroversen, darunter der Streit zwischen Ovulisten (wie Swammerdam) und Animalkulisten über die Priorität des weiblichen Eis bzw. männlichen Samens beim Zeugungsvorgang, machen sich im Streit um die Immen bemerkbar. John Thorley schreibt den Drohnen weiterhin die zentrale, aber prestigelose Funktion von Brutbienen und -ammen zu.[36] Wären sie tatsächlich zeugungsfähige Männchen und Väter der nächsten Generation, wie inzwischen zahlreiche "Gentlemen" behaupteten, so müsse ihre miserable Stellung im Bienenstaat dem Gebildeten unbegreiflich bleiben:

Why must the Female be crowned with Honour and regal Dignities, and all the Ensigns of Royalty; when at the same Time the Males are degraded, treated with the utmost Contempt, triumphed over, and trampled upon by the Populace and Commonality; expelled and banished, and, in a Word, slain without Mercy? Or

---

[35] Alfred G. Steer Jr.: *Goethe's Science*. S. 138-39.
[36] John Thorley: *Melisselogia*. S. 101.

have these Gentlemen quite forgot what they were taught when School-boys, that the Masculine Gender is more worthy than the Feminine?[37]

Die Gleichung "früher Tod", "unnütz Leben", "Frauenschicksal" wird in Goethes Werk am deutlichsten von Iphigenie ausgesprochen.[38] Ihre Entsprechung in der Kulturgeschichte der Bienen ist die menschliche Geringschätzung der kurzlebigen Drohnen (auch "Tränen") im Bienenstaat, die Verachtung ihrer subordinierten, von den Arbeiterinnen auf Gedeih und Verderb abhängigen Existenz, was, wie u. a. Lucas feststellt, auch für die Königin zutrifft, die ihren Stachel zur nahezu permanenten Eiablage, selten als Waffe benutzt. Der Leben und Tod bringende Bienenstachel erinnert nicht nur an die Zuschneiderin Philine, die beim Anblick der Tuchvorräte der Auswanderer die reiche "Ernte für Sichel und Sense" (WJ 442) antizipiert, sondern auch an die bei Goethe häufig anzutreffende Konstruktion des Weiblichen als Gebärerin und Zerstörerin. Den romantischen Typus der *femme fatale*, der für den Mann todbringenden Frau, gibt es weder in den *Lehr-* noch in den *Wanderjahren*, obwohl Hersilies schwankende Haltung zwischen Vater und Sohn fast zur Katastrophe führt und die von ihr suggerierte Verbindung Schlüssel/Bienenstachel zu solchen Vorstellungen reichlich Stoff bietet. Die jährlichen Drohnenmassaker sind, bei unterschiedlicher Deutung, seit der Antike bekannt, seit dem späten achtzehnten Jahrhundert kursieren Vermutungen über das später weitläufig beschriebene "Zurückbleiben abgerissener Theile der männlichen Geschlechtswerkzeuge im Innern der weiblichen Scheide nach vollzogener Begattung".[39] Der Bienenkopulation folgt "der augenblickliche Tod der Drohne", ein Faktum, gegen das sich "fast alle Bienenzüchter ganz gewaltig [spreizten] und meinten, es sei doch gar zu grausam vom Schöpfer, wenn er also mit der Drohne verführe".[40] Entsprechend bezahlen in den *Lehr-* und *Wanderjahren* ausschließlich Frauen den Sexualakt mit dem Leben: Mariane stirbt an den Folgen von Felix' Geburt und teilt dieses zeitgenössisch verbreitete Frauenschicksal mit der Schwester der schönen Seele (die Mutter Lotharios, Natalies und Friedrichs) sowie Thereses (biologischer) Mutter. Selbst Philine äußert sich in den *Lehrjahren* ausgesprochen negativ zum Thema Natur, Schwanger- und Mutterschaft: "Wenn ich nur nichts mehr von Natur und Naturszenen hören sollte" (LJ 101). "Wenn ich nur [...] keine Frau mehr guter Hoffnung sehen sollte" (LJ 203). Frau Melinas und ihre eigene Schwangerschaft beschreibt sie als "Mißgestalt" (LJ 203) und "niederträchtig[e]" (LJ 559) Verunstaltung des Leibes, die Kinder möchte sie am liebsten ohne Leibesopfer "von den Bäumen" (LJ 204) schütteln. Mütter sind in beiden Romanen auffallend

---

[37] Ibid. S. 90.
[38] HA 5. S. 10.
[39] Berlepsch: *Die Biene*. S. 29.
[40] Ibid. S. 28f.

selten: In den *Lehrjahren* kommen sie nur als schattenhafte Randfiguren und Mütter erwachsener Kinder vor (z. B. Wilhelms Mutter, die Mutter der schönen Seele, Hilaries Mutter), die Brotschneideszene der *Wanderjahre* findet unauffällig im Kohlenmeiler statt (WJ 38). Andere den Geburtsvorgang überlebende Frauen geben mehr oder weniger tragische, melancholische Figuren ab (Frau Melinas Totgeburt, Mignons Mutter Sperata, Lotharios Jugendliebe Margarethe). Die *Wanderjahre* präsentieren geglückte Mutterschaft als Extremfall zwischen 'Heiliger' (Marie) und 'Hure' (Philine), ansonsten als unglückselige Pflichtübung untergehender Adels- und Zwergengeschlechter in nur zwei Erzähleinlagen (*Nicht zu weit, Die neue Melusine*). Durch die Präsentation des Mannes als "Zuchtbulle[n]",[41] als von der Frau ausgehaltener exogamer Samenspender zur Rettung einer inzestuösen uralten Zwergenmonarchie göttlichen Ursprungs – auch Bienenstöcke sind, von gelegentlicher Befruchtung durch fremde Drohnen abgesehen, reine Inzestbetriebe – erinnert das Melusinen-Märchen an die traditionelle Gegenüberstellung von harmonischer 'Bienenmonarchie' und militanter 'Ameisenrepublik', an die seit der Antike konstatierte Feindschaft zwischen Bienen und Ameisen, die derselben Familie der Hymenoptera angehören und in Goethes Novelle als Feinde und Verbündete präsentiert werden.

An dieser Stelle kann die Interpretation des Schlüssels zum Kästchen im Zusammenhang mit der von Steer zu Recht geltend gemachten Differenz zwischen Bild und Beschreibung, zwischen Signifikant und Signifikat vervollständigt werden. Die Zeichnung sieht nicht nur einem gewöhnlichen Pfeil, sondern auch einem gewöhnlichen Schlüssel auffallend unähnlich. In den Katalogen historischer Schlüsselsammlungen finden sich häufige Rückgriffe auf antike Motive in der Griffornamentik (z. B. die *cista mystica*), doch die eindeutig dominierende Form des Schlüssels von der Antike zur Moderne verfügt über einen *einseitigen*, abgewinkelten Bart (vgl. Abb. 3). Sieht man von der inversiven Verdoppelung der beidseitigen "Widerhaken" ab (vermutlich die nicht genau bezeichnete magnetisch verbundene, glatte Bruchstelle des Schlüssels am Halm, WJ 457-58), so gleicht Goethes Abbildung von Halm und Bart T-förmigen keltischen Sichelschlüsseln, die es ebenfalls in der später üblicheren L-Form gibt (Abb. 4).[42] Dieser Befund stimmt mit dem hohen Alter des antiken Kästchens überein und bestätigt Steers Hinweis auf die sehr ähnlichen Phalluszeichnungen Goethes. Allerdings stehen solche Schlüssel in der Antike oft in einem weiblichen und religiösen Kontext, worauf die erste Erwähnung von Schlüsseln in den *Wanderjahren* – "laß mir den Schlüssel. Tun Sie einen Blick hinein, Lucidor!" (WJ 104) – einen Hinweis gibt. Der betreffende Absatz in der Erzähleinlage erinnert in mehrfacher Spiegelung an die spätere Übergabe des Kästchens

---

[41] Henriette Herwig: *Das ewig Männliche*. S. 277 (über den Barbier).

[42] Dazu Bert Spilker und Nancy Aahre (Hg.): *Keys and Locks in the Collection of the Cooper-Hewitt Museum*. Mit einem Vorw. von Lisa Taylor. New York 1987.

im "Haus von alter, ernster Bauart" (WJ 144) des Sammlers. Während das Kästchen dort mit dem christlichen Symbol des Kruzifixes in Verbindung gebracht wird (vgl. das Kreuz im Zentrum des Schlüsselgriffs), bleibt Lucidor "nicht verborgen, daß hier eine alte, stattliche Hauskapelle zum Dienste der Themis, bei veränderten Religionsbegriffen, verwandelt sei" (WJ 104). Die von Hersilies Schlüsselbeschreibung eröffneten Assoziationsfelder Insekt, Biene, Stachel weisen in dieselbe Richtung. Bei den Griechen und Römern finden sich Darstellungen von Priestern und Priesterinnen als "Schlüsselträger[n]", deren hakenförmige Tempelschlüssel einerseits den einfachen T- oder L-förmigen Keltenschlüsseln gleichen,[43] andererseits den seit Swammerdam geläufigen Illustrationen des Bienenstachels ähnlich sehen (Abb. 5-7). Als Symbol der reinen, dreifaltigen Mutterbiene (Demeter, Artemis, Persephone), als Priesterinnen bei den Griechen, Römern und Juden (Melissa, Debora) gilt die Biene "als Darstellung der weiblichen Naturpotenz", "des Erdstoffes nach seiner Mütterlichkeit, seiner nie rastenden, kunstreich formenden Geschäftigkeit" und "Bild der demetrischen Erdseele in ihrer höchsten Reinheit".[44] Hinweise auf die Goethe bekannte Verbindung von (summenden) Bienen, Mysterienkult und Erleuchtung ("Lucidor") finden sich in der bereits von Ohly ausführlich besprochenen, dem Demetermythos huldigenden 12. Römischen Elegie: "Vielbedeutend gebärdeten sich die Priester und summten / Ungeduldig und bang harrte der Lehrling auf Licht".[45]

Von einer Irreführung des Lesers durch Hersilie kann besonders im Hinblick auf das weibliche Zentrum des Romans, Makarie (dazu unten), keine Rede sein. Vielmehr vervollständigt und berichtigt Hersilies Kommentar die von der volkstümlichen Vulgärsprache nahegelegte Symbolik des Schlüssels als männliches Genital in einfacher sexueller Bedeutung.[46] Sowohl die Bienen als auch die Titanin Themis verhalten sich sperrig gegenüber einer phallozentrischen Verherrlichung physischer Zeugung und Fruchtbarkeit. Als Göttin des Gesetzes und der Ordnung in menschlichen Gemeinschaften vereinigt sich in Themis die auch bei Artemis, Demeter, Persephone (und im Bienenstock) anzutreffende Präsentation von Leben und Tod, Keuschheit und Fruchtbarkeit, von Jungfrau, Mutter und Zerstörerin als dialektische

---

[43] Erich Pfeiffer-Belli: *Schlüssel und Schloß. Schönheit, Form und Technik im Wandel der Zeiten.* Aufgezeigt an der Sammlung Heinrich Pankofer, München. Fotos Fritz Nüssel. Texte Erich Pfeiffer-Belli. 2. durchges. Aufl. München 1974. S. 11, vgl. S. 29.

[44] Johann Jakob Bachofen: *Das Mutterrecht. Eine Untersuchung über die Gynaikokratie nach ihrer religiösen und rechtlichen Natur.* Eine Auswahl hrsg. von Hans-Jürgen Heinrichs. 7. Aufl. Frankfurt/M. 1989. S. 86.

[45] Friedrich Ohly: Zum Kästchen in Goethes *Wanderjahren.* In: *Zeitschrift für deutsches Altertum und deutsche Literatur* 91 (1961/1962). S. 255-262, hier S. 255.

[46] Louis Zara: *Locks and Keys.* New York 1969. S. 21

Einheit. Das auf Fortpflanzung und Familiengründung beschränkte Verständnis von *oikos* ist mit der weit umfassenderen, globalen Ökologie der Themis unvereinbar. Themis bat Zeus um einen großen Krieg zur Entlastung ihrer eigenen Mutter, der übervölkerten Gaia/Erde.[47] Als Alternativen bieten sich der Liebesbegriff der vor allem in Natalie personifizierten christlichen *caritas* als Opferung des Leibes an: kinderlose Ehen, Adoption statt Zeugung und ein Frauentypus, dem die Kinderlosigkeit zur zweiten Natur wird. Von daher ergibt sich auch eine Verbindung zwischen Sammler und Pädagogischer Provinz, Schlüssel/Kästchen und Kruzifix: "Im Leben erscheint er [Christus] als ein wahrer Philosoph – stoßet Euch nicht an diesem Ausdruck –, als ein Weiser im höchsten Sinne" (WJ 163). Die Bezeichnung Christi als "Weiser" im Sinne von Philosoph und "der Weise" (WJ 163) ist konventionell und steht im Einklang mit der übrigen Schilderung des Christentums als höchste Steigerungsform des Ethischen, dennoch soll der erstgenannte Begriff dem Leser auffallen. Der bienenkundliche Nebensinn (Weiser oder Weisel als Bezeichnung des Bienenkönigs bzw. der –königin) präsentiert den ohne männlichen Samen durch Jungfrauengeburt in die Welt gekommenen 'König der Juden', der (wie die Bienen im antiken Mythos) "göttlichen Usprung" (WJ 163) in Anspruch nimmt. Er ist die nach erfolgter geistiger Befruchtung des Juden- und Heidentums gnadenlos gekreuzte Über-Drohne. Der Mythos der jungfräulichen Geburt ist im Bienenstock (als Drohnenproduktion) der Normalfall. Gleichzeitig nährt der den unfruchtbaren Leib segnende und die homogene Menschheit predigende Religionsstifter beim Abendmahl "einen Verräter, der ihn und die Bessern zugrunde richten wird" (WJ 163). Auch das konkrete Leibesopfer der Bienenkönigin führt (bei abnehmender Fruchtbarkeit bzw. 'Drohnenbrütigkeit') dazu, dass sie von ihren eigenen Töchtern (Arbeiterinnen und neue Königinnen) 'verraten' bzw. verlassen wird. Die Bienen spielen in der christlichen Mythologie und Ikonographie eine bedeutsame Rolle – als Symbole der Keuschheit, der Fruchtbarkeit im weiteren Sinne, der harmonisch verbundenen und patriarchalisch strukturierten christlichen Gemeinde. Erst ab dem 17. Jahrhundert verbreitete sich die Sicht des Bienenstocks als "entire female Monarchie"[48] und der Honigbienen als "True Amazons"[49] in der eu-

---

[47] Konrat Ziegler et al. (Hg.): *Der Kleine Pauly. Lexikon der Antike.* Auf der Grundlage von Pauly's Realencyclopädie der classischen Altertumswissenschaft. München 1975. Bd. 5. Sp. 676.

[48] Richard Remnant: *A Discourse or Historie of Bees. Shewing Their Nature and usage, and the great profit of them. Whereunto is added the causes [...] of smutty Wheat: All which are very usefull for this later age.* London 1637. Nachdr. London 1982 (International Bee Research Association Series). S. 1.

[49] Im Titel des in zahlreichen Auflagen und Übersetzungen kursierenden Bienen-Bestsellers von Joseph Warder: *The True Amazons: Or: the Monarchy of Bees.*

ropäischen Bienenkunde, ohne die alte Auffassung völlig zu verdrängen. Noch Zedlers *Universal-Lexikon* preist unverdrossen die Effizienz des ohne wahrnehmbaren Zwang und Befehl geheimnisvoll regierenden Bienenkönigs ("Weiser", "Apum Rex") – ein Herrschaftsmodus, der in den *Lehr-* und *Wanderjahren* der 'wahren Amazone' Natalie[50] und der Seherin Makarie zugeschrieben wird:

> Er weiß auch seinen Stock so weislich zu regieren, daß man nicht genugsam bewundern kann, wie an einem so kleinen und sonst gering scheinenden Thierlein dem Menschen ein so vollkommenes Muster einer wohl angeordneten und glückseligen Gemeine vorgestellet worden. Denn da ist keine Biene, die nicht ihre angewiesene Arbeit habe, und sorgfältig verrichte.[51]

Bienenstock und Erotik in den *Lehr- und Wanderjahren*

Das neuzeitliche Bienenschrifttum zeichnet sich durch zahlreiche Umdichtungen vorgängiger Erdichtungen aus, wie im Falle Joseph Warders, der, subversiv und huldigend zugleich, mehrere Strophen aus dem Bienenkapitel (4. Buch) von Vergils *Georgika* zitiert. Die Vorlage (in Drydens englischer Übersetzung: "Besides, not Egypt, India, Media, more / With servile Awe their Idol King adore") wird zu "No Amazonian Dames, nor Indians more / With loyal Awe their Idol Queen adore".[52] Das neue Paradigma stellte auch für die Vertreter der Königin-These eine Provokation dar. Richard Remnants Epilog ("Bees and women compared") richtet sich dementsprechend nicht nur an Naturwissenschaftler und Imker: "Out of the experience of ruling Bees may be learned how to rule most women: for there is some resemblance between them".[53] Die ungebührliche Weiberherrschaft im Bienenstock wird als notwendige Folge männlicher Dekadenzerscheinungen dargestellt, die Drohnenverachtung der Bienenkundler gipfelt in der Feststellung,

---

Being a new Discovery and Improvement of those wonderful Creatures [...]. 7. Auflage. London 1742.

[50] Der Begriff der Amazone taucht vor allem in den *Lehrjahren* auf, wo die vielfache Verwendung des Begriffs sich vor allem auf Natalie bezieht (vgl. LJ 226, 235, 240, 293, 426, 428, 435, 439, 441, 445, 471, 511, 512, 513, 516, 568). In den *Wanderjahren* tritt der Begriff explizit nur noch einmal auf: "Männliche und weibliche Kraftgestalten in gewaltsamen Stellungen erinnerten an jenes herrliche Gefecht zwischen Heldenjünglingen und Amazonen, wo Hass und Feindseligkeit zuletzt sich in wechselseitig-traulichen Beistand auflöst" (WJ 253).

[51] Zedler: *Universal-Lexikon*. Bd. 2. S. 840.

[52] Joseph Warder: *The True Amazons*. S. 94f.

[53] Richard Remnant: *A Discourse or Historie of Bees*. S. 33.

das antriebslose Geschlecht müsse durch aufwendige Bemühungen der Weibchen erst zu zeugenden Männern gemacht werden:

> [...] wie sich denn selbst der Umstand, daß kein Männchen keines der Weibchen mißbrauchen kann, dadurch näher erkläret, weil die Begattung verkehrt geschiehet, das Weibchen den Mann besteigt, und diese faulen Männer, die nicht einmal Wasser – wie die Alten glaubten – tragen, geschweige andere Geschäfte verrichten, sogar zur Begattung durch hunderterlei Liebkosungen von ihnen erst angereizt und gleichsam gezwungen werden müssen.[54]

Um eine repräsentative Darstellung der kontrovers diskutierten Drohneninstinkte und -funktionen handelt es sich dabei nicht. Eher ließe sich eine Verbindung zum, so Henriette Herwig, "größten Interpretationsproblem" der Meister-Romane herstellen: Wilhelms "Wahrnehmungsblokade dort, wo er aufrichtig geliebt wird".[55] Drohnen werden auch als "individuell belebte Begattungsmaschine[n]" dargestellt, die "ausschließlich dem Minnedienst leben; sie werden geschlechtsreif geboren, begatten sich und sterben".[56] Für Wilhelm besteht ebensowenig ein zwingender Grund, auf die von Hersilie halbherzig abgeschossenen "Pfeile mit Widerhaken"[57] zu reagieren, wie es Natalie freisteht, die Gesellschaft ihres Bruders und Thereses derjenigen ihres zur freiwilligen Wanderschaft gezwungenen ewigen Bräutigams Wilhelm vorzuziehen. "Sie sind ein rechter Stock!" (LJ 133) lautet Philines doppeldeutige Replik auf Wilhelms energische Zurückweisung ihrer Liebkosungen in den *Lehrjahren*. Angesichts der übervölkerten Landstriche der *Wanderjahre* erscheint der bis zur Unnatur sublimierte Eros geradezu als natürlich-historische Notwendigkeit und literarisches Gegenmodell zur expansiven Bevölkerungspolitik der Goethezeit und, wie wir sehen werden, der Kolonialisten der *Wanderjahre*. Daneben betreffen die von Bienenkundlern angeführten Gründe für die Frigidität der Drohnen beim Menschen (wie an den Frauenfiguren und Müttern des Romans verdeutlicht wird) ausschließlich das weibliche Geschlecht:[58]

---

[54] J. S. Ersch, J. G. Gruber (Hg.): *Allgemeine Encyclopädie der Wissenschaften und Künste*. Erste Sektion, Teil 10. Nachdr. der Ausgabe von 1818-89 (Leipzig: Johann Friedrich Gleditsch). Graz 1970. S. 120.

[55] Herwig: *Das Ewig Männliche*. S. 366.

[56] Berlepsch: *Die Biene*. S. 9.

[57] Vgl. Herwig: *Das ewig Männliche*. S. 363.

[58] Zur von Rousseau betonten anatomischen Basis der 'weiblichen Schamhaftigkeit' vgl. das 4. und 5. Buch seines einflußreichen Erziehungsromans, z. B. die Darstellung der Schwangerschaft als potenziell tödlich verlaufende Krankheit: "'Mama', sagte der kleine Wirrkopf, 'woher kommen die Kinder?' Ohne zu zögern, antwortete die Mutter: 'Die Frauen schlagen sie ab wie du den [Nieren-]Stein, unter Schmerzen, die ihnen oft das Leben kosten.' Narren mögen lachen und Dummköpfe empört

One single female should in the midst of seven or eight hundred males, one would think, be incessantly assailed. But nature has provided against that inconvenience, by making them of a constitution extremely frigid. The Female chooses out one that pleases her; she is obliged to make the first advances, and excite him to love by her caresses. But this favour proves fatal to him: scarce has he ceased from amorous dalliance, but he is seen to perish. The pleasure of these observations may be taken, by putting a female with several males into a bottle.[59]

Im Zusammenhang mit dem Kästchen bekunden der Sammler, sein Gehilfe und der Oheim ein entschiedenes Desinteresse an enthistorisierten, herrenlosen Kunstprodukten (WJ 377). Aus Hersilies Sicht, die sich angesichts des zufällig ihrem Zugriff ausgelieferten Schlüssels und Kästchens in einen "Kriminalfall" verwickelt sieht, fällt die Öffnung dem rechtmäßigen Besitzer Felix zu. Der Goldschmied des Oheims resümiert anlässlich der kompetenten Öffnung des Kästchens, an "solche Geheimnisse" sei "nicht gut rühren" (WJ 458). Aufforderung und Warnung kennzeichnen auch und besonders Hersilies Verhalten. Sie, die neugierigste und ungeduldigste aller Kästchenverwahrer, erweist sich gleichzeitig als selbstbeherrschte Pandora, die einer eigenhändigen Öffnung des Kästchens ("Gott sei uns gnädig!") trotz der sich anbietenden Gelegenheit eisern widersteht. Die geglückte, das Geheimnis bewahrende (der Goldschmied), als auch die unterlassene oder verunglückte, an der Lüftung des Geheimnisses gar nicht ernsthaft interessierte Öffnung (der Gehülfe, Felix) bleibt Männersache, soll jedoch im (auf der Handlungsebene nicht realisierten) Idealfall im Dreieck Hersilie, Felix, Wilhelm stattfinden. Ebenso gerät der Versuch, Schlüssel und Kästchen als einfache erotische Phallus- und Weiblichkeitssymbole zu deuten, durch die Assoziation der Bienen in die für die *Lehr-* und *Wanderjahre* typische Geschlechterverwirrung. Der vermeintliche Schlüssel/Phallus/Stachel des *Rex Apum* ist das eindeutige Geschlechtsmerkmal der teils fruchtbaren, teils unfruchtbaren Weibchen. Dasselbe gilt für die weiblich konnotierten Behältermetaphern. Der noch von Swammerdam verkannte Beutel im Geschlechtsapparat der Königin enthält, nach der einmaligen Befruchtung durch die Drohne, den für alle zukünftigen Eiablagen der Königin erforderlichen männlichen Samen, der für die Produktion neuer Weibchen sorgt.[60] Und schließlich wäre angesichts der zahlreichen Warnungen mit Bezug auf die

---

sein. Der Weise aber möge versuchen, eine bessere Antwort zu finden, die genauer ins Ziel trifft." In: Jean-Jacques Rousseau: *Emil oder Über die Erziehung.* Hg. von Ludwig Schmidts. 10. Aufl. Paderborn 1991. S. 218.

[59] *Encyclopaedia Britannica* (1797). S. 126. Das Zitat stammt aus der entomologischen Literatur des späten 18. Jahrhunderts.

[60] Zur Forschungsgeschichte der einmaligen Befruchtung der Königin seit Swammerdam vgl. Berlepsch: *Die Biene.* S. 19f.

Öffnung des Kästchens die Doppelfunktion des Bienenstachels als Legröhre und Giftspritze zu beachten, die von Swammerdams mikroskopischer Offenbarung der königlichen Geschlechtsteile bezeugt wurde.[61] Der auf den ersten Blick phallisch-männliche, bei näherer Betrachtung mann-weibliche (Steer) Schlüssel bzw. Stachel gibt sich in vollkommener Weiblichkeit zu erkennen.

Wer oder was ist weiblich (W) oder männlich (M), vorherrschend oder subordiniert, relevant oder irrelevant in einem Romanwerk, in dem die das Problem auf den Punkt bringenden Initialen des bürgerlichen Helden, WM, ausdrücklich als mit dem Monogramm einer Gräfin, "der Chiffer einer Freundin" (LJ 201) identisch herausgestellt werden? Die Stelle befindet sich im 3. Buch der *Lehrjahre*. Hier macht Wilhelm nicht nur nähere Bekanntschaft mit seinem auf Geschlechterverwirrung spezialisierten Namensvetter und "Paten" Shakespeare (LJ 210). Bezeichnenderweise findet sich dort auch die einzige Erwähnung der Bienen in den *Lehrjahren*:

> Endlich war der Prinz angekommen; die Generalität, die Stabsoffiziere und das übrige Gefolge, das zu gleicher Zeit eintraf, die vielen Menschen [...] machten das Schloß einem Bienenstocke ähnlich, der eben schwärmen will (LJ 175).

In Übereinstimmung mit dem Bienenwissen seiner Zeit bestimmt Goethe Überbevölkerung ("die vielen Menschen") als Anlass zur Spaltung des Bienenstocks und der Bildung neuer Kolonien – das sog. "Schwärmen" als ein Hauptmotiv der *Wanderjahre*, das an dieser Stelle der *Lehrjahre* angedeutet wird. Bei der Teilung der Auswanderer in Vor- und Nachschwärme, Binnen- und Überseeprojekte handelt es sich um reguläres Bienenverhalten, nur die Besiedlung Amerikas blieb für die Honigbienen (*apis mellifera*) ohne menschliche Transporthilfen unerreichbar. Hauptanlass des Geschwärms (bei den Bienen die Anwesenheit einer oder mehrerer neuer Königinnen) ist in den *Lehrjahren* die entfernt an den Bienenkönig erinnernde Ankunft des Prinzen. Die zeitgenössische apistische Literatur interpoliert die Vorgänge innerhalb und außerhalb des Bienenstocks unterschiedlich, indem entweder die neue Königin – als Anlass und Ziel des Geschwärms – oder die zahlreichen um deren Befruchtung rivalisierenden Drohnen als erste Anzeichen des Schwärmens bezeichnet werden. Auch in *Dichtung und Wahrheit* produziert die Ankunft des Grafen, seiner Offiziere und Adjutanten in dem "nur für eine Familie eingerichteten" väterlichen Haushalt des jungen Goethe "eine Bewegung und ein Gesumme wie in einem Bienenkorbe, obgleich alles sehr gemäßigt, ernsthaft und streng zuging".[62] Die französische Besatzung des Elternhauses und Verwirrung väterlicher Autorität und Ordnung liefert dem jungen Goethe eine Gelegenheit, sich durch die vorwitzige Öffnung eines

---

[61] Ibid. S. 21.
[62] HA 9. S. 84.

Kästchens im Besitz des Grafen "unverhofft Einblick[e] in die Geheimnisse des Geschlechts"[63] zu verschaffen. Politik und Erotik werden bereits in der Bienen-Episode der *Lehrjahre* verflochten. Das Treiben im Schloss und Wilhelms "Konfrontation mit der Adelswelt" steht "im Dienst der produktiven Desillusionierung, der Emanzipation von einem gesellschaftlichen Ideal, das gleichzeitig auch die Stelle des Elternideals vertritt".[64] Die vom Grafen für den Prinzen geplante Überraschung (vgl. LJ 175) besteht vor allem darin, dass die diversen "Ordre" von Wilhelm und dem Baron mit Hilfe der adligen Damen unterminiert werden, ohne dass das Täuschungsmanöver vom Grafen wahrgenommen wird. Insofern ergibt sich hier ein kompliziertes Netzwerk von Herrschaft und Subversion, dessen Dynamik von den Beteiligten weder durchschaut noch eigentlich kontrolliert wird. Die Durchsetzung eigener Interessen gelingt nur als Selbsttäuschung und Illusion (der Graf), oder als geschickte Manipulation fremder Interessen und Kompetenzen für die eigenen Zwecke (der Baron, Wilhelm und die adligen Frauen). Die in diesem Kapitel am Beispiel einer geselligen Theateraufführung geschilderten politischen Machtverhältnisse lassen sich am besten durch das von Philine formulierte Beispiel aus dem Bereich der Erotik (und Ästhetik) in "diesem vierfach verschlungenen Romane" (LJ 249) illustrieren, nach dem der Herrschende und Verfolger zugleich der Beherrschte und Verfolgte, der Verräter und Betrüger zugleich der Verratene und Betrogene ist. Die Einleitung der komödienhaften Episode durch den Vergleich mit schwärmenden Bienen erscheint also kaum zufällig oder nur konventionell: Von den Ägyptern bis Napoleon waren Bienen nicht nur bevorzugte Embleme der Monarchie (die Ankunft des Prinzen in den *Lehrjahren*), der Bienenstock ist auch seit ihrer Gründung durch Ludwig XIV. das bekannte Emblem der *Comédie Française*.[65]

---

[63] Herwig: *Das ewig Männliche*. S. 49.

[64] Brigitte Kohn: *"Denn wer die Weiber haßt, wie kann der leben?"Die Weiblichkeitskonzeption in Goethes "Wilhelm Meisters Lehrjahren" im Kontext von Sprach- und Ausdruckstheorie des ausgehenden 18. Jahrhunderts*. Würzburg 2001. (Epistemata. Würzburger Wissenschaftliche Schriften. Reihe Literaturwissenschaft 356). S. 305-306.

[65] Zur Analogisierung von Schauspieler-Ensemble und "Stock" vgl. LJ 21 und 275. In den Beschreibungen der Webertechniken finden sich subtile Hinweise auf die 1794 zur Nationalflagge erklärte *tricolore*, die die Flagge der französischen Monarchie (goldfarbene *fleurs-de-lis* auf weißem Hintergrund, die nach der Restauration 1814 wieder eingeführt, 1830 im Zuge der Julimonarchie wieder abgeschafft wurde) ersetzte. Napoleon ersetzte die Lilien mit seinem persönlichen Emblem, den Bienen. In den von Lenardo aufgezeichneten Webetechniken werden die Farben und Symbole der französischen Republik und Revolution (rot, blau, Streifen) und der Bourbonen-Monarchie und Restauration (weiß, Blumen) miteinander versponnen und mit dem doppeldeutigen Begriff 'Mugge' (umgangssprachlich für Insekt) ver-

Namensverwechslungen: Hummeln, Seidenspinner und Frau Susanne

Je nachdem, welcher Grad der Stilisierung dem Leser zulässig erscheint, kann der Bienenstachel samt den bei Königinnen und Arbeiterinnen mehr oder weniger ausgebildeten Ovarien als natürliches Vorbild des Schlüssels zum Kästchen der *Wanderjahre* bezeichnet werden: Bart und Schlüsselrohr als eigentlicher Stachel/Legröhre, die Ovarien als Entsprechung zur in den Mysterienkulten das weibliche Geschlechtsteil verhüllenden *cista mystica* als Schlüsselgriff. Die kunstreiche Verwebung und Vertextung von Bienenkunde, Religionsgeschichte, Gesellschafts- und Geschlechtertheorie legt es nahe, den weder pfeil-, noch schlüsseltypischen Doppelbart der Abbildung mit einer im Roman zwar angekündigten, aber nicht gelieferten zweiten "Zeichnung" zu verbinden. Beschrieben wird die Differenz zwischen "links und rechts gedrehtem Garn" in der Spinnerei/Weberei/Texterei:[66]

> [J]enes ist gewöhnlich feiner und wird dadurch bewirkt, daß man die Saite, welche die Spindel dreht, um den Wirtel verschränkt, wie die Zeichnung nebenbei deutlich macht (die wir leider wie die übrigen nicht mitgeben können) (WJ 341).

Spindel und Wirtel sind nicht nur Begriffe aus der Spinnereitechnik, sondern gehören, als Bezeichnungen von Pflanzenstengel und Blattansatz, auch zur botanischen Fachsprache der Goethezeit.[67] Das Gespräch mit Eckermann über den Bienenkönig im Zusammenhang mit die Pflanzen- und Tierwelt bis zur Poesie und kulturellen Produktion regelnden Triebkräfte sowie die botanischen Zeichnungen Goethes (Abb. 8) verdeutlichen, dass die fehlende "Zeichnung" bereits in der Abbildung des Schlüssels enthalten sein dürfte. Das thematische Geflecht wird von Hersilies vorausdeutender Bezeichnung der Besitzerin und Leiterin dieser Pflanzenfasern verarbeitenden Weberwerkstätten, Susanne, als "wilde Hummel" bestätigt.[68] Eine etymologisch-entomologische Verbindung der zur weitläufigen Bienenfamilie gehörenden Hummeln mit Spinn- und Webstuben ergibt sich aus der von

---

bunden: "Der Eintrag von getretener sowohl als gezogener Weberei geschieht, je nachdem das Muster es erfordert, mit weißem, lose gedrehtem sogenannten *Muggengarn*, mitunter auch mit türkischrot gefärbten, desgleichen mit blauen Garnen, welche ebenfalls zu Streifen und Blumen verbraucht werden" (WJ 418, Hervorhebung im Text).

[66] Zur bei Goethe häufigen Präsentation der "Gedankenfabrik" als "Weber-Meisterstück" vgl. *Faust* I, V. 1922-1927.

[67] Vgl. Jacob und Wilhelm Grimm: *Deutsches Wörterbuch*. Bearb. von Ludwig Sütterlin. Leipzig 1960. Abt. II, Bd. 14. Sp. 651ff.

[68] Zum Zusammenhang von Geschlechtertheorie und Botanik vgl. Astrida Orle Tantillo: Goethe's Botany and His Philosophy of Gender. In: *Eighteenth-Century Life* 22.2 (1998). S. 123-138.

den antiken Schriftstellern herrührenden terminologischen Verwirrung und Verwechslung von *bombylios* und *bombykion*, von Hummeln (Genus *Bombus*) und Seidenwürmern (Genus *Bombyx*).[69] Hersilies Neugierde auf die Hintergründe von Lenardos Verwechslung Nachodines (das unter mehreren Namen auftretende nussbraune Mädchen/Susanne/die Gute-Schöne oder Schöne-Gute) mit Valerine wird nur durch ihr Interesse am Inhalt des Kästchens übertroffen:

> Sagen Sie mir, was will der Vetter in seiner Nachschrift mit Valerinen? [...] Wie er sich der blonden Schönheit so genau erinnern und sie mit der Tochter des liederlichen Pachters, einer wilden Hummel von Brünette verwechseln kann, die Nachodine hieß und die wer weiß wohin geraten ist, das bleibt mir völlig unbegreiflich und intrigiert mich ganz besonders. Denn es scheint doch, der Herr Vetter, der sein gutes Gedächtnis rühmt, verwechselt Namen und Personen auf eine sonderbare Weise (WJ 76).

Lenardos Verwechslung wiederholt sich auf hermeneutischer Ebene in der verbreiteten Charakterisierung der jungfräulichen Susanne als Witwe und Parallelfigur zur keinesfalls jungfräulichen Marie in der Josephs-Novelle, die nach dem Trauerjahr als Mutter eine zweite, glückliche Ehe eingeht. Die Rechtssprache des 18. Jahrhunderts, in der sich Goethe auskannte, versteht unter einer Witwe im "uneigentlichem Verstande" eine Frau, "der ihr Mann unvermögend oder abwesend [ist], oder endlich auch eine jedwede Weibsperson, die keinen Mann hat, noch jehmals gehabt hat; folglich auch eine Jungfer".[70] Der Garnbote kündet Lenardo in Susanne "eine junge Witwe" an, die "in guten Umständen ein reichliches Gewerbe mit den Erzeugnissen des Gebirges betreibe" (WJ 352). Dies widerspricht nicht nur der später von Susanne geschilderten Verarbeitung importierter Baumwolle (s. unten), sondern auch der rückblickenden Schilderung ihrer Eheschließung. Susanne stellt trotz und wegen der Verschleierung klar, dass diese Ehe nie als *copula carnalis* vollzogen werden konnte. Lenardos sonst unverständliche Bemerkung – "ich fühlte mich sehr zufrieden, sie nicht als Witwe denken zu dürfen" (WJ 427) – betont den Gegensatz zu seinem vermeintlichen *alter ego*, dem unheiligen Joseph ("ich gönnte und wünschte dem guten Ehemann das Leben, und doch mochte ich sie [Marie] mir so gern als Witwe denken" WJ 25), und wird von Susannes Bericht bestätigt:

> Und nun lassen Sie mich einen Schleier über das Nächstfolgende werfen; durch einen Zufall ward meines Verlobten kostbares Leben, seine herrliche Gestalt plötzlich zerstört; er wendete standhaft seine letzten Stunden dazu an, sich mit

---

[69] Dazu Ian C. Beavis: *Insects and Other Invertebrates in Classical Antiquity*. Exeter 1988. S. 197.

[70] Zedler: *Universal-Lexikon*. Bd. 6. S. 1938.

mir Trostlosen verbunden zu sehen und mir die Rechte an seinem Erbteil zu sichern (WJ 423-24).

Der Ehemann stirbt, in Umkehrung des Drohnenschicksals, nicht unmittelbar *nach*, sondern *vor* der Begattung. Laertes wird durch eine ähnliche Erfahrung zum ausgesprochenen Weiberfeind,[71] die Parallele zum ungewöhnlichem Fall einer Eheschließung, der die 'Verwitwung' unmittelbar folgt, sollte, trotz offenkundiger Differenzen, bei der Deutung von Susannes Absage an zwei potenzielle neue Ehemänner (der Faktor, Lenardo) nicht übersehen und mit der Geschichte von Joseph und Marie verwechselt werden.[72] Auch Susannes Beziehungen zum anderen Geschlecht sind von leidvollen Erfahrungen geprägt. Ihre Entwicklung zur selbständigen, kompetenten Unternehmerin ist nicht das Resultat zielstrebig-intentioneller Selbstverwirklichung, sondern notgedrungene Folge der Unfähigkeit der Männer in ihrem Leben, ihre materielle und soziale Existenz zu sichern: "Und so bedurfte ich denn freilich in der größten Not und Absonderung jener Selbständigkeit, in der ich mich, glückliche Verbindung und frohes Mitleben hoffend, frühzeitig geübt" (WJ 424). Ihr Vater, ein schlechter Wirtschafter, verursacht jene Bedrängnis, die sie zur Bittstellerin des jungen Lenardo macht, der "das Unmögliche" (WJ 131) nicht zu tun vermag und, bei wachsenden Gewissensqualen, seinen Männer- und Adelsprivilegien verpflichtet bleibt. Mit ihrem späteren Ehemann verband Susanne gerade das, was andere Paare zu trennen pflegt:

Wir waren wirklich ein ganz wunderliches Paar, welches auf einsamen Spaziergängen sich nur von solchen Grundsätzen unterhielt, welche den Menschen selbständig machen, und dessen wahrhaftes Neigungsverhältnis nur darin zu bestehen schien, einander wechselseitig in solchen Gesinnungen zu bestärken, wodurch die Menschen sonst voneinander völlig entfernt werden (WJ 421).

---

[71] Vgl. LJ 219: "'Wer wird ihm übelnehmen, [...] daß er ein Geschlecht haßt, das ihm so übel mitgespielt hat und ihm alle Übel, die sonst Männer von Weibern zu befürchten haben, in einem sehr konzentrierten Tranke zu verschlucken gab? Stellen sie sich vor: binnen vierundzwanzig Stunden war er Liebhaber, Bräutigam, Ehmann, Hahnrei, Patient und Witwer! Ich wüßte nicht, wie man's einem ärger machen wollte'". "Witwer" hier im Sinne eines von seiner Frau verlassenen Ehemannes.

[72] Vgl. Herwig: *Das ewig Männliche*. S. 153: "Frau Susanne ist Witwe. Rechtlich ist sie im Moment, da Lenardo sie wiederfindet, frei. Psychisch ist sie wie Marie, als Sankt Joseph der Zweite sie trifft, noch an ihren verstorbenen Gatten gebunden". Angesichts der nie vollzogenen Ehe war Susanne im rechtlichen Sinne nie verheiratet. Vgl. Kants *Metaphysik der Sitten*. Rechtslehre § 27. In: Immanuel Kant: *Werke in zehn Bänden*. Hg. von Wilhelm Weischedel. Nachdruck der Studienausgabe von 1960. Darmstadt 1983. Bd. 7. S. 329f.

Sublimierter Eros, die "Leidenschaft zu irgendeinem Wahren, Guten" (WJ 422) verbindet dieses Paar, das sich zum Eheversprechen erst durch die Intervention Dritter durchringt. Wilhelm, der nach der katastrophal verlaufenden sinnlichen Passion mit Mariane rein platonisch mit Natalie verbunden wird, betreibt das Verlöbnis, das vom Vorsteher mit einer feurigen Rede über "die große Gefahr der Lauheit" (WJ 423) zelebriert wird. Natalie hat, ihrem Bruder Friedrich zufolge, von der Liebe keine Ahnung, das gebrannte Kind Wilhelm scheut das Feuer. Insofern ist die für Lenardo enttäuschende Aktivität Wilhelms als Ehevermittler nicht unbegreiflicher[73] als die Verwechslung der Ehe Susannes mit der glücklichen (legitimen) Ehe der kinderlosen Valerine oder der verwitweten Mutter Marie bei den Interpreten dieser verhüllt offenbarten fiktiven Eheverhältnisse.

Das Motiv der Eheschließung auf dem Sterbelager des Bräutigams ist die Vermögensübertragung als Sicherung der Zukunft der geliebten Frau. Das Scheitern des nächsten Ehebewerbers (der Faktor) wird in der Forschung mit dessen angeblichem Mangel an Entsagungsbereitschaft, Dezenz und Feingefühl, einem unlauteren Ehemotiv (Vermögensübertragung) bzw. anrüchigen Fall von "Heiratsschwindelei" erklärt.[74] Aus niedrigen Verhältnissen wie Susanne, gewänne der Faktor durch die Heirat nicht mehr und nicht weniger als Susanne selbst. Die Legitimität ihrer Erbschaft kann sich nicht auf die Eheschließung, sondern nur auf die Adoption durch ihre Schwiegereltern berufen. Die 'Heiratsschwindlerin' Nachodine tritt an die Stelle der ebenfalls verstorbenen Tochter, erhält den Vornamen der Schwägerin (Susanne) und nach dem Tod der Eltern den Familienbesitz. Der durchaus entsagungsbereite Faktor, der Susanne schon lange verehrte, stand ihrer Verbindung mit seinem Freund nicht im Wege (WJ 431). Erst die Konfrontation mit dem Rivalen Lenardo, eben von Susannes Vater als rein brüderlicher, himmlischer Bräutigam der Tochter eingesegnet (WJ 434), bringt den Faktor in Rage. In leidenschaftlicher Erregung, doch zugleich "ruhig mit einer gewissen frommen Hoheit" (WJ 435), klagt er seine Rechte ein und besteht auf einer augenblicklichen Entscheidung Susannes. Die Entschlossenheit des Faktors bildet einen scharfen Kontrast zu Susannes "geteilte[m] Selbst" (WJ 447). Sie kann sich weder für den Faktor noch für Lenardo entscheiden, doch auch Lenardos "Leidenschaft aus Gewissen" (WJ 448) reicht nicht, sich über eine mögliche gemeinsame Zukunft im geringsten zu äußern (WJ 447). Was steht dem Liebespaar im Wege?

Der Faktor erscheint in seiner leidenschaftlichen Entschlossenheit nicht nur als Negativfolie. Darauf gibt in diesem Erzählstrang, in dem Namen und Verwechslungen eine besondere Rolle spielen, besonders der Vorname des Faktors, Daniel (WJ 416), einen Hinweis. "Wie die Susanna des apokryphen Zusatzes zum Buch Daniel hält sie, von zwei Männern bedrängt, einem

---

[73] Dagegen Herwig: *Das ewig Männliche*. S. 148.
[74] Ibid. S. 159.

Dritten die Treue, ihrem verstorbenen Gatten".[75] Doch im Anspielungstext tritt Daniel als strahlender Retter der von falschen Zeugen der Unkeuschheit bezichtigten Susanna auf, die von den leichtgläubigen Israeliten zum Tode verurteilt wurde. In Goethes Roman sind Liebe und Leidenschaft, Sexualität und Schwangerschaft ein potenzielles Todesurteil für die Frau. Goethes Daniel hat eine dem biblischen Vorbild verwandte Funktion. Susannes heiliger Schwur gegenüber dem Faktor – ihr Verhältnis zu Lenardo sei ein absolut reines, geschwisterliches (WJ 434) – bezeugt die Keuschheit dieser jungfräulichen Witwe, die ihren Platz vorerst im Dienst Makaries, nicht des Wanderers Lenardo findet, dessen Bund sich wie ein "Ameisengeschlecht" (WJ 386) in Amerika verbreiten soll. "Von der Frage der Jungfräulichkeit sieht Goethe vollständig ab; seine Männerfiguren sind nicht fixiert auf die Unschuld der Frau",[76] trifft auf den von Hersilie als "verzogene[r] Neffe" Makaries identifizierten Lenardo keinesfalls zu. Seine "Hauptneigung" auf "unbebaute[m] und unbewohnte[m] Land" "ganz von vorne anzufangen" (WJ 242), "kein Pferd" zu mögen, das er "nicht selbst zugeritten" (WJ 142), korrespondiert mit seiner Erleichterung über die jungfräuliche Witwenschaft Susannes und den patriarchalischen Gesetzen des alten Testaments, nach denen Jungfräulichkeit zur Garantie der Vaterschaft vorausgesetzt wird, was mit Susannes urchristlichen Vorstellungen von ehelicher Gemeinschaft jedoch unvereinbar ist. Lenardos "Leidenschaft aus Gewissen", sein (uneingestandenes) Verständnis von Ehe und Vaterschaft als Pflicht und Mittel zum Zweck (Fortpflanzung bzw. Kolonialisierung) steht nicht nur in unüberbrückbarem Gegensatz zu seinem paradoxen Ausschluss der Juden in einem christlichen Auswandererbund, der "Ursprung und Herkommen" dieser "höchsten Kultur" tatsächlich in doppeltem Sinne verleugnet (WJ 405), sondern auch zu den einzigen glücklichen Ehemännern und Vätern des Romans, Joseph und Friedrich, für die Vaterschaft auf Liebe und Überzeugung, nicht auf Zeugung und Pflicht beruht. Angesichts des Keuschheitsgelöbnisses von Susanne erschaudert Lenardo dann auch "bis tief ins Innerste" (WJ 434).

Der bei der Interpretation Susannes ebenfalls meist übersehene, von Hersilie verliehene Beiname – "wilde Hummel" – wäre also ernst zu nehmen. Wie bei den Bienen hängt das Geschlecht der Weibchen (als fruchtbare Königin oder jungfräuliche Arbeiterin) bei den Hummeln von der Zellenbeschaffenheit und Ernährung der Maden ab.[77] Susannes Entwicklung von der

---

[75] Ibid. S. 155.

[76] Ibid. S. 44.

[77] Vgl. die ausführliche Abhandlung über die Hummeln (trotz des englischen Titels handelt es sich hier um einen Beitrag in französischer Sprache) von Pierre Huber (der Sohn des oben erwähnten schweizer Bienenforschers François Huber): Observations on Several Species of the Genus Apis, Known by the Name of Humble-bees,

femme naturelle ("wild und unbändig" WJ 420) zur Guten-Schönen wird bestimmt von ihrer sozialen Herkunft, ihrer religiösen Erziehung durch den Vater, der Überdosis von "Hallers 'Alpen', Geßners 'Idyllen', Kleists 'Frühling'" (WJ 422) an der Seite ihres verstorbenen Mannes, dessen Familie zu den Glaubensbrüdern des Vaters gehörte. Bei den Hummeln wie den Menschen wird die Frau als Frau geboren, Mütterlichkeit hängt von Umweltfaktoren, der *educatio* als Ernährung und Erziehung ab.[78] Das Vorbild der emanzipierten, selbständigen Vorsteherin der Weberei in den *Wanderjahren* ist ein wabenbauendes Insekt, das die Konflikte der Reproduktions- und Produktionssphäre durch die effiziente Arbeitsteilung der Weibchen, ihre Spaltung in Mütter und Arbeiterinnen, gelöst hat und die Männchen (vom Hochzeitsflug abgesehen) nur als Brüder und Söhne im Stock duldet. Als Ehefrau der Ehebewerber Daniel oder Lenardo stünde der "wilden Hummel" Susanne das "Maschinenwesen" als Industrieproduktion und/oder bienen- oder ameisenkönigliche Gebärmaschine bevor. Ist die Leiterin der Weberwerkstätten als Vorbild weiblicher Emanzipation und Selbstbestimmung oder als Bienenjungfer mit verkümmerten Geschlechtsorganen, als Rädchen im Getriebe, zu verstehen?

Unverheiratete und unabhängige Frauen, die sich als Näherinnen und Spinnerinnen ihren Lebensunterhalt verdienten, wurden als "Eigenbrötlerinnen" bezeichnet; die pejorative moderne Bedeutung – als eigensinniger, exzentrischer Mensch – setzt sich erst im Verlauf 19. Jahrhundert durch. Doch schon im 17. Jahrhundert wurde die Unabhängigkeit der Spinner- und Weberinnen "zum Brennpunkt von Ängsten über den sozialen Wandel in einer Gesellschaft, deren Produktionsweisen in diesem Bereich kapitalistische Züge annahmen".[79] Die Spinnstuben Susannes werden als "[h]äuslicher Zustand, auf Frömmigkeit gegründet" beschrieben, und zwar "im glücklichsten

and called Bombinatrices by Linnæus. In: *Transactions of the Linnean Society* 6 (1802). S. 214-298, hier S. 286.

[78] Vgl. *Encyclopaedia Britannica* (1797). S. 130: "all the common or working bees were originally of the female sex; but that when they have undergone their last metamorphosis, they are condemned to a state of perpetual virginity, and the organs of generation are obliterated; merely because they have not been lodged, fed, and brought up in a particular manner, while they were in the worm state". Die Stelle bezieht sich auf die auch bei Goethes "philosophische[m] Bienenfreund" Lucas diskutierten und kritisierten Quellen.

[79] Eine zeitgenössische Quelle (1642) beschreibt die Spinnstuben als Versammlung von "müssigen finstern Eigenbrötlerinnen, die am Licht und öffentlichen Diensten nicht eingehen, oder schaffen mögen, sondern ein faules geschwätziges, und gemeiniglich leichtfertiges Gesind, hin und wieder in denen Winkeln stecken, die Kirchen und öffentlichen Gottesdienst gar selten besuchen, auch junge unschuldige Herzen an sich hängen und verführen". Zitiert nach Ulinka Rublack: *Magd, Metz' oder Mörderin. Frauen vor frühneuzeitlichen Gerichten.* Frankfurt/M. 1998. S. 222.

Verhältnis der Pflichten zu den Fähigkeiten und Kräften" (WJ 351). Laut Wilhelm befindet sich Susanne in einem Kreis "von Handarbeitenden im reinsten, anfänglichsten Sinne", gekennzeichnet durch "Umsicht und Mäßigung, Unschuld und Tätigkeit" (WJ 351). Doch in Lenardos Beschreibung des Haushalts der Susanne tauchen zwei weibliche "Figuren" (Gretchen und Lieschen) auf, die ihn "ganz irre" machen und an die negative Charakterisierung der Eigenbrötlerin erinnern. Gretchen erscheint als "gesetztes, freundliches Kind", ihre Interaktion mit Lenardo beschränkt sich darauf, ihm "verständig und ruhig" die rein "mechanischen Verfahren" der Spinnstube zu erläutern (WJ 417-18). Ganz anders das unruhestiftende Lieschen: Sie unterbricht ihre Arbeit und die Konversation Gretchens mit Lenardo, "ist geschäftig, dreinzureden, und zwar auf eine Weise, um jene durch Widerspruch nur irrezumachen" (WJ 418). Nach Gretchens Auffassung stiftet der "Schalk" Lieschen "nichts Gutes"; sie belausche Susannes Privatgespräche, teile letztere heimlich dem Faktor mit, mit dem sie ein undurchsichtiges Verhältnis hinter dem Rücken ihrer Arbeitgeberin anspinnt (WJ 433). Lieschen ist damit mitverantwortlich für den Eifersuchtsausbruch des Faktors gegenüber Susanne und Lenardo. Auch das Gespräch zwischen Lenardo und Gretchen stört sie erst mit verwirrendem Geplapper, dann durch verhüllt erotische Signale, indem sie "ohne durch die Enge des Raums genötigt zu sein, mit ihrem zarten Ellenbogen zweimal merklich" Lenardos Arm streift, was ihm "nicht sonderlich gefallen wollte" (WJ 418). Der 'Wink mit dem Ellenbogen'[80] ist in Goethes *Faust* eine eindeutig sexuelle Pantomime, der Vergleich liegt außerdem wegen der Namen der Dienstmägde nahe, wobei ein gewisser Rollentausch zwischen Lieschen und Gretchen auffällt, die sich in *Faust* nicht in der Spinnstube, sondern am Brunnen begegnen. Für die kleinbürgerlichen Töchter und Hausmägde in der Tragödie wäre ökonomische Unabhängigkeit von Haus und Familie nur als Nonnen-, Bettler- und Prostituiertenexistenz vorstellbar. Lieschens scharfe Moralpredigt und strenge Forderung der Bestrafung leichtfertiger Frauenzimmer richtet sich dort gegen die nicht-eheliche Schwangerschaft. In den *Wanderjahren* fordert das gute Gretchen die Züchtigung (durch Susanne, WJ 433) der Unruhestifterin Lieschen: Kommunikative Verwirrung, Überschreitung der Rangordnung und korrespondierender Kompetenzen, sowie die Anfachung erotischer Leidenschaften stören den reibungslosen Ablauf des Spinnstubenmechanismus. Das Gretchen der *Wanderjahre* ist keine sexuelle Figur. Im Gegensatz zu Lieschen nimmt sie die Männer (Lenardo, Faktor) nicht als potenzielle Liebhaber oder Ehemänner zur Kenntnis. Durch Ausschaltung der Störfaktoren Sexualität und Familiengründung entspricht Gretchen dem idealen Frauentypus der Spinnindustrie, deren Kritiker seit dem 17. Jahrhundert die Unab-

---

[80] Vgl. HA 3. *Faust I*, V. 959-972; *Faust II*, V. 5191.

hängigkeit der Eigenbrötlerinnen zwangsläufig in moralische Dekadenz münden sahen, ohne auf ihre Arbeitskraft verzichten zu können.[81]

Die Befreiung der Frau vom Haus erscheint so betrachtet als soziale Revolution, die einem Rückfall in den Naturzustand gleichkommt – die im Bienenstaat perfektionierte Zusammenarbeit Geschlechtsloser zum Nutzen des Gemeinwohls. Das von Susanne gefürchtete "überhandnehmende Maschinenwesen" (WJ 429) ist nicht der Beginn, sondern die Steigerung dieser Entwicklung, die man als emanzipatorischen Fortschritt gegenüber den geschlechtsspezifischen, familienwirtschaftlichen Produktionsweisen der traditionellen Agrargesellschaft oder als veloziferischen Prozess der Instrumentalisierung und Entmenschlichung auffassen kann. Im Rahmen zeitgenössischer Diskurse über Versorgungskrisen durch Überbevölkerung entspricht Susannes Keuschheitsgelöbnis der Lösung von Malthus (Enthaltsamkeit, Verzicht auf Fortpflanzung), die dem "Maschinenwesen" misstrauisch entgegensehende Unternehmerin korrespondiert mit der Position Condorcets (Steigerung der Produktivität, Bildung und Emanzipation der Frau), beide Positionen vereinigen sich im Bienenstaat in den Arbeiterinnen. Bemerkenswert ist die aus Gretchens Sicht übertriebene Nachsicht Susannes mit der Quertreiberin Lieschen. Erläutert wird sie nur beiläufig und andeutungsweise im Zusammenhang mit einigen in umherstehenden Töpfen aufkeimenden Baumwollpflanzen:

So nähren und pflegen wir die für unser Geschäfte unnützen, ja widerwärtigen Samenkörner, die mit der Baumwolle einen so weiten Weg zu uns machen. Es geschieht aus Dankbarkeit, und es ist ein eigen Vergnügen, dasjenige lebendig zu sehen, dessen abgestorbene Reste unser Dasein beleben (WJ 418-19).

Die Stelle ist im Zusammenhang mit Goethes Diskurs über die Vollendung der Pflanze im Samen und den Bienenkönig in mehrfacher Hinsicht bemerkenswert: Hier deutet sich eine Differenz zu den – wie in der apistischen Literatur betont wird – auf Reinlichkeit und Nutzen bedachten Bienen an. Susanne bekundet eine gewisse ökologische Ehrfurcht vor dem aus betriebsökonomischer Sicht Unnützen und Widerwärtigen, die der höchsten (christlichen) Bildungsstufe in der Ehrfurchslehre der pädagogischen Provinz entspricht. Die Hummeln, von denen nur die befruchtete Königin überwintert, legen sich keinen Wintervorrat an Honig an, den der Mensch für seine Zwecke hätte plündern (in der euphemistischen Sprache der Bienenzucht 'zei-

---

[81] Vgl. Ulinka Rublack: *Magd, Metz' oder Mörderin.* S. 326: "Man benötigte die Arbeitskraft lediger, flexibler Frauen. An dieser Produktionsweise war neu, daß Produktionsort und Wohnung getrennt waren, der Lohn vor allem monetär war sowie die Beziehung zwischen Arbeitgeber und Arbeitnehmer rein funktional. Die Nachfrage nach solchen Arbeitsstrukturen unterhöhlte ein Ordnungsgefüge, das auf dem Haus als Kern der Sozialverfassung basierte".

deln') können. Anders als die Biene baut die Hummel ihre unregelmässigen Waben, nicht "winkel- und waagerecht, als Meister und Geselle".[82] Die Hummeln (als "wilde Bienen") standen deshalb im Ruf der Faulheit und Liederlichkeit, wurden als Ungeziefer, Honigdiebe in den Stöcken der Honigbienen verdächtigt oder (aufgrund ihrer Größe) mit den Drohnen (als Schmarotzer oder Brutbienen) im Bienenstock verwechselt, wie in der oben zitierten Stelle aus Swammerdams *Bibliae Naturae* deutlich wurde.[83] Im Kontext der *Wanderjahre* hat der Vergleich Susanne/wilde Hummel eher positive Konnotationen. Susannes Toleranz gegenüber dem Nutzlosen, Widerwärtigen erscheint als Symptom wahrer Menschlichkeit, personifiziert im legitimen Kästchenbesitzer und ehemaligen Kind Felix:

> Der Knabe war mit einem neuen Spielwerke beschäftigt, der Vater suchte es ihm besser, ordentlicher, zweckmäßiger einzurichten; aber in dem Augenblicke verlor auch das Kind die Lust daran. "Du bist ein wahrer Mensch!" rief Wilhelm aus; "komm, mein Sohn! Komm, mein Bruder, laß uns in der Welt zwecklos hinspielen, so gut wir können!" (LJ 569).

Goethes oben zitierte formale Beschreibung der *Wanderjahre* als "in einem Sinne" verfasstes heterogenes "Geschlinge" oder "Aggregat" kommt einem Hummelnest (Abb. 9) näher als dem exakt hexagonalen Wabenbau der Honigbienen. Die Analogie Hummel/Künstler findet sich häufiger in der zeitgenössischen Literatur.[84] Daneben deutet sich in Susannes Kommentar der vegetativ keimenden Samen im abgestorbenen menschlichen Dasein ein

---

[82] *Novelle*. HA 6. S. 507.

[83] Auch bei Goethe finden sich unschmeichelhafte Erwähnungen der Hummeln. Über Kotzebues Monatsschrift *Die Biene* heisst es abfällig, sie werde "mit Recht nicht einer Biene, sondern einer Hummel zugeschrieben" (Brief an F. A. Wolf, 28. September 1811).

[84] Vgl. Andrew Cooper: *The Apian Way*. S. 161: "the domesticated classical honeybee could image the longing of Romantic writers for patronage and acceptance by the rising middle class, as well as their nostalgia for feudal olden days [...]. This may explain why early nineteenth century writers show so little interest in the 'surly Humble Bee', that solitary, potentially Byronic wanderer who in John Day's drama some hundred years earlier 'hath too long / Liv'd like an outlaw, and will neither pay / Honey nor wax, do service or obey': any similarities here would only reemphasize the Romantic writer's failure to achieve an accepted social role. On the other hand, the honeybee's capacity to feed on its own honey connotes a self-sufficiency that could seem to solve the poet's task, in an age largely lacking the traditional forms of patronage [...]". Die Hummeln unterscheiden sich in ihrer Fähigkeit, vom eigenen Honig zu leben, nicht von den Honigbienen. Die Hummelkönigin ist wesentlich unabhängiger und vielseitiger als die Bienenkönigin: sie überwintert in der Erde und gründet im Frühjahr eigenständig neue Kolonien.

'Stirb und Werde' an, das die auch in der Bienenliteratur (z. B. bei Lucas) umstrittene irreversible Fixierung der Arbeiterinnen auf Sterilität in Frage stellt. In Hersilies ironischer Umkehr der Oheim-Sprüche wird das "Wahre[..]" und "Nützliche[..]" der weiblichen Existenz als Ehe und Mutterschaft bezeichnet (WJ 66). Susanne, die "Schöne-Gute" übergibt ihr gesamtes Vermögen dem Faktor Daniel, der dadurch instand gesetzt wird, eine Familie zu gründen und "die Bewohner des arbeitslustigen Tales" mit Fabriken, neuem Reichtum und (vermutlich) Bevölkerungswachstum zu versorgen. Susanne selbst wird vollkommen abhängig von Makarie, deren Absicht es ist, die junge Frau früher oder später dem Neffen zuzuführen. Welche Beziehung besteht zwischen der todgeweihten Stifterin steriler Ehen und der zyklischen Fruchtbarkeit der demetrischen Erdseele?

Makarie, das "terrestrische Märchen" und der Auswandererbund

Die überragende, sozusagen ranghöchste und von allen verehrte Frauenfigur der *Wanderjahre* ist keine Mutter, sondern eine alte Jungfer, gekennzeichnet vom Zerfall des Körpers bei blühendem Geist. Wie eine Bienenkönigin thront und regiert sie versteckt im Allerheiligsten der *Wanderjahre*-Topographie, bewacht und umsorgt von Jungfrauen (wie Angela) sowie einem Arzt und Mathematiker. Der Makarienbereich erinnert an die religiösmythische Bedeutung der Bienen als Priesterinnen der Muttergöttinnen und die alte Vorstellung ihrer jungfräulichen Zeugung. Makaries Fruchtbarkeit ist nicht körperlich, sondern geistig definiert, sie ist nicht der Erde, sondern dem All verbunden: Apis, die Biene (auch als Musca, die Fliege) bezeichnete ein kleines südliches ("die südische Fliege") sowie ein nördliches Gestirn.[85] Aufgrund ihrer Eigenschaften als Honigproduzenten, Wetterboten und geometrisierende Wabenbauer wurden die Bienen oft mit den Bereichen der Medizin, Astronomie und Mathematik assoziiert. Makaries Gedanken (Eier) werden im Archiv (Zellen) abgelegt, von Jungfrauen geordnet, kopiert und versorgt – die Bienenkönigin als das von den eigentlichen Honigbienen (Arbeiterinnen) vollkommen abhängige Zentrum des Bienenstocks. Nach ältesten Vorstellungen bedarf der Dichter der Gunst der traditionell in Bienengestalt auftretenden Musen oder Musenvögel.[86] Inhaltlich und formal betont Makaries Archiv nicht nur die Abhängigkeit des Dichters von den gängigen Diskursen bei der Werkgenese, sondern auch der Werkrezeption

---

[85] Johann Heinrich Zedler: *Grosses vollständiges Universal-Lexikon aller Wissenschaften und Künste* (1732-54). Nachdr. Graz 1961-64. Bd. XI, Sp. 1352. Als südliche Konstellation aus vier Sternen beschrieben bei J. S. Ersch, J. G. Gruber: *Allgemeine Encyclopädie der Wissenschaften und Künste*. Erste Sektion, Teil 10. Nachdruck der Ausgabe Leipzig 1818-89. Graz 1970. S. 129.

[86] Zum Topos des von Bienen umschwärmten neugeborenen Dichters, hier Pindar, vgl. Goethes Aufsatz *Philostrats Gemälde und Antik und Modern*.

und Überlieferung an die Nachwelt, wie im oben zitierten Bienen-Diskurs mit Eckermann angedeutet wurde. Beim in Makaries Archiv ausgebreiteten Zitatenschatzes handelt es sich um eine eigenwillige Zusammenstellung und Kommentierung disparater Gedanken, die bereits von anderen gedacht wurden. Makaries Archiv kann schon zu ihren Lebzeiten nur durch die Arbeitskraft der ihr huldigenden Jungfrauen bestehen. Zwischen der Beziehung Makarie-Angela und derjenigen Goethes zu seinem auf den Junggesellenstand verpflichteten Gesprächspartner und Archivar Eckermann besteht eine gewisse Verwandtschaft. Makaries skeptischer Hausfreund erinnert, in ironischer Brechung, zugleich an den im Archiv erwähnten Georg Christoph Lichtenberg.[87]

In der Fortsetzung des Bienenkönig-Gesprächs mit Eckermann ist von Naturforschern die Rede, "denen es vor allem nur daran liege, ihre Meinung zu beweisen", die durch geschickte Leserlenkung bestimmte Assoziationen erwecken, womit "dem arglosen Leser die Schlinge des Irrtums über den Kopf gezogen wird, er weiß nicht wie".[88] In der *Wanderjahre*-Forschung finden sich dazu zahlreiche Parallelen, die, wie im Fall der Jungfrau-Witwe Susanne, mit den Assoziationsfeldern der Bienen und Hummeln verknüpft werden. Der letzte hier zu besprechende Fall betrifft Makaries Antithese, die terrestrische Person, die in der Forschung allgemein als "terrestrische Frau" präsentiert wird, eine durch die Kommentare und Inhaltsverzeichnisse zahlreicher Werkausgaben fortgepflanzte Verzerrung des im Text geschilderten Sachverhalts. Der Einführung dieses sehr bienenhaften Wesens wird in den *Wanderjahren* eine umfangreiche, hier nur verkürzt zitierbare erkenntnistheoretische Belehrung vorangestellt:

> Bei dem Studieren der Wissenschaften, besonders derer, welche die Natur betreffen, ist die Untersuchung so nötig als schwer: ob das, was uns von alters her überliefert und von unseren Vorfahren für gültig geachtet worden, auch wirklich gegründet und zuverlässig sei [...]? Oder ob ein herkömmliches Bekenntnis nur stationär geworden und deshalb mehr einen Stillstand als einen Fortschritt veranlasse? (WJ 443).

Dieser epistemologischen Reflexion folgt ohne nähere Erläuterung – "unbegreiflich" und "wunderseltsam" – die "Eröffnung Montans" über "eine Person [...] welche ganz wundersame Eigenschaften und einen ganz eigenen Bezug auf alles habe, was man Gestein, Mineral, ja sogar was man überhaupt Element nennen könne" (WJ 443). Dies erinnert an die in der Bienenliteratur vieldiskutierten Instinkte der Bienen, ihrer Intelligenz und Sprache,

---

[87] Zu Lichtenberg und Makaries Hausfreund vgl. Aeka Ishihara: *Makarie und das Weltall*. Köln 1998 (Kölner Germanistische Studien 42). S. 16-21.
[88] Gespräch mit Eckermann, 13. Februar 1829.

die Goethe als 'offenbares Geheimnis' der Natur darstellte.[89] Die Assoziation 'Gesteinsfühlerin' liegt angesichts der angeblich spezifisch weiblichen Intuition der gleich anschließend erwähnten 'Gestirnsfühlerin' Makarie nahe. Dieser erste Eindruck wird durch den permanenten, geradezu exzessiven Einsatz des femininen Personalpronomens bestätigt, das sich jedoch ausnahmslos auf das grammatische ("die Person"), nicht das biologische Geschlecht bezieht:

> *Sie* ["diese Person", K.B.] fühle nicht bloß eine gewisse Einwirkung der unterirdisch fließenden Wasser, metallischer Lager und Gänge, sowie der Steinkohlen und was dergleichen in Massen beisammen sein möchte, sondern, was wunderbarer sei, *sie* befinde sich anders und wieder anders, sobald *sie* nur den Boden wechsele. Die verschiedenen Gebirgsarten übten auf *sie* einen besonderen Einfluß, worüber er sich mit *ihr*, seitdem er eine zwar wunderliche, aber doch auslangende Sprache einzuleiten gewußt, recht gut verständigen und *sie* im einzelnen prüfen könne, da *sie* denn auf eine merkwürdige Weise die Probe bestehe, indem *sie* sowohl chemische als physische Elemente durchs Gefühl gar wohl zu unterscheiden wisse, ja sogar schon durch den Anblick das Schwerere von dem Leichtern unterscheide. *Diese Person, über deren Geschlecht er sich nicht näher erklären wollte*, habe er mit den abreisenden Freunden vorausgeschickt und hoffe zu seinen Zwecken in den ununtersuchten Gegenden sehr viel von *ihr* (WJ 443-444, Hervorhebung K.B.).

Der Leser wird ebenso eindeutig dazu verführt, das biologische Geschlecht mit dem grammatischen zu verwechseln, wie ihm durch die Weigerung Montans, das Geschlecht dieser "Person" zu bestimmen, eine deutliche Warnung vor dieser besonders aus der Bienenkunde geläufigen Fehlzeugung zukommt. Zudem ist anschließend von der "Ähnlichkeit der hier eintretenden Fälle bei der größten Verschiedenheit" (WJ 444) die Rede, was sich intratextuell auf die zugleich suggerierte und geleugnete Parallelität der doppelgeschlechtlichen Paarungen Makarie/Astronom, terrestrische Person/-Montan bezieht. Die Formulierung "Abschied Montans und seiner Frauenzimmer" bringt keine Aufklärung, da hier ausdrücklich nur von Lydie und Philine die Rede ist (WJ 445). Spiegelbildlich folgt im nächsten Kapitel die Beschreibung der terrestrischen Person einer ausführlichen Erwähnung der unweiblich-weiblichen Makarie[90] (WJ 452): Erstere sei, wie Montan "mit

---

[89] Gespräch mit Eckermann. 8. Oktober 1827: "Wir stecken in lauter Wundern, und das Letzte und Beste der Dinge ist uns verschlossen. Nehmen wir nur die Bienen. [...] Sie gehen wie an einem unsichtbaren Gängelband hierhin und dorthin; was es aber eigentlich sei, wissen wir nicht. [...] Alle diese äußeren Dinge liegen klar vor uns wie der Tag, aber ihr inneres geistiges Band ist uns verschlossen".

[90] Zur Forschungsdiskussion der unsinnlichen Weiblichkeit Makaries s. Herwig: *Das ewig Männliche*. S. 379f.

dem größten Anschein von Ehrlichkeit" angibt, "schon mit den ersten Wanderern in die weite Ferne gezogen" (WJ 452). Damit verbietet es sich einerseits, die terrestrische Person Montans nach wie vor anwesenden "Frauenzimmer[n]" (Lydie, Philine) zuzurechnen, andererseits wird Montan hier als nicht ganz ehrlich, die Information als "unwahrscheinlich" ausgewiesen, so dass die Sache weiterhin in der Schwebe bleibt. Die widersprüchlichen Angaben heben sich gegenseitig auf, ein Verfahren, das auch den letzten der terrestrischen Person gewidmeten Abschnitt kennzeichnet. Unter dem Gesinde verbreiten sich Gerüchte, die Montans angeblich abgereiste terrestrische Frau mit einer vermeintlichen "Dienerin" in Verbindung bringen:

> Philine nämlich und Lydie hatten eine Dritte mitgebracht, unter dem Vorwand, es sei eine Dienerin, wozu sie sich aber gar nicht zu schicken schien; wie sie denn auch beim An- und Auskleiden der Herrinnen niemals gefordert wurde (WJ 452).

Die Person erscheint erst hier als eindeutig weiblich ("eine Dritte", "Dienerin"), zugleich wird diese Eindeutigkeit noch einmal als "Vorwand" ausgewiesen. Warum sollten Philine und Lydie eine weibliche Dienerin nicht beim An- und Auskleiden beanspruchen? Noch dazu zeigt die angebliche "Dienerin", die zwei- bis dreifache Männerarbeit leistet,

> keine gesellige Bildung, wovon die Kammermädchen immer die Karikatur darzustellen pflegen. Auch fand sie gar bald unter der Dienerschaft ihren Platz; sie gesellte sich zu den Garten- und Feldgenossen, ergriff den Spaten und arbeitete für zwei bis drei. Übrigens hielt sie sich still und gewann gar bald die allgemeine Gunst. Sie erzählten sich von ihr: man habe sie oft das Werkzeug niederlegen und querfeldein über Stock und Steine springen sehen, auf eine versteckte Quelle zu, wo sie ihren Durst gelöscht. Diesen Gebrauch habe sie täglich wiederholt, indem sie von irgendeinem Punkte aus, wo sie gestanden, immer ein oder das andere rein ausfließende Wasser zu finden gewußt, wenn sie dessen bedurfte (WJ 452-53).

Seit der Antike wurden die Honigbienen (Arbeiterinnen) als 'Wasserträger' mit besonderer Begabung für das Auffinden von Quellen geschildert, die sie für Honigproduktion und Brutpflege benötigen.[91] Die wunderbare Erschei-

---

[91] U. a. Aristoteles. HA 625b:19; Callimachus: *Hymne an Apollo* 110; Vergil: *Georgika*. IV, 54. Im *Haushaltsbuch* von J. Colerus (Ende 16. Jahrhundert) findet sich folgende Anweisung zur erfolgreichen Bienenhaltung: "So soll auch Wasser in der Nähe sein, besonders fein reines, liebliches Born- oder Quellwasser soll man im Garten nicht weit von den Stöcken haben oder muß es sonst in Röhren hineinführen [...], daß sie nicht weit nach Wasser zu fliegen brauchen und die Honigarbeit desto fleißiger pflegen können". Zitiert nach Bodenheimer: *Geschichte der Entomologie*. II, S. 53.

nung der terrestrischen "Person" erinnert einerseits an das Masken- und Rollenspiel des Schauspielers (*dramatis personae*), andererseits an die schwankende Geschlechtlichkeit und flexible Arbeitsteilung der Honigbienen.[92] Diese werden von der zeitgenössischen Entomologie als tendenziell (anatomisch) weiblich, aber prinzipiell geschlechtslos beschrieben, verrichten, von der Brutpflege bis zur bewaffneten Verteidigung, alle Arbeiten im Stock und (wie Lucas es formulierte) bestimmen ihre Geschlechtlichkeit als unbegreifliche "Intelligenzen" selbst. Entsprechend befindet sich die terrestrische Person "anders und wieder anders, sobald sie nur den Boden wechsel[t]". Im Gegensatz zu den auf Honig und Wachs spezialisierten Bienen (wichtige Produkte der traditionellen Agrarökonomie) besteht der vielversprechende Nutzen der mysteriösen Instinkte der terrestrischen Person für den Auswandererbund in deren Fähigkeit, die für die industrielle Produktion unverzichtbaren Rohstoffe (Metalle, Mineralien) auszuspüren. Die allgemeine Gunst (des einfachen Dienstpersonals) erwirbt sie durch ihre wünschelruten- und bienenhafte Affinität zu Wasserquellen – die unverzichtbare Basis jeder Form menschlicher Existenz und Sozietät.

Für den Plan der Auswanderer, Amerika mit Europäern und Manifakturen zu besiedeln, ist das Wasser so unverzichtbar wie das Gebären (zur Analogie von Wasserschöpfen und Gebären vgl. LJ 541). Philine, die gemeinsam mit Lydie die Zurichtung der Bräute übernimmt, kommt damit nicht nur die symbolische Aufgabe zu, die "neuen Kolonien mit Kleidungsstücken" (WJ 442), sondern auch mit Menschen zu versorgen. Als einzige Mutter unter den Auswanderern wird sie vom Erzähler abschätzig als Fremdkörper in der hohen Kultur des Makarienbezirks dargestellt. Makaries Segen erhalte sie nur, weil man sie "desto eher loszuwerden hoffte", die engelhafte Angela, selbst im Brautstand, weicht entsetzt vor der Zuschneiderin zurück (WJ 440-41). Die Wanderer sind sich der Tatsache wohl bewusst, dass "ein einziges Glied, das in einer großen Kette bricht, [das Ganze] vernichtet" (WJ 412). Gegenläufig zum Erzählerkommentar rehabilitiert wird die "wahre Eva" und "Stammutter des weiblichen Geschlechts" (LJ 100) nicht nur vom Leiter des Binnenprojekts (Odoard) und seinen wenig erbaulichen Erfahrungen als Vater (*Nicht zu weit*), sondern auch von Friedrich, der die Treffsicherheit der intuitiven Schneiderei seiner Frau hervorhebt: "Solltet ihr wohl denken [...], daß das unnützeste Geschöpf von der Welt, wie es schien, meine Philine, das nützlichste Glied der großen Kette werden wird?" (WJ 335).

Die "gefräßige[..] Schere" der deshalb als "lästig" empfundenen Philine kennt "weder Maß noch Ziel" (WJ 440), Lydie sieht "ihre Schülerinnen sich ins Hundertfache vermehren und ein ganzes Volk von Hausfrauen zu Genauigkeit und Zierlichkeit eingeleitet und aufgeregt" (WJ 442). Auch die

---

[92] Zum flexiblen Rollentausch der Arbeiterinnen im Bienenstaat vgl. Oliver Goldsmith: *An History of the Earth*. S. 69-70.

überragende Bedeutung der "grosse[n] Bienenmutter" und "wahre[n] Stammmutter aller Bienen"[93] leitet sich aus deren phänomenaler Fruchtbarkeit ab, von ihr hängt die Produktion neuer Weibchen, von den Arbeiterinnen die differenzierende Aufzucht der Larven als Arbeiterinnen und Mütter ab. Aus bienenkundlicher Sicht wäre demnach folgerichtig, dass nicht nur die Mutter Philine, sondern auch ihr absoluter Gegenpol, die Jungfrau Natalie, "eine besondere Neigung" für die "Ausstattung" von "Bürgermädchen an ihrem Brauttage" mit ihren "besten Stoffen" demonstriert (LJ 418). "Man muß sich", lautet einer von Philines Sprüchen, "beizeiten aufs Kuppeln legen, es bleibt uns doch weiter nichts übrig, wenn wir alt werden" (LJ 344). Handelt es sich nicht auch bei den Aktivitäten der helfenden und heilenden Makarie um Kuppelei? Schon bei ihrer ersten Erwähnung im Roman wird sie als "Schutzgeist der Familie" (WJ 65) bezeichnet. Zwischen Lenardo und der Tante bestehen seit Antritt seiner mehrjährigen Kavalierstour geheime Verabredungen, die Lenardos erster Brief andeutet, vom Brief Makaries an die Nichten jedoch verschleiert werden und sich am Ende des Romans als (durch den "Handelsfreund" Werner verwaltete und übermittelte) finanzielle Unterstützung von Lenardos Überseeprojekt durch das beträchtliche Vermögen Makaries herausstellen.[94] Montan stellt vorausweisend klar, dass in den geplanten Kolonien alte Sitten herrschen werden: "wenn du nicht kuppeln und Schulden bezahlen kannst, so bist du unter ihnen nichts nütze" (WJ 33). Handelt es sich beim Makarienbereich um eine bienenhafte Jungfrauenschleuse, die unfruchtbare Weibchen angesichts neuer Siedlungsräume in potenzielle Mütter verwandelt? Angelas Verlobung mit der "zweibeinige[n] Rechenmaschine" (WJ 335) wird als langgehegter, heimlicher Plan Makaries offenbart (WJ 446), Angela selbst macht Wilhelm beim Besuch der Sternwarte – die Parallelkonstruktion zur Männerausbildung in der pädagogischen Provinz – auf die "hübsche, lebenstätige Kolonie" aufmerksam, die dort ausgebrütet wird: junge Mädchen, die für ein "tätiges Leben", in den meisten Fällen als "wackere Gattin", ausgebildet werden (WJ 123). Die ans Wunderbare grenzende Ehestifterei Makaries durch Umleitung von Privatbriefen oder segnendes Handauflegen meint bei der Verabschiedung der Auswanderer am Ende des Romans die Gründung von Familien. Was ist von dieser unheiligen Heiligen zu halten, deren Bedeutung etymologisch aus griechischen und lateinischen Namen für Seligkeit, Ruhe, oder aus dem ägyptischen "*maacheru: was sinngemäß Mitte zwi-*

---

[93] Ersch/Gruber: *Allgemeine Enzyklopädie.* S. 118-119.

[94] Vgl. WJ 72: "Endlich erhalten Sie nach drei Jahren den ersten Brief von mir, liebe Tante, unserer Abrede gemäß, die freilich wunderbar genug war". Dazu Makaries Überraschung vortäuschender Brief an die Nichten: "Endlich, liebe Kinder, ein Brief von dem dreijährigen Schweiger" (WJ 74). Zur Beziehung zwischen Werner, Makarie, Lenardo vgl. S. 445.

schen dem Fließenden und dem Ruhenden heißt", abgeleitet wurde?[95] Ebenso ließe sich unter Berücksichtigung des besonderen Verhältnisses Makaries zur Sonne eine Brücke zum altägyptischen, bei Griechen und Römern populären Fruchtbarkeitsgott Apis schlagen (der die Sonne zwischen den Hörnern trägt), dessen Kultstätten sich in *Memphis* und *Sakkara* befinden: Apis als Stier und Fruchtbarkeitssymbol, oder Apis als Biene, die zufolge alter Mythen spontan aus verwesenden Stierleichen entsteht und über besondere astronomische Instinkte verfügt? Herwigs Feststellung im Zusammenhang mit ihrer Analyse der Novelle *Die pilgernde Törin* könnte auch auf den Makarienmythos zutreffen:

> Der Witz der Erzählung besteht darin, daß aus Unkenntnis der Sprache des andern die Parodie nicht als solche verstanden, das Profane für das Heilige genommen wird. Sie zeigt aber auch, wie nah die Parodie des Sakralen beim Erotischen liegen und damit an heidnische Begriffe des Sakralen anknüpfen kann.[96]

Der Name der "Glückselige[n]" ist "zugleich Anagramm für Amerika"[97] und damit ein Hinweis auf die keinesfalls nur astralen und erdabgewandten Interessen Makaries, die als "Schutzgeist" ihrer Familie offenbar auch nach rein diesseitiger, genealogischer Unsterblichkeit strebt. Nach Auffassung des von Makarie besonders geliebten "verzogenen Neffe[n]" (WJ 74, vgl. 77) Lenardo ist die Welt nur für den Menschen da, was besonders die Wanderlieder betonen: "bleibe nicht am Boden heften, / frisch gewagt und frisch hinaus" – "wo wir uns der Sonne freuen, / sind wir jede Sorge los: / daß wir uns in ihr zerstreuen, / darum ist die Welt so groß" (WJ 318, vgl. 388, 392). Soll Makaries Gestirnsfühlerei im Verbund mit der wissenschaftlichen Überprüfung ihrer Intuitionen durch den skeptischen Hausfreund im weiteren Kontext darauf hinweisen, dass dem Menschen nach der früher oder später erreichten Überbevölkerung der entdeckten und besiedelten Weltteile nur noch die zweifelhafte Besiedlung der "neu entdeckten Planeten" (WJ 475) bleibt?[98]

In den demagogischen Reden der Führer des Auswanderungsprojekts finden sich deutliche Anklänge an die Verachtung der Adligen und Reichen in der politischen Drohnenrhetorik der Goethezeit.[99] Die "Drohnenschlacht" wird von den Bienenkundlern als notwendige Beseitigung "unnütze[r] Fres-

---

[95] Herwig: *Das Ewig-Männliche*. S. 380.

[96] Ibid. S. 73.

[97] MA 17. S. 1119 (zu S. 313).

[98] Zu Goethes Kenntnis der phantastischen Spekulationen des Astronomen Gruithuisen über die "Entdeckung deutlicher Spuren der Mondbewohner" und Fontenelles *Entretiens sur la pluralité des mondes* (1686) vgl. Aeka Ishihara: *Makarie und das Weltall*. S. 87, 131-138 in passim.

[99] Dazu Andrew Cooper: The Apian Way. S. 163-164.

ser" durch die Arbeiterinnen, als "Zeichen der Vollkommenheit eines Stockes"[100] dargestellt. Identische Grundsätze vertritt der von Männern dominierte und vor allem durch Lenardo – "das Band" (WJ 352) – repräsentierte
Auswandererbund in den *Wanderjahren*, der die seit Jahrtausenden dem
Menschen als hervorragende Eigenschaften der Bienen gepredigte Tugenden preist: Wandern (Schwärmen), effiziente Arbeitsteilung, Einseitigkeit,
Nützlichkeit, Fleiß und Subordination des Individuums zugunsten des Gemeinwohls.[101] Der mit großem rhetorischem Aufwand erzeugte Ausblick
auf den Segen ewigen Wanderns, auf Nutzung ohne Besitz, gesellschaftliche
Harmonie ohne Rivalität wird aus der Perspektive des aus Amerika zur europäischen Kultur zurückgekehrten Oheims als Gewalt, Betrug und Selbstbetrug entlarvt:

> Überall bedarf der Mensch Geduld, überall muß er Rücksicht nehmen, und ich
> will mich doch lieber mit meinem Könige abfinden, [...] als daß ich mich mit den
> Irokesen herumschlage, um sie zu vertreiben, oder sie durch Kontrakte betrüge,
> um sie zu verdrängen aus ihren Sümpfen, wo man von Moskitos zu Tode gepei
> nigt wird (WJ 82).

Das Mephistophelische in den *Wanderjahren* macht sich unaufdringlich –
und angesichts des Insektengottes Mephistopheles folgerichtig – trotz und
wegen der 'Heiligen' Makarie durch die Einblendung von Insekten bemerkbar. Die Assoziation Makaries mit Bienen, Venus, Morgenstern und Luzifer-Mythos[102] findet sich auch in der anakreontischen Tradition und Goethes
Liebeslyrik. Die transatlantischen Schwärmer erinnern aus der Moskito-
Perspektive an die Gegenüberstellung von Teufeln und Bienen in Miltons
Paradise Lost, den Versuch, auch noch der Hölle durch Bearbeitung Gewinne zu entlocken.[103] "Jede Revolution", notiert Goethe in vieldeutig-
stichwortartigen Zusammenhängen mit Hussitenkriegen, Klösterzeidlern
und Bienenstöcken, "geht auf Naturzustand hinaus".[104]

---

[100] *Allgemeine Encyclopädie*. S. 121. Vgl. auch Berlepsch: *Die Biene*. S. 108: "Im
gesunden Bienenvolk wird kein Wesen geduldet, das unnütz wäre".
[101] Z. B. WJ S. 386, als universalistische Deutung des Horazischen *prodesse et delectare* S. 353: "Niemand tritt in unsern Kreis, als wer gewisse Talente aufzuweisen
hat, die zum Nutzen oder Vergnügen einer jeden Gesellschaft dienen würden". Zur
Geschichte der Bienenkunde als Verbindung des "Angenehme[n] mit dem Nützlichen" vgl. Lucas: *Über den wissenschaftlichen Gang der Bienenzucht*. S. 545.
[102] Zur Motivkette Makarie, Venus, Morgenstern und Luzifer vgl. Aeka Ishihara:
Makarie und das Weltall. S. 229-235 und Herwig: *Das ewig Männliche*. S. 390-394.
[103] Dazu Andrew Cooper: The Apian Way. S. 165.
[104] WA I 42/1. S. 401 (Paralipomena). Vgl. Maximen und Reflexionen. HA 12. S.
380: "Jede Revolution geht auf Naturzustand hinaus, Gesetz- und Schamlosigkeit.
(Picarden, Wiedertäufer, Sansculotten)".

Schlussbetrachtung: Kästchen und Arztbesteck

Analog zur kontroversen Rezeption der *Wanderjahre* zeigt die Kulturgeschichte der Bienen, dass sich nicht nur das religiöse und philosophische (z. B. der "Weiser" Christus), sondern auch das animalische Modell zur Sanktionierung der widersprüchlichsten Auffassungen verwenden lässt: zur Rechtfertigung der Fruchtbarkeit und Unfruchtbarkeit, der feudalen Hierarchie, des Königsmords oder Wahlkönigtums,[105] der Superiorität des männlichen oder weiblichen Geschlechts, der konkurrenzlosen Allharmonie oder Eliminierung gemeinschaftsschädlicher Schmarotzer im perfektionierten Staatswesen. Wilhelms "Pate" Shakespeare präsentiert die Honigbienen einerseits als "creatures that by a rule in nature teach / The act of order to a peopled kingdom" (*Henry V* I.2), andererseits in Analogie zu Ariel, der seine Befreiung aus menschlichen Frondiensten mit einem Lied über die harmonische und beglückende Ordnung der Natur zelebriert: "Where the bee sucks, there suck I / In a cowslip's bell I lie" (*The Tempest* V.1). Ariels bevorzugte Blume, die Schlüsselblume, spielt in Wilhelms rückblickender Schilderung seiner sexuellen und beruflichen Initiation eine bedeutsame Rolle. In der Fischerknaben-Episode tritt eine "alte, wohlgesinnte" (WJ 271) Tante Wilhelms auf, die sich ausschließlich für den medizinischen und politischen Nutzen dieser Blumen (als Heiltee, WJ 277) und jener mit dem Leben des Fischerknaben und mehrerer Dorfkinder teuer bezahlten kulinarischen Delikatesse interessiert. Letztere, die Krebse, dienen der Tante zur verblümten Bestechung eines einflussreichen Beamten als Durchsetzung ihres Wunsches, "eine[m] Unwürdigen" (WJ 278) eine Stellung zu verschaffen. In mehrfacher Hinsicht erinnert die Charakterisierung des Bestochenen und dieser "sittlich" fragwürdigen, aber der Familie und Gemeinde "bürgerlich und politisch" nützlichen Aktionen (WJ 276f.) an den Oheim und Makarie. Der Egoismus und Altruismus verbindende, auf Bewahrung seines Besitzes bestehende Oheim kann wie der hohe Beamte in dieser Episode als ebenso geizig und mitunter skrupellos (i.e. die Vertreibung zahlungsunfähiger Pächter durch den Oheim) wie die Tante beschrieben werden, ist wie der Oheim jedoch zugleich "speiselustig", "genäschig" und gewohnt, allein zu speisen (WJ 278, zur auserlesenen Feldküche des Oheims vgl. WJ 70).

Die Charakterisierung von Wilhelms Tante liefert sozusagen das Schattenbild Makaries, die trotz der ihr zur Verfügung stehenden Mittel zum Zeitpunkt von Nachodines/Susannes Vertreibung durch den Oheim nicht als

---

[105] *Encyclopaedia Britannica* (1797). S. 130: "the kingdom of the bees is not, if the expression may be used, a *jure divino* or hereditary monarchy, but an elective kingdom, in which the choice of their future ruler is made by the body of the people, while she is yet in the cradle, or in embryo; and who are determined by motives of preference which will perhaps for ever elude the penetration of the most sagacious naturalists".

Mittlerin und Helferin fungiert, und deren Enthusiasmus für Lenardo besonders von Hersilie als Begünstigung eines Unwürdigen nahegelegt wird. Wie
Hersilies Tante (Makarie) fungiert Wilhelms Tante als Ehestifterin, "das
Innere der Familien" ist ihr durch Indiskretionen ("Klatschereien") "genau
bekannt", als Hauptmotiv ihrer nicht alle Parteien beglückenden Ehe- und
Berufsvermittlung wird der "Stolz, für eine bedeutende, einflußreiche Person gehalten zu werden" (WJ 277), angegeben. In Wilhelms Erinnerungen
an das "erste Aufblühen der Außenwelt als die eigentliche Originalnatur"
(WJ 273f.) in der Fischerknaben-Erzählung findet sich zudem die größte
Dichte von Insekten und Pflanzen in den Meister-Romanen: "Grashupfer",
"Ameisen", "bunte Käfer" und "goldschimmernde Sonnenjungfern" tum-
meln sich im Umfeld der homoerotischen Attraktion zwischen Wilhelm und
dem Fischerknaben, der sich "im höheren Sonnenschein" (WJ 272) abtrock-
net. Wilhelms Vision einer "dreifachen Sonne" beim Anblick des schönen,
nackten, jugendlichen Männerkörpers übertrifft die 'doppelte Sonne' (WJ
449) der Greisin Makarie. Als sterile Liebe erscheint die Knabenliebe im
Zwielicht von zweckentbundener Natur- und Kunstschönheit, außerge-
wöhnlichem sinnlichen Genuss und Todessymbolik als Kontrastmodell zum
Makarienbereich wie auch zum planvoll arrangierten frühlingshaften Ziergarten ("Tulpenbeete[n]", "gereihte[n] Narzissen" WJ 273) in Wilhelms
zweiter erotischer Begegnung innerhalb der Fischerknaben-Episode. Sein
Spaziergang mit der Amtmannstochter – "schön, blond, sanftmütig", "etwas
jünger als ich" (WJ 273) – beschreibt das ideale Paarungsmuster einer auf
gegenseitiger Zuneigung und physischer Attraktion beruhenden heterosexuellen Verbindung, die durch Jugend und Charakter der Frau den Bestand
künftiger Generationen zu garantieren sucht. Im blühenden Ziergarten und
menschlichen Lustgarten ist für "die folgenden Jahreszeiten gesorgt"; die
"auf zahlreiche Nelkenstöcke verwendete Sorgfalt versprach den mannig-
faltigsten Flor", die unter den konventionellen Liebesblumen ("Rosen") ver-
teilten "vielblumige[n] Lilienstengel" (WJ 273) verweisen zugleich auf das
in den *Lehrjahren* vom Harfner zitierte vegetative Vorbild unkonventionel-
ler, inzestuöser Fortpflanzungsmodelle (LJ 584), oder die gemischte Familie
der Josephs-Novelle (WJ 25-28). Wie die erste Liebe seines Vaters (zum
Fischerknaben oder Mariane) droht Felix' Liebe zu Hersilie in den *Wanderjahren* an Vorurteilen und falschen Reaktionen zu scheitern. Nicht die
Natur (Wasser, Krebse), sondern die Maßnahmen der Lebensretter führen,
Wilhelms fortschrittlichem Vater zufolge, zum Tod des Fischerknaben und
der Dorfkinder (WJ 279). Hersilie selbst stellt ihre psychologisierende
Theorie über die Gründe der "geheimnisvolle[n] Neigung jüngerer Männer
zu älteren Frauen" – "eine Erinnerung an die Ammen- und Säuglingszärt-
lichkeit" – als ungebührliche Infantilisierung von Felix' Leidenschaft und
boshafte Präsentation der älteren Geliebten heraus (WJ 267). Eine wesentlich vorteilhaftere Darstellung findet sich u. a. bei Ovid, der die unkonven-
tionelle Attraktion in seiner Hetärenpoesie (z. B. *Ars Amatoria*, 2. Buch)

ohne jede Geheimniskrämerei als Sinnenlust feierte, die Bedrohungen des Liebesglücks durch Schwangerschaften ausschließt. Die Verbindung Hersilies zum "artige[n] Taugenichts" (WJ 81) Felix kann daher als heterosexuelle Parallele zur sterilen Knabenliebe, als zumindest potenziell nicht-generative, sinnliche Liebe aufgefasst werden, als, wie es Hersilie formuliert, 'Entschädigung' der Frau durch Männer der "folgende[n] Generation" (WJ 81). Hersilie befindet sich zwar keinesfalls jenseits des durchschnittlichen Heiratsalters, doch auch bei der Eheschließung ihrer älteren Schwester Juliette spielt die Familiengründung keinerlei erkennbare Rolle. Aus der Perspektive der Generationensicherung als Ehemotiv, die in der Begegnung des jungen Wilhelm mit der Amtmannstochter anklingt, wäre es demnach gleichgültig, ob sich Hersilie mit dem vermutlich gleichaltrigen Wilhelm oder mit Felix verbindet. Kommt Makarie deshalb weder der zwischen Vater und Sohn schwankenden Nichte, noch dem "geteilten Selbst" (WJ 447) der Witwe Susanne, der nicht mehr ganz jungen früheren Spielkameradin ihres auswandernden Neffen Lenardo, mit 'brünstigen Küssen' zu Hilfe?

Mit der Einblendung von Bienen und Hummeln bringt Goethe nicht nur das respektable Kunststück zustande, fruchtbare und unfruchtbare Weiblichkeit als Produkt der Erziehung und Kultur und als Bestimmung der Natur zu bestätigen. Die Honigbienen, neben den Seidenwürmern die ältesten und kleinsten Haustiere des Menschen, beleuchten durch ihre hybride Stellung zwischen domestiziert-gezüchteter und wilder Natur zahlreiche Aspekte und Widersprüche der diversen historischen Versuche, nicht nur die äußere, sondern auch die innere (und besonders die geschlechtliche) Natur des Menschen den jeweils herrschenden Vorstellungen und Bedürfnissen anzupassen. Am Instinkt der Bienen wird vor allem die Anpassung der Reproduktions- bzw. Aufzuchtsrate an die zur Verfügung stehenden Ressourcen und Arbeitskräfte bewundert, was in Makaries Rolle als selektive Ehestifterin und Familiengründerin wiederkehrt. Das Schwärmen, als Fortpflanzungsakt des Bienenstocks, geschieht 'freiwillig' und 'zufällig' oder kann vom Züchter reguliert werden, was auch die unterschiedlichen menschlichen Ehe- und Zeugungsmodelle des Roman-Zyklus bestätigen. Die absichtslose und unerwartete Zeugung wird nicht nur im Umfeld des Kästchens bzw. Finden des Schlüssels (der Sammler) empfohlen, sondern betrifft auch dessen (Hersilie zufolge) rechtmäßigen Besitzer, Felix, mit dem weder die pädagogische Provinz, der Auswandererbund noch Makarie etwas anzufangen weiß. Das nutzlose Drohnengeschlecht wird in der Erklärung des schönen und leidenschaftlichen Jünglings zum "herrlich[en] Ebenbild Gottes" (WJ 460) durch den zu Beginn der *Lehrjahre* zufällig zeugenden und am Ende der *Wanderjahre* zufällig rettenden Vater voll rehabilitiert. Angesichts der am Ende der *Lehrjahre* im Kontext der Harfner-Geschichte als lebensrettend präsentierten intuitiven Verweigerung gesellschaftlicher Normen (das unzivilisierte Trinken aus der Flasche) durch das Kind Felix muss man sich fragen, ob der verunglückte Sohn wegen oder trotz der fragwürdigen Heilkünste (Aderlass) seines Vaters überlebt. In der Fischerknaben-Episode ergreift das Kind Wilhelm jedenfalls intuitiv die richtige Maßnahme (Beatmung, WJ 276) zur Wiederbelebung des geliebten Freundes, die in diesem Fall zu spät kommt. Wilhelms Vater setzte bei dieser Gelegenheit auf den Aderlass zur "Wiederbelebung der für tot Gehaltenen, auf welche Weise sich auch die äußeren Zeichen des Lebens möchten verloren haben" (WJ 279). Der Aderlass ist, besonders im Hinblick auf die Rettung Ertrunkener, zum Zeitpunkt des Romanendes bereits so anachronistisch wie die Annahme eines Bienenkönigs, was Goethe zweifellos wusste.[106] Trotzdem handelt es sich bei dieser fragwürdigen Rettung des "von innen oder von außen" (WJ 460) verletzten Sohnes durch den Vater ebensowenig wie beim gegenüber Eckermann erwähnten "Bienen-König" um einen einfachen Lapsus Goethes oder die absichtslose Beibehaltung der herkömmlichen medizinischen Praxis oder entomologischen Terminologie trotz besseren Wissens. Im Gegensatz zur von Goethes Farbenlehre attackierten Newtonschen Optik war die Vorurteilsstruktur des Erkennens antiker, mittelalterlicher und neuzeitlicher Bienenkundler und Mediziner zu Beginn des 19. Jahrhunderts ebenso offenkundig wie die Möglichkeit langfristiger praktischer Erfolge – als Honigproduktion oder Heilungserfolg – auf der Basis falscher oder unvollständiger Theorien über die Gesetze der Natur. Felix' Wassersturz am Ende der *Wanderjahre* führt zurück zu deren Beginn, dem Dialog zwischen Vater und Sohn an "grauser, bedeutender Stelle": Erst durch die "Kulturleistungen der Menschen" ist "der Uferweg, der sonst als Leinpfad benutzt werden konnte, gefährlich geworden".[107] Ohne das zeittypische Ammenmärchen, das die Liebe zur älteren Frau als infantile Fixierung tabuisiert und Hersilie den Weg zu Felix versperrt, wäre das sinnlose Ausbluten des auf Leben und Tod dem Minnedienst verschriebenen Sohnes durch den frigiden Vater gar nicht nötig gewesen.

Wie gezeigt wurde, steht das thematische Geflecht der *Wanderjahre* als "in Einem Sinne" verfasster "Verband der disparatesten Einzelheiten" in engem Zusammenhang mit den religiösen, literarischen, politischen und naturwissenschaftlichen Diskursen über die Bienen und der historischen Nutzung ihrer Produkte, so auch im Bereich von Arztbesteck und Medizin (z. B. als anatomische Wachsmodelle WJ 326) sowie den übrigen Kästchen-Motiven des Romans: das Kästchen im Melusinen-Märchen als Geschichte einer von exogamen Samenspendern aufgefrischten uralten Zwergenmonarchie göttlichen Ursprungs, oder der kosmetische Koffer des Verjüngungskünstlers in *Der Mann von fünfzig Jahren*, wo die Beschreibung des Majors als "mumienhaft" (WJ 178) Einbalsamierten einen deutlichen Hinweis auf den kosmetischen und präservativen Einsatz von Honig und Wachs seit den

---

[106] Dazu ausführlich Herwig: *Das Ewig Männliche*. S. 243-247.

[107] Claudia Schwamborn: *Individualität in Goethes "Wanderjahren"*. Paderborn 1997. S. 162.

Ägyptern gibt. Die Analogie Christus/"Weiser" in der Pädagogischen Provinz, wie diejenige zwischen Schlüssel/Kästchen und dem Kruzifix des Sammlers sowie die christologische Überzeichnung von Felix' Rettung aus dem Wasser,[108] lässt sich vielleicht durch eine Reflexion des Bienenforschers Berlepsch verdeutlichen:

> Die modischen Versuche der Wissenschaft, die Thiere alles Geistes zu entkleiden und zu willenlos getriebenen Maschinen, wie Wollspindeln einer Manchester Krämerseele herabzudrücken, dünkt mich eine selbstige Verblendung des Menschengeistes, der in Hegelscher Selbstvergötterung, allen Geist im All sich anmaßt und weder fühlt noch sieht, daß der mittheilungsselige lebendige Gott am Schöpfungsmorgen nicht blos Adam, sondern Allem, das da lebet auf Erden, Odem aus sich gnädig eingeblasen hat [...]. Das ist weder Pantheismus noch Materialismus, sondern es ist der ächte Christianismus der unbedingten Dependenz und Unterschiedenheit der Geschaffenen vom Schaffer [...].[109]

Der "Kopf des Ganzen", der "Bienen-König" Goethe, zeigt in seinem esoterischen Altersroman und den diesbezüglichen Konversationen mit Eckermann also keinerlei Spur von Senilität, die Perspektive des Autors ist mit der Perspektive einzelner Romanfiguren nicht identisch. Begriffe wie "Weiser", "Stock", "Ehe" oder "Witwe" sind in ungewohnten Schattierungen erkennbar, die anthropozentrisch-symbolischen Geschlechtszuschreibungen an nicht-geschlechtliche Gegenstände (Kästchen, Schlüssel) geraten durch die subtil eingeblendete Bienenanatomie hoffnungslos durcheinander. Der in Hersilies inkongruenter Beschreibung des Schlüssels angedeutete Bienenstachel als Leben und Tod bringendes Instrument trifft daher nicht nur ins Zentrum apistischer Kontroversen. Das im Zusammenhang mit dem Schlüssel zum Kästchen verhüllt offenbarte Bienengleichnis beleuchtet schlaglichtartig ein zentrales Interpretationsproblem im Hinblick auf das in den *Lehr-* und *Wanderjahren* in weit verstreuten Episoden und Motiven präsentierte poetische Welttheater, den in übervölkerten Gebieten nützlichen und lebenserhaltenden sterilen Lieben, asexuellen Fortpflanzungsmethoden (Adoption, geistige Zeugung), zwitterhaften Gestalten und terrestrischen Wunderwesen, die, je nach Bodenbeschaffenheit, in Frauen- oder Männerrollen agieren:

> It has been a Controversy in all past Ages of the World, and is disputed in the present age, whether in Strictness they are Male or Female; or consist of both, and propagate their Species, as do other Insects, by Copulation. And if so, which is the Male, and which the Female.[110]

---

[108] Vgl. ibid.

[109] Berlepsch: *Die Biene*. S. 62.

[110] John Thorley: *Melisselogia*. S. 81.

Abb. 1

HA 8. S. 321

160

Abb. 2

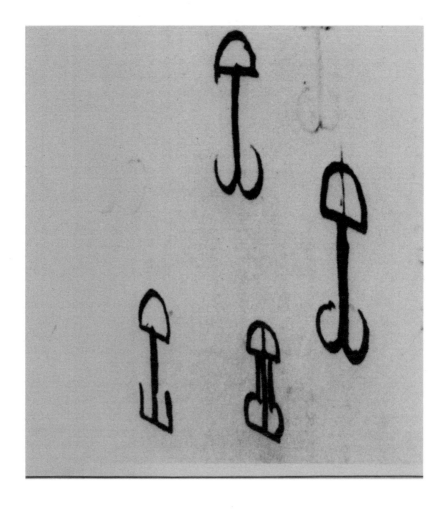

Gerhard Femmel (Hg.). *Corpus der Goethezeichnungen*. Leipzig 1958. Bd. 6A.
S. 66

Abb. 3

CLEFS (*Anciennes*) : 1. Romaine ; 2. Mérovingienne ; 3. Du VIIe siècle ; 4. Du XVIe siècle ;
5. Du XVIIe siècle ; 6. Du XVIIIe siècle ; 7. Japonaise. — (*Modernes*) : 8. Diamant ; 9. Bénarde ;
10. Forée ; 11. De pendule ; 12. Fichet ; 13. De coffre-fort ; 14. De montre ; 15 et 16. De
cadenas ; 17. De loqueteaux.

Nouveau Larousse illustré. Dictionaire universel Encyclopédique. Hg. unter der Leitung von Claude Augé. 3. Bd. Paris 1897. S. 47.

Abb. 4

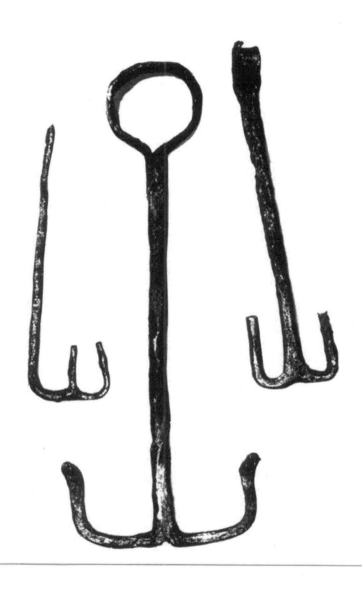

Heinrich Pankofer. *Schlüssel und Schloß. Schönheit, Form und Technik im Wandel der Zeiten aufgezeigt an der Sammlung Heinrich Pankofer.* 2. Aufl. München 1974. S. 33

Abb. 5

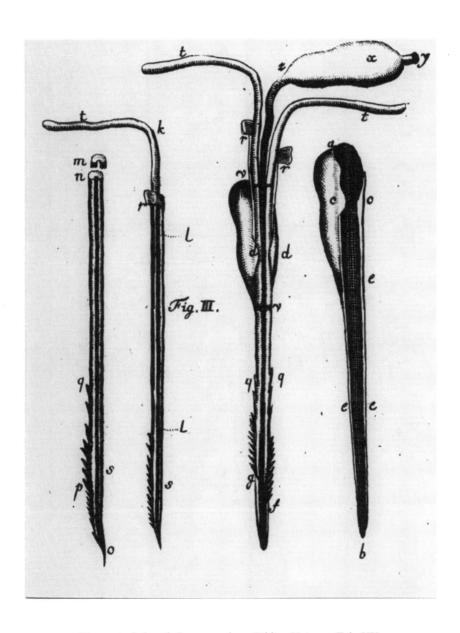

Bienenstachel nach Swammerdam. *Bibliae Naturae*. Tab. XX.

Abb. 6

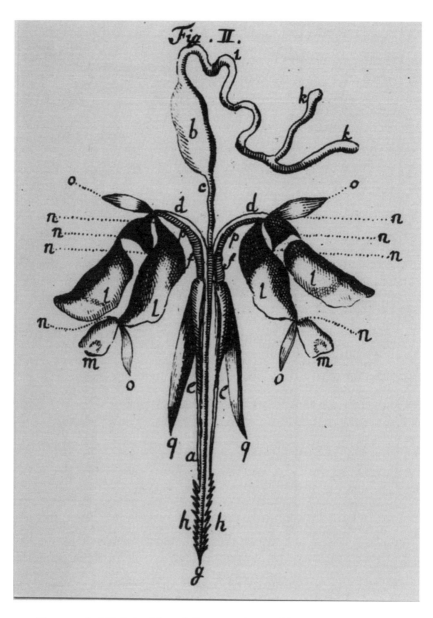

Bienenstachel (Arbeiterin) nach Swammerdam. *Bibliae Naturae*. Tab. XX.

Abb. 7

Bienenstachel und Ovarien (Königin) nach Swammerdam. *Bibliae Naturae.*
Tab. XIX

Abb. 8

Morphologische Zeichnung Goethes. HA 13. S. 61.

Abb. 9

Pierre Huber: Observations on Several Species of the Genus Apis.
In: *Transactions of the Linnean Society* 6 (1802). S. 238.

Stefani Engelstein

Reproductive Machines in E. T. A. Hoffmann

I analyze Hoffmann's story Der Sandmann *in conjunction with the work of contemporary naturalists who were engaged in research on the mechanism of reproduction and regeneration. By examining issues of gender and generation, and by focusing attention on the character of Clara, my reading restores to Hoffmann's story the full measure of anxiety over the relation between the physical nature of the body and volition, creativity, and mechanicity.*

"Losing the head is not a mortal mutilation", proclaimed John Graham Dalyell in his introduction to the 1803 English translation of Lazzaro Spallanzani's *Tracts on the Natural History of Animals and Vegetables*, and he further assured his readers that "in the prosecution of these experiments, distrust will gradually wear away: when we see the fins, flesh, bones, claws, feet, eyes, and jaws of an animal regenerated, and behold an animal survive after being divided in pieces, it is not so repugnant to think that it may reproduce the head".[1] This volume was published 37 years after Spallanzani first demonstrated that snails could re-grow their heads and a full 63 years after Abraham Trembley made the shocking discovery of the first radically regenerative animal, the polypus, about which the Paris Academy of Sciences rhapsodized, "The story of the Phoenix which is reborn from its ashes, fabulous as it is, offers nothing more marvellous than the discovery of which we are going to speak. [...] here is Nature which goes farther than our chimeras".[2] The continued existence of disbelief and repugnance surrounding regeneration shows the extent to which these revelations disturbed accepted truths about nature, particularly those concerning mortality, reproduction, and gender relations.

It was not only texts from scientific disciplines, however, that struggled to distinguish and relate nature, mechanism, and imagination. Their intertwining is nowhere better encapsulated and interrogated than in the work of

---

[1] Lazzaro Spallanzani: *Tracts on the Natural History of Animals and Vegetables.* Ed. by Charles Bonnet. Trans. by John Graham Dalyell. Edinburgh and London 1803. P. ixx.

[2] Quoted in Virginia P. Dawson: Regeneration, Parthenogenesis, and the Immutable Order of Nature. In: *Archives of Natural History* 18 (1991). No. 3. Pp. 309-321, here p. 317f.

E. T. A. Hoffmann, whose intrusive stories constantly traverse the boundaries between text and reality, paradoxically both fragmenting and fusing art, artifice, artist, offspring, and procreator. Hoffmann firmly links his concerns to those of natural history in works from *Der Sandmann* and *Das öde Haus* to *Meister Floh* by incorporating naturalists and their experimental subjects into elastic narratives that defy neat divisions between internal and external elements. Hoffmann's tendency to usurp the names, biographies, and technologies of not only long-dead naturalists, but also of near contemporaries, accentuates the vertigo produced by shifting representations of the "natural" within his texts. In *Der Sandmann* the character Nathanael guides the reader toward natural history with his comment that his professor at the university, "wie jener berühmte Naturforscher Spalanzani heißt."[3] Spalanzani's namesake, Lazzaro Spallanzani (1729-1799) is now most frequently remembered for the first successful artificial insemination, which he performed via syringe on a dog. This accomplishment, the Catholic priest wrote, "gave me more pleasure than I have ever felt in any of my other scientific researches".[4] During his lifetime, however, he was known for a wide variety of research interests ranging from the ability of bats to navigate in the dark, to a refutation of John Turberville Needham's demonstration of spontaneous generation, to his most famous and controversial findings: those regeneration experiments which we will revisit in this article.[5]

---

[3] All quotes from E. T. A Hoffmann will be taken from E. T. A. Hoffmann: *Poetische Werke*. Berlin 1957. Here volume III page 16. All future references will be parenthetical by volume and page number.

[4] Quoted in Clara Pinto-Correia: *The Ovary of Eve. Egg and Sperm and Preformation*. Chicago 1997. P. 203. As she notes, "Quoting his statement about this last experiment [...] is almost mandatory in all secondary literature on this subject". I see no need to part with tradition here.

[5] Hoffmann's more than casual interest in Spallanzani can be derived not only from his appearance in *Der Sandmann*, but also from the appellation, "Du Spalanzanische Fledermaus!" (*Werke* III 189), applied to the narrator in *Das öde Haus*. This story was also published in the *Nachtstücke* volume in which *Der Sandmann* appeared. Spallanzani had erroneously concluded that bats have an unknown sixth sense which gives them a unique access to reality, forming a parallel to Hoffmann's artist/narrator. For an overview of the debate about spontaneous generation and Spallanzani's contribution see the following: Charles E. Dinsmore: Lazzaro Spallanzani: Concepts of Generation and Regeneration. In: *A History of Regeneration Research*. Ed. by Charles E. Dinsmore. Cambridge 1991. Pp. 67-89. Paula Gottdenker: Three Clerics in Pursuit of "Little Animals". In: *Clio Medica* 14 (1980). No. 3/4. Pp. 213-224. Shirley Roe: Needham's Controversy with Spallanzani: Can Animals Be Pro-

In their writings, eighteenth-century naturalists quite explicitly displayed their investment in the philosophical, moral, and religious presuppositions of their theories and consequences of their findings. By analyzing in some detail Spallanzani's regeneration experiments and the naturalist discourse surrounding regeneration, this article will trace the enormous cultural stakes of the controversy before proceeding to a reevaluation of Hoffmann. Understanding the terms of this conflict will restore to *Der Sandmann* the full force of the anxiety over the physical nature of the body which permeates the text, an anxiety that far exceeds the specificity of the castration anxiety and concomitant fragmentation anxiety posited by the psychoanalytic interpretations that have dominated its reception. While this present analysis will therefore resituate Hoffmann's concerns about the body in a debate that stretched across disciplines, it will also situate the naturalist texts themselves within this debate, rather than at its origin. The experiments that naturalists chose to perform and their own interpretations of the findings were embedded in the same framework of cultural significance that Hoffmann manipulated to such dramatic effect. Although a handful of critics such as Hanne Castein, Sarah Kofman, and Dieter Müller have noted the explicit reference to Spallanzani in *Der Sandmann*, no serious attempt has been made to understand the connections between Hoffmann's work and that of the naturalist.[6] My reading of *Der Sandmann*, together with a closer examination of Lazzaro Spallanzani and the scientific culture in which he participated, will expose the ways in which both disciplines grappled with the same issues and anxieties: the threatened correspondence between reality and intuitive conceptions of the "natural", the challenges to a gendered understanding of the universe, and the fundamental and disconcerting conflation of nature and machine.

The shock of the original discovery that the organism then known as the polyp or polypus, and now known as the fresh-water hydra, could regenerate into a new whole from any fragment of its simple tubular body was augmented by each new and startling addition to the list of organisms capable of such feats of healing (see Fig. A). While the capabilities of the salamander and the snail were more limited in scope, the complexity of these ani-

duced from Plants. In: *Lazzaro Spallanzani e la Biologia del Settecento.* Ed. by Walter Bernardi and Antonello La Vergata. Florence 1982. Pp. 295-303.

[6] Hanne Castein: "Zerrbilder des Lebens". E. T. A. Hoffmann's *Der Sandmann* and the Robot Heritage. In: *Publications of the English Goethe Society.* N.S. 67 (1997). Pp. 43-54. Sarah Kofman: *Freud and Fiction.* Trans. by Sarah Wykes. Cambridge 1991. Dieter Müller: Zeit der Automate. Zum Automaten-Problem bei Hoffmann. In: *Mitteilungen der E. T. A. Hoffmann Gesellschaft* 12 (1966). Pp. 1-10.

mals and of the components they could replace provided new grounds for astonishment. Spallanzani recorded the re-growth of limbs and eyes in salamanders, but achieved his greatest sensation with snails, which he demonstrated capable of replacing their entire heads, complete with tongue, tooth, jaw, feelers, eye-stalks, eyes, and rudimentary brain (see Figs. B and C). While his findings were supported by such naturalists as Laura Bassi, Charles Bonnet, Antoine-Laurent Lavoisier, Jakob Christian Schäffer, and even Voltaire, several experimenters, particularly Michel Adanson and Valmont de Bomare vehemently repudiated his results.[7] Even researchers who were able to reproduce the experiment had a low success rate. In fact, out of the 423 snails that Spallanzani decapitated, a full 36% died, 34% developed monstrous structures in place of the lost ones, and only 22% regenerated perfect heads over the course of several months. The remaining 8% had neither died nor begun regeneration within a year of the operation. In no other organism was regeneration so unreliable and unpredictable. Most perplexing of all was the pattern of re-growth, which varied wildly even in those individuals who survived. The healing process generally involved multiple areas of tissue developing on the surface of the laceration in isolation from each other before joining into a whole, which only occasionally came to resemble the lost appendage (see Fig. D). This creation of monstrosity even in the progress to normal healing distinguished the snail from other regenerative animals, and demanded an explanation from theorists.

The controversy over regeneration was indivisible from the dominant research objective of natural history in the eighteenth century, discovering the mechanism that would explain reproduction. The dissection of a polyp into numerous fragments, which resulted in the same number of new organisms, established regeneration as a form of externally induced procreation and further complicated speculations about the role of sex in reproduction. Although the debate over procreation was framed in terms of the two competing schools of preformationism and epigenesis, these groups were by no means uniform. Nor was their opposition so complete as to preclude common ground.[8] The dominant theory of preformation, adhered to most nota-

---

[7] For an excellent overview of the debate surrounding snail regeneration, see Marguerite Carozzi: Bonnet, Spallanzani, and Voltaire on Regeneration of Heads in Snails: a Continuation of the Spontaneous Generation Debate. In: *Gesnerus* 42 (1985). Pp. 265-288. The best source of information on the topic is, however, Spallanzani's *Tracts* itself.

[8] For more on the debate over whether regeneration amounted to reproduction, as well as for a more detailed discussion of the connection between regeneration and reproductive theories, see Charles W. Bodemer: Regeneration and the Decline of

bly by Spallanzani, Trembley, Charles Bonnet, and Albrecht von Haller, posited pre-existing germs as the origin of new limbs as well as the origin of progeny. According to this theory, all generations of humanity until the end of history had been encased in the ovary of Eve (or by a less popular theory, in the testes of Adam). Sex stimulated this process, but provided no true fusion of maternal and paternal traits in producing offspring. Spallanzani himself, in spite of his success with artificial insemination and in vitro fertilization, believed that the particles swimming in spermatic fluid, named spermatozoa by the like-minded Karl Ernst von Baer in 1827, were parasites and irrelevant to generation. The competing theory of epigenesis, on the other hand, which was championed by Caspar Friedrich Wolff and Johann Friedrich Blumenbach, postulated that both parents were necessary not only for the development, but also for the inception of new life.[9] However, adherents of epigenesis posited vague and conflicting accounts of the mechanism responsible. In the case of asexual reproduction, epigenesists offered a still hazier hypothesis in the form of an unspecified internal mechanism. The strength of epigenesis as a theory lay less in its explanatory power than in its exposure of the weaknesses of its rival. Its eventual success owed as much, however, to an increased receptivity to its insistence on the intrinsic capacity of nature to produce truly new life and to organize matter.

Regeneration challenged both theories, but ultimately hastened the demise of preformationism. While preformationists believed that only germs already stipulating the correct relationship of internal structures could account for the precision of regenerated body parts, epigenesists objected that exactly this precision disproved the germ theory, since the germs would have to be woven into the entirety of the tissue, infinitely and minutely varied to account for their exact position. Preformationists and epigenesists alike, however, were shocked by the possibility that an animal as complex as the snail could survive so drastic a mutilation, particularly because the head was afforded a certain priority as the point where soul and body were

Preformationism in Eighteenth Century Embryology. In: *Bulletin of the History of Medicine* 38 (1964). No. 1. Pp. 20-31. Clara Pinto-Correia's *The Ovary of Eve* provides an excellent overview of theories of reproduction in the eighteenth century and Spallanzani's place in them. For a good if brief summary of the history of the pre-formation–epigenesis debate from the perspective of regeneration, see Beate Moeschlin-Krieg: *Zur Geschichte der Regenerationsforschung im 18. Jahrhundert.* Basel 1953.

[9] Caspar Friedrich Wolff: *Theorie von der Generation in zwei Abhandlungen erklärt und bewiesen* (1759). Hildesheim 1966. Johann Friederich Blumenbach: *Über den Bildungstrieb und das Zeugungsgeschäfte.* Göttingen 1781.

joined. Unlike the tiny polypus, the snail was well known and ubiquitous, allowing every amateur experimenter in Europe to participate in this particular debate. It is amazing that the snail population of Europe survived the ensuing onslaught. In reply to this overwhelming response, Spallanzani wrote,

> I know not whether in our days there has been any natural phenomenon which, from novelty and singularity, has made as great a noise in the physical world, has given birth to so many experiments, and altogether to results so various and opposite as the reproduction of the heads of snails. Since the publication of my *Prodromo*, and the translation of it into the French, German and English languages, it is incredible how many of these reptiles have been decollated.[10]

Spallanzani's language is striking for the way in which it binds the work of the experimenter to the nature he investigates. He describes a process that begins with a natural phenomenon that "gives birth to" the experiments that then, in turn, like the decapitated snails themselves, produce varying results. In fact, experimentation preceded knowledge of most regenerative phenomenon, including snail regeneration, as researchers sought sequels to the feats of the polyp, which had themselves been discovered in a laboratory rather than in a natural setting. By reversing this process in his description, Spallanzani naturalizes experimentation. The goal of these attempts, meanwhile, was the clarification of the process of generation and birth, whose opacity left it suspended, as in this passage, at the juncture between the natural, the supernatural, and the mechanical.

Faced with the seemingly impenetrable mystery of reproduction, epigenesists and preformationists actually agreed on the crucial language of organic processes, establishing an analogy with machines while simultaneously denying the possibility of purely mechanical explanations for life. Both sides were, and still continue to be, plagued by accusations of mechanical materialism, although the evaluation of this characteristic has changed; in the eighteenth century the charge of resorting to an entirely mechanistic account was strictly pejorative, while today we favor such explanations as properly scientific. As Thomas Hall insightfully notes, "Much confusion has arisen from historians' attempts to separate preformation from epigenesis on the basis that one was mechanistic, the other vitalistic – alas

---

[10] Spallanzani: *Tracts*. P. 257.

with little agreement in regard to which of the two was which".[11] Charles Bonnet, the leading proponent of preformationism, insisted:

> ich will nur sagen, daß wir, nach unsern gegenwärtigen physikalischen Kenntnissen, kein vernünftiges Mittel entdecken können, die Bildung eines Thieres, oder auch nur des allergeringsten Organons, mechanisch zu erklären. Ich habe es daher der gesunden Philosophie für gemäßer gehalten, wenn man wenigstens für höchst wahrscheinlich annähme, daß die organischen Körper, gleich vom Anfange an, vorher da gewesen sind.[12]

Bonnet here expresses an intense prejudice against mechanical explanations, which leads him to the conclusion that the organism cannot be formed, cannot *become*. The organism is instead astonishingly described as pre-existing the ultimate beginning, "already from the beginning, previously there". Johann Friedrich Blumenbach, on the other hand, who published one of the most influential epigenetic texts in addition to his more famous work on comparative anatomy and physical anthropology, also railed against "chemischen Fermentationen und der blinden Expansion, oder andern blos *mechanischen* Kräften die einige zum Zeugungsgeschäfte angenommen haben".[13] Blumenbach is here criticizing the vegetative force, which John Turberville Needham postulated could spontaneously generate life, and Caspar Friedrich Wolff's *vis essentialis*, which purported to explain generation and re-growth. Both of these naturalists, however, would have in turn rejected the notion that their theories were "merely mechanical". This nearly universal aversion to mechanical forces, however, did not carry over to the related words "mechanism" and "machine".[14] Blumenbach did not scruple

---

[11] Thomas S. Hall: Spallanzani on Matter and Life. With Notes on the Influence of Descartes. In: *Lazzaro Spallanzani e la Biologia del Settecento*. Ed. by Walter Bernardi and Antonello La Vergata. Pp. 67-82, here p. 75.

[12] Charles Bonnet: *Betrachtungen über die Natur*. Trans. by Johann Daniel Titius. Leipzig 1772. Pp. liii.

[13] Blumenbach. P. 14.

[14] There were of course some self-proclaimed mechanical materialists at this time, most notably Julien Offray de la Mettrie. Julien Offray de La Mettrie: *Man a Machine and Man a Plant*. Trans. by Richard A. Watson and Maya Rybalka. Introd. by Justin Leiber. Indianapolis 1994. For a discussion of the connection between Trembley's discovery of regeneration and La Mettrie, see Aram Vartanian: Trembley's Polyp, La Mettrie, and Eighteenth-Century French Materialism. In: *Journal of the History of Ideas* 11 (1950). No. 3. Pp. 259-286. See also Leiber's introduction to *Man a Machine*.

to call the organism a "belebte[..] Maschine"[15] while even Bonnet could not help but refer to organisms as "beseelte[..] Maschinen".[16] While there is, of course, a crucial distinction between a machine that is "ensouled" and one that is merely "vivified", Bonnet and Blumenbach suddenly seem less than polar opposites on the question of mechanicity. This language testifies to the irrevocable bond that had already been forged between nature and machine by the mid-eighteenth century. Only in the context of an increasingly mechanized world could physicians, surgeons, and naturalists begin to recognize the regularity and reciprocal activity of the parts of the living body. Nature was thus, from at least the seventeenth century, irreversibly intertwined with mechanism, and organic function could not be conceived of without reference to machinery.

A clear distinction between the theories emerges, however, from the gender roles they assigned. While observations in the eighteenth century complicated the preformationist vision of reproduction as primarily a female affair, the ovist conviction that gave the mother complete ownership of the preformed fetus still dominated when Hoffmann wrote *Der Sandmann* in 1816, as well as when the story was set in 1789 or 1790.[17] Dalyell, in his commentary on Spallanzani, confidently declared in 1803: "But it is now universally known that the foetus belongs to the mother alone".[18] This prevalent sentiment was mimicked by Gotthilf Heinrich Schubert in his popularizing 1808 *Ansichten von der Nachtseite der Naturwissenschaft*, a volume with which Hoffmann was familiar.[19] Schubert's formulation ren-

---

[15] Blumenbach. P. 71.

[16] Bonnet. P. 92.

[17] The only information in the story which indicates a date is Nathanael's comparison of Spalanzani to a picture of Cagliostro which is said to have appeared in a Berlin pocket calendar. The picture actually appeared in *Berliner genealogischer Kalender* of 1789, assigning the date of Nathanael's student year to not earlier, and presumably not much later, than this date. See Michael Rohrwasser: *Coppelius, Cagliostro und Napoleon. Der verborgene politische Blick E. T. A. Hoffmanns*. Basel 1991. P. 36.

[18] Dalyell (trans.). In: Spallanzani: *Tracts*. P. xvi.

[19] The relationship between Hoffmann and Schubert has been explored by Christine Staninger, Peter von Matt, and Gisela Vitt-Maucher. Christine Staninger: E. T. A. Hoffmann's *The Sandman* and the Night Side of the Enlightenment. In: *Subversive Sublimities: Undercurrents of the German Enlightenment*. Ed. by Eitel Timm. Columbia, SC 1992. Pp. 98-104. Peter von Matt: *Die Augen der Automaten. E. T. A. Hoffmanns Imaginationslehre als Prinzip seiner Erzählkunst*. Tübingen 1971. Gisela Vitt-Maucher: E. T. A. Hoffmanns *Die Königsbraut*. In: *Mitteilungen der E. T. A. Hoffmann-Gesellschaft* 30 (1984). Pp. 42-58.

ders the ideological stakes of this gender differentiation strikingly visible, clearly revealing the entanglement of cultural expectations and scientific observation. "Unser Geschlecht, [war] anfangs nur ein Theil der Mutter, aus welcher es der höhere Einfluß gezeuget", he explains.[20] Further,

> Der göttliche Keim, dessen zartes Beginnen die Mutter gepflegt, wird im Gemüth des Menschen stark, und siehe! der Brust und des Bedürfnisses der Mutter entwachsen, fragt der junge Knabe nach seinem Vater, und nach jenem göttlicheren Ideal, durch welches diese Natur, und aus ihr der Mensch geworden. Hierauf sehen wir in der Geschichte der Naturwissenschaft, welche mit der Urgeschichte unsres Geschlechts Eins ist, den alten Bund des Menschen mit der Natur übertreten.[21]

Following analogical reasoning which would reach its height in Ernst Haeckel's evolutionary and Freud's psychoanalytic theorizing, ontogeny here repeats phylogeny; the origin of the human in the mother forms a parallel to the origin of humanity in nature. The germ belonging to the mother may be godly, but the ideal towards which the *boy* strives with the help of his *father* is godlier. Schubert's passage also implies, through a strange use of "Naturwissenschaft", that this story is not applicable just to individuals and to humanity, but also to the science of nature itself, which begins with direct observation of nature and concludes with abstract philosophy, moving from feminine material to masculine *Geist*. This parallel suggests that naturalists are no longer subject to nature, but master over it, a suggestion that, as we will see, plays a large role, but is ultimately rejected, in *Der Sandmann*.

Schubert thus embeds sexual division not only in reproductive strategies, but also in the interaction of theorist and object of study. The shocking observation of asexual reproduction first among aphids and polyps and later among microscopic "animalculae", however, called sexual division itself into question, opening a space in which speculation about the nature of gender became not only possible, but necessary. The revolutionary impact of Bonnet's discovery of parthenogenesis in aphids was somewhat mitigated by the fact that aphids, which are sexually differentiated, are also capable of reproducing sexually. The complete asexuality of polyps and microscopic organisms, however, undermined notions of gender division as fundamental to nature. Abraham Trembley, confronted with this asexuality for the first

---

[20] Gotthilf Heinrich Schubert: *Ansichten von der Nachtseite der Naturwissenschaft* (1808). Eschborn 1992. P. 8.
[21] Schubert. Pp. 8-9.

time, nonetheless referred to his creatures as "mothers" in relation to their young. Femaleness existed for him not in relation to maleness, i.e., to sexual differentiation, but in relation to reproductive capacity.[22] Opinion on this point, however, was not unanimous. Julien Offray de La Mettrie, writing about the polyps in *L'Homme machine*, commented, "if someone had announced to the universe that reproduction can take place without eggs and females, would he have found many partisans? Mr. Trembley, however, discovered such reproduction, which takes place by division alone without coupling".[23] For La Mettrie, to be female is to be marked by gender; in the absence of sexual reproduction, no marking appears and the female vanishes. Implicitly this reasoning leaves the male as the unmarked state of the organism. Spallanzani offered a third opinion, proclaiming, the "polypus is a perfect hermaphrodite without sex".[24] Interestingly, Spallanzani considered organisms like the snail and earthworm, recently discovered to possess the organs of both sexes simultaneously, *less* hermaphroditic than the sexless polyp because of their dependence on a second individual to reproduce.

The diversity of origins in Hoffmann's *Der Sandmann* amplifies these concerns, calling into question the role of the female body in generation and intensifying the ambivalence of the genitals as simultaneously a source for the uncanny and an antidote for it. Hoffmann exposes the contradictions in Schubert's attempt to insist on the dominance of reason over nature, while simultaneously appealing to nature as the immutable foundation of a traditional social hierarchy. Confronting the threat of mechanical materialism that was so central to naturalist debates, Hoffmann at the same time grasps at the radical potential of collapsing boundaries between male and female, human and animal, animal and machine, and animate and inanimate that arise, as Donna Haraway has so powerfully posited, from the cyborg's merging of the organic and the mechanic. This breakdown of categories is fraught with anxiety for Hoffmann, but nonetheless opens up a space for productive irony and a healthy rejection of origin myths and gender expectations.[25] While Haraway claims to be describing newly emergent late

---

[22] Abraham Trembley: *Memoirs Concerning the Natural History of a Type of Freshwater Polyp with Arms Shaped like Horns*. Trans. by Sylvia G. Lenhoff and Howard M. Lenhoff. In: *Hydra and the Birth of Experimental Biology - 1744*. Ed. by Sylvia G. Lenhoff and Howard M. Lenhoff. Pacific Grove, CA 1986. Book II.

[23] La Mettrie. P. 40.

[24] La Mettrie. P. 189.

[25] Donna Haraway: A Manifesto for Cyborgs. Science, Technology, and Socialist Feminism in the 1980s. In: *Socialist Review* 15 (1985). No. 2. Pp. 65-107.

twentieth-century conditions, the cyborg, as she defines it, has been lurking in the shadows since the modern constitution of "nature" two centuries ago.

Hoffmann presents two competing humanoid genealogies in *Der Sandmann*, the first in the presentation of a normal or "*natural*" family; the second in the chemical and technological creation of an automaton by a series of male *naturalists*. These heritages, however, fail to remain distinct over the course of the story, and their collapse reveals a deep ambivalence in the concept of "nature", as the nurturing mother blends into the inexorable master. The family of the child Nathanael is portrayed as a precarious, but internally sound unit. The reproductive success of the parents is indicated by the presence of several children of both sexes who, like their parents, remain nameless, identified only by their familial relationship to Nathanael. Within this nuclear family, the act of birth forestalls uncanniness, representing the epitome of normalcy, the ultimate declaration of a "Heim". Olimpia's lineage as the product of technical collaboration appears in stark contrast to the close-knit family pictured above. However, Spalanzani reveals that the project of creating Olimpia has lasted over twenty years, a time frame that not only gives the machine Olimpia an age consistent with that of the young woman she purports to be, but also suggests that Nathanael's father was involved in the same project when observed by his son at the age of ten. Olimpia, in other words, is more closely related to Nathanael than we may have expected, since they share at least one parent. The similarity in generation between Olimpia and Nathanael would seem to end there. While female reproduction familiarizes, the masculine production of Olimpia is designed to look illicit, suspect. Like the nanny's gruesome fairy-tale sandman, Coppelius is a father with no female bearer for his offspring, stealing eyes for these illegitimate creations. And indeed, Coppelius himself chooses a masculine myth of origin. While examining, disassembling, and reassembling Nathanael's limbs, in the course of which he "setzte sie bald hier, bald dort wieder ein" (*Werke* III 10), Coppelius refuses to credit a feminized Mother Nature for the human form. Musing admiringly, "'Der Alte hat's verstanden!'" (*Werke* III 10), he prefers a creation story that features a conscious male creator after which he can model himself.

In spite of the conceit of addressing Coppelius as "Meister", however, there are no masters in this text, and no privileged positions, neither the naturalist profession of Coppelius nor the natural status of Nathanael. Manipulated like an automaton by Coppelius, Nathanael is reconstituted according to Coppelius's will and skill. This passage also calls into question Nathanael's original condition. A child who can survive the unscrewing and replacement of both hands and feet hardly seems human, and yet hopes for just such reconstitutative abilities fueled research into the regenerative powers of other organisms, drawing the human simultaneously closer to both animal and machine. As early as his 1712 paper on crayfish, René-Antoine Réaumur noted that he might be more willing to serve as a soldier if humans could regenerate limbs.[26] The ironic tone of this insight lessened, however, as time went on. Dalyell proclaimed in his introduction, "There is much reason to think that some part of a mutilated limb might be reproduced, was it not from the methods practiced in healing the wounds".[27] This optimistic perspective, according to which the most fantastic developments in medical possibility lay just around the corner, exudes from Blumenbach's *Über den Bildungstrieb*, which concludes with the following hope:

> allein wahrscheinlich hat man auch die Reproductionskraft[28] der leztern [warm blooded animals], über die man bisher zu sparsame Versuche angestellt, nur allzu gering angeschlagen, und ich gebe die Hoffnung noch nicht auf, daß wenn man nur erst durch Versuche alle die Hindernisse wird ausgefunden haben, die die Reproduction bey diesen Thieren erschwehren, daß nicht alsdenn der menschliche Verstand auch Mittel ausfindig machen sollte, sie wenigstens grossentheils zu überwinden.
>
> Reproduction ist der grosse Zweck der ganzen Chirurgie! Und man sieht also leicht was jene Hoffnung für Aussichten zur Erweiterung der Grenzen dieser Wissenschaft und folglich zur Milderung des menschlichen Elendes öffnet, und wie durch eine solche Anwendung der Naturgeschichte, diese anmuthigste und lehrreichste aller menschlichen Kenntnisse auch immer mehr zur wohlthätigsten und nutzbarsten erhoben werden könnt.[29]

A formative drive, Blumenbach posits, unites growth, healing, and procreation, and is inherent in all life (see Fig. E). If this is the case, regenerative capacity should belong, at least latently, to all organisms. Blumenbach proposes an expansion of vivisection experiments to include warm-blooded organisms, in order to determine, and then eliminate, the obstacle to this latent regenerative capacity. We might think that Coppelius has taken this advice a bit too far.

It is thus not Nathanael's origins within an established dichotomy of nature/artifice, but this distinction itself, which falls victim to Coppelius's, as

---

[26] Dorothy M. Skinner and John S. Cook: New Limbs for Old. Some Highlights in the History of Regeneration in Crustacea. In: *A History of Regeneration Research*. Ed. by Charles E. Dinsmore. Cambridge 1991. Pp. 25-45, here p. 31.

[27] Dalyell (trans.). In: Spallanzani: *Tracts*. P. lxv.

[28] Blumenbach here follows a common eighteenth-century usage of "Reproduction" to refer to what we now call regeneration. The later shift in the word's meaning not only highlights the conflation of the two processes, but also forcefully links propagation to replacement, rather than new generation.

[29] Blumenbach. Pp. 86-87.

to Blumenbach's and Spallanzani's, manipulations. Coppelius's own entanglement in this conflation of nature and artifice can be gleaned from his relationship to repetition. It is worth noting that while Olimpia does nothing but repeat, almost all of the story's characters are marked by repetition to a large extent. Coppola himself stutters "'Nu – Nu –Brill – Brill'" (*Werke* III 26), while Coppelius salivates over "'Augen – Augen'" (*Werke* III 10). Even Spalanzani, who speaks only once, manages to squeeze three repetitions into a short, if agitated, entreaty to Nathanael to chase down Coppelius. Most striking is the doubling of Coppelius/Coppola himself. While the question of identity between the two is seemingly settled by Spalanzani's address to Coppola under the name of Coppelius, the more important connotations of doubling still remain. In this story of sliding *Doppelgänger*, each character is linked to others in a mimetic chain that finally ensnares the narrator, author, and the reader herself. Françoise Meltzer, while analyzing the frequency of repetition in the speech of Olimpia, has redeployed the claim of the "Professor der Poesie und Beredsamkeit", who announces "'[d]as Ganze ist eine Allegorie – eine fortgeführte Metapher!'" (*Werke* III 40). Meltzer finds Olimpia to be an allegory "of the machinery of psychoanalysis – for at the basis of Freud's science is repetition compulsion".[30] Repetition need not lead us back only to Freud, however, but has implications that extend to science in general as dependent upon the repetitive regularity of natural law. The importance of repeatability in scientific experiments was emerging in the late eighteenth century and Spallanzani was dedicated to this idea.[31] Paul de Kruif in his canonical 1926 work, *Microbe Hunters*, paints a portrait of Spallanzani that, while it may be only slightly less fictional than *Der Sandmann*, resonates remarkably with its main concerns. Describing Spallanzani's character, de Kruif notes the incongruity of his experimental doggedness with his normal impatience. "He was not the lively sparkling Spallanzani now. He was slow, he was calm. Like some automaton, some slightly animated wooden man he put one drop of seedsoup after another before his lens".[32] Repetition is the sign of both the mechanical devise and its creator, both natural law and its investigator.

---

[30] Françoise Meltzer: The Uncanny Rendered Canny: Freud's Blind Spot in Reading Hoffmann's *The Sand Man*. In: *Introducing Psychoanalytic Theory*. Ed. by Sander Gilman. New York 1982. Pp. 218-239, here p. 233.

[31] Spallanzani also invented the practice, now considered indispensable, of establishing a control group for each experiment, i.e. an experimental double with the test factor missing (Pinto-Correia 191).

[32] Paul de Kruif: *The Microbe Hunters*. New York 1926. P. 34.

After the scene in the study Nathanael's family loses its aura of normalcy, opening up the possibility that Coppelius intervenes much more extensively in Nathanael's life after his original investment in his physical constitution. Most dramatically, Nathanael's father is killed in an explosion while working with Coppelius, who escapes before he can be held to account. More quietly, Nathanael's multiple siblings simply vanish. Their last appearance in *Der Sandmann* is the mourning tableau around the body of their father. They are replaced in the household "bald darauf, als Nathanaels Vater gestorben" (*Werke* III 19) by Lothar and Clara, distantly related orphan children who become Nathanael's closest companions. The origin of these relatives remains an unsolved mystery. As John Ellis convincingly argues, Nathanael's paranoia is more than justified by the series of suspicious events after his arrival in the university town G.[33] Coppola's immediate visit, the raised curtain that allows Nathanael to peek at Olimpia, the *chemical* fire that destroys his apartment in his absence, his friends' choice of new lodgings directly across from Olimpia's now uncurtained room, and finally Coppola's sale of the pocket perspective lead Nathanael progressively toward a specific lascivious objective. Spalanzani and Coppola's choice of Nathanael as a potential mate for Olimpia is anything but coincidental. Nathanael is crucial to their experiment; so crucial that they not only engineer his interaction with Olimpia after his arrival, but from all appearances follow him to G. in order to captivate him. The hapless Nathanael writes Lothar after his arrival, "Ich höre bei dem *erst neuerdings angekommenen* Professor der Physik [Spalanzani] ... Kollegia" (*Werke* III 16, my emphasis).

Why are Spalanzani and Coppola so dependent on Nathanael for the culmination of their twenty-year project? He is the not-quite-natural counterpart of their not-quite-machine. Nathanael and Olimpia are paired cyborgs linked through their transplanted and regenerated eyes. Only the quarrel between Spalanzani and Coppola that dismembers Olimpia prevents the desired endpoint of the courtship orchestrated by the two men. Their feud is necessary for the narrative as a means of forestalling the coupling of Olimpia and Nathanael and the closure of speculation about the mechanics of reproduction that such a sexual act would entail.

Coppelius aspires to a control over nature that, according to the rhetoric of Schubert, should release him from it. The more he attempts to align human nature with orderly machinery, however, the more he reveals his own tie to the bestiality he despises, so that he occupies the middle of a collaps-

---

[33] John Ellis: Clara, Nathanael and the Narrator. Interpreting Hoffmann's *Der Sandmann*. In: *The German Quarterly* 54 (1981). No. 1. Pp. 1-18.

ing triangle of human, beast, and machine. During the traumatic scene in which Nathanael is caught spying, Coppelius uses his habitual appellation for children "'kleine Bestie! – kleine Bestie!' meckerte er zähnefletschend" (*Werke* III 10). Coppelius's bleating reaction to the "little beasts" exposes his own kinship with them, even as his activities illustrate the fragility of the distinction between human and artifice. The constant conjunction of "kleine" with the noun "Bestie" deserves further attention. Children are Coppelius's nemesis. Childhood is not only impossible for an automaton, but indeed also superfluous for a purely mechanical method of reproduction. Children provoke feelings of inadequacy in Coppelius by their mere presence. He responds to them by inducing precisely the irrational emotions that demonstrate human deviance from efficient machinery.

Indeed, the word "Kind" in a variety of forms plays a large and unacknowledged role in *Der Sandmann*. Clara and Nathanael each project the charge of childishness into the mouth of the other as they worry about how their fears and suggestions will be received. Far from finding Clara simpleminded, however, Nathanael is instead annoyed at the depth of her analysis, and complains to Clara's brother Lothar that, "In der Tat, man sollte gar nicht glauben, daß der Geist, der aus solch hellen holdlächelnden *Kindes*augen, oft wie ein lieblicher süßer Traum hervorleuchtet, so gar verständig, so magistermäßig distinguieren könne" (*Werke* III 16, my emphasis). In this exchange both characters use the same language that the narrator will employ in his description of Clara a few pages later, where he not only attributes to her the fantasy of a "kindischen Kindes", but twice combines a depiction of her child-like qualities with that of her "scharf sichtenden Verstand", and her "tiefes weiblich zartes Gemüt" (*Werke* III 20).[34] If the combination of a childlike quality, a feminine disposition, and an acute understanding strikes us, as well as Nathanael, as unusual, we have only to return to the Schubert citation above to see why. The child, who insofar as he becomes rational at all is seen as male, is supposed to gain the faculty of reason by turning away from the mother towards the father in the process of growing up. It is this image of the child as irrational and feminine to which

---

[34] In the same paragraph in which these three characteristics are juxtaposed, the narrator repeats all three terms again, praising her as "das gemütvolle, verständige, kindliche Mädchen" (*Werke* III 20). The frequent use of the word "Kind" continues throughout the story, with both positive and negative connotations: Nathanael is ashamed of his "kindischen Gespenterfurcht" (*Werke* III 26), after the dismemberment of Olimpia and Nathanael's ensuing illness, he returns to Clara "milder, kindlicher geworden" (*Werke* III 41), and, of course, the story closes with the image of Clara and her "zwei muntre Knaben" (*Werke* III 44).

both characters appeal when they worry about appearing childish. But by refusing to set childishness and understanding in opposition to each other, the narrator gives this trait a much more positive connotation, one which he moreover applies across genders.

Equipped with this new picture of childhood and with a recognition of the confusion of nature and machine that permeates the story, we must reevaluate Clara's character. Readings of Clara run the gamut from Ellis's overblown claim that she is the dark force who destroys Nathanael's life by not providing enough unconditional love and support; to Meltzer's depiction of her as a mindless conformist; to Ruth Ginsburg's self-proclaimed identification with Clara as level-headed seeker of her own happiness.[35] I believe that in Clara, Hoffmann has created a much more nuanced and complex character than any of these readings suggest, a woman at once sympathetic and flawed. Clara has a sense of humor; she not only enjoyed the funny tales we are told that Nathanael once wrote, but calls Nathanael in frustration "'das böse Prinzip [...], das feindlich auf meinen Kaffee wirkt'" (*Werke* III 22). She combines this wit with a healthy libido when she insists in a sly reference to her lover that Coppelius will not spoil her "Näscherei" (*Werke* III 15). She is loyal to Nathanael in spite of what is described as a radical change in personality coupled with neglect, insult and finally unfaithfulness. While this constancy might seem masochistic, we have no reason to assume it springs from any source other than sincere affection built over a lifelong acquaintance. Finally, Clara has a mind of her own. She dislikes being bored and is incapable of feigning interest. She commands an intelligent and sophisticated reasoning, but is insecure about revealing it, an insecurity rendered comprehensible by the postulated incompatibility of femininity and rationality highlighted by Nathanael's irritation with her advice.

This advice is generally taken to reflect a dismissive attitude towards her fiancé's fears. In contrast, I believe that her attempt to minimize the effect of the horror he experiences is part of a consistent strategy on Clara's part in response to the serious challenge of Coppola's appearance, a strategy that is simultaneously desperate, devious, and self-deceptive. Like Nathanael, Clara equates the dark forces that control life with a principle, one that she situates internally in an attempt to render it governable by the will, while nonetheless identifying it as foreign and alien. In her letter to Nathanael, Clara gives an analysis of these dark forces and a prescription for deterring them that deserves close attention:

---

[35] Ellis, see note 32. Meltzer, see note 29. Ruth Ginsburg: A Primal Scene of Reading. Freud and Hoffmann. In: *Literature and Psychology* 38 (1992). No. 1/2. Pp. 24-46.

Gibt es eine dunkle Macht, die so recht feindlich und verräterisch einen Faden in unser Inneres legt, […] so muß sie in uns sich wie wir selbst gestalten, ja unser Selbst werden […]. Haben wir festen, durch das heitre Leben gestärkten Sinn genug, um fremdes feindliches Einwirken als solches stets zu erkennen und den Weg, in den uns Neigung und Beruf geschoben, ruhigen Schrittes zu verfolgen, so geht wohl jene unheimliche Macht unter in dem vergeblichen Ringen nach der Gestaltung, die unser eignes Spiegelbild sein sollte. (*Werke* III 14-15)

Clara chides Nathanael for externalizing interior forces, but she concludes precisely by advising him to cast them out as alien and hostile. In fact, her entire theory is suffused both with the language of a hostile invasion that would vindicate Nathanael's fears of an external force, and with the contradictory language of betrayal that locates the force as truly a part of the self. These "dark forces" haunting Hoffmann's *Nachtstücke*, the volume in which *Der Sandmann* appeared, simultaneously internal and external, which threaten not only to control, but to usurp the place of the individual, are strongly reminiscent of descriptions of the laws by which nature not only regulates but *is* humanity. In another famous Hoffmann text, in fact, Kater Murr rhapsodizes about just these forces: "Ich meine nämlich, die geistige Kraft, die unbekannte Macht, oder wie man sonst das über uns waltende Prinzip nennen mag […]. O Natur, heilige hehre Natur!" (*Werke* IX 9). Hoffmann's œuvre thus joins a tide of speculation on the purview of these forces and their impact on freedom and creativity ("in Kunst und Wissenschaft nach selbsttätiger Willkür zu schaffen" [*Werke* III 21], to use Nathanael's expression).

Nathanael responds to Clara by equating the forces with diabolical powers and turning the message into the messenger, Coppelius. Clara's approach, which is more subtle, but not therefore entirely successful, lies in an exertion of the slandered will power. Much like Samuel Johnson's famous rebuttal of George Berkeley's challenge to reality by kicking a stone, Clara's strategy deals only with superficial appearance. She encourages Nathanael to regain faith in the freedom of his will by exercising it. In fact, Clara is aware of the weakness of her own argument, worrying that she will be seen as one who "'über die goldgleißende Frucht [sich freut], in deren Innerm tödliches Gift verborgen'" (*Werke* III 14). Nonetheless, she remains faithful to a policy of denial, swearing that the poison concealed in the fruit can be rendered harmless by ignoring it. Her plea to Nathanael "Sei heiter – heiter!" (*Werke* III 15), stands out as a motto of self-delusion.

Throughout most of the story Clara occupies this ambiguous psychological position between the careful strategy born of self-awareness and the repression of any knowledge that upsets her worldview. This precarious equanimity never fails her, but she maintains it at a high cost and sometimes only through the most blatant refusal to acknowledge reality. The incident on the tower is the most obvious example. As the story draws to a close with Clara and Nathanael once again planning marriage, Clara calls Nathanael's attention to a strange object, "'Sieh doch den sonderbaren kleinen grauen Busch, der ordentlich auf uns loszuschreiten scheint'" (*Werke* III 41). Even before Samuel Weber made the connection between the gray bush and Coppelius's gray bushy eyebrows, the object had been taken to represent Coppelius, who in fact arrives at the base of the tower shortly afterward.[36] Why, however, Clara should perceive Coppelius as a bush is a question that, far from being answered, has never even been posed. After all, it is Nathanael's mental health, not Clara's, that has been the main subject of critical debate. Her transference of the powers of nature to the interior realm of a domesticated psyche forces her to reject the identity of Coppelius and Coppola and the notion of a plot against her fiancé. This rejection explains her refusal to connect Coppelius causally to the death of Nathanael's father. Instead, she makes him responsible for his own foolishness and for the consequences of his actions, just as she would like to convince Nathanael that we all are. Coppelius, as far as Clara is concerned, was an inconsequential dabbler in alchemy who vanished for good after the accidental death of Nathanael's father. His reappearance would be too large a coincidence for her to integrate into her theory. She is therefore incapable of perceiving him and transforms him into a non-threatening, domesticated, natural object – a bush. In spite of Coppelius's bushy gray eyebrows, this is not the vision of a psychologically healthy woman.[37] Moreover, even without recognizing Coppelius consciously, she is aware of the object as a threat, a threat which manifests itself in her perception of movement towards the market place in the center of town as "coming straight towards us" (my translation).

When Nathanael looks through the pocket-glass at Clara, he responds to two simultaneous observations. He sees in her, on the one hand, the micromachines of the human body that convince him of the inescapability of mechanism. Mechanicity has become a kind of contagious disease in the

---

[36] Samuel Weber: The Sideshow or: Remarks on a Canny Moment. In: *Modern Language Notes* 88 (1973). No. 6. Pp. 1102-1133, here p. 1122.

[37] Rohrwasser notes the interesting allusion to the movement of Birnam Wood in *Macbeth*, an allusion which he justifies by speculating on Nathanael's feelings of guilt in the death of his father (63). I would point the allusion in another direction, since it is not Nathanael who perceives the phenomenon. Macduff, whose army approaches hidden behind trees, was born by Caesarian section, thus fulfilling the second requirement of the prophecy that "none of woman born shall harm Macbeth" (IV.i.80). Macbeth is thus destroyed not only by his own guilt, but also by a man who is simultaneously human himself and constructed by human artifice. William Shakespeare: *Macbeth*. Ed. by Sylvan Barnet. New York 1987.

story. Traveling from character to character and indeed from the narrator to the reader, the epidemic even induces tea-party society within the story to break models of conformity to prove that they are not infected. Nathanael's terror before Clara emanates from his suspicion that he is himself an automaton, provoking the cry, "'Holzpüppchen, dreh' dich – Holzpüppchen, dreh' dich'" (*Werke* III 42), which is primarily self-directed, a description of his own behavior as he "sprang hoch in die Lüfte" (*Werke* III 43). But that is not all Nathanael sees; what suddenly strikes him in Clara's eyes must be her fear, her own approach to madness in the face of indisputable evidence that the outside world is neither as benign nor as distinct as she wishes. The final surreal happy-ending image of Clara allows her a refuge from the difficult questions of reality; in spite of her name, she has turned, finally, away from self-awareness. It is her world as much as Nathanael's that is a fantasyland.

While allying nature and artifice, Hoffmann has thus subtly disentangled familial relations from nature. The identity of parentless relatives remains undisclosed; childhood is divorced from youth; and wooden progeny becomes the object of a custody battle between fathers. In analyzing the motherless production that ties Hoffmann's *Der Sandmann* to other tales such as Mary Shelley's *Frankenstein*, feminist critics from Anne Mellor to Margaret Homans and Elissa Marder have exhibited a wariness of the usurpation of the one realm over which women have traditionally been granted sovereignty.[38] Fantasies of male reproduction that project La Mettrie's description of the paternal polypus into the human world threaten, if successful, to render females superfluous. For Freud, however, whose article on *Das Unheimliche* has become intrinsic to our reading of *Der Sandmann*, it is not masculine production but feminine reproduction in its discomfiting and estranging familiarity, that is uncanny.[39] Gender and female generation are issues inhabiting only the subtext of this interpretation, however. Ruth Ginsburg concludes that "What remains repressed in Freud's text, haunting the margins of his reading, is woman; not as castration, but as origin, as beginning and possibly, as end" (44). Ginsburg rightly argues that Freud represses the crucial role of the feminine in Hoffmann's text. However, Gins-

[38] Anne Kostelanetz Mellor: A Feminist Critique of Science. In: *Frankenstein/Mary Shelley*. Ed. by Frank Botting. New York 1995. Pp. 107-139. Margaret Homans: *Bearing the Word. Language and Female Experience in Nineteenth-Century Women's Writing*. Chicago 1986. Elissa Marder: The Mother Tongue in *Phedre* and *Frankenstein*. In: *Yale French Studies* 76 (June 1989). Pp. 59-77.
[39] Sigmund Freud: Das Unheimliche. In: *Gesammelte Werke*. Vol. 12. London 1955. Pp. 229-268.

burg's reading, like those of Mellor, Homans, and Marder with regard to *Frankenstein*, takes too much biology for granted. The elimination of privilege is also liberation from the assumption of biological expectations. At the site of an always already breached boundary between nature and machine we are confronted once again with Haraway's cyborg as our own disconcerting but potentially revolutionary double, a cyborg who is "suspicious of the reproductive matrix and of most birthing [...] [who requires] regeneration, not rebirth".[40]

In his reading of *Der Sandmann*, Freud focuses not on female organs of reproduction, but on the male organ, which he claims is represented by the threatened eyes in *Der Sandmann*. The eyes are privileged organs, baffling early naturalists with their complexity, and mediating between external and internal, between matter and spirit. By insisting on the eyes as substitutes for the phallus Freud loses this connection to mental activity and experience. To use Meltzer's language, "It is Freud, then, who is the real Sandman of the Hoffmann story, for he 'robs' it of the cognitive value of its eyes".[41] She turns the tables on Freud, reading *Der Sandmann* as, in effect, a commentary on Freud and his longings to create a reductionist psychological science, free of uncertainty. It should come as no surprise to us that Hoffmann is so perceptive a reader of Freud. From Freud's language of drives, influenced by Blumenbach, to his erasure of free will, Freud himself is a product of the internalization of mechanism into nature that characterized the late eighteenth and early nineteenth centuries. And Freud's focus on the reproductive organs is reminiscent of a much earlier thinker. In his 1651 *Disputations Touching the Generation of Animals*, William Harvey commented that, "each particular individual, both male and female alike, seems to exist for the producing of eggs so that the same species may persist, though its authors perish".[42] By transforming the story's eyes, its cognitive symbols, into replacement phalluses Freud restages the reproductive fears that pervade *Der Sandmann*. Always one step ahead of Freud, Hoffmann forces us to consider the possibility of a meta-castration anxiety: the fear of returning always to the phallus. Our greatest worry is no longer over the potential loss of an organ, a mere instrument, but the anxiety that our organs are themselves the unconscious sovereigns of which the subject is merely an instrument.

---

[40] Haraway. P. 100.

[41] Meltzer. P. 232.

[42] William Harvey: *Disputations Touching the Generation of Animals*. Ed. and trans. by Gweneth Whitteridge. Oxford 1981. P. 150.

Fig. A

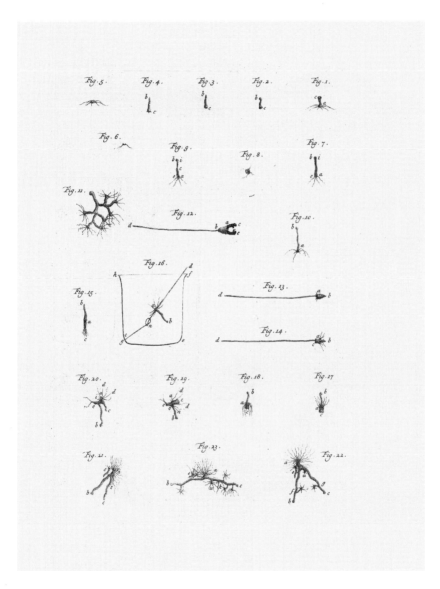

Regenerating Polyps, Abraham Trembley: *Mémoires, Pour Servir à l'Historie d'un Genre de Polypes d'eau douce, à bras en forme de cornes*. Figs. 1 and 2 show the anterior and posterior halves of a bisected polyp. The regenerative progress of the posterior is shown in Figs. 3 and 4. Fig 7 displays a polyp bisected lengthwise. Its healing process is exhibited in Figs. 9 and 10.

Fig. B

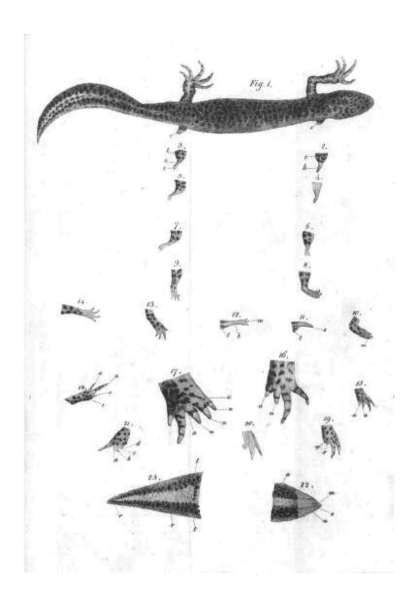

Regenerating salamanders, Lazzaro Spallanzani: *Tracts on the Natural History of Animals and Vegetables*. Successful and systematic progress toward complete healing.

Fig. C

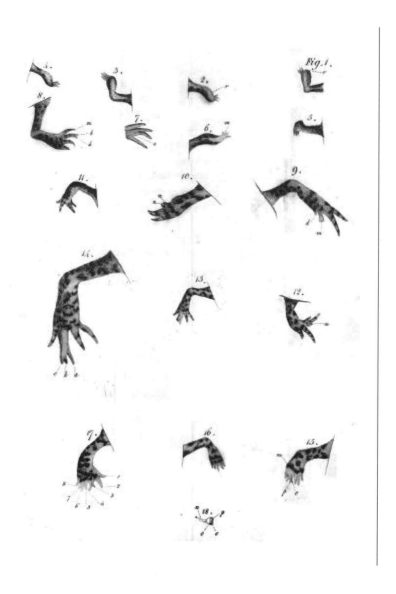

Salamander deformities, Lazzaro Spallanzani: *Tracts on the Natural History of Animals and Vegetables*. Figs. 1 -17 display various deformations resulting from faulty regeneration. Fig. 18 illustrates the anatomy of a regen erated salamander's eye.

192

Fig. D

Regenerating snails, Lazzaro Spallanzani: *Tracts on the Natural History of Animals and Vegetables*. Fig. 1 depicts a decapitated snail head while Fig. 2 shows the remaining stump. The uneven progress of successful regeneration can be seen in Figs. 3-11. The remaining Figs 12-21 display monstrous deformities.

Fig. E

Frontispiece, Johann Friedrich Blumenbach: *Über den Bildungstrieb und das Zeugungsgeschäfte*. This image juxtaposes all of the vital functions united by Blumenbach's postulated drive: grafting, reproduction, growth and healing. The missing limb of the infant who grows into the child and then the old man in the background points to the as yet unrealized potential of research into regeneration.

Sophie Boyer

"Das Mark aus meinem Rückgrat trank / Ihr Mund mit wildem Saugen": le corps vampirique chez Heinrich Heine ou l'échange symbolique de l'amour et de la mort

This essay provides an exploration of the vampiric body in Heinrich Heine's works as the site where the experience of love blends with the experience of death. The analysis begins with an examination of the emergence and significance of the vampire in the realm of Enlightenment fiction. In an age marked by a growing interest in anatomy, the vampire defies all rationalistic theories and embodies the unresolved enigma posed by the dead body. It will be shown that, in Heine's poetry, the erotic encounter with the vampire's infected body leaves the poet ultimately facing his own death. Particular attention will be focused on the motif of decapitation, an apotropaic ritual which, in Heine's poetry and Memoiren, *manifests erotic and political dimensions.*

Lorsque Heinrich Heine voit le jour le 13 décembre 1797 à Düsseldorf, le grand Goethe termine de quelques mois seulement la composition d'un poème qu'il qualifie de "vampirique": il s'agit de sa ballade 'Die Braut von Korinth', désormais célèbre.

Un jeune Athénien débarque de nuit à Corinthe, où il trouve refuge chez une famille récemment convertie au christianisme. Cette famille est celle de sa future épouse. Tous dorment dans la maison sauf la mère, qui conduit le jeune homme dans une pièce confortable où il pourra manger et dormir. Apparaît soudain une jeune fille au teint pâle, sa promise, qu'il ne reconnaît pas dès l'abord. Attiré par sa beauté, le jeune homme entreprend de la séduire mais elle lui résiste, lui expliquant que sa mère a décidé pour elle un destin de recluse, conformément à une promesse solennelle faite au Sauveur. Le jeune Athénien reconnaît alors en la jeune fille celle qui lui était promise. Il l'invite à partager son repas. Or, comme ils en viennent bientôt aux caresses, l'amoureuse se révèle froide comme le marbre!

> Liebe schließet fester sie zusammen,
> Tränen mischen sich in ihre Lust;
> Gierig saugt sie seines Mundes Flammen,
> Eins ist nur im andern sich bewußt.
> Seine Liebeswut
> Wärmt ihr starres Blut,
> Doch es schlägt kein Herz in ihrer Brust.[1]

Mais qu'à cela ne tienne: la mère les surprend bientôt à leurs ébats amoureux. La

---

[1] Johann Wolfgang von Goethe: *Goethes Werke.* Hamburger Ausgabe. Tome 1. Éd. Erich Trunz. Hamburg 1969. P. 271.

fiancée, en alarme, se répand en paroles pour justifier son amour. Or, le plaidoyer révèle son identité de morte amoureuse, cadavre échappé le jour même de son cercueil. La vampire qu'elle est devenue se nourrit du sang de celui qu'elle aime et à qui elle reste liée par les lois imprescriptibles de l'antique religion païenne. Leur liaison sera de courte durée: son amant mourra des suites du mal qu'elle lui a insufflé. Quant à elle, elle est condamnée à errer toujours en quête de sang, pour se maintenir perpétuellement entre la vie et la mort.

Nous sommes au plus fort de l'époque classique. L'étonnant est que Goethe choisit pour sujet central de sa ballade la figure du vampire, une forme imaginaire héritée du folklore païen, vouée par ailleurs à l'avenir qu'on lui connaît dans le champ de la littérature et des diverses créations artistiques, jusqu'à nos jours. Ce choix étrange pour l'époque n'a d'ailleurs cessé de déconcerter la critique, au point que celle-ci a préféré longtemps ignorer la dimension "vampirique" du poème. Ainsi, Walter Müller-Seidel va-t-il jusqu'à refuser tout fondement sociohistorique susceptible pourtant de nous éclairer sur la motivation de Goethe à nous représenter un vampire: "Gespenstermotive, Geistererscheinungen und Vampyrsagen haben unmittelbar mit Geschichte und Gesellschaft wenig zu tun, und die Frage nach dem geschichtlichen Ort wird durch ihre Teilhabe am Gedicht nicht erleichtert, sondern erschwert".[2] Ayant écarté le vampire de son interprétation, Müller-Seidel peut engager son analyse sur la voie d'une identification des idéaux que le classicisme a su illustrer, tels du moins qu'ils s'inscrivent dans la poétique générale et la mouvance goethiennes: nommément dans 'Die Braut von Korinth', le concept d'autonomie et le droit inaliénable de l'individu à l'autodétermination.[3] Évacuer le vampire comporte l'avantage indéniable, si l'on veut, de préserver et de maintenir la réputation de l'humanisme classique. Wolfgang Schemme, pour sa part, dénonce ce refus de traiter du vampire, ou alors, de l'appréhender simplement comme métaphore de la critique sociale généralement articulée par Goethe. Dans un cas comme dans l'autre, l'analyse en profondeur du personnage central de la ballade demeure en souffrance – situation à laquelle Schemme remédie avec succès. Or, si Schemme a su reconnaître la fascination qui commençait de s'exercer, à l'époque, pour le vampire – expression populaire d'un surnaturel morbide –, le critique fait néanmoins du vampire une forme de véhicule propre à servir la pensée humaniste de Goethe, qui s'insurge contre les empêchements à l'amour: "die Tragik der Liebe, die in einer gewandelten Welt zum Untergang verurteilt ist – ja, die Tragik einer Liebe, die gerade den in den Tod zwingen muß, auf den diese Liebe gerichtet ist".[4]

Toutes ces interprétations se perdent en abstractions qui, sans être fausses en soi, nous mènent cependant bien loin du point nodal – très concret lui – où

[2] Walter Müller-Seidel: Johann Wolfgang von Goethe. 'Die Braut von Korinth'. In: *Geschichte im Gedicht: Texte und Interpretationen. Protestlied, Bänkelsang, Ballade, Chronik.* Éd. Walter Hinck. Frankfurt/M. 1979. P. 80.

[3] Ibid. P. 84-85.

[4] Wolfgang Schemme: Goethe. 'Die Braut von Korinth'. Von der literarischen Dignität des Vampirs. In: *Wirkendes Wort* 36 (1986). P. 343.

s'entrecroisent jusqu'à s'y confondre l'expérience de l'amour et l'expérience de la mort. Et ce point nodal n'est autre que le corps vampirique, phénomène d'une *inquiétante étrangeté* toute freudienne dont nous retracerons d'abord l'origine pour ensuite en observer les nombreux avatars chez celui qui se désignait comme *le grand païen no 2* – "der große Heide Nr. 2" – après Goethe: Heinrich Heine. La tâche sera de démontrer comment le vampire se trouve éminemment ancré dans un contexte sociohistorique précis, reflet sensible de préoccupations marquées dans l'histoire. Au-delà des pratiques usuelles de vampirisation (morsure, succion, aspiration de l'âme, etc.), une attention particulière sera accordée au thème récurrent de la décapitation chez Heine ainsi qu'à ses implications érotiques et politiques. Nous verrons que la décapitation, par son ritualisme morbide et la symbolique qui s'y joue, se présente chez Heine comme une extension de sens à la vampirisation proprement dite.

Le vampire entre dans la composition des faits divers, à travers les journaux du XVIIe siècle. Il est d'abord et essentiellement objet de curiosité. Traités et dissertations abondent bientôt sur le sujet, et c'est avec la diffusion de rapports médico-policiers sur des cas de vampirisme dans les journaux de l'époque que s'ensuit un véritable intérêt public, aux proportions étonnantes, pour ce phénomène. L'année 1732 marque un point tournant avec pas moins de 35 publications, dont la plus célèbre est le *Visum et Repertum* ou "rapport Flückinger", d'après le nom du chirurgien militaire chargé de mener une commission d'enquête sur un cas de vampirisme dans un village de Serbie.[5] Suite à ce fameux rapport, la composition du vampire et sa démultiplication dans l'univers fictionnel ne se fait pas attendre: la première oeuvre recensée, dont le personnage central est un vampire, date de 1748. Il s'agit du poème de Heinrich August Ossenfelder, 'Der Vampir'. Ainsi, si Goethe n'est pas le premier à s'emparer du sujet, il innove du moins en introduisant, avec 'Die Braut von Korinth', le tout premier vampire arborant un visage et un corps de femme.

Le vampire, monstre né du merveilleux païen, sinon d'un folklore superstitieux, fait donc sa véritable apparition en plein coeur des Lumières. L'antinomie apparente de cette situation dans l'histoire s'explique pourtant, comme s'empresse de le souligner la critique la mieux avisée sur cette question.[6] Au coeur des interrogations scientifiques sur les origines de la vie et de la création, le corps mort devient matière à explorer. Cette perspective nouvelle, comme nous l'indique l'historien Philippe Ariès, nous montre ses premiers signes au XVIIe siècle, à travers l'étude de l'anatomie, dans la dissection des cadavres. Ainsi, les Encyclopédistes affirment

---

[5] Antoine Faivre: Du vampire villageois aux discours des clercs (Genèse d'un imaginaire à l'aube des Lumières). In: *Les Vampires: Colloque de Cerisy*. Sous la dir. de Antoine Faivre et Jean Marigny. Paris 1993 (Les Cahiers de l'Hermétisme). P. 49-51.
[6] À ce sujet, voir Jean-Claude Aguerre: Résistance de la chair, destitution de l'âme. In: *Les Vampires: Colloque de Cerisy*. P. 76. Voir également Schemme op. cit. P. 339, ainsi que Silvia Volckmann: 'Gierig saugt sie seines Mundes Flammen': Anmerkungen zum Funktionswandel des weiblichen Vampirs in der Literatur des 19. Jahrhunderts. In: *Weiblichkeit und Tod in der Literatur*. Éd. Renate Berger et Inge Stephan. Köln 1987. P. 156.

avec sérieux que "la connaissance de l'anatomie importe à tout homme",[7] affirmation que Balzac se permettra de persifler quelques années plus tard, étalant avec zèle, sous la rubrique "Catéchisme conjugal" de sa *Physiologie du mariage* (1829), la profession de foi suivante: "Un homme ne peut se marier sans avoir étudié l'anatomie et disséqué une femme au moins".[8] Ironie balzacienne mise à part, les cadavres laissent l'expert-anatomiste souvent perplexe devant la multitude de questions troublantes qu'ils suscitent. Au centre des préoccupations soulevées, la question sur l'existence de l'âme tourne à l'obsession, pour conduire éventuellement à la conclusion que "l'âme n'aurait rien de divin mais ne serait qu'un subtil rouage du corps".[9]

Étrange coïncidence donc, que parallèlement à cette "sécularisation de l'âme",[10] le vampire surgisse comme symptôme d'un trouble général qui sévit à la frontière même opposant et délimitant vie et mort: principe de raison, clôture d'appartenance au monde, principe du vivant. En effet, on défie la pensée rationnelle, les théories mécanistes et toutes les lois de la médecine. Ce revenant reste un mort, dont l'âme revient errer sur terre, et dont la chair résiste à la putréfaction: "a demonic spirit in a human body who nocturnally attacks the living, a destroyer of others, *a preserver of himself*".[11] Parallèlement à l'engouement pour le vampire règne donc un enthousiasme nouveau pour l'étude du corps en général. Or, autre coïncidence *cruciale,* en réponse à l'oxymoron d'une mort vivante telle qu'incarnée par le vampire: la même époque voit apparaître également, sous une forme qu'on ne lui connaissait pas – et proprement morbide – la rencontre d'Éros et de Thanatos dans l'imaginaire européen. En effet, Ariès démontre comment littérature et peinture du XVIIe siècle abondent en descriptions où l'agonie est poussée à l'extrême limite de la jouissance; phénomène nouveau, particulièrement palpable, dans la représentation des supplices des saints et martyres:

> Ces extases mystiques sont des extases d'amour et de mort. Ces vierges saintes meurent d'amour, et la petite mort du plaisir est confondue avec la grande mort corporelle: Douce est la mort qui vient en bien aimant. La confusion entre la mort et le plaisir est telle que la première n'arrête plus le second, mais au contraire l'exalte. Le corps mort devient à son tour objet de désir.[12]

Cette percée du sadisme se veut d'abord discrète, voire inconsciente; elle connaîtra cependant une explosion fulgurante aux XVIIIe et XIXe siècles. En plein coeur du siècle des Lumières donc, à une époque où la raison semble vouloir régner

[7] Article "Anatomie" de l'*Encyclopédie*, cité dans Philippe Ariès: *L'homme devant la mort*. Tome 2. Paris 1977. P. 75.

[8] Honoré de Balzac: *Physiologie du mariage*. Paris 1971. P. 87.

[9] Aguerre op. cit. P. 85.

[10] Ibid. P. 87.

[11] James B. Twitchell: *The Living Dead: A Study of the Vampire in Romantic Literature*. Durham 1981. P. 7.

[12] Ariès op. cit. P. 82.

sur l'ordre des choses, l'inévitable retour de la sauvagerie dans la civilisation est annoncé par l'apparition du monstre bicéphale: l'amour et la mort; "Ce rempart dressé contre la nature avait deux points faibles, l'amour et la mort, par où suintait toujours un peu de la violence sauvage".[13] Pour apprivoisée qu'elle fût, la mort devient "ensauvagée": ce changement de perspective voit naître, de la part du clergé, la tentative de diminuer l'intensité de la mort ainsi que de ritualiser, et donc de contrôler, cette dernière. Les corps médical et policier, pour leur part, travailleront de concert afin d'endiguer les excès de la sexualité; avec le développement de la métropole, ils tenteront de soumettre le monde prostitutionnel à un contrôle strict.[14] Or, la volonté d'endiguer les débordements de la sexualité et de la mort révèle surtout l'intention de juguler le sentiment de peur que cette nature menaçante et hostile éveille en l'homme moderne. Il en va alors, pour le maintien de l'ordre social et l'équilibre mental, de canaliser cette peur abyssale.

Pour familière ou apprivoisée qu'elle fût, la mort devient d'une inquiétante étrangeté, *unheimlich*. Signalons que le préfixe "un", comme nous l'explique Freud dans son essai éponyme, n'annule en rien le caractère familier de la mort: il marque plutôt le moment où cette familiarité, devant la peur qu'elle suscite soudain, se voit refoulée dans l'inconscient collectif:

> [...] denn dies Unheimliche ist wirklich nichts Neues oder Fremdes, sondern etwas dem Seelenleben von alters her Vertrautes, das ihm nur durch den Prozeß der Verdrängung entfremdet worden ist. [...] Das Unheimliche ist also [...] das ehemals Heimische, Altvertraute. Die Vorsilbe «un» an diesem Worte ist aber die Marke der Verdrängung.[15]

Pour grave qu'elle fût, la mort devient un superficiel jeu d'apparences, une pure représentation: "[...] cette mort n'est plus la mort, elle est une illusion de l'art. *La mort a commencé à se cacher* [...] *sous la beauté*".[16] Reprenant cette théorie d'Ariès pour mieux en explorer toutes les implications, Elisabeth Bronfen se penche dans *Over Her Dead Body: Death, Femininity and the Aesthetic* sur la représentation picturale et littéraire de la mort s'opérant à partir du corps de la femme. Ces représentations remplissent, selon Bronfen, la double fonction d'exprimer une peur de la mort en même temps qu'une fascination pour celle-ci. Fascination naturellement troublante, voire dangereuse, puisque la mort cèle une connaissance qu'il ne nous est permis de posséder qu'au prix de notre propre anéantissement. Devant une telle menace de destruction, l'appareil psychique et son instinct de conservation refouleront cette soif de connaissance (cette "volonté de savoir") et l'assouviront sur un objet *autre* dans une ultime tentative de mise en

---

[13] Ibid. P. 102.

[14] À ce sujet, voir Alain Corbin: *Les filles de noce: Misère sexuelle et prostitution (19e siècle)*. Paris 1982.

[15] Sigmund Freud: *Gesammelte Werke: chronologisch geordnet*. Éd. Anna Freud et al. Tome 12. Frankfurt/M. 1973. P. 254-259.

[16] Ariès op. cit. P. 182.

scène, d'esthétisation. Or, le résultat de ce déplacement, source de jouissance, inspire une peur qui, paradoxalement, fascine et déroute, l'influx se voyant par trop détourné de sa voie d'origine. Ainsi, le processus de refoulement n'est que partiellement réussi puisque la peur que provoque l'objet de substitution laisse toujours déjà entrevoir, à la surface trouble des apparences, l'éternel retour du même: "If symptoms are failed repressions, representations are symptoms that visualise even as they conceal what is too dangerous to articulate openly but too fascinating to repress successfully".[17]

Si, tel qu'affirmé par Ariès, l'amour et la mort constituent les deux domaines qui menacent à tout moment de pénétrer dans l'enceinte civilisée des hommes, alors leur représentation esthétique doit être interprétée comme une riposte stratégique dont le but est de réprimer la menace et de maintenir l'ordre établi. Or, le cadavre féminin symbolise à lui seul le lieu où vient se cristalliser la rencontre d'Éros et de Thanatos. Sous sa pâleur morbide, la belle mort accuse des traits définitivement féminins: "Since it combines these two disruptive elements [love and death], the dead body of a woman served as a particularly effective figure for this triumph over 'violent nature' and its failure to expulse the Other completely; a superlative figure for the inevitable return of the repressed".[18] Cet éternel retour du même par lequel la mort reflue à l'orée du vivant devient, chez Jean Baudrillard, hantise d'une mort omniprésente qu'il tente de définir avec le concept de "mort équivalente". Dans *L'échange symbolique et la mort*, Baudrillard explique avec quelle énergie la société moderne s'emploie à établir une nette séparation entre la vie et la mort; séparation tout à fait illusoire quand c'est plutôt d'une "ligne de partage" qu'il s'agit, par laquelle la vie se trouve toujours déjà investie de la mort. Ainsi, si la mort est officiellement niée, refoulée, elle hante sans cesse le vivant et "devient, à chaque instant, l'objet d'un désir pervers".[19]

Le cadavre fascine, il est vrai, mais le cadavre féminin, lui, devient, pour quiconque s'y mire ou s'y attarde, une véritable hantise. Il est un moment où la séparation, toute commode, opposant le spectateur vivant à la belle morte se dissout au profit d'une expérience autre, où vient sévir alors le pur effroi. Ce moment coïncide avec celui de la rencontre et de l'échange amoureux avec la femme-vampire. De par sa nature même de revenant, le vampire n'est, en effet, jamais tout à fait mort: il se voit plutôt impliqué dans une "dialectique de l'échange";[20] le vampire forme en lui-même cette "ligne de partage" que mentionne Baudrillard et qui participe à la fois du royaume des vivants et de celui des morts. C'est justement cette position liminale qu'il occupe qui fait du vampire une figure symptomatique de l'ambivalence éprouvée face à la mort, comme l'a montré Bronfen:

[17] Elisabeth Bronfen: *Over her Dead Body: Death, Femininity and the Aesthetic*. New York 1992. P. xi.

[18] Ibid. P. 86.

[19] Jean Baudrillard: *L'échange symbolique et la mort*. Paris 1976. P. 226.

[20] Voir à ce sujet Jean Marigny: Dialectique de l'échange dans les histoires de vampires. In: *Échanges: Actes du Congrès de Strasbourg*. Paris 1982. P. 309-319.

Representations of the vampire or the revenant fascinate, it seems, because here the ambivalence towards death is embodied in one and the same figure. On the one hand the revenant incorporates a kind of triumph over death in the sense of eternal survival, of repeated resurrection out of death. On the other hand the fear that the vampire inspires has to do with the fact that it undoes safe and secure boundaries between the living and the dead, and thus between survival and destruction.[21]

Semblable ambivalence peut se vérifier à la lumière du rapport que Heine entretient à la *femme noire*. D'ailleurs, son poème n'est pas sans évoquer l'étreinte représentée par la lithographie *Le Vampire*, du peintre norvégien Edvard Munch. La femme noire, un des nombreux avatars du vampire heinien, caresse tendrement le poète et lui extrait par son baiser toute énergie vitale:

> Es hatte mein Haupt die schwarze Frau
> Zärtlich ans Herz geschlossen;
> Ach! meine Haare wurden grau,
> Wo ihre Thränen geflossen.
>
> Sie küßte mich lahm, sie küßte mich krank,
> Sie küßte mir blind die Augen;
> Das Mark aus meinem Rückgrat trank
> Ihr Mund mit wildem Saugen. (III/1, 198)[22]

Nul doute que la femme noire incarne ici la Maladie revendiquant elle-même son butin: la santé du poète – laissant ce dernier paralysé, malade, aveugle. En effet, tout contact avec le corps vampirique s'avère fatal car, bien que combattant sans cesse sa propre décomposition, il n'en demeure pas moins investi de la puissance mortelle: "The [...] illness contained in the vampire motif revolves around a more explicit pathologizing of death, by virtue of designating the dying/decomposing body as dangerous and polluted, as the carrier of a fatal contagious disease".[23] Bien que la critique soit encore aujourd'hui divisée sur la question de la cause précise du décès de Heine, ce qu'il nous importe ici de retenir est qu'il se *croyait* atteint d'une maladie contagieuse: *lues cerebrospinalis* ou syphilis, maladie sexuellement transmise, qu'il *croyait* avoir contractée au contact de prostituées.

Retraçant l'iconographie de la syphilis à travers les âges, Sander Gilman cons-

---

[21] Elisabeth Bronfen: The Vampire: Sexualizing or Pathologizing Death. In: *Disease and Medicine in Modern German Cultures*. Éd. Rudolf Käser et Vera Pohland. Ithaca 1990. P. 72.

[22] Les citations de Heinrich Heine renvoient au texte de la *Historisch-kritische Gesamtausgabe der Werke*. Éd. Manfred Windfuhr. Hamburg 1973-1997. Entre parenthèses sont indiqués le volume d'abord, la page ensuite.

[23] Bronfen: *The Vampire*. P. 73.

tate le changement de perspective selon lequel nous passons d'une représentation où l'homme, en martyre isolé, personnifie la maladie et apparaît stigmatisé par la vérole, à la représentation de la syphilis cette fois sous la forme d'une femme elle-même source d'infection, précisément à partir des Lumières. Déjà présente au Moyen-Âge dans le mythe de Dame Fortune, alias Frau Welt,[24] la perception du corps féminin comme centre de corruption et transmetteur de maladie resurgit donc dans l'image du vampire séducteur. Gilman résume le regard incriminant qu'on porte sur la femme, à l'époque de la modernité: "The female is seen as the source of pollution, but also as the outsider, the prostitute, the socially deviant individual".[25] En faisant commerce de son corps, la "vamp", la femme *fatale*, quand bien elle ne penserait jamais à mal, offre un corps-marchandise qui n'en demeure pas moins pollué. Affirmer que la prostituée se donne à son client n'est pas tout à fait juste puisqu'elle ne "le fait" jamais gratuitement; l'échange qui unit le couple prostitutionnel ne s'arrête pas au simple don du corps féminin moyennant une somme versée par l'homme. Le corps prostitutionnel, porteur du mal vénérien, appelle un contre-don beaucoup plus engageant que l'argent: *Rends-moi plus que je ne te donne*. La femme vénale donne sa maladie en gage et exige de l'autre qu'il la reçoive, qu'il accepte ce don en rendant, à son tour, sa propre mort en échange:

> Le danger le plus grave que constitue le malade, ce en quoi il est véritablement asocial et comme un fou dangereux, c'est son exigence profonde d'être reconnu comme tel et *d'échanger sa maladie*. Exigence aberrante et irrecevable du malade (et du mourant) de fonder un échange sur cette différence – non pas du tout de se faire soigner et rectifier, mais de *donner* sa maladie, et qu'elle soit *reçue*, donc symboliquement reconnue et échangée.[26]

Ainsi, malgré la fascination objective qu'elle exerce, la femme noire du poème 'Es hatte mein Haupt die schwarze Frau', sous quelque aspect (créature maligne, sorcière, prostituée, vampire) renvoie d'abord et avant tout à l'homme, comme en un miroir, l'image ravie de sa propre mort. Il est face à sa soeur compagne de toujours – la mort –, qui n'est autre que lui, image personnifiant au sens fort l'éternel retour du Même. Le seuil de cette (re)connaissance franchi, aucun échange à proprement parler n'est plus possible. Comme le révèlent les deux dernières

---

[24] Dame Fortune peut quelquefois frapper de maladie. À preuve, dans le poème de Walter von der Vogelweide ('Frô Welt, ir sult dem wirte sagen'), Dame Fortune agit comme une tentatrice menaçant de corruption, corps et âme, le poète lui-même. Notons que la Frau Welt et la prostituée, loin de se confondre, ne peuvent être comparées en fait que sous l'oeil de l'opprobre public tendant à les "démoniser" toutes deux. Pour une étude des représentations de la Frau Welt, du Moyen-Âge à nos jours, voir également Barbara Becker-Cantarino: "Frau Welt" und "femme fatale": Die Geburt eines Frauenbildes aus dem Geiste des Mittelalters. In: *Das Weiterleben des Mittelalters in der deutschen Literatur*. Éd. James F. Poag et Gerhild Scholz-Williams. Königstein/Ts. 1983. P. 61-73.

[25] Sander L. Gilman: *Disease and Representation: Images of Illness from Madness to AIDS*. Ithaca 1988. P. 256.

[26] Baudrillard op. cit. P. 278.

strophes du poème, l'homme s'est en effet laissé prendre au jeu de l'amour, et son corps, transformé en cadavre, littéralement vampirisé, reflète l'impression d'un emprisonnement invincible à son esprit:

> Mein Leib ist jetzt ein Leichnam, worin
> Der Geist ist eingekerkert –
> Manchmal wird ihm unwirsch zu Sinn,
> Er tobt und rast und berserkert.
>
> Ohnmächtige Flüche! Dein schlimmster Fluch
> Wird keine Fliege tödten.
> Ertrage die Schickung, und versuch
> Gelinde zu flennen, zu beten. (III/1, 199)

Mais, fait à remarquer, contrairement au sort habituel que la production littéraire masculine réserve à la femme-vampire[27] ou à la femme fatale,[28] c'est-à-dire la mort, la femme est ici épargnée. En effet, le poète ne la condamne en aucun temps, mais la déleste plutôt de son aura maléfique. La mise à mort qui devrait lui être réservée n'a pas lieu; le poète étant trop faible pour tuer – même une mouche. La mise à mort sera cependant déplacée sur le corps du poète autour duquel tourne tout le poème. Les deux pôles contradictoires qui déterminent l'expérience amoureuse, *fatalité* et *liberté*,[29] gravitent autour du corps individuel. Ne ressentant ni remords, ni rancoeur, le poète accepte le destin. La femme fatale est ce *fatum*, "die Schickung", dont il porte aujourd'hui sans regrets les stigmates.

Telle la figure du *Doppelgänger* évoqué par Freud dans son essai sur l'inquiétante étrangeté, le vampire personnifie à la fois une scission et un redoublement du sujet qui déroutent et effraient.[30] S'il se qualifie comme vampire, c'est qu'il est mort. Or, voilà qu'il refuse de se laisser fixer dans cette mise à mort et qu'il la transcende; il devient dès lors le mort-vivant qui menace à son tour de mise à mort son vis-à-vis, il devient le double et le miroir de l'homme à qui il renvoie toujours déjà sa propre mort. L'épigraphe au "poème dansant", *Der Doktor Faust*, illustre bien cette dialectique de l'échange propre au vampire. Celle qui était morte s'adresse à l'homme qui, grâce à ses pouvoirs magiques et à ses caresses voluptueuses, l'a littéralement réanimée. Mais inversement, cette réanimation coûtera à l'homme sa propre âme, *anima*, souffle de vie dont le vampire insatiable a besoin pour sans cesse se maintenir dans une zone limitrophe entre la vie et la mort. Car il s'agit bien ici d'un vampire qui *boit* le souffle, la substance gazeuse jouant ici en surimpression avec le sang comme véhicule de l'énergie vitale:

---

[27] Volckmann op. cit. P. 167.

[28] Carola Hilmes: *Die femme fatale: Ein Weiblichkeitstypus in der nachromantischen Literatur*. Stuttgart 1990. P. 10.

[29] À ce sujet, voir Octavio Paz: *La flamme double: Amour et Érotisme*. Paris 1994. P. 116-119.

[30] Bronfen: *The Vampire*. P. 73-74.

> Du hast mich beschworen aus dem Grab
> Durch deinen Zauberwillen,
> Belebtest mich mit Wollustgluth –
> Jetzt kannst du die Gluth nicht stillen.
>
> Preß deinen Mund an meinen Mund,
> Der Menschen Odem ist göttlich!
> Ich trinke deine Seele aus,
> Die Todten sind unersättlich. (IX, 84)

Même silencieuse, voire absente, la femme-vampire se révèle comme assassine, vindicative: force agissante. Le bel objet, même immobile, n'est jamais tout à fait passif; le cadavre se venge, l'Autre donne la mort. Et dans un inquiétant revers de fortune, il semblerait même que les différentes méthodes apotropaïques pour "achever" le vampire – soit l'empalement et la décapitation[31] – se voient utilisées chez Heine par le vampire lui-même contre sa proie. Ainsi, dans un poème de jeunesse, 'Traumbilder V', le poète assiste à la cérémonie de mariage de sa fiancée avec un autre homme. Impuissant à renverser le cours des événements, "immobile et muet", il ne peut que demeurer le témoin passif de son échec sentimental et de sa propre fin. En effet, ce cauchemar confronte le poète à la triple inscription de sa mort. Comme en un crescendo, la douleur ressentie est exprimée chaque fois par un cri jusqu'au baiser ultime de la mort:

> Der Bräut'gam füllt den Becher sein,
> Und trinkt daraus, und reicht gar fein
> Der Braut ihn hin; sie lächelt Dank, –
> O Weh! mein rothes Blut sie trank.
>
> Die Braut ein hübsches Aepflein nahm,
> Und reicht es hin dem Bräutigam.
> Der nahm sein Messer, schnitt hinein, –
> O Weh! das war das Herze mein.
>
> Sie äugeln süß, sie äugeln lang,
> Der Bräut'gam kühn die Braut umschlang,
> Und küßt sie auf die Wangen roth, –
> O Weh! mich küßt der kalte Tod. (I/1, 29)

La fiancée participe activement à ce rituel cannibale où le sang du poète est bu, son coeur empalé, puis dévoré. Ainsi, la mort de soi n'est pas seulement projetée sur le corps de l'Autre; l'Autre pose également en grande Faucheuse s'abattant puis-

---

[31] Pour une discussion de ces différentes méthodes, voir Paul Barber: *Vampires, Burial, and Death: Folklore and Reality*. New Haven 1988.

samment sur l'homme traqué. 'Traumbilder II' met en scène le poète dans un décor merveilleux, digne des contes de fées. Il y rencontre une jeune fille – "so fremd und doch so wohlbekannt" (I/1, 19); l'inquiétante étrangeté en personne – en train de laver un tissu blanc qui s'avèrera être le linceul du poète. Puis, l'écho d'une hache; c'est la même fille qui s'affaire à construire son cercueil. Enfin, elle lui apprend que la fosse qu'elle creuse n'est destinée à nul autre qu'à lui.

Hache, cercueil, couteau: ce sont tous les instruments de la destruction et de la mort qui sont mis en place pour préparer au spectacle de la décapitation du poète. Recensé par la critique, notamment par Lesli Bodi, ce "leitmotiv" de la décollation demeure encore aujourd'hui aussi mystérieux qu'inquiétant. En guise de point de départ à l'analyse de ce thème récurrent dans l'oeuvre de Heine, Bodi se sert de l'épisode de la "rotes Sefchen", tiré des mémoires du poète. Parmi ses souvenirs de jeunesse, le poète se rappelle en effet de la fille du bourreau qu'il embrassa, scène déterminante pour celui qui devait, sa vie durant, entretenir deux passions: "die Liebe für schöne Frauen und die Liebe für die französische Revoluzion" (XV, 99). Mais, à part constater la rencontre des sphères érotique et politique, du désir et de la peur, "Erotik und Aggression",[32] la thèse de Bodi nous laisse sur notre faim.

Sans perdre de vue la tendance heinienne à l'auto-mise en scène, une lecture attentive des *Memoiren* révèle cependant un subtil scénodrame de la castration. Ainsi, passant en revue les personnages qui ont marqué son enfance, le poète s'attarde sur le cas de la sorcière Göchinn, de qui il aurait appris une fois adulte "l'art secret" de la sorcellerie. Liée d'amitié avec la nourrice de Heine, Zippel, la Göchinn aurait aidé celle-ci à se venger d'une rivale amoureuse, lui jetant un sort qui la rendit stérile. Quant à l'amoureux infidèle qui aurait préféré une autre femme à Zippel, la sorcière lui réserve également un sort peu enviable, la castration:

> Die Ceremonien welche bey der Entmannung beobachtet werden, sind so schmutzig und haarsträubend grauenhaft, daß ich sie unmöglich mittheilen kann. Genug der Patient wird nicht im gewöhnlichen Sinne unfähig gemacht, sondern in der wahren Bedeutung des Wortes seiner Geschlechtlichkeit beraubt, und die Hexe welche im Besitze des Raubes bleibt, bewahrt folgendermaßen dieses *corpus delicti* dieses Ding ohne Namen, welches sie auch kurzweg das Ding nennt (XV, 92).

Puis, le poète enchaîne *immédiatement* avec le personnage de Josepha, nièce de la Göchinn, qui l'initiera au plaisir macabre des sens. Maigre, blanche comme la cire, la jeune Sefchen a de longs cheveux roux comme le sang qui, lorsqu'attachés sous son menton, donnent l'impression "als habe man ihr den Hals abgeschnitten und in rothen Strömen quölle daraus hervor das Blut" (XV, 93). Scénarisant à l'aide de sa chevelure diabolique sa propre décapitation, la jeune fille qui, indéniablement, attire le poète, le confronte à l'éveil de sa sexualité et à la crainte latente de la castration, symptôme d'une crise identitaire imminente. Pour ajouter au processus

---

[32] Lesli Bodi: Kopflos – ein Leitmotiv in Heines Werk. In: *Internationaler Heine-Kongreß 1972*. Sous la dir. de Manfred Windfuhr. Hamburg 1973. P. 230.

de projection de cette angoisse naissante, Sefchen la Rouge, véritable *Doppelgänger*, a une voix éteinte, métallique qui ressemble à s'y méprendre à celle du poète: "Wenn sie sprach, erschrak ich zuweilen und glaubte mich selbst sprechen zu hören und auch ihr Gesang erinnerte an Träume wo ich mich selber in derselben Art und Weise singen hörte" (XV, 93). Fille et petite-fille de bourreau, Sefchen est une paria, vivant en retrait de la société; tels les vampires, la caste des bourreaux se frotte de près au royaume des morts et devient par le fait même intouchable. Élevée par son grand-père, elle raconte comment une nuit celui-ci reçut une douzaine de bourreaux des régions avoisinantes pour une cérémonie mystérieuse à laquelle elle assista à leur insu. Au pied d'un arbre, les hommes rassemblés enterrèrent un paquet mystérieux. C'est sa tante, la Göchinn, qui lui en révèle le contenu quelques années plus tard: tel que la coutume l'exige, un bourreau doit se débarrasser de son épée une fois que celle-ci a servi à décapiter cent condamnés. En effet, une telle épée possède une connaissance secrète, "ein heimliches Bewußtseyn" (XV, 98), parfois même – qualité vampirique – un goût du sang incontrôlable. Faisant fi du danger que cette épée représente, seul comptant à ses yeux l'attrait magique de l'arme, la sorcière s'empresse de la déterrer et de la conserver précieusement dans son armoire.

Curieux, le poète demande un jour à Sefchen de bien vouloir lui montrer l'épée en question. Et c'est avec cette histoire en toile de fond que la jeune fille se présente à lui avec l'épée, en chantant: "Willst du küssen das blanke Schwert, / Das der liebe Gott bescheert?" (XV, 98), à quoi le poète répond qu'il préfère embrasser Sefchen la Rouge. Ce baiser échangé avec la fille du bourreau, l'intouchable, est donc à l'origine de ses deux passions mentionnées plus haut, les belles femmes et la Révolution française.

Or, la préférence exprimée pour Sefchen la Rouge n'est qu'une figure de rhétorique feignant l'exclusion car, en fait, le poète embrasse *à la fois* la jeune fille et la lame lisse et brillante, exprimant ainsi sa solidarité avec la paria et démontrant par son geste sa précocité tant sexuelle que politique:

> [...] mit großer Herzhaftigkeit umschlang ich die feinen Hüften und küßte ich die trutzigen Lippen, ja, trotz dem Richtschwert, womit schon hundert arme Schelme geköpft worden, und troz [sic] der Infamia womit jede Berührung des unehrlichen Geschlechtes jeden behaftet, küßte ich die schöne Scharfrichterstochter, ich küßte sie nicht bloß aus zärtlicher Neigung sondern auch aus Hohn gegen die alte Gesellschaft und alle ihre dunklen Vorurtheile (XV, 98-99).

Afin de se rire tant et plus de la vieille société et de son système de castes, le poète ose l'infamie suprême de toucher l'intouchable. *Malgré* l'épée? Non, plutôt *séduit par* l'épée, symbole d'une prise de pouvoir politique et d'une érotique sauvages.

Aux lendemains de la Révolution, la décapitation devient la sentence universelle dans les cas de peine capitale. Plus noble que la pendaison et donc réservée jusque là à l'aristocratie, cette sentence rend maintenant tous citoyens égaux devant la mort. L'appareil inventé par Joseph Ignace Guillotin devient l'emblème de la Révolution et assure à tous une mort également juste, rapide, voire humanitaire.

La mort se civilise, s'institutionnalise et, dernière étape de sa domestication, se féminise. Mais de façon paradoxale, cette féminisation marque l'inévitable retour de la sauvagerie dans la civilisation: la "veuve", la "guillotine", "Louisette" ou la "petite Louison" (d'après le nom du docteur Antoine Louis qui perfectionna l'idée de Guillotin) sont les nombreux surnoms donnés à une invention qui revêt soudain une dimension indéniablement érotique, perceptible dans la littérature et l'iconographie de l'époque. Tel qu'avancé par Regina Janes dans son essai sur les différentes pratiques de décapitation au temps de la Révolution, la lunette de la guillotine où est insérée la tête du condamné représente l'angoissante *vagina dentata* qui castre et dérobe à l'homme son identité:

> The man who flirts with her [la guillotine] attempts to retain or assert his sexual dominance. [...] In a few explicit eroticizations of the guillotine, the guillotine is replaced by [...] or, more usually, linked with a sexually inviting female body. Such depictions emphasize the parallels between female anatomy and guillotine geometry and set up a tense oscillation between desire and destruction.[33]

Or, le rapport évident qui lie la décapitation à la castration, confirmé dans l'équation freudienne "Kopfabschneiden=Kastrieren", est mis en doute ici par Janes qui insiste sur une nuance de taille entre ces deux formes de mutilation. En effet, les organes génitaux ne coïncident pas avec l'identité: "Once they have been detached, there is no way to tell whose they were".[34] Cette chose sans nom, "dieses Ding ohne Namen", que la sorcière vole à l'amoureux infidèle dans les *Memoiren*, c'est, nous l'avions deviné, son membre viril qui s'avère effectivement non identifiable et donc, interchangeable; phénomène aboutissant chez Heine à une situation aussi farfelue qu'un chanoine qui, moyennant dédommagement financier, se voit remettre le membre d'un Turc plutôt que d'un chrétien (XV, 92). La tête, cependant, parle et révèle notre identité, toute notre histoire. Tranchée et exhibée, la même tête marque l'appropriation du pouvoir par le meurtrier; les aristocrates à la lanterne deviennent le butin du peuple et le symbole de son triomphe et de sa souveraineté sur ses anciens bourreaux: "The prestige of the head is mirrored in contempt for the body without a head. The body without a head is a body without a name".[35]

L'adage féministe selon lequel la sphère privée est l'enjeu véritable du politique ("the personal is the political") se voit ici confirmé; l'heure fatale où le poète se laisse prendre au jeu de la séduction sonne son arrêt de mort. La femme, véritable puissance révolutionnaire, s'approprie alors la tête de celui qu'elle a aimé d'un amour sanglant. "Wird ein Weib das Haupt begehren/ Eines Manns, den sie nicht liebt?" (IV, 59) demande le poète à propos de Salomé, offrant ainsi une nouvelle version à la légende biblique dans laquelle, aux enjeux politiques, viennent

---

[33] Regina Janes: Beheadings. In: *Death and Representation*. Éd. Elisabeth Bronfen et Sarah Webster Goodwin. Baltimore 1993. P. 255-256.
[34] Ibid. P. 249.
[35] Ibid. P. 250.

s'ajouter des enjeux érotiques.

Mais si la femme est assez puissante pour dérober son identité à l'homme, les blessures qu'elle inflige à sa victime ont, inversement, le pouvoir de lui rendre cette identité perdue ou même, de lui en offrir une nouvelle. Heine illustre on ne peut mieux ce pouvoir salvateur dans 'Schlachtfeld bey Hastings' où il donne sa version de la conquête de l'Angleterre par les Normands. Défait par Guillaume le Conquérant, le roi Harold est mort au champ de bataille. L'abbé de Waltham dépêche deux moines sur la scène du massacre, mais ils reviennent bredouille; la dépouille du roi est introuvable, les cadavres sauvagement mutilés par l'ennemi sont méconnaissables, toute trace de leur identité s'en trouvant effacée. L'abbé envoie alors les deux moines à la recherche d'Edith au Col-de-Cygne, l'ancienne maîtresse du roi, car seule la mémoire du corps sait reconnaître celui qu'elle a aimé:

> [...] der König Harold,
> Er liebte die junge Schöne.
>
> Er hat sie geliebt, geküßt und geherzt,
> Und endlich verlassen, vergessen.
> Die Zeit verfließt; wohl sechzehn Jahr'
> Verflossen unterdessen.
>
> Begebt euch, Brüder, zu diesem Weib
> Und laßt sie mit euch gehen
> Zurück nach Hastings, der Blick des Weib's
> Wird dort den König erspähen. (III/1, 23)

Comme chez l'animal de proie, le regard perçant de la femme saura repérer le roi parmi les cadavres. Edith est décrite en ces termes: comme un être mi-sauvage, mi-civilisé; mi-animal, mi-humain. Pieds nus, les cheveux au vent, muette, l'image même de la sorcière, elle se révèle une force sauvage de la nature. Quand soudain, elle trouve la dépouille du roi, sa réaction est à la mesure de sa douleur et elle pousse alors le cri strident de l'animal blessé:

> Sie suchte schon den ganzen Tag,
> Es ward schon Abend – plötzlich
> Bricht aus der Brust des armen Weib's
> Ein geller Schrey, entsetzlich.
>
> Gefunden hat Edith Schwanenhals
> Des todten Königs Leiche.
> Sie sprach kein Wort, sie weinte nicht,
> Sie küßte das Antlitz, das bleiche. (III/1, 24-25)

Dans son étude sur Guillaume le Conquérant, Paul Zumthor relate l'épisode de la bataille de 1066 où le duc de Normandie, "der Bankert", défait le roi Harold près de Hastings:

> On découvrit, auprès des corps de Gyrth et de Leofwine, un troisième cadavre, nu, au visage effroyablement mutilé, au point qu'on ne put l'identifier d'abord. C'était Harold. Selon une tradition anglo-saxonne, il aurait été reconnu, à quelques marques corporelles, par sa maîtresse, Edith au Col-de-Cygne.[36]

Ces marques deviennent chez Heine la trace d'une morsure laissée par la femme-vampire: "Drey kleine Narben, Denkmäler der Lust, / Die sie einst hinein gebissen" (III/1, 25). Sans elles, le roi Harold serait mort au champ de bataille, le corps réduit en bouillie par l'ennemi, sa chair se mêlant à celle de ses frères d'armes. Mais un roi ne peut se fondre ainsi dans la masse en vulgaire chair à canon car alors, il se voit réduit à l'anonymat, et, au-delà de la mort physique, à une mort sociale. Il ne suffisait pas qu'il ait été anéanti par un bâtard, il fallait que ce dernier commette le sacrilège ultime de refuser au roi que sa dépouille repose dans l'abbaye de Waltham, selon les rites dignes de son rang. Ce n'est pas la blessure béante qu'il porte à la poitrine – "auf des Königs Brust/ Die Wunde blutumflossen" (III/1, 25) – qui vaudra au roi Harold de passer du charnier de Hastings à l'histoire de son peuple, mais la trace de la morsure laissée par Edith au Col-de-Cygne en souvenir indélébile de leur histoire d'amour. Or, la femme-vampire, par sa morsure, n'extrait pas cette fois la vie à sa victime, mais lui permet au contraire de recouvrer son identité. Éros triomphe de Thanatos: les trois petites cicatrices à l'épaule scellent l'identité morcelée. L'érection de ces "monuments du plaisir" à la mémoire des amants, l'expérience de volupté inscrite jusque dans la chair, redonnent au corps son caractère unique et sacré.

Sans doute une avenue se fait jour, chez Heine, en faveur d'un dépassement, d'ordre dialectique, au conflit mettant aux prises Éros et Thanatos. Le poète en effet témoigne par avance d'un problème qui intéressera l'histoire des réprésenta-tions: d'où vient cette possibilité, pour l'homme moderne, de vivre et d'éprouver à travers la femme "vampire" un amour tel de la mort? Suivant une logique de la découverte propre à l'aventure du langage, Heine, voire Goethe avant lui, ouvrent une catégorie nouvelle parmi l'ordre du pensable. Le désir de tout connaître – même la mort – devient, poussé à l'extrême, une soif et une jouissance qui en-traînent l'homme des Lumières aussi loin qu'au divorce d'Éros d'avec l'éthos: l'homme qui s'éprouve comme puissance, plus qu'à nulle autre époque ne tient déjà plus dans les bornes de l'éthique prescrivant sa conservation. La Révolution, vers laquelle pointe Heine en de nombreux passages de son oeuvre, culmine dans la mort même, celle du roi, indirectement institution de Dieu. Faire la révolution, en ce sens, revient à connaître la mort, du moins la vivre par procuration, et jouir de sa lame – la serrant de près. Les énergies de liaison du moi, d'élévation inhéren-tes à l'Éros (aspiration au bien, au beau, au vrai selon une volonté d'appropriation personnelle) épousent Thanatos et se trouvent entraînées à la déperdition identitaire.

---

[36] Paul Zumthor: *Guillaume le Conquérant*. Paris 1964. P. 272.

Conjuguant avec le péril de mort, Heine esquisse une voie d'évitement à la déperdition, avec les armes d'un dialogue qui le confronte à la peur. Lors-même se
trouve réaffirmée l'identité du sujet en proie précisément à la mort, cette mort qui,
étrangement – historiquement – s'est faite belle.

Gaby Pailer

"... was verliert das Vaterland durch ein Weib?"
Krieg, Körperpolitik und Gender in Wilhelmine von Gersdorfs Drama *Die Horatier und Curiatier* (1790)

The "Horatier" story, chronicled by the ancient Roman historian Livius, has been dramatized in various ways over time and was especially popular in the 17ᵗʰ and 18ᵗʰ centuries. This paper focuses on a recently discovered version by the German writer Wilhelmine von Gersdorf from 1790. As the analysis of the play shows, on the one hand Gersdorf radicalizes the versions from the era of French Classicism (Pierre Corneille) and German Enlightenment (Georg Behrmann) and on the other, merges allusions of Greek myths into the Roman story. Her play presents a critical view of the instrumentalization of bodies under the laws of war: the male body as the fighting machine, the female body as the victim. This is framed by the discourses of the father, who represents Rome as the leader of all nations, and the mother, who refuses to victimize her children for blind patriotism and finally turns her back to the symbolic order of the "fatherland".

I.

Aus der mythischen Frühgeschichte Roms ist eine Episode überliefert, in der die Söhne zweier verwandter Familien, die Horatier und Curiatier, einen lange schon während Krieg durch einen repräsentativen Waffengang entscheiden müssen. Begleitet wird der Kampf von Tränen und Wahnsinn der Frauen. Über Jahrhunderte lieferte diese Episode den Stoff für Dramatisierungen, so dass, entgegen der Annahme Elisabeth Frenzels, das Material selbst eröffne keine große Variationsbreite dramaturgischer Möglichkeiten,[1] von einem bemerkenswerten intertextuellen Prozess zu sprechen ist. Im 17. und 18. Jahrhundert – am Kreuzungspunkt absolutistischer Politik, aufklärerischer Philosophie und revolutionärer Praxis – scheint der Stoff besonders geeignet, um einen Konflikt zwischen Staatstreue, Kriegsbegeisterung, Todesmut auf der einen und Partnerliebe, Familiensinn, Lebenserhaltung auf der anderen Seite zu gestalten. Die beiden Achsen Staat-Krieg-Tod und Familie-Liebe-Leben verbinden sich nun mit der Nationalidee, mit dem

---

[1] Elisabeth Frenzel: *Stoffe der Weltliteratur. Ein Lexikon dichtungsgeschichtlicher Längsschnitte.* 9. überarb. und erw. Aufl. Stuttgart 1998. S. 347-349, hier S. 348. Sie argumentiert, dass mit dem Erlöschen barocker Staatsgläubigkeit auch die Möglichkeiten dieses Stoffes sich erschöpften. Interessanterweise sind die hier behandelten Texte aus dem 18. Jahrhundert von Behrmann und Gersdorf bei ihr nicht erfasst.

Diskurs des Vaterlandes. Ins Zentrum rückt zunehmend der Aspekt der 'Körperpolitik' in Verbindung mit dem des 'Gender'. Wie die Terminologie erkennen lässt, bewegt sich die folgende – in ihrem Kern textnahe – Lektüre von Horatier-Dramen vor dem Hintergrund von Michel Foucaults Denkfigur der sich im ausgehenden 18. Jahrhundert formierenden modernen 'Bio-Macht', der Regulierung sexueller Praktiken und des Umgangs mit dem eigenen Körper in Familie und Staat, mit der die Instrumentalisierung des Einzelnen im 'Volkskörper' wie auch die Hysterisierung des weiblichen Körpers einhergehen.[2] Judith Butler hat Foucaults Ansatz vor allem im Hinblick auf die Gender-Thematik vertieft und mit Lacan Identitätsbildung als eine Art Beitrittspflicht zur heterosexuellen Norm interpretiert.[3] Für den vorliegenden Zusammenhang der Mythen-Rezeption verdient ihre neuere Studie *Antigone's Claim. Kinship between Life and Death* Beachtung. In Auseinandersetzung mit Hegel und Foucault versteht Butler Antigone als eine Figur, die gegen diese heterosexuelle Norm für sexualpolitische Freiheit eintritt.[4] Inwiefern rebellische weibliche Figuren in den Horatier-Dramen ein ähnliches Widerstandspotential entwickeln, wird weiter unten auszuführen sein.

Die Untersuchung nimmt ihren Ausgangspunkt bei einem erst kürzlich wiederentdeckten Drama, Wilhelmine von Gersdorfs *Die Horatier und Curiatier* (1790),[5] das Körperpolitik in der Geschlechtscharaktere ausdifferenzierenden Form des späten 18. Jahrhunderts im Kern thematisiert. Die Motive Krieg und Familie werden bei Gersdorf in ihrer Funktion für den Staat angeklagt und mit dem Gender-Diskurs verbunden, indem der männliche Körper als Aktionsmedium, der weibliche Körper als Repräsentationsmedium der kriegerischen Politik konnotiert wird. Um die Radikalität dieser Stoffbearbeitung zu verdeutlichen, wirft der Beitrag weiter, gewissermaßen textarchäologisch, einen Blick zurück auf Vorläuferdramen der französischen Klassik und der deutschsprachigen Frühaufklärung, Pierre Corneilles

[2] Michel Foucault: *Sexualität und Wahrheit I: Der Wille zum Wissen.* Übers. von Ulrich Raulff und Walter Seitter. Frankfurt/M. 1983. Für die Darstellung und Diskussion von Foucaults Theorie sei verwiesen auf Hans Herbert Kögler: *Michel Foucault.* Stuttgart, Weimar 1994, insbesondere Kap. II: Genealogie: Eine Analytik moderner Macht.

[3] Judith Butler: *Bodies that Matter.* New York 1993.

[4] Judith Butler: *Antigone's Claim. Kinship between Life and Death.* New York 2000.

[5] Wilhelmine von G.[ersdorf]: *Die Horatier und Curiatier, eine dramatische Skizze aus der römischen Geschichte.* In: *Museum für Frauenzimmer von einigen ihrer Mitschwestern.* Zweites Quartal 1790. S. 1-62. Im Text zitiert mit der Sigle "G". Uneinheitlichkeiten in den Zitaten werden nicht gesondert vermerkt. S. auch die Neuedition des Dramas in diesem Band: Wilhelmine von Gersdorf: *Die Horatier und Curiatier.* Hg. von Gaby Pailer.

Horace (1640/1641)[6] und Georg Behrmanns *Die Horazier* (1733/1751).[7] Bemerkenswert ist dabei, wie sich von Corneille über Behrmann zu Gersdorf ein Paradigmenwechsel abzeichnet, der zugleich im Zusammenhang mit der sich wandelnden politischen Situation zu sehen ist. Während in Corneilles Bewunderungsdramaturgie männlicher Kampfesmut belohnt, die 'vaterlandslosen' Warnungen der Frauen dagegen bestraft werden, lässt Behrmanns Drama – entgegen der expliziten intentio auctoris – die kriegskritische Tochter zur heimlichen Heldin werden. Gersdorf schließlich erteilt dem herrschenden kriegerischen System eine Absage.

Da die Darstellung bei Livius vor allen dramatischen Bearbeitungen den grundlegenden Referenztext bildet, sei die Episode aus seinem Geschichtswerk *Ab urbe condita*[8] vorab in ihren wesentlichen Komponenten referiert. Hervorgehend aus der von Æneas gegründeten ersten Ansiedlung Alba Longa, wird Romulus zum Gründer und ersten König Roms, der – auf wundersame Weise in die Wolken entrückt – seinem Volk den Auftrag erteilt, die Weltherrschaft zu erringen. Unter Tullus Hostilius, der wenige Jahrzehnte später zum König gewählt wird, kommt es zu einem Streit mit der älteren Stadt Alba, mit der man bis dahin in friedlicher Nachbarschaft gelebt hat. Gegenseitige Plünderungsaktionen albanischer und römischer Bauern nimmt der kriegslüsterne Tullus zum Anlass, Alba den Krieg zu erklären. Nach zahlreichen erbitterten Gefechten schlägt der albanische Heerführer Mettius Fufetius[9] einen repräsentativen Kampf zwischen je drei Kämpfern beider Seiten vor, um die Kräfte der Heere für den weiteren Krieg gegen einen gemeinsamen Feind, die Etrusker, zu sparen. Die aus dem Stellvertretungskampf siegreich hervorgehende Partei soll die allein herrschende Nation werden. Die Wahl fällt auf die Drillingssöhne zweier Familien, die römischen Horatier und die albanischen Curiatier. Vor den Augen der versam-

---

[6] Pierre Corneille: *Horace. Tragédie.* In: *Œuvres complètes.* Texte erstellt und mit Anm. versehen von George Cuton. Bd. 1. Tours 1980. S. 831-901. Im Text zitiert mit der Sigle "C". Eine frühaufklärerische Übertragung ins Deutsche stammt von Friedrich Ehrmann Freyherr von Glaubitz: *Die Horazier, ein Trauerspiel.* In: *Die Deutsche Schaubühne.* Hg. von Johann Christoph Gottsched. Faksimiledruck nach der Ausgabe von 1741-1745. Mit einem Nachwort von Horst Steinmetz. Bd. 1. Stuttgart 1972. S. 1-78.

[7] Georg Behrmann: *Die Horazier. Ein Trauerspiel.* Hamburg 1751. In: *Das deutsche Drama des 18. Jahrhunderts in Einzeldrucken.* Hg. von Reinhart Meyer. Gruppe 1: Das Repertoire bis 1755. Bd. 1: Das Trauerspiel 1. München 1981. S. 203-326. Im Text zitiert mit der Sigle "B". Zitiert wird nach der Paginierung des Originals. Uneinheitlichkeiten in den Zitaten werden nicht gesondert vermerkt.

[8] Titus Livius: *Ab Urbe Condita.* Tomus I. Libri I-V. Hg. von Robert Seymour Conway and Carl Flamstadt Walters. Bd. 1. Nachdr. London 1966. S. 22-26.

[9] In einigen Ausgaben auch: Metus Suffetius. Vgl. z. B. den Auszug, den Pierre Corneille in seinem Widmungsschreiben an Richelieu zitiert: Pierre Corneille: *Titus Livius.* In: *Œuvres complètes.* Bd. 1. Tours 1980. S. 835-838.

melten Truppen kann Horatius, der älteste der römischen Streiter, den Kampf durch eine List für Rom entscheiden. Nachdem seine beiden Brüder getötet wurden, wendet er sich scheinbar zur Flucht, jedoch nur um zurückzukommen und die drei Curiatier in Einzelkämpfen zu töten. Nach dem Kampf kommt ihm seine Schwester Horatia entgegen und klagt ihn an, ihren Verlobten, den ältesten der Curiatier, erschlagen zu haben, worauf er sie in Rage ersticht. Er soll zuerst für den Mord hingerichtet werden, doch seinem Vater gelingt es, Tullus davon zu überzeugen, dass die Tat gerechtfertigt war. So erwirkt er Horatius' Begnadigung und die Rehabilitation als Befreier Roms.

II.

Gersdorfs Drama, das bis vor kurzem völlig vergessen war, erschien 1790 in der Zeitschrift *Museum für Frauenzimmer von einigen ihrer Mitschwestern*, von der selbst nur ein Quartalsband erhalten ist.[10] Das Drama wurde bisher lediglich in Susanne Kords Überblickswerk *Ein Blick hinter die Kulissen*[11] verzeichnet, das eine Vielzahl vergessener Dramen von Autorinnen erfasst und analysiert, und es wurde kursorisch im Zusammenhang der Frauenzeitschriften im späten 18. Jahrhundert von Ulrike Weckel[12] behandelt. Hier wird das Stück erstmals einer ausführlichen Lektüre unterzogen. Auf zwei Besonderheiten wird dabei zu achten sein: Zum einen verschärft Gersdorfs Version die thematischen Aspekte Krieg und Liebe gegenüber den älteren Stoffadaptionen, zum zweiten rekurriert sie für das ausgehende 18. Jahrhundert in ungewöhnlicher Weise auf einen Plot aus der römischen Frühgeschichte, versetzt ihn aber zugleich, der gräzisierenden Mode ihrer Zeit nachkommend, mit Allusionen griechischer Mythen.

Ohne Exposition, die zunächst die Vorgeschichte und Handlungszusammenhänge vermitteln würde, setzt Gersdorfs Stück unmittelbar ein mit dem römischen Vater Horatius und seiner Frau Horatia, die über Sinn und Nutzen des anstehenden Kampfes der römischen und albanischen Drillinge streiten. Horatius wirft seiner Frau vor, eine schlechte "Heldenmutter" (G 5) zu sein,

---

[10] Über die Herausgeberinnen ist wenig bekannt. In den zwanziger Jahren entschlüsselte Carl Wilhelm von Schindel zwei der in der Vierteljahrsschrift von 1790 verwendeten Pseudonyme. Demnach war eine der Herausgeberinnen die Lehrerin Karoline Keller, verheiratete Weinich, eine weitere Wilhelmine von Gersdorf. S. Ulrike Weckel: *Zwischen Häuslichkeit und Öffentlichkeit. Die ersten deutschen Frauenzeitschriften im späten 18. Jahrhundert und ihr Publikum.* Tübingen 1998 (Studien und Texte zur Sozialgeschichte der Literatur 61). S. 111-115.

[11] Susanne Kord: *Ein Blick hinter die Kulissen. Deutschsprachige Dramatikerinnen im 18. und 19. Jahrhundert.* Stuttgart 1992 (Ergebnisse der Frauenforschung 27). S. 368. Das Erscheinungsdatum bei Kord (1796) ist unzutreffend.

[12] Weckel. S. 584.

da sie ihre Söhne nicht für Rom bereitstellen will. Den Grund ihrer Weichlichkeit und Weinerlichkeit sieht er darin, dass sie keine gebürtige Römerin ist, sondern aus Alba stammt. Die Tochter (die hier den Namen Julia trägt) fleht den Vater im Einklang mit der Mutter an, ihre Brüder, vor allem aber ihren Verlobten Albanus, den ältesten der drei Curiatier, zu schonen. Doch umsonst, denn Horatius macht sich bereits Vorwürfe, eine Albanierin geheiratet zu haben, und ist alarmiert bei der Vorstellung, dass weitere 'gemischte' Verbindungen daraus hervorgehen werden. Als der Vater unerbittlich bleibt, versucht Julia den albanischen Heerführer (hier Suffetius genannt), der sich früher für sie interessiert hat, zum Verzicht auf den repräsentativen Waffengang zu bewegen; doch dieser wendet sich höhnisch ab. Die drei Horatier-Brüder treten auf, um sich von Mutter und Schwester zu verabschieden, und es erweist sich, dass nur einer von ihnen, der älteste (hier Fulvius genannt), vom Kampf für Rom durch und durch überzeugt ist, während die beiden jüngeren, Lucius und Aurelius, den Waffengang für grausam und unmenschlich halten und Julia versprechen, die Gegner zu schonen. Schließlich kommt Julias Verlobter Albanus selbst. Auch er fügt sich in den für ihn absurden Kampf, ohne siegen zu wollen. Sein Tod scheint ihm beschlossen, und Julia erkennt nun, dass es auch für sie nur noch den Tod als Lösung gibt. Nach dem Kampf irrt sie vor den Toren der Stadt umher, wo sie auf Fulvius trifft, umringt von Volk, das ihn für seinen listreichen Sieg bejubelt. Als sie den Leichnam ihres Geliebten sieht, verflucht sie ihren Bruder, und er ersticht sie. Julia stirbt, ihm dankend für den von ihr ersehnten Tod, und ihm verzeihend – während er sich vorwirft, seinen Sieg durch den Schwestermord entehrt zu haben. Nacheinander kommen die Mutter und der Vater auf das Schlachtfeld. Horatia sieht sich nun all ihrer Kinder beraubt. Während Horatius seinen Sohn trotz der Ermordung Julias schützen will, verstößt sie ihr letztes noch lebendes Kind und will selbst zum "Grabmahl" (G 62) ihrer Kinder werden.

Gegenüber der Darstellung bei Livius hat Gersdorf die Namen geändert und neue Figuren hinzugefügt. Der römische Vater, der im Geschichtsbuch erst nach dem Kampf erwähnt wird, wird jetzt zur tragenden Figur und erhält eine Gattin; neben dem ältesten Sohn als Helden werden auch seine jüngeren Brüder mit Vornamen versehen. Die zentrale Figur ist die Tochter Julia. Das Stück hat keine Akteinteilung, sondern besteht aus neun Szenen, in denen diese durchgängig präsent ist und, lebend oder als Leichnam, inmitten unterschiedlicher Konstellationen zu sehen ist. Die Anordung der Szenen ist symmetrisch. Zu Beginn und Ende (1. und 9. Szene) treten Vater und Mutter als Figurationen antagonistischer Prinzipien auf. Im Zentrum des Stückes steht Julias Entschluss, mit ihrem Geliebten und ihren Brüdern zu sterben (5. Szene). Die Szenen bis zu diesem Entschluss zeigen sie als noch Hoffende – vor Suffetius kniend oder ihre Brüder und Albanus um Kampfesverweigerung bittend –, die Szenen danach führen vor, wie sie stirbt und wie ihr Tod von Vater und Mutter unterschiedlich aufgenommen und interpretiert wird. Insgesamt wirkt das Stück wie eine Abfolge von Tableaux und lässt an die Kunstform der "lebenden Bilder" denken, wie sie im ausgehenden 18. Jahrhundert insbesondere durch Lady Hamilton in Mode kamen.[13] Wie Dagmar von Hoff in ihrem Buch *Dramen des Weiblichen* darlegt, eignet vielen Dramen von Autorinnen um 1800 eine solche Tableauhaftigkeit, wodurch sie einen neuen und anderen

> Aktionsradius des Dramatischen sichtbar [machen], der gerade auch vor dem Hintergrund fremder Diskurse eine Bedeutung erhält. Denn das, was in den Texten zu entdecken ist, ist interessanterweise weniger die Formulierung von 'Ganzheit', 'Liebesfähigkeit', 'Natürlichkeit', als vielmehr eine seelische und konfliktuale Besessenheit, die eine Nähe zum hysterischen Diskurs hat [...]. So ist der Dynamik des Handlungsgewinns zugleich immer schon der Umschlag: die Begrenzung und Hemmung eingeschrieben. Die Wortergreifung der Autorinnen kommt als Wortergriffenheit in den Blick.[14]

Die Auseinandersetzung mit dem Weiblichkeitsideal der Ganzheit, Liebesfähigkeit und Natürlichkeit im privaten Raum, verbunden mit dem Griff zum Drama als öffentlichster Literaturgattung, mündet häufig in eine Unbewegtheit äußerer Handlung und eine Verlagerung der Konflikte auf den Körper der Heldin als *Ver*körperung des seelischen Innenraums. So erscheint auch Gersdorfs Mittelpunktsfigur Julia wie ein 'lebendes Bild' inmitten wechselnder 'Gruppen'. Unterstrichen wird dies durch die Sprachform: Gersdorf verwendet nicht die typischen Tragödienverse der Frühaufklärung (Alexandriner) oder der Weimarer Klassik (Blankvers), sondern Prosa, die jedoch durch die dominierenden Daktylen einen antikisierenden Duktus erhält.[15] Der in Julia verkörperte Konflikt, der sich nicht in einer äußeren Handlung entladen darf, verweist auf den ihm ursächlichen Verblendungszusammenhang, dem die – ausnahmslos männlichen – handlungsmächtigen Figuren sich unerbittlich unterstellen.

Der Grund für den Krieg bleibt völlig ausgespart. Als Motivation nennt der alte Horatius seine römisch-albanische 'Mischehe', die weitere Vermischungen der beiden Völker nach sich ziehe. Stoffgeschichtlich ist der As-

---

[13] Hannelore Schlaffer: Laienspiel und "Lebende Bilder". In: *Klassik und Romantik 1770-1830*. Stuttgart 1986 (Epochen der deutschen Literatur in Bildern). S. 49-58, 256-257.

[14] Dagmar von Hoff: *Dramen des Weiblichen. Deutsche Dramatikerinnen um 1800.* Opladen 1989 (Kulturwissenschaftliche Studien zur Literatur). S. 17f.

[15] Den Vergleich zu Christa Wolfs *Kassandra* mit ihrem Erzählgeflecht aus antikisierenden Metren zu ziehen, wäre allzu verführerisch auch angesichts dessen, dass die Protagonistin eine Kassandra ähnliche Figur ist, deren Warnungen ungehört bleiben. Diesem Zusammenhang nachzugehen, muss indessen einer späteren Arbeit vorbehalten bleiben.

pekt, die Rassenverhältnisse bereinigen zu wollen, als Kriegsbegründung neu. Livius betont umgekehrt, dass dieser Krieg einem Bürgerkrieg gleichgekommen sei. Da Alba wie Rom letztendlich von Troja her stammte und Rom selbst aus Alba hervorging, kämpften gewissermassen Eltern und Kinder gegeneinander.[16] Dass Gerdorfs Drama ein Jahr nach der Französischen Revolution erschien, mag für diese stoffliche Verschärfung eine Erklärung abgeben. Möglicherweise wird hier schon die Revolution im Nachbarland als potentiell völkertrennend und kriegsauslösend empfunden. Damit freilich würde das Stück die Kriegsfurcht zu einem relativ frühen Zeitpunkt ins Zentrum stellen, als in weiten Teilen der deutschsprachigen Publizistik noch Revolutionsbegeisterung oder zumindest ein sachlich-analysierender Umgang mit der Revolution vorherrscht.[17] Erst ab 1792 verschärft sich der Diskurs der Feindschaft der 'Vaterländer' Frankreich und Deutschland, der sich im 19. Jahrhundert zementieren wird.[18] Krieg, so viel steht fest, fungiert in diesem Stück als Behauptung eines Nationalcharakters, der sich selbst als stark und männlich versteht, gegenüber einem als schwächlich und weiblich markierten Nationalcharakter des Feindes. Dies wiederum erinnert an die Nationalstereotype, die sich im Anschluss an die Französische Revolution im deutschen Raum verfestigten, und die mit spezifischen Temperamenten und Geschlechtscharakteristika versehen wurden. So galt der französische Nationalcharakter als schwach, sanguinisch und weiblich, der deutsche dagegen als stark, cholerisch und männlich.[19] Fulvius etwa beschimpft seine weniger kriegsbegeisterten Brüder als "Weiber in Waffenrock" (G 31).

---

[16] "Et bellum utrimque summa ope parabatur, ciuili simillimum bello, prope inter parentes natosque, Troianam utramque prolem, cum Lauinium ab Troia, ab Lauinio Alba, ab Albanorum stirpe regum oriundi Romani essent" (Livius I. S. 22).

[17] Zu publizistischen Quellen: *Deutschland und die Französische Revolution 1789-1806*. Hg. von Theo Stammen und Friedrich Eberle. Darmstadt 1988 (Quellen zum politischen Denken der Deutschen im 19. und 20. Jahrhundert 1). S. 19-21. Der Band zitiert Auszüge aus Revolutionsbriefen und Diskussionen, ohne indessen auf die Frauenzeitschriften einzugehen. Texte aus den Jahren 1790 stammen etwa von Wieland, Campe, Moser, Schubart (vgl. ebd. S. 27-109).

[18] Für die Bedeutung von 'Feindschaft' als konstituierendem Moment nationaler Identitätsbildung s. Michael Jeismann: *Das Vaterland der Feinde. Studien zum nationalen Feindbegriff und Selbstverständnis in Deutschland und Frankreich 1792-1918*. Stuttgart 1992 (Sprache und Geschichte 19).

[19] Ruth Florack: "Weiber sind wie Franzosen geborne Weltleute". Zur Verschränkung von Geschlechter-Klischees und nationalen Wahrnehmungsmustern. In: *Nation als Stereotyp. Fremdwahrnehmung und Identität in deutscher und französischer Literatur*. Hg. von Ruth Florack. Tübingen 2000. S. 319-338; Gudrun Loster-Schneider: "Die Ordnung der Dinge ist inzwischen durch keine übergeschäfftige Hand gestört worden". Zur Interaktion von National- und Geschlechterstereotypen in Theodor Fontanes *Kriegsgefangen*. In: *Theodor Fontane. Am Ende eines Jahr-*

Hervorzuheben ist die Unerbittlichkeit, mit der die Behauptung des eigenen Volkscharakters durchgeführt werden muss: um den Preis nämlich der vollständigen Auslöschung des Anderen. Gemeinsam mit den Körpern der Feinde werden auch die Körper der eigenen Helden auf ihren Gebrauchswert als Waffe reduziert. Harsch fordert Horatius von seiner Frau, ihre drei Söhne für "Rom, die Herrscherin der Nationen" (G 7), zu opfern. Deutlicher noch spricht sein Mustersohn Fulvius aus, worum es geht: "Ich habe nicht Mutter, nicht Schwester, nicht Freunde, ein Vaterland hab ich, das Alles mir ist! Roms Herrschaft will ich gründen, und Albanien in Fesseln werfen!" (G 30f.). Um Missverständnisse auszuschließen, fügt er hinzu, dass er, sobald er Julias Verlobten "erwürgt" habe, sie einem Edlen des eigenen Volkes zuführen werde (G 31).

Die Abwertung des Weiblichen durch die Kriegstreiber wird dabei so begründet, dass der weibliche Körper als Waffe untauglich sei: "[...] was verliert das Vaterland durch ein Weib?" (G 12) herrscht Horatius seine Tochter an, und Fulvius verbietet ihr zornig jede Kritik an seiner Heldentat: "Wie? – Ein Weib? Ein elendes Weib soll meine Thaten wägen? Soll mir meinen Muth brandmarken, und ins Geschrei meines Sieges heulen, während daß mein Volk mich seinen Retter preiset, und Ehrensäulen mir sezzen will?" (G 50). Freilich heißt das nicht, dass Frauenkörper nicht dem Krieg zum Opfer fallen können. Was Horatia zu Beginn fürchtet, dass ihre Tochter gleichfalls dem Krieg geopfert werde – "Wollt ihr auch diese Einzige mir rauben, da ihr Geschlecht sie sichert?" (G 12) –, bewahrheitet sich am Ende durch deren Ermordung. Dass ihr Geschlecht unter vaterländischen Gesichtspunkten indessen ohne Wert ist, beweist die Sanktionierung des Mordes durch den Vater, die eine groteske Steigerung gegenüber Livius darstellt. Der König wird erst gar nicht gefragt, denn Horatius – obschon er um seine Tochter trauert – schreibt den Mord kurzerhand einem Unbekannten zu, damit man Fulvius als Helden feiern kann: "Ein Fremdling hat meine Tochter erschlagen, und ich will sie betrauern; mein Sohn hat Rom errettet, und ich will ihn schüzzen!" (G 61).

Im Kontrast zu den Kriegstreibern im Stück, Horatius als Verkörperung Roms sowie dessen albanischem Gegenstück, dem Heerführer Suffetius, tritt neben Julia vor allem die Mutter als Warnfigur auf. Eine Besonderheit ist in Gersdorfs Version, dass sie sich am Ende mit Grausen von der Szenerie verabschiedet. Das Stück endet mit ihren, an Horatius gerichteten Worten:

> Nehmt euern Liebling, euern Stolz! das Ungeheuer der Natur! – vergeßt uns alle unter dem Schatten seiner Lorbeern! ich kenn' ihn nicht! – ich habe keine Kinder mehr! nehmt euern Sohn, und laßt mir die Leichen meiner Kinder im Stande der Vernichtung, im Staube selbst mir noch werther, als dieser Unmensch im mörde-

hunderts. Hg. von Hanna Delft von Wolzogen in Zusammenarbeit mit Helmuth Nürnberger. Würzburg 2000. S. 227-239.

rischen Daseyn! – Eine unglükliche Mutter nimmt nicht Theil an euerm Jubel! –
alles was ich begehre ist: daß ich ruhig bleibe bei meinen Todten, und alles was
ich bettle, ist: ein Almosen von Erde für ihren Staub! – Auf ihrem Grabe will ich
bleiben und o – daß die Götter mein Flehn erhörten! daß sie mich verwandelten
in ein Grabmahl meiner Kinder! (G 61f.)

Horatia, die sich als Mutter aller 'Kinder' im Stück ansieht und den Verbo-
ten zum Trotz als Weib die Stimme gegen die martialische Instrumentalisierung ihrer Kinder erhebt, begibt sich zu deren toten Körpern auf das
Schlachtfeld. Als die Fortschreibung des Typus der 'femme forte' sowie als
Negation weiblicher Mythisierungen und Allegorisierungen des Vaterlandes[20] scheint die Horatia-Figur insbesondere auf Mutterfiguren der Frühaufklärung zu referieren, wie etwa *Cornelia, die Mutter der Gracchen* von
Luise A. V. Gottsched (bzw. Anne de Barbier).[21] Im Unterschied zu Cornelia, der Tochter Scipios, die sozusagen als Mutter Roms nach dem Tod des
Tiberius ihren zweiten Sohn Caius ebenso unerbittlich zum Kampf und Tod
für das republikanische Rom anheizt, repräsentiert Horatia nicht Rom allein,
sondern steht als römisch-albanische Mutter für das Prinzip der Völkerver-
ständigung beider Städte. Dies verdeutlicht sich auch, wenn von ihrer
Schwester, der Mutter der drei Curiatier die Rede ist, die sich – so höhnt
Suffetius – im albanischen Lager nicht anders als Horatia im römischen
gebärde: "Wie? – winselt ihr auch wie eure albanische Schwester Curiatia,
und klagt mich an: ich nähme euch eure Lieblinge?" (G 21). Wenn Horatia
am Ende ein "Grabmahl" werden möchte, erinnert das an die verschollene
Cornelia-Statue, von der antike Autoren berichten.[22] Indessen steht Horatia

---

[20] Zur Vorstellung des Vaterlandes als Mutter bei Rousseau: Sidonia Blättler: "Nation" und "Geschlecht" im Diskurs der Moderne. Die politischen Schriften Jean-
Jacques Rousseaus. In: *Die Zukunft des Wissens. XVIII. Deutscher Kongress für
Philosophie.* Konferenzunterlagen. Hg. von J. Mittelstraß. Konstanz 1999. S. 995-
1002, hier: S. 1002. Leider ist der Beitrag im publizierten Kongressband nicht veröffentlicht.

[21] Luise Adelgunde Victorie Gottsched: *Cornelia, die Mutter der Grachen, ein
Trauerspiel. Aus dem Französischen der Madlle Barbier, übersetzt.* In: *Die Deut-
sche Schaubühne.* S. 163-230. Gottsched übersetzte ein Drama von Mademoiselle
[Anne] de Barbier: *Cornélie, Mère des Gracques.* Paris 1703.

[22] Von einer Bronzestatue, die die sitzende Cornelia dargestellt habe, berichten sowohl Plutarch als auch Plinius. Die Statue selbst ist verschollen, der Sockel wurde
1878 bei Kanalisationsarbeiten entdeckt. Die Inschrift der ca. 100 v. Chr. errichteten
Statue wurde später von "Cornelia Mater Gracchorum" in "Cornelia Africani. F.
Gracchorum" geändert, was darauf hindeutet, daß sich das Cornelia-Bild bereits in
der Antike von der gebildeten, politisch engagierten Mutter von Revolutionären zur
kinderreichen Mutter aus allererster Familie wandelt, eine Tendenz, die auch die
spätere Rezeptionsgeschichte der Cornelia in der bildenden Kunst kennzeichnet.
Vgl. Barbara Hornberger: *Cornelia die Mutter der Gracchen als Thema der bilden-*

als Statue für anderes. Ist Cornelia – freilich innerhalb eines differenten historischen Kontexts – die Allegorie eines republikanisch aufgeklärten Roms, so symbolisiert Horatia die Verweigerung einer weiblichen Indienstnahme für die Stadt, deren kriegerische Aktivitäten in falschem Ehrbegriff und Nationaleifer wurzeln.

Indem Horatia vor der Stadt bei den Leichen bleiben will, vollzieht sie einen Schritt, der durch Julia vorbereitet wurde. Als die Tochter sich auf den Kriegsschauplatz vor der Stadt begibt, übertritt diese das Gesetz des Königs, wie Fulvius ihr vorwirft: "Wie? du hier? – Eine römische Jungfrau umherirrend vor dem Thore? – Wekte dich der Widerhall meines Siegs, oder jagte Wahnsinn der Liebe dich von dannen, daß du, Kühne! das Gesez übertratest?" (G 46). Das erinnert an die Sophokleische Antigone, die sich dem toten Körper ihres Bruders Polyneikes vor der Stadt zuwendet und damit ein Prinzip erinnernder Geschichte praktiziert, während Kreon diesen Körper einer Symbolisierung, der Unterscheidung von Freund und Feind im Namen des Gesetzes unterwirft.[23] Denkt man diesen Symbolisierungszwang weiter als Installierung eines binären kulturellen Codes und einer heterosexuellen Norm, so lässt sich Antigones Agieren darüber hinaus als Akt des Widerstandes gegen diese Norm lesen.[24] Die Antigone-Tragödie gibt ein Beispiel der unterschiedlichen kulturellen Positionen des 'Männlichen' und 'Weiblichen' zur Stadt. Grundsätzlich beschreibt Sigrid Weigel ein Funktionsmuster antiker Gründungsmythen, demzufolge

> die Gründung einer Stadt mit der Errichtung einer Mauer verbunden [ist], mit deren Hilfe das Weibliche aufgespalten wird in einen wilden, dämonisierten Anteil draußen und in eine domestizierte Frau, Gattin und Mutter im Innern der Stadt. In der mythischen Urszene der Stadtgründung beispielsweise, wie sie uns von den antiken griechischen Mythen in vielfältigen Variationen erzählt wird, läßt sich die Stadtmauer leicht als Schutzwall erkennen, mit dem die neu errichtete Ordnung (die Polis) gegen die wilde, ungebändigte Natur draußen abgegrenzt wird, gegen jenen Raum, in dem sich der Heros im Kampf gegen das Chaos als Drachentöter beweist.[25]

den Kunst. Magisterarbeit (masch.) am Institut für Kunstgeschichte der Universität Stuttgart 1990. S. 26f.; Hornberger bezieht sich u. a. auf Filipo Coarelli: La statue de Cornélie, mère des Gracques, et la crise politique à Rome au temps de Saturnius. In: *Le dernier siècle de la république romaine et l'époque augustéenne.* Strasbourg 1978. S. 13-27.

[23] Sigrid Weigel: "Antigone" und der "Engel der Geschichte" – zwei Denkbilder. In: *Topographien der Geschlechter. Kulturgeschichtliche Studien zur Literatur.* Reinbek bei Hamburg 1990. S. 9-13, hier S. 10.

[24] Judith Butler: *Antigone's Claim.* Butler stellt den Widerstand gegen die heterosexuelle Norm ins Zentrum.

[25] Weigel. S. 157.

Diese mythische Urszene kehrt auch in der Horatier-Episode wieder. Topographisch gibt es schon bei Livius eine Trennung von Stadt und Marsfeld durch die Mauer. Der Kampf gilt aber nicht dem Drachen als Figur, sondern der eigenen, zum neuen nationalen Auftrag nicht mehr passenden Vergangenheit. Alba ist ein Störfaktor im neuen homogenen Selbstbild Roms als Herrscherin der Welt. Entsprechend muss die Tochter, die die Grenze zwischen dem Ort der Domestizierung und der Wildnis überschreitet, getötet, die Stadt Alba als Ort ausgelöscht und ihre Bevölkerung Rom einverleibt werden.[26] Bei Gersdorf ist der Kriegsanlass indessen diesem Gründungszusammenhang ganz enthoben und lediglich in einem im Drama selbst unerklärten Feindbild motiviert. Der Sieg Roms und die Unterwerfung Albas gelingt den Kriegstreibern zwar, was aber misslingt, ist die Einverleibung des Weiblichen, da sich die Mutter dieser eindeutig verweigert, wenn sie sich – eine neue, politisch motivierte Niobe[27] – als Mahnmal zu den Schlachtopfern begibt und damit den von der Tochter begonnenen Weg vor die Mauer, also aus dem Rahmen des Gesetzes, vollendet.

Während die Tochter das System des Vaters zwar anprangert, aber nicht wirklich durchschaut, und so vor allem zu dessen Opfer wird, erscheint die Mutter als Verstehende und Wissende, die aus der Opferung ihrer Kinder die Konsequenz zieht. Dieser Unterschied kommt insbesondere zum Ausdruck, wenn Julia auf die Idee verfällt, mit frisch aufgestecktem Haar vor Suffetius zu knien, um ihn zur Einlenkung gleichsam zu 'verführen'. Das, was Horatia bereits weiß, dass Schönheit als mythisierte Waffe der Frau versagt, wo hartes Männergeschäft angesagt ist, muss Julia erst noch erfahren, als Suffetius sie höhnisch abweist (G 20-26). Am Ende wird ihr selbst das Frauenopfer mit seinem symbolischen Verweis auf die unerträglichen Zustände aberkannt,[28] indem der Vater den Mord einem Fremdling anlastet. Ihr persönlich bringt er freilich den gewünschten Tod – und dafür dankt sie ihrem Mörder. Dieser erkennt seinerseits seine vorherige Verblendung, sieht Julias Kassandra-Worte erfüllt und erwartet das Geschrei des Volkes nach seinem Blut. Der Vater beschwichtigt ihn: "Laß es schreien – bin ich nicht dein Vater? – bist du nicht der lezte Zweig meines Stammes [...]?" (G 61), da er den Helden feiern will. Für den Körper der Tochter, die er zuvor kurz unter Hinweis auf ihre Jungfräulichkeit und Schönheit betrauert hat (G 60), verzichtet er

---

[26] Livius. I. S. 29.

[27] Eines der "lebenden Bilder" Emma Hamiltons zeigt sie als Niobe, mit einer Hand die Augen verhüllend, mit der anderen den Leichnam ihrer Tochter schleppend. Vgl. Schlaffer. S. 53.

[28] Prototypisch hierfür ist Iphigenie, die in dreifacher Kodierung als Opfer bestimmt ist: kultisches Opfer des Vaters, Opfer ihrer Sozialposition, Opfer des Thoas. Vgl. Sigrid Lange: *Spiegelgeschichten. Geschlechter und Poetiken in der Zeit um 1800.* Frankfurt/M. 1995. S. 105.

auf eine symbolische Deutung; dieser wird einfach negiert. Zeichenhaft verstehen kann ihn nur die Mutter, und zwar als Kritik an der väterlichen Definitionsmacht, die ihr als Pervertierung der Natur erscheint. Der zum "Ungeheuer der Natur" erklärte Sohn steht für die Ungeheuerlichkeit des Krieges in nuce. Zu dieser Naturberufung von Mutter und Tochter fügen sich die Tiermetaphern, die im Stück vielfach anklingen, um zu unterstreichen, dass das 'zivilisatorische' menschliche Treiben jeder Natur hohnspricht: Julia als Lamm oder Reh, Horatia aber als Löwenmutter gegenüber den kampfeswütigen Männern, die sich schlimmer als reißende Löwen oder Tiger gebärden.

Beachtung verdient, dass im Drama auch solche männlichen Figuren auftreten, die lieber der Mutter als dem Vater folgen. Dies zeigt insbesondere jene Szene, in der die drei Brüder zu Julia und Horatia kommen, um Abschied zu nehmen. Während Fulvius sich mit Stolz auf seine Kriegspflicht beruft, weist ihn Lucius zurecht: "Grausamkeit ist keine wahre Heldenpflicht!" (G 28), und Aurelius nennt den Kampf "unmenschlich" (G 28). Horatia lobt die beiden daraufhin: "Dies ist die Sprache meiner Söhne! – kommt an eurer Mutter Herz ihr meine beiden Kinder! – – laßt euch – ach vielleicht zum leztenmal! an ihre Brust drükken! – empfangt ihren besten, schönsten Segen" (G 29). Wie die folgende Szene sichtbar macht, steht auch Albanus dem Kampf skeptisch gegenüber. Immer kehrte er, so sagt er, "willig zur blutigen Arbeit fürs Vaterland zurük! Heute, zum erstenmal, schleicht fieberhafter Abscheu durch meine Adern, und die Ehre der man mich würdigt, verstummt vor der stärkern Uebermacht der Liebe und Freundschaft!" (G 37). Und deutlicher noch: "dein Curiatius geht den Weg seiner Pflicht, aber seinen Sieg zu wünschen, den Sieg über Julias Brüder, dies vermag seine Seele nicht!" (G 40). Unterstrichen wird die Absurdität des Krieges somit dadurch, dass, zumindest von den Kämpfern, die als Figuren im Drama auftreten, nur einer wirklich siegen will: Fulvius Horatius. Alle anderen wollen ihre Feinde schonen. Zu den an die Kriegstreiber gerichteten Bitten und Klagen auf der Figurenebene tritt dadurch ein kriegsstörendes Moment auch auf der Handlungsebene auf, da der Sieg des Helden durch die kampfeskritische Haltung seiner Mit- und Gegenstreiter fragwürdig erscheint. Im Nebentext wird unmittelbar nach dem Siege des Fulvius ein weiterer kritischer Hinweis gegeben, wenn das Volk "verworren" hinter dem Helden herjauchzt (G 46).

Das Drama ist unterzeichnet mit dem abgekürzten Namen "Wilhelmine von G..." (G 62), hinter dem erstmals Carl Wilhelm von Schindel Wilhelmine von Gersdorf vermutete,[29] die wohl Mitherausgeberin des *Museums für Frauenzimmer* und überdies Autorin zahlreicher weiterer dramatischer

---

[29] Carl Wilhelm Otto August von Schindel: *Die deutschen Schriftstellerinnen des neunzehnten Jahrhunderts*. 3 Bde. Leipzig 1823-1825. Nachdr. Hildesheim, New York 1978. Bd. 2. S. 406f. Vgl. hierzu auch Weckel. S. 111-115.

Texte war.[30] Über die dramatische Absicht der Autorin – die freilich ohnehin nicht die entsprechende Umsetzung garantiert, sondern bestenfalls eine Interpretation darstellen würde – wissen wir nichts. Als Hinweis in diese Richtung kann allenfalls das Motto angesehen werden, das dem Drama vorangeht:

> Ruhe beglücke die Seelen der Helden!
> Nahmhaft war in Gefahren ihr Muth!
> Sie sollen von Wolken getragen
> Schweben um mich! (G 3)

Als Quelle wird im Paratext *Oßians Fingal* benannt.[31] Das im Motto postulierte Heldenlob scheint auf den ersten Blick der hier vorgetragenen Lesart des Dramas zu widersprechen, jedoch mag es bei genauem Hinsehen ebenso gut einen alternativen Heldenbegriff propagieren. Zum einen ist nämlich die Rede von toten Helden – während Fulvius Horatius überlebt –, zum anderen legt die Pluralform nahe, unter den "Helden" dessen jüngere Brüder, den Geliebten Albanus und die Tochter zu verstehen. Da die von Macpherson als gälische Originale edierten Ossian-Gesänge in der deutschsprachigen Literatur vor allem als empfindsame Lektüre verortet sind – Goethes Werther ist unter den Lesern –, liegt die Anwendung auf die sterbenden Figuren des Stückes sogar mehr als nahe. Das Motto könnte so gezielt änigmatisch formuliert sein, um die anti-patriotische Tendenz zu verschleiern oder zumindest abzuschwächen. Damit würde sich das Stück in einer Tradition von (nicht nur weiblichen) Mottos und Vorworten positionieren, die mit Verbeugungen vor herrschenden moralischen und politischen Auffassungen von dem radikaleren Inhalt ihres nachfolgenden Werks abzulenken versuchen. Gerade für den Horatier-Stoff ist eine solche Tradition besonders auffällig, klaffen doch schon bei Pierre Corneille explizite und implizite Dramaturgie auseinander, was sich bei Georg Behrmann noch steigern soll. Ein kursorischer Blick auf die beiden älteren Fassungen vermag die radikale Wende, die Gersdorfs Version unternimmt, zu verdeutlichen.

III.

Corneilles *Horace*, uraufgeführt 1640 und veröffentlicht 1641, war eines seiner erfolgreichsten Stücke. Im Zentrum steht der älteste der drei römi-

---

[30] Bislang liegen weder zuverlässige Lebensdaten noch ein über Autopsie geprüftes Werkverzeichnis vor.

[31] Das Gedicht referiert *The Works of Ossian, Son of Fingal*, die James Macpherson 1762 als angebliche Originale eines gälischen Volksdichters herausgab. Vgl. *James Macpherson's Ossian. Faksimile-Neudruck der Erstausgaben von 1762/63 mit Begleitband: Die Varianten.* Hg. von Otto L. Jiriscek. Heidelberg 1940.

schen Söhne, Horace, der als vorbildlicher Held für Vater und Vaterland kämpft und siegt, kontrastiert durch den albanischen Curiace, der am Sinn des Kampfes zweifelt, obwohl auch er gehorcht. Leidend und kritisch verhalten sich die Frauen im Stück. Neben Camilla (so lautet hier der Name der Schwester des Horace und Verlobten des Curiace) ergänzt Corneille das Personal um Sabine, die Schwester des Curiace und Frau des Horace. In den wesentlichen Plot-Elementen Livius folgend, lässt Corneille im vierten Akt den rückkehrenden Helden die Rom verfluchende Schwester töten und zeigt im fünften Akt die Diskussion um die Begnadigung des Helden angesichts seiner patriotischen Tat.

Der Dramaturgie der französischen Klassik verpflichtet, setzt das Drama mit Horace als alleinigem Titelhelden auf Heldenbewunderung, kontrastiert durch abschreckende Figuren. So erscheint es auf den ersten Blick als ein royalistisches Paradestück im Frankreich Richelieus. Eine Widmung, die die Einschwörung auf den Staat und die Unterdrückung persönlicher Leidenschaft propagiert, ist an denselben gerichtet.[32] Indessen sahen schon die Zeitgenossen diese Intention nicht vollständig verwirklicht. Dies verdeutlicht sich insbesondere in Corneilles späterem *Examen*, das die Hauptkritikpunkte der Académie Française an seinem Stück aufnimmt und diskutiert. Corneille räumt hier ein, die Tragödie nicht auf eine einzige Aktion des Helden konzentriert, sondern die Einheit der Gefahr für denselben verdoppelt zu haben, wenn diesem nach dem Mord an Camilla die Hinrichtung drohe: "[...] que cette mort fait une action double par le second péril où tombe Horace après être sorti du premier".[33]

In welcher Weise Corneille immer wieder versuchte, sich gegenüber der 'doctrine classique' Freiheiten zu nehmen, zeigen etwa seine *Trois Discours sur le Poème Dramatique*,[34] die eine Auseinandersetzung mit den klassischen Einheiten und den Wirkungszielen der Tragödie führen, unter wechselnder Berufung auf Aristoteles einerseits und Corneilles eigene Dramen andererseits. Sein *Horace* lässt darüber hinaus eine implizite Dramaturgie erkennen, die von der explizit formulierten abweicht. Corneille verdoppelt nämlich nicht allein die Gefahr für den Helden oder eröffnet eine zweite Handlung, vielmehr führt er mit Camille eine neue Heldin ein. Dadurch aber rückt die Haltung der Frauen im Stück ins Zentrum. Camille erfüllt die ihr zugedachte Abschreckungsfunktion, insofern sie sich von ihren Affekten fortreißen lässt und diese über die positiv dargestellten Kriegsziele stellt. Ihr Fluch auf Rom ist nicht politisch, sondern wurzelt in persönlicher Leidenschaft:

---

[32] Pierre Corneille: À Monseigneur, Monseigneur le Cardinal Duc de Richelieu. In: *Œuvres complètes*. Bd. 1. S. 833-835.

[33] Pierre Corneille: Examen. In: *Œuvres complètes*. Bd. 1. S. 839-834, hier S. 840.

[34] Pierre Corneille: Les Trois Discours sur le Poème Dramatique. In: *Œuvres complètes*. Bd. 3. Tours 1987. S. 115-190.

Rome, l'unique objet de mon ressentiment!
Rome, à qui vient ton bras d'immoler mon Amant!
Rome, qui t'a vu naître et que ton cœur adore!
Rome, enfin que je hais parce qu'elle t'honore! (C 887).

Erst nach dieser Begründung ihres Hasses auf Rom wünscht sich Camille die Nachbarvölker, den Orient, die ganze Welt herbei, um Rom zu zerstören. Damit mag Camille übertrieben wirken, ihr Tod erscheint jedoch nicht rundheraus gerechtfertigt. Unterstrichen wird dies dadurch, dass auch ihre emotional gezügeltere und staatstreuere Schwägerin Sabine sich nicht mit der Situation abfinden kann und ihren Brüdern in den Tod folgen will. Dabei münzt sie ihre Todessehnsucht zur vaterländischen Tat um, wenn sie anstelle des ihr verhasst gewordenen Mannes sterben und dem Land so den Helden erhalten will. Zum König spricht sie:

La mort que je demande et qu'il faut que j'obtienne
Augmentera sa peine, et finira la mienne.
Sire, voyez l'excès de mes tristes ennuis,
Et l'effroyable état où mes jours sont réduits.
Quelle horreur d'embrasser un homme don't l'épée
De toute ma famille a la trame coupée
Et quelle impieté de haïr un époux
Pour avoir bien servi les siens, l'État, et vous! (C 897)

Obschon als explizite Botschaft die vaterländische Tat des Horace gelobt wird, rücken die Frauenfiguren als Sympathieträgerinnen zunehmend ins Zentrum, so dass im Subtext ein Bruch mit der "Verherrlichung absolutistischer Staatsräson"[35] aufscheint.

Dies verschärft sich bei Georg Behrmann, dessen sehr freie Adaption des Corneille-Dramas schon Ansätze einer emotionalistischen Ästhetik zeigt, die auf kathartische Wirkung setzt.[36] Behrmann, ein bürgerlicher Autor aus

---

[35] Jürgen Grimm: Das 'klassische' Jahrhundert. In: *Französische Literaturgeschichte*. Unter Mitarbeit von Elisabeth Arend-Schwarz, Karlheinz Biermann, Brigitta Coenen-Mennemeier u. a. hg. von Jürgen Grimm. 3., um die frankophonen Literaturen außerhalb Frankreichs erweiterte Auflage. Stuttgart, Weimar 1994. S. 136-180, hier S. 159.

[36] Alberto Martino beschreibt diese Entwicklung anhand poetologischer Entwürfe. Demnach setzt sich im Laufe des 18. Jahrhunderts die Ästhetik des Emotionalismus gegen die klassizistische Ästhetik der Bewunderung durch; auch die heroische Tragödie verwandelt sich der auf Gefühlsregung ausgerichteten Dramaturgie an: *Geschichte der dramatischen Theorien in Deutschland im 18. Jahrhundert*. Bd. 1: *Die*

Hamburg,[37] ist heute nahezu vergessen. Zeitgenossen waren der Meinung, dass sein Stück *Timoleon, der Bürgerfreund* und nicht Johann Christoph Gottscheds *Sterbender Cato* die erste deutsche Originaltragödie sei.[38] Sein zweites Stück *Die Horazier*, 1733 verfasst, wurde im selben Jahr von Friederike Caroline Neubers Truppe in Hamburg und 1747 in einer überarbeiteten Version von der Schönemannschen Truppe, gleichfalls in Hamburg, aufgeführt. Überlebt hat es nur in einer Überarbeitung des Autors von 1751. Wie Behrmanns eigene Beschreibung der Änderungen in seiner *Vorrede* vermuten lässt, hat er den Diskurs der Empfindsamkeit adaptiert, was auch das Wirkungsziel seines Trauerspiels beeinflusste.[39] In einem gereimten Epilog zum Stück bezieht sich Behrmann ausdrücklich auf Corneille, dessen Fehler einer gedoppelten Handlung er vermeiden möchte.[40] Gleich dem französischen Autor intendiert er den siegenden jungen Horaz als ein bewunderungswürdiges Tugendmuster, die Frauen aber als Negativbeispiele zu gestalten:

> [...] So lang Exempel lehren,
> Und ein Horaz sich hebt, in Söhnen Helden weckt,
> Die feige Tochter straft, und durch Camilla schreckt;
> So lange Kunst und Witz und Sitten nicht verschwinden:
> So lange hoffen wir Vertheidiger zu finden. (B 112)

Allerdings führen Behrmanns dramaturgische Eingriffe nachgerade zu einer gegenläufigen Aussage. Mehr noch als in Corneilles Fassung wird nun die Tochter zur Sympathieträgerin und heimlichen Heldin des Stückes. Schon die Exposition gibt ihr den Raum, Rom als Aggressor zu beschreiben, der sich von seinen eigenen historischen Wurzeln trennt, indem er die Schwesterstadt Alba zerstört. Im eröffnenden Gespräch mit Valerius argumentiert sie, dass Rom in Alba die eigene Herkunft auslöschen wolle; in den folgenden Akten gelingt es ihr, das Volk gegen den geplanten Kampf aufzubringen; und am Ende steht nicht ihr Tod als Strafe, sondern sie wird rasend und verflucht die Vaterstadt:

> Daß dir, glorsüchtigs Rom, dein heutigs Siegsgeschrey

Dramaturgie der Aufklärung (1730-1780). Aus dem Italienischen von Wolfgang Proß. Tübingen 1972.

[37] Eine der wenigen Quellen zu Behrmann ist Johann Friedrich Schützes *Hamburger Theater-Geschichte.* Hamburg 1794. S. 221-228.

[38] Albert Meier: *Dramaturgie der Bewunderung. Untersuchungen zur politisch-klassizistischen Tragödie des 18. Jahrhunderts.* Frankfurt/M. 1993 (Das Abendland. NF 23). S. 133.

[39] Behrmann: Vorrede. In: *Die Horazier.* S. 205-211.

[40] Vgl. dazu auch Behrmanns Ausführungen. Ebd. S. 208-211.

> Der Anfang deines Fluchs und dein Verderben sey,
> Damit dein Untergang noch schleuniger geschehe,
> Als ich zu deiner Schand um Curiaz vergehe!
> Mein Bruder mordet ihn; und ich? Ich bleibe nach?
> Für mich, für meine Wuth sey Rom und er zu schwach!
> Ich eil, und will in ihm auch meinen Mörder suchen,
> Und bis er mich entleibt, ihn sehn, und ihn verfluchen.
> Verwünscht, vermaledeyt sey der Albansche Krieg!
> Verflucht der Römer Glück, der Sieger und der Sieg! (B 110).

Dies sind, wohlgemerkt, die letzten Worte des Dramas. Der Fluch auf den Staat und seine Ruhmsucht steht unkommentiert dort, wo traditionell die Moral formuliert wird. Auf diese Weise verstärkt Behrmanns Revision der "action double" gerade nicht das Wirkungsziel der Bewunderung, sondern macht aus der bei Corneille von persönlicher Leidenschaft fortgerissenen weiblichen Kontrastfigur eine positive Heldin, deren Fluch im Verlauf des Stückes historisch-politisch motiviert wird und ihr Gelegenheit gibt, ihren herbeigewünschten Tod vorausschauend als Schande Roms zu deuten.

Ist Behrmanns Text überhaupt komplexer, was das Personal und dessen Konstellation betrifft, so verhandelt er auch an zentraler Stelle das Thema zweier unterschiedlicher politischer Systeme, eines älteren, tendenziell friedvollen, und eines jüngeren, tendenziell kriegerischen Systems. Dazu führt er eine weibliche Figur in der Elterngeneration ein, Secienia, Mutter des Curiaz und der Sabina. Der alte Horiaz und sie stehen wie die Verkörperung zweier Prinzipien im Stück. Beide sind der Meinung, dass der Kampf stattfinden muss, jedoch aus verschiedenen Gründen. Will Horaz die Vernichtung Albas, so erhofft sich Secienia von dem Waffengang das Wiedererstehen eines goldenen Zeitalters, eines römisch-albanischen Friedensreiches, das dem gemeinsamen Feind "Hetrurien" (B 14), also den Etruskern, trotzt:

> Und nun erleben wir die alte güldne Zeit.
> Von ihr entfernen sich der Mißgunst und der Neid.
> Drey Helden sollen euch, drey Helden uns beschützen,
> Durch ihrer Waffen Glück den Frieden unterstützen,
> Der ewig dauern soll, den der bedrängte Staat
> Entehrt, gehofft, gewünscht, und nun erlanget hat. (B 15)

Diese Hoffnung wirkt allerdings verfehlt, angesichts dessen, dass sie sich als die Mutter beider Völker fühlt und um die albanischen und die römischen 'Kinder' gleichermaßen bangt. Secienia markiert eine merkwürdige Mutterposition, wenn ihre Hoffnung auf die Errichtung eines Friedensreiches auf der Basis des unmenschlichen Zweikampfes an keiner Stelle begründet erscheint. So wirkt es überzeugend, wenn Camilla ihre Hoffnung als Verblendung begreift:

> Euch glänzt kein treues Glück, es ist ein leerer Schatten,
> Umsonst verlasst ihr euch auf euren Friedensbund.
> Ihr hofft den Frieden schon, und hofft ihn ohne Grund.
> Um einen einz'gen Kampf, um dreyer Helden Leichen,
> Wird kein verfluchtes Heer, kein Staat dem Sieger weichen. (B 15)

Auf dramaturgischer Ebene ist zu beachten, dass Behrmann vorgibt, Corneilles Version nachzubessern, was dem Drama aber unter der Hand eine neue Wirkungsdimension gibt. Zur Bewunderung des ältesten der römischen Brüder tritt als konkurrierendes Wirkungsziel nun eine kathartische Reaktion mit Camilla als positiver tragischer Heldin, deren Warnungen ungehört bleiben. Hatten die weiblichen Figuren schon bei Corneille größeren Spielraum erhalten als die starren männlichen Helden, so werden sie hier noch mehr zu den plausiblen Figuren gemacht, deren Emotionen, Beweggründe und Handlungen zur Einfühlung auffordern. Wichtig ist dabei, dass nun eine Mutter im Stück auftritt, die sich für die Bevölkerung beider Städte einsetzt. Figuriert diese Mutter zugleich das ältere und friedlichere Alba, so bedeutet dies, dass schon bei Behrmann Horaz als Vater Roms ein kriegerisches System verkörpert, das mit dem Krieg gegen die ältere Stadt die Auslöschung des eigenen mütterlichen Erbes betreibt.

Der Ausflug zu den beiden früheren Dramen mag deutlich gemacht haben, welche Komponenten dem Stoff von Corneille über Behrmann zuwachsen, die dann bei Gersdorf radikal zugespitzt werden: Corneilles "action double" propagiert vordergründig die Heldenbewunderung und mithin die Unterwerfung unter absolutistische Kriegsziele. Der Körper der Frau soll hier als Zeichen der Abschreckung gegen übertriebene individuelle Leidenschaftlichkeit fungieren, doch bereits unter der Hand wird er zum Zeichen der Kritik am Heldenkult. Behrmann will Corneilles Handlung vereinfachen, generiert aber auf diesem Wege vor allem eine Gefahr für die heimliche Heldin, die am Ende (noch) nicht hingerichtet wird, sondern Rom verflucht. Unterstützt wird deren nun historisch-politisch begründete Absage an Rom dadurch, dass Rom und Alba, figuriert in dem alten Horaz und Secienia, wie zwei unvereinbare Systeme erscheinen: der Vater als Statthalter des symbolischen Gesetzes, die Mutter als Figuration eines uneinlösbaren Friedensphantasmas. Obschon auch Wilhelmine von Gersdorf durch das Ossian-Motto weiterhin den Schein des expliziten Heldenlobs wahrt, wird in ihrem Stück der männliche Sieger nun vollends zur blinden Kriegsmaschine, die unter absurden Voraussetzungen kämpft, denn seine Brüder *wollen* nicht mitkämpfen, seine Gegner ihn nicht besiegen. Vor allem aber erwacht er angesichts der toten Schwester aus seiner Verblendung, das Ausmaß der Unmenschlichkeit wird ihm bewusst, und er sieht Julias vorherige Kassandra-Rufe bestätigt. Der Vater ist es, der ihn zum "Helden" definiert und den Tod der Schwester zur Quantité négligeable erklärt. Damit wird bei Gersdorf Bevölkerung über Blutsbande und der Körper des Sohnes als Waffe zur Erhaltung der Volksreinheit bestimmt. Den Frauen bleibt nur hysterisch-machtloses Aufbegehren, da ihre Schönheit zugleich ihre Überflüssigkeit repräsentiert. Ganz abgesehen davon, dass sie das störende Element per se sind, da sie zu 'Mischehen' und neuen Formen von Verwandtschaftsbeziehungen verführen. Mit Butler gedacht, formuliert das Stück aber gerade über die Frauenfiguren ein erstaunliches Widerstandspotential gegen das binäre Freund-Feind-Modell, das eine neue Form von Gender-Differenz begründet und frühere Formen von Verwandtschaftsbeziehungen ausschaltet. Bemerkenswert ist in dieser Hinsicht vor allem, dass der Körper der Tochter vom Vater gerade nicht zur jungfräulich-schönen Leiche stilisiert und der eigenen kulturellen Symbolik einverleibt wird. Vielmehr setzt die Mutter den Weg der rebellischen Tochter fort und steigert ihn noch, indem sie das 'Weibliche' in seiner Bestimmung zur 'Funktionslosigkeit' innerhalb der väterlichen Definitionsmacht markiert.

Kupferstiche der Erstausgabe im *Museum für Frauenzimmer von einigen ihrer Mitschwestern*. Zweites Quartal 1790.

Museum für Frauenzimmer

von

einigen ihrer Mitschwestern.

Zweites Quartal. 1790.

Weißenfels und Leipzig,

bei Friedrich Severin.

Vte Scene

pag: 35

Stirb nicht, Albanus! —

Der Abdruck der Kupferstiche erfolgt mit freundlicher Erlaubnis der Sächsischen Landesbibliothek – Staats- und Universitätsbibliothek Dresden (Signatur 3.A.857 R.S.).

Daniel J. Kramer

Winckelmann's Impact on Drama Prior to Goethe's *Iphigenie*: Joseph Bernard Pelzel's *Das gerächte Troja*

Scholarship on Winckelmann's early impact on the German stage has focused on Goethe and Weimar. An analysis of Das gerächte Troja *(1780) by the Viennese playwright Joseph Bernard Pelzel reveals that Winckelmann's influence was more extensive than previously considered. Pelzel recasts two of the drama's lead characters, Hecuba and Cassandra, who are traditionally portrayed as hysterical, emotionally overwrought women, into self-controlled stoics, who conform to Winckelmann's view of Greek Classicism.*

The publication of Goethe's *Iphigenie auf Tauris* in 1787, with its ancient Greek setting and its focus on a stoic character, is treated by scholars as if it were a bolt of lightning on the literary landscape of the "Spätaufklärung". Indeed, *Iphigenie* arrived at a time when the German stage was dominated by foreign translations and tragic operas, and more innovative works fell chiefly into the categories of the *bürgerliches Trauerspiel* and *Sturm und Drang* tragedies. Against the unrestrained emotional displays typical of these newer plays, Iphigenie's serene and august demeanor posed a startling contrast. Goethe's contemporaries took note of it immediately and recognized in his titular heroine a new character type – one that was the embodiment of Johann Joachim Winckelmann's notion of "edle Einfalt und stille Größe". By 1787, this formula, which the art historian had used to characterize the Laocoon group in his renowned 1755 essay *Gedanken über die Nachahmung der griechischen Werke in der Malerei und Bildhauerkunst*, would have been well-known to virtually any German artist or intellectual of that period. With Goethe's dramatic interpretation of Winckelmann's study of the ancient Greek aesthetic, began a new era in drama, which scholarship since the 19th century has canonized as the German Classical period.[1]

The 32-year gap between Winckelmann's first essay and Goethe's play, however, raises the question of whether Winckelmann's writings inspired German playwrights other than Goethe to publish dramas with a classical

---

[1] Both the notion of Goethe's *Iphigenie* (along with his well-documented trip to Italy) as the start of the *Deutsche Klassik* and that of Winckelmann's influence on Goethe have become commonplace. *The Oxford Companion to German Literature* notes that this play "is the first important work manifesting [Goethe's] classicism" and that "[t]he classicism of Winckelmann [...] provided a basis" for it. Henry and Mary Garland: *The Oxford Companion to German Literature*. New York 1986. Pp. 442 and 493 respectively.

setting and stoic heroes. One answer to this question lies in a little known tragedy, *Das gerächte Troja*, published in 1780 by Joseph Bernhard Pelzel. This drama, which treats the tragic situation of the female survivors of Troy's defeat, provides evidence that Goethe may in fact *not* have been the first playwright to adapt Winckelmann's ideas. But before we examine the extent to which Pelzel's play made use of Winckelmann's notion of "noble simplicity and quiet grandeur", it is important to recall briefly the degree to which Winckelmann's works influenced a wide variety of disciplines and to discuss the reasons why drama remained in large part impervious to that influence despite the fact that Winckelmann's ideas themselves drew from the dramatic genre.

The impact of Winckelmann's essay and of his later work *Geschichte der Kunst* (1764), in which he expands the main points of the *Gedanken* essay, was widespread and has been the focus of a number of scholarly studies. Foremost among them are Walther Rehm's *Griechentum und Goethezeit*, which treats the relationship between Winckelmann and well-known writers of the Age of Goethe and E. M. Butler's study, an attempt "to measure the intensity and the nature of the tyranny of the Greeks over some great outstanding minds".[2] In *Winckelmann and His German Critics*, Henry Hatfield examines "the impact of [Winckelmann's] dogmas upon literary criticism and production during this period [of 1755-1781]" and gives "an account of the reception which greeted his major works and the esteem in which he was held".[3] Most recently, Ludwig Uhlig's *Griechenland als Ideal* presents primary texts – chiefly essays – that illustrate the German reception of Winckelmann's image of Greece.[4] In addition to studies that focus on Winckelmann's influence in literary criticism and philosophy of aesthetics, there has been no dearth of scholarly inquiry into the impact of Winckelmann in fields, such as art history, history, and music.[5] Regarded

---

[2] Walther Rehm: *Griechentum und Goethezeit*. Bern 1951, and E. M. Butler: *The Tyranny of Greece Over Germany*. Cambridge 1935. P. 7.

[3] Henry Hatfield: *Winckelmann and His German Critics*. New York 1943. P. 1.

[4] Ludwig Uhlig: *Griechenland als Ideal*. Tübingen 1988. Other significant studies include Adolf Beck: *Griechisch-deutsche Begegnung*. Stuttgart 1947; Martin Brück: *Antikerezeption und frühromantischer Poesiebegriff. Studien zur "Gräkomanie" Friedrich Schlegels und ihrer Vorgeschichte seit J. J. Winckelmann*. Diss. Konstanz 1981; Rosemarie Elliot: *Wilhelm Heinse in Relation to Wieland, Winckelmann, and Goethe*. New York 1996; H. B. Nisbet: Laocoon in Germany. The Reception of the Group since Winckelmann. In: *German Studies* 10 (1979). Pp. 22-63; Walther Rehm: *Götterstille und Göttertrauer*. Bern 1951; Arthur Schulz: *Winckelmann und seine Welt*. Berlin 1962; and Rudolf Sühnel: *Die Götter Griechenlands und die deutsche Klassik*. Würzburg 1935.

[5] See Daniel Aebli: *Winckelmanns Entwicklungslogik der Kunst*. New York 1991; M. Kay Flavell: Winckelmann and the German Enlightenment. On the Recovery and Uses of the Past. In: *Modern Language Review* 74 (1979). Pp. 79-96; and Simon Richter: Sculpture, Music, Text. Winckelmann, Herder and Gluck's *Iphigénie en*

as a whole, the scholarship leaves little doubt as to the extent to which Winckelmann's ideas were accepted and employed by prominent figures across the spectrum of intellectual thought and artistic endeavor.

The field of drama, however, was slow to embrace the tenets of the *Gedanken*. Winckelmann's first publication faced almost immediate opposition from Gotthold Ephraim Lessing. Throughout his letters on tragedy to Friedrich Nicolai and Moses Mendelssohn (1756-57) and most succinctly in his essay *Laokoon* (1766), Lessing found fault with the stoical figure of the heroic French tragedy and its manifestation in the Gottschedian *Trauerspiel*. According to Lessing's argument, Winckelmann's hero follows in this tradition of a character with which the German audience could no longer identify. Instead, Lessing advocated the protagonist of the *bürgerliches Trauerspiel*. When in 1756 Mendelssohn writes to Lessing asking his impression of Winckelmann's first essay, Lessing answers with emphatic disapproval.[6] According to E. H. Gombrich, *Laokoon* is Lessing's response to the fear that Winckelmann's *Gedanken* essay and his major work *Geschichte der Kunst* might bring about a return in Germany to the theatrical tradition of Voltaire and French classicism.[7] Therefore, in *Laokoon*, Lessing first attacked Winckelmann's notion of the stoic as "untheatrical" before providing an alternative:

> Alles Stoische ist untheatralisch; und unser Mitleiden ist allezeit dem Leiden gleichmäßig, welches der interessierende Gegenstand äußert. Sieht man ihn sein Elend mit großer Seele ertragen, so wird diese große Seele zwar unsere Bewunderung erwecken, aber die Bewunderung ist ein kalter Affekt.[8]

As a solution, Lessing presented, both in this text and throughout his later arguments in the *Hamburgische Dramaturgie*, a different model: tragic characters with whom the audience could identify, and who expressed their emotions (though not excessively), thereby moving the audience to feel pity for them. It is this model, along with a more extreme version conceived by the *Sturm und Drang* writers, that inspired German playwrights up until the appearance of Goethe's *Iphigenie* in 1787. Since Lessing appears to have been so successful in stultifying Winckelmann's concept of "edle Einfalt und stille Größe" with regard to drama, it is not surprising that scholars might overlook Winckelmann's influence in this genre, assuming that playwrights of the late Enlightenment fell in line with Lessing's argument and ignored Winckelmann's ideas.

Tauride. In: *Goethe Yearbook* 8 (1996). Pp. 157-171.

[6] Gotthold Ephraim Lessing, Moses Mendelssohn, and Friedrich Nicolai: *Briefwechsel über das Trauerspiel*. Ed. by Jochen Schulte-Sasse. München 1972. P. 73ff.

[7] Lecture on a Master Mind: Lessing. In: *Proceedings of the British Academy* (1957). Pp. 136-156, here, pp. 140-143.

[8] Gotthold Ephraim Lessing: *Laokoon*. Stuttgart 1964. P. 11.

Before Winckelmann can be discounted, however, a closer examination of the ways in which his *Gedanken* essay might be applicable to tragic drama is warranted. In his study of Greek art, sculpture and painting, Winckelmann asserts that, for German artists, the path to greatness lies in the imitation of Greek art. Since Winckelmann does not distinguish between the plastic and the literary arts in his aesthetic theory, German playwrights could easily have interpreted his model to mean that the path to great drama, too, lies in the imitation of the Greeks. For Winckelmann, arts of ancient Greece, whether as text or as image, carry the same distinct features, which he encapsulates in his famous formulation as "edle Einfalt und stille Größe".[9] These characteristics, he writes, are exhibited not only in the Laocoon sculpture but also in Sophocles' drama *Philoctetes*: "Laokoon leidet, aber er leidet wie des Sophokles Philoktet".[10] From this specific case of the shared features, Winckelmann then posits a general principle: "Die edle Einfalt und stille Größe der griechischen Statuen ist zugleich das wahre Kennzeichen der griechischen Schriften aus den besten Zeiten".[11] Winckelmann's work thus could easily be read as suggesting to German dramatists that if they are to imitate the Greek tragedies, they must include in their *dramatis personae* characters that evince the primary features of "edle Einfalt und stille Größe". Any study of Winckelmann's influence on German drama of the Classical Period must therefore ascertain whether these particular characteristics are present in the tragedies written in that period.

It is critical, of course, to determine exactly what Winckelmann meant by his famous formulation, and, more importantly, the ways in which it was applicable to tragic figures. Although Winckelmann offers no formal definition, he does provide three contextual means for defining the phrase: an extended simile, a clear definition of what it is not, and concrete examples of what it is. Winckelmann first uses the image of the calm ocean depths to concretize his idea: "So wie die Tiefe des Meers allezeit ruhig bleibt, die Oberfläche mag noch so wüten, ebenso zeiget der Ausdruck in den Figuren der Griechen bei allen Leidenschaften eine große und gesetzte Seele".[12] With this image, he establishes a chain of binary oppositions – raging surface and calm depth, strong passions and a composed soul, painful suffering and restrained emotion – that culminate in the illustrative examples of Laocoon and Philoctetes. Winckelmann further defines the idea of the poised, self-controlled soul by describing what it is *not*, namely,

---

[9] *Winckelmanns Werke in einem Band.* Ed. by Helmut Holtzhauer. Berlin 1969. P. 20.

[10] Ibid. P. 18. The sharing of these primary features between the plastic arts and tragedies is not surprising since the Laocoon story was also the subject of an unfortunately lost tragedy by Sophocles.

[11] Ibid. P. 22.

[12] Ibid. P. 18.

"parenthyrsus" – a term used by Pseudo-Longinus to describe the exaggerations of the sublime style in rhetoric.[13] Winckelmann employs the term to depict all actions and positions that are "zu feurig und zu wild". Like "edle Einfalt und stille Größe", the concept of "parenthyrsus" also becomes clear first through an analogy and then through two concrete examples. Winckelmann likens this rhetorical concept to "eine Seele [...], die wie ein Komet aus ihrem Kreise weichet",[14] i.e., something lacking control and careening beyond its normal orbits. Winckelmann's reference to the figures of Ajax and Capaneus offers two examples of such overzealous, uncontrolled action on the Greek stage.[15] In Sophocles' tragedy *Ajax*, the title character falls into a fit of jealous rage when he is denied Achilles' armor during the Trojan war. In his madness, he slaughters sheep and cattle, mistaking them for his rivals Agamemnon and Menelaus; and after being thoroughly disgraced upon the discovery of his error, he kills himself. In Aeschylus' *Seven Against Thebes*, Capaneus, one of the seven chieftains waging war on Thebes, boasts that not even Zeus himself could stop him from scaling the city walls. Zeus responds by striking the overconfident Capaneus down with a thunderbolt. Thus, Ajax and Capaneus help to further define the concept of "edle Einfalt und stille Größe" by functioning as foils to the two positive examples of Laocoon and Philoctetes.

In Winckelmann's view, these two tragic figures, Laocoon and Philoctetes, are the quintessential embodiment of "noble simplicity and quiet grandeur". Laocoon, the main character in a lost tragedy by Sophocles, is the Trojan priest of Apollo who warns his people against accepting the Greek's gift of the Wooden Horse. When his warnings fall on deaf ears, he throws a lance into the side of the horse in order to expose its true purpose. But in doing so, Laocoon unknowingly offends Athena, the goddess of wisdom and the guardian of the Greeks, who, as punishment, sends two enormous sea serpents to strangle not only Laocoon, but his two sons. In the same way, Philoctetes, a renowned Greek archer en route to Troy along with an army of other Greeks, makes a stop at the island of Lemnos. There, he mistakenly wanders into an unmarked sacred grove and, as a result of this offense, a snake, the symbol of divine power, bites him in the foot. The wound leaves Philoctetes a cripple and emits such an odor that his friends abandon him in his agony on the island. Though ignorant of their transgressions, Philoctetes and Laocoon are made to suffer terrible afflictions.

It is this moment of suffering and the manner in which the characters endure their misery that are immortalized in the *Gedanken*. According to Winckelmann, a character must remain a stoic in his agony. A stoic, he writes, maintains an inner calm despite any external disturbances, threats, or

---

[13] For a discussion of this rhetorical term, see Max L. Baeumer: Winckelmanns Formulierung der klassischen Schönheit. In: *Monatshefte* 65 (1973). Pp. 64ff.

[14] *Winckelmanns Werke in einem Band*. P. 19.

[15] Ibid. P. 19

injury; he does not cry out but remains silent and endures his pain with fortitude. In doing so, he achieves greatness and nobility. It is this type of stoicism that in Winckelmann's view links Laocoon and Philoctetes:

> Diese Seele schildert sich in dem Gesichte des Laokoon, und nicht in dem Gesichte allein, bei dem heftigsten Leiden. Der Schmerz, welcher sich in allen Muskeln und Sehnen des Körpers entdeckt und den man ganz allein, ohne das Gesicht und andere Teile zu betrachten, an dem schmerzlich eingezogenen Unterleibe beinahe selbst zu empfinden glaubt, dieser Schmerz, sage ich, äußert sich dennoch mit keiner Wut in dem Gesichte und in der ganzen Stellung. Er erhebt kein schreckliches Geschrei, wie Virgil von seinem Laokoon singt. Die Öffnung des Mundes gestattet es nicht; es ist vielmehr ein ängstliches und beklemmtes Seufzen, wie es Sadolet beschreibt. Der Schmerz des Körpers und die Größe der Seele sind durch den ganzen Bau der Figur mit gleicher Stärke ausgeteilt und gleichsam abgewogen. Laokoon leidet, aber er leidet wie des Sophokles Philoktetes: sein Elend geht uns bis an die Seele, aber wir wünschten, wie dieser große Mann das Elend ertragen zu können.[16]

Clearly, Winckelmann is part of a stoic tradition in Germany that extends back as far as the Baroque with Martin Opitz' translation of Seneca's *Trojan Women* in 1625. The neo-Stoics of the Baroque fused Christian morality with Stoic ethics;[17] that is, they read the stoic term *constantia* to mean the ability to maintain not only a constant emotional state but also a steadfast commitment to specific high-minded principles, in their case, Christian tenets. Hence, the martyr play was a favored Baroque genre. In the early Enlightenment, Gottsched and his followers fashioned stoical heroes, beginning with Cato, who were committed to Enlightenment's ideals, such as freedom and virtue, but did not always maintain calm or composed under duress.[18] Winckelmann's understanding of stoicism, however, differs dramatically from that of his immediate predecessors: he breaks the tie with Christian morality and Enlightenment principles and focuses exclusively on that part of the stoic tradition that champions emotional restraint.

---

[16] Ibid. P. 18.

[17] Thomas G. Rosenmeyer: *Senecan Drama und Stoic Cosmology*. Berkeley 1989. P. 13.

[18] While it is true, as Robert Heitner argues, that Cato "sets virtue and republican ideals above every other consideration [... and] is called a hero [...] because he has clung firmly to virtue in spite of many misfortunes", his love of freedom gives way to fanaticism, and his stoic demeanor to suicide. "The act of suicide", which Heitner points out, "was completely out of harmony with the philosophy of the German Enlightenment, because it was the most overt admission possible that [...] one's emotions had run away with reason". Robert Heitner: *German Tragedy in the Age of Enlightenment*. Berkeley 1963. Pp. 27 and 29 respectively.

In *Geschichte der Kunst*, Winckelmann offers another – perhaps his most extreme – example of a tragic figure who embodies the concept of "edle Einfalt und stille Größe". In contrast to the two Sophoclean characters Laocoon and Philoctetes, Niobe consciously defies the gods. Niobe, the title character of a tragedy by Aeschylus of which we have only fragments,[19] is the queen of Thebes and the mother of 14 children. The pride she derives from bearing so many offspring leads her to commit an act of hubris. Boasting that she is superior to the goddess Leto, who had only two children, Queen Niobe refuses to worship Leto and even suggests that the women of Thebes worship her, their queen, instead of their guardian goddess. Leto's children, Apollo and Artemis, avenge this insult to their mother's honor by eliminating Niobe's children one by one. Although it is Niobe's overblown pride that is the cause of her punishment, she bears her tragic losses with as much stoicism as Sophocles' two protagonists Laocoon and Philoctetes. In fact, she is the epitome of the silent stoic: her suffering causes her to turn to stone, voiceless and motionless. Thus, Winckelmann offers up Niobe, along with Laocoon, as a prime example of the stoic figure.[20] It is her silence that Winckelmann finds so remarkable in Aeschylus' tragedy:

> [D]aher führte Aeschylus die Niobe stillschweigend auf in seinem Trauerspiele. Ein solcher Zustand, wo Empfindung und Überlegung aufhört, und welcher der Gleichgültigkeit ähnlich ist, verändert keine Züge der Gestalt und der Bildung, und der große Künstler konnte hier die höchste Schönheit bilden, so wie er sie gebildet hat: denn Niobe und ihre Töchter sind und bleiben die höchsten Ideen derselben.[21]

In his discussion of the ancient Greeks, Philoctetes, Laocoon, and Niobe emerge as the three examples of the types of characters Winckelmann considers to be the highest achievement of Greek art and Greek tragedy. And it is through these three paradigmatic examples that Winckelmann offers clearly defined models for German dramatists to emulate in their own struggles to produce "great art".

Although the tendency among scholars has been to analyze Winckelmann's work on Greek art in terms of its relevance to aesthetic theory, sculpture, and literature, his texts make plain reference to the tragedies as

---

[19] For a discussion of the Niobe tragedy by Aeschylus, see Wolfgang Schadewaldt: Die Niobe des Aischylos. In: *Sitzungsberichte der Heidelberger Akademie der Wissenschaften* 24 (1933). Pp. 3-32.

[20] Winckelmann considered these two works (the Laocoon group and Niobe) "[zwei] der schönsten Werke des Altertums: von welchen das eine ein Bild der Todesfurcht, das andere des höchsten Leidens und Schmerzes ist". *Winckelmanns Werke in einem Band*. P. 214.

[21] Ibid.

well, in particular those of Aeschylus and Sophocles. The one 18th-century dramatic work that is routinely regarded as a response to and a representation of Winckelmann's tenets is, of course, Goethe's *Iphigenie*. Here, the heroine, torn between conflicting loyalties and facing both her own imminent execution and that of her brother and her cousin, responds to the challenge with courage and tranquility.

Before turning our attention to Goethe's portrayal of *Iphigenie*, however, we must examine yet another exemplary figure of Greek tragedy, the one who graces the cover of Winckelmann's *Gedanken* essay, Iphigenia at Aulis. Winckelmann, to my knowledge, does not discuss Euripides' play *Iphigenia at Aulis* or its eponymous protagonist in either his writings or his letters. We can only speculate as to why he chose to have his artist friend Adam Friedrich Oeser decorate the essay's cover with an engraving that depicts the sacrifice of Iphigenia, Agamemnon's daughter.[22] But read in the context of the other three dramatic figures just mentioned, the story of Iphigenia at Aulis offers many similarities. While Iphigenia, like Niobe, is punished for an act of hubris, it is her father's, not her own. While waiting for the Greek fleet to gather at Aulis before sailing to Troy, Agamemnon shoots one of Artemis' sacred deer. Pleased with his marksmanship, the King boasts that Artemis herself could not have done better. To punish Agamemnon, Artemis calms the winds, thereby hindering the Greeks' voyage to Troy. The winds, she promises, will not blow again until Agamemnon agrees to sacrifice his oldest and most cherished daughter, Iphigenia. In Euripides' tragedy, Iphigenia, like the other dramatic figures Winckelmann holds in high esteem, accepts her punishment with dignity

---

[22] Winckelmann mentions the frontispiece in two letters, but in neither of them does he discuss the subject of Iphigenia. In one letter (dated 3 June 1755) to Konrad Friedrich Uden, a fellow student at Halle, Winckelmann identifies the subject of the vignette as Iphigenia: "Das erste Kupfer ist das Opfer der Iphigenia. Wie aber kommt das Opfer zu dieser Schrift? Man weiß nicht warum ich das gethan habe: und ich weiß es wohl, und habe es Sr. Majest. schriftlich erkläret. Der Mahler ist Timanthes – die griechischen Worte werden es erklären". *Briefe*. Ed. by Hans Diepolder and Walther Rehm. 4 Vols. Berlin 1957. Vol I. P. 172. Unfortunately, the written explanation that Winckelmann indicates here did not survive. However, another explanation did. In a letter (dated 4 June 1755) to Hieronymus Dietrich Berendis, another close friend from Winckelmann's student days at Halle, he writes that this Iphigenia engraving, which depicts a painter at work, represents the act of imitation: "Das erste Kupfer ist die Nachahmung. Der Mahler ist Timanthes" (*Briefe* I. P. 177). But this letter, too, indicates nothing regarding Winckelmann's opinion of the painting's subject matter.

The essay also includes two other vignettes by Oeser. One depicts the Persian Sinetas offering a handful of water to the Persian King; the other shows Socrates at the entrance to the Acropolis. For a further discussion of these engravings, see Walther Rehm's notes in his edition of *Johann Joachim Winckelmann. Kleine Schriften, Vorreden, Entwürfe*. Berlin 1969. Pp. 325 and 424.

and resolves to die well and gloriously to "[put] away from [her] whatever is weak and ignoble".[23] And like Laocoon and Niobe, Iphigenia demonstrates serene resolve in the end, announcing to her father: "Silent, unflinching, I offer my neck to the knife".[24] The chorus of women praises Iphigenia for playing her part with "nobleness";[25] and Achilles calls her "a noble heart".[26] Although one can only surmise Winckelmann's intentions when he chose or agreed to this illustration for the cover of the *Gedanken*, one must characterize as striking the similarities between this Iphigenia, a noble figure suffering in silence, and the other dramatic figures that Winckelmann privileges in his work.

Just as we can only speculate on Winckelmann's reasons for using the Iphigenia engraving, we must also leave unanswered the question as to the influence this image might have had on Goethe's choice of Iphigenia as the main character for his like-named play. Although much has been written both on *Iphigenie*, which Goethe revised in Rome in 1786 while reading Winckelmann,[27] and on Winckelmann's influence on Goethe, there is, to my knowledge, no comment by Goethe on this illustrated cover. Nor has any scholar remarked on the image's relevance to Goethe's play.[28] We do know, however, that during his student days at Leipzig (1765-68), Goethe became a friend of the director of the Leipziger Akademie, Adam Friedrich Oeser. We also know from letters and from Goethe's comments in his autobiographical text *Dichtung und Wahrheit* that Oeser introduced him to Winckelmann's views of ancient Greece. But whether the two ever discussed Oeser's engraving on the cover of Winckelmann's text is a mystery. The fact remains, however, that when Goethe read Winckelmann's *Gedanken* or referred to it while writing his own tragedy, he would have had before him Oeser's image of a stoic Iphigenia at Aulis.

---

[23] Euripides: *Iphigenia at Aulis*. Trans. Charles R. Walker. In: *The Complete Greek Tragedies*. Ed. by David Grene and Richard Lattimore. Chicago 1958. P. 290.

[24] Ibid. Pp. 304-305.

[25] Ibid. P. 291.

[26] Ibid. P. 292.

[27] Goethe began writing in the final weeks of 1778, completing a prose-version in 1779. For a general chronology of the play's composition, see Trevelyan's *Goethe and the Greeks*. Cambridge 1941. Pp. 94-148.

[28] For Goethe's comments on his *Iphigenie*, see the appendix "Goethe und seine Zeitgenossen über *Iphigenie auf Tauris*" in volume 5 of the Hamburger Ausgabe of Goethe's works, pp. 403-410. For Goethe's comments on Winckelmann, see *Winckelmann und Goethe* edited by Die Nationalen Forschungs- und Gedenkstätten der klassischen deutschen Literatur in Weimar. Erfurt no date. Pp. 61-124. For an analysis of the role of Winckelmann in Goethe's writing, see Walther Rehm: *Griechentum und Goethezeit*. 2nd ed. Bern 1968. Pp. 114-190; E. M. Butler: *The Tyranny of Greece Over Germany*. Cambridge 1935. Pp. 85-154; and Humphrey Trevelyan: *Goethe and the Greeks*. Cambridge 1941.

Let us now turn from speculation to what we *do* know about Winckelmann's influence on drama, that is, on Goethe's one completed tragedy set in Greece.[29] The history of Goethe's rewriting of *Iphigenie* during his sojourn in Rome while reading Winckelmann's *Geschichte* is well documented.[30] We do not need to retrace this history but simply to highlight how the play presents Winckelmann's ideas for the stage.[31]

The title character , Iphigenie, fits the Winckelmannian model well. Like Laocoon, Philoctetes, and Iphigenia at Aulis, Goethe's Iphigenie is forced to suffer, but in her case, the pain stems from an internal struggle as opposed to an external injury. While Laocoon struggles with deadly snakes and Philoctetes suffers from an incurable wound, Iphigenie agonizes over a seemingly intractable dilemma. In this version of the myth, Iphigenie is not killed at Aulis but whisked away unharmed by the goddess Diana (the Roman name for Artemis) and brought to the shores of Tauris. There Iphigenie serves as the priestess to Diana and helps civilize both Thoas, the king who has befriended her like a father, and the Taurians, whose laws demand they kill any foreigner who lands on their shores. Thus, when Iphigenie's brother, Orestes, and his friend and cousin Pylades arrive at Tauris to kidnap Iphigenie secretly and to bring her back to Argos, they are in immediate danger. Aware of the rescue attempt and of Orestes' ploy to take the sacred icon of Diana with them, Iphigenie must choose between two sets of loyalties: loyalty to her brother or to her surrogate father, Thoas,[32] and

---

[29] In addition to *Iphigenie auf Tauris*, Goethe did attempt other dramas set in Greece (*Nausikaa*, *Elpenor*, and *Pandora*), but all three remained unfinished.

[30] See footnotes 27 and 28.

[31] Johann Wolfgang von Goethe. *Iphigenie auf Tauris. Goethes Werke.* Hamburger Ausgabe in 14 Bänden. Ed. by Lieselotte Blumenthal and Eberhard Haufe. München 1988. Vol. 5. Pp. 7-67.

[32] Goethe makes Iphigenie's dilemma more difficult by suggesting the bond of hospitality is just as strong as the bond to her family. The text makes this comparison most clearly when Orestes begins to narrate the final episodes of the House of Atreus and Iphigenie responds so emotionally. Her emotional outburst causes Orestes to ask: "Bist du gastfreundlich diesem Königshause, / Bist du mit nähern Banden ihm verbunden / Wie deine schöne Freude mir verrät". Goethe: *Iphigenie*. P. 34.

The dramatic irony here is clear enough since we, and not Orestes, know how closely she is connected to the House of Atreus. But Orestes asks if her joy at the news that Electra and he are still alive stems from a guest-host relationship with his family, not whether she is a distant relative. His question signals the importance in this story of the bond between guest and host. If the guest-host relationship is likened to the ties that bind a family, the choice that Iphigenie must make later between Orestes and Thoas is necessarily akin to a choice between brother and father. Iphigenie even refers to her host as a "zweiter Vater" (1641) and tells him that he is as dear and valued as her father (2156). But the fact that Orestes' first guess at the cause of her emotional outburst is the bond of hospitality suggests that this bond between guest and host is

loyalty to her beloved homeland or to the Taurians whom she has helped to civilize.[33] In the end, she overcomes this struggle and rises to greatness and nobility by performing an "unerhörte Tat": she confesses to Thoas her brother's plan of deception and puts her trust in the King. In doing so, Iphigenie sets a new standard for humanity, as summarized in Orestes' final four lines:

> Gewalt und List, der Männer höchster Ruhm,
> Wird durch die Wahrheit dieser hohen Seele
> Beschämt und reines kindliches Vertrauen
> Zu einem edeln Manne wird belohnt. (2142-45)

By coming to terms with her dilemma, Goethe's Iphigenie achieves an internal serenity similar to that reached by Laocoon, Philoctetes, Oedipus, Niobe, and Euripides' Iphigenia.

Although Goethe's play does not contain the phrase "edle Einfalt und stille Größe", his contemporaries recognized how his Iphigenie implicitly embodied Winckelmann's ideas. A review of the play in the *Gothaische gelehrte Zeitungen* (20 October 1787) praises the drama in Winckelmann's terms: "Welch eine Simplizität, und doch zugleich welch ein Interesse im Gang und Plane des Ganzen, welch eine Wahrheit und edle Einfalt in den Charakteren und Gesinnungen!"[34] In his "Über die *Iphigenie auf Tauris*" (1789), Schiller echoes similar sentiments: "Man findet hier die imponierende große Ruhe".[35] In a letter (dated 21 December 1797) to Christian Gottfried Körner, Wilhelm von Humboldt stresses the external simplicity of the play and the internal peace that Iphigenie achieves: "Hier nun ist der Stoff ganz antik, großenteils sogar die Charaktere und Ideen, und der deutsche Dichter hat dem Stück gar keine Pracht, gar keinen äußeren Glanz gegeben. Er hat alles allein in den inneren Gehalt gelegt [...]. [D]ie hohe, stille und bescheidene Größe des Innern wird immer ihr Recht behaupten".[36]

---

nearly as strong as the bond between family members. This comparison then implies that her choosing between Orestes and Thoas is similar to choosing between brother and father. Goethe: *Iphigenie*. P. 52 and p. 67 respectively.

[33] In his article "On Bringing Statues to Life", R. C. Ockenden makes a similar argument concerning the consequences of Iphigenie's decision to hide Orestes' plan from Thoas: "By not telling Thoas the truth and appealing to his humanity, she is relegating him forever to the rank of barbarian". In: *Publications of the English Goethe Society* 51 (1980). Pp. 69-106, here p. 76.

[34] *Goethes Werke*. P. 412.

[35] Ibid. P. 413

[36] Ibid. P. 413. This practice of employing Winckelmannian terms without explicitly mentioning his name to describe *Iphigenie* was not, of course, confined to Goethe's contemporaries. For example, in Hermann Hettner's comprehensive *Geschichte der deutschen Literatur im XVIII. Jahrhundert* (Leipzig 1929), concepts such as

Twentieth-century scholars have been more explicit in drawing the connection between Winckelmann and Goethe's *Iphigenie*. In *Griechentum und Goethezeit*, Rehm points out that it is Winckelmann's ideas that make Goethe's play possible: "Ohne [Winckelmann] und seinen begeisternden Hinweis auf die adlig-vollkommenen Menschen der griechischen Kunst, ohne sein Wort von der edlen Einfalt und stillen Größe wäre die Iphigenie nicht möglich gewesen".[37] Butler too makes clear the relationship of Winckelmann and Goethe in *The Tyranny of Greece Over Germany*: "Goethe created in *Iphigenie* what Winckelmann had seen in Laocoon: noble simplicity and serene greatness in the heroine, and the conquest of pain and suffering by sublimity of soul".[38] In an article on the prehistory of Winckelmann's formulation of "edle Einfalt und stille Größe", Alfred Kamphausen adds his voice to those who view Goethe's title character as the fulfillment of Winckelmann's ideas: "'Edle Einfalt und stille Größe', der Tiefe des unermeßlichen Meeres gleichgesetzt, diese trotz aller Vorwegnahmen in ähnlich klingenden Postulaten doch Winckelmannsche Setzung wurde in Goethes Iphigenie erfüllt und trug somit ihre köstliche Frucht".[39] And as recently as 1990, F. J. Lamport in his *German Classical Drama* describes the Greece of *Iphigenie* as "the Greece of the 'edle Einfalt und stille Größe' [...] praised by the art historian Winckelmann as the hallmark of Greek art and Greek humanity".[40]

These remarks assume that Goethe's play was the first example of Winckelmann's influence on German drama. But any examination of the link between Goethe's *Iphigenie* and Winckelmann's two key works should seriously consider an important question: Given Winckelmann's effect on Goethe during the latter's trip to Italy in 1786-87 and the fact that Winckelmann's ideas were so well known before that date, could not other playwrights prior to Goethe have been similarly influenced?

The answer to this question is yes. In the remainder of this paper, I will show that the type of Winckelmannian stoic heroine Goethe presents in his *Iphigenie*, which others have viewed as revolutionary, had already been anticipated by the Viennese playwright Joseph Bernhard Pelzel in 1780, seven years before the publication of the seminal work of German Classicism. In *Das gerächte Troja*, Pelzel's radical adaptation of *The Trojan Women*, Pelzel's treatment of Hecuba, the wife of Priam and the mother of Hector, breaks from a long-held tradition (established by such writers as Euripides,

"plastische Ruhe", "veredelte und vertiefte" (p. 40), and "anmutige Einfachheit" (p. 41) are used to demonstrate the differences between the 1779 prose-version and the 1786 verse-version of Goethe's play.

[37] Rehm: *Griechentum*. Pp. 126-127.

[38] Butler: *Tyranny*. P. 101

[39] Alfred Kamphausen: Johann Joachim Winckelmann. In: *Beiträge zur Kunst- und Kulturgeschichte* 38 (1969). Pp. 7-17, here, pp. 10-11.

[40] F. J. Lamport: *German Classical Drama*. Cambridge 1990. P. 81.

Ovid, and Dante) of portraying the Trojan queen as what Dante called a "yelping bitch", a woman who exhibits no restraint in her suffering. In contrast, Pelzel makes a significant change to Hecuba's character – transforming her from an hysterical, emotionally overwrought mother into a self-controlled, stoical figure who can endure grief and horror with Job-like patience.

Since the only review of Pelzel's *Das gerächte Troja* was extremely critical,[41] it is not surprising that scholars have virtually ignored the play.[42] But Pelzel himself was not an unknown playwright in Vienna in his day. Although his first tragedy *Yariko* (1770), a one-act rendition of the tragic tale of the American-Indian woman Yarico and her beloved Englishman Inkle, was not met with critical praise, it did enjoy commercial success. As Lawrence Marsden Price points out in his *Inkle and Yarico Album*, "[w]hatever the critics may have thought, this one-act tragedy seems to have been one of the most popular German dramas on the subject. It was reprinted four times between 1776 and 1778".[43] Moreover, the recently opened Burgtheater staged the play 23 times between 1776 and 1794.[44] Although none of his other ten plays (seven comedies and three tragedies, including *Das gerächte Troja*) ever attained the same level of popular acclaim, three of them had a combined total of eight performances at the Burgtheater.[45] *Das gerächte Troja*, however, was not among them and never reached the stage there or anywhere else. Thus, it is understandable that this particular play of Pelzel's has gone virtually unnoticed until now. But a closer look – in the context of the play's role as a precursor to German Classicism – may well cast Pelzel's work in a different light.

Pelzel's tragedy *Das gerächte Troja*, as the title suggests, centers on the fall of Troy. Similar to Euripides' two surviving plays on the same subject (*Hecuba* and *The Trojan Women*), Pelzel's drama treats the plight of the

---

[41] The reviewer in *Allgemeine deutsche Bibliothek* 52 (1782) praises Pelzel for his choice of subject and meter, but bemoans the flat characters:
> [a]ber das wäre dann auch wohl alles Lob, was diesem Dichter gebühret, dessen Scenen mehr Deklamation als Handlung enthalten, dessen Situationen zwar für das Auge ganz gute Gemälde geben, aber meistentheils das Herz kalt lassen, dessen Personen sich all äußerst gleichförmig und monotonisch ausdrücken, und dessen Iamben fast durchgehends hart und ungeschmeidig sind. (137)

[42] The only scholarly treatment of this play is contained in Tadeus Kachlak's brief study of the reception of *The Trojan Women*, which includes Euripides, Seneca, Opitz, and Johann Elias Schlegel, but Kachlak limits his analysis of Pelzel's version to two paragraphs: *Die Troerinnen* – eine antike und moderne Warnung vor dem Krieg. In: *Schriften zur Geschichte und Kultur der Antike* 6 (1973). Pp. 139-54, here pp. 151-152.

[43] Lawrence Marsden Price: *Inkle and Yarico Album*. Berkeley 1937. P. 114

[44] Otto Rub: *Das Burgtheater*. Wien 1913. P. 5

[45] Ibid. P. 227.

defeated Trojan women as they are about to leave their destroyed city. As in the Greek originals, the Trojan women here are forced to witness the executions of both Hecuba's daughter Polixena and Andromacha's son Astianax, as well as the spectacle of the Greeks as they divide the surviving women among themselves as spoils of war. Although the female characters are obviously not Greek and thus could fall outside the scope of this paper on technical grounds, these women and their tragedy have been so intimately intertwined with the Greeks since the time of Homer and so integrally a part of the Greek theatrical repertoire since Euripides (415 B.C.) that they are virtually inseparable from the Greek tradition.

The first half of *Das gerächte Troja* is typical of many of the *Sturm und Drang* plays written during the mid-1760s to mid-1780s. As in the Greek originals, the women, wailing in terse, exclamatory language, lament the loss of their fathers, husbands, children, and city. The scene in which Andromacha first appears after a failed search for her missing son Astianax is a prime example:

Andromacha:		Hekuba!
Hekuba:	Andromacha!	
Andromacha:	Ach!	
Hekuba:		Ach! [...] von deinem Mund
		Erwartete ich diese Thräne nicht![46]

Moreover, the play concentrates on the emotions the women experience and discloses their emotional states both through their own words and through the stage directions. The depth of Andromacha's anguish is revealed as she recalls her reaction seeing Pirrhus, the son of Achilles, who instigated the sacrifice of Hekuba's daughter Polixena: "Es / Empörete sich da mein ganzes Blut! / Und ich warf einen Blick dem Pirrhus zu, / In dem ich ihm den ganzen Abscheu wies".[47] When Pirrhus then appears before Hekuba, the stage directions also underscore the Trojan queen's distress: "Sie war geflohn, und ruft jetzt mit Thränen, und hastig".[48] In the strength of the characters' emotional reactions, Pelzel not only follows here the example of typical dramas of this period but also adheres to the emotional tone of Euripides' original.

At the same time, however, Pelzel breaks with both traditions by presenting heroines of a more stoical type, as suggested by his first reviewer. In the midst of the above-mentioned scene, the outwardly expressed emotions of Andromacha and Hekuba are juxtaposed with the strong, stoic stance of Kassandra. Andromacha reports to the other women that she observed the doomed prophetess surrounded by the Greeks, as if ringed by

---

[46] Joseph Bernhard Pelzel: *Das gerächte Troja*. Wien 1780. (not paginated) II.5.

[47] Ibid.

[48] Ibid.

tigers, yet completely silent ("stum"): "sie sprach kein Wort, / Das ein Wehmut angezeigt; es floß / Vom Auge keine Thräne, welche mich / Willkommen hieß ... / In eines Aeaziden schrecklicher Gewalt! umringt von hundert Tiegern, des / Achilles Kriegern, die gelagert sind / Um sie".[49]

In her silence, Pelzel's Trojan priestess stands in stark contrast to her Euripidean counterpart. When Cassandra first appears in Euripides' *The Trojan Women*, she has just learned that she is to become a Greek's slave and is in a state of bacchanalian frenzy, symbolized by the flaming torch that she cannot carry upright. Her mother describes Cassandra as "crazed, passionate" and announces that her "fate is intemperate as [she is], always".[50] Thus, if Pelzel's play had wanted to emphasize highly emotional states, it could easily have incorporated the traditional Euripidean portrayal of Cassandra. But Andromacha's report of Kassandra's stoic stance in her struggle against the Greeks points to another tradition. To compare Kassandra's silence while at the mercy of "tigers" with Laocoon's stoic struggle with the snakes might initially appear overly ambitious. But if one recalls Kassandra and Laocoon's common history, then the connection between the two figures seems much less coincidental. According to Homer, when the Greek wooden horse first appeared at the gates of Troy, only two people urged the Trojans to reject the Greek gift and destroy it: the priest Laocoon and Priam's daughter, the priestess Cassandra. Both of their warnings were ignored. Laocoon was then attacked on the shore by two giant sea serpents and, after a stoic struggle (at least in Winckelmann's view), was strangled as the snakes tightened their coils around him. Note the similarities in Kassandra's plight, surrounded as she is by metaphorical tigers, on the very same shore upon which Laocoon succumbed to the sea serpents.

Pelzel's treatment of Hekuba also breaks from another long-standing tradition that portrays the Trojan queen as a tormented woman lacking self-control. In the introduction to his translation of Euripides' *Hecuba*, William Arrowsmith highlights the traditional presentation of the Trojan queen:

Along with Croesus, Oedipus, and Priam, the figure of Hecuba, the *mater dolorosa* of Troy transformed by suffering into the "bitch of Cynossema", survived in classical imagination as a supreme example of the severest degradation the reversal of human fortune can inflict. From Euripides on, through Ovid, medieval literature, and Dante to the "mobled queen" of Hamlet's players, the image persists with extraordinary purity, untampered with, almost unchanged.[51]

Pelzel's Hekuba initially adheres to this well-established model. Before her appearance on stage, one of the Trojan women reports that Hekuba was

[49] Ibid.

[50] Euripides: *Iphigenia*. P. 140.

[51] In: *The Complete Greek Tragedies*. Ed. by David Grene and Richard Lattimore. Chicago 1958. P. 2.

moved to tears at the loss of her daughter Polixena: "Wie hingesenkt! [...] Vielleicht die harte Thrän' / an ihrem Auge noch nicht trocken, die / Bey Polixenens Scheiden floß!".[52] When Hekuba does arrive, the stage directions also underscore her disturbed state: "Sie birgt ihr Antlitz, und läßt dem Schmerzen freyen Lauf".[53]

Hekuba's emotional reaction to her plight remains unchecked throughout the second and third acts, which is understandable considering what then occurs. Achilles' son, Pirrhus, who sacrificed Polixena at his father's grave, apparently has had a change of heart when he appears before Hekuba and the other Trojan women. His aim now is to help the remaining Trojan women escape. Hekuba, however, is skeptical and Pirrhus attempts to prove his sincerity by gathering forces loyal to him and staging an attack on Uliß and his Greek army. Meanwhile, Uliß pretends to have undergone a similar conversion. He announces to the Trojan women that he wishes to help Andromacha spare her son Astianax by presenting him before the Greek assembly. In truth the wily Greek actually plans to throw the child off the ramparts of Troy and, in doing so, completely extinguish Hector's line.

Throughout these maneuvers by the Greek leaders, Andromacha, who functions as Hekuba's foil, is unable to control her emotions – even when her child's life depends on it. Uliß, who has been searching for Astianax among the surviving Trojan children, finds a boy but is uncertain of his identity. To establish it, Uliß has the child paraded out unexpectedly while he is talking with Andromacha. Her maternal feelings overwhelm her, as indicated by the stage directions: "sie [...] ruft wild und ungestüm".[54] It is this emotional outburst that allows Uliß to identify Astianax which eventually results in her own and her son's undoing.

Beginning with the fourth act, Hekuba, unlike Andromacha, undergoes a transformation. In the first scene, Andromacha and Hekuba prepare to hand over Astianax to Uliß, who has promised to protect him. Whereas Andromacha weeps, the stage directions indicate that Hekuba is silent: "Hinter [Andromacha] mit ruhigem, aber rührend traurigem Gang, Hekuba".[55] The contrast between the two becomes more evident as the scene develops. On the one hand, Andromacha regrets that she can no longer control her emotions: "Ich wäre ruhiger! [...] / Ich kann nicht! / [...] ich habe zittern gelernt, / Und flehn, und heiße Thränen weinen".[56] On the other hand, Hekuba remains calm and stoic as she explains to Andromacha how she must learn to bear her terrible fate. To emphasize the difference between the two women, Pelzel employs Winckelmannian language in the stage directions to

[52] Pelzel: *Troja*. II.3.
[53] Ibid. II.4.
[54] Ibid. III.3.
[55] Ibid. IV.1.
[56] Ibid.

describe Hekuba: "Mit stiller Größe und ruhiger Trauer".[57] By imitating almost precisely the structure of Winckelmann's famous phrase, Pelzel immediately removes his Hekuba from the Euripidean tradition and places her alongside the heroes that Winckelmann had chosen as models. Hekuba then departs to comfort the other Trojan women and encourage them also to bear their lot with fortitude and grace.

Hekuba's advice and example have no effect whatsoever on Andromacha, however, which is understandable and fitting for her character. Uliß appears and convinces her to give up Astianax with the promise that he will protect the young boy. Shortly after Uliß departs with Astianax, Pirrhus arrives with the Cretan King, Idomeneus, and announces that they are ready to set sail and to bring the Trojan women to safety on Crete. When the two Greeks discover that Astianax has been handed over, Idomeneus reveals to Andromacha that Uliß plans to break his word and execute her son. He then offers to take Andromacha with him. Since she does not want Hekuba to see her suffering, she accepts Idomeneus' offer and departs with the following words: "führt mich / Aus Mitleid fort, Cretenser!"[58]

Andromacha's final words suggest that her character will not accept Hekuba's advice; consequently she remains the queen's foil. Through these two characters, Pelzel presents two distinct visions of the tragic heroine. Andromacha's emotional outbursts, historically typical for the portrayal of her character, seem intended to move the audience to pity her, as Idomeneus does. Thus, her character fits easily into the *Sturm und Drang* tradition. But the fact that Andromacha departs the stage in act IV suggests that it is not her character but rather Hekuba's that Pelzel wants his audience to identify with and imitate in the end.

Pelzel's preference for Hekuba is evident, as it is she who commands the stage for the remainder of the play. Immediately following Andromacha's departure, Hekuba reappears to discover Andromacha and Astianax disappeared. Once more Pelzel tests his main character by subjecting her to trying circumstances, and once again she proves her mettle. While the other women cry in their grief, Hekuba "bezwingt ihre Empfindungen".[59] Moreover, even though she finds this latest blow to be devastating, she tells her fellow Trojans that she "will / Ihn überwinden".[60]

The final test comes at the end of act IV, when Pirrhus' forces fall to Agamemnon's. Although this means that Hekuba's last hope for escape have been dashed, the Trojan queen remains stoic to the end and encourages the other women to do the same. As a model for them to follow, she suggests her daughter Polixena:

---

[57] Ibid. IV.1.
[58] Ibid. IV.8.
[59] Ibid. IV.9.
[60] Ibid. IV.10.

Führt ihr das Loos der Polixena zu
Gemüthe […] Polixenen am Altar!..
Wie groß die Edle litt! wie groß sie starb
Die ganz Unglückliche … daß ohne Klag'
Auch sie vor ihrem Loos erschien', und den
Olimp beschäme, welcher über sie
Solch schweres Loos verhängt.[61]

Since Hekuba's invocation of Polixena is Pelzel's innovation (it does not occur in Euripides' *Trojan Women*), the reference to the child supports the argument that Pelzel is attempting to cast Hekuba in a new light by rewriting her character according to Winckelmannian notions. Polixena's death closely resembles that of Iphigenia, who, as pointed out earlier, graces the cover of Winckelmann's *Gedanken* essay. The parallels between the two women are striking. Like Iphigenia at Aulis, Polixena is sentenced to death to make amends for a crime that she did not commit. In Polixena's case, the legend tells us that Achilles, upon seeing her during a truce between the Greeks and Trojans, falls in love with Polixena and agrees to try to bring about peace if Priam will give her to him as a wife. It is when Achilles goes to the temple of Apollo in Troy to marry Polixena that her brother Paris kills him. Achilles' ghost later appears and demands the sacrifice of Polixena. Thus, in the same way that Iphigenia is sacrificed to atone for Agamemnon's transgression in shooting one of Artemis' sacred deer, so too is Polixena sacrificed to avenge the death of Achilles by Paris' deadly arrow. In both instances, the two women accept their fate willingly and silently. Their stoic demeanor in turn causes observers to remark on their noble bearing. The words by the chorus of Greek women and by Achilles on Iphigenia's noble deeds in Euripides' *Iphigenia at Aulis*[62] are echoed by Coryphaeus, one of the Trojan women in Euripides' *Hecuba*, who describes Polixena's heroic actions: "Nobility of birth / is a stamp and seal, conspicuous and sharp. / But true nobility allied to birth is a greatness and a glory".[63] Thus, it would not be incorrect to call Polixena the "Iphigenia" of Troy.

With Polixena, then, serving as a model, it comes as no surprise that as Agememnon approaches to carry off Hekuba, she prepares to receive him "[e]insam, und ruhig".[64] The stoicism of Pelzel's Hekuba is in stark contrast to her Euripidean counterpart, who neither calls up the image of Polixena nor exhibits any signs of composure. To underscore this new paradigm shift, Polixena's name is invoked by the other key stoic figure, Kassandra. As the Trojan priestess departs for Sparta as Menelaus' slave, she nevertheless consoles her mother and encourages her to be strong:

[61] Ibid. V.2.
[62] See my earlier discussion of this point.
[63] Euripides: *Hecuba*. p. 25.
[64] Pelzel: *Troja*. V.2.

> Betrüb dich nicht.
> Du sollest sehn, wie ich in mein Geschick
> Mich füg'. Ich denk' an Polixenens Loos:
> Und dein nicht unwerth, Königinn, trink ich
> Den bittern Kelch […]
> Und ohne Klage will
> Ich scheiden […]
> Du sollst Kassandrens Wehmut nicht
> Mehr hören.[65]

Thus, in the same way that Hekuba employed Polixena's model of stoic behavior as means to console the Trojan women, Kassandra uses her sister's name and example to comfort her mother and to serve as a source of strength.

At first Hekuba is unable to follow her own advice or that of her daughter. The sight of Astianax's broken body proves too much. Hekuba lashes out at the Greeks, her fellow Trojan women, and, as the stage directions indicate, even the gods: "Sie blickt den Olimp an, als klagte sie die Götter an, daß sie so einen Mord gestattet" (V.8). Although these outbursts cause her initially to appear weak and inconsistent, they do add depth to her character. Moreover, they prevent her from seeming distant, cold, and unapproachable. Most importantly, in allowing these emotions to be expressed, Pelzel, like Goethe with Iphigenie, is able to emphasize the effort it takes for his character to bring those feelings of anger and despair under control. Hekuba's ability to overcome these powerful human emotions places her squarely alongside the other heroes whom Winckelmann so admires.

The stage directions in Pelzel's play show Hekuba's evolution as it occurs. As Uliß approaches to take Hekuba away as a slave, she undergoes her final transformation:

> Als [Hekuba] vernahm, daß sie Ulissens Sklavinn werde – bebte sie – aber schnell hörte ihr Seufzen auf. Sie sank auf ihren Sitz, und saß, das Antlitz offen, die Hand mit Stolz, und Stärke gestützt. Hier sah man an ihr nicht mehr die wilde Wut, die Verzweiflung, und ein vor Wehmuth schluchzend Herz: Man sah den stolzen Schmerz, das Aug voll Empörung, und Hochmut. Da Uliß eintritt, […] tritt [sie] mit stillem Schmerz in ihrer ganzen Majestät vor ihn.[66]

In essence, Pelzel's Hekuba is another Laocoon, the embodiment of Winckelmann's "stille Größe". Even when Uliß orders his men to put her in chains and bring her to his ship, Hekuba maintains her self-control: "Ihnen

---

[65] Ibid. V.2.
[66] Ibid. V.9.

entgegen eilend, und sich in ihrer ganzen Grösse darstellend".[67] And when Pirrhus' forces attack Uliß' and the other Greeks flee, Hekuba tells the other Trojan women to scatter and hide; she, however, will remain to face her fate with dignity: "nicht weinen – sterben da – als Mutter, die / Nur Helden Ilion gebahr".[68] Not only does she now follow the example set by her daughter Polixena, but she also provides the proper model for the other women to emulate – a connection immediately made clear through a comment by Theone, one of Hekuba's companions: "Ihr Mund schweigt. Ahmen wir ihr Schweigen nach".[69] Theone's comment echoes the title of Winckelmann's first essay as well as his central idea of imitating the Greek characteristic of "edle Einfalt und stille Größe", and suggests that Pelzel's Hekuba might be a model for future Winckelmannian-like heroes on the German stage.

In the final scene of Pelzel's tragedy, Andromacha reappears on stage before departing with the rest of the Cretans. Unlike Hekuba, Andromacha remains the same impassioned woman in her suffering. As she passes by Hekuba and the other Trojan women and she continues to cry out – "Ach! ach! o Königinn!" – Hekuba reprimands her for such lamenting: "Du thust nicht gut, Andromacha, daß du / Die Wehmuth so vor mir erschallen läßt".[70] Hekuba, resigned to her fate, is resolved not to metamorphose into the "bitch of Cynossema", as in the classical tradition, but to remain a stoic queen.

Through Hekuba's transformation, Pelzel provides—seven years prior to Goethe—an outstanding example of the type of character that Winckelmann's writing on Greek statues championed. In doing so, Pelzel's play demonstrates that Winckelmann's influence, despite Lessing's repeated counter-arguments, was more extensive than scholars have previously thought. Moreover, the drama suggests that a more thorough examination of other plays written between 1755 and 1787 and set in antiquity may reveal to an even greater extent the impact of Winckelmann's ideas on drama prior to *Iphigenie auf Tauris*. Regardless of the findings of such future studies, Pelzel's treatment of the characters in *Das gerächte Troja* shows the same clear response to and adoption of Winckelmann's "edle Einfalt und stille Größe", as Goethe's handling of Iphigenie.

---

[67] Ibid. V.12.
[68] Ibid. V.13.
[69] Ibid.
[70] Ibid. V.15.

Andrea Heitmann

"und jeder Tag nimmt etwas von dem lodernden Feuer hinweg". Körperlichkeit und Sexualität in Sophie von La Roches *Geschichte des Fräuleins von Sternheim*

This article investigates to what extent a new, sensitive concept of physicality, in which the body serves the expression of the inner processes of the beautiful soul, is manifested in the novel Geschichte des Fräuleins von Sternheim *by Sophie von La Roche. On the basis of gender relations, the article analyses the power structures underlying this concept of physicality. It is argued that control exercised over sexuality constitutes a moral superiority of women, which ultimately allows them a certain freedom.*

Der von Selbstanalyse und psychologischem Einfühlungsvermögen gekennzeichnete Roman der Sophie von La Roche hat zunächst zu einer Auseinandersetzung mit dem tugendhaften, empfindsamen Frauentyp als einem der zentralen Ansatzpunkte geführt. "Allein alle die Herren irren sich, wenn sie glauben, sie beurtheilen ein Buch – – es ist eine *Menschenseele*", so Merck in einer Rezension vom 14. Februar 1777.[1] Caroline Flachsland erkennt – wie sie Herder 1771 schreibt – in dem Fräulein von Sternheim ihr "ganzes Ideal von einem Frauenzimmer";[2] für Herder wiederum erbringt der Roman den Beweis, daß "es außer der bloß *leichten* Schönheit einer menschlichen Seele, wahrhaftig eine höhere, ernsthaftere, rührende[re] Grazie"[3] gibt. Mit der *Geschichte des Fräuleins von Sternheim* war "die 'schöne Seele' geboren, ein Frauentyp, der als Vorläuferin von Goethes Iphigenie bezeichnet worden ist".[4]

Während literaturwissenschaftliche Auseinandersetzungen seit den 60er Jahren häufig das Œuvre der Sophie von La Roche im Hinblick auf die Rolle der Frau als Schriftstellerin[5] sowie das Verhältnis der Autorin zu

---

[1] Zitiert nach: Dokumente zur Wirkungsgeschichte. In: Sophie von La Roche. *Geschichte des Fräuleins von Sternheim.* Hg. von Barbara Becker-Cantarino. Stuttgart 1983. S. 367.

[2] Ebd. S. 365.

[3] Ebd.

[4] Barbara Becker-Cantarino: Nachwort. In: Sophie von La Roche. *Geschichte des Fräuleins von Sternheim.* S. 402.

[5] Vgl. Monika Nenon: *Autorschaft und Frauenbildung. Das Beispiel Sophie von La Roche.* Würzburg 1988; sowie Ingrid Wiede-Behrendt: *Lehrerin des Schönen, Wahren, Guten. Literatur und Frauenbildung im ausgehenden 18. Jahrhundert am Beispiel Sophie von La Roche.* Frankfurt/M. 1987.

Wieland[6] analysiert haben, wendet diese Arbeit sich wieder dem Frauentyp des Romans zu. Es wird untersucht, wie sich Körperlichkeit vor der Folie des unweigerlich als zentral erlebten Seelenthemas des Romans abzeichnet. Nicht das Psychogramm der Seele des 'papiernen Mädchens', sondern das empfindsame Konzept von Körperlichkeit steht im Mittelpunkt der Betrachtung. Ausgehend von der vornehmlich sozial determinierten Entwicklung einer neuen Körperlichkeit, wie sie Koschorke in *Körperströme und Schriftverkehr* darstellt,[7] wird untersucht, inwieweit der empfindsame, dem Ausdruck von Seelenvorgängen dienende Körper eine – im 18. Jahrhundert vermeintlich eher dem weiblichen Geschlecht mögliche – Beherrschung der Leidenschaften und der sexuellen Triebe impliziert und inwieweit sich aus dieser über die Sexualität ausgeübten Kontrolle eine moralische Überlegenheit konstituiert. Eine solche Prävalenz bedeutet, daß der Frau "im Sinne der Doppelmoral der Zeit [...] die Verantwortung für die Tugend, besonders im Bereich der Liebe, zugeschoben"[8] wird. Es gilt zu untersuchen, ob Sophie von La Roche, als Teil der Gesamtkategorie 'Mensch', auf den die Forderungen Kants sich nicht beziehen und somit, wie Bovenschen es bezeichnet, "als 'Zuschauerin[..]' der Geschichte in den Vorzimmern der Moral"[9] verharren muß, in ihrem Roman dieses Idealbild bürgerlicher Weiblichkeit reproduziert.

Darüber hinaus wird die soziale Dimension der neuen Körperlichkeit verdeutlicht, die in dieser Arbeit "als Signifikant innerhalb sich verschie-

---

[6] Vgl. Verena Ehrich-Haefeli: Gestehungskosten tugendempfindsamer Freundschaft. Probeme der weiblichen Rolle im Briefwechsel Wieland – Sophie La Roche bis zum Erscheinen der *Sternheim*. In: *Frauenfreundschaft – Männerfreundschaft. Literarische Diskurse im 18. Jahrhundert*. Hg. von Wolfgang Mauser und Barbara Becker-Cantarino. Tübingen 1991. S. 75-135; Barbara Becker-Cantarino: Muse und Kunstrichter. Sophie La Roche und Wieland. In: *Modern Language Notes* 99 (1984). S. 571-588; sowie Gabriele von Koenig-Warthausen: Sophie La Roche, geb. Gutermann. Schriftstellerin, Jugendliebe Wielands. 1730-1807. In: *Lebensbilder aus Schwaben und Franken*. Hg. von Max Miller und Robert Unland. Bd. 10. Stuttgart 1966. S. 101-125.

[7] Vgl. insbesondere Kapitel I bis III in Albrecht Koschorke: *Körperströme und Schriftverkehr. Mediologie des 18. Jahrhunderts*. München 1999. Koschorke beschreibt die mit der aufklärerischen Sittenreform einhergehende Neumodellierung des menschlichen Körpers, indem er dem Wechsel des medizinischen Paradigmas den Umbruch der Kommunikationsverhältnisse gegenüberstellt. Die sich daraus ergebenden Umbesetzungen werden im dritten Kapitel anhand der empfindsamen Literatur untersucht.

[8] Barbara Becker-Cantarino: *Der lange Weg zur Mündigkeit. Frau und Literatur (1500 - 1800)*. Stuttgart 1987. S. 295.

[9] Silvia Bovenschen: *Die imaginierte Weiblichkeit. Exemplarische Untersuchungen zu kulturgeschichtlichen und literarischen Repräsentationsformen des Weiblichen*. 6. Aufl. Frankfurt/M. 1990. S. 231.

bender symbolischer Systeme"[10] der Analyse von Machtstrukturen dient. Von der ästhetischen Enteignung des Fräuleins von Sternheim durch die Blicke der Männer bei Hofe über den vermeintlichen Höhepunkt ihrer Tugendlosigkeit auf dem Maskenball bis zum Absterben ihrer Sexualität in den 'Bleygebürgen' wird das wechselseitige Verhältnis von Macht und neuer Körperlichkeit untersucht. Es gilt letztlich zu beurteilen, inwieweit das empfindsame Konzept von Körperlichkeit der Sicherung eines männlichen Machtanspruchs dient, inwieweit die Protagonistin des Romans sich diesem Anspruch unterwirft und ob der Rolle der tugendhaften Frau letztlich ein bedingter Freiraum immanent ist.

Wenn mit der *Geschichte des Fräuleins von Sternheim* "die (erzwungene?) Identifikation der Frau mit der ihr vorgegebenen entsexualisierten Geschlechtsrolle"[11] beginnt, dann geschieht dies auf der Grundlage einer neuen Körperlichkeit, die sich in der "Neumodellierung der Verhältnisse zwischen Körper und Körperumgebung"[12] manifestiert. Der Körper als beseelter Leib hat dabei die Aufgabe, die inneren Vorgänge der 'schönen Seele' zum Ausdruck zu bringen. Diese sich qua Körper ausdrückende Innerlichkeit ist – insbesondere für die empfindsame Frau – stark reglementiert. Erlaubt und erwünscht sind Tränen, die der körperlichen Reinigung dienen. Ein trockenes Auge bedeutet Härte und Rohheit, "Sittlichkeit hingegen ist mit der Fähigkeit zu weinen untrennbar verknüpft".[13] Daraus ist allerdings keinesfalls zu schließen, daß die Frau sich ihrem Körpergefühl überlassen möge, vielmehr wird ihr Auftreten gänzlich von der damit verbundenen Wirkung determiniert. Die Außenwirkung und die sich darin manifestierende Fremdbestimmung, die "eine Art ästhetischer Enteignung des Körpers"[14] darstellt, sind dabei nicht an aktives Wirkenwollen der Frau gebunden, sie sind vielmehr unvermeidlich – wird doch die weibliche Schönheit "von vornherein,

---

[10] Sigrid Schade: Körper und Macht. Theoretische Perspektive bei Adorno und Foucault. In: *Flaschenpost und Postkarte. Korrespondenz zwischen kritischer Theorie und Poststrukturalismus.* Hg. von Sigrid Weigel. Köln 1995. S. 117-126, hier S. 117.

[11] Stephan Schindler: *Eingebildete Körper. Phantasierte Sexualität in der Goethezeit.* Tübingen, 2001. S. 167. Sexualität bezieht sich dabei – wie Irmgard Roebling schreibt – nicht nur auf "den *Geschlechtsakt* selbst und die von ihm beeinflußten *Körpererfahrungen*, sondern [...] ist Teil *politischer Reflexion und Praxis*, da sie in beinahe alle Bereiche des gesellschaftlichen Lebens reicht". Irmgard Roebling: Die Rolle der Sexualität in der Neuen Frauenbewegung und der feministischen Literaturwissenschaft. Versuch einer Bestandsaufnahme. In: *Literarische Entwürfe weiblicher Sexualität.* Hg. von Johannes Cremerius. Würzburg 1993. S. 21-51, hier S. 21.

[12] Koschorke. S. 42.

[13] Ebd. S. 88.

[14] Verena Ehrich-Haefeli: Zur Genese der bürgerlichen Konzeption der Frau. Der psychohistorische Stellenwert von Rousseaus Sophie. In: *Literarische Entwürfe weiblicher Sexualität.* Hg. von Johannes Cremerius. Würzburg 1993. S. 89-134, hier S. 107.

ohne Zutun der Person, ein Einsatz in der Zirkulation und als solcher Gegenstand sozialer Verhandlungen".[15] Selbstbestimmung ist somit unmöglich. Die Erfahrungen des Fräuleins von Sternheim am Hof des Fürsten in D. machen dies deutlich. Die anwesenden Männer betrachten – zum Ärger der Sternheim – ziemlich ungeniert die versammelte Weiblichkeit: "Manche Augen gafften nach mir, aber sie waren mir zur Last, weil mich immer dünkte, es wäre ein Ausdruck darin, welcher meine Grundsätze beleidigte" (75).[16] Die Grundsätze der Hofdamen hingegen sind nicht so schnell zu beleidigen, fordern sie doch die Blicke der Männer häufig heraus. Das Fräulein von Sternheim schließt daraus, daß die Eitelkeit der Damen in D. sehr heißhungrig sein müsse (vgl. 62). Auch ihre neue Freundin, das Fräulein von C., beteiligt sich zum Befremden des Fräuleins von Sternheim an diesem Spiel der Blicke: "Sie ist sehr liebenswürdig, [...] nur manchmal, dünkte mich, wären ihre freimütige, ganz liebreiche Augen zu lang und zu bedeutend auf die Augen der Mannsleute geheftet gewesen" (66). Im Gegensatz zu den Hofdamen bemüht sich das Fräulein von Sternheim, "die passive Wirkung ihres Körpers durch die aktive Wirksamkeit ihres keuschen Blicks zu konterkarieren", sie versucht, "sich in den Besitz auch ihrer optischen Außenseite zu bringen und damit die Exzentrierung ihrer Person durch die Blicke der anderen rückgängig zu machen".[17] Derby, der in einem Brief an seinen Freund in Paris schreibt, daß "ein Blick, ein einziger ungekünstelter Blick ihrer Augen", die Blicke "zu verscheuchen" (102) scheint, überschätzt damit jedoch die Möglichkeiten des Fräuleins von Sternheim, sich der begehrlichen Blicke zu erwehren. Der Besitz "ihrer optischen Außenseite" bleibt ihr bei Hofe verwehrt, und ihre Abneigung gegen diese Blicke nimmt zu. "Was für Blicke, meine Liebe! [...] Der bitterste Schmerz durchdrang mich bei dem Gedanken, der Gegenstand so häßlicher Blicke zu sein" (98), so schildert sie ihren Widerwillen in einem Brief an ihre Vertraute. Nur der Blick Mylord Seymours ist ihr angenehm:

> [D]as durch etwas Melancholisches gedämpfte Feuer seiner schönen Augen, den unnachahmlich angenehmen und mit Größe vermengten Anstand aller seiner Bewegungen, und, was ihn von allen Männern, deren ich in den wenigen Wochen, die ich hier bin, eine Menge gesehen habe, unterscheidet, ist (wenn ich mich schicklich ausdrücken kann) der tugendliche Blick seiner Augen, welche die einzigen sind, die mich nicht beleidigten, und keine widrige antipathetische Bewegung in meiner Seele verursachten (71).

[15] Koschorke. S. 39.

[16] Sophie von La Roche: *Geschichte des Fräuleins von Sternheim*. Hg. von Barbara Becker-Cantarino. Stuttgart 1983. Alle Zitate nach dieser Ausgabe im Text.

[17] Koschorke. S. 41.

Da das Fräulein von Sternheim, wie Derby es beschreibt, "die begierigen Blicke aller Mannsleute" (134) auf sich zieht, weckt sie die Mißgunst ihrer Geschlechtsgenossinnen.

> Der weibliche Neid gilt der Begierde der Männer, die sich auf eine andere Frau richtet, ist also selbst Begierde, die Haupttriebkraft der höfischen Gesellschaft, sobald sie der Sternheim ansichtig wird. Um sich ihr zu entziehen, müßte sie sich unsichtbar machen können.[18]

Verunsichert von den Vorkommnissen bei Hofe beschließt das Fräulein von Sternheim, sich von jeglichem Spiel der Blicke – selbst in seiner tugendhaften und unschuldigen Form – loszusagen. Sie will ihren Augen auch "das Vergnügen versagen, Mylord Seymour anzuschauen", obwohl ihre Blicke "ohnehin flüchtig genug" (99) waren. Die Bemühungen des Fräuleins von Sternheim, sich der voyeuristischen Enteignung zu widersetzen und die ihr unverständlichen Ressentiments der Hofdamen abzubauen, sind vergebens. "Sie fällt in zweifacher Hinsicht der Optik zum Opfer: Sie scheint die Mätresse des Fürsten zu sein, und sofort erscheint ihre zur Schau gestellte Tugend falsch. Einmal wird dem Anschein geglaubt, das andere Mal dem Schein mißtraut".[19] In einer absolutistischen Hofkultur, in der sämtliches Verhalten darauf ausgerichtet ist, "die Affekte zu erschüttern, die Leidenschaften zu erregen, [...] den Menschen in einen erotischen Erregungszustand zu versetzen, der nach Befriedigung der Begierden verlangt",[20] kann das Fräulein von Sternheim – will es ihre Tugendhaftigkeit bewahren – nur scheitern. In dieser "Kultur der körperlichen Exhibition" geht alles, was "sich nicht, im Rahmen rhetorischer Angemessenheitskriterien, auf der sichtbaren Oberfläche des Körpers darstellt, [...] für den Tauschverkehr der Zeichen verloren".[21] Paradoxerweise gelingt es gerade dem 'Bösewicht',[22] Mylord Derby, diese kommunikativen Strukturen letztlich zu durchschauen. Er schildert seinem Freund die Begegnung mit dem Fräulein von Sternheim, die auf ihn einen großen Eindruck gemacht hat, und weiht ihn in seine Pläne ein: "So weit es zu meinen Absichten dient, mag es sein; aber, beim Jupiter, sie soll mich schadlos halten!" (102). Derby möchte das Fräulein von Stern-

---

[18] Ursula Naumann: Das Fräulein und die Blicke. Eine Betrachtung über Sophie von La Roche. In: *Zeitschrift für deutsche Philologie* 107 (1988). S. 488-516, hier S. 508.

[19] Christine Lehmann: *Das Modell Clarissa. Liebe, Verführung, Sexualität und Tod der Romanheldinnen des 18. und 19. Jahrhunderts.* Stuttgart 1991. S. 43.

[20] Nenon. S. 87f.

[21] Koschorke. S. 16.

[22] Naumann weist darauf hin, daß in keinem anderen Werk Sophie La Roches "dem Bösen als Widerpart der Tugend so viel Macht – und Recht eingeräumt" wurde. Nach Ansicht Naumanns hängt die Qualität des Werkes damit "wohl wesentlich zusammen" (S. 506).

heim "besitzen", sie soll sein "Eigentum werden" (121). Er betrachtet sie als Objekt, sie ist sein "Täubchen", das noch nicht "kirre" genug ist, das "Feuer [s]einer Leidenschaft in der Nähe zu sehen" (121). Um sie "kirre" zu machen, versucht er, ihren Idealen von selbstloser Wohltätigkeit zu entsprechen. Er erkennt, daß alle "Anstalten, die man dem Fürsten zu Ehren macht", nur dazu dienen, "das schöne schüchterne Vögelchen in [s]ein verstecktes Garn zu jagen" (134). Die mit "Täubchen" (121) und "Vögelchen" (134) bezeichnete Frau wird nicht nur zum jungfräulichen Objekt, sie wird zur Beute, zum tierischen und triebhaften Lebewesen, das eingefangen werden muß.

Obwohl Derbys Interesse sich auf das 'Geschlechtswesen Sternheim' zu richten scheint, ist er fasziniert von der Tugendhaftigkeit des Fräuleins. Ihr Verhalten stärkt seinen Eroberungsdrang; ob Derby allerdings, nachdem er zeitweilig an der Tugendhaftigkeit der Sternheim zweifelte, "im Glauben an die Wahrheit ihres tugendhaften Charakters, den Schein des Lasters auf diese Wahrheit hin zu durchschauen" beginnt, wie Naumann argumentiert,[23] oder ob er das tugendhafte Verhalten der Sternheim letztlich für ein Spiel hält, kann nicht mit Bestimmtheit entschieden werden. Sicher ist jedoch, daß nicht die Sorge um die verlorene Ehre der tugendhaften Frau, sondern Neugier und Ehrgeiz in dem Wettbewerb um die Sternheim Derby dazu bringen, Nachforschungen anzustellen. Er findet heraus, daß die Sternheim – entgegen der allgemeinen Annahme – die Pläne ihrer Tante, sie zur Mätresse des Fürsten zu machen, nicht durchschaut. Damit ist Derby "das scharfe Auge des Romans: intellektuelle Sehschärfe und hoch entwickelter ästhetischer Sinn verbinden sich mit dem Jagdinstinkt des Raubtiers und machen ihn zu dem gefährlichsten aller Jäger".[24] Während Seymour, der die Sternheim liebt und an ihre durch und durch asexuelle Persönlichkeit glaubte, außer sich gerät "über ihre vorgespiegelte Tugend" (136), ist es für Derby nicht entscheidend, ob es sich um vorgespiegelte oder wirkliche Tugend handelt, da sein Interesse an dem Fräulein von Sternheim auf einem anderen Konzept von Körperlichkeit basiert. Für ihn manifestiert sich in der physiognomischen Transparenz, mit Hilfe derer die im Innern des Körpers verborgene Seele gezeigt wird, auch die (vorübergehende) Unterdrückung der Sexualität. Er vermutet in der Sternheim gemäß seiner Vorstellung von Körperlichkeit eine letztlich triebhafte Frau. Und gerade das macht ihn für sie so gefährlich. Bei Seymour hingegen ruft die vermeintliche Tugendlosigkeit der Sternheim Wut und tiefe Enttäuschung hervor: "Itzt hingegen verachte, verfluche ich diese Sternheim und ihr Bild" (145). Seymours Dilemma besteht nach Naumann darin, daß er vor lauter Tugendbildern die Tugend des Fräuleins nicht mehr sehe.[25]

---

[23] Naumann. S. 511.

[24] Ebd.

[25] Vgl. ebd. S. 510.

Die vermeintliche Tugendlosigkeit der Sternheim erreicht ihren Höhepunkt auf dem Maskenball. Während "die Maskerade als Versteckspiel der Individuen [...] für das höfische Sozialgefüge im ganzen keine Bedrohung bedeutet", da es "eines weitgehenden Diskretionsschutzes seiner Gesellschaftsschicht sicher sein" kann, verhält es sich "in der Welt der bürgerlichen Normen gerade umgekehrt".[26] Der Verlust eindeutiger Zuordnungen und Zugehörigkeiten ist heikel und potentiell katastrophal. Nachdem der tugendhafte Gesichtsausdruck hinter einer Maske verschwindet, bleibt das Geschlechtswesen übrig – so auch im Fall des Fräuleins von Sternheim, deren die durch die Maskierung hervorgerufene Veränderung Derby wie folgt schildert:

Doch machte ich noch in Zeiten die Anmerkung, daß unser Gesicht, und das, was man Physionomie nennt, ganz eigentlich der Ausdruck unsrer Seele ist. Denn ohne Maske war meine Sternheim allezeit das Bild der sittlichen Schönheit, indem ihre Miene und der Blick ihrer Augen eine Hoheit und Reinigkeit der Seele über ihre ganze Person auszugießen schien, wodurch alle Begierden, die sie einflößte, in den Schranken der Ehrerbietung gehalten wurden. Aber nun waren ihre Augenbrauen, Schläfe und halbe Backen gedeckt, und ihre Seele gleichsam unsichtbar gemacht; sie verlor dadurch die sittliche charakteristische Züge ihrer Annehmlichkeiten, und sank zu der allgemeinen Idee eines *Mädchens* herab. Der Gedanke, daß sie ihren ganzen Anzug vom Fürsten erhalten, ihm zu Ehren gesungen hatte, und schon lange von ihm geliebt wurde, stellte sie uns allen als würkliche Mätresse vor (185f).

Durch die Maskierung fallen "Schein und Sein auf beunruhigende Weise"[27] zusammen. Das Gesicht der Sternheim, das – wie sie überaus tugendbewußt schreibt – "allezeit die Empfindungen meiner Seele ausdrückt" (115), "zwingt den Mann dazu, seine Aufmerksamkeit auf die spirituelle Transparenz statt auf die Oberflächenschönheit des weiblichen Körpers zu richten".[28] Durch die nach Lavaters Hierarchie der drei Gesichtszonen den Mittelteil – also die Augen- und Nasenpartie – verdeckende Maske, verschwindet der Ausdruck der Persönlichkeit. Sind die Empfindungen der Seele nicht mehr erkennbar, so läßt sich auch eine tugendhafte Unschuld wie das Fräulein von Sternheim auf erotische Attraktivität und somit auf rein sexuelle Körperlichkeit reduzieren. Da Derby in dem Fräulein von Sternheim nie nur eine "leibhaftige Unschuld" gesehen hat, gelingt es ihm, in der maskierten Frau mehr als rein sexuelle Körperlichkeit zu erkennen. Er bemerkt, daß das Fräulein von Sternheim beim Tanz auf dem Maskenball versucht, sich der Nähe des Fürsten zu erwehren.

[26] Koschorke. S. 28.
[27] Naumann. S. 510.
[28] Koschorke. S. 29.

da [...] darauf der Fürst in einer Maske von nämlichen Farben als die ihrige kam, und sie, da eben deutsch getanzt wurde, an der Seite ihrer Tante, mit der sie stehend redte, wegnahm, und einen Arm um ihren Leib geschlungen, die Länge des Saals mit ihr durchtanzte. Dieser Anblick ärgerte mich zum Rasendwerden, doch bemerkte ich, daß sie sich vielfältig sträubte und loswinden wollte; aber bei jeder Bemühung drückte er sie fester an seine Brust (186).

Seymour hingegen, der dem Fräulein von Sternheim anfänglich "eine holde Ernsthaftigkeit in ihrem Gesicht, eine edle anständige Höflichkeit in ihrem Bezeugen, die äußerste Zärtlichkeit gegen ihre Freundin, eine anbetungswürdige Güte und die feinste Empfindsamkeit der Seele" (91) zuschreibt, ist nicht in der Lage, im Vertrauen auf die Tugendhaftigkeit der Sternheim, die Intrigen des Hofes zu durchschauen. Vielmehr scheint die vermeintlich tugendhafte Frau – lediglich dadurch, daß sie Begehren erweckt – bereits über eine sexuelle Körperlichkeit zu verfügen. Da Seymour jegliches Verhalten der Sternheim entsprechend interpretiert, kann es ihm im Gegensatz zu Derby nicht gelingen, die Maske zu durchschauen.

Der tiefste Schmerz war in meiner Seele, als ich sie singen hörte, und mit dem Fürsten und mit andern Menuette tanzen sah. Aber als er sie um den Leib faßte, an seine Brust drückte, und den sittenlosen, frechen Wirbeltanz der Deutschen mit einer aller Wohlstandsbande zerreißenden Vertraulichkeit an ihrer Seite daherhüpfte – da wurde meine stille Betrübnis in brennenden Zorn verwandelt (204).

Der durch die Maskierung verdeutlichte Zusammenhang zwischen Persönlichkcit und Scxualität spicgclt das von Koschorke den damaligen Lebensführungslehren entnommene "umgekehrt proportionale [...] Verhältnis zwischen 'Lust' und 'Empfindungen'"[29] wider, wonach die Bewahrung des empfindsamen Nervensystems körperliche Enthaltsamkeit erfordert. Derby hingegen scheint eher ein proportionales Verhältnis zwischen ausgedrückter Empfindsamkeit und unterdrückter Lust anzunehmen. Er erwartet, nachdem er die Situation bei Hofe ausgenutzt und mit dem Fräulein von Sternheim eine Scheinehe eingegangen ist, einen Ausbruch der Leidenschaften. Das Fräulein von Sternheim hingegen, das auf Derbys leidenschaftliche Stimme und Blicke bereits vor der vermeintlichen Hochzeit mit Übelkeit reagierte (vgl. 177), hofft auf eine Normalisierung ihrer Beziehung. Sie "will keine Gefälligkeit, keine Bemühung versäumen, [ihrem] Gemahl angenehm zu sein" (218). Unterschiedliche Charaktereigenschaften lassen sie bereits Konflikte antizipieren; sie vermutet, sie werde "oft ausweichen" müssen, hofft abcr, dabei nicht gcnötigt zu sein, ihren "Charakter" und ihre "Grundsätze" aufzuopfern (218). Da das Fräulein von Sternheim zu diesem Zeitpunkt von Derbys Intrigen und der vorgetäuschten Eheschließung nichts ahnt, kann

[29] Ebd. S. 99.

ihre Angst vor körperlicher Nähe nicht direkt auf sein unmoralisches Verhalten zurückgeführt werden. Vielmehr ist ihre Furcht auf Derbys Konzept von Körperlichkeit zurückzuführen, welches weibliche Lust und weibliches Verlangen beinhaltet und somit den Überzeugungen der Sternheim widerspricht. Derby will das Fräulein von Sternhein – wie Wiede-Behrendt schreibt – "zu seinen Konditionen lieben"[30] und das heißt leidenschaftlich; und er möchte – was in diesem Kontext von noch größerer Bedeutung ist – ihrer Leidenschaft zum Ausbruch verhelfen und ebenso leidenschaftlich geliebt werden. Dieses Konzept bietet keinen Raum für die Sternheimsche Tugendleistung der Affekt- und Triebbeherrschung, da Derby keine Kontrolle ihrer und damit letztlich auch seiner Leidenschaften fordert. Dem Fräulein von Sternheim droht eine Entdeckung und Aktivierung ihrer bisher erfolgreich unterdrückten Sexualität. Die "leidenschaftliche Liebe" wird damit – wie Becker-Cantarino im Nachwort zu Sophie La Roches *Geschichte des Fräuleins von Sternheim* schreibt – "als *die* Bedrohung der Heldin gesehen, die als Frau die sexuellen Triebe zu kanalisieren und zu sublimieren hat".[31]

Lord Derby, der sich bei der vermeintlichen Hochzeit am Ziel seiner Wünsche wähnt, wird enttäuscht. Die erhoffte sexuelle Erfüllung bleibt aus. Zunächst erwidert die Sternheim "die feurigen Umarmungen ihres Liebhabers bloß mit der matten Zärtlichkeit einer frostigen Ehefrau" und gibt ihm "kalte – mit Seufzern unterbrochene Küsse" (219). Als Derby die Sternheim einige Tage später mit offenen Haaren an ihrem Nachttisch sitzen sieht und sich an Miltons Eva in *Paradise Lost* erinnert fühlt, bittet er das Fräulein von Sternheim, "sich auf einen Augenblick zu entkleiden, um [ihn] so glücklich zu machen, in ihr den Abdruck des ersten Meisterstücks der Natur zu bewundern" (222). Sie versagt ihm seine Bitte und sträubt sich, bis "Ungeduld und Begierde" ihm eingeben, "ihre Kleidung vom Hals an durchzureißen, um auch wider ihren Willen zu [s]einem Endzweck zu gelangen" (222). Die Interpretationen dieses Vorfalls sind unterschiedlich. Während Touaillon der Ansicht ist, daß in dieser Szene "ein Mann durch ein Netz von Intrigen ein Mädchen um seine körperliche Unschuld bringt",[32] verweist Naumann auf den Symbolcharakter der Handlung: "Daß Derby ihr Gewand zerreißt [...], steht für eine Vergewaltigung".[33] Lehmann hingegen mutmaßt, daß „Sophie in der Entkleidungsszene unberührt geblieben"[34] ist. Es soll an dieser Stelle nicht weiter darüber spekuliert werden, ob das Zerreißen der Kleider eine Vergewaltigung andeutet, ob Derbys Beschreibung der matten Zärtlichkeit einer frostigen Ehefrau (219) auf die Erfüllung 'ehelicher

---

[30] Wiede-Behrendt. S. 167.

[31] Becker-Cantarino: Nachwort. S. 403.

[32] Christine Touaillon: *Der deutsche Frauenroman des 18. Jahrhunderts.* Wien 1919. S. 106f.

[33] Naumann. S. 515.

[34] Lehmann. S. 46.

Pflichten' hinweist oder ob Sophies Bemerkung, Derby erst in Florenz lieben zu können (221f), sexuelle Enthaltsamkeit bedeutet, denn schließlich
hat das Fräulein von Sternheim "seine seelische Unschuld bewahrt".[35] Ihr
Herz ist "unschuldig und rein" (236), wie sie selbst in einem Brief an ihre
Vertraute Emilia schreibt. Wenn in der Empfindsamkeit gemäß der Darstellung Koschorkes "das Postulat der Jungfernschaft der Braut [...] von außen nach innen getragen und auf diese Weise gleichsam verdoppelt"[36] wird,
somit also Leib *und* Seele unberührt bleiben sollen, dann zeigt sich am Beispiel des Fräuleins von Sternheim, daß die Reinheit von Körper und Psyche
nicht gleichberechtigt nebeneinander stehen, sondern letzterer eine größere
Bedeutung zukommt.

Während sich in den Briefen der Sternheim kein Hinweis auf die (vermeintliche) Vergewaltigung findet, schildert Derby den Vorfall in einem
Brief an seinen Freund in allen Einzelheiten. Er rechtfertigt sein Verhalten
mit der rhetorischen Frage, ob es nicht die Pflicht der Sternheim gewesen
sei, sich nach seinem Sinne zu schicken, da sie sich für seine Ehefrau halte
(vgl. 224). Auch der Versuch des Fräuleins von Sternheim, ihrem vermeintlichen Ehemann ihre heftige Reaktion zu erklären, scheitert. Ihr Geständnis,
"daß sie mit Vergnügen bemerkte, wenn man von ihrem Geist, und von ihrer
Figur vorteilhaft urteile; dennoch [...] lieber dieses Vergnügen entbehren, als
es durch ihre eigene Bemühung erlangen" (223) wolle, kann Derby nicht
verstehen, erwartete er doch, dem Fräulein von Sternheim zu schmeicheln
mit seiner Aufforderung, sich zu entkleiden, damit er sie bewundern könne.
Er kann nicht nachvollziehen, "daß ein Weib ihre vollkommenste Reize
nicht gesehen, nicht bewundert haben will" (223). Auch Wieland erscheint
die Erläuterung der Sternheim nicht einleuchtend, wie er in einem Kommentar als Herausgeber ausführt: "In der Tat löset diese Antwort das Rätsel
gar nicht auf. Mylord Derby ersparte ihr ja diese eigene Bemühung. – Warum wurde sie dennoch so ungehalten? Warum sagte sie, er zerreiße ihr Herz,
da er doch nur ihr Deshabille zerriß?" (223).[37] Beide Männer, "der fiktive
und der reale, sind sich einig, daß der nackte Frauenkörper als Bild von
klassischen Proportionen nicht unschicklich ist".[38] Wieland vermutet in seiner Anmerkung schließlich, das Verhalten des Fräuleins von Sternheim sei
darin begründet, daß diese Derby nicht liebe (vgl. 223). Der Vorwurf man-
gelnder Liebe weist auf das empfindsame Konzept ehelicher Liebe hin, in
welchem die Gefühle der Frau „aus der dankbaren Erwiderung der jeweils
auf ihre Person gerichteten Männergefühle" bestanden und somit "Spiegel,

---

[35] Touaillon. S. 106.

[36] Koschorke. S. 32.

[37] Für Naumann, die das Zerreißen des Gewandes als Vergewaltigung interpretiert,
deutet Wielands Anmerkung darauf hin, daß dieser den Vorfall für ein "Kavaliers-
delikt" halte, das er "witzelnd" kommentiere. Vgl. Naumann. S. 515.

[38] Lehmann. S. 45.

nicht Quelle"[39] waren. Bedenkt man Derbys leidenschaftliche Gefühle für das Fräulein von Sternheim, so deutet die Bemerkung Wielands auf die aus damaliger männlicher Perspektive begangene Unterlassungssünde der Sternheim hin. Naumann knüpft an den Vorwurf der Lieblosigkeit an, wenn sie die Frage aufwirft, ob nicht Derby "Liebe für Körper *und* Seele des Fräuleins" empfunden habe, und die Sternheim – da sie Derby zu heiraten beschließt, ohne ihn zu lieben – "ihn mehr als er sie betrogen hat".[40] Die Frage, wer letztlich dem anderen mehr falsche Hoffnungen gemacht habe, bleibt offen, aber es wird deutlich, daß die Sternheim sich nicht allein auf ihre – in diesem Fall naive – Tugendhaftigkeit berufen kann, sondern für die Eskalation der Situation mitverantwortlich ist. Allerdings ist es weniger ein Mangel an Liebe als vielmehr die Sozialisation der Sternheim, die ein nicht unerhebliches eheliches Konfliktpotential in sich birgt. Indem das Fräulein von Sternheim sich der Blicke ihres vermeintlichen Ehemanns verweigert, versucht sie, sich der Enteignung ihres Körpers zu widersetzen. Dieser Widerstand ist – wie Naumann ausführt – mehr als 'nur' ein Kampf um die Unschuld. Die Sternheim, die dazu erzogen wurde, ihren bekleideten Körper als Ausdruck ihrer schönen Seele "zur Schau zu stellen, ihn durch passend gewählte Kleider, durch anmutige Bewegungen im Tanz zur Geltung zu bringen und den Männern reizend zu machen",[41] wird durch die gewaltsame Entkleidung gezwungen, ihre eigene Körperlichkeit wahrzunehmen. Sie muß erkennen, daß Derby die dem empfindsamen bürgerlichen Konzept von Weiblichkeit inhärente Kontrolle der Leidenschaften in Frage stellt. Da für das Fräulein von Sternheim somit auch die tugendhafte eheliche Liebe die Gefahr unkontrollierbarer Affekte in sich birgt, versucht sie auch diese zu vermeiden. "Statt der Liebe pflegt sie die Nächstenliebe".[42]

Das Ziel, andere Menschen glücklich zu machen, bleibt auch nach der von Derby inszenierten Entführung in die schottischen 'Bleygebürge' handlungsbestimmend. Das Fräulein von Sternheim findet erneut den Sinn des Lebens in der Nächstenliebe und den übenden Tugenden. Als eine abermalige Intrige Derbys schließlich ihren sicheren Tod zu bedeuten scheint, kann sich das Fräulein von Sternheim – da es "der Tugend getreu" (321) war – ruhig und vertrauensvoll auf den Tod vorbereiten. Allerdings verdeutlichen die Tagebucheintragungen aus der Zeit in der Abgeschiedenheit der 'Bleygebürge' nicht nur – im Sinne eines Romanschemas der Prüfungen – die Fähigkeit der Sternheim zur Nächstenliebe und die Kraft, die sie aus den übenden Tugenden schöpft, sondern auch die erfolgreiche Unterdrückung ihrer Sexualität. Das Fräulein von Sternheim durchläuft in der Isolation "eine Phase der Entsagung bis hin zur symbolischen Tötung".[43]

---

[39] Koschorke. S. 33.

[40] Naumann. S. 513.

[41] Ebd.

[42] Lehmann. S. 46.

[43] Koschorke. S. 41.

Diese Entwicklung ist notwendig, da die "neuen Liebenden [...] nur im Zeichen eines durchgestrichenen Begehrens"[44] zueinander finden können. Nach der Erfahrung in der völlig entsexualisierten Welt der 'Bleygebürge' stellt auch die tugendhafte, aber dennoch leidenschaftliche Liebe des guten Helden, Lord Seymour, keine Gefahr mehr für das Fräulein von Sternheim dar.

Die Leidenschaft Seymours offenbart sich auf dessen Reise nach Schottland. Seymour sucht zunächst das Wirtshaus auf, in dem das Fräulein von Sternheim mit Derby wohnte und wirft sich "unausgekleidet mit halb zerrütteten Sinnen auf das Bette, worin Sternheim so kummervolle Nächte zugebracht hatte" (263). Er genießt "ein schmerzhaftes Vergnügen [...] bei dem Gedanken: daß [s]eine verzweiflungsvolle Tränen noch die Spuren der ihrigen antreffen, und sich mit ihnen vereinigen würden" (263). Er kauft das "kleine Hauptküssen" (264) vom Sohn der Wirtin.

[I]hr Kopf hatte sich mit der nämlichen Bedrängnis darauf gewälzt wie meiner; ihre und meine Tränen haben es benetzt; ihr Unglück hat meine Seele auf ewig an sie gefesselt, von ihr getrennt, vielleicht auf immer getrennt, mußten sich in dieser armen Hütte die sympathetischen Bande ganz in meine Seele verwinden, welche mich stärker zu ihr als zu allem, was ich jemals geliebt habe, zogen (264).

Seymours sexuell konnotiertes Verhalten ist möglich, da er zu diesem Zeitpunkt annimmt, das Fräulein von Sternheim sei tot: "Unter der Prämisse, sie als Tote zu denken, kann er sie begehren".[45] Seymour beschreibt seinen Umgang mit dem Kissen auf eine Art, "in der die Moralzeitschriften gewöhnlich den Onanisten beschreiben"[46]: "aber nachts hielt mich mein Küssen schadlos; ich zehrte mich ab, und erschöpfte mich" (264). Körperliche Liebe wird bei Abwesenheit möglich, sie wird "gewissermaßen in effigie vollzogen".[47] Da der Tod – auch der symbolische – die größtmögliche Sicherheit bietet, das begehrte Objekt zu verfehlen, bedarf es einer symbolischen Kastration oder eines symbolischen Todes des geschlechtlichen Körpers, um affektive Ströme zu erzeugen.[48] Mortifikation und Fetischisierung bilden eine Einheit; das wahre Objekt der Begierde muß notwendigerweise verfehlt werden, an seine Stelle tritt ein Fetisch.

Während der Tod des Fräuleins von Sternheim in den 'Bleygebürgen' nur symbolisch ist, erscheint das Absterben ihrer Sexualität in der Isolation der schottischen Bergwelt real. Damit ist die Voraussetzung für ein glückliches Ende an der Seite Mylord Seymours und seines Bruders Rich geschaffen. Von beiden Brüdern geliebt, beschließt das Fräulein von Sternheim zunächst, allein zu bleiben, um niemanden zu kränken. Rich, dessen Liebe

[44] Ebd.

[45] Ebd. S. 142.

[46] Ebd.

[47] Ebd. S. 143.

[48] Vgl. ebd.

"von der Art Anhänglichkeit" ist, "welche ein edeldenkender Mann für *Rechtschaffenheit, Weisheit,* und *Menschenliebe*" (328) fühlt, kann das Fräulein von Sternheim jedoch davon überzeugen, dem Werben seines Bruders Seymour nachzugeben, der sie leidenschaftlich liebt. Ehrich-Haefeli vermutet in der Entscheidung des Fräuleins von Sternheim für Seymour den vielleicht unbewußten Versuch der Autorin, ihre eigene Biographie zu korrigieren: "die Sternheim darf den jungen, unpraktischen Schwärmer heiraten, der ältere, edle, tüchtige, aber etwas trockene Lord Rich wird der entsagende Freund".[49] Das mag so sein; allerdings ist Lord Seymour nicht nur aufgrund des biographischen Hintergrunds der Autorin, sondern auch infolge seiner emotionalen Disposition im Roman prädestiniert für die Rolle des Ehemanns. Seine leidenschaftliche Liebe garantiert der Sternheim, daß sie ihrer tugendhaften ehelichen Aufgabe, nämlich der Affekt- und Triebbeherrschung, nachkommen kann. Da Seymours Konzept von (weiblicher) entsexualisierter Körperlichkeit mit dem des Fräuleins von Sternheim übereinstimmt, überläßt er ihr die Kontrolle seiner Leidenschaften. Die ihr damit übertragene Verantwortung für die Tugend, birgt nach der Phase der Entsexualisierung in den 'Bleygebürgen' keine Gefahren mehr. So nimmt dann mit Hilfe des Fräuleins von Sternheim "jeder Tag [...] etwas von dem lodernden Feuer hinweg" (349), welches die Empfindungen ihres Gemahls durchströmt. Das Leben der Sternheim ist gemäß den empfindsamen Maßstäben vorbildlich, wie sie – nun als Lady Seymour – ihrer Freundin berichtet: "Emilia, ich bin glücklich; ich bin es vollkommen, denn ich kann die seligsten, die heiligsten Pflichten alle Tage meines Lebens erfüllen" (344). Der Glückszustand manifestiert sich für die neue Lady Seymour darin, den Mann geheiratet zu haben, der ihr ein ihrem Konzept von empfindsamer Körperlichkeit entsprechendes Leben ermöglicht.

Der Weg der Protagonistin führt aus der von ihr abgelehnten und gefürchteten Welt der sexualisierten Körperlichkeit bei Hofe in die von unkontrollierter Leidenschaftlichkeit und sexuellen Reizen befreite Gesellschaft an der Seite von Mylord Seymour und Lord Rich. Stellt man – wie beispielsweise Foucault es getan hat – einen Zusammenhang her zwischen Sexualität und Macht, dann spricht dieser Werdegang eine eindeutige Sprache. Der für das männliche Geschlecht einfachste Weg, seinen Machtanspruch zu sichern, besteht darin, die Frauen zu überzeugen, ihren potentiellen 'Wert' zu steigern, indem sie sich jeglichen Machtanspruchs enthalten. Die Notwendigkeit, ihren Machtanspruch zu sichern, leitet das männliche Geschlecht – wie Ehrich-Haefeli schreibt –, daraus ab, daß die Sexualität der Frauen nicht natürlich eingeschränkt ist. Auf der Grundlage der ständigen sexuellen Bereitschaft des weiblichen Geschlechts wird das Schreckensszenario einer Gesellschaft entworfen, in der "die Frauen in kurzer Zeit die Männer zu Tode brauchen und alle zusammen durch das Mittel der Fort-

---

[49] Ehrich-Haefeli: Gestehungskosten tugendempfindsamer Freundschaft. S. 128.

pflanzung aussterben würden".[50] Aus männlicher Perspektive muß daher im Dienste der Menschheit weibliches Begehren sublimiert werden. Die Entwicklung des Fräuleins von Sternheim paßt sich diesem patriarchalischen Konzept von weiblicher Sexualität an.[51]

Prämisse für die Domestizierung der ungebändigten Triebhaftigkeit und Leidenschaftlichkeit der Frauen und somit gleichzeitig "diskursive Voraussetzung für das Entstehen empfindsam-viktorianischer Liebeskonzepte" ist die "Abtrennung der sexuellen Lust vom Fortpflanzungsgeschehen".[52] Nur wenn der weibliche Orgasmus nicht mehr die notwendige Voraussetzung für die Empfängnis darstellt, kann der an Nachkommen interessierte Mann die Existenz einer triebhaften Sexualität der Frau negieren. Entsprechend vermutet Seymour in seiner tugendhaften Frau weder Triebhaftigkeit noch Leidenschaftlichkeit, ihre Sexualität nimmt er nur in "ihrer biologischen Funktion als Gebärerin von Söhnen"[53] wahr. Die empfindsame Ehe der Sternheim hat "mit sinnlichem Liebesglück nichts zu tun",[54] ihre weibliche Sexualität bleibt unterdrückt. Das Idealbild der asexuellen Ehefrau wird auf die Mutterrolle projiziert; das Fräulein von Sternheim gebiert nicht, sie wird Mutter (vgl. 347). Auch das Stillen wird seiner körperlichen Funktion beraubt, wenn Lord Rich die Seligkeit seines Bruders beschreibt, als dieser "seinen Sohn an der Brust der besten Frau, Tugend einsaugen sieht" (349). Ebenso wie der Körper der Frau dem Ausdruck der schönen Seele dient, manifestiert sich im Stillen des Kindes die Übermittlung der inneren Werte der Mutter. Der zweitgeborene Sohn [sic], der bereits vor der Geburt des ersten Kindes Lord Rich versprochen wurde, wird diesem von Lady Seymour mit folgenden Worten übergeben: "'Hier haben Sie Ihren jungen Rich; Gott gebe ihm mit Ihrem Namen Ihren Geist, und Ihr Herz!'" (347). Lord Rich hat die Erziehung und Ausbildung 'seines' Sohnes bereits geplant:

---

[50] Ehrich-Haefeli: Zur Genese der bürgerlichen Konzeption der Frau. S. 119.

[51] Die moralische Erziehung und berufliche Ausbildung junger Mädchen, derer die Sternheim sich zuwendet, stellt im Ansatz den Versuch zu einer Erziehung zur Unabhängigkeit dar. Daraus jedoch – wie Nenon in *Autorschaft und Frauenbildung* – zu schlußfolgern, daß "die La Roche letztlich von einem egalitären Geschlechtsverhältnis" (83) ausgehe, erscheint überzogen. Wenn das Frauenbild Sophie von La Roches auch keinesfalls mit den Extrempositionen Rousseaus gleichgesetzt werden kann, so erkennt die Schriftstellerin doch letztlich eine von der sozialen Klasse bestimmte Rolle der Frau in Abgrenzung zum Mann an. Nicht ein egalitäres oder nicht-egalitäres Geschlechtsverhältnis, sondern vielmehr eine biologisch respektive sozial determinierte Geschlechterdifferenz unterscheiden die Konzepte Rousseaus und La Roches.

[52] Koschorke. S. 101.

[53] Becker-Cantarino: *Der lange Weg zur Mündigkeit*. S. 3.

[54] Ehrich-Haefeli: Zur Genese der bürgerlichen Konzeption der Frau. S. 122.

[W]enn ich das Leben behalte, soll dieser Knabe keinen andern Hofmeister, keinen andern Begleiter auf seinen Reisen haben als mich. – Alle Ausgaben für ihn
sind meine; seine Leute sind doppelt belohnt; ich schlafe neben seinem Zimmer;
ja ich baue ein Haus am Ende des Gartens, in das ich mit ihm ziehen werde,
wenn er volle zwei Jahre alt sein wird (347f.).

Indem Zuwendung und Erziehung Elternschaft konstituieren, wird der Fortpflanzungsakt und damit jede Körperlichkeit verdrängt. Auch die Rolle der
Frau als Gebärerin wird auf ein Minimum reduziert.

In dem Roman Sophie von La Roches manifestiert sich vor dem Hof als
Negativfolie das Bild einer neuen empfindsamen Körperlichkeit. Der Körper dient dem Ausdruck der tugendhaften Innerlichkeit, jegliche Form unkontrollierter Gefühlsäußerungen wird – mit Ausnahme des Weinens – ab-
gelehnt. Darin zeigt sich eine Kritik am Hofleben, wobei insbesondere das
Verhalten der Hofdamen das Mißfallen des Fräuleins von Sternheim erregt.
Denn obwohl die Protagonistin versucht, sich der begehrlichen Blicke zu
erwehren, begegnet sie dem Verhalten der Männer bei Hofe letztlich weniger kritisch als dem der Frauen. Sophie von La Roche leistet damit einerseits dem patriarchalischen Konzept von Weiblichkeit Vorschub, andererseits gelingt es ihr, gerade aus dem Unvermögen der Männer, ihre Leidenschaft zu kontrollieren, einen bedingten Machtanspruch der tugendhaften
Frau zu deduzieren. Damit weist sie der empfindsamen Frau einen Bereich
zu, aus dem sich nicht nur eine Überlegenheit gegenüber den Hofdamen
ableitet, sondern aus dem sich darüber hinaus die Verantwortung für das
tugendhafte Leben des Mannes konstituiert. Allerdings kann dieser teils aus
Anpassung teils aus Überlegenheit bestehende Bereich der Frau nur wahrgenommen werden, wenn der Mann die weibliche Rolle ebenfalls gemäß
dem empfindsamen Konzept von Tugendhaftigkeit und Körperlichkeit definiert. Die Verbindung mit Derby muß daher notwendigerweise scheitern.
Seymour hingegen ermöglicht es dem Fräulein von Sternheim innerhalb des
vordergründig auf die Unterdrückung weiblicher Sexualität ausgerichteten
Konzepts von Körperlichkeit, eine gewisse Eigenständigkeit zu entwickeln.
Indem das Fräulein von Sternheim dazu beiträgt, daß "jeder Tag [...] etwas
von dem lodernden Feuer" (349) hinwegnimmt, nutzt sie einen bedingten,
durch Anpassung entstandenen, Freiraum ihrer Weiblichkeit.

Alexander Mathäs

Colonising the German Body: Self and Other in *Sturm und Drang* Drama

By linking immutable intellectual and moral properties to physical appearance and ethnic origin, late-eighteenth-century German intellectuals anticipated later "justifications" for race and gender hierarchies. Two central figures connected to such thinking were Johann Caspar Lavater (1741-1801) and Johann Gottfried Herder (1744-1803), who associated human character traits to national characteristics. My analysis of Götz von Berlichingen *and* Julius von Tarent *will show, however, that the literary enactment of the colonialist imagination in* Sturm und Drang *drama not only asserted but also questioned its claims to validity.*

This analysis brings together concepts belonging to seemingly unrelated topics. What does colonialism, generally referred to as "the implanting of settlements on distant territory",[1] have to do with a late eighteenth-century German literary movement that called for aesthetic innovation and successfully contributed to the establishment of a German national culture? Germany did not even exist as a nation state during the period of the *Sturm und Drang* in the 1770s and therefore could not have been involved in any colonialist endeavours at that time. Or can we assume that Germany's geopolitical fragmentation in the eighteenth century produced "a sense of moral superiority, a moral highground for judging the performance of others" which was to be expressed in "ethnocentric, exclusive, eventually even aggressive fantasies", as Susanne Zantop suggests?[2]

Before one can confirm any such assertions, the relationship between nationalism, colonialism, and racism needs clarification. In other words, what does the promotion of German national literary and cultural values possibly have to do with racism or colonialism? According to Etienne Balibar's hypothesis, racism is based on "a historical system of complementary exclusions and dominations which are mutually interconnected".[3] This entails the systematic oppression of "various social groups – not just ethnic groups, but women, sexual deviants, the mentally ill, subproletarians and so on" – based on the "naturalization of differences".[4] Such discriminatory practices are

---

[1] Edward Said: *Culture and Imperialism*. New York 1994. P. 9.

[2] Susanne Zantop: *Colonial Fantasies: Conquest, Family, and Nation in Precolonial Germany, 1770-1870*. Durham, NC 1997. P. 8.

[3] Etienne Balibar: Racism and Nationalism. In: *Race, Nation, Class: Ambiguous Identities*. Ed. by Etienne Balibar and Immanuel Wallerstein. London, New York 1991. P. 49.

[4] Ibid. P. 48.

brought about by the production of a fictive ethnicity through the fantasies, discourses, and behaviours that constitute a national community. In short, nationality is intrinsically linked to racism because it is the result of a selection process that is based on a fictitious ethnicity.

Nationalism is connected to colonialism because of its territorial claim. For nationality is always defined against the outside world. While Germany did not exist as a national territory within fixed borders until 1871, nationalism did exist in the form of an 'ideology'. In fact, many historians have argued that German nationalism was induced by Germany's geo-political fragmentation.[5] Consequently, the absence of national unity provoked the yearning for it, as can be seen in *Sturm und Drang* literature. In view of this background, Zantop's hypothesis of literature as a *"Handlungsersatz*, as a substitute for the real thing, as imaginary testing ground for colonial action" becomes understandable.[6]

My analysis does not focus on an imaginary colonialist settlement of distant territory but rather on the literary colonisation of the German body as a spatial metaphor that became available for the inscription or – in Albrecht Koschorke's term – "alphabetisation" of nationalist cultural yearnings.[7] Koschorke presents his notion of the imaginary inscription of the body in the context of the paradigm shift from the oral communication practices of the feudal order to the written discourses of late-eighteenth-century society. The shift from an established feudal order, with its consecrated hierarchical structures embodied by the physical presence of authority, to the complex legal structures of the new civil state required new discursive practices.[8] The power that once had been personified by political and spiritual authority figures became diversified and was eventually substituted by an anonymous set of legal regulations that privileged the written word over oral discourses. The absence of personified authority in written communication put the integrity of the body of the state into question. Yet Koschorke asserts that the deterritorialisation of the state's body also initiated literary practices that recreated the body through fantasies of national cohesion, and thus compensated for the loss of its physical presence. This so-called process of "alpha-

[5] Hans-Ulrich Wehler: *Aspekte des Nationalismus*. Göttingen 2000; Wolfgang J. Mommsen: *Bürgerliche Kultur und künstlerische Avantgarde: Kultur und Politik im deutschen Kaiserreich 1870-1914*. Frankfurt/M. 1994; Karl-Dietrich Bracher: *The German Dictatorship: The Origins, Structure, and Consequences of National Socialism*. New York 1991; Jürgen Kocka: Assymetrical Historical Comparison: The Case of the German 'Sonderweg'. In: *History and Theory* 38 (1999). Vol. 1. Pp. 40-51.

[6] Zantop. P.6.

[7] Albrecht Koschorke: *Körperströme und Schriftverkehr: Mediologie des 18. Jahrhunderts*. München 1999.

[8] Ibid. Pp. 264-265.

betisation" filled in the spaces where the old body had been amputated.[9] To be more precise, fantasies that imagined the ideal body as a complete and organic unit with distinct physical boundaries compensated for the loss of actual national and social identity.

This cultural fantasy of a "natural" body served *Sturm und Drang* writers as a model for the nation's anatomy and character. The analogy between body and nation functioned, on the one hand, to legitimate claims to national autonomy and, on the other hand, to define the nation in terms of innate characteristics. A central figure connected to such thinking was Johann Caspar Lavater (1741-1801). By establishing a direct correspondence between physical appearance and human behaviour, Lavater's *Physiognomische Fragmente zur Beförderung der Menschenkenntnis und Menschenliebe* (1775-1778) prepared the body for the inscription of bourgeois ethics. He colonised the human body, as it were, by constructing it as a space with distinct boundaries that was to be appropriated, defined, idealised, and endowed with meaning. In this respect, colonising the German body means investing it with moral, political, and patriotic values and presenting them as natural.[10]

A particular interest of this analysis lies in the spatial and visual imagery that links Lavater's pseudo-scientific method to *Sturm und Drang* drama. The tropes, metaphors, and images of that period call attention not only to the fear of Germans being colonised by their European neighbours but also to a power struggle within the emerging bourgeois subject. Germany's political fragmentation during the eighteenth century as well as the psychological insecurities of the emerging middle class inspired a literary and philosophical discourse that expressed a longing for spiritual and national unity. The desire of German bourgeois intellectuals to overcome a depressing political reality – a reality that could not live up to the Enlightenment promise of individual autonomy and social equality – manifested itself in the creation of a national myth that presented Germany as a naturally grown organism.[11] Yet the promotion of this national character created an interior battleground for a perpetual power struggle between imagined unity and

---

[9] Ibid. P. 267: "In gewisser Weise dehnt sich der alte Leib als Entstehungsort und Durchzugsgebiet von Fluida auf das Territorium der Schriftlichkeit aus. Mit dem gleichen Recht kann man sagen, daß er kommunikationstechnisch amputiert wird und das Schicksal einer fortschreitenden Deterritorialisierung erfährt. Denn die Schrift ist der Ort, wo der Körper nicht ist, und die Ausnutzung dieser simplen Tatsache bietet gerade der Empfindsamkeit vielfältige Variationsmöglichkeiten".

[10] Ibid. Pp. 267-268. Koschorke points out the discrepancy between the increasing fluidity of the written discursive practices and the binary contrast of literary fantasies, such as Lavater's silhouettes.

[11] Johann Gottfried Herder: Auch eine Philosophie der Geschichte zur Bildung der Menschheit. In: *Werke:* Vol. 4. Ed. by Jürgen Brummack and Martin Bollacher. Frankfurt/M. 1994. Pp. 9-107.

political reality. The literary enactment of these internal tensions engendered a colonialist metaphysics that, on the one hand, anticipated the political realities of nineteenth-century imperialism and, on the other, metamorphosed into a powerful conceptual dialectics to challenge it.

Götz von Berlichingen, for example, likens his mutilated body to the fractured nation when he compares his own fate to that of the *Kaiser*: "Ich lieb ihn, denn wir haben einerlei Schicksal [...]. Ich weiß, er wünscht sich manchmal lieber tot, als länger die Seele eines so krüppligen Körpers zu sein".[12] Götz's crippled body is viewed against the background of an ideal national body that is infused with so-called indigenous character traits, such as honesty, vigour, sincerity, simplicity, and originality. Such character traits permeate the *Sturm und Drang* literature of all genres, from the essay-collection *Von deutscher Art und Kunst* (1773) to Goethe's *Die Leiden des jungen Werther* (1774) to Bürger's poems, to dramas by Goethe, Klinger, and Leisewitz. By linking immutable intellectual and moral properties to physical appearance and ethnic origin, this discourse anticipated the justification for race and gender hierarchies that would later gain such notoriety. My investigation concentrates on the literary metaphors that paved the way for an explicitly German colonial imagination.

While recent German scholarship has attempted to rescue the literature of the *Sturm und Drang* era from false claims of national-socialist researchers, who attempted to exploit these works to promote their ideological agenda,[13] it might be of interest to examine the reasons that made such misguided readings possible. This analysis will therefore attempt to shed light on the distinction between what Balibar called "'good' and 'bad' nationalism",[14] by comparing the naturalisation of moral values in Lavater's and Herder's writings on physiognomy to the enactment of those values in some of the most well-known *Sturm und Drang* dramas, such as Goethe's *Götz von Berlichingen* (1774), J. A. Leisewitz's *Julius von Tarent* (1776), and F. M. Klinger's *Die Zwillinge* (1776). These dramas present the German national character as embodied by a certain type of manliness that both secures and yet exceeds its boundaries. To illuminate the discursive practices of the colonial imagination, I will first delineate the recurring metaphors connected to the colonisation of the body. In a second step I will discuss how Lavater and Herder helped shape these discursive practices in their attempts to define national characteristics. A closer examination of *Götz von Berlichingen* and *Julius von Tarent* will show, however, that the literary enactment of the colonialist imagination not only asserts but also questions its consequences.

---

[12] Johann Wolfgang Goethe: *Götz von Berlichingen*. In: *Werke*. Hamburger Ausgabe. Vol. 4. München 1996. Pp. 141.

[13] Matthias Luserke: *Sturm und Drang*. Stuttgart 1997. Pp. 40-41.

[14] Balibar. P. 47.

Both the dramas of the *Sturm und Drang* as well as Lavater's *Physiognomische Fragmente* construct the boundaries of male subjectivity by using spatial imagery, such as confinement, penetration, damarcation, that is reminiscent of colonial discourse. In their endeavours to preserve male autonomy as the bourgeoisie struggles for emancipation, they create an ideal form of the body that acts in compliance with the laws of nature rather than those of an authoritarian ruler. While the outside of the bodily contour is determined by the exigencies of empirical reality, the inside must be preserved and defended as a sanctuary of divine nature.[15] Under the overwhelming pressures of the outside world that threaten to infringe on the freedom of the individual, nature in these texts emancipates itself from its confined space and transcends the borders of its quasi "unnatural" confinement. This impulse to break free from incarceration finds expression in almost all the *Sturm und Drang* plays from Gerstenberg's *Ugolino* (1768) to *Götz von Berlichingen* to *Urfaust* (1775) to Lenz's *Der Hofmeister* (1774) to *Julius von Tarent*. In all of these plays the protagonists find themselves in positions of spatial confinement and isolation, which they try to overcome. Yet the borders of their confinement are also part of an identity that provides them with a sense of safety and inner freedom. In their attempts to defend their autonomy, the boundaries are invested with ambiguous meanings. They can be represented as both real and ideal, both natural and unnatural. For the protagonists assume roles of both the coloniser and the colonised.

The spatial imagery in the *Sturm und Drang* dramas under analysis here illustrates how images of the body and its confinement give a sense of unity to the individual by evoking scenarios of conquest, expansion, occupation, and surrender. For example, the male protagonists emphasise an unwavering integrity and moral firmness, which also finds expression in their physical vigour and rigidity. In the process of erecting borders between the outside and the self, moral attributes are infused with gender-specific qualities. Similarly, Sigrid Weigel and Susanne Zantop point out the discursive analogies that exist between colonialist descriptions of nature and those of women in eighteenth-century travel literature. They show that toward the end of the great geographical discoveries of the eighteenth century, "woman" as a symbol for the unknown or irrational replaced the foreign or the exotic.[16] In the absence of further geographical territories to be discovered, women figures in literature were assigned the same characteristics as

---

[15] Hartmut Böhme: *Natur und Subjekt.* Frankfurt/M 1988. Pp. 198-204. Böhme points out the idealised nature of the silhouette by referring to its mystical origins in Swedenborg's writings. See also Koschorke pp. 148-153.

[16] Sigrid Weigel: Die nahe Fremde – das Territorium des 'Weiblichen': Zum Verhältnis von Wilden und Frauen im Diskurs der Aufklärung. In: *Die andere Welt: Studien zum Exotismus.* Ed. by Thomas Koebner and Gerhard Pickerodt. Frankfurt/M. 1987. P. 173.

the "foreign" used to have. Both pure yet deceitful, both chaste yet seductive, both tame yet savage, both restrained yet uncontrollable, women figures came to suggest the ambiguities that male explorers had projected onto the unknown.

Yet colonial imagery is not reserved for the characterisation of Woman as Other. The ambiguity of the coloniser's attitude toward the "foreign" is also apparent in the *Stürmer and Dränger's* characterisation of the male body. Regarded at the time as a divine creation, the body is also the site where an idealised nature and a vilified reality collide. In this dual capacity, the body's boundaries parallel Germany's geopolitical reality. For they signify both the desire for a unified German identity and the despondence over a constricting political reality. The *Stürmer und Dränger's* focus on the definition and maintenance of male autonomy intersects with an awareness that the borders between the male subject and its Other are unsustainable. In view of a superior power that encroaches upon the male subject's individuality, the protagonists follow a double-edged strategy of constriction and expansion – a strategy that protects the individual autonomy from its own restrictions in the name of an inner freedom. This tactic becomes obvious when Götz von Berlichingen is confronted with imminent defeat in his final hour. For as soon as the borders that protect his autonomy break down, Götz transcends the confinement of his earthly prison and becomes part of an all-embracing universe: "Löse meine Seele nun. – Arme Frau. Ich lasse dich in einer verderbten Welt. [...] Himmlische Luft – Freiheit! Freiheit! *Er stirbt*".[17] Such fantasies of spiritual self-extension anticipate the dream of territorial expansion.

The affirmation of a male gender identity is also very much part of this period's double-edged body politics. Correspondingly, male protagonists strive to protect themselves from "threatening" female attractions by assuming an impenetrable firmness. Femininity, on the other hand, is depicted as a penetrating, devouring force that can invade the borders of male identity. Götz von Berlichingen and Guido of *Julius von Tarent*, for example, are obsessed with manly resolve in their attempts to counteract fears of being intruded upon by forms of weakness, effeminate self-indulgence or political deceitfulness.[18] Their readiness to defend their gender territory is expressed in their physical appearance. Götz's armour, for example, signifies both his moral firmness and his fears of penetration. Guelfo of *Die Zwillinge* is also a knight who prides himself on his heroic actions on the battlefield,[19] and Guido brags about his resolve and inner steadfastness.[20] On the one

---

[17] Goethe: *Götz*. P. 175.

[18] Johann Anton Leisewitz: *Julius von Tarent*. Ed. by Werner Keller. Stuttgart 1965. P. 11.

[19] Friedrich Maximilian Klinger: *Die Zwillinge*. Stuttgart 1972. P. 27.

[20] Leisewitz. P. 15.

hand, rigidity is supposed to provide protection against the intrusion of weak, yet uncontrollable forces that threaten to undermine the male protagonists' individuality. At the same time, this rigidity prevents these heroic overachievers from extending their limits and taking advantage of their full potential. Götz's armour is both protection and confinement. It signifies the knight's firmness of conviction, but it also allows for little flexibility. One of his main tragic flaws, for example, is his inability to adapt to the changing times.

The male protagonists of these dramas are depicted as afraid of being subjugated and yet eager to transcend their limits in order to colonise what lies beyond. Guido seeks to augment his glory as heroic knight by fighting in a crusade and feels like a prisoner in a cage at home.[21] Faust in his relentless striving to discover life also reveals the avarice of the coloniser. Götz dreams of fighting wolves, Turks, the foxes, and the French even beyond the borders of the German lands.[22] The juxtaposition of wolves and Turks or foxes and French equates foreigners with ferocious, cunning beasts. According to Balibar such "systematic 'bestialization' of individuals and racialized groups" is typical of racist xenophobia which "endlessly rehearses the scenario of a humanity eternally leaving humanity behind and eternally threatened with falling into the grasp of animality".[23]

The heroes' efforts to exceed their bodily limitations are provoked by their longing to be "whole". Like Götz, who lost both his right hand and his best friend, Guido and Guelfo also feel bereft. Guido, for example, competes with his brother Julius for Blanca. Guido compares her to a trophy that he wants to possess in order to feel complete. For Blanca, as her name already suggests, is simply a generic substitute for the male heroes' narcissistic zeal.

While their desire for completion persists, the male protagonists' borders are contested from both outside and within. For they feel restricted and besieged. Götz, Guido, and Guelfo also feel limited by their brothers and *alter egos* who simply represent what they are not: soft, yielding, effeminate, opportunistic, and, in their eyes, deviating from nature's path. While the protagonists depend on these Others to define their own individualities, their existence prevents them from living up to their potential. Thus the male heroes are confined by the very borders that set them apart from their *alter egos* and determine their individuality. Götz, for example, feels threatened by the dawning new age and its restricting laws that will no longer grant him autonomy as a free knight. At the same time he is not satisfied with a peaceful existence in his castle but strives to fight for his cause outside his home turf. Guido feels restricted by his brother's success, effeminacy, and

---

[21] Ibid. Pp. 13-14.
[22] Goethe. *Götz*. Pp. 142-143.
[23] Balibar. P. 57.

276

intellectual superiority. He seeks compensation for his insufficiencies by trying to gain recognition on the battlefield in foreign countries. In view of these pressures that threaten the borders of male individuality, questions of identity become subject to negotiation in spite of the protagonists' commitments to inner stability. Such challenges to the male sense of self were being widely discussed among intellectuals at the time. This is why the definition of the individual's contours receives so much attention in both Lavater's physiognomy and *Sturm und Drang* drama.

The ambiguity of such limiting borders comes across most clearly in *Götz von Berlichingen* when Götz hears about the captivity of his men, and Elisabeth answers to his angry reaction: "Laß sie gefangen sein, sie sind frei!"[24] In exchange for their imprisonment Götz's men gain an inner freedom that is absolute. The same transformation from outer confinement to inner sovereignty occurs at the end of the drama when Götz finally leaves his worldly prison.[25] The dialectics between freedom and confinement are also at play when Götz is sentenced to stay put in his own castle. This time the knight acts against his inclinations and obeys the emperor's orders to save the lives of his men. If he had followed his own leanings he would have broken his vow of loyalty toward the emperor. Yet the decision to obey the emperor is also a decision against himself. The border that once limited the knight's freedom only from the outside now becomes internalised and compromises his integrity. Georg, his young admirer, expresses Götz's dilemma rather succinctly: "Ach, ich vergaß, daß wir eingesperrt sind – und unsere Haut davonzubringen, setzen wir unsere Haut dran?"[26] By restoring Götz's fighting spirit and sending him into battle, Goethe pushes the borders out again and thus rescues Götz's individuality. Ironically the knight's tragic flaws, his inflexibility and outmoded patriarchal egotism, predicate his personal autonomy. Seen from this perspective, Götz is free at the end when he is thrown into prison. For he can stay true to his nature and must yield only to pressures from outside. This is why Elisabeth is right when she exclaims: "Laß sie gefangen sein, sie sind frei!" The age of cunning and deceit, as Götz calls it, brings about his ultimate physical defeat and sets him internally free.

Lavater's *Physiognomische Fragmente* can be viewed as an attempt to define the borders of the male bourgeois subject in order to preserve his internal freedom. In the following I will sketch out the basic principles of Lavater's physiognomy because they illustrate some of the figurative strategies of proto-colonialist discourse in the 1770s – strategies that parallel those in *Sturm und Drang* drama. Lavater relied on an enormous amount of drawings, silhouettes, and engravings on which he based his character stud-

---

[24] Goethe. *Götz*. P. 145.
[25] Ibid. P. 175.
[26] Ibid. P. 143.

ies. Among the various styles of depiction Lavater preferred the silhouette because he believed that it was both the truest and most truthful rendition of a human face ("das wahreste und getreueste Bild das man von einem Menschen geben kann"[27]): "Was kann weniger Bild eines ganz lebendigen Menschen seyn, als ein Schattenriß? und wie viel sagt er! wenig Gold; aber das reinste!"[28] Lavater wanted to get as close to nature as possible. For nature was for the *Stürmer and Dränger* the most reliable source when it came to detecting the divine principle that was supposedly at work in all creatures. Lavater's dual specification of the silhouette, as both the truest and most faithful rendition of the human face, refers to the double perspective that meets in the contour of the silhouette – just as the borders in *Sturm und Drang* drama are also always subject to twofold scrutiny. While "das wahreste" refers to the truth in an ideal sense, "das getreueste" describes the mimetic qualities of the contour and thus refers to empirical reality. In this sense physiognomy was more than a science because it was supposed to reveal the divine language of creation beneath the surface appearance of the human body.[29] Defining the limits of the subject in drama follows the same objectives as Lavater's interpretations of silhouettes: to reveal the line where, according to Goethe's words, "das Eigentümliche unsres Ichs, die prätendierte Freiheit unsres Wollens, mit dem notwendigen Gang des Ganzen zusammenstößt".[30] (See Plate XXVII, Figs. 1 to 5)

The silhouette marks a distinct border that defines an individual's uniqueness. As an imprint of divine nature, it represents an undistorted, measurable identification that allows the physiognomist to describe a human being in an objective manner. At the same time, silhouettes leave the interior of the facial area undefined. The interior blank space gives the physiognomist enough room to be creative and idealise his object – just as Goethe idealises Götz when he sends him back into battle and reconstructs his internal dilemma as a fight against the outside world in order to rescue his individual autonomy. The silhouette proves ideal for Lavater's purposes because it is both a precise and undetermined rendition of nature: "Die Natur ist scharf und frei".[31] In other words, the "ideal" and the "natural" meet in the contour of the silhouette. The physiognomist has to focus on specific points of reference in a human being's body that permit him to get to the bottom of a person's basic character traits.[32] For Lavater a person's bone structure or con-

---

[27] Johann Caspar Lavater: *Physiognomische Fragmente zur Beförderung der Menschenkenntnis und Menschenliebe*. Ed. by Christoph Siegrist. Stuttgart 1984. P. 152.

[28] Ibid.

[29] Ibid. Pp. 95-96.

[30] Johann Wolfgang Goethe: Zum Shakespeares-Tag. In: *Werke*. Hamburger Ausgabe. Vol. 12. München 1998. P. 226.

[31] Lavater. P. 153.

[32] Ibid. P. 161.

tour of face tells much more than the surface of the skin.[33] His predilection for silhouettes results from his method of distilling the essence from the surface. The identification of the "ideal" with the "natural", is found in countless literary and cultural documents of the 1770s and 1780s. The simple plain contours of Götz von Berlichingen's armor resemble those of Lavater's silhouettes. It is both an integral part of his identity and symbolizes the line where his individual freedom and the pressures of the outside world collide. The metaphor of the *silhouette* (*Schattenriß* or *Sonnenriß*) occurs time and again in the literature of this period. Both Herder and Lessing, for example, use this metaphor to signify the congruity between the divine origin of nature and true-to-nature art.[34]

While creative accomplishment replaces birthright, bourgeois values still need a quintessential justification. The attempt to determine the nature of people by categorising them according to their physical appearance can be attributed to a lack of stability in a rapidly changing empirical reality. Despite the *Stürmer und Dränger's* plea for individual autonomy, their philosophies reveal a resistance toward secularisation by clinging to absolute laws, accessible only to the high priest of culture: the genius. The promotion of the genius as a naturally gifted individual is inextricably linked to the idealisation of nature. By naturalising bourgeois ideals, Herder, Lavater, Goethe and other members of the *Sturm und Drang* were cultivating a natural order that imitated the God-given hierarchy of feudal society. The consecrated right of the noble ruler is now rivalled by the divine right of the genius. This interpretation would also explain the *Stürmer und Dränger's* belief in firm character traits that can withstand the superficial whims of the times. Lavater, for example claims that each individual is equipped with a different physiognomy and consequently specific character traits: "Jeder muß bleiben, wer er ist".[35] The loss of the belief in a divine order during the secularisation process created a spiritual vacuum that could readily be filled with pseudo-scientific or metaphysical explanations. Hence the need for essential truths and reliable belief systems. Physiognomy is one example of the desire to classify and categorise empirical phenomena in order to create fundamental laws that could explain human nature. According to Balibar, "classification and hierarchy are operations of naturalisation *par excellence*" and as such mark the shift from historical and social differences to "natural", genealogical, or racial characteristics.[36]

---

[33] Christoph Siegrist: Nachwort. In: *Physiognomische Fragmente*. Stuttgart 1984. P. 383.

[34] Gotthold Ephraim Lessing: Hamburgische Dramaturgie. In: *Werke und Briefe*. Vol. 6. Ed. by Klaus Bohnen. Frankfurt/M. 1985. Pp. 577-578; Herder: Shakespeare. In: *Werke*. Vol. 2. Frankfurt/M. 1993. Pp. 510-512.

[35] Lavater. P. 310.

[36] Balibar. P. 56.

The dangers of such classifications become obvious in Herder's essay "Ist die Schönheit des Körpers ein Bote von der Schönheit der Seele?" published in the *Gelehrten Beiträgen zu den Rigischen Anzeigen aufs Jahr 1766*.[37] While Herder attempts to replace a classicist aesthetics of a beautiful and idealised nature by a more historically and culturally differentiated system, he adheres to essentialist categories of beauty. These categories are modified, however, according to the cultural, social, geographical, and historic needs of specific ethnic groups. That is, the standards of beauty vary among the different nations and even among individual people. Yet Herder still recognises a hierarchy of aesthetic categories ranging from external skin colour as the lowest, to the physical shape or bone structure of the face, to the spiritual beauty (*geistige Schönheit*) as the highest:

> Der *niedrigste* Geschmack läßt sich an der bloßen *Völligkeit* begnügen, und urteilt höchstens nach *Munterkeit* und dem Anstrich der Wangen. Der feinere erhebt sich, um *Regelmäßigkeit* bis in den feinsten Zügen zu empfinden; der dritte ist auf die *geistige Schönheit* aufmerksam, die sich in den Augen, den Wangen und den Stellungen und Nuancen des ganzen Körpers entdecket.[38]

Herder is careful not to push too far with such generalisations. He concedes that these categories are only an indication of certain character dispositions or inclinations toward moral decency and cannot be considered as reliable proof for a person's deep intellect (*tiefen Verstand*) or strong and really virtuous soul (*starke und wirklich tugendhafte Seele*).[39] Yet he universalises certain European beauty ideals, such as white skin colour, by remarking that even black people find lighter colour of skin desirable and respect the white God always as a good God.[40] While Herder shows an awareness of cultural differences, he reaffirms the connection between the beauty of the body and the beauty of the soul. He also judges different ethnic groups from a eurocentric point of view. In citing a famous quote by David Hume, he maintains that black people are not ingenious by alleging that they resemble apes in both body and spirit.[41] Herder attributes the spiritual and mental inferiority of so-called Negroes and Eskimos to the extremities of the climate, which prevents mental and physical development: "Nur die mittlere [sic] Gegenden sind Werkstätten der Natur, wo sie die Schönheit des Körpers und

---

[37] Herder: Ist die Schönheit des Körpers ein Bote von der Schönheit der Seele? In: *Werke*. Vol. 1. Ed. by Ulrich Gaier. Frankfurt/M. 1985. Pp. 135-151.

[38] Ibid. P. 143.

[39] Ibid. P. 146.

[40] Ibid. Pp. 143-144.

[41] Ibid. P. 140.

Geistes gemeinschaftlich zur Reife bringen, ausbilden und erheben kann".[42]
(See Plate LVIII, Figs. 3 to 6)

Such condescending judgements are not uncommon among European thinkers at the time. Kant, for example, refers to the same citation by Hume in his "Beobachtungen über das Gefühl des Schönen und Erhabenen".[43] Apart from allocating "Negroes" to the lowest positions of humankind, he invokes natural law in his warnings against racial intermixture.[44] Lavater also classifies different nationalities by linking physical appearance to behaviour. He assumes that the eyes of the Chinese are somehow an indication of indulgence, voluptuousness, and sloth[45] and characterises black people as "geil, diebisch, rachgierig, Lügner und Schmeichler".[46] What lends these physiognomic generalisations credibility to his contemporaries is the appearance of objectivity. By connecting so-called natural laws to empirical observations that are verifiable, such hypotheses gain a legitimacy that is further fuelled by nationalist sentiments: "What theoretical racism calls 'race' or 'culture' (or both together) is therefore a continuation of the nation, a concentrate of the qualities which belong to the nationals as their own".[47]

In sketching out the anthropological contours of different races and nationalities, Lavater and Herder create a space which allows them to define the essential character traits of the German bourgeois individual. Values like distinctness, integrity, purity, righteousness, honesty, stability, and decisiveness were paired with a gendered physique that matched these internal qualities. Götz is characterised as the archetype of an individual who ideally could make use of his human potential and carry out his calling as an exemplary knight.[48] He could be in tune with himself, were it not for his missing right hand. His physical handicap does not prevent him from fulfilling his knightly duties, however. As the result of a combat injury, his mutilation does not affect his "natural" knightly talents. Thus the missing hand signifies the difference between the "real" and the "natural". While Götz's personality stays true to his "natural" disposition, the reality of his life no longer conforms to this inner ideal. (See Plate LVIII, Figs. 8 to 11)

The male protagonists compensate for the threat of being colonised by outside forces with megalomaniac fantasies of self-expansion and domination. When the outside pressures on the individual increase to a point that it

---

[42] Ibid. P. 141.

[43] Immanuel Kant: Beobachtungen über das Gefühl des Schönen und Erhabenen. In: *Gesammelte Schriften.* Ed. by Artur Buchenau. Vol. 2. Berlin 1912. P. 253.

[44] Paul Gilroy: *Against Race: Imagining Political Culture Beyond the Color Line.* Cambridge, Mass. 2000. P. 58.

[45] Lavater. P. 317.

[46] Ibid. P. 325.

[47] Balibar. P. 59.

[48] Goethe: *Götz.* Pp. 80-82, 156.

becomes difficult to maintain the subject's autonomy, the protagonists' freedom recedes deeper into their interior and takes an abstract quality. Guido in *Julius von Tarent*, for example, seeks refuge in his internal powers that transcend the realm of the natural:

> Was wäre Guido ohne diese Stetigkeit – Macht, Stärke, Leben, lauter Schalen, die das Schicksal abschälet, wenn es will – aber mein eigentliches Selbst sind meine festen Entschließungen – und da bricht sich seine Kraft. Und warum sollte ich meine Entwürfe nicht ausführen? Gehorsam beugt sich die leblose Natur unter die Hand des Helden [...].[49]

These heroes defend their inner freedom even beyond their graves. When Götz realises that the approaching age of reason encroaches on the boundaries of his personal territory, – which also mark the territory of his male identity – he embraces death because it offers an escape from his worldly prison and promises freedom from all.[50] As soon as the empirical reality confronts the protagonists with their own mortality and threatens to penetrate the walls of their existence, the *Sturm und Drang* heroes view the assault as a chance to break free of all "natural" limitations.

Defining the borders of the national character means to contrast the Ideal to its Other. In the dramas of the *Sturm und Drang* the contours of the perfect male German subject re-emerge most clearly through interactions and conflicts with other social groups. In *Götz von Berlichingen,* for example, Götz and his men are contrasted to courtly society at the Bishop of Bamberg's palace. The play leaves no doubts that the German princes are interested only in augmenting their own power at the expense of the national cause. In a scene that exposes the pompous vacuity of courtly society, Olearius is introduced as one of many German courtiers who study law in Italy because Roman law is considered superior to traditional German law. The fact that he denies both his social and national origins presents him as the spineless opportunist that his name seems to suggest. The "oil" of his name characterises him as obscure as opposed to pure, fluid as opposed to firm, slick as opposed to honest. Thus he fits right into the *Sturm und Drang* typology that associates German nationality with purity, simplicity, firmness, vigour, distinctiveness, homogeneity, vitality, originality, practicality, straightness and everything foreign with the opposites of these terms.

The *Sturm und Drang* typology cannot really be called racist, however, because inherited character traits do not determine a person's life. According to Lavater, there is room for improvement as well as for deterioration in a person's development.[51] In *Sturm und Drang* drama this potential for

---

[49] Leisewitz. P. 15.

[50] Goethe: *Götz*. P. 175.

[51] Lavater. P. 145.

change is illustrated by the fraternal-strife motif. In these plays the two antagonists share a common family background. Weislingen and Götz, Guido and Julius, Guelfo and Ferdinando, Franz and Karl Moor are either twins or brothers in spirit who grow apart. Because the ability to change one's behavior also entails the possibility for deception, the physiognomist must be able to differentiate empirical reality from the underlying truth:[52] *"Ueberhaupt drückt die Silhouette vielmehr die Anlage, als die Würklichkeit des Charakters aus"*.[53] Despite the *Stürmer und Dränger's* caution in hypostatising the body-mind correspondences, both Lavater's *Physiognomische Fragmente* and the *Sturm und Drang* dramas contain practical tips that teach the reader or spectator to distinguish false pretences from true characteristics.

Such practical guidance aimed at the uncovering of deceptive human behaviour is, however, based on essentialist notions and occurs frequently with reference to gender issues. Lavater generally adopts the aesthetic principles of Plato by equating beauty with moral goodness: "Je moralisch besser; desto schöner. Je moralisch schlimmer; desto häßlicher".[54] This raises the question why Weislingen, as a morally weak character, is explicitly characterized as good-looking.[55] Weislingen is well built, makes a very friendly, pleasing impression and bears a close resemblance to *Kaiser Maximilian*. He reveals a "halb traurige[n] Zug auf seinem Gesicht"[56] that indicates a melancholy disposition. Adelheid, who knows Weislingen best, links his appearance to his character traits and describes him as rather effeminate:

> Endlich gingen mir die Augen auf. Ich sah statt des aktiven Mannes, der die Geschäfte des Fürstentums belebte, [...] den sah ich auf einmal jammernd wie einen kranken Poeten, melancholisch wie ein gesundes Mädchen, und müßiger als einen alten Junggesellen.[57]

According to Lavater's aesthetics, Weislingen's attractive appearance does not correspond to his rather non-masculine character, or does it? While Götz is depicted as the epitome of masculinity in spite of his "mutilated" body, Weislingen's character traits also seem to contradict his handsome looks. According to Goethe's play, masculinity is a quality that comes across through one's actions. Good looks per se, on the other hand, do not reveal any distinct personality traits. In actuality they seem to indicate a lack of

---

[52] Ibid. P. 111.
[53] Ibid. P. 161.
[54] Ibid. P. 53.
[55] Goethe: *Götz*. P. 108.
[56] Ibid. P. 108.
[57] Goethe: *Götz*. P. 117.

character as turns out to be the case for Weislingen. The mere fact that Weislingen's good looks are mentioned as an outstanding feature in itself makes him appear unmanly or even effeminate. Adelheid's maid, who describes Weislingen as "gewachsen wie eine Puppe",[58] underlines this gender anomaly. Herder, who in principle agrees with Lavater's premises, notes in his essay "Ist die Schönheit des Körpers ein Bote von der Schönheit der Seele?": "Ein Mann, der an Körper und Seele schön wie ein Weib sein will, ist eben so unleidlich als eine Henne, wenn sie kräht".[59] He also emphasises that great men often possess irregular features that signify distinctness and passion.[60] Thus Weislingen's moral deficiencies are "naturalised" by making him appear simply beautiful like a woman, yet lacking any other distinctive features.

Not only the male characters' gender deviance corresponds to moral deficiency. The same holds true for the women characters, such as Adelheid. Characterized as a beautiful woman, she has all the physical attributes that could make her predestined to be morally good, according to Lavater's aesthetics. Yet as an unscrupulous political strategist with a superior intellect that outsmarts all the men around her, she is the anathema to the female virtue of her time. For "die weiblichen Seelen", according to Lavater, simply "denken nicht viel". Thinking is men's power ("Denken ist Kraft der Mannheit"), feeling is women's power ("Empfindung ist Kraft der Frauen"), he adds.[61] Lavater admits to not knowing much about women but does not want to forgo the opportunity to warn others of degradation and self-degradation ("vor Erniedrigungen seiner selbst und anderer"). More explicitly, he wants to use physiognomy to discover the border between flesh and spirit ("die Gränze zwischen Fleisch und Geist entdecken") and to alert his fellow men, for example, to the harmful effects of women's immodest breasts ("euch verwahren gegen allen schädlichen Reiz ihrer schamlosen Brust!").[62]

Lavater treats the opposite sex like a foreign continent. While he mystifies women's angelic innocence, their "natural" ability to suffer, and their capacity to make men's lives more pleasant, he also senses a seductive danger that women's bodies exude. Thus the object of discovery becomes dubious because of the subject's expectations. Whereas masculine body characteristics are generally presented as direct expressions of moral qualities, feminine body qualities are often associated with deception. Such a naturalisation of gender norms marks a first step towards a 'racialisation' directed against women and deviants.

---

[58] Ibid. P. 108.
[59] Herder: Schönheit. P. 146.
[60] Ibid. P. 144.
[61] Lavater. P. 264
[62] Ibid. Pp. 260-262.

In Goethe's play the naturalisation of gender norms is highlighted by the contrasting figures of Maria and Adelheid. Maria has the humble, caring, and kind-hearted qualities that Lavater praises in his idealization of women. After all, she forgives Weislingen for betraying her and stays with him in his dying hour.[63] Adelheid's beguiling appearance, on the other hand, teaches the male physiognomist to look beyond the surface of women's bodies in order to discover their soul ("in dem Leibe die Seele zu sehen").[64] Had Weislingen been able to recognise Adelheid's cold-hearted, scheming character, he would have been forewarned. By presenting the vamp as an intellectually superior politician, Goethe follows the prevailing demonization of domineering women. According to the gender discourse of the time, women who engage in power politics are considered to be anomalous.[65] Adelheid violates the gender norms not only by venturing into the male domain of politics but also by luring Weislingen away from Maria and destroying the seeds for their "healthy" family-life. Lavater calls such domineering women, who rule "mit Zorn und Donnerwort" like men, "Mißgeburten" – a word choice that shows how gender and moral deviance intersect and become biological deviance.[66]

The characterisation of women figures in Leisewitz's *Julius von Tarent* is also suggestive of a colonial imagination. Blanca is the object of desire of the two inimical twins, Guido and Guelfo. As her name already suggests, she has no function other than being a blank screen for the projection of male longing. While the women figures in *Götz von Berlichingen* are typecast in a social context that permits them to either represent or violate the moral principles of their day and age, the women in Leisewitz's play lack any distinctive character traits that would make them come to life as individuals. We know them simply as potential brides-to-be. However, the focus of attention in *Sturm und Drang* drama is not directed toward these objects of desire but toward the narcissistic hegemony of the male self. The fact that Julius replaces his commitment toward his *fatherland* with his longing for Blanca, reveals how easily the object of desire can be associated with a territorial claim: "Vater und Vaterland will ich in ihr [Blanca] lieben".[67] In other words, territorial or colonial appropriation is driven by the same underlying motivation as erotic yearning: the satisfaction of male longing for completeness. Woman and *Fatherland* are both exchangeable as objects of desire that promise to compensate for the male subject's feelings of insufficiency.

---

[63] Goethe: *Götz*. Pp. 169-171.

[64] Lavater. P. 262.

[65] Kant. Beobachtungen. Pp. 228-253.

[66] Lavater. P. 265.

[67] Leisewitz. P. 51.

Gender deviations in *Sturm und Drang* drama usually signify moral shortcomings from the patriarchal ideals of the time, including those laid out in Lavater's physiognomy. The efforts to naturalise and safeguard male autonomy are, however, modified by more probing explorations into the male psyche. While the conflicts of *Sturm und Drang* drama are based mostly on extreme contrasts of character that highlight the protagonists' physiognomic typification, the naturalisation of bourgeois ideals never quite succeeds. Since the definition of the body promises internal autonomy and yet entails confinement, the process of colonisation can never be regarded as completed. For its dialectic implies that individual and national autonomy are restricted by the demarcation of their borders. The protagonists caught up in this dilemma in Goethe's *Götz von Berlichingen* and Leisewitz's *Julius von Tarent*, reveal this contradiction. At this juncture, the plays leave open whether individual and national autonomy can be salvaged by restoring a naturalised code of honour, as proposed later by the nationalist, colonialist, and racist ideologies of nineteenth-century Germany.

Yet the plays do not end by advocating such nationalist ideas, for what leads to the *Sturm und Drang* heroes' downfall is not their deviation from their convictions but their stubborn adherence to an outdated albeit idealised code of moral values. Goethe's dual perspective on his hero's masculine borders, which on the one hand idealises the patriarchal order and on the other reveals its limitations, abandons a colonial point of view that simply promotes male expansion. In retrospect, Götz's defence of his male boundaries is presented in a rather dubious light, for it comes at the price not only of his own life but at the lives of those who were loyal to him. The male protagonists of Leisewitz's *Julius von Tarent* and Klinger's *Die Zwillinge* are looked upon even less favourably. While Götz still reveals stature and courage in standing up for principles and ideals that are worth defending, his younger successors appear merely immature in their destructive attempts to act according to their impulses. By putting the "große Kerl" to the test and confronting him with the demands of the outside world, the plays leave no doubts about the limitations of individual autonomy. The fact that self-domination rather than domination over others seems the only way out of the protagonists' dilemmas foreshadows the idealist path that German literature would take in upholding individual autonomy as an ideal while revealing its actual impossibility. Consequently, the political demand for freedom was thwarted and turned back against the self. In this respect the bourgeois subject ended up colonising itself rather than others.

Yet this preoccupation with the bourgeois self, commonly known as *Verinnerlichung*, supports some of the assumptions connected to the so-called *Sonderweg*-theories: namely that the increasingly unpolitical and escapist nature of German intellectual life precipitated the totalitarianism and irrationalism of the Nazi regime. On the other hand, it is precisely the idealist turn away from politics that stopped short of pushing the nationalist agenda. For when literature replaced politics as a testing ground for bourgeois aspirations toward national and social liberation, the complexities, even contradictions behind the high expectations connected to the emancipation of the individual became obvious. Goethe, Klinger, and Leisewitz show an awareness of the paradoxical nature of male autonomy by revealing the close ties between individual autonomy and an uncompromising male egotism that forms the basis of colonial domination over its Other. Consequently, their dramas disclose a conceptual dialectic that both anticipated and challenged the political realities of nineteenth century imperialism. This said, one might add that the *Stürmer und Dränger* did not speak out against the nationalist and patriarchal value system of their time but left its conceptual framework intact. Moreover one could even argue that the spiritualisation of these values contributed to their preservation and made them unassailable. Regardless of the outcome of such critical inquiries, my analysis has shown that while the *Stürmer und Dränger* relied on classifications and hierarchies that by today's standards might be called racist or sexist, these attempts to naturalise a national bourgeois ethics could not withstand the test of literary enactment.

Illustrations

The illustrations and captions are published with the permission of Ross Woodrow (ed.): "Digital Lavater" available at http://www.newcastle.edu.au/discipline/fine-art/pubs/lavater/index.htm

Plate XXVII:
Source of character descriptions: Johann Caspar Lavater: *Essays on Physiognomy*. Transl. by Thomas Holcroft. 4th ed. London 1844. Pp. 197-200.

1

Fig. 1:
An original countenance, that will, to hundreds, speak sensibility, timidity, perspicuity, wit, and imagination. Not to be numbered among the strong, bold, unshaken, and enterprising; but very considerate, cautious to timidity; a countenance which often says much with a cold, yet excellent aspect.

2

Fig. 2:
A man of business, with more than common abilities. Undoubtedly possessed of talents, punctual honesty, love of order, and deliberation. An acute inspector of men; a calm, dry, determined judge. I do not know the man, not even so much as by name; but, to the middle of the mouth, is an advancing trait, which speaks superiority in common affairs.

Fig. 3:

A good head. – Cannot be mistaken, not even in shade. Conceal the under part, and leave only the nose and forehead visible, and signs of attention, love of order, and certainty, are apparent. The forehead, altogether, is too perpendicular for a productive mind. – The acute, the cheerful, the subtle, uncultivated wit of the original is difficult to be discovered in this shade; yet the outline of the lips gives reason to suspect these qualities.

Fig. 4:

Those who have never studied the man, and men in general but little, still cannot but respect this profile; although the forehead is not so entirely exact and pure as to discover the whole capacity of his understanding. The harmony of the whole, especially the nose, mouth, and chin, denote a mind of extraordinary observation, research, and analysis.

Fig. 5:

A noble forehead, a miracle of purity, the love of order, I might say, the love of light. – Such the nose, such is all. How capable of cultivation must such a profile be! I am unacquainted with the man, yet am I certain as that I live, that he is capable of the calmest examination, that he feels the necessity of, and delights in, clear conceptions, and that he must be an attentive observer.

Plate LVIII:

Fig. 3:

A German countenance, indubitably; concentered to one visible, limited purpose; full of phlegmatic patience, fidelity, and calm observation; formed to learn, imitate and finish: civil, ready to serve, most capable of works of art, without great sensibility, or creative genius.

Fig. 4:

An equally indubitable Italian countenance, apparent in the forehead, eyes, nose, mouth, and chin: candid, pious, eloquent, and intuitive; not inquiring comprehension, sublime free-thinking, nor the creative power of system-building, but an inexhaustible expansion of heart, humility, and serious exhortation, appear to me visible in this face.

Fig. 5:
This head is visibly Russian. At least there will be no hesitation in answering the question – Is it English, French, Italian, or Russian? The retreating of the upper parts, the high eyebrows, shallow eyes, short, somewhat turned up nose, and the large under part of the countenance, show the Russian. Worthy, faithful, good, brave; one to whom all wish well.

Fig. 6:
Manifestly a Turk, by the arching and position of the forehead, the hind part of the head, the eyebrows, and particularly the nose. The aspect is that of observation with a degree of curiosity. The open mouth denotes remarking, with some reflection.

Figs. 8, 9, 10, 11:
That these are neither French, Italian, German, nor English countenances will easily be seen; but not so easily that they are northern characters, employed in hunting and soothsaying, under the wide ruling Russian sceptre. The sleepy eye, the short thick nose, and the rather large mouth, especially the very remarkable under lip, and the inclination to breadth, in the full face, are manifestly the chief marks of their national character. Indolence and limited sensuality are apparent throughout.

Source of readings of national characters: Johann Caspar Lavater: *Essays on Physiognomy*. Transl. by Thomas Holcroft. 4th ed. London 1844. Pp. 429-432.

K. F. Hilliard

Atemübungen: Geist und Körper in der Lyrik des 18. Jahrhunderts

The paper examines poems by Brockes and Goethe in which breathing is either a topic of discussion, or a marked feature of viva voce performance, or both. It places the poems in the context of ideas about breathing in the medical (dietetic) discourse of the period, as well as the more familiar context of poetic inspiration. Brockes disciplines, Goethe liberates breath. The contrast illustrates changing attitudes to the body and to embodied spirit in the 18th century.

I.

Herder, der bekanntlich ein fleißiger und erfolgreicher Verfasser von Preisschriften war, machte in seiner selbst aus einer Preisschrift hervorgegangenen Abhandlung *Vom Erkennen und Empfinden der menschlichen Seele* (1778) die Anregung: "Ich bin auf die Preisfrage begierig: 'was das Othemholen eigentlich für Würkungen im lebendigen Körper hervorbringe?'"[1] Dass er offensichtlich meinte, damit ein Problem von großer Tragweite angerissen zu haben, gibt uns einigen Aufschluss über den Stellenwert physiologischer Fragen im 18. Jahrhundert. Sie waren kaum weniger dringend als philosophische; ja, man erhoffte sich von ihrer Beantwortung grundsätzliche anthropologische und philosophische Einsichten über Wesen und Bestimmung des Menschen. Herders *Vom Erkennen und Empfinden* oder seine späteren *Ideen* (1784-91) sind in diesem Sinne als physiologisch-philosophische Untersuchungen zu betrachten.

Im letzten Drittel des 18. Jahrhunderts wurden u. a. durch Haller, Priestley und Lavoisier bedeutende Fortschritte in der naturwissenschaftlichen Erforschung der Respiration gemacht. In den Horizont der Alltagserfahrung rückte die Atmung allerdings weniger im Zusammenhang mit der Anatomie oder der sogenannten "pneumatischen Chemie",[2] umso mehr aber als Gegenstand der am eigenen Leib erfahrenen diätetischen Medizin. Auch Herder macht sogleich die diätetische Nutzanwendung, wenn er in *Vom Erkennen und Empfinden* in den sich im Ein- und Ausatmen manifestierenden "Gesetzen" von "Anziehung und Ausbreitung, Tätigkeit und Ruhe" weise Maßnahmen der "Natur" erkennt, "Gesundheit und Glück des Lebens" zu befördern und "unsre Maschine [...] mit

[1] Johann Gottfried Herder: *Werke in zehn Bänden.* Bd. 4: *Schriften zu Philosophie, Literatur, Kunst und Altertum 1774-1787.* Hg. von Jürgen Brummack und Martin Bollacher. Frankfurt/M. 1994 (Bibliothek deutscher Klassiker 105). S. 327-393, hier S. 334.
[2] James C. Riley: *The Eighteenth-Century Campaign to Avoid Disease.* Basingstoke 1987. S. 98-99; Roy Porter: *The Greatest Benefit to Mankind. A Medical History of Humanity from Antiquity to the Present.* London 1997. S. 254.

Lebensgeist an[zu]hauchen".[3]

Die folgenden Überlegungen zu Gedichten des 18. Jahrhunderts wollen diese u. a. als diätetische Erscheinungen erfassen und greifen deshalb an entscheidenden Punkten auf diätetische Denkfiguren zurück. Zunächst sei also die Bedeutung der Diätetik für die Lebenshaltung des 18. Jahrhunderts in allgemeinen Worten umrissen.

Die Medizin des 18. Jahrhunderts verstand sich, in Übereinstimmung mit der hippokratischen Überlieferung, weniger als Wissenschaft denn als praxisnahe, prophylaktische und vor allem diätetische Kunst (wobei "Diät" im damaligen Sprachgebrauch "nicht nur das Speise-Regiment", sondern auch den "rechte[n] Gebrauch der Lufft, der Bewegung und Ruhe, derer Gemüths-Bewegungen, des Schlafens und Wachens, auch derer Dinge, welche man zur Gesundheit entweder von sich geben, oder behalten muß" beinhaltet).[4] Im Jahrhundert der Philanthropie entfaltete die Medizin in diesem Sinne mit der Verbreitung einer populärwissenschaftlichen "gemeinnützigen Arzneikunde" und dem Aufkommen einer staatlich gelenkten "medizinischen Polizey" eine neue gesellschaftliche Wirksamkeit.[5] Und im Jahrhundert der Aufklärung, des Selbstdenkens wie der Selbstbeobachtung, konnte man die Erfüllung der in der Schulmedizin tradierten Forderung erwarten, dass jeder für sein eigenes Wohl zu sorgen habe.[6] Zu den selbsternannten "Vormündern", gegen die die Aufklärung mit ihrem "Sapere aude!" ins Feld zieht, gehört deshalb neben dem "Seelsorger, der für mich Gewissen hat", auch der "Arzt, der für mich die Diät beurteilt".[7] Stattdessen gelte es, zur Selbsthilfe zu greifen: "Wenn man nicht ganz fremd in der Physik, dabei ein wenig bewandert in medizinischen Büchern ist, sein Temperament kennt und weiß, zu welchen Krankheiten man Anlage hat und was Wirkung auf uns macht, so kann man auch oft bei wirklichen Krankheiten sein eigener Arzt sein".[8]

---

[3] Herder: *Vom Erkennen und Empfinden der menschlichen Seele.* In: *Werke.* Bd. 4. S. 334.

[4] *Großes vollständiges Universal-Lexicon aller Wissenschaften und Künste.* Bd. 1-64. Halle und Leipzig 1732-50. Bd. 7 (1734). Sp. 733-734.

[5] Vgl. *Archiv der medizinischen Polizey und der gemeinnützigen Arzneikunde.* Hg. von Johann Christian Friedrich Scherf. Bd. 1-6. Leipzig 1783-87.

[6] Vgl. *Encyclopédie, ou Dictionnaire raisonné des sciences, des arts et des métiers.* Bd. 1-17. Hg. von Denis Diderot und Jean le Rond d'Alembert. Paris und Neufchastel 1751-1765. Bd. 8 (1765). S. 384-388, Artikel "Hygiene": Die Meinung, bei Beobachtung der Hauptregeln der Hygiene könne man "se servir de medecin à soi-même", wird dort der Schule von Salerno zugeschrieben (S. 387). – Hier wie in anderen Zitaten aus Texten des 18. Jahrhunderts, französischen wie deutschen, ist darauf hinzuweisen, dass die Orthographie (Akzentsetzung, Groß- und Kleinschreibung usw.) nicht immer heutigen Normen entspricht. Es wird hier und im weiteren Verlauf grundsätzlich nach dem Original zitiert.

[7] Immanuel Kant: Beantwortung der Frage: Was ist Aufklärung? In: *Was ist Aufklärung? Thesen und Definitionen.* Hg. von Ehrhard Bahr. Stuttgart 1981. S. 9.

[8] Adolph Freiherr von Knigge: *Über den Umgang mit Menschen.* 3. erw. Aufl. 1790.

Unter diesem Blickwinkel wurde der Körper des einzelnen zum Gegenstand einer diätetischen Selbstbeobachtung, wie sie uns etwa im 3. Abschnitt von Kants Spätschrift *Der Streit der Fakultäten* (1798) vorgeführt wird, wo von der "Macht des Gemüts, durch den blossen Vorsatz seiner krankhaften Gefühle Meister zu sein", gehandelt wird.[9] Nach einer allgemeinen Einführung zur Diätetik kommen an körperlichen Vorgängen der Schlaf, das Essen und Trinken und das Atmen zur Sprache, an psychologischen die Hypochondrie und das "krankhafte Gefühl aus der Unzeit im Denken".[10] In einem umfassenderen Sinne aber ist es das Ich, das als Objekt diätetischer Beobachtung und als Subjekt des autobiographischen Krankenberichts zur Sprache kommt: "Im dogmatisch-pragmatischen Vortrage, z. B. derjenigen Beobachtung seiner selbst, die auf Pflichten abzweckt, die jedermann angehen, spricht der Kanzelredner nicht durch *Ich*, sondern *Wir*. In dem erzählenden aber der Privatempfindung (der Beichte, welche der Patient seinem Arzte ablegt) oder eigener Erfahrung an sich selbst muß er durch Ich reden".[11] Wo von Gesundheit und Krankheit die Rede ist, wird also das Ich gleichsam aus dem Hinterhalt des neutralen wissenschaftlichen Diskurses hervorgelockt. Die Anfälligkeit von Körper und Seele ruft ein Subjekt auf den Plan, dem die Aufgabe zuwächst, sich selbst zu beobachten, um dann als redendes Ich über das "innere Experiment oder Beobachtung"[12] sich selbst und anderen Bericht abzustatten und Rechenschaft zu geben.

Das Ich wäre somit ein Nebenprodukt des Krankenberichts. Nun ist aber die medizinische Diätetik im 18. Jahrhundert keineswegs das einzige Gebiet, auf dem Selbstbeobachtung und die "Beichte" über die "Privatempfindung" angesagt sind. Daneben gibt es eine moralisch-seelsorgerische Diätetik, die sich auf der einen Seite mit der medizinischen überschneidet (da für die Gesundheit des Körpers die des Geistes die Voraussetzung bildet, und umgekehrt: *mens sana in corpore sano*), auf der anderen mit einer homiletisch-theologischen, wie sie sich im Erbauungsschrifttum der Zeit niederschlägt. Und aus diesen Diskursen fließt einem anderen Diskurs Nahrung zu, in dem zunehmend die "Privatempfindung" und ihre "Beichte" ihren Platz finden: der Dichtung, die ja nicht nur bei Goethe die "Generalbeichte" als probates "Hausmittel" benutzt und "Bruchstücke einer großen Konfession" in sich aufnimmt und verarbeitet.[13] Nicht von ungefähr behandelt das 7. Buch von *Dichtung und Wahrheit* den Einfluß, den in der Zeit um 1760 "Predigten und Abhandlungen" zur "Religion und der ihr so nah verwandten Sittenlehre" und Schriften der "Ärzte" auf die "allgemeine Bildung"

Hg. von Gert Ueding. Frankfurt/M. 1977. S. 358.

[9] Immanuel Kant: *Der Streit der Fakultäten*. 2. Aufl. Leipzig 1992. S. 95-115.

[10] Ebd. S. 107

[11] Ebd. S. 96.

[12] Ebd. S. 96.

[13] Johann Wolfgang Goethe: *Aus meinem Leben. Dichtung und Wahrheit*. In: *Sämtliche Werke. Briefe, Tagebücher und Gespräche. Erste Abteilung*. Bd. 14. Hg. von Klaus-Detlef Müller. Frankfurt/M. 1986 (Bibliothek deutscher Klassiker 15). S. 639 und 310.

ausübten, und speziell auf diejenigen, "welche sich mit deutscher Literatur [...] abgaben".[14]

Nicht zuletzt für die Lyrik dürfte diese Durchdringung der Diskurse befruchtend gewesen sein. Im Mittelpunkt der folgenden Erörterungen stehen denn auch lyrische Gedichte, in denen der Körper und das Ich zur Sprache kommen. Diese sollen (wie oben bereits angedeutet) vor dem Hintergrund diätetischer Denkgewohnheiten durchleuchtet werden. Denn wo vom Körper und seinem Ich die Rede ist, bildet die Diätetik, die der Zeit in so hohem Maße ihr Gepräge gibt, gleichsam eine unausgesprochene Vorgabe, als Verständnishorizont, innerhalb dessen auch heterodoxe Äußerungen ihren Stellenwert bekommen.[15]

Speziell geht es in den folgenden Textbeispielen um die Atmung. Das ist zunächst nur eine Körperfunktion unter vielen. Welche Bedeutung sie jedoch im 18. Jahrundert erlangen konnte, haben wir bereits an Herders Vorschlag zu einer Preisfrage über das "Othemholen" gesehen. Unter diätetischem Gesichtspunkte hatte sie als "fonction maîtresse" zu gelten.[16] Darüber hinaus aber wuchsen ihr aus einer langen Tradition Assoziationen zu, die aus ihr das Bindeglied zwischen Körper und Geist, Physiologischem und Metaphysischem machten.[17] Schon die Vorsokratiker meinten aus naheliegenden Gründen im Atem das Lebensprinzip schlechthin zu erkennen,[18] und in der biblischen Schöpfungsgeschichte bläst Gott dem ersten Menschen den "lebendigen Odem" ein, um ihn zum Leben zu erwecken (1. Buch Mose, 2. 7). Damit wurde die Atmung metaphysisch auf folgenschwere Weise aufgeladen. Hatte sie schon als Körperfunktion im Vergleich etwa zur Verdauung etwas Unstoffliches an sich, so spielten nun ihre sekundären Bedeutungen, die sich aus der Gleichbedeutung mit dem griechischen *pneuma* und *psyche* und dem lateinischen *spiritus* und *anima* ergeben, vollends ins Geistige und Geistliche hinüber: "Nos mots grecs et latins, πνεῦμα, anima, spiritus ne signifient originairement que l'air ou vent qu'on respire, comme une des plus subtiles choses qui nous soit connue par les sens: et on commence par les sens pour mener peu à peu les hommes à ce qui est au dessus des sens".[19] Auch Sprache und Sprachfähigkeit des Menschen werden

---

[14] *Dichtung und Wahrheit*. S. 276-277.

[15] Zur "Diätetisierung der Poesie" in der Aufklärungszeit s. Wolfgang Mauser: *Konzepte aufgeklärter Lebensführung. Literarische Kultur im frühmodernen Deutschland*. Würzburg 2000. S. 244-329, hier S. 258. Vgl. besonders den Abschnitt "Diätetik und Literatur" (S. 304-308).

[16] Respiration. In: *Encyclopédie*. Bd. 14 (1765). S. 184.

[17] M. H. Abrams: The Correspondent Breeze: A Romantic Metaphor. In: *English Romantic Poets. Modern Essays in Criticism*. Hg. von M. H. Abrams. 2. Aufl. London 1975. S. 37-54, hier S. 44-46.

[18] F. Ricken u. a.: Seele. In: *Historisches Wörterbuch der Philosophie*. Hg. von Joachim Ritter und Karlfried Gründer. Bd. 9 (1995). Basel 1971f. Sp. 1-89, hier Sp. 1-3.

[19] Gottfried Wilhelm Leibniz: *Nouveaux essais sur l'entendement human* (1765). Hg. von der Leibniz-Forschungsstelle der Universität Münster. In: *Sämtliche Schriften und Briefe*. Hg. von Preußische Akademie der Wissenschaften/Akademie der Wissenschaften der DDR. 6. Reihe. Bd. 6. Berlin 1990. S. 39-527, hier S. 104. Zu *psyche* und

durch diese Bedeutungserweiterung als Atmungsphänomene begriffen. Denn wenn der Atem schon rein materiell gesehen das Substrat der Rede ist ("la voix est une action qui dépend entièrement de la *respiration*"),[20] so kommt über die Verbindung mit *pneuma* und *spiritus* hinzu, dass die göttliche Eingebung, in der menschlicher und göttlicher *logos* gleichsam ineinanderfließen, damit der Laut zu Sprache werde und sich mit (höchstem) Sinn fülle, bildlich als Atmungsvorgang vorgestellt wird, als "Inspiration", und zwar sowohl für den Einzelnen, in der *parole*, wie für die Gattung in der *langue* selbst: "Mit der Organisation zur Rede empfing der Mensch den Atem der Gottheit, den Samen zur Vernunft und ewigen Vervollkommnung, einen Nachhall jener schaffenden Stimme zu Beherrschung der Erde".[21]

So ist das Atmen in seiner Bedeutung überdeterminiert und bietet sich eben deshalb zur Untersuchung an, um den Vorstellungen, die sich das 18. Jahrhundert über das Verhältnis von Geist und Körper machte, auf den Grund zu kommen. Und was schliesslich das lyrische Gedicht angeht, wird man nicht vergessen dürfen, dass jedes solche Gebilde ganz konkret ein Atmungsvorgang ist, in dem durch Zeilenlänge, Metrum und Cäsur dem Atem des Lesers gleichsam eine Partitur untergelegt wird. So kann auch da, wo das Atmen nicht ausdrücklich thematisiert wird, dennoch davon die Rede sein. Das muss nicht in jedem, kann aber im Einzelfall durchaus Bedeutung haben.

II.

Wie weit die aufklärerische Disziplinierung des Körpers im Namen der Diätetik getrieben wurde, lässt sich an Kants bereits erwähnten Ausführungen zur Atmung erkennen. Kant war der Überzeugung, dass durch "den Vorsatz im Atemziehen […], mit festgeschlossenen Lippen durchaus die Luft durch die Nase zu ziehen" (und nicht durch den Mund), der Schnupfen zu verhüten sei.[22] Die dazu erforderliche geistige "Aufmerksamkeit"[23] müsse freilich ihre Herrschaft auch über die Nacht- und Schlafenszeit ausdehnen, da ja sonst die segensreiche Wirkung der tagsüber praktizierten Selbstkontrolle nachts durch den unbotmäßigen Körper aufgehoben würde. Dass diese diätetische Aufmerksamkeit auch während des Schlafs anhalten könne, sei aber aus seiner eigenen Erfahrung zu beweisen:

Das ist aber von der größten diätetischen Wichtigkeit, den Atemzug durch die

---

Atem, s. Ricken u. a. Sp. 1.

[20] Albrecht von Haller: Respiration. In: *Supplément au Dictionnaire raisonné des sciences, des arts et des métiers*. Hg. von Jean Baptiste Robinet. Bd. 4. Amsterdam 1776-1777. S. 613-623, hier S. 623.

[21] Herder: *Ideen zur Philosophie der Geschichte der Menschheit*. In: *Werke*. Hg. von Martin Bollacher. Bd. 6. Frankfurt/M. 1986 (Bibliothek deutscher Klassiker 41). S. 142.

[22] *Der Streit der Fakultäten*. S. 109.

[23] Ebd. S. 110.

Nase bei geschlossenen Lippen sich so zur *Gewohnheit* zu machen, daß er selbst im tiefsten Schlaf nicht anders verrichtet wird und man sogleich aufwacht, sobald er mit offenem Munde geschieht, und dadurch gleichsam aufgeschreckt wird; wie ich das anfänglich, ehe es mir zur Gewohnheit wurde, auf solche Weise zu atmen, bisweilen erfuhr.[24]

So gründlich hat der sklavische Leib zu parieren gelernt, dass ihn das diätetische Gewissen auch aus dem "tiefsten Schlaf" erwecken kann. Offenbar fühlt er sich dabei ertappt; denn er "schreckt" bei solchen Gelegenheiten solange "auf", bis ihn die "Aufmerksamkeit" sich vollkommen gefügig gemacht und ihn in Form der "Gewohnheit" ihrem Gesetz unterworfen hat.

Damit ist ein Grundmuster aufklärerischen Denkens über den Körper auf den Begriff gebracht. Brockes etwa hätte den sich in Kants Überlegungen äußernden Gedanken sofort anerkannt und gebilligt. Sechzig und mehr Jahre vor Kant sann auch er auf Mittel, den Körper dem Geist gefügig zu machen. Die Augen und der Mund z. B. waren ihm

> [...] drey rege Glieder, von denen wir ihr schnelles Regen
> Und ihr uns nimmer wiederspenstig, nie ungehorsames, Bewegen
> Zu leiten, zu regieren, taugen.[25]

Demgemäß könne man, "wenn man nur [...] Acht auf sich [...] nehmen wollte", seine Mienen "so in Ordnung führen", dass man ihnen einen freundlichen und einnehmenden Ausdruck zur Gewohnheit machte.[26] Selbst im Schlaf dürfe die dabei aufzubringende "Mühe"[27] nicht nachlassen:

> Man darf, wenn man sich schlaffen legt, nur blos ein wenig sich bemühn
> Und Augen-Brauen etwas auf-, den Mund ein wenig rückwärts ziehn;
> So wird vermuthlich das Gesicht in dieser Stellung lange bleiben,
> Und ohne Müh, ein süsser Zug dem Angesicht sich einverleiben.[28]

Hier wird der Leib noch bis in den Schlaf hinein dressiert und dem Willen des Geistes unterworfen. Dieser wiederum ist bloß ausführendes Organ gesellschaftlicher Anforderungen, geht es doch hier um das 'Mittel gefällig zu werden' (so der Titel des Gedichts),[29] um die Kunst also, "uns den Menschen angenehmer

---

[24] Ebd. S. 109.
[25] Barthold Hinrich Brockes: 'Mittel gefällig zu werden'. In: *Irdisches Vergnügen in GOTT, bestehend in Physicalisch- und Moralischen Gedichten, Fünfter Theil*. Hamburg 1736. Nachdr. Bern 1970. S. 389.
[26] Ebd. S. 390.
[27] Ebd. S. 391.
[28] Ebd.
[29] Ebd. S. 389.

[…] zu machen".[30]

Mit sich uneins scheint sich Brockes nur darüber zu sein, ob diese Dressur mit oder "ohne Müh" zu absolvieren sei. Als ob sich die Kreatur vor dem Zahmwerden noch einmal aufbäumte, ist von "Mühe" zunächst die Rede, bevor diese dann schrittweise ("Mühe" – "ein wenig sich bemühn" – "ohne Müh") zum Verschwinden gebracht wird. So ganz ausgemacht ist es also offenbar nicht, daß der Körper "uns nimmer wiederspenstig" und "nie ungehorsam" sei, wie Brockes zu Anfang behauptet hatte. In einem anderen Gedicht zum gleichen Thema spricht er denn auch vom Widerstand, den die Mienen im Banne der Leidenschaften der Vernunft entgegensetzen, so daß wir, um ihrer Herr zu werden, z. B. gezwungen sind, mitten im trübenden Affekt "gleichsam mit Gewalt die Augen aufzuklären".[31]

In der Gesamtkonzeption des *Irdischen Vergnügens in GOTT* spielt die durch die "Gewalt" der Vernunft zu überwindende geistige wie körperliche Trägheit eine große Rolle. Brockes sieht es als seine Aufgabe an, Sinn und Geist einer "gantz unempfindlichen und gleichsam schlafsüchtigen Welt"[32] "aufzumuntern".[33] Er selbst will "nicht müde" werden, ihr die Wunderwerke der Schöpfung "anzupreisen".[34] Dass er so viel schreibt – das *Irdische Vergnügen* schwoll zuletzt auf neun Bände an, die über eine Zeitspanne von 28 Jahren zwischen 1721 und 1748 erschienen – geht auf die Rechnung der "Unempfindlichkeit"[35] seiner Leser ("ihr [seyd] selber Schuld daran", erklärt er ihnen rund heraus).[36] Weil *ihre* Sinne so stumpf sind, muss *er* einen langen Atem haben. Ihm, dem Nimmermüden, fällt die Aufgabe zu, die anderen zu erwecken: aufwachen sollen seine Leser aus dem "gewohnten Schlaf",[37] der sie umfängt und ihre Sinne benebelt.

Dem wachen Bewusstsein wird somit aller Wert zugesprochen. So ist es also nur konsequent, wenn Brockes sich darüber Gedanken macht, wie man ihm auch über die unbewussten Zustände des Körpers die Herrschaft geben könnte (und

---

[30] Ebd. S. 391.

[31] Brockes: 'Bewährtes Mittel, Gemühts-Bewegungen zu stillen'. In: *Verdeutschte Grund-Sätze der Welt-Weisheit des Herrn Abts GENEST, nebst verschiedenen eigenen theils Physicalischen theils Moralischen Gedichten, als des Irdischen Vergnügens in GOTT Dritter Theil.* 3. Aufl. Hamburg 1736. Nachdr. Bern 1970. S. 702. Auch wenn es nicht so gemeint ist – "aufklären" bedeutet hier bloß "aufhellen", "freundlich dreinblicken" –, klärt uns diese Stelle doch auch unfreiwillig über die Dialektik der Aufklärung auf. – Zu den beiden zuletzt genannten Gedichten vgl. Mauser. S. 290-291.

[32] Christian Friedrich Weichmann: Widmung an August Wilhelm, Herzog zu Braunschweig und Lüneburg. In: Barthold Hinrich Brockes: *Irdisches Vergnügen in GOTT, bestehend in Physicalisch- und Moralischen Gedichten, Erster Theil.* 6. Aufl. Hamburg 1737. Nachdr. Bern 1970. o. S.

[33] Brockes: *Irdisches Vergnügen in GOTT [...] Fünfter Theil.* S. 158 und 221.

[34] Ebd. S. 511.

[35] Ebd. S. 244.

[36] Ebd. S. 511.

[37] Ebd.

wenn es auch nur wäre, dass man vor dem Schlafengehen die Mienen in die richtigen Falten legte). Die unbewussten Prozesse des Körpers sollen auf ein Mindestmaß an Wirksamkeit eingeschränkt werden. Das geschieht nun hauptsächlich dadurch, dass man ihnen das bewusste Erleben zugesellt, als Wächter, der (ganz dem Wortsinne gemäß) die Aufgabe hat, den Geist zu wecken, den Körper aber zu überwachen. So ist es etwa mit den Sinnen:

> Laßt uns die Sinnen, GOtt zum Ruhm, der sie uns giebt, gebrauchen lernen!
> Dieß kann nun GOtt-gefälliger auf andre Weise nicht geschehn,
> Als wenn durch des Verstandes Licht wir würcklich sehen, daß wir sehn;
> Empfinden daß und was wir riechen; vernünftig schmecken, wenn wir *schmecken*;
> Nicht ohn Gefühl seyn, wenn wir fühlen; auch deutlich hören, wenn wir hören.[38]

Es genügt also nicht, bloß Sinneseindrücke in sich hineinströmen zu lassen, sondern man muss sie mit Bewusstsein aufnehmen, und noch dieses Aufnehmen selbst bewusst erleben. Die Wortwiederholungen in den zitierten Zeilen machen selber auf "vernünftig-sinnliche" Weise deutlich, dass es dabei um eine Verdopplung der Sinnesfunktion durch eine ihr übergeordnete Verstandesfunktion geht. Ohne diese Verdopplung wäre, so Brockes, "der Mensch [...] nicht besser, als ein Vieh".[39]

Es ist freilich ein fast schon wieder übermenschliches Vorhaben, alle unbewussten Prozesse des Körpers ins Bewusstsein heben zu wollen. So läßt sich womöglich erklären, dass Brockes erst im fünften Teil des *Irdischen Vergnügens* ausführlich auf das "Othem-hohlen" zu sprechen kommt, wobei er sich selbst Vorwürfe macht, diesen Vorgang, dem wir, eben weil er uns "so nah" und alltäglich ist, allzu leicht "unempfindlich" gegenüberstehen, nicht schon früher bedacht und besungen zu haben.[40] Sein Meisterstück in dieser Gattung ist aber wohl dieses 1743 im siebten Teil des *Irdischen Vergnügens* erschienene Gedicht:

> Der vernünftige Geruch.
>
> Mit inniglich-gerührter Brust,
> Und gleichsam überschwemmt von Lust,
> Roch ich jüngst mehr als hundertmahl
> Den kräftig-recht durchwürzten Duft
> Von der Violen Matronal.
>
> Um recht gesättiget zu seyn,

---

[38] Brockes: 'Vernünftig-sinnlicher Gottes-Dienst'. In: *Irdisches Vergnügen in GOTT [...] Fünfter Theil.* S. 398-399.
[39] Brockes: *Irdisches Vergnügen in GOTT [...] Fünfter Theil.* S. 398.
[40] Ebd. S. 323.

Zog ich die balsamirte Luft,
Mit stets erneuertem Vergnügen,
In kurzen unterbrochnen Zügen,
Bald hauchend und bald schnaufend, ein.
Um Lust und Dank nun auch zu fügen,
Beschloß ich, wenn ich roch und blies,
Den Athem zog und von mir ließ,
Bei jedem Anziehn, jedem Hauchen
Mich einer Silbe zu gebrauchen
Von diesem Liedchen, welches man
Auch leicht, wie ich, verrichten kann.

Dir – riech' – ich – die–se – schö–ne – Bluh– me,
O – GOtt, – Der – sie – mir – schenkt, – zum – Ruh–me.
Ich – riech' – und – freu' – mich – Dein – in – ihr;
Denn – Du – al–lein – for–mierst – und – gie–best,
Zur – Pro–be, – wie – so – stark – Du – lie–best,
Der – Bluh–men – Pracht, – Ge–ruch – und – Zier.
Die – Kraft – zu – rie–chen – schenkst – Du – mir.[41]

Hier überbietet sich die Diätetik der Aufklärung selbst. Dreierlei soll hier unter Kontrolle gebracht, d. h. sowohl beaufsichtigt als auch gelenkt werden: der Körper (die Atmung), das Denken, und die Sprache. Und das nicht nur oder nicht einmal hauptsächlich beim Dichter selbst: der ist nur unser Vorredner, und auf uns als Leser ist es eigentlich abgesehen. Auch wir sollen uns das erbauliche "Liedchen" zu eigen machen. Ganz "leicht" soll es uns gemacht werden (Z. 17). Doch können wir gar nicht anders, als das "Liedchen" nachzusprechen, wenn wir das Gedicht zu Ende lesen wollen. Und schon wird uns vorgeschrieben, wie wir zu atmen und was wir uns dabei zu denken haben – ein Schulbeispiel für die sanfte Gewalt der Aufklärung, mit der wir aus unserem "Gewohnheits-Schlaff"[42] erweckt und zu unserem Glück gezwungen werden sollen.

Das Einatmen des Blumendufts ist buchstäblich die Inspiration des Gedichts; von Gottes Natur geht der Hauch aus, den wir hier ein- und ausatmen. Das Gedicht will uns belehren, die sinnliche Empfindung des Geruchssinns mit dem Gedanken an den Schöpfer zu verknüpfen, der sie uns "geschenkt" hat, und macht, indem es den Geruch damit einem höheren Zweck unterordnet, die sinnliche Tätigkeit zu einer "vernünftigen" (wie es im Titel heißt). Doch nicht nur durch den physikotheologischen Unterricht wird unsere sinnliche Natur der Dis-

---

[41] Brockes: *Land-Leben in Ritzebüttel, als des Irdischen Vergnügens in GOTT Siebender Theil.* Hamburg 1743. Nachdr. Bern 1970. S. 139. Im Original ist der Schriftsatz des "Liedchens" (der letzten sieben Zeilen also) größer als der des einleitenden Teils.
[42] Brockes: *Irdisches Vergnügen in GOTT [...] Fünfter Theil.* S. 667.

ziplin vernünftiger Religion unterworfen. Darüber hinaus ist das Gedicht eine Anleitung zum "vernünftigen" Atmen, *d. h.* zu einem Atmen, in dem die bloß natürliche Tätigkeit durch einen Akt des Bewußtseins begleitet, ja von ihm geradezu aufgesogen wird. Der Schriftsatz der letzten sieben Zeilen zwingt uns, die Atmung in die vorgeschriebene Bahn zu lenken und sie in einen Akt der Andacht zu verwandeln. Die mit Gewalt die Silben auseinanderreißenden Gedankenstriche geben in der Tat den Gedanken Raum, indem sie dem natürlichen und daher gedankenlosen Dahinfließen der Worte Einhalt gebieten. Stattdessen müssen die Silben bewußt artikuliert oder vielmehr im Ein- und Ausatmen "aspiriert" werden. Der natürliche Rhythmus der Atmung wird der Artikulation des *logos* dienstbar gemacht; *physis* schlägt um in *logos*. Die Atemübung wird damit zu einer geistlichen Übung. Jeder Atemzug wird mit geistlichem Sinn angefüllt: kein Hauch, der nicht Gottes Lob kündete. So wird das kreatürliche Leben restlos in Gebet überführt. Der Atem wird erlöst, indem er zu Geist wird.

In einem anderen, berühmteren Blumengedicht von Brockes wird diese Übersetzung des gedankenlosen Atmens in geisterfüllte Anbetung beschrieben:

> Zwar lässt die blinde Welt so Zucker-süssen Duft,
> Im Athem, acht-los von sich schiessen,
> Und wieder in die Luft,
> Woraus er stammet, fliessen;
> Ich aber schwinge mich, auf Flügeln reiner Triebe,
> Zu GOTT, und opfer' Ihm den süssen Hauch,
> Von Brunst und Dank entflammt, als einen Opfer-Rauch,
> In heissen Seufzern auf.[43]

Im 'Vernünftigen Geruch' aber wird der Vorgang nicht nur *be*schrieben, sondern dem Sprachleib des Gedichtes auch *ein*geschrieben. Und indem wir die Worte des in ihm enthaltenen "Liedchens" nachhauchen, atmen auch wir den Geist, der jede Silbe desselben trägt und durchdringt. Für die Dauer des Gedichts zumindest ist damit unser leibliches Dasein geheiligt und in einem höheren, geistigen Dasein aufgehoben.

Der vorhergehende sinnliche Genuss wird uns leider vorenthalten. Den haben wir uns bloß zu denken. Die Blume, die für den Dichter eine wirkliche war und deren Duft ihn mit "Lust" "überschwemmte", ist für uns nur eine gedachte. Aber das macht nichts: desto "vernünftiger" ist für uns denn auch ihr Geruch.

III.

Der 'Vernünftige Geruch' zeichnet sich u. a. dadurch aus, dass in ihm die Atemführung von geradezu metronomischer Regelmäßigkeit ist. Das entspricht einem diätetischen Ideal, nach dem die Extreme zu vermeiden sind ("Il faut éviter tout

---

[43] Brockes: 'Die Rose.' In: *Irdisches Vergnügen in GOTT [...] Erster Theil.* S. 88.

excès" ist die erste Maxime der Hygiene)[44] und insbesondere die Atmung gleichmäßig zu sein hat: "Plus un homme se porte bien, plus la *respiration* est libre, & plus elle est lente, toute chose égale".[45] Freilich wusste auch Brockes, dass es Gelegenheiten gibt, wo der Atmung mehr abverlangt wird. In 'Die Rose' entzückt den Dichter der Duft so sehr, dass es ihm vorkommt, als ob das Herz "vor Vergnügen / Nicht mehr so eng verschrencket liegen" könne:

> Drum dehnt sich die gewölbte Brust,
> So weit ihr möglich, aus,
> Die durch die holde Duft
> So lieblich balsamierte Luft
> Nicht anderwärtig hinzulassen,
> Nein sie, wo möglich, gantz zu fassen.[46]

So macht sich das Herz unmittelbar nach diesen Worten nicht mehr in einem "Liedchen", sondern in einer "Aria" Luft. Die höhere Gattung stellt auch höhere Anforderungen an die Atemorgane. Es bleibt bei Brockes aber noch bei einem Lippenbekenntnis. Die auf die zitierten Zeilen folgende Aria setzt sich allenfalls durch ein etwas gewagteres Reimschema vom einfacheren Lied ab. Von einem *Lungen*bekenntis aber – von den Wirkungen einer in Bewegung geratenen, die Lungenkapazität strapazierenden Atmung also – ist darin nichts zu spüren.

Das sollte sich erst nach der Jahrhundertmitte ändern. Wie alle anderen physikalischen und physiologischen Erscheinungen ordnet Brockes die Atmung der vernünftig-frommen Betrachtung unter, und lässt sie nur unter dieser Bedingung gelten. Eine andere Stimme meinen wir zu hören, wenn ein junger, zwei Jahre nach Brockes' Tod geborener Dichter einem Freund in einem Brief über seinen Gesundheitszustand schreibt: "Mein Husten fährt fort, ich binn zwar sonst wohl, aber man lebt nur halb, wenn man nicht Athemhohlen kann. Und doch mag ich nicht in die Stadt. Die Bewegung und freye Luft hilfft wenigstens was zu he[l]ffen ist".[47] Zwar ist auch das diätetisch gedacht. In der Gleichsetzung des (unbehinderten) "Athemhohlens" mit dem Leben schlechthin drückt sich aber eine Einstellung aus, in dem sich im Vergleich zu Brockes oder Kant das kör-

---

[44] Hygiene. In: *Encyclopédie*. Bd. 8. S. 386: das sei die erste Regel der Hygiene des "célèbre Hoffmann". Zu Friedrich Hoffmann (1660-1742) s. Riley. S. 51; zu Hoffmann und Brockes, s. Mauser. S. 283.

[45] Haller: Respiration. S. 619.

[46] Brockes: *Irdisches Vergnügen in GOTT [...] Erster Theil*. S. 87. Nach Adelung kommt "Duft" als Femininum bei "einigen Meißnern" vor. Johann Christoph Adelung: *Grammatisch-kritisches Wörterbuch der hochdeutschen Mundart*. Bd. 1. 2. Aufl. Leipzig 1793-1801. S. 1568.

[47] Goethe an J. D. Salzmann, 5. 6. 1771. In: *Von Frankfurt nach Weimar. Briefe, Tagebücher und Gespräche vom 23. Mai 1764 bis 30. Oktober 1775*. Hg. von Wilhelm Große. In: *Sämtliche Werke. Zweite Abteilung*. Bd. 1. Frankfurt/M. 1997 (Bibliothek deutscher Klassiker 139). S. 229.

perliche Wohlgefühl zu einem Wert an sich potenziert hat.

Über Krankheit und Gesundheit war der junge Goethe aus eigener Erfahrung unterrichtet, seitdem er Ende Juli 1768 einen Blutsturz erlitten hatte, an dessen Folgen er dann über mehrere Monate hinweg laborierte. Die Ärzte verordneten "diätetsche Ruh".[48] Der Genesende vertrieb sich u. a. die Zeit, indem er medizinische Literatur las.[49] Einer der Ärzte, der ihn 1768-69 in Frankfurt behandelte, war Johann Philipp Burggrave (1700-1775), dessen Schrift *De aere, aquis & locis urbis Francofurtanae ad Moenum commentatio* (Frankfurt 1751) schon im Titel zu erkennen gibt, in welchem Maße sie der hippokratischen, d. h. der in der Hauptsache der Diät und den Umwelteinflüssen, und erst in zweiter Linie der Arznei vertrauenden Medizin, verpflichtet war.[50] Goethes Vater pflegte denn auch das englische Scherzwort zu zitieren: "Dr. Diet, Dr. Quiet and Dr. Merry-Man are the best physicians".[51] Sein Sohn wird sich also in Theorie und Praxis in der Diätetik der Aufklärung ausgekannt haben.

Dennoch scheint Goethe sich Anfang der 1770er Jahre selbsttherapeutisch von dem diätetischen Ideal des Maßhaltens in allen Dingen abgekehrt zu haben. Im Einklang mit dem Kraftkult des Sturm und Drang wird nun ein forscherer, energischerer Ton angeschlagen: "Ich bin sehr in der Lufft. Schlafen Essen Trincken Baden Reiten, war so ein Paar Tage her der seelige inhalt meines Lebens".[52] Man wird Einflüsse von außen vermuten dürfen, an erster Stelle wohl Rousseaus *Émile*, mit dem er sich in der Straßburger Zeit intensiv auseinandersetzte und dessen Lehre körperlicher Abhärtung in der Pädagogik und Medizin gerade um diese Zeit Epoche machte.[53] Zu diesem neuen Gesundheitsideal gab aber das, was er am eigenen Leib erfuhr, den Kommentar ab, etwa bei seinen häufigen Fußmärschen zwischen Frankfurt, Bad Homburg und Darmstadt, die ihm bekanntlich im Bekanntenkreis den Namen des "Wanderers" eintru-

---

[48] Goethe: 'Zueignung' (1769). In: *Gedichte 1756-1799*. Hg. von Karl Eibl. In: *Sämtliche Werke. Erste Abteilung*. Bd. 1. Frankfurt/M. 1987 (Bibliothek deutscher Klassiker 18). S. 95.

[49] In den *Ephemerides* (1770) ist die Lektüre der *Aphorismi de cognoscendis et curandis morbis* (1709) von Herman Boerhaave belegt (Goethe: *Von Frankfurt nach Weimar*. S. 190). In *Dichtung und Wahrheit* werden neben Boerhaave weitere führende Ärzte wie Tissot, Haller, Unzer und Zimmermann genannt (S. 303, 376).

[50] Burggrave war Hausarzt der Familie Goethe: Siehe *Von Frankfurt nach Weimar*, S. 665 und 668. *De aere aquis locis* ist der lateinische Titel eines berühmten, dem Hippokrates zugeschriebenen Werkes. Zu Burggraves Stellung innerhalb der neohippokratischen Bewegung des 18. Jahrhunderts, s. Riley. S. 36-38.

[51] Goethe spielt darauf an im Brief an Cornelia vom 12.-14. 10. 1767. In: *Von Frankfurt nach Weimar*. S. 94. Vgl. auch den Kommentar S. 655.

[52] An Johanna Fahlmer, 5. 6. 1775. In: *Von Frankfurt nach Weimar*. S. 454.

[53] Typisch ist der Rat zur Kindererziehung aus dem 1. Buch: "Endurcissez leurs corps aux intempéries des saisons, des climats, des éléments, à la faim, à la soif, à la fatigue". Jean-Jacques Rousseau: *Émile ou de l'éducation*. Hg. von François und Pierre Richard. Paris 1964. S. 20. Schon in Leipzig war Goethe indirekt mit Rousseaus Vorstellungen konfrontiert worden: s. *Dichtung und Wahrheit*. S. 360.

gen.[54]

Das alles wäre allenfalls von biographischem oder medizingeschichtlichem Interesse, wenn diese neue Leiblichkeit (wenn man es so nennen kann) nicht auch auf die Dichtung übergegriffen hätte. Auch da wehte ab Mitte des Jahrhunderts ein anderer Wind. Man wollte jetzt im lyrischen Gedicht die Leidenschaft atmen hören: "Poetry [...] is indebted for its origin, character, complexion, emphasis, and application, to the effects which are produced upon the mind and body, upon the imagination, the senses, the voice, and respiration by the agitation of passion", meinte Herders Gewährsmann Lowth schon 1741.[55] Auf den Rezipienten bezogen hob Lichtenberg ebenso die physiologische Materialität von Lyrik hervor, indem er aphoristisch erklärte "Oden, wenn man sie liest, so gehen einem mit Respekt zu sagen Nasenlöcher und Zehen auseinander".[56] Man wollte sympathetisch zu einem anderen, einem affektbestimmten, körperbetonten, biologischen Rhythmus in der Lyrik mitgerissen werden. Der physiologische Ort der Ode lag nun an der Grenze zur Atemlosigkeit: "Die reinen [...] Empfindungen der Lust, gehören, so wie ihr Gegenteil, wenn sie die Seele nicht ganz übermannet, und ihr zum Ausdruck gleichsam den Atem benommen haben, für die Ode".[57] Die Ode sollte daher "in kurzem Odem jauchzen, oder donnern, oder seufzen und weinen".[58] "In dem warmen Odem des Affekts" bestand "das ganze Verdienst der heutigen Dichtkunst".[59]

Hervorgebracht und zugleich erfüllt wurden solche Erwartungen vor allem durch Klopstocks Lyrik. Die eben zitierten Bemerkungen von Herder und Claudius stehen im Kontext von Würdigungen seiner dichterischen Leistung. In den Mittelpunkt des Interesses rückt dabei das "Klopstockische freie Silbenmaß".[60] Der Vorteil des von Klopstock in die deutsche Dichtung eingeführten freien Verses lag eben darin, dass er sich dem wechselnden Atemrhythmus des Dichters anschmiegte, um dann dem Vorleser denselben Rhythmus vorzuschreiben. Schon Lessing hatte im Versduktus von Klopstocks 'Allgegenwärtigem' diese neuen Möglichkeiten für die *mimesis* natürlicher Atmung erkannt: "Wie viel Vorteile auch der Schauspieler daraus ziehen könnte, will ich itzt gar nicht er-

---

[54] *Dichtung und Wahrheit.* S. 567.

[55] *Lectures on the Sacred Poetry of the Hebrews; translated from the Latin of the Right Rev. Robert Lowth, D. D. [...] by G. Gregory [...]. To which are added, the Principal Notes of Professor Michaelis, and Notes by the Translator and Others.* Bd. 1. London 1787. S. 366.

[56] Georg Christoph Lichtenberg: *Sudelbücher, Fragmente, Fabeln, Verse.* In: *Schriften und Briefe.* Hg. von Franz H. Mautner. Bd. 1. Frankfurt/M. 1983. S. 224.

[57] Thomas Abbt in *Briefe, die neueste Litteratur betreffend*, 212. Brief; zitiert von Herder in *Von der Ode* (1765) und *Über die neuere deutsche Literatur* (1767). Herder: *Frühe Schriften 1764-1772.* In: *Werke.* Hg. von Ulrich Gaier. Bd. 1. Frankfurt/M. 1985 (Bibliothek deutscher Klassiker 1). S. 65 und 484.

[58] Herder: *Über die neuere deutsche Literatur.* In: *Werke.* Bd. 1. S. 232.

[59] Matthias Claudius: *Sämtliche Werke.* 8. Aufl. Darmstadt 1996. S. 51.

[60] Herder: *Über die neuere deutsche Literatur.* In: *Werke.* Bd. 1. S. 168.

wähnen; wenn sich nämlich der Dichter bei der Abteilung dieser freien Zeilen nach den Regeln der Declamation richtete, und jede Zeile so lang oder kurz machte, als jener jedesmal viel oder wenig Worte in einem Atem zusammen aussprechen müßte".[61]

Diese teils sachlich, teils rhapsodisch vorgetragenen Meinungen zum Affekt, zur Atmung und zum freien Vers bilden eine physiologische Ergänzung der Pneumatologie der Geniebewegung. Der klassizistische Dichter entschuldigt sich noch dafür, daß "die Respiration der Empfindung, wenn ich's so nennen darf, [...] den Ausdruck stolpernd [und] unkorrekt" mache.[62] Das Genie dagegen setzt bekanntlich die Begeisterung über Korrektheit und Kalkül. Die Metapher der Inspiration erborgte man sich von der Theologie:

> Kam [...] der Geist über eine Seele, so war das Aushauchen seiner Fülle das erste notwendige Atmen eines so gewürdigten Herzens [...]. [...] Paulus setzt die zur Empfindung des Geists bewegte Seele [...] dem ruhigen Sinn [...] entgegen, nebeneinander vielmehr, nacheinander! Wie ihr wollt! Es ist Vater und Sohn, Keim und Pflanze. πνευμα! πνευμα! was wäre νους ohne dich![63]

Was aber *auch* Metapher war, konnte schwerlich *nur* Metapher bleiben, wo doch die Atmung nichts Weithergeholtes, sondern eine in jedem Augenblick am eigenen Leibe lebendig gemachte Erfahrung war. Das Genie wurde damit zu einer physiologischen Größe. Die "Veränderungen des Odems"[64] markierten Ebbe und Flut der Inspiration und mußten auch und gerade in der Sprache ihre deutlichen Spuren hinterlassen. Im Sprachduktus der Stürmer und Dränger wurde daher der sprunghafte Atem zur Signatur der Eingebungen von Genie und Leidenschaft. Typisch ist eine Stelle wie diese, aus Goethes Rede "Zum Schäkespears Tag" (1771):

> Die meisten von diesen Herren, stoßen auch besonders an seinen Charakteren an.
> Und ich rufe Natur! Natur! nichts so Natur als Schäkespears Menschen.
> Da hab ich sie alle überm Hals.
> Lasst mir Luft daß ich reden kann![65]

---

[61] Gotthold Ephraim Lessing: *Briefe, die neueste Literatur betreffend.* In: *Werke und Briefe.* Bd. 4. Hg. von Gunter E. Grimm. Frankfurt/M. 1997 (Bibliothek deutscher Klassiker 148). S. 621.

[62] Johann George Scheffner: *Erotische Gedichte.* Berlin 1780. S. A2ᵛ.

[63] Goethe: Zwo wichtige bisher unerörterte biblische Fragen (1773). In: *Sämtliche Werke. Erste Abteilung.* Hg. von Fricdmar Apel. Bd. 18. Frankfurt/M. 1998 (Bibliothek deutscher Klassiker 151). S. 138-139.

[64] Georg Friedrich Meier: *Theoretische Lehre von den Gemüthsbewegungen überhaupt.* Halle 1744. Nachdr. Frankfurt/M. 1971 (Athenäum Reprints). S. 402.

[65] Goethe: *Sämtliche Werke nach Epochen seines Schaffens.* Bd. I.2. *Der junge Goethe 1757-1775.* Hg. von Gerhard Sauder. München 1987. S. 413.

Vier Sätze, und ebenso viele Absätze: exakt hält sich Goethe an die Beobachtung der Physiologie, wonach "in den Leidenschaften" das "Odemholen [...] beschwerlich, unterbrochen und starck, und die schnell wiederholten Absätze desselben [...] überaus kurtz" werden.[66] Der Eindruck wird erweckt, als ob dem Redner im Sturm der Erregung die Luft knapp würde, so dass er nur zu abgerissenen Ausrufen fähig wäre, deren letzte diese seine Notlage auch noch kommentiert – überflüssigerweise, hat er sie uns doch im selben Atemzug schon zu Gehör gebracht.

Das sind die Grundlagen für Goethes Experimente mit der Atemtechnik des Verses in seiner Lyrik. Einige seiner bekanntesten Gedichte sind in diesem Sinne als Atemübungen zu verstehen.

Im Gegensatz zur moderaten aufklärerischen Diätetik eines Brockes vertritt der junge Goethe eine Diätetik des lebenssteigernden Überschwangs, des im Frühwerk so vielfach beschworenen "Muts".[67] "Wie gibt das Othemholen Mut", ruft Herder aus;[68] "Mut hebt die Brust, Lebensothem die wehende Nase".[69] Das Herz soll schneller schlagen ('Es schlug mein Herz [...]'),[70] soll "glühen" ('Wandrers Sturmlied').[71] Und da "die Lunge [...] das Bette [ist], in welchem das Hertz ruhet[, ...] muß [sie] an den Bewegungen des Hertzens Theil nehmen".[72] Schon bei Galenus geht das tiefe Atemholen mit Wärme in der Brust einher.[73] Das goethesche Gedicht macht sich diese energische Diätetik zu eigen; es möchte gleichsam so viel Luft in sich fassen wie möglich, und nimmt dabei auch Atemstörungen in Kauf – ja, diese werden der Stimmführung des Gedichts einverleibt, als Gnadenzeichen von Affekt, Genie und Begeisterung.

'Maifest' führt uns zunächst vor, was es heißt, einen langen Atem zu haben. Das von Lebensfreude überbordende Lied macht es dem Leser atemtechnisch

---

[66] Meier: *Theoretische Lehre von den Gemüthsbewegungen.* S. 402.

[67] Siehe 'Maifest', 'Pilgers Morgenlied', 'Wandrers Sturmlied', 'Eislebens Lied' (später u. d. T. 'Mut'). In: *Gedichte 1756-1799.* S. 130, 138, 145, 206 und "Von deutscher Baukunst". In: *Ästhetische Schriften 1771-1805.* S. 118.

[68] Herder: *Vom Erkennen und Empfinden der menschlichen Seele.* In: *Werke.* Bd. 4. S. 334.

[69] Ebd. S. 332. "Mut" im Sinne von "Hochherzigkeit" ist im Sprachgebrauch Herders vielfach zu belegen. Siehe *Ueber die Wirkung der Dichtkunst auf die Sitten der Völker in alten und neuen Zeiten* (1777). In: *Werke.* Bd. 4. S. 149-214, hier S. 167, 184, 185, 189. Dieser Herdersche und Goethesche "Mut" ist gleichzusetzen mit dem *thymos* Platons, der im Brustkorb seinen Sitz hat. S. Ricken u. a. Sp. 3. Vgl. auch J. M. R. Lenz: 'Lied zum teutschen Tanz': "O Mut, den Busen geschwellt [...] Kürzer die Brust / Atmet in Lust". Jakob Michael Reinhold Lenz: *Werke. Dramen, Prosa, Gedichte.* Hg. von Karen Lauer. München 1992. S. 482.

[70] Goethe: *Gedichte 1756-1799.* S. 128.

[71] Ebd. S. 144. Paul Stöcklein bezeichnet Goethes "Denk- und Sprechstil" als "kardiozentrisch" bzw. "kardiographisch". Paul Stöcklein: *Wege zum späten Goethe. Dichtung, Gedanke, Zeichnung. Interpretationen um ein Thema.* 2. Aufl. Hamburg 1960. S. 328-329.

[72] Meier: *Theoretische Lehre von den Gemüthsbewegungen.* S. 402.

[73] Respiration. In: *Encyclopédie.* Bd. 14 (1765). S. 185.

nicht ganz einfach. An mindestens drei Stellen kann es passieren, dass einem entgegen der Erwartung, die sich aus dem Schriftbild kurzer Zeilen und Strophen ergibt, nicht genug Luft bleibt, den Satzbogen zu Ende zu führen. Das ist auch dann der Fall, wenn die Satzglieder an sich kurz sind:

> Es dringen Blüten
> Aus jedem Zweig,
> Und tauschen Stimmen
> Aus dem Gesträuch,
>
> Und Freud und Wonne
> Aus jeder Brust.
> O Erd o Sonne
> O Glück o Lust!
>
> O Lieb' o Liebe [...][74]

Kommt es schon beim Strophenwechsel nach "Gesträuch" unerwartet, dass der Satz noch nicht zu Ende ist, und dass der durch die Wiederkehr des Reims markierte Abschluss nur scheinbar war, so wiederholt sich das Ganze noch einmal am Umbruch zur folgenden Strophe, wo man zunächst meint, mit dem vierfachen Ausruf und dem emphatischen "o Lust!" einen Schlußpunkt setzen zu können, um dann durch die alliterierende Fortsetzung der Ausrufe eines Besseren belehrt zu werden. Hatte man in beiden Fällen zunächst mit vier Einheiten (Zeilen bzw. Vokativen) gerechnet, so muss man den Atem nun über sechs spannen. Noch mehr wird uns in der zweiten Hälfte des Gedichts abverlangt:

> O Mädchen Mädchen,
> Wie lieb' ich dich!
> Wie blinkt dein Auge!
> Wie liebst du mich!
>
> So liebt die Lerche
> Gesang und Luft,
> Und Morgenblumen
> Den Himmels Duft,
>
> Wie ich dich liebe
> Mit warmem Blut,
> Die du mir Jugend
> Und Freud und Mut

---

[74] Goethe: *Gedichte 1756-1799*. S. 129.

Zu neuen Liedern,
Und Tänzen gibst![75]

"So liebt die Lerche" usw. glaubt man zunächst als Apodosis zu "Wie liebst du mich" in der vorhergehenden Zeile lesen zu können. In Wirklichkeit stellt es sich aber als Protasis für die folgenden Zeilen heraus. Wieder fließt also die erwartete vierzeilige Einheit in eine sechszeilige über (bis hinunter zu "Blut" also). Aber auch da ist die Periode nicht zu Ende; weitere vier Zeilen müssen noch aufgenommen werden, bevor man wieder Atem schöpfen kann.

Wir müssen uns hier also erst den langen Atem aneignen, über den der Dichter in seinem "neuen Lied" so mühelos verfügt. Die Lektüre des Gedichts gibt uns die Anleitung dazu. Will es in seinen Übergängen und Perioden gleichsam in einem begeisterten Zug gelesen werden, so dehnt es uns die Lungen und schenkt uns die Luft, die wir dazu brauchen. Die Lektüre des Gedichts wird damit zur Begeisterung, von der es spricht.

Der Dichter selbst schöpft aus dem 'Maifest' der Liebe Atem und "Mut" nicht nur zu diesem einen, sondern gleich zu mehreren "neuen Liedern, / Und Tänzen". Da fragt es sich, wo er denn an die Grenzen seiner Begeisterung stoße und ihm der Atem ausgehe.

"La carriere qu[e le poëte] doit fournir est si courte, qu'il n'aura pas le temps de perdre haleine [...]: c'est là l'*ode* pindarique".[76] Wenn Goethe diese Stelle kannte, hätte er ihr gewiss widersprochen. In der erhabenen lyrischen Gattung ging es geradezu darum, außer Atem zu kommen: so tief Luft und Inspiration zu schöpfen, dass einem zuletzt der Atem ausging. So wäre z. B. an den "eratmenden Schritt / Mühsam Berg hinauf" in 'An Schwager Kronos' zu erinnern.[77] Auf die höchste Probe stellt Goethe jedoch sein dichterisches Atmungsvermögen in 'Wandrers Sturmlied'[78] – einer pindarischen Ode, wohlgemerkt[79] –, wo er, auf freier Flur der Gewalt der Elemente ausgesetzt, Muskelkraft und Lungenkapazität gegen die der "sturmatmende[n] Gottheit" (Z. 93), "Jupiter Pluvius" selbst (Z. 75), misst.

Damit ist eigentlich schon vorprogrammiert, dass er unterliegen muss. Nur auf das Früher oder Später kommt es an. Lange Zeit, in den weit ausholenden Perioden der Invokationen des schutzgewährenden "Genius" und der "Musen" im ersten Drittel des Gedichts (der "Strophe" des pindarischen Vorbilds), geht alles gut (Z. 1-38). Erste Gedanken an eine Umkehr (Z. 39) werden in der Antistrophe noch unterdrückt (Z. 39-70). In der Epode, dem letzten Drittel, rafft sich das Gedicht noch einmal zu einer grandiosen Anrufung des Sturmgottes auf. Damit ist aber sein Atem fast schon verbraucht. Das von Anfang an hinausgezö-

---

[75] Ebd. S. 130.

[76] Ode. In: *Encyclopédie*. Bd. 11 (1765). S. 346.

[77] Goethe: *Gedichte 1756-1799*. S. 202.

[78] Ebd. S. 142-145.

[79] Zum Nachweis s. den Kommentar in *Gedichte 1756-1799*. S. 855-858.

gerte Unterliegen führen uns die letzten Zeilen der Ode eindrucksvoll vor:

> Wenn die Räder rasselten Rad an Rad
> Rasch ums Ziel weg
> Hoch flog siegdurchglühter Jünglinge Peitschenknall
> Und sich Staub wälzt
> Wie vom Gebürg herab sich
> Kieselwetter ins Tal wälzt
> Glühte deine Seel Gefahren Pindar
> Mut Pindar – Glühte –
> Armes Herz –
> Dort auf dem Hügel –
> Himmlische Macht –
> Nur so viel Glut –
> Dort ist meine Hütte –
> Zu waten bis dort hin. (Z. 104-17)

In den ersten sieben Zeilen des Auszugs ist als Substrat der in kurzem Abstand aufeinander folgenden beschwerten Silben (z. B. "Rad an Rad / Rasch", "Tal wälzt / Glühte") ein schwer kämpfender, in kurzen Stößen ausgepresster Atem zu betrachten. Die extrem harte Fügung am Zeilenumbruch von Z. 108-109 ("Wie vom Gebürg herab sich / Kieselwetter") macht uns in plastischer Weise ein momentanes Aussetzen des Atems vor. Dann versagt er aber fast völlig. Es reicht nur noch zu abgerissenen Satzfetzen. Die Gedankenstriche, die nun die Rede unterbrechen, haben hier eine ganz andere Funktion als im 'Vernünftigen Geruch' von Brockes. Dort fügten sie dem vom Atem getragenen Wort die Gedankenpause hinzu, hier sind sie als Verschnaufpausen der Ort, an dem der Atem versucht, wieder zu sich kommen; für Gedanken und Worte bleibt da nicht viel übrig. Dort dienten sie dem Gedanken, hier hat der Dichter alle Not, überhaupt noch einen Gedanken zu fassen. Dort gaben sie dem Bewußtsein Raum, die körperliche Tätigkeit zu durchdringen und zu sich hinaufzuziehen, hier sind sie im entgegengesetzten Sinn als Einbrüche des Körperlichen zu lesen, dem das Bewußtsein nur noch so weit standhält, als es sich auf das existentiell Notwendigste beschränkt; und auch das ist mühevoll genug.

Der Kommentar von Wilkinson und Willoughby merkt ganz richtig an: "The broken sentences reflect [the poet's] breathless exhaustion". Aber auch dies ist richtig: "Yet he is not back where he started".[80] Der Ertrag ist keineswegs negativ. Im Kräftemessen mit den sich im Unwetter manifestierenden Göttern erschöpft sich der Wanderer zwar bis auf den letzten Atemzug (wobei wieder die Exaktheit der physiologischen Beobachtung besticht: Zu allem Überfluß geht es zum Schluß auch noch *bergauf* [Z. 113]). Aber nur indem er bis an diese

---

[80] E. M. Wilkinson und L. A. Willoughby: *Wandrers Sturmlied*. A Study in Poetic Vagrancy. In: *Goethe. Poet and Thinker*. London 1962. S. 35-54, hier S. 51.

Schmerzensgrenze vorstößt, kommen Herz, Blut und Gedanken so in Bewegung, dass sich enfalten kann, was an "Mut" in ihm steckt, und zum Ausdruck gelangt, was er an Genie besitzt.

Nach dem Ein- kommt das Ausatmen. "Ein Atem, den man in sich zeucht, stärket, ein Atem, den man von sich läßt, erfreuet das Leben: in jedem Atemzuge sind zweierlei Gnaden".[81] Verschreibt sich 'Wandrers Sturmlied' der Inspiration, so wird man 'Wandrers Nachtlied' ("Über allen Gefilden") als expirierendes Pendant dazu betrachten dürfen. Bekanntlich "an die Wand der Jagdhütte auf dem Kickelhahn bei Ilmenau geschrieben",[82] ist hier die "Hütte" erreicht, der der Wanderer im "Sturmlied" noch entgegenstolperte. Es ist die Ruhe nach dem Sturm, das Ausruhen von den Strapazen der Wanderung:

> Über allen Gefilden
> Ist Ruh,
> In allen Wipfeln
> Spürest du
> Kaum einen Hauch;
> Die Vögel schweigen im Walde.
> Warte nur, balde
> Ruhest du auch.[83]

Hier hat man Zeit zum Ausatmen. Die Kürze der zweiten Zeile im Vergleich zur ersten schafft eine kleine Lücke im Text, der dort gleichsam Halt macht, damit Herz- und Atmungsrhythmus sich beruhigen und ins Gleichgewicht kommen können. Die vierte Zeile gibt noch einmal Anlass zum tieferen Einatmen, da die Ergänzung des Sinnes noch aussteht; diese aber, in der fünften Zeile, bringt atemtechnisch ein wohliges Ausatmen mit sich. Nach der langen sechsten Zeile tritt in den letzten zwei Zeilen die endgültige Beruhigung ein. Kürzere Zeilen schließen das Gedicht, das im Reimwort "auch" lautmalerisch mit einem letzten Aushauchen des Atems endet.[84]

---

[81] Herder: *Vom Erkennen und Empfinden der menschlichen Seele.* In: *Werke.* Bd. 4. S. 334. Herder zitiert hier den persischen Dichter Sadi. Derselben Stelle liegt Goethes Gedicht 'Im Atemholen sind zweierlei Gnaden' aus dem *Divan* zugrunde. Goethe: *West-östlicher Divan. Teil 1.* In: *Sämtliche Werke. Erste Abteilung.* Hg. von Hendrik Birus. Bd. 3/1. Frankfurt/M. 1994 (Bibliothek deutscher Klassiker 113). S. 15. Die alternative Naturheilkunde moderner Prägung macht sich (auf freilich unpoetische Weise) denselben Grundsatz zu eigen: Siehe James E. Loehr, Ed. D. und Jeffrey A. Migdow, M. D.: *Breathe In Breathe Out. Inhale Energy and Exhale Stress by Guiding and Controlling Your Breathing.* Alexandria, VA 1999. — Zum Komplex des Atmens im *Divan* s. George F. Peters: "'Wind', 'Atem', and 'Geist' in Goethe's *West-östlicher Divan*". Diss. Stanford 1971.
[82] Goethe: *Gedichte 1756-1799.* S. 1072.
[83] Hier nach der Originalfassung zitiert. Goethe: *Gedichte 1756-1799.* S. 388.
[84] Vgl. Engels Beschreibung der idealen Elegie: "Längere [...] Zeilen [...] mit kürzern abwechselnd, in welchen der bis dahin ausgehaltne gezogene Athem sanft verhaucht:

"Kaum einen Hauch" spürt der Wanderer in den "Wipfeln" der Bäume; auch hierin ist der Gegensatz zum "Sturmlied" offenbar. So wie es der Dichter dort mit einer "sturmatmenden Gottheit" aufnahm, passt er sich hier dem kaum spürbaren Atem einer zur Ruhe gekommenen Natur an. Seine verklingende Rede ist selbst "kaum ein Hauch". Die das Gedicht umgebende, atemlose Stille, die vor allem am Ende der zweiten, fünften, sechsten und letzten Zeile hörbar wird, ist ihm ebenso wesentlich, wie die auf einem leisen Lufthauch getragenen Worte selbst. Hier ist also ein anderer, der entgegengesetzte Grenzzustand erreicht, als im 'Sturmlied'. War dort der "*Donner* der Ode" zu hören,[85] so ist es hier gleichsam sein Fehlen, das uns aufhorchen lässt; war dort von höchster Anstrengung die Rede, so sind hier Körper und Geist zur Ruhe gekommen.

Indem aber in beiden Gedichten der Atem das tragende Element bildet, in dem sie sich bewegen, sind sie beide in gleichem Maße auch an die körperliche Erfahrung gebunden. "Eine Ode besteht nicht an und für sich, sie muß aus einem schon bewegten Elemente hervorsteigen".[86] Dieses Element ist hier der Körper des Dichters. Diesem gibt er in der *mimesis* des Gedichts ein zweites Dasein. Wenn wir uns von ihm leiten lassen, unseren Atem seinem Takt anpassen, können auch wir ein Stück körperlicher Erfahrung wiedererwecken und unserer eigenen Erfahrung einverleiben.[87] Und wenn es in der Dichtungsauffassung des 18. Jahrhunderts ein Gemeinplatz ist, dass die Rührung des Dichters auf den Leser zu übertragen sei – "A man […] may be called eloquent, who transfers the passion or sentiment with which he is moved himself, into the breast of another"[88] – so darf man hier behaupten, dass das Ideal tatsächlich erfüllt ist, handelt es sich doch im wörtlichsten Sinne um eine Übertragung aus einer Brust in die andere: einer Atembewegung nämlich, die aber zugleich auch ganz Gefühlsregung ist.

IV.

"Zum guten Diät-halten [gehört] der rechte Gebrauch der Lufft [und] der Bewegung und Ruhe".[89] Auch bei Goethe findet, wenn auch über einen längeren Zeit-

---

wie sehr können sie der wehmütigen schmelzenden Empfindung des elegischen Dichters gemäß seyn!" J. J. Engel: *Ideen zu einer Mimik*. Bd. 2. Berlin 1786. S. 138.

[85] Herder: *Über die neuere deutsche Literatur*. In: *Werke*. Bd. 1. S. 487.

[86] Goethe: Theilnahme Goethes an Manzoni (1827). In: *Sämtliche Werke. Erste Abteilung*. Bd. 22: *Ästhetische Schriften 1824-1832. Über Kunst und Altertum V-VI*. Hg. von Anne Bohnenkamp. Frankfurt/M. 1999 (Bibliothek deutscher Klassiker 160). S. 781-813, hier S. 801.

[87] Zu diesem Komplex s. Peter von Matt: Lyrik und Körperlichkeit: Das lyrische Reden als Wiedergewinn ausgegrenzter Erfahrung. In: *Verlust und Ursprung: Festschrift für Werner Weber*. Hg. von Angelika Maass and Bernhard Heinser. Zürich 1989. S. 179-194.

[88] Oliver Goldsmith: *The Bee* (VII, 17. November 1759). In: *The Collected Works of Oliver Goldsmith*. Hg. von Arthur Friedman. Bd. 1. Oxford 1966. S. 477.

[89] *Großes vollständiges Universal-Lexicon*. Bd. 7 (1734). Sp. 733.

raum hinweg, vom 'Sturmlied' bis zum 'Nachtlied', ein Wechsel zwischen den Polen von Bewegung und Ruhe statt. Ansonsten aber hat seine (voritalienische) Diätetik wenig von der "vernünfftigen Ordnung" der Frühaufklärung. Seine Gesundheit holt er sich von den Extremen her, auch den körperlichen. Wo Brockes den Körper dem Geist untertan machen wollte, läßt ihm Goethe seinen Lauf und gibt sich seinen Regungen hin. Und wo Brockes den Atem reglementierte, war für Goethe, dem schönen Wort Herders entsprechend, das "Othemholen durch seinen Druck auf die Maschine zugleich der Takt [...], der die Modulation der Gedanken regier[te]".[90]

Es ging hier darum, in welcher Form der Körper im lyrischen Gedicht des 18. Jahrhunderts in Erscheinung tritt und wie ihm mit dessen Kunstmitteln ein virtuelles Dasein über das Leben des Dichters hinaus verschafft werden kann. Man wird daraus über die literarhistorische Einordnung der beiden behandelten Dichter nichts Neues gelernt haben. Wohl ist aber zu hoffen, dass unter dem Blickwinkel einer Pneumatologie der Lyrik ihre Eigenart sich klarer profiliert hat, wie auch die der literarischen Strömungen, denen sie angehören. Welchen Geist das 18. Jahrhundert atmete, dürfte nicht zuletzt an der Art und Weise, *wie* es atmete, abzulesen sein.

---

[90] Herder: *Vom Erkennen und Empfinden*, 1. Fassung (1774). In: *Werke*. Bd. 4. S. 1094.

Heather Merle Benbow

Goethe's *Die Wahlverwandtschaften* and the Problem of Feminine Orality

In this article I examine the figure of Ottilie in Goethe's 1809 novel Die Wahlverwandtschaften. *The focus of my analysis is orality, the gendered values and taboos
which pertain to the oral as it is manifested in speech, food consumption, and sexuality. I argue that the Enlightenment gender hegemony dictates a femininity which is
impoverished with respect to oral functions; the much-lauded feminine modesty
stands for lack of appetite, desire, and will. Ottilie appears as an ideal of modest
bourgeois femininity yet her wasting is perhaps a problematisation of the Enlightenment feminine ideal.*

> Die Weiber, auch die gebildetsten, haben mehr
> Appetit als Geschmack.
> (Johann Wolfgang von Goethe)[1]

The polyfunctionality of the mouth did not escape the attention of peda-
gogues of the early nineteenth century: "Man kann den Mund öffnen und
schließen; man kann mit dem Mund essen, trinken und reden; man kann
durch den Mund speyen und bluten".[2] As the organ of discourse production
as well as of appetite, both gastronomic and sexual, the mouth unites apparently divergent intellectual and physical activities. As Rosalind Coward remarks, orality is deeply problematic, particularly for women: "Complicated
taboos and prohibitions surround the sensual pleasures of the mouth. In fact,
the mouth appears to be the organ where the tightest controls are placed on
women's behaviour, where women's sensual life is most closely policed".[3]
In Goethe's 1809 novel, *Die Wahlverwandtschaften*, the contradictions and
paradoxes in attitudes to feminine appetites are brought into relief. A consideration of the heroine's virtues leads to the conclusion that Ottilie is "un-
mouthed" in all respects: she renounces all oral manifestations of appetite –
gastronomic, sexual, and intellectual/metaphorical. For these qualities she is
praised and desired by Eduard.[4] Yet Ottilie's oral modesty also stands for

---

[1] Friedrich Wilhelm Riemer: *Mitteilungen über Goethe.* Leipzig 1921. P. 247.
[2] Johann Heinrich Pestalozzi: *Das Buch der Mütter oder Anleitung für Mütter ihre
Kinder Bemerken und Reden zu lehren.* Zürich 1803. P. 90.
[3] Rosalind Coward: *Female Desire.* London 1984. P. 118.
[4] Johann Wolfgang von Goethe: *Die Wahlverwandtschaften.* In: *Werke.* Hamburger
Ausgabe. Ed. by Erich Trunz. Vol. 6. Hamburg 1948. P. 281. Hereafter referred to
as WV.

her inability to situate herself in the world as a speaking subject, to nourish her body, to express her intellect, to act upon her sexual desires, and is implicated in her demise.

In a novel originally intended by the author to form part of the *Bildungsroman, Wilhelm Meisters Lehrjahre*,[5] the educational program of which Ottilie is a product is foregrounded, inviting an analysis of prevailing educational perspectives of feminine orality in which the despised figure of the immodest, educated woman serves to highlight the desirability of a femininity based on the threefold roles of wife, mother, and domestic worker. The figure of the "Pedantin oder Amazone" (as the learned woman is dubbed in Kant's *Beobachtungen über das Gefühl des Schönen und Erhabenen*[6]) haunts much of the late Enlightenment writing on feminine virtue; the education to feminine *modesty* implies the presence of an inherent appetitive *excess* and this is conflated with anxieties aroused by the emancipatory tendencies of the early Enlightenment. Orality is, in its feminine manifestation, fraught with danger for the gender hegemony of the Enlightenment, always threatening to subvert the order of feminine modesty. The natural excess ascribed to the feminine is nowhere more apparent than in the image of the maternal and reproductive female body. Ottilie's idealisation as "mother" in the novel and her death of self-denial reveal the paradox inherent in pedagogical and biomedical femininities; fecundity and modesty cannot be reconciled.

This article will first examine modesty – primarily as the containment of appetite[7] – in the context of the bourgeois feminine role, then three tiers of appetitivity: gastronomic, intellectual (i.e. the "hunger" for knowledge), and sexual. Then the intensification of the paradox of a desiring/modest femininity, around the maternal feminine, will be interrogated. Finally, late-twentieth century discourses surrounding *anorexia nervosa* will be considered in the context of the persistent problematisation of feminine appetitivity.

The Enlightenment ushered in a cult of feminine modesty. It was praised by philosophy, identified by medicine, required by pedagogy, enforced by so-

[5] A. G. Steer: *Goethe's Elective Affinities. The Robe of Nessus.* Heidelberg 1990. P. 222.

[6] Immanuel Kant: Beobachtungen über das Gefühl des Schönen und Erhabenen. In: *Immanuel Kants sämtliche Werke.* Ed. by Felix Gross. Vol. 1. Leipzig 1921. P. 49.

[7] Modesty has various shades of meaning, ranging from a sense of shame (corresponding more closely to the German *Schamhaftigkeit*), to humility, to moderation. It will be argued here that prescriptions of feminine modesty focus on the curtailment of appetites deemed excessive in their 'natural' form.

cial treatises.[8] Modesty was to be apparent in all aspects of feminine activity – in outward appearance, in demeanour, and particularly in appetite. This characterisation of femininity was commensurate with the prescriptive roles of "beglückende Gattinnen, bildende Mütter und weise Vorsteherinnen des inneren Hauswesens"[9] to which all bourgeois women were expected to conform. Barbara Duden sees the employment of "erstickendes Lob"[10] of bourgeois femininity to this end, but the saccharine depictions of feminine domesticity are matched by the brutal rhetoric invoked to condemn alternatives, such as education and engagement in the public sphere or even merely the desire to shape one's own destiny.[11] The latter half of the eighteenth century saw what might be called a backlash – inspired by Rousseau – against the emancipatory tendencies of the early Enlightenment.[12] Much of the censorious language converged on the danger of giving free reign to feminine desire (both physical and metaphorical). Goethe's *Die Wahlverwandtschaften* appears at a time when the consensus on the appropriate role of bourgeois woman was apparent, and the characterisation of Ottilie falls clearly within this trajectory. She emerges as an idealised figure in contrast to her Amazonian cousin, Luciane.

Ottilie's is a femininity which serves as a "Mittel zum Zweck der Befriedigung des Mannes";[13] she is defined by an extreme selflessness and desire to please. It is precisely her lack of desire – and her constant readiness to fulfil the desires of others, in particular, Eduard – which defines her as a feminine role model for Goethe's era. The timid girl comes into her own in the novel as she gains familiarity with the household chores which come to define her existence; Ottilie is tirelessly servile, ever-responsive to the needs of those around her:

---

[8] See for example Kant: Beobachtungen. P. 42, and Joachim Heinrich Campe: *Väterlicher Rath für meine Tochter. Ein Gegenstück zum Theophron.* Paderborn 1988 (Quellen und Schriften zur Geschichte der Frauenbildung 3). Pp. 172-181.

[9] Campe. Pp. 16-17.

[10] Barbara Duden: Das schöne Eigentum. Zur Herausbildung des bürgerlichen Frauenbildes an der Wende vom 18. zum 19. Jahrhundert. In: *Kursbuch* 47 (1977). Pp. 125-142, here p. 126.

[11] See Kant: Beobachtungen. P. 35; Jean-Jacques Rousseau: *Émile.* London 1974. P. 371-372 [hereafter referred to as E]; Ernst Brandes: *Betrachtungen über das weibliche Geschlecht und dessen Ausbildung in dem geselligen Leben.* Hannover 1802. Pp. 3:38, 2:200.

[12] Heidemarie Bennent-Vahle: Einleitung der Herausgeberin. In: *Grundriss einer Weltweisheit für das Frauenzimmer.* Ed. by Heidemarie Bennent-Vahle. Aachen 1995. P. 13.

[13] Duden: Das schöne Eigentum. P. 139.

die Dienstbeflissenheit Ottiliens [wuchs] mit jedem Tage. Je mehr sie das Haus, die Menschen, die Verhältnisse kennenlernte, desto lebhafter griff sie ein, desto schneller verstand sie jeden Blick, jede Bewegung, ein halbes Wort, einen Laut. Ihre ruhige Aufmerksamkeit blieb sich immer gleich, so wie ihre gelassene Regsamkeit. Und so war ihr Sitzen, Aufstehen, Gehen, Kommen, Holen, Bringen, Wiederniedersitzen, ohne einen Schein von Unruhe, ein ewiger Wechsel, die ewige angenehme Bewegung. (WV 283-284)

Ottilie's ability to understand the barely articulated needs of others contrasts to her own lack of desire. For Duden the bourgeois revolution results in a revaluation of feminine work, which becomes both eroticised and conceived in terms of "duty".[14] The result is woman as "eine Person ohne Ich",[15] an apt description for Ottilie, whose servitude is augmented by an at best ephemeral presence: "Dazu kam, daß man sie nicht gehen hörte, so leise trat sie auf" (WV 284).

A comparison of Ottilie with the equally fictional Sophy of Rousseau's iconic pedagogical work, *Émile* (1762), is enlightening. Rousseau self-consciously calls Sophy full-grown into being when his fictitious pupil, Émile, is ready to marry: "Let us call your future mistress Sophy; Sophy is a name of good omen" (E 294). Sophy has impeccable bourgeois credentials, and, like Ottilie, she is modest and exceedingly competent in housework:

Needlework is what Sophy likes best; and the feminine arts have been taught her most carefully [...]. She has also studied all the details of housekeeping; she understands cooking and cleaning; she knows the prices of food, and also how to choose it; she can keep accounts accurately, she is her mother's housekeeper. [...] she can take the place of any of the servants and she is always ready to do so. (E 357)

Rousseau then proceeds to invent a history for the girl, thereby portraying the correct upbringing for the bourgeois girl-child which he has neglected in the rest of his educational treatise. In this history it becomes apparent that Sophy's modesty is anything but a natural feminine virtue, rather it is a behaviour to be inculcated into the unruly girl-child. Whereas Rousseau insists upon the rightness of absolute physical freedom for the boy – "Do not make him sit still when he wants to run about [...]. Let them run, jump and shout to their heart's content. All their own activities are instincts of the body" (E 50) – the girl's physical movements are to be strictly curtailed. Submission goes hand-in-hand with modesty for Rousseau, who writes that girls "ought to have little freedom [...], enthusiasm must be kept in check, because it is

---

[14] Duden: Das schöne Eigentum. Pp. 135-136.
[15] Ibid. P. 125.

the source of several vices commonly found among women [...], do not leave them for a moment without restraint. Train them to break off their games and return to their other occupations without a murmur" (E 333). This passage is reminiscent of Ottilie's uncomplaining "Sitzen, Aufstehen, Gehen, Kommen, Holen, Bringen, Wiederniedersitzen" (WV 283). For Rousseau such restraint is necessary to train the girl for a future of domestic servitude: "for she will always be in subjection to a man, or to man's judgment, and she will never be free to set her own opinion above his" (E 333).

But the harshest sanctions are reserved for the area of appetite in the girl-child's upbringing. The goal of such sanctions is modesty in the adult woman, which – once inculcated – will be deemed a 'natural' feminine trait, as exemplified by the figures of Sophy and Ottilie. Ottilie represents an ideal feminine characterised not merely by a lack of appetites; it is orality generally which is suppressed in her. Eduard is immediately captivated by the shy Ottilie and remarks to his wife, Charlotte:

"Es ist ein angenehmes, unterhaltendes Mädchen."
"Unterhaltend?" versetzte Charlotte mit Lächeln; "sie hat ja den Mund noch nicht aufgetan."
"So?" erwiderte Eduard, indem er sich zu besinnen schien: "das wäre doch wunderbar!" (WV 281)

That Eduard develops an instant liking for Ottilie even though (perhaps because) she fails entirely to situate herself as a speaking subject is testament to the desirability of a femininity which is un-mouthed.

Ottilie's modesty finds its apparently logical culmination in an almost complete lack of appetite, which is lamented by the governess of the *Pension* where Ottilie is educated:

"Sie ist nach wie vor bescheiden und gefällig gegen andere; aber dieses Zurücktreten, diese Dienstbarkeit will mir nicht gefallen [...]. Auch kann ich ihre große Mäßigkeit im Essen und Trinken nicht loben. An unserem Tisch ist kein Überfluß; doch sehe ich nichts lieber, als wenn die Kinder sich an schmackhaften und gesunden Speisen satt essen. [...] Dazu kann ich Ottilien niemals bringen. Ja sie macht sich irgendein Geschäft, um eine Lücke auszufüllen, wo die Dienerinnen etwas versäumen, nur um eine Speise oder den Nachtisch zu übergehen." (WV 263-264)

Ottilie's is an apparently natural modesty, one to which she adheres even in the face of official disapproval. Rousseau's Sophy, too, "eats sparingly" (E 358), but in his account of her upbringing it becomes apparent that this was not always so. A note of urgency is tangible in Rousseau's exhortation: "Little girls are not to be controlled, as little boys are, to some extent, by their greediness. This tendency may have ill effects on women and it is too dangerous to be left unchecked" (E 358). There are regulatory practices recommended by Rousseau to ensure Sophy develops sufficiently "feminine tastes" including the withholding of meals: "When Sophy was little, she did not always return empty handed if she was sent to her mother's cupboard, and she was not quite to be trusted with sweets and sugar-almonds. Her mother caught her, took them from her, and made her go without her dinner" (E 358). The inherent greediness (and cunning, "a natural gift of woman, and so convinced am I that all our natural inclinations are right, that I would cultivate this among others, only guarding against its abuse" [E 334]) of the girl-child is epitomised for Rousseau in the following anecdote:

> Children are commonly forbidden to ask for anything at table [...]. [...] this is what I saw done by a little girl of six; the circumstances were much more difficult, for not only was she strictly forbidden to ask for anything directly or indirectly, but disobedience would have been unpardonable, for she had eaten of every dish; one only had been overlooked, and on this she had set her heart. This is what she did to repair the omission [...]; she pointed to every dish in turn, saying, "I've had some of this; I've had some of this;" however she omitted the one dish so markedly that some one noticed it and said, "Have not you had some of this?" "Oh, no," replied the greedy little girl with soft voice and downcast eyes. (E 334)

Rousseau's strident condemnation of the little girl, coerced by a strict etiquette to employ cunning – a behaviour of the powerless – to get what she desires, stands in stark contrast to his *laissez faire* attitude to the little boy's appetites: "whatever food you give your children, provided you accustom them to nothing but plain and simple dishes, let them eat and run and play as much as they want; you may be sure they will never eat too much and will never have indigestion [...]. Our appetite is only excessive because we try to impose upon it rules other than those of nature" (E 120). The reader should be in no doubt that, despite the gender-neutral language used, the "children" of whom Rousseau here writes, are boys. The failure of nature's rules to regulate an inherently excessive feminine appetite, rather than constituting a crisis for Rousseau's faith in mother nature, by whom he otherwise sets such great store, invites the implementation of a strict and punitive regulation of this excess. The goal of this regulation is the acquisition of "feminine tastes", retrospectively deemed inherent to the femininity of the adult Sophy: "Sophy has preserved her feminine tastes; she likes milk and sweets; she likes pastry and made-dishes, but not much meat. She has never tasted wine or spirits; moreover, she eats sparingly; women, who do not work so hard as men, have less waste to repair" (E 358). The long-standing association of meat with masculine virility has been noted by Carol J. Adams: "a mythology permeates all classes that meat is a masculine food and meat eating a male activity [...]. Most food taboos address meat consumption and they place more restrictions on women than on men".[16] Adams's analysis of meat-eating as the behaviour of sexual dominance[17] provides a clue to Rousseau's characterisation of a lack of appetite for meat as feminine. The medical doctor Carl Gustav Carus, in his rules for the nourishment of woman, is also concerned about the sexual connotations of certain foods; he warns against allowing women to eat "erhitzende, stark reizende Getränke und Speisen [...] und alle starken Gewürze".[18] It seems such foods might awaken the dormant passions in the woman tamed by feminine eating.

Ottilie expresses as little desire for the acquisition of scholarly knowledge as she does for food. She arrives in Eduard's household after the shame of failure in the public examination, in which her cousin Luciane has shone. The *Gehülfe* knows "'wie wenig die gute Ottilie zu äußern imstande ist, was in ihr liegt und was sie vermag'" (WV 278), and indeed her silence and selflessness, praised by Eduard, is a liability in the public educational machinery. The *Gehülfe* praises Ottilie as one who learns "'nicht als Schülerin, sondern als künftige Lehrerin'" (WV 265), which for Friedrich Kittler situates Ottilie in the bourgeois maternal role, itself the product of Enlightenment pedagogy: "Es geht also um die pädagogische Produktion von Beamten und Müttern [...]. [...] die Zweiheit von Beamten- und Mutterschaft [begründet] das Machtsystem der Goethezeit".[19] Luciane, who is, as her mother notes "'für die Welt geboren'" (WV 251) and Ottilie, who prefers silent domestic servitude, are two sides of a discussion about the role of women – with Luciane standing for the emancipated "Pedantin oder Amazone" and Ottilie for the much-praised wife and mother. Goethe is known to have taken a conservative position in the debates surrounding women's emancipation towards the end of the eighteenth century[20] and Wolf Kittler sees Ottilie as a clear favourite in the eyes of the author.[21] For Friedrich Kittler,

---

[16] Carol J. Adams: *The Sexual Politics of Meat: A Femininst-Vegetarian Critical Theory.* New York 1990. Pp. 26-27.

[17] Ibid. Pp. 39ff.

[18] Carl Gustav Carus: *Lehrbuch der Gynäkologie, oder thematische Darstellung und Behandlung eigenthümlicher gesunder und kranker Zustände, sowohl der nicht schwangeren, schwangeren und gebärenden Frauen, als der Wöchnerinnen und neugeborenen Kinder.* Vol. 1. Leipzig 1820. P. 81.

[19] Friedrich A. Kittler: Ottilie Hauptmann. In: *Goethes Wahlverwandtschaften: Kritische Modelle und Diskursanalysen zum Mythos Literatur.* Ed. by Norbert Bolz. Hildesheim 1981. Pp. 260-275, here p. 262

[20] Helmut Fuhrman: *Der androgyne Mensch: "Bild" und "Gestalt" der Frau und des Mannes im Werk Goethes.* Würzburg 1995. P. 11.

[21] Wolf Kittler: Goethes Wahlverwandtschaften. Soziale Verhältnisse symbolisch dargestellt. In: *Goethes Wahlverwandtschaften: Kritische Modelle und Diskursana-*

Ottilie's failure in the public examination is assured *because* of her idealisation as mother: "In öffentlichen Prüfungen kann eine Mutter selbstredend nur durchfallen"[22] because of her confinement to the private sphere ("Innerlichkeit") as opposed to the public realm ("Öffentlichkeit"). Public speech is incompatible with this confinement: "Die Tiefe einer Innerlichkeit aber ist nur am Grad ihres Schweigens zu ermessen".[23]

In Kant's "Beantwortung der Frage: Was ist Aufklärung?" (1783), his contribution to the debate in the *Berlinische Monatsschrift* on the meaning of Enlightenment, the role of *speech* is clear; it is an act of Enlightenment "in seiner eigenen Person zu sprechen".[24] Jonathan Hess has commented upon the proliferation of corporeal metaphors in Kant's essay, particularly oral metaphors: "The enlightenment essay [...] define[s] the human being [...] as a being capable of language, that is, capable of *Mündigkeit*, speaking for oneself, using its own mouth (*Mund*)".[25] The claim of an etymological link between *Mund* (mouth) and *Mündigkeit*[26] is false (it in fact refers to the archaic middle high German *munt*, meaning "Schutz") but perhaps accords to a popular etymology linking the organ of speech and self-representation with Enlightened maturity. Certainly, allusions to gastronomy abound in Kant's work: "thought is the 'food' of the philosopher's mind".[27]

Intellectual inquiry is an appetite commonly imagined in terms of physical hunger. Maud Ellmann writes of the prevalence of hunger as a metaphor for the desire for knowledge, and the comparison of the digestive and thought processes:

> Kierkegaard is only one of many thinkers who implicate digestion in cognition, for the analogy between these processes is integral to Western thought. Indeed, it is ingrained into our very language. To "ruminate," for instance, means to think but also means to chew one's cud; we speak of "chewing over" an idea, of "devouring" a book, of "food for thought".[28]

lysen zum Mythos Literatur. Ed. by Norbert Bolz. Hildesheim 1981. Pp. 230-259, here p. 248.

[22] Kittler: Ottilie Hauptmann. P. 264.

[23] Ibid. P. 264.

[24] Immanuel Kant: Beantwortung der Frage: Was ist Aufklärung? In: *Immanuel Kants sämtliche Werke.* Ed. by Felix Gross. Vol. 1. Leipzig 1921. P. 167.

[25] Jonathan M. Hess: *Reconstituting the Body Politic: Enlightenment, Public Culture and the Invention of Aesthetic Autonomy.* Detroit 1999. P. 201.

[26] Ibid. P. 201:N11.

[27] Susan Meld Shell: *The Embodiment of Reason: Kant on Spirit, Generation, and Community.* Chicago 1993. P. 295.

[28] Maud Ellmann: *The Hunger Artists. Starving, Writing, and Imprisonment.* Cambridge 1993. P. 29.

Ellmann turns to psychoanalysis for a ready explanation of the phenomenon; she traces the association to "the early months of life, when the infant gets to know external objects by inserting them into its mouth".[29] Yet surely the role of the mouth as the organ of discourse production is a more compelling explanation for the conflation of gastronomic and intellectual appetites. Friedrich Kittler writes of the intersection of hunger and learning in the early nineteenth century, typified by Johann Basedow's use of edible letters in literacy teaching: "Alphabetisierung zielt also auf eine kulinarische Oralität".[30] He identifies a "revolution" in the discursive system of the nineteenth century: "Die Revolution des europäischen Alphabets ist seine Oralisierung".[31] This "oralisation" of the European alphabet is typified by Heinrich Pestalozzi's *Buch der Mütter* in which the polyfunctionality of the mouth is described: "Man kann den Mund öffnen und schließen; man kann mit dem Mund essen, trinken und reden".[32]

The inherent excess of the feminine appetite extends also into this realm, as Ernst Brandes points out in his three-volume treatise, *Betrachtungen über das weibliche Geschlecht*: "Die Exaltationen des Geistes durch den unmäßigen Genuß derjenigen Schriften, die ausschließend oder vorzüglich die Einbildungskraft in Bewegung setzen [...] sind dem andern Geschlechte noch verderblicher, wie dem unsrigen".[33] For Brandes, who is scathing of women's encroachment into the intellectual realm, the seemingly inexhaustible feminine appetite for intellectual nourishment has deleterious consequences for the household economy and therefore the comfort of the husband:

Hat die Frau aber wirklich viele Anlagen, viele Einbildungskraft, viele Lebhaftigkeit des Geistes, dann wächst vollends die Gefahr. [...] durch die Unruhe des Mannes, einer solchen Frau immer mehr Nahrung für den Geist [...] zu verschaffen, geschieht das Schlimmste, was geschehen kann: – die natürliche Unruhe des Geistes und des Charakters der Frau wird vermehrt. Der größte geistige Genuß, den der Mann darbringen, anschaffen kann, wird nicht haushälterisch ausgetheilt, sondern verschwelget, gleichsam im Gallop verzehrt. Eigenes und fremdes geistiges Vermögen muß bey einem so übertriebenen lebhaften Gebrauche bald zu Ende gehen, und woher soll das Surrogat kommen, das dieses ersetzt? Die natürliche Stimmung der Frau ging schon dahin, viel Genuß der Art zu verlangen.[34]

[29] Ellmann. P. 30.
[30] Friedrich A. Kittler: *Aufschreibesysteme 1800/1900*. München 1985. P. 36.
[31] Ibid. P. 38.
[32] Pestalozzi. P. 90.
[33] Brandes. P. 3:74-75.
[34] Ibid. Pp. 2:160-161.

Woman's "natürliche Unruhe des Geistes" is multiplied as it is satisfied; it makes a meal of any intellectual nourishment. This situation is characterised by Brandes as "das Schlimmste, was geschehen kann"! The feminine approach to reading is categorised by Brandes in terms reminiscent of accounts of the modern disease *bulimia*; reading has the potential to become a gluttonous indulgence for the young girl:

> Die Neigung zum Lesen wird bey jungen Mädchen, die viel Lebhaftigkeit des Verstandes oder viel warme Empfindung haben, gewöhnlich sehr groß seyn [...]; aber sie werden leicht zu viele Bücher verschlingen [...]. [...] es ist höchst nöthig, daß dahin gesehen werde, daß junge Mädchen nicht zu viel und mit der gehörigen Auswahl für ihre Jahre lesen.[35]

Even allowing for a level of hyperbole in Brandes's writing, it seems the containment of woman's appetites (physical *and* metaphorical) and the restriction of her access to knowledge (designated as of the "highest" necessity) are of urgent concern. Woman's appetite for knowledge finds more mundane expression in curiosity, in German: "Neugier". The etymology of the word is as it appears: "die gier etwas neues kennen zu lernen, eine neuigkeit zu erfahren, meist nur um des neuen willen",[36] a *greed* for *knowledge*. By now we will not wonder that Brandes deems the feminine to be characterised by this negatively connoted trait:

> Ob die Weiber neugieriger sind wie wir, darüber ist freylich viel gestritten. Es scheint jedoch ausgemacht, daß man im Allgemeinen ihnen einen größeren Grad der Neugier beylegen müsse. [...] Der Grad der Neugier ist im Allgemeinen bey dem andern Geschlechte stärker, wie bey dem unsrigen, und die Feinheit seines Geistes gibt ihm bessere Mittel, diese Begierde zu befriedigen.[37]

The late-eighteenth century climate is one of strident condemnation of the idea of the education of woman to any end other than that of wifedom, maternity and domestic servitude. Any learning which goes beyond these ends is decried as an abandonment of feminine duty:

> I would a thousand times rather have a homely girl, simply brought up, than a learned lady and a wit who would make a literary circle of my house and install herself as its president. A female wit is a scourge to her husband, her children, her friends, her servants, to everybody. From the lofty height of her genius she

---

[35] Brandes. Pp. 2:280-281.
[36] Jacob and Wilhelm Grimm: *Deutsches Wörterbuch*. Leipzig 1971. P. 7:666.
[37] Brandes. Pp. 3:149-150.

scorns every womanly duty and she is always trying to make a man of herself. (E 371)

Kant also saw learned women usurping the masculine role; the woman who indulges in "mühsames Lernen oder peinliches Grübeln",[38] is depicted as encroaching on a naturally masculine domain:

> Ein Frauenzimmer, das den Kopf voll Griechisch hat, wie die Frau Dacier, oder über die Mechanik gründliche Streitigkeiten führt, wie die Marquisin von Chastelet, mag nur immerhin noch einen Bart dazu haben; denn dieser würde vielleicht die Miene des Tiefsinns noch kenntlicher ausdrücken, um welchen sie sich bewerben.[39]

It is a theme reiterated with predictable regularity; to illustrate the absurdity of woman's "Schriftstellerey" (seen as a means "öffentlich aufzutreten" and therefore immodest) Brandes notes: "die Anmaßungen, die nicht ihren Grund in den natürlichen Anlagen der Weiber haben, wirken, wenn sie sich bey dem Geschlechte zeigen, grade des Unnatürlichen wegen, so einen Eindruck hervor, wie ein Mann, der sich schminkt".[40]

In a treatise directed at his then fifteen-year-old daughter, Joachim Heinrich Campe (1796) discourages her from intellectual endeavour, for the same reasons as Kant, Rousseau et al., for this would necessarily imply the rejection of the approved domestic role of the bourgeois woman. He warns against the "Belesenheit und Vielwisserei"[41] of women, making explicit the ancient convergence of gastronomic and intellectual appetites in the biblical myth of the fall from Paradise:

> Oder glaubst du, daß ein Frauenzimmer, welches von dem, eurem Geschlechte verbotenen Baume der gelehrten Erkenntniß einmal gekostet hat, nicht gegen jede einfachere Nahrung des Geistes und Herzens, welche von der Natur und der menschlichen Gesellschaft euch recht eigentlich angewiesen ward, einen geheimen Ekel und Widerwillen empfinden werde?[42]

The banishing of the hungry woman from the realm of knowledge is an enduring theme in Western culture and society. Gerhard Neumann sees in the early nineteenth century "das eucharistische Prinzip der Verwandlung des Trivial-Materiellen ins Erhabene-Geistige [...] säkularisiert und in durch-

---

[38] Kant: *Beobachtungen*. P. 35.
[39] Ibid. P. 36.
[40] Brandes. P. 3:38.
[41] Campe. P. 51.
[42] Ibid. Pp. 52-53.

gängiger Geltung".[43] At issue here is woman's access to the non-material, the realm of the intellect; but the sphere of the woman's influence does not go beyond (and must not be permitted to go beyond) the care for the *material* wellbeing of others: "Glaubst du, daß ihr Gatte für die versalzenen, angebrannten oder unschmackhaften Gerichte, die sie ihm vorsetzt [...] sich durch ein gelehrtes Tischgespräch, durch ein Gedichtchen, einen Roman oder desgleichen, aus der Feder seiner geistreichen ehelichen Hälfte geflossen, werde entschädigt halten?"[44] Where woman infiltrates the masculine intellectual domain, things get out of hand; men are served unappetising food and – as Brandes's account of woman's natural tendency to intellectual-appetitive excess shows – household economies are destroyed. The invocation of orality as a metaphor for intellectual pursuit comes with gendered socio-cultural baggage; when Kant speaks of food for the intellect, it is a food for masculine consumption only – the fruits hanging from the Tree of Knowledge. When the feminine ambushes this lofty discursive realm images of unstoppable and destructive excess proliferate. Such images draw their power from the prevalence of the idea of the abundance of feminine bodily appetites.

Observations by the gynaecologist Carus will serve as an introduction to a consideration of the third tier of "appetites" to be explored here, namely – sexual appetite. Carus is writing in his *Lehrbuch der Gynäkologie* (1820) on the unfortunate condition of "Mutterwuth, Manntollheit (*Nymphomania, Andromania, Furor uterinus*)".[45] It is, he notes in a tone redolent of both pity and horror: "Eine traurige, der auf Sitte und Schamhaftigkeit gegründeten weiblichen Natur hohn sprechende, und eben deshalb einen höchst widrigen Anblick gewehrende Krankheit, welche in übermäßig hervorbrechendem, Verstand und Gewissen fast oder vollkommen überwältigendem Triebe zur Geschlechtslust sich zu erkennen giebt".[46] This condition offends acceptable notions of a femininity which is – paradoxically – understood to be *naturally* subject to the *social* convention of feminine sexual modesty. The first degree of the illness is characterised by "die Geilheit (*Salacitas*), wo [...] theils das Aeußere des Körpers (das erhitzte Gesicht, die schwimmenden Augen, die stark gerötheten aufgeworfenen Lippen u.s.w.) die angeregte Sinnlichkeit offenbaret".[47] One barely need refer to the analogies common in the Enlightenment which compare the va-

---

[43] Gerhard Neumann: Das Essen und die Literatur. In: *Literaturwissenschaftliches Jahrbuch im Auftrage der Görres Gesellschaft* 23 (1982). Pp. 174-190, here p. 183.

[44] Campe. P. 53.

[45] Carus. P. 216.

[46] Ibid. P. 216-217.

[47] Ibid. P. 217.

gina and the mouth[48] to notice the conflation of the two in Carus's description of the "stark gerötheten aufgeworfenen Lippen"; the then prevalent term for the vagina – *Muttermund* – points to its widespread acknowledgement. Among the causes of nymphomania Carus counts the "Genuß stark nährender und zugleich erhitzender, Congestionen nach den Geschlechtsorganen herbeyführender Speisen und Getränke".[49] There is here a complete collapse of the distinction between sexual and gastronomic appetites; for Carus it is apparent that, given a taste of "heating" food (associated with sexual pleasure), the woman may demand the object of her appetite in excess. Coward notices the same association in her contemporary analysis of feminine appetite: "Terms of endearment frequently refer to food: honey, sweetheart, peach, sugarplum [...]. Do we detect a note of cannibalism here? Certainly. Something about the sensations of sexual familiarity seems to evoke memories of food".[50] The potential for feminine sexual excess is a grave matter for Rousseau and underscores the necessity for women's subordination in the marriage relationship: "if philosophy ever succeeded in introducing this custom [equality between the sexes] into any unlucky country, especially if it were a warm country where more women are born than men, the men, tyrannised over by the women, would at last become their victims, and would be dragged to their death without the least chance of escape" (E 322). It is only feminine modesty which saves men from this ugly fate at the hands of desirous women: "Female animals are without this sense of shame, but what of that? Are their desires as boundless as those of women, which are curbed by this shame? [...] what would take the place of this negative instinct in women if you rob them of their modesty?" (E 322).

In the figure of Luciane, Goethe offers us a portrayal of immodest femininity; scholastically successful, gregarious, Luciane is an enthusiastic participant in those unfeminine activities disdained by the conservative social engineers of the late Enlightenment. Compared to her selfless cousin, Luciane's presence is an actively consuming one in the gastro-sexual sense discussed above; at one of many social gatherings held for Luciane's benefit, an admirer offers up his provisions and himself to Luciane: "Man scherzte einmal ziemlich laut, daß Charlottens Wintervorräte nun bald aufgezehrt seien, als der Ehrenmann [...] von Lucianens Vorzügen hingerissen, denen er nun schon so lange huldigte, unbedachtsam ausrief: 'So lassen Sie es uns auf polnische Art halten! Kommen Sie nun und zehren mich auch auf!'" (WV 395).

---

[48] See for example Thomas Laqueur: *Making Sex: Body and Gender from the Greeks to Freud.* Cambridge 1990. P. 36, and Barbara Duden: *Geschichte unter der Haut: Ein Eisenacher Arzt und seine Patientinnen um 1730.* Stuttgart 1987. P. 166.
[49] Carus. P. 220.
[50] Coward. P. 87.

Fuhrmann, noting Goethe's sympathy for "häusliche Mädchen" such as Ottilie,[51] characterises the author as "ein schwankender Paris" in relation to the "emancipated" and "domestic" models of femininity.[52] Noting the juxtaposition of Luciane's desire with Ottilie's lack of the same, Wolf Kittler interprets Goethe's disdain for Luciane thus: "Was ihn an dieser Frau verwirrt, das ist ihr hemmungslos geäußertes Begehren".[53] Luciane, though recently betrothed, preys upon men: "es [schien] bei ihr Plan zu sein, Männer, die etwas vorstellten, Rang, Ansehen, Ruhm oder sonst etwas Bedeutendes vor sich hatten, für sich zu gewinnen [...]; jeder hatte sein Teil, seinen Tag, seine Stunde, in der sie ihn zu entzücken und zu fesseln wußte. So hatte sie den Architekten schon bald ins Auge gefaßt" (WV 379). Luciane does not drag the Architect to his death (as in Rousseau's nightmarish fantasy of feminine emancipation), he instead manages to silence and immobilise her in passive representations in *tableaux vivants*; Luciane portrays Poussin's Jewish queen Esther unconscious before Ahasverus and a compliant prostitute in Ter Borch's euphemistically titled *Väterliche Ermahnung*: "und hätte sie nun gar gewußt, daß sie schöner aussah, wenn sie still stand, als wenn sie sich bewegte, indem ihr im letzten Falle manchmal etwas störendes Ungraziöses entschlüpfte, so hätte sie sich mit noch mehrerem Eifer dieser natürlichen Bildnerei ergeben" (WV 392). Her casting in roles of subordinated femininity (and sexual passivity) are a prelude to her quiet disappearance from the novel altogether.

The sexually voracious Luciane is contrasted to passionless Ottilie, destined for chaste motherhood, yet an association between maternity and a voracious sexuality lies dormant in Carus's observation that nymphomania can occur "sogar während der Schwangerschaft".[54] Carus's amazement at this possibility (he seems to overlook entirely the linguistic clues in his own names for the illness – *Mutterwuth* and *Furor uterinus*), demonstrates to what extent maternity and active sexuality have become severed in the early nineteenth century. Femininity, characterised above all in its maternal aspect by extreme receptivity,[55] forbids a desiring maternal body. Yet Carus's horror at the prospect of an excessively desiring maternal is a product of a late-Enlightenment innovation in gender relations. For, as Laqueur writes, sexual pleasure and feminine fecundity were until the late eighteenth century intimately intertwined:

---

[51] Fuhrman. P. 44.

[52] Fuhrman. P. 91.

[53] Kittler: Goethes Wahlverwandtschaften. P. 248.

[54] Carus. P. 217.

[55] Ibid. P. 42.

Near the end of the Enlightenment [...], medical science and those who relied on it ceased to regard the female orgasm as relevant to generation. [...] The old valences were overturned. [...] Women, whose desire knew no bounds in the old scheme of things, and whose reason offered so little resistance to passion, became in some accounts creatures whose whole reproductive life might be spent anaesthetised to the pleasures of the flesh. When, in the late eighteenth century, it became a possibility that "the majority of women are not much troubled with sexual feelings," the presence or absence of orgasm became a biological signpost of sexual difference.[56]

Accordingly, there emerges from Duden's analysis of the medical histories of early-eighteenth century women an image of a *necessarily* appetitive maternal body in which mouth – the organ of desire *par excellence* – and vagina are analogous. According to Duden the placenta was removed by midwives with haste due to a fear the womb would consume it:

Muttermund und Mund gleichen sich im Bild der gierigen Öffnung. [...] Der Muttermund saugt in der Konzeption den Samen an sich, so daß, was in der Geburt als heller Schleim abgeht, für einen noch in sich behaltenen männlichen Samen angesehen wird: "welches auch denen erfahrenen Heb-Ammen nicht unbekannt ist, und daher denen Weibern die öfteren Congressus verrücken" [sic].[57]

Rousseau's pedagogy is situated midway between these two texts, in the space in which desire as an accepted feminine attribute disappears, if not completely.

If the maternal body, and the social role of motherhood, is imagined in the early nineteenth century as entirely passive, the stigma of feminine appetitivity is transposed into a metaphorical register; it is the learned woman – the woman who rejects the Enlightenment social commandment of feminine modesty – whose desire (for intellectual nourishment) is imagined to be endless. Friedrich Kittler writes that the scholastically gifted Luciane is "verzogen"[58] in a culture in which, says the pedagogical assistant: "'Man erziehe die Knaben zu Dienern und die Mädchen zu Müttern'" (WV 410). The passive and undesiring Ottilie better represents the motherly ideal of which the pedagogical assistant speaks and she is the true success of Enlightenment pedagogy; her failure in the public exam, as Wolf Kittler observes,[59] is her strength. As Friedrich Kittler writes: "Ottilie ist die erzogene Erzieherin und, weil alle Erziehung mit der mütterlichen anzuheben hat, die

---

[56] Laqueur. P. 3-4.
[57] Duden: *Geschichte unter der Haut.* P. 190.
[58] Kittler: Ottilie Hauptmann. P. 263.
[59] Kittler: Goethes Wahlverwandtschaften. P. 234.

ideale Mutter".[60] Ottilie's passivity, her passionlessness, makes her the ideal subject for pedagogical coercion; Friedrich Kittler sees her caught "ein Leben lang im Bann der Pädagogenmacht".[61] It is apt that Ottilie's idealisation as mother should culminate in her portrayal on Christmas Eve ("Muttertag *avant la lettre*" for Friedrich Kittler[62]) as the Virgin Mary (WV 403-04) – the symbol of the dignity of passionless maternity – and in an immaculate conception of her own: "Wenn schließlich die Augen des Kindes, das Charlotte ausgetragen hat, Ottilies Augen sind, dann wird klar, wer hier Mutter wird [...]. Ottilie wird Mutter, und Charlotte gebiert das Kind. So verkehrt sich der Mythos von der unbefleckten Empfängnis in die Geschichte einer stellvertretenden Geburt".[63] The immaculate conception is the ultimate goal of an Enlightenment pedagogy which seeks to create a maternal femininity in which appetites can have no place. The spectacular failure of this ideal in the figure of Ottilie must, then, be accounted for.

If, as Friedrich Kittler claims, the nineteenth-century feminine *is* the maternal, then Ottilie is increasingly idealised as maternity is foisted upon her, but the structural weaknesses of this idealisation are soon exposed. Ottilie performs a resistance to the role of ideal mother, one staged at the level of orality, beginning with her refusal to speak and culminating in her anorectic death. In her perfection of feminine modesty Ottilie takes the exhortations of Enlightenment pedagogy too far and dies the death which is the natural consequence of a complete lack of appetite. Jochen Hörisch turns to the "Goethe-Bewunderer Schopenhauer" in his interpretation of Ottilie's starvation as the "einzig angemessene Weise der Verneinung des Willens";[64] in *Die Welt als Wille und Vorstellung* Schopenhauer writes of starvation:

Es scheint jedoch, daß die gänzliche Verneinung des Willens den Grad erreichen könne, wo selbst der zur Erhaltung der Vegetation des Leibes, durch Aufnahme von Nahrung, nöthige Wille wegfällt. [...] ein solcher völlig resignierter Asket (hört) bloß darum auf zu leben, weil er ganz und gar aufgehört hat, zu wollen. Eine andere Todesart als die durch Hunger ist hiebei nicht wohl denkbar [...], weil die Absicht, die Qual zu verkürzen, wirklich schon ein Grad der Bejahung des Willens wäre.[65]

[60] Kittler: Ottilie Hauptmann. P. 264.

[61] Ibid. P. 263.

[62] Ibid. P. 265.

[63] Kittler: Goethes Wahlverwandtschaften. P. 246.

[64] Jochen Hörisch: Die Himmelfahrt der bösen Lust. In: *Goethes Wahlverwandtschaften. Kritische Modelle und Diskursanalysen zum Mythos Literatur.* Ed. by Norbert Bolz. Hildesheim 1981. Pp. 308-322, here p. 317.

[65] Arthur Schopenhauer: Die Welt als Wille und Vorstellung. In: *Werke in zehn Bänden.* Ed. by Arthur Hübscher. Vol. 2. Zürich 1977. P. 495.

The censure of feminine appetites, as has been shown, converges on orality and, in her absolute conformity to the ideal of an "un-mouthed" femininity, Ottilie's orality becomes a corporeal frontier to be defended: "ihr Mund als das Organ, das den Austausch zwischen dem Inneren und dem Äußeren vollzieht, bleibt nicht nur für die Sprache geschlossen. Durch Schweigen und durch die Weigerung zu essen – eins ist die Kehrseite des anderen – schirmt sich Ottilie gegen irdische Wünsche ab".[66] Paradoxically, her determination to control the oral frontier appears as a kind of perverse will in itself; her refusal to be owned by Eduard's desire – "'Eduards werd ich nie!'" (WV 463) – is emphatic. The social seclusion necessitated by Ottilie's complete renunciation of orality (for she neither speaks nor participates in the social ritual of meals) is incongruent with her previous wish to please, yet she defends her actions in the imperative: "Dringt nicht in mich, daß ich reden, daß ich mehr Speise und Trank genießen soll, als ich höchstens bedarf!'" (WV 477)[67] Can Ottilie's radical conformity to feminine ideals of passionlessness in fact represent a farcical repudiation of those ideals?

In an article for the *Journal of the Royal Society of Medicine* Bahnji *et al.* – in an attempt at literary diagnosis – claim: "Ottilie's sex, age and social class are consistent with the epidemiology of *anorexia nervosa*".[68] To presume a transhistorical epidemiology of any illness (let alone a psychological disorder) is fraught with problems which are beyond the scope of this article, but the debates around the meaning of *anorexia* draw directly upon the history of feminine appetitivity which has been explored here; they will be considered in this light.

As Hilde Bruch remarks of early scholarship on the disorder: "Under the influence of psychoanalytic teaching the rejection of food was equated with the rejection of and disgust with sex. The explanation of the syndrome was reduced to one complex which was considered to be specific, namely a defence against unconscious fear of impregnation".[69] Whilst Bruch rejects this

---

[66] Kittler: Goethes Wahlverwandtschaften. P. 251.

[67] As Anna Richards has noted, the verb "dringen" has connotations of sexual intercourse; Ottilie's refusal to be penetrated is also a rejection of the "oral" appetites of sexuality. Anna Richards: Starving for Identity. Wasting Women in German Literature 1775-1820. In: *Gendering German Studies. New Perspectives on German Literature and Culture*. Ed. by Margaret Littler. Oxford 1997. Pp. 39-50, here p. 49.

[68] S. Bahnji, F. E. F. Jolles and R. A. S. Jolles: Goethe's Ottilie. An Early Nineteenth-Century Description of Anorexia Nervosa. In: *Journal of the Royal Society of Medicine* 83 (1990). Pp. 581-85, here p. 583.

[69] Hilde Bruch: *Eating Disorders. Obesity, Anorexia Nervosa, and the Person Within*. New York 1973. P. 276. See also: Joan Jacobs Brumberg. *Fasting Girls. The Emergence of Anorexia Nervosa as a Modern Disease*. Cambridge 1988. P. 28, and Noelle Caskey: Interpreting Anorexia Nervosa. In: *The Female Body in Western*

as an issue in most cases, Ottilie's refusal to be penetrated, coupled with her refusal of Eduard's advances and the death of "her" child at her own hands, seem to indicate a problematisation of the pedagogical maternal construct which is thematised in Goethe's novel. The association of eating and impregnation is certainly alive in Goethe's era, as Novalis's encyclopaedic fragments (written in 1798-99) show: "Empfangen ist das weibliche Genießen – Verzehren das männliche [...]. Das Befruchten ist die Folge des Essens – es ist die umgekehrte Operation – dem Befruchten steht das Gebären, wie dem Essen das Empfangen entgegen".[70] As Richards writes of this fragment: "Men choose to consume and conquer; women receive or are invaded".[71] Thus Ottilie's refusal to allow anything into her mouth may constitute a challenge to the oral economy which posits woman as receptor, a metaphorical resistance to impregnation.[72] Ottilie's refusal to eat, in the context of a passionless, yet compulsorily maternal, late-Enlightenment femininity, reveals the contradiction inherent in this construction. In Ottilie – as in the Enlightenment feminine – jurisdiction over orality is at issue, and her policing of this boundary is both a compliance with "feminine tastes" and a rejection of the "forced-feeding" of passive feminine sexuality and maternity. As Caskey writes: "Refusing to eat is supremely defiant and supremely obedient at the same time".[73]

When Ottilie renounces desire completely, both gastronomic and sexual, the Enlightenment construction of an "un-mouthed" femininity is stillborn. The impossibility of inhabiting such an identity becomes apparent as Ottilie is cast in the final *tableau vivant* as the Virgin; her composure is destroyed when, under the gaze of the pedagogical assistant – he who has idealised her as a future mother and groomed her for the role – she becomes aware of a gulf between her self and the maternal ideal as which she is cast:

> Mit einer Schnelligkeit, die keinesgleichen hat, wirkten Gefühl und Betrachtung in ihr gegeneinander. Ihr Herz war befangen, ihre Augen füllten sich mit Tränen, indem sie sich zwang, immerfort als ein starres Bild zu erscheinen; und wie froh war sie, als der Knabe sich zu regen anfing und der Künstler sich genötigt sah, das Zeichen zu geben, daß der Vorhang wieder fallen sollte! (WV 406)

Culture. Contemporary Perspectives. Ed. by Susan Rubin Suleiman. Cambridge 1986. P. 187.

[70] Novalis: Die Fragmente. In: *Briefe und Werke.* Ed. by Ewald Wasmuth. Vol. 3. Berlin 1943. Pp. 523-524.

[71] Richards. P. 48.

[72] See also Ellmann's interpretation of the forced feeding of the English suffragette hunger strikers as "force-feeding as an oral rape" (p. 33).

[73] Caskey. P. 181. See also Brumberg. P. 29.

Hans-Günther Schwarz

"Welle" und "Locke". Goethes *déréaliser* im *West-östlichen Divan*

Germanists consider Goethe to be the poet of the concrete, visible world. However, in the Divan *Goethe withdraws from reality and creates a poetic universe inspired solely by the imagination, as Hafis had done before. Following the Persian poet, Goethe anticipates the* déréaliser *and* déformer *of the French symbolists. Like them, Goethe ornamentalizes the world. The parallels between the* Divan *and the works of Gautier and Baudelaire are astonishing. Goethe foreshadows the anti-mimetic spirit of modernity.* *

Ganz im Sinne der orientalischen Dichtung und Kunst schafft Goethe im *Divan* keine zweite Welt, sondern eine neue Welt, die einzig und allein von der Phantasie bestimmt ist. Wie schon das Eingangsgedicht 'Hegire' zeigt, ist Realitätsvermeidung das Ziel seines Orientalisierens.

> Nord und West und Süd zersplittern,
> Throne bersten, Reiche zittern,
> Flüchte du, im reinen Osten
> Patriarchenluft zu kosten;
> Unter Lieben, Trinken, Singen
> Soll dich Chisers Quell verjüngen.[1]

In einer Zeit, wo die individuelle Freiheit durch Krieg und Politik gefährdet war, sicherte sich Goethe durch seine fiktive orientalische Existenz persönliche und künstlerische Freiheit. Diesen Aspekt betont Théophile Gautier, der Vater der modernen französischen Dichtung, in seinem "Préface" zu *Émaux et Camées*:

> Pendant les guerres de l'empire
> Goethe, au bruit du canon brutal,
> Fit le *Divan occidental*
> Fraîche oasis où l'art respire.[2]

---

*Der Verfasser bedankt sich bei seiner Kollegin Brigid Garvey für ihre Hilfe bei der Abfassung des englischen Abstrakts.

[1] Johann Wolfgang Goethe: *West-östlicher Divan*. Hg. von Hans-J. Weitz. Frankfurt/M. 1988. S. 9. Im folgenden immer als "Goethe" zitiert.

[2] Théophile Gautier: *Poésies complètes*. Bd. 3. Paris 1970. S. 3.

Die Symbolisten bewundern Goethes Fähigkeit, sich durch sein Dichten einer bedrohlichen Realität zu entziehen und ihr zu trotzen. Gautier ahmt Goethes distanzierende Haltung gegenüber der Realität nach und etabliert diese als sein künstlerisches Programm.

> Comme Goethe sur son divan
> A Weimar s'isolait des choses
> Et d'Hafiz effeuillait les roses,
>
> Sans prendre garde à l'ouragan
> Qui fouettait mes vitres fermées,
> Moi, j'ai fait *Émaux et Camées*.[3]

Realitätsvermeidung charakterisiert die islamische Kunst. Ihr Ziel ist nicht Abbildung der Welt, sondern Entwirklichung. Das Prinzip der Entwirklichung findet sich in der weltlosen Ornamentik des Teppichs ebenso wie in der Dichtung des Hafis. Goethe beschreibt in einem Brief an Zelter vom 11. Mai 1820 die von Hafis inspirierte Haltung: "Unbedingtes Ergeben in den unergründlichen Willen Gottes, heiterer Überblick des beweglichen, immer kreis- und spiralartig wiederkehrenden Erdetreibens, Liebe, Neigung zwischen zwei Welten schwebend, alles Reale geläutert, sich symbolisch auflösend".[4] Mit der Läuterung und symbolischen Auflösung des Realen, die er im *Divan* dichterisch verwirklicht, antizipiert Goethe zwei Schlüsselelemente der modernen Ästhetik: das *déréaliser* und *déformer* des französischen Symbolismus. Entwirklichung bestimmt die Dichtung von Gautier, Baudelaire und Mallarmé ebenso wie die Malerei von Cézanne bis zu Matisse. Ihr künstlerisches Ziel ist eine totale Abkehr von der gegebenen Realität. So formuliert der Maler und Theoretiker Maurice Denis in seinen *Nouvelles théories sur l'art moderne 1914-1921*: "c'était de tout refuser à l'objectivité. Nous renoncions au réel".[5]

Goethes Realitätsverzicht drückt sich darin aus, daß er eine Kunst des Lieblichen, Schönen und Ewigen schaffen will. Es wäre ein Mißverständnis Goethescher Intention, darin ein Echo von Klassizismus oder Idealismus zu sehen. Der Schönheitskult des Symbolismus deutet sich an. Die am Ende des ersten Buches ausgedrückte Hoffnung "Möge meinem Schreibe-Rohr / Liebliches entfließen"[6] ist programmatisch. In dem 'Liebliches' betitelten Gedicht[7] gibt Goethe eine aufschlußreiche Interpretation dessen, was er unter "Liebliches" und "Schönes" versteht. Dort wird die in Nebel getauchte Landschaft um Erfurt durch eine Orientvision "entwirklicht". Die Land-

---

[3] Gautier. S. 3.

[4] Goethe. S. 294.

[5] Maurice Denis: *Nouvelle théories sur l'art moderne 1914-1921*. Paris 1922. S. 27.

[6] Goethe. S. 21.

[7] Goethe. S. 16.

schaft wird durch den Traum – ein wesentliches Element des Symbolismus – der Natur entzogen; sie wird zu einer imaginären Zeltstadt, zu "Teppiche des Festes";[8] sie verwandelt sich gar in Schiras, die Vaterstadt des Hafis, ehe die Empirie den Tagträumer wieder in die Wirklichkeit zurückholt. Der Farbeindruck der imaginierten Teppiche wird mit einem "Wüßt ich Schöneres nicht zu schauen"[9] kommentiert. Das "Liebliche" und "Schöne" zeigt sich nicht im Blick auf die Welt, sondern in einem "inneren Sehen" über ihre äußeren Gegebenheiten hinweg! Das innere Sehen ist das Verfahren der persischen Dichter. Es geht dem Dichter darum, die durch Logik, Empirie, Alter, Lebensumstände etc. gesetzten Grenzen durch die Phantasie zu überschreiten, die Materialität und Realität der Welt durch den Geist zu überwinden und zu beherrschen. In diesem Sinne ist der Dichter "grenzenlos"[10] und Hafis, wie es im gleichnamigen Gedicht heißt, "unbegrenzt".[11] Zeit und Raum definieren den Dichter nicht, wie wir es von der westlichen Literatur gewohnt sind. Der orientalische Dichter oder Künstler erfasst nicht, was in der Welt ist, sondern was über ihr ist. Der erlebte Augenblick, der Körper, die Liebe und die Dichtung müssen in Analogie zum Unbegrenzten der dichterischen Phantasie ins Ewige überführt werden.

Das Ewige kennzeichnet die Dichtung von Hafis, wie sie Goethe im Gedicht 'Unbegrenzt', das im Wiesbadener Register noch den Titel 'Hafis Dichtercharakter' trug, beschreibt:

> Daß du nicht enden kannst das macht dich groß,
> Und daß du nie beginnst das ist dein Los.
> Dein Lied ist drehend wie das Sterngewölbe,
> Anfang und Ende immerfort dasselbe,
> Und was die Mitte bringt ist offenbar
> Das was zu Ende bleibt und anfangs war.[12]

Hafis, als "Musterbild" des Dichters, hat ein "Lied" geschaffen, das jeder Kontingenz und Zeitbedingtheit enthoben ist. Dies ist im geschichtlich denkenden 19. Jahrhundert ein wichtiger Gesichtspunkt: man denke an Herders Furcht, daß Shakespeare veralte, oder an Baudelaires in 'Les phares'[13] geäußerte Überzeugung, daß es keine Vorbilder in Dichtung und Kunst mehr gibt. Das die Zeiten überdauernde "Meisterwerk" verschwindet im 19. Jahrhundert, wie Hans Belting in *Das unsichtbare Meisterwerk*

---

[8] Ebd.
[9] Ebd.
[10] Goethe. S. 145.
[11] Goethe. S. 25.
[12] Ebd.
[13] Charles Baudelaire: *Œuvres complètes*. Hg. von Claude Pichois. Paris 1961. S. 12f.

gezeigt hat.[14] Hafis' Dichtung ist im Gegensatz zur westlichen Dichtung ewig wie der Kosmos. Sie stellt, genau wie das islamische Ornament, das Ewige dar und ist so Teil des Ewigen, wie Goethe erkannt hat. "Vor Gott muß alles ewig stehn",[15] kommentiert Suleika vor dem Spiegel die Augenblickswirkung ihrer Schönheit. Von der Dichtung wird verlangt: "Jede Zeile soll unsterblich, / Ewig wie die Liebe sein".[16] Die Liebe ist aber nur ewig in der durch den Dichter geschaffenen und bewahrten überpersönlichen Form, den "Musterbildern",[17] denen auch Hatem und Suleika nacheifern: "Musterhaft in Freud' und Qual"[18] soll ihre Liebe sein. Nicht das Erlebnis, nicht der Augenblick zählt in der Kunst, sondern die durch den Dichter geschaffene typisierende und symbolische Transformation, die nie Kopie, sondern immer Verwandlung ist. Diese Verwandlung wird in 'Freude des Daseins' thematisiert.

> Wenn du, Suleika,
> Mich überschwenglich beglückst,
> Deine Leidenschaft mir zuwirfst
> Als wärs ein Ball,
> Daß ich ihn fange,
> Dir zurückwerfe
> Mein gewidmetes Ich -
> Das ist Ein Augenblick![19]

Es ist die Aufgabe des Dichters, dem zeitbedingten "Hier und Jetzt" der Realitätserfahrung durch den Prozess der Vergeistigung Überhöhung und Ewigkeitswert zu verleihen:

> Aber Tage währts,
> Jahre dauerts, daß ich neu erschaffe
> Tausendfältig deiner Verschwendungen Fülle,
> Auftrösle die bunte Schnur meines Glücks,
> Geklöppelt tausendfadig
> Von dir, o Suleika.[20]

Der Prozess der Vergeistigung führt weg vom Abbild hin zur Überhöhung und Verewigung. Er geschieht durch die Entwirklichung der vorgegebenen

---

[14] Hans Belting: *Das unsichtbare Meisterwerk*. München 1999.
[15] Goethe. S. 45.
[16] Goethe. S. 32.
[17] Goethe. S. 29.
[18] Goethe. S. 87.
[19] Goethe. S. 73.
[20] Ebd.

Realität. Als Folge der dichterischen Entwirklichung löst sich das
dichterische Wort aus seiner Materialität. Nicht mehr an Ton und Buchstabe
gebunden, wird es im Anklang an die Mythen zum Sternbild, damit Teil des
ewigen Kosmos:

> Das Wort erreicht, und schwände Ton und Schall.
> Ists nicht der Mantel noch gesäter Sterne?
> Ists nicht der Liebe hochverklärtes All?[21]

Nicht das Erlebnis, wie es die Goetheforschung – fasziniert von der Beziehung Goethes zu Marianne von Willemer – von Grimm bis Korff in den
Mittelpunkt der *Divan*-Studien stellte, ist entscheidend, sondern eine von
Hafis gelernte Entgrenzung des Augenblicks hin zum Ewigen. Ganz in
Übereinstimmung mit den Zielen islamischer und moderner Kunst stellt sich
der Orient im *Divan* nicht als eine persönliche Erfahrung dar, sondern als
eine Idee, die mit dem gelebten Leben des Dichters überhaupt nichts zu tun
hat. Kunst und Leben sind getrennt.

Die Negierung des Biographischen ist für den *Divan* ebenso programmatisch wie für *Les fleurs du mal*. Wir erinnern uns an Baudelaires Worte im
ersten "Préface": "On m'a attribué tous les crimes que je racontais".[22] In
beiden Fällen wurde die dichterische Methode verkannt, da sie einen Bruch
mit der westlichen Tradition der Subjektivität darstellt. Goethe bereitet das
künstlerische Ideal des Symbolismus vor. Dieses wird von Lord Hallward in
Oscar Wildes *The Picture of Dorian Grey* als ein "absolute sense of beauty"
bezeichnet: "an artist should create beautiful things, but should put nothing
of his own life into them. We live in an age when men treat art as if it were
meant to be a form of autobiography. We have lost the absolute sense of
beauty".[23] Um diesen absoluten Sinn für das Schöne geht es Goethe im *Divan*, ihn beschreibt er mit den Adjektiven "lieblich" und "schön". Der
Zweck der Kunst im *Divan* und im Symbolismus ist Schönheit.

Goethes *Divan* antizipiert Oscar Wildes Begriff von Kunst als "charmed
circle", die die Realität ausschließt. Kunst hat die Aufgabe, das Unwirkliche
und Nicht-Existierende darzustellen: "what is unreal and non-existent".[24]
Die symbolistische Kunst folgt Goethes *Divan*, indem sie Weltflucht und
Weltlosigkeit besonders betont. Goethes von Hafis inspiriertes "Lieben,
Trinken, Singen" liegt ebenso außerhalb des normalen Lebens und seiner
Wirklichkeit wie das von den Symbolisten verkündete Lebensideal von
"luxe, calme et volupté". Auch dieses Lebensideal ist vom Orient inspiriert,
wie Baudelaires 'L'invitation au voyage' zeigt:

---

[21] Goethe. S. 82.
[22] Baudelaire. S. 184.
[23] Oscar Wilde: *Complete Works*. Hg. von Vyvyan Holland. London, Glasgow
1967. S. 25.
[24] Wilde. S. 978.

> La splendeur orientale,
>   Tout y parlerait
>   A l'âme en secret
> Sa douce langue natale.
>
> Là, tout n'est qu'ordre et beauté,
> Luxe, calme et volupté.[25]

Goethe drückt die Welt- und Zeitenthobenheit der Dichtung des Hafis durch das ornamentale Symbol der Welle aus:

> Du bist der Freuden echte Dichterquelle,
> Und ungezählt entfließt die Well auf Welle.[26]

Die Welle – bei aller Veränderung doch immer gleichbleibend, sich immer wiederholend – wird Goethes Symbol für die Dichtung des Hafis. Dies ist ein folgenreicher Schritt, der erst im Symbolismus und im Jugendstil voll zum Tragen kommt. Dort wird alles Gegenständliche, besonders der menschliche Körper, durch die Linie – gewellt und geschlängelt – in die Fläche überführt, also entwirklicht. Wolfdietrich Rasch spricht im Anklang an Goethes Worte vom "unendlichen Fließen der Dinge und Gestalten".[27] Die Welle ist das Gegenteil einer geschlossenen Form, sie kennt keine Mitte, wie die symbolischen Kreis- und Quadratformen im westlichen ästhetischen Denken; sie verbindet Bewegung, Mannigfaltigkeit, Wiederholung und Ewigkeit der Form. Die Welle symbolisiert in den Worten von Rasch "den Fluß des Lebens selbst, in dem die Dinge unaufhörlich werden und vergehen, der aber selbst ewig und immer der Gleiche ist"[28] – eine Thematik, wie sie etwa Goethe in 'Selige Sehnsucht' behandelt. Anstelle westlicher Statik, herrscht im Orient die Idee der Dynamik. Im Gegensatz zum westlichen Denken ist es aber keine Dynamik des Fortschritts und damit des Vergehens, sondern eine Wiederholung dessen, "was immer ist". Die Dichtung des Hafis gehört für Goethe zum Urelement des Flüssigen. Seine Lieder sind "Ein Brustgesang der lieblich fließet".[29] Ihnen haftet nichts Körperliches an; sie sind der konkreten Anschauung nicht zugänglich und so geeignet, Weltvergessenheit zu induzieren.

> Und mag die ganze Welt versinken,

---

[25] Baudelaire. S. 51.

[26] Goethe. S. 25.

[27] Wolfdietrich Rasch: Fläche, Welle, Ornament. In: *Studien zur deutschen Literatur seit der Jahrhundertwende.* Stuttgart 1967. S. 200.

[28] Rasch. S. 220.

[29] Goethe. S. 25.

Hafis, mit dir, mit dir allein
Will ich wetteifern![30]

Weltvergessenheit, Weltlosigkeit, Realitätsvermeidung kennzeichnen orientalische Kunst und den von ihr inspirierten *Divan* Goethes. Der Geist setzt sich über die Realität hinweg, über die Welt der Zwecke und der Empirie. Der orientalische Dichter verfolgt im Gegensatz zur westlichen Poetik keinen Zweck, wie Goethe im Kapitel "Mahomet" der *Noten und Abhandlungen* feststellt. Der Dichter "sucht mannigfaltig zu sein, sich in Gesinnung und Darstellung grenzenlos zu zeigen".[31]

Dichtung und Ornament berühren sich in der Zweckfreiheit. Das orientalische Ornament ist Ausdruck der Überlegenheit des Geistes über das Gegebene; es ist welt- und grenzenlos. Aus diesem Grund gehört das Ornamentalisieren zum Orientalisieren Goethes. Es bestimmt in Antizipation von Jugendstil und Symbolismus selbst die Menschendarstellung. Dabei spielen die "Locken" bei den Frauengestalten eine besondere Rolle. Poetologisch setzen sie die Wellenthematik fort. Die "Locke" nimmt als literarisches Motiv im Werk von Hafis einen bedeutenden Platz ein. Wie Goethe beobachtet: "Unaufhörlich finden wir den Dichter, wie er mit *Locken* spielt".[32] Die Locke, genau wie die Welle, ist aber von ihrer "Materialität" her gesehen unwichtig, denn das Ziel persischer Dichtung und Kunst ist eine durch die Einbildungskraft bewirkte Entgegenständlichung. Die Natur wird durch den Geist negiert. Dieser sucht "was immer ist", wie die Teppichknüpferin in Hofmannsthals *Die Frau ohne Schatten* treffend sagt.[33]

"Welle" und "Locke" manifestieren im *Divan* Goethes Faszination mit dem Ornament. Beide können als Formen der Arabeske bezeichnet werden, wenn auch dieser Begriff in der Germanistik oft ohne Bezug auf den Orient gebraucht wird. So bezeichnet von Graevenitz den *Divan* als "arabeske Lyrik", verankert aber diese Form fest im linear-perspektivischen Konstruktivismus westlicher Kunst. Die von von Graevenitz invozierte Triade von *constructio, simulatio,* und *significatio* ist aber ein Produkt des von Empirie und Zweckdenken geleiteten westlichen Blicks, der aus der Betrachtung der Welt eine zweite Wirklichkeit aufbaut. Von Graevenitz spricht von einem "Ornament des Blickes"[34], während Goethe ein Ornament des Geistes in der Tradition der Weltlosigkeit orientalischer Kunst schafft. Um die Terminologie des Symbolismus zu gebrauchen: westliches *reproduire* steht östlichem

---

[30] Ebd.

[31] Goethe. S. 145.

[32] Goethe. S. 184.

[33] Hugo von Hofmannsthal: *Die Frau ohne Schatten.* In: *Gesammelte Werke. Erzählungen.* Frankfurt/M. 1973. S. 215.

[34] Gerhart von Graevenitz: *Das Ornament des Blickes: Über die Grundlagen des neuzeitlichen Sehens, die Poetik der Arabeske und Goethes "West-östlicher Divan".* Stuttgart 1994.

déréaliser gegenüber. Von Graevenitz' Argument bleibt im Rahmen des *reproduire*, dem Goethe, von Hafis beeinflußt, entfliehen will. Goethes Abstand von der Nachahmungsästhetik zeigt sich in seinem Kommentar zum *Buch der Liebe*: "Der geistreiche Mensch, nicht zufrieden mit dem, was man ihm darstellt, betrachtet alles, was sich den Sinnen darbietet, als eine Vermummung, wohinter ein höheres geistiges Leben sich schalkhaft-eigensinnig versteckt, um uns anzuziehen und in edlere Regionen aufzulocken".[35] Hier zeigt sich eine verblüffende Nähe zu Baudelaires 'Correspondances'. Den Verzicht des Orients auf die beobachtende *simulatio* und ihre Illusionswirkung hat Oscar Wilde besser verstanden. Lord Hallward in *The Picture of Dorian Gray* sieht seine schriftstellerischen Ambitionen in den weltlosen Formen des Teppichornaments erfüllt: "I should like to write a novel certainly; a novel that would be as lovely as a Persian carpet and as unreal".[36] Die von Goethe im Orient entdeckte Welt- und Gegenstandslosigkeit wird zum eigentlichen Impetus für die moderne Kunst. In unserem Kontext muß eine Äußerung von Maurice Denis über ein Gemälde Gauguins genügen, um die Faszination der Moderne mit der Weltlosigkeit und ihren arabesken Formen zu beweisen: "A l'origine, l'arabesque pure".[37]

Wie programmatisch der Bruch mit der sichtbaren Natur auf Grund der Hafis-Erfahrung für Goethes Dichtung im *Divan* geworden ist, zeigt sich im Gedicht 'An Hafis'. In Vorwegnahme der Flächenordnung der symbolistischen Malerei und des Jugendstils wird der weibliche Körper ornamentalisiert und in einen "Zusammenhang der Dinge" überführt, die auf "totale Einheit"[38] deuten. Der in der persischen Lyrik häufige Zypressenvergleich ist Ausdruck dieser Ornamentalisierung. Der Zypressenvergleich entwirklicht und überhöht zugleich, denn im Orient ist die Zypresse Symbol des Ewigen ebenso wie Symbol weiblicher Schönheit. Das pflanzliche Element ist immer grundlegend für den Prozeß der Ornamentalisierung. Es weckt Assoziationen von ewiger Wiederkehr und Paradies. Die schlanke Zypresse ist durch ihre auf die Ewigkeit hinweisende vegetale Form ein "Musterbild" des weiblichen Körpers.

> Wenn sie das Auge nach sich reißt
> Die wandelnde Zypresse.
>
> Wie Wurzelfasern schleicht ihr Fuß
> Und buhlet mit dem Boden;
> Wie leicht Gewölk verschmilzt ihr Gruß,
> Wie Ost-Gekos' ihr Oden.

[35] Goethe. S. 200.
[36] Wilde. S. 45.
[37] Maurice Denis: *Théories 1890-1910*. Paris 1912. S. 7.
[38] Rasch. S. 191.

Das alles drängt uns ahndevoll,
Wo Lock an Locke kräuselt,
In brauner Fülle ringelnd schwoll,
So dann im Winde säuselt.[39]

Durch die Ornamentalisierung wird die jugendliche Gestalt der Geliebten aus dem vergänglichen Augenblick, aus der körperlichen Erscheinung und Kontingenz, in das ewig bestehende "Musterbild" überführt und so deformiert und entgrenzt. Goethe erfüllt hier den Ewigkeitsanspruch, den van Gogh an die von ihm gemalten Gestalten stellt: "Je voudrais peindre des hommes ou des femmes avec ce je ne sais quoi d'éternel, dont autrefois le nimbe était le symbole".[40] Die Transformation und Deformierung des Körpers in die Formen der Zypresse, der Wurzeln, der Wolken und Locken, entspricht dem Vorgang der Linearisierung. Dieser ist wesentlich für die Gestaltung von Teppichmustern und Miniaturgemälden und wird zum Vorbild für die Flächenkunst des Symbolismus. Die Vegetalisierung des Körpers demonstriert die "Verkettung alles Irdischen". "Wie Wurzelfasern schleicht ihr Fuß" verbindet den Körper mit dem Boden, den er betritt. Goethe ersetzt die Abbildung des Körpers durch eine Zusammenhangsfunktion ganz im Sinne der vom Symbolismus inspirierten Hofmannsthalschen "Verkettung" in der *Frau ohne Schatten*.[41] Diese darf aber keinesfalls als ein Gebundensein an die Erde verstanden werden. Himmel und Erde treffen sich in der Zeichnung der Geliebten, denn ihr Gruß weckt Assoziationen mit den Wolken, ihr Atem mit dem Morgenwind. Der Körper ist in der Tat zwischen "zwei Welten schwebend", existiert in einem Weltzusammenhang: "le rapport entre toutes les parties et entre chaque partie des parties", den Maurice Denis von der modernen Malerei fordert.[42] Der Körper wird durch Bezüge auf außerkörperliche Phänomene entkonkretisiert und geht so in einem größeren, nicht mehr analysierbaren Bezugsrahmen auf: "dans cette cohésion indéfinissable, presque inanalysable".[43] Das Undefinierbare der Moderne berührt sich mit dem Mehrdeutigen der orientalischen Kunst und Dichtung. Goethe verweist explizit auf die Mehrdeutigkeit des Wortes in der persischen Lyrik: "Denn daß ein Wort nicht einfach gelte / Das müßte sich wohl von selbst verstehen / Das Wort ist ein Fächer!"[44] Die Mehrdeutigkeit gehört zum Ornament und, wie Hegel meint, ganz allgemein zu den sym-

---

[39] Goethe. S. 27.

[40] Vincent van Gogh: *Lettres à son frère Théo*. Hg. von Georges Philippart. Paris 1937. S. 230.

[41] Hofmannsthal. S. 267.

[42] Maurice Denis: *Journal*. Bd. 1. Paris 1957. S. 134.

[43] Ebd.

[44] Goethe. S. 26.

bolischen Künsten des Morgenlandes[45] und natürlich auch zum Symbolismus. Mallarmé ersetzt das eindeutige *nommer* durch ein unbestimmtes und mehrdeutiges *suggérer*. Anstelle der westlichen Konkretisierung des Körpers im Hier und Jetzt, wie sie Goethes Schilderung von Friederike Brion in *Dichtung und Wahrheit* exemplarisch zeigt,[46] entgrenzt sich der Körper in der persischen Lyrik in die Natur und das Überirdische. Nicht das von Hegel an der griechischen Skulptur gewürdigte Konkrete, sondern das Grenzenlose der Bezüge zeichnet persische Lyrik und besonders Hafis aus. Der Dichter ist "grenzenlos",[47] er ist keinem Zweck untertan, sein Ziel ist die "Mannigfaltigkeit" der Bezüge. "Mannigfaltigkeit" ist das von Goethe am häufigsten benutzte Charakteristikum arabischer und persischer Dichtung.[48]

Es geht nicht um die zu ordnende, konkrete und empirische Mannigfaltigkeit des westlichen Beobachter-Blickes, wie sie J. M. R. Lenz in den *Anmerkungen übers Theater* definiert ("aller der Dinge, die wir um uns herum sehen, hören, etc."[49]) oder, analog dazu, wie von Graevenitz zu beobachten glaubt, um den perspektivischen Blick, der von den Objekten dieser Welt geleitet sich eine ihnen ähnliche zweite Welt aufbaut. Goethe, um wieder Maurice Denis zu zitieren, "fermait décidément la *fenêtre ouverte sur la nature*".[50] Goethe antizipiert Serusiers Kunstkonzeption der "déformation subjective", die sich auf wenige arabeske Elemente und Wellenformen beschränkt: "La synthèse [...] consiste à faire rentrer toutes les formes dans le petit nombre de formes que nous sommes capables de penser, lignes droites, quelques angles, arcs de cercle et d'ellipse: sortis de là nous nous perdons dans l'océan des variétés".[51] Dies ist das Verfahren des Teppichknüpfers und des Hafis. Beide ersetzen die Vielfalt des Materiellen durch wenige Symbole des Ewigen, den "équivalents" eines Cézanne.[52]

Die Abkehr von der gegenständlichen Welt der Körper, von der Objektwelt als dem imitativen Ziel der Kunst ("copie" in der Sprache der Symbolisten) beschreibt Goethe programmatisch in 'Lied und Gebilde'. Das "Gebilde" manifestiert die von den Griechen ererbte Menschennachahmung.

---

[45] Georg Friedrich Wilhelm Hegel: *Vorlesungen über die Ästhetik*. Hg. von Rüdiger Bubner. Stuttgart 1971. S. 422.

[46] Johann Wolfgang von Goethe: *Dichtung und Wahrheit III*. In: *Werke*. Hamburger Ausgabe. Hg. von Erich Trunz. Bd. 9. München 1982. S. 505: "ich sah sie nun zum erstenmal in städtischen, zwar weiten Zimmern, aber doch in der Enge in Bezug auf Tapeten, Spiegel, Standuhren und Porzellanpuppen".

[47] Goethe. S. 23.

[48] Goethe. S. 131, 143, 145, 158, 165, etc.

[49] J. M. R.Lenz: *Anmerkungen übers Theater*. Hg. von H.-G. Schwarz. Stuttgart 1999. S. 9.

[50] Denis: *Nouvelles théories*. S. 66f.

[51] Denis: *Théories 1890-1910*. S. 251.

[52] Hans-Günther Schwarz: *Orient-Okzident*. München 1990. S. 306.

Sie wird zum Vorbild westlicher Kunst, die in der Darstellung des Menschen ihren Mittelpunkt findet. Der Symbolismus bricht mit dem Kult der griechischen Skulptur, wie Gautiers Gedicht 'Le Poème de la Femme' zeigt: "lasse d´art antique, De Phidias et de Vénus".[53] Das unbegrenzt fließende orientalische "Lied" ist dem statischen, imitativen Wirken des griechischen Künstlers entgegengesetzt. Es konkretisiert nicht, es verbindet Alles mit Allem. Wie Goethe im Kapitel "Allgemeinstes" bemerkt: "Jene Dichter haben alle Gegenstände gegenwärtig und beziehen die entferntesten Dinge aufeinander".[54] Die von Winckelmann und Hegel zum Ideal westlicher Kunst erhobene konkrete Darstellung des menschlichen Körpers weicht im *Divan* einer Kunst, die die irdische Beschränktheit des Körpers auflöst. Für sie ist das flüssige Element charakteristisch. Dessen Symbol ist wiederum die Welle; sie steht auch hier für Entgrenzung.

> Mag der Grieche seinen Thon
> Zu Gestalten drücken,
> An der eignen Hände Sohn
> Steigern sein Entzücken;
>
> Aber uns ist wonnereich
> In den Euphrat greifen,
> Und im flüßgen Element
> Hin und wider schweifen.
>
> Löscht ich so der Seele Brand,
> Lied es wird erschallen;
> Schöpft des Dichters reine Hand,
> Wasser wird sich ballen.[55]

Das "Hin und wider schweifen", die Hand des Dichters im Wasser, verursacht die Wellen, Grundform jeder Ornamentik. Die Verbindung mit der "Locken"-Thematik wird in dem Gedicht 'Versunken' augenscheinlich:

> Voll Locken kraus ein Haupt so rund! –
> Und darf ich dann in solchen reichen Haaren
> Mit vollen Händen hin und wider fahren.[56]

Locken sind mehr als erotische Symbole. "Locken-Schlangen / Hals und Busen reizumhangen / Tausendfältige Gefahr!"[57] spiegeln zwar ebenso wie

---

[53] Gautier. S. 8.
[54] Goethe. S. 168.
[55] Goethe. S. 18.
[56] Goethe. S. 31.
[57] Goethe. S. 70.

"Locken! haltet mich gefangen / In dem Kreise des Gesichts!"[58] die Wirkung von weiblicher Schönheit auf den männlichen Betrachter. Durch ihren ornamentalen Charakter sind Locken aber auch sichtbarer Ausdruck der ewigen Schönheit des Ornaments, das der menschlichen Gestalt zusätzlichen Reiz und Überhöhung verschafft. Diesen Aspekt betont Goethe am Schluß des Gedichts 'Versunken':

> Man wird in solchen reichen Haaren
> Für ewig auf und nieder fahren.
> So hast du, Hafis, auch getan,
> Wir fangen es von vornen an.[59]

Goethes "Locke" als Teil der "Wellen"-Thematik fungiert als ein Symbol für Entgrenzung. Hugo Friedrich weist auf ähnliche Zusammenhänge im Werk Baudelaires. Dort spielt die Locke ihre ornamentale Rolle. In 'La chevelure' wird die Locke zu einem Symbol der Entgrenzung: "l'oasis où je rêve".[60] Baudelaires "Kurvenbewegungen des Wortes",[61] die die Dichtung mit Mathematik und Musik verbinden, spiegeln im Bild der steigenden und fallenden Linien die Welle. In der modernen Malerei wird die Welle zu einem der wichtigsten Mittel der Bildgestaltung, wie wir schon in der Beschreibung der Bildelemente Serusiers durch Maurice Denis gesehen haben.

Der *Divan* beweist, daß Goethe von der ornamentalen Schönheit islamischer Kunstwerke fasziniert war. Teppiche und Kalligraphie ("Die schön geschriebenen, / Herrlich umgüldeten")[62] sind wichtige Motive im *Divan*. Sie sind durch Linie und Farbe charakterisiert – beides Grundelemente der Welterfassung symbolistischer Malerei. Das Transzendieren der sichtbaren Welt durch Linie und Farbe ist als Vergeistigung zu verstehen, "la recherche de l'absolu", wie Denis sagt.[63] Die Leidenschaft des Symbolismus für die Entgegenständlichung mittels der Teppichideale "ligne, surface, couleur"[64] ist ebenfalls als Prozeß der Vergeistigung zu betrachten, wie Kandinskys Schrift *Über das Geistige in der Kunst* beweist. Die Farbwirkung von Orientteppichen brachte Walter Pater zu seinen revolutionären Einsichten in das Wesen der Malerei. In *The Renaissance* gibt er den Farben eines Gemäldes mehr Gewicht als der inhaltlichen Darstellung. Damit beginnt die Entgegenständlichungstendenz der Moderne, die Goethe im *Divan* an-

---

[58] Goethe. S. 77.

[59] Goethe. S. 31.

[60] Baudelaire. S. 26.

[61] Hugo Friedrich: *Die Struktur der modernen Lyrik*. Reinbeck 1985. S. 9.

[62] Goethe. S. 73.

[63] Denis: *Théories*. S. 200.

[64] Schwarz. S. 9.

tizipiert: "In its primary aspect, a great picture has no more definite message for us than an accidental play of sunlight and shadow for a few moments on the wall or floor; is itself, in truth, a space of such fallen light; caught as the colours are in an Eastern carpet, but refined upon, and dealt with more subtly and exquisitely than by nature itself".[65] Wilde in *The English Renaissance* drückt Paters Einsicht noch radikaler aus. Ein Gemälde "is a beautifully coloured surface, nothing more".[66] Abstrakte, rein von der Farbwirkung her definierte Kunst fand hier ihre theoretische Rechtfertigung.

Goethe antizipiert diese Betonung der Farbe in seinem Gedicht 'Liebliches'. Sein Farbensehen, seine Beschreibung eines Farbeindrucks in der trüb-nebligen Landschaft um Erfurt nimmt sich den Orientteppich als Vergleichspunkt. Hier antizipiert er Gautier, von dem Baudelaire in seinem Aufsatz *Théophile Gautier* sagt: "il a introduit dans la poésie un élément nouveau, que j'appellerai la consolation par les arts, par toutes les objets pittoresques qui réjouissent les yeux".[67] Die Kunstwerke des Orients, seine Preziosen, Teppiche, Shawls und Parfums inspirieren den *Divan* ebenso wie den Symbolismus. Der Farbeindruck: "Was doch Buntes dort verbindet / Mir den Himmel mit der Höhe?"[68] löst eine Teppichassoziation aus: "Sind es Teppiche des Festes / Weil er sich der Liebsten traute?"[69] Die Farbe ist das wichtigste Element in Goethes Teppichfantasie: "Rot und weiß, gemischt, gesprenkelt / Wüßt ich Schönres nicht zu schauen".[70] Lange vor Delacroix und Victor Hugo, die die Aufmerksamkeit auf die Farben des Orients lenkten, war Goethe bereits vom Farbenreichtum des Orients fasziniert. Die klaren und leuchtenden Farben des Orients wurden zum Vorbild der modernen Malerei. Ähnlich wie in Goethes Teppichvision verselbständigt sich dort die Farbe; sie wird zu einem vom Gegenstand unabhängigen Ausdrucksmittel. Sie dissoziiert sich von der Objektwelt und weckt so neue Assoziationen. Wieder zeigt sich bei Goethe der Prozeß der Entwirklichung zuerst. Das Auge wird entmachtet. Durch das von der Orientvision provozierte innere Sehen wird eine so nicht existierende Welt "erfunden". Goethe antizipiert in 'Liebliches' die Träume eines Baudelaire, so z. B. 'Le rêve d'un curieux'. Goethes Tagtraum in 'Liebliches' endet mit der Bestätigung westlicher Realität: "Ja, es sind die bunten Mohne"[71]. Baudelaires 'Rêve parisien' folgt diesem Muster – freilich mit einem wesentlich unangenehmeren Erwachen: "j'ai vu l'horreur de mon taudis".[72]

---

[65] Walter Pater: *The Renaissance*. London 1961. S. 130.

[66] Wilde. S. 463.

[67] Baudelaire. S. 698.

[68] Goethe. S. 16.

[69] Ebd.

[70] Ebd.

[71] Ebd.

[72] Baudelaire. S. 98.

Die Entwirklichung wird zum entscheidenden Formprinzip der modernen Kunst und Literatur. Im *Divan* zeigen sich antizipatorisch anti-mimetische Elemente, wie die Linie, in Gestalt von Welle und Locke, und Farbe. Im Verbund mit der Fläche prägen sie als die grundsätzlichen Gestaltungselemente die moderne Kunst und markieren das Ende der perspektivischen Sicht der Welt. Die von der Phantasie gestaltete Fläche ersetzt den an die Objektwelt gebundenen perspektivischen Blick und die Dreidimensionalität des "Gebildes". Beobachtung und Nachahmung weichen der Ornamentalisierung. Natur und Körper werden entwirklicht. Die Phantasie siegt über die Wirklichkeit, der Orient über die westliche Mimesis.

Elisabeth Krimmer

"Die allmähliche Verfertigung des Geschlechts beim Anziehen" Epistemologies of the Body in Kleist's *Die Familie Schroffenstein*

This article investigates the complex interrelation between gender, the body, and epistemology in Kleist's early drama Die Familie Schroffenstein. *Although Kleist's drama appears to take recourse to gender and the body as guarantors of truth, it ultimately insists that the question of gender must not be confounded with that of truth or moral law, and that the body cannot serve as a foundation for epistemologically correct statements.*

> Ich weiß nicht, was ich Dir über mich unaussprechlichen Menschen sagen soll. – Ich wollte ich könnte mir das Herz aus dem Leibe reißen, in diesen Brief packen, und Dir zuschicken. – Dummer Gedanke!
> (Heinrich von Kleist to Ulrike von Kleist, March 13, 1803).

From his Kant crisis to his preference for "it seems" and "as if" constructions,[1] the Kleistian trauma of the epistemological inaccessibility of the world has become commonplace in scholarship about this fascinating and unusual early nineteenth-century author.[2] Kleist's textual universe is haunted by the anxiety that all knowledge will ultimately remain uncertain. The fear that the truth not only about the constitution of the world and the nature of moral law but also about the core of one's personal identity can never be grasped informs many of Kleist's dramas and stories.

To Kleist, however, unattainability does not equal undesirability. Even though the Kleistian world is such that "wir können nicht entscheiden, ob das, was wir Wahrheit nennen, wahrhaft Wahrheit ist, oder ob es uns nur so scheint",[3] Kleist's texts are driven by the desperate and often ferocious de-

---

[1] Norbert Alternhofer: *Der erschütterte Sinn. Hermeneutische Überlegungen zu Kleists* Das Erdbeben in Chili. Munich 1985. P. 45.

[2] See Anthony Stephens: *Heinrich von Kleist. The Dramas and Stories*. Oxford 1994. P. 3. See also Robert E. Helbling: *The Major Works of Heinrich von Kleist*. New York 1975. P. 88.

[3] To Wilhelmine von Zenge, March 22, 1801. In: *Heinrich von Kleist: Briefe 1805-1811*. Vol. 6: *Sämtliche Werke und Briefe in sieben Bänden*. Ed. by Helmut

sire to stabilize cognition and prove the validity of "natural" moral laws. In order to do so, they attempt to deduce the moral teleology of the world from its physical facts.[4] More often than not, the body is singled out as privileged signifier and guarantor of stability, certainty, and truth. Raimar Zons even claims that Kleist's texts are addressed not to souls, but to nerves.[5] One need only think of the numerous instances of swooning, blushing, and stammering in which the body seems to promise access to the truth of the Other. But Kleistian characters are not content to limit their search for truth to the surface of the body. When in dire straits, only the sacrifice of the body can restore order and stability. In *Die Hermannsschlacht* (1808), for example, the bodies of Hermann's sons are pledged to guarantee the truth of his message, and the despoiled dead body of the rape victim Hally becomes the instrument with which national unity is restored.[6] As the second example indicates, it is especially the female body which is called upon as the last reliable repository of truth. Again and again, Kleist's "nostalgia for a preverbal, pre-discursive realm",[7] for a truth that has not yet been corrupted by language, attaches itself to the female body. Thus, one might be tempted to conclude that, if Kleist's metaphysical arch does not tumble, it is not because all stones are pressing downwards – as Kleist claims in a letter to Wilhelmine von Zenge[8] – but because it rests on the female body of the caryatid.

However, such a conclusion would fail to do justice to Kleist's philosophical sophistication. Just like Kleist is no advocate of a Rousseauistic return to nature,[9] he is also unwilling to endow the body with the task of redemption. The figure of the Doppelgänger in *Amphitryon*, for instance,

Sembdner. Munich 1964. P. 163. All subsequent quotations from Kleist are taken from this edition.

[4] Robert Labhardt: *Metapher und Geschichte. Kleists dramatische Metaphorik bis zur Penthesilea als Widerspiegelung seiner geschichtlichen Position.* Kronberg 1976. P. 160.

[5] Raimar Zons: Von der Not der Welt zur absoluten Feindschaft. Kleists *Hermannsschlacht.* In: ZfdPh 109.2 (1990). Pp. 175-199, here p. 182.

[6] Barbara Kennedy: For the Good of the Nation. Woman's Body as Battlefield in Kleist's *Die Hermannsschlacht.* In: *Seminar* 30.1 (1994). Pp. 17-31, here 17.

[7] Chris Cullens and Dorothea von Mücke: Love in Kleist's *Penthesilea* and *Käthchen von Heilbronn.* In: DVjS 63.3 (1989). Pp. 461-493, here p. 479.

[8] "Da ging ich, in mich gekehrt, durch das gewölbte Tor, sinnend zurück in die Stadt. Warum, dachte ich, sinkt wohl das Gewölbe nicht ein, da es doch keine Stütze hat? Es steht, antwortete ich, weil alle Steine auf einmal einstürzen wollen und ich zog aus diesem Gedanken einen unbeschreiblich erquickenden Trost, der mir bis zu dem entscheidenden Augenblicke immer mit der Hoffnung zur Seite stand, daß auch ich mich halten würde, wenn alles mich sinken läßt". To Wilhelmine von Zenge, November 16, 1800. In: Sembdner: Briefe. P. 125.

[9] Peter Horn: *Heinrich von Kleists Erzählungen.* Königstein 1978. P. 126.

might be cited as an example that proves the instability of the body as guarantor of truth. Similarly, my reading of Kleist's *Die Familie Schroffenstein* will demonstrate that, even though Kleist's first drama appears to take recourse to the body in order to stabilize meaning and identity, it ultimately reflects the futility of such an endeavor. In the end, the hoped-for naturalness of the body turns out to be nothing but another cultural sign. The empirically given body and the socially constructed body turn out to be inseparable after all.[10] Not even gender inheres in the body. Rather, gender itself, like truth, is a product of cultural inscription. Thus, we might infer that, analogous to the "allmähliche Verfertigung der Gedanken beim Reden" – the title of one of Kleist's famous essays –, Kleist also believed in the "allmähliche Verfertigung des Geschlechts beim Anziehen".

In order to understand Kleist's epistemological quest, it is helpful to turn to the motif of cross-dressing. The figure of the cross-dresser, more precisely the death of the cross-dresser, functions as a linchpin in the conflicted relationships between body and text, nature and culture, and truth and gender. In order to set the stage for my analysis and to explain why Kleist chose the figure of the cross-dresser as companion on his hermeneutical journey, this analysis begins with a discussion of the privileged relationship between cross-dressing, death, and epistemology.

I.

In May 1810 a rather peculiar group gathered in the apartment of the widow Cole in London. Ten men, among them a professor of anatomy, two surgeons, a lawyer, and a journalist, had been asked to inspect the body of Mrs. Cole's roommate of fourteen years, a certain Chevalière d'Eon. To their great surprise, they discovered that the Chevalière was anatomically male.[11] Clearly, such a discovery is sensational in and of itself. But it is even more so in d'Eon's case whose gender had been the subject of speculation for quite some time. Charles Geneviève Louise Auguste André Thimothée d'Eon was born the son of a Burgundian nobleman in 1728. He served with distinction in the Seven Years' War, was awarded the prestigious Cross of Saint-Louis, and became a diplomat and spy for King Louis XV. His brilliant career took a piquant turn when rumors that the Chevalier was a woman were confirmed by an official declaration of Louis XVI in 1776. For the rest of his life, the Chevalier himself would insist that he was born a woman but was forced by his parents to assume the identity of a boy. But even though d'Eon wanted his contemporaries to believe that he had always

---

[10] Veronica Kelly and Dorothea Mücke (eds.): *Body and Text in the Eighteenth Century*. Stanford 1994. P. 3.

[11] See Gary Kates: *Monsieur d'Eon is a Women: A Tale of Political Intrigue and Sexual Masquerade*. New York 1995.

been a woman, he continued to puzzle them by refusing to wear women's clothing as the King's orders demanded. For several years, d'Eon's gender was the subject of numerous bets and legal proceedings. But in spite of such keen public interest, his "real" sex remained hidden until his death.

D'Eon's story teaches us that as long as we live and breathe, the culturally mediated body is an unreliable agent of truth. It took the rigor of death to harden the fluid indeterminacy of the Chevalier's gender identity into an unambiguous fact. And the Chevalier's story is not the only one of its kind. Death also led to the discovery of Mary Lacey – alias Happy Ned – who, as a sailor, participated in the American Civil War. Lacey's anatomical gender remained a secret until she died in 1887. Another case in point is that of Dr. James Barry (1795-1865), who finished his studies of medicine in Edinburgh in 1812 and subsequently worked in the colonies for the remainder of his life. It was only after his death that a newspaper article revealed that the doctor's anatomy was that of a woman. In all these cases as in numerous other stories about cross-dressing, the riddle of a dubious gender identity was to be solved only postmortem.[12]

In fiction as in history, death and cross-dressing entertain a rather intimate relationship. When the exposure of the cross-dresser occurs at the moment of his/her demise, death is defined as a privileged moment of truth. But death may also be a means of moral retribution meted out as punishment for the cross-dresser's transgressions. In both versions – as moment of truth and as punishment – death is not only at the center of the narrative, but also imparts authority to the particular interpretations of truth and gender that these stories present. In fact, one often encounters a mixture of these two narrative patterns in which the death or killing of the cross-dresser becomes the guarantor of an order that defines both truth and gender as newly accessible and unambiguous.

A recurrent element of literary and historical accounts of cross-dressing from the eighteenth century to the present is the murder or legal execution of gender-benders. The most famous example of such Draconic punishment imposed on a gender-bender is the sentence of death pronounced against the Virgin of Orléans. The fact that Jeanne d'Arc had put on men's clothing informed almost all accusations leveled against her. Cross-dressing was mentioned in no less than five points of her indictment.[13] Significantly,

[12] Julie Wheelwright: *Amazons and Military Maids. Women Who Dressed as Men in the Pursuit of Life, Liberty and Happiness*. London 1989. P. 19. Vern L. Bullough and Bonnie Bullough: *Cross-Dressing, Sex, and Gender*. Philadelphia 1993. P. 51. Marjorie Garber: *Vested Interests. Cross-Dressing and Cultural Anxiety*. New York 1993. P. 203.

[13] Cf. Bullough and Bullough. P. 57f.; Garber. P. 215; Valerie R. Hotchkiss: *Clothes Make The Man. Female Cross-Dressing in Medieval Europe*. New York 1996. Pp. 49-68.

when Jeanne d'Arc first recanted, she also put on women's clothing. It was her return to men's clothes that brought about her final conviction.

Though Jeanne d'Arc's story seems to suggest the opposite, the wearing of male clothing per se was not generally considered a capital offense by legal authorities. Rudolf M. Dekker and Lotte C. van de Pol claim that if the cross-dresser was motivated by patriotism or family feelings – praiseworthy sentiments in women – she might be judged mildly.[14] But if a cross-dresser laid claim to the privilege of desiring another woman – especially if a marriage had been performed – capital punishment would invariably be enforced. A well-documented case of this kind is that of Catharina Lincken, who was executed by sword in Halberstadt in 1721. When she entered the bond of matrimony, Catharina Margaretha Lincken, alias Peter Wannich, alias Anastasius Lagrantinus Rosenstengel, alias Caspar Beuerlein, alias Cornelius Hubsch, could already look back on a rather adventurous life. Wearing men's clothing, Lincken joined a group of religious zealots in Halle and traveled through the countryside as their prophet. Following this spiritual interlude, Lincken became a musketeer with the Hannoverian troops, then with the Royal Prussian troops and finally with the Royal Polish regiment. Her subsequent career as a dyer and manufacturer of cotton was crowned by her marriage with Catharina Margaretha Mühlhahn in 1717. To perform her matrimonial duties, Lincken used a "stuffed male member, made of leather, to which a pouch out of a pig's bladder and two stuffed testiculi made of leather had been attached".[15] The sexual details of her intimate relationship of four years with Mühlhahn stimulated much interest during the investigation and trial that followed upon her arrest. Lincken was eventually sentenced to death while Mühlhahn got off with a fairly mild penalty.

As different as the story of the death of the Chevalier d'Eon and the account of the execution of Catharina Lincken may seem, they share a common element. Both stories depict the death of a cross-dresser as a turning point that puts an end to a situation that is epistemologically unstable and morally dubious. Over his/her dead body, truth is again knowable and transgressions are again punishable. By immobilizing the fluid gender identity of the cross-dresser through his/her death, epistemological and ontological instabilities can be solved by proxy.

In order to understand how death and cross-dressing came to function as privileged topoi for the resolution of a hermeneutical dilemma, it is necessary to discuss their relation to the sign system of language. An association

---

[14] Rudolf M. Dekker and Lotte von de Pol: *The Tradition of Female Transvestism in Early Modern Europe*. New York 1989. P. 74.

[15] F. C. Müller: Ein weiterer Fall von conträrer Sexualempfindung. In: *Friedreich's Series for Forensic Medicine. Criminal Investigation*. Nürnberg 1891. Pp. 91-112, here p. 96.

of death and language was postulated by Jacques Lacan, who defined language as the "murderer of the soma". Lacan based his claim on the notion that linguistic signs designate that which is absent. They constitute substitutes for – are "murderers" of – material reality. As arbitrary signs – signifiers whose relation to their signified is not determined by inherent similarities, correspondences or causalities – they rely on an indirect production of meaning. Bodies, on the other hand, can be understood as immediate and pure signs which, due to their fusion of signifier and signified, defy all attempts at distortion.

The arbitrariness of linguistic signs is at the heart of the ability of language to convey meaning independent of whether it describes 'real' facts or whether that, to which it refers, exists in the realm of language only. It is because signs are independent of their referent that we can talk about dreams and fantasies as easily as we talk about our daily experiences. However, it is also due to this arbitrariness that language, and thereby literature, lacks every inherent guarantee of truth and thus any inherent moral justification.

Consequently, the cross-dresser who has transformed his/her body – the quintessential agent for a direct production of meaning – into an arbitrary sign becomes a metaphor for language itself. S/he marks the entry into the symbolic.[16] In the figure of the cross-dresser, just as in linguistic systems of meaning, signifier and signified have fallen apart. As long as characters are cross-dressed, their body and its clothing cannot speak the truth of gender. However, the figure of the cross-dresser not only expresses an epistemological crisis, it is also instrumental in solving it. By projecting the split of language onto the split of the gender-bender, an illusory harmony of signifier and signified can be reestablished through the death and subsequent unmasking of the cross-dresser. Over his/her dead body, appearance and reality are joined in a seemingly natural embrace.

By portraying the cross-dresser's death as a necessary and inevitable consequence of his/her 'false', made-up appearance, the connection between signifier and signified, which in language must always be an estranged one, is redefined as a quasi-natural unity. In the end, so we are to believe, truth and true gender will always triumph over false appearances. Interestingly, it is through the naturalization of gender that the validity of truth is stabilized.

Moreover, it is not accidental that it is the *death* of the cross-dresser that facilitates the fusion of appearance and reality, of signifier and signified, and of truth and gender. Philippe Ariès claims that, in the eighteenth century, the preoccupation with one's own death gradually replaced the fascination with the death of the other (*la mort de toi*), and that, accompanying

---

[16] Garber. P. 354.

this change, death became a privileged moment of truth.[17] According to Elisabeth Bronfen, this privileged relation to truth is based in the fact that in death the body becomes its own sign. Because it is in a state of transition, the corpse can be thought of as an auto-icon. While it preserves its identity with the living person, it is also transformed into a sign that points to the absence of this person.[18] During this liminal phase, in which signifier and signified are identical, death brings a material dimension to the realm of the symbolic. Because it is identical with and yet different from the deceased, the corpse opens up the possibility of a 'true' sign.[19] Thus, the corpse seems to present an answer to the fear that the cross-dresser raises: the fear that there is no naturalness to the sign.[20]

The question whether truth, especially the truth of gender, can be glimpsed from the dead body is central in Kleist's *Familie Schroffenstein*. Kleist's drama intertwines the search for truth and the interrogation of the body with the concept of gender identity. The nature and naturalness of the sign are inextricably linked with the nature and naturalness of gender. Because of this slippage, Kleist is able to employ the gender dichotomy to stabilize other systems of order.[21] But even though it might seem as though the murder of the cross-dresser succeeds in establishing identity and naturalizing the gender hierarchy, this is not actually the case. There simply is no panacea for the philosophical and political uncertainties that characterize Kleist's text.

II.

Die Familie Schroffenstein is a drama about lovers whose families are engaged in a feud. Kleist's lovers, unlike Shakespeare's *Romeo and Juliet*, belong to different branches of the same clan, the Rossitz and the Warwand line of the Schroffenstein dynasty. The cause of the conflict between the families is an old testamentary contract which decrees that, should one of the family lines become extinct, the other line stands to receive possession of all property, thus fostering an atmosphere of mistrust between the two households. New fuel is added to this fire of hatred as two Warwand ser-

---

[17] Philippe Ariès: *Western Attitudes Toward Death. From the Middle Ages to the Present*. Trans. by Patricia M. Ranum. Baltimore 1974. Pp. 55-82.

[18] Elisabeth Bronfen: *Over Her Dead Body. Death, Femininity, and the Aesthetic*. New York 1992. P. 96f.

[19] Bronfen. P. 84f., p. 314f.

[20] Garber. P. 40.

[21] Cf. Helmut Kreuzer: Die Jungfrau in Waffen. Hebbels Judith und ihre Geschwister von Schiller bis Sartre. In: *Untersuchungen zur Literatur als Geschichte. Festschrift für Benno von Wiese*. Ed. by Vincent J. Günther u. a. Berlin 1973. Pp. 363-384, here p. 364.

vants are found next to the corpse of Peter, the youngest son of Rupert of Rossitz. Under torture one of the two pronounces the name of Sylvester, the master of Warwand. Rupert, already convinced of Sylvester's guilt in the death of his son, sends a messenger to Warwand to declare war. Sylvester, frightened by the news, suffers a fainting spell during which his men kill the messenger. Meanwhile a meeting between Johann of Rossitz and Agnes, Sylvester's daughter, is misinterpreted, and Johann is wounded and incarcerated. Rupert now wants revenge and maliciously kills Jeronimus, a Schroffenstein of the line Wyg, who had been sent by Sylvester in order to mediate between the two houses. When Rupert learns that his oldest son Ottokar is engaged in a clandestine love affair with Agnes, he makes preparations to kill Agnes. But Ottokar anticipates him. In order to protect his beloved, he and Agnes exchange their clothes. Rupert, mistaking his own son for Agnes, stabs Ottokar to death. Sylvester, wanting to take revenge for Agnes, kills his cross-dressed daughter. Only Agnes' blind grandfather Sylvius recognizes the true identity of the two corpses. Finally, Rupert's pain over the loss of his son Ottokar is aggravated by the news that his son Peter was not murdered but drowned in a brook in the forest.

A number of critics consider *Die Familie Schroffenstein* to be Kleist's most inferior drama. Peter André Block refers to it as the "product of a madman"[22] and Peter Szondi calls it a "poetic failure".[23] Interestingly, many scholars connect this failure with the cross-dressing scene and the following murders. Hinrich Seeba, for example, refers to Kleist's attempts to revise the last act as evidence of its failed design.[24] Such a negative evaluation of the last act, however, is completely contrary to its importance for Kleist's own creative process. According to Ernst von Pfuehl, Kleist wove the entire drama around the exchange of clothes:

> Ihm war eines Tages die seltsame Auskleideszene des letzten Aktes, rein als Szene, in den Sinn gekommen, und da die Situation ihn anzog, hatte er sie wie eine zusammenhanglose Phantasie niedergeschrieben. Dann erst fiel ihm ein, sie mit andern Fäden der Erfindung, vielleicht auch mit einem zufällig entdeckten Stoff zusammenzuspinnen, und so wob sich allmählich um diese Szene die ganze Tragödie herum.[25]

---

[22] Peter André Block: *Walter Muschg. Pamphlet und Bekenntnis. Aufsätze und Reden*. Freiburg 1968. P. 357.

[23] Peter Szondi: *Versuch über das Tragische*. Frankfurt/M. 1964. P. 97.

[24] Hinrich Seeba: Der Sündenfall des Verdachts. Identitätskrise und Sprachskepsis in Kleists *Die Familie Schroffenstein*. In: DVjS 44 (1970). Pp. 64-100, here p. 69f.

[25] Qtd. in Helmut Sembdner (ed.): *Heinrich von Kleists Lebensspuren. Dokumente und Berichte der Zeitgenossen*. Bremen 1957. P. 45f.

George Howe names Wieland's *Ein Pulver wider die Schlaflosigkeit, in einer dramatischen Erzählung* as a possible source for the "accidentally discovered" plot.[26] Wieland later developed this theme in his *Novelle ohne Titel* (1803). The young Kleist's predilection for Wieland as well as the fact that Wieland ended his story with the remark that it would be an excellent subject for a drama corroborate this assumption. Furthermore, Wieland's story, too, relies on the motif of a cross-dressed woman.[27] Given that Kleist's cross-dressing scene had been written before the rest of the plot, it is possible that it was this common motif that prompted him to adopt Wieland's idea of a testamentary contract as the missing link for his own drama. A comparison with the earlier versions of *Die Familie Schroffenstein* demonstrates that Kleist's original choice of Spain as location can also be traced to Wieland's story. Following the advice of his friends, Kleist later changed the location to medieval Swabia.

The testamentary contract – and the Rousseauistic concept of the Fall of Man due to worldly properties and possessions,[28] for which the contract is said to stand – was not Kleist's only or even primary preoccupation in conceiving his drama. Although the contract plays a prominent role in the first act, it is hardly mentioned afterwards. Rather, as the genesis of the drama suggests and as further analysis will bear out, it is the question of personal, and hence gendered, identity that is at the heart of the drama.

That questions of gender are of great importance in Kleist's early drama is even more evident if we remember that Kleist started working on *Die Familie Schroffenstein* in 1801 in Paris; he finished it during his stay on the Swiss Aare-island. His companion on this journey to Paris was his half-sister Ulrike, who was wont to travel in men's clothing. However, it is not only Ulrike's cross-dressing that emerges as an important reason for the author's interest in gender-bending.[29] Rather, his sister's entire being stood in stark contrast to everything that Kleist deemed proper in a young woman. Puzzled by his sister's "manly" behavior, Kleist seeks to reconcile Ulrike's heroic soul with her female body:

[26] George Howe: The Possible Source of Kleist's *Familie Schroffenstein*. In: MLN 38.3 (1923). Pp. 148-153, here p. 150.
[27] In Wieland's earlier version of the story, the rich Don Pedro promises his brother Don Felix that the latter's second child, provided it is a boy, would become his sole heir. When Felix's wife gives birth to a girl, the parents decide to conceal the gender of the child, call it Pedro and raise it as a boy. After several intricacies of plot, "Pedro" finally marries Ferdinand, the relative who was deprived of his rightful inheritance by Pedro's gender masquerade.
[28] Ernst Fischer: Heinrich von Kleist. In: *Heinrich von Kleist. Aufsätze und Reden*. Ed. by Walter Müller-Seidel. Darmstadt 1967. Pp. 459-562, here p. 480.
[29] The assumption that Kleist's first drama represents his attempt to come to terms with his sister's gender defiance would also explain why he did not want her to read this "miserable trashy book", i.e., his first drama. In: Sembdner: *Briefe*. P. 254.

Ich wäre auf dieser Rheinreise sehr glücklich gewesen, wenn – wenn – Ach, gnädigste Frau, es giebt wohl nichts Großes in der Welt, wozu Ulrike nicht fähig wäre, ein edles, weises, großmüthiges Mädchen, eine Heldenseele in einem Weiberkörper, u ich müßte von Allem diesen nichts sein, wenn ich das nicht innig fühlen wollte. Aber – ein Mensch kann viel besitzen, vieles geben, es läßt sich doch nicht immer, wie Göthe sagt, an seinem Busen ruhen – Sie ist ein Mädchen, das orthographisch schreibt u handelt, nach dem Tacte spielt und denkt, ein Wesen, das von dem Weibe nichts hat, als die Hüften, und nie hat sie gefühlt, wie süß ein Händedruck ist – Aber sie mißverstehen mich doch nicht –? O es giebt kein Wesen in der Welt, das ich so ehre, wie meine Schwester. Aber welchen Mißgrif hat die Natur begangen, als sie ein Wesen bildete, das weder Mann noch Weib ist, u gleichsam wie eine Amphibie zwischen zwei Gattungen schwankt?[30]

Kleist is both impressed and frightened by Ulrike's courage, level-headedness and determination, all of which he considers unfeminine qualities. During their journey to Paris, he tries to fend off his insecurity by engaging in a frantic search for Ulrike's "feminine" traits. And to Kleist, the privileged site for such an endeavor is the body. Thus, when Ulrike's actions attest to her "manly" spirit, when she attends lectures in men's clothing, or when she is the only one who keeps her cool when a storm turns a family boat trip into a dangerous adventure, Heinrich recalls Ulrike's bodily weakness and takes note of the "contradiction between will and strength".[31] Again, the body is called upon as the last resort that can guarantee the gender identity of his half-sister. But the fact that Kleist feels compelled to repeat this manoeuvre over and over again is ample evidence of its unsatisfactory nature. Moreover, what if it is precisely this body, hidden under men's clothing, that cannot be identified as female?

Kleist's experience with his sister Ulrike's gender obfuscation certainly contributed to how the author fashioned the cross-dressing scene in *Die Familie Schroffenstein*. During their journey to Paris, Ulrike von Kleist and her brother encountered a blind flute player, who, unaware of her male outfit, was not fooled by Ulrike's masquerade. The parallel to the blind Sylvius, the first character to recognize the true identity of his cross-dressed granddaughter, is obvious. Kleist's fascination with this scene was motivated by his ardent wish that, by interrogating the body, he could snatch from it the absolute truth of a person's identity and gender. Thus, his quest for truth is inseparably linked with an inquiry into the naturalness of gender. In *Die Familie Schroffenstein*, Kleist probes the epistemological consequences of a transgression against the "natural" boundaries of the gender dichotomy.

---

[30] To Adolphine von Werdeck, July 28, 1801. In: Sembdner: *Briefe*. P. 202.
[31] Sembdner: *Briefe*. P. 202.

From the very beginning, Kleist's drama toys with the idea of a natural order, from which man's moral order derives its validity. Both natural and moral order are then linked to the truth of gender. In the first act, Rupert, convinced that his relative Sylvester is the murderer of his son, believes that this atrocious crime has destroyed the natural order. He calls upon his wife Eustache to take part in his revenge. When Eustache refers to her feminine tenderness, he objects:

> Ich weiß, Eustache, Männer sind die Rächer –
> Ihr seid die Klageweiber der Natur.
> Doch nichts mehr von Natur.
> Ein hold ergötzend Märchen ists der Kindheit,
> Der Menschheit von den Dichtern, ihren Ammen,
> Erzählt. Vertrauen, Unschuld, Treue, Liebe,
> Religion, der Götter Furcht sind wie
> Die Tiere, welche reden. – Selbst das Band
> Das heilige, der Blutsverwandtschaft riß, […]
> Und weil doch alles sich gewandelt, Menschen
> Mit Tieren die Natur gewechselt, wechsle
> Denn auch das Weib die ihrige – (40-59)

Here, the destruction of the moral order is portrayed as inseparable from the disintegration of the gender code. A comparison of the printed version with its predecessors suggests that the link between natural order and "natural" gender that Rupert invokes was of some importance to Kleist. In *Die Familie Ghonorez*,[32] Elmire, later named Eustache, is portrayed as a cold, calculating and vengeful character – all attributes that do not conform to stereotypical notions of proper femininity. Thus, one might claim that the transformation of the harsh wife into a soft, conciliatory character is connected to the desired concatenation between natural order and 'natural' gender. Seen in this light, Eustache's feminine nature functions as a guarantee for the intactness of the natural order; an order which, as the reader later learns, has not yet been despoiled by the murder of a relative. Rupert's inability to appraise the facts correctly would then be a result of his moral blindness.

---

[32] *Die Familie Schroffenstein* has come down to us in three different versions. The first version, entitled *Die Familie Thierrez*, is merely a rough sketch of the plot. The second manuscript, entitled *Die Familie Ghonorez*, bears traces of several stages of revision. Some of the alterations, even though rejected by Kleist, entered the printed version of 1803, entitled *Die Familie Schroffenstein*, whose authenticity must thus remain questionable. While some scholars assume that the editors Ludwig Wieland and Heinrich Geßner changed Kleist's manuscript without prior authorization, it is now commonly accepted that the variations are mostly due to mistakes by typesetters and copyists. See Thomas Wichmann: *Heinrich von Kleist*. Stuttgart 1988. P. 53.

However, accepting moral blindness as the root cause of the misunderstanding would be tantamount to falling for Rupert's flawed logic. Superficially, Rupert's error consists in the failure to recognize the intactness of the natural order. Fundamentally and epistemologically, it consists in the problematic assumption that there is such a direct correlation between nature, natural gender, and moral law to begin with. But Kleist's first act presents a world in which any such concatenation is conspicuously absent. Indeed, in the first act of *Die Familie Schroffenstein*, it is a deviation from the "natural" gender order that accounts for the intactness of the moral order. Peter was not murdered precisely because Sylvester is not an avenger – as Rupert claims all men "naturally" are – but a conciliatory neighbor and concerned father. He might even be characterized as effeminate. Far from plotting revenge, Sylvester is first introduced as swatting flies. He occupies himself with gardening and swoons when overwhelmed by his enemy's accusations. Moreover, Sylvester, unlike Rupert, does not confuse natural order with moral law. When Aldöbern wrongly accuses Sylvester of murder, he replies:

> – Sieh, wenn du mir sagtest,
> Die Ströme flössen neben ihren Ufern
> Bergan, und sammelten auf Felsenspitzen
> In Seen sich, so wollt – ich wollts dir glauben;
> Doch sagst du mir, ich hätt ein Kind gemordet,
> Des Vetters Kind – (629-633)

To the wise Sylvester, the order of nature and the laws of human morality are two distinctly different categories. Changes in one order do not affect the organization of the other.

The second scene in the third act provides a further example of how *Die Familie Schroffenstein* first posits a connection between gender and truth that it then proceeds to deconstruct. In trying to establish the whereabouts of his messenger and his illegitimate son Johann, Rupert is confronted with contradictory reports. Eustache claims that the messenger was beaten to death, while Santing wrongly informs his master that Johann was killed. As Rupert identifies unfounded rumors with femininity – "RUPERT: Erschlagen, sagst du? EUSTACHE: Ja so spricht das Volk. RUPERT: Das Volk – ein Volk von Weibern wohl?" (1503-1504) – the question of truth is again confounded with that of true gender:

> RUPERT: Wer von euch beiden ist das Weib?
> SANTING: Ich sage, Johann [wurde getötet, EK]; und ists der Herold,
> wohl, so steckt die Frau ins Panzerhemd, mich in den Weibsrock.
> [...]
> SANTING: Hier ist der Wanderer, Herr, er kann dir sagen,
> Ob ich ein Weib, ob nicht. (1512-1514)

The reader, knowing that Johann is still alive, is called upon to take Santing for a woman. Thus, unlike Rupert, the reader realizes that the gender dichotomy cannot possibly function as the foundation for epistemologically correct statements. Rupert, on the other hand, continues to confuse the gender order with moral law. Consequently, and in spite of his inquisitive interrogation, he learns neither that Johann is still alive nor that Sylvester had no part in the murder of the messenger. Interestingly, both Rupert and Santing define gender not as a natural entity but as a category that has yet to be determined. Does Kleist suggest that it is Rupert and Santing's alienation from the "natural" order, manifest in their inability to read gender correctly, that leads to their distortion of basic facts? Does Eustache's superior knowledge signify that woman is a vessel of truth? Although Kleist teases his readers with these options, a careful reading of *Die Familie Schroffenstein* suggests that in Kleist's drama truth is not distributed according to gender lines. In the Warwand household, it is Sylvester's wife Gertrude who is full of suspicion and unwilling to face the truth whereas both Sylvius and Sylvester are portrayed as conciliatory and trustful.

The gender confusion reaches a peak in the fifth act when Ottokar takes advantage of the general chaos in order to protect his beloved Agnes. Aware that his father is roaming through the forest in search of Agnes, Ottokar betakes himself to the cave that has long been his and Agnes' secret meeting place. He finds Agnes and attempts to calm her nerves by narrating the fantastic tale of their future wedding. As he describes the wedding night, he takes off Agnes' coat and wraps his own coat around her. Then, taking her hat and replacing it with his helmet, he urges Agnes to flee while he himself dons Agnes' clothes and awaits the arrival of his father. Tragically, however, Ottokar's plan effects the very opposite of what he had intended. Both Ottokar and Agnes die through the hands of their fathers. Interestingly, it is Ottokar's consciously devised perversion of nature, embodied in the exchange of gender roles, that brings about the final catastrophe. Again, we might be tempted to conclude that for Kleist the illegibility of the gender order must necessarily lead to the impossibility of finding truth. Or does it?

Some critics have interpreted the exchange of clothing as a positive utopia. To Seeba, Kleist's cave transvestism represents "a mystery play of reconciled identity".[33] To Zons, it symbolizes "the political coup of the overthrow of the dynasty- and gender-hierarchy".[34] However, a reading of the cave scene as a positive utopia of a fusion of identities must ignore the fact that Ottokar and Agnes are not equal partners. Ottokar does not share his

---

[33] Seeba. P. 92.

[34] Raimar Zons: Der Tod des Menschen. Von Kleists *Familie Schroffenstein* zu Grabbes *Gothland*. In: *Grabbe und die Dramatiker seiner Zeit. Beiträge zum II. Internationalen Grabbe-Symposium 1989*. Ed. by Detlev Kopp and Michael Vogt. Tübingen 1990. Pp. 75-102, here p. 92.

knowledge with Agnes but uses his poetic fantasies to manipulate her. Similarly, Ingeborg Harms' interpretation that Ottokar and Agnes transcend death in their willingness to sacrifice themselves is problematic.[35] A textual reference, that Harms herself points out, suggests that there is no resurrection in Kleist's drama. When visiting the cave where Jesus is buried, the biblical Maria finds the grave empty. Agnes, however, after remarking that "the cave is empty, as you say", discovers Ottokar in it (107). Far from portraying a positive utopia, the cave scene embodies the martyrdom of self-inflicted alienation. It is "the real and final fall into the difference of reality and appearance".[36]

The inability to see the truth is taken to its extremes when neither fathers nor mothers recognize the true identity of their disguised children. But while both parents mourn at the site of the wrong body, Agnes' blind grandfather Sylvius realizes that a mistake has been made. Does Kleist suggest to his readers that, in spite of deceitful appearances and in the midst of utter confusion, truth – and truth is again the truth of gender – can be discerned by touching the body? It is of interest to note that the murder of Rupert's younger son is also solved through the truth that his body tells. The old Ursula, a witch-like character, had cut off a finger from the body of the drowned boy. In the last scene, when presented with this limb, Eustache recognizes a characteristic pock mark and identifies the finger as that of her son. In fact, allusions to the truth-telling power of the body permeate the entire drama. Rupert, looking at his mirror image in the river, perceives the face of a devil, and Sylvester's swooning indicates that he is innocent of murder. Indeed, one might wonder why Kleist's drama is fraught with so many misunderstandings if the body tells the truth so loquaciously.

Although Kleist's play repeatedly teases its readers with the idea of the body as a vessel of truth, it is never wholly committed to it. In fact, readers are alerted to the problematic nature of bodily signs at the very beginning of the play. The origin of the entire Schroffenstein feud can be traced to the misinterpretation of a bodily state: when the sick Rupert was wrongly taken for dead (188-195), Sylvester laid claim to the estate. All further misunderstandings follow from this. Moreover, even if bodily symptoms are diagnosed correctly, their meaning is anything but straightforward. Agnes' swooning, for example, is caused by fear but is mistaken for a reaction to physical pain. Sylvester's vomiting is a reaction to spoilt food, but is believed to be the result of poisoning. Thus, at the origin of all confusion in the play, and of the split in Kleist's world, is not the psychosomatic dyslexia

---

[35] Ingeborg Harms: Wie fliegender Sommer. Eine Untersuchung der Höhlenszene in Heinrich von Kleists *Die Familie Schroffenstein*. In: *Jahrbuch der deutschen Schillergesellschaft* 28 (1984). Pp. 270-314, here p. 294.

[36] Bettina Schulte: *Unmittelbarkeit und Vermittlung im Werk Heinrich von Kleists*. Göttingen 1988. P. 89f.

of the characters but the precarious relationship between signifier and signified.

In his essay on bodily signs and legal codes, Manfred Schneider claims that Kleist has strayed from the tradition of the Christian councils, which was guided by the belief in a strict juridical relation between letter and spirit. Schneider maintains that Kleist is part of a 'Jewish' tradition that does not believe in any pre-ordained assignment of signifier and signified. According to this tradition, signs can be read adequately only if put in their proper context. The meaning of signs can never be separated "from the surface of their contiguous relationships".[37] Thus, Sylvester's name, pronounced under torture by his servant (235), may signify Sylvester's guilt or a last attempt to exonerate an innocent master. The fact that Sylvester's servants are found near the corpse of Peter also has no intrinsic meaning. Even the finger of the dead child can be interpreted only if inserted into a narrative context.

In Kleist's drama, disjointed signs lead to wrong conclusions. Meaning can be established only if the isolated signifiers are re-contextualized correctly. However, there seems to be one exception to this rule. When Agnes and Ottokar meet in the forest, Agnes accepts water from Ottokar's hands although she believes it to be poisoned. Offering her body as a pledge for the truth of her affection, she is willing to stake her life on Ottokar's word. Thus, one might be tempted to conclude that Agnes' body becomes the new agnus dei that heals the breach caused by Rupert's perversion of the holy communion in Act I. Moreover, whatever its consequences, Agnes' action is the logical result of her general inability to separate body and spirit. Her firm belief in the unity of body and identity is already evident when Agnes first appears on the scene. Mourning the death of her brother, Agnes takes no comfort in the words of the priest, who assures her that her brother is well even though his body is in the grave. For Agnes, such a split of bodily and spiritual well-being is not possible:

> Wie ich muß lachen, eh ich will, wenn einer
> Sich lächerlich bezeigt, so muß ich weinen
> Wenn einer stirbt.
> [...]
> Zwar der Pater sagt,
> Er sei nicht in dem Grabe. – Nein, daß ichs
> Recht sag, er sei zwar in dem Grabe – Ach.
> Ich kanns dir nicht so wiederbeichten. Kurz,
> Ich seh es, wo er ist, am Hügel. Denn

---

[37] Manfred Schneider: Die Inquisition der Oberfläche. Kleist und die juristische Kodifikation des Unbewußten. In: *Heinrich von Kleist. Kriegsfall – Rechtsfall – Sündenfall.* Ed. by Gerhard Neumann. Freiburg 1994. Pp. 107-126, here p. 125.

Woher, der Hügel? (396-409)

Unwilling to separate her brother's corpse from his soul, Agnes is also prepared to sacrifice her own body in order to answer "Kleist's cardinal question regarding the truth of the feelings of the other";[38] an act that Hugo Dittberner calls "the horrible initiation of the future through the sacrifice of a woman".[39] But if Agnes' sacrifice in Act III initiates the future, what is the purpose of her death? Should we conclude that it is only when this child of nature is alienated from her (cross-dressed) body that the catastrophe can ensue? Does Agnes live in perfect harmony with her natural gender until she becomes the weak-willed object of Ottokar's gender manipulation?[40] Does her death restore the "natural" order? After all, Agnes' alienation, that is, the disassociation of body and identity, is brought about by the agency of a man. Ottokar not only induces a trance-like state in Agnes but also takes off her coat and clothes her with his. And it is precisely because of Agnes' "natural" unity of body and identity that Ottokar has to resort to artfulness in order to take from Agnes the outer trappings of her gender. Contrary to Ottokar's claim that he is "the helpmate of nature" (2486), who restores a primeval state, Ottokar's "allmähliche Verfertigung des Geschlechts beim Anziehen" leads to the greatest imaginable alienation from nature. However, to conclude that Kleist posits the existence of a "natural" femininity that is destroyed by man's interference would be rash. Rather, any such interpretation must take into account Kleist's tendency toward "ideological self-deconstruction".[41] Kleist's *Die Familie Schroffenstein* questions not only the "naturalness" of nature and gender but also the assumption that death is a privileged moment of truth.

Although Agnes is portrayed as a child of nature, her "natural" instincts are not always correct. Initially, Agnes is convinced that the Rossitz relatives are her enemies and must be shunned. Innocence, so it would appear, is not "naturally" conciliatory. Moreover, one might claim it is not Agnes' body that is the foundation of trust between Ottokar and the young maiden, but the lengthy conversation between the two lovers that succeeds in dispelling all doubt. More importantly, given that Agnes and Ottokar have deduced the facts correctly and could have communicated them to their families, their death is not the necessary foundation of a better order but a meaningless sacrifice. In fact, their dead bodies do not even tell the truth any-

---

[38] Gerhard Neumann: Skandalon. Geschlechterrolle und soziale Identität in Kleists *Marquise von O ...* und in Cervantes' Novelle *La Fuerza de la sangre*. In: *Heinrich von Kleist. Kriegsfall – Rechtsfall – Sündenfall.* Pp. 149-192, here p. 160.

[39] Hugo Dittberner: Der Sensationsdichter. Zu Kleist. In: *Heinrich von Kleist.* Ed. by Heinz Ludwig Arnold. Munich 1993. Pp. 5-25, here p. 17.

[40] Stephens: *Dramas and Stories.* P. 24.

[41] Labhardt. P. 162.

more. Interestingly, Kleist's stage directions for the last scene demand that Agnes be equipped with two sets of clothing. Thus, when Ottokar claims to remove the alien cover and restore original nature, he is merely taking off Agnes' coat (*Überkleid*). Consequently, it remains undecided whether Sylvius recognizes the true identity of the dead because he touches the actual bodies or because he touches the first set of clothing hidden underneath Ottokar's coat and Agnes' *Überkleid*. In the end, the hoped-for naturalness may be nothing but another cultural sign, enacting an infinite deferral in which the truth of the body will always remain hidden.

In the fifth act of *Die Familie Schroffenstein*, Kleist distances himself from the Christian tradition in which the body of the crucified stands in for the truth of his message. Agnes and Ottokar's deaths do not authenticate "the word turned flesh"[42] nor do they function as foundation for a new and better order. Indeed, the joy of having deprived his readers of a clear-cut solution in spite of all appearances to the contrary might also explain why Kleist and his friends could not help but break out in laughter when reading the final scene. Although Kleist may have wished that personal identity, "that unspeakable being", could be spoken by the (dead) body, he also made fun of such a "stupid thought". Kleist was acutely aware that such an epistemological "emergency brake" must remain unsatisfactory because the authentication of truth is identical with the death of the testifying subject. In order to discover the truth about each other, humans need to rely on communication. The body in and of itself is an unreliable agent of truth. Kleist may have wished to send his heart in a package, but he knew very well that such a gift would never do.

---

[42] Wolf Kittler: Militärisches Kommando und tragisches Geschick. Zur Funktion der Schrift im Werk des preußischen Dichters Heinrich von Kleist. In: *Heinrich von Kleist. Studien zu Werk und Wirkung*. Ed. by Dirk Grathoff. Opladen 1988. Pp. 56-68, here p. 64.

Matthew Pollard

Reading and Writing the Architecture of the Body in Kleist's *Penthesilea*

Although Kleist's Penthesilea *has both antagonized and fascinated numerous critics, it is nonetheless striking that most scholarship has not discussed its depiction of the body in any great detail. This essay provides a reading of how this play deploys and represents the body as a construct, rendering and rending it as a site of displacement, fragmentation and inscription. By examining the relationship between the body and metaphors of architecture, this essay draws further connnections between the body, the forging of meaning, and the act of writing.*

As a "geniales Ärgernis"[1] for both contemporaries and critics, Kleist's tragedy *Penthesilea* has both endured outright rejection and enjoyed extensive critical attention since its inception. Ranging from Goethe's refusal to accept the play's foreignness to his understanding of antiquity[2] to our modern validation of the work as one of German literature's most puzzling,[3] *Penthesilea* offers to the reader an interpretative challenge, a provocation accurately summed up by Ruth Angress: "[Kleist] preferred to entertain an audience by shocking them into awareness rather than edifying them with idylls and ideals. Perhaps the time has come when we can appreciate the boldness of a combination of classical and popular/sensational ingredients in serious literature rather than deplore it".[4] While its near-unperformability – despite Kleist's deployment of teichoscopic effects to relate rather than show physical violence – has frequently consigned it to the invisible theater, its calculated yet passionate affront to theatrical taste has promoted rather than hindered its status as an object of interpretive and performative experimentation. With his *Penthesilea*, Kleist "wußte, daß er [...] Grenzen überschritt und Tabus verletzte: Grenzen der Bühne und

[1] Helmut Sembdner (ed.): *Heinrich von Kleists Lebensspuren. Dokumente und Berichte der Zeitgenossen*. Frankfurt/M. 1992. P. 232.

[2] Cf. Peter Goldammer: Heinrich von Kleists *Penthesilea*. Kritik der Rezeptionsgeschichte als Beitrag zur Interpretation. In: *Impulse. Aufsätze, Quellen, Berichte zur deutschen Klassik und Romantik*. Ed. by Peter Goldammer and Walter Dietze. Berlin and Weimar 1978. Pp. 200-231; Helmut Sembdner: *Lebensspuren*. Pp. 228-238; Helga Gallas: Antikenrezeption bei Goethe und Kleist: Penthesilea – eine Anti-Iphigenie. In: *Momentum dramaticum. Festschrift for Eckehard Catholy*. Ed. by Linda Dietrick and David John. Waterloo 1990. Pp. 209-220.

[3] Jost Hermand: Kleists *Penthesilea* im Kreuzfeuer geschlechtsspezifischer Diskurse. In: *Monatshefte* 87.1 (1995). Pp. 34-47, here p. 34.

[4] Ruth Angress: Kleist's Nation of Amazons. In: *Positionen I. Beiträge zur Germanistik. Heinrich von Kleist 1777-1811*. Ed. by Peter Horn. Capetown 1977. Pp. 5-28, here p. 9.

Schauspielkunst seiner Zeit, [und ...] des Einfühlungsvermögens der Zuschauer".[5] In light of its depiction of a strong female figure, described by Emmel as a "gigantisches Bild der erotischen Maßlosigkeit",[6] Jost Hermand's critical account (in both senses) of *Penthesilea* scholarship has recently evoked the spectacle of a "Kreuzfeuer geschlechtsspezifischer Diskurse". In his rejection of "wilden Interpretationen" which rely largely on Kleist's few and cryptic remarks on his play, Hermand recognizes the effectiveness of a feminist approach that links the drama to Kleist's ideological position, without retreating to the timeless ahistory of the mythological, archetypal, psychological, or biological.[7] Helga Gallas further testifies to the play's richness, by outlining at least six prevalent ways of viewing the text: as "Staatskritik", "Kampf der Deutschen mit Napoleon-Achill", "Widerspiegelung des Kampfes Goethe – Kleist" (cf. Mommsen), "Manifestation des mörderischen Wesens von Liebe und Sexualität", "Manifestation von Homosexualität" and finally "Ausdruck verschiedener narzißtischer Störungen".[8] While this work continues to provoke psychoanlytical readings of the characters' mental processes,[9] it is also clear that *Penthesilea* foregrounds the creation and destruction of the body.

Nutz's insight, that *Penthesilea* is a "Körperdrama" built around the readings and misreadings of bodily signifiers, serves as this reading's point of departure. This drama depicts the reading, misreading, and appropriation of bodily sign systems. Such sign systems function through Penthesilea's omnivorous gaze fixed on the body of Achilles, which on the one hand constructs Achilles and then, on the other, transforms the hungry eye into the hungry mouth in a process of increasingly deadly proximity.[10] This essay exegetically itemizes *Penthesilea*'s discourse of the body, drawing out the broader implications of such collisions, interactions, and stigmata for the politicized body and the Amazonian body politic. Finally, the architectural metaphors of suspension and collapse serve as building blocks for an analysis of the protagonists' self representation. This drama performs a paradox: the return of the body, in and through language and visual presentation as the center of dramatic action, and

[5] Maximilian Nutz: Lektüre der Sinne. Kleists *Penthesilea* als Körperdrama. In: *Heinrich von Kleist. Studien zu Werk und Wirkung.* Ed. by Dirk Grathoff. Opladen 1988. Pp. 163-185, here p. 163.

[6] Felix Emmel: *Das ekstatische Theater.* Prien 1924. P. 154.

[7] Jost Hermand: Kleists *Penthesilea.* P. 44.

[8] Helga Gallas: Kleists *Penthesilea* und Lacans vier Diskurse. In: *Kontroverse, alte und neue. Akten des VII. Internationalen Germanistenkongresses Göttingen.* Ed. by Inge Stephan and Carl Pietzcker. Tübingen 1986. Pp. 203-212, here p. 203.

[9] Cf. Helga Gallas: Kleists *Penthesilea*; Joachim Pfeiffer: Kleists *Penthesilea.* Eine Deutung unter den Aspekten von narzißtischer und ödipaler Problematik. In: *Kontroverse, alte und neue.* Pp. 196-202; Gerhart Pickerodt: Penthesilea und Kleist. Tragödie der Leidenschaft und Leidenschaft der Tragödie. In: *Germanisch-Romanische Monatsschrift* 37 (1987). Pp. 52-67.

[10] Michel Chaouli: Devouring Metaphor: Disgust and Taste in Kleist's *Penthesilea.* *German Quarterly* 69.2 (1996). Pp. 125-143.

its opposing effacement and erasure. The following reading of the politics of
the body recognizes two factors: that a drama actualizes an action, that is a
movement of a body through time and through space, and that an approach
attempting to integrate the body in all its manifestations need not necessarily
reduce itself to the ecstatic rhetoric of sensation, by celebrating, for example,
Penthesilea's cannibalism according to "lust-betont-postmodernen Sehwei-
sen".[11] Secondly, the body of Kleist cannot be arbitrarily severed from the sign
of the state or from claims to power, a relationship further examined where the
drama begins and ends: in the construction and destruction of Achilles' body.

The first three scenes of the drama demonstrate Kleist's gift for teichoscopic
representation, in which "Auge und Zunge, Schauen und Sprechen", fundamental elements of theater, attain ascendancy over the representation of such action.[12] The narration of the Amazons' intervention and Penthesilea's reaction to
the sight of Achilles overcomes the visual representation, and could be seen as
more authentic and dramatically effective.[13] The gradual appearance of Achilles on the horizon is described in the following way by a Myrmidon:

> Seht! Steigt dort über jenes Berges Rücken,
> Ein Haupt nicht, ein bewaffnetes empor?
> Ein Helm, von Federbüschen überschattet?
> Der Nacken schon, der mächtige, der es trägt?
> Die Schultern auch, die Arme, stahlumglänzt?
> Das ganze Brustgebild, o seht doch, Freunde,
> Bis wo den Leib der goldne Gurt umschließt? (I 356-362)[14]

Firstly, the twice-repeated phatic "seht" emphasizes the pleasure of seeing and
recognition, although the identity of the emerging figure is revealed eight lines
later. Secondly, the itemized body parts are coupled with attributes: a helmeted
"Haupt", a "Helm" overshadowed by plumage, a powerful "Nacken", "Arme"
and "Schultern" sheathed in steel. Kleist cuts off this homoerotic inventory of
body and steel at the waist, in that the belt reins in the spectators' view of the
hero, which is impelled in an almost cinematic fashion towards the heads of the
horses (I 364-365). Achilles, however, is attributed no distinguishing facial
features. He exists and is recognized under the gaze of the Greeks as a con-
glomerate of gradually assembled body parts, weapons, and armour. This re-
membering evokes for Chaouli the Lacanian mirror stage, by which the body

---

[11] Jost Hermand: Kleists *Penthesilea*. P. 38.
[12] Volker Klotz: Aug um Zunge – Zunge um Aug. Kleists extremes Theater. In: *Kleist-Jahrbuch* 1985. P. 129.
[13] Ibid. P. 139.
[14] All citations from Kleist's works are taken from the following edition and are marked by volume and page number (for letters) and by volume and verse number (for plays) or page number (for variants) within the body of the essay: Heinrich von Kleist: *Sämtliche Werke und Briefe*. Ed. by Helmut Sembdner. 9th ed. 2 vols. Munich 1993.

parts come together and are then allocated a signifier, as well as foreshadowing his final dismemberment.[15] Mohammad Kowsar describes Achilles' emergence as embodying a perceptual paradox: "On the one hand the subject of the vision is flesh emerging into a perceptible form, on the other it is all the emblems that shape armatures around flesh itself".[16] However, as the appearance of the marked body of Achilles in scene four visually demonstrates, what the male gaze has brought together can also be taken apart.

The arm wound of Achilles physically and visually characterizes him before he speaks. Although its limited material meaning for the drama's action has caused most critics to neglect this incident, it is clear that "Kleist does not want us to miss this wound: for seventy-five lines of text [...] two medics busy themselves with bandaging Achilles".[17] Achilles seems concerned with military matters, the care of the horses, and finally the prospect of Penthesilea, and refuses to acknowledge the medical attention. During Achilles' first appearance on stage, returning from his first encounter with Penthesilea, he fails to notice the treatment of his wound according to the following stage direction: "*Zwei Griechen ergreifen, ihm unbewußt, einen seiner Arme, der verwundet ist, und verbinden ihn*" (I 491-492). While being treated by the two, Achilles becomes angered at their distracting attentions ("Was neckt ihr" [I 505]) and subsequently expresses his indifference: "Nun ja" (I 507). The following discussion among the Greeks brings three elements into focus: the associative imagery of the plumes, the wound that is conclusively bound, and Achilles' state of distraction:

> ACHILLES *in die Ferne hinaus schauend.*
> Steht sie noch da?
> DIOMEDES.   Du fragst? –
> ANTILOCHUS.   Die Königin?
> DER HAUPTMANN.
> Man sieht nichts – Platz! Die Federbüsch hinweg!
> DER GRIECHE *der ihm den Arm verbindet.*
> Halt! Einen Augenblick.
> EIN GRIECHENFÜRST.   Dort, allerdings!
> DIOMEDES. Wo?
> DER GRIECHENFÜRST.
>   Bei der Eiche, unter der sie fiel.
> Der Helmbusch wallt schon wieder ihr vom Haupte,
> Und ihr Mißschicksal scheint verschmerzt. –
> DER ERSTE GRIECHE.   Nun endlich!
> DER ZWEITE. Den Arm jetzt magst du, wie du willst, gebrauchen.

[15] Chaouli: Devouring Metaphor. P. 141.

[16] Mohammad Kowsar: Fugitive Desire. The Figural Component in Heinrich von Kleist's *Penthesilea*. In: *Theatre Journal* 40.1 (March 1988). Pp. 61-76, here p. 66.

[17] Chaouli: Devouring Metaphor. P. 131.

DER ERSTE. Jetzt kannst du gehen. (I 558-565)

Firstly, the "Federbüsche", whose traditional implications of "aggressive virility" have already been explicated by Reeve,[18] inhibit the mens' view of Penthesilea, while her "Helmbusch wallt schon ihr vom Haupte" (I 566) once the Greeks have moved their helmet plumes, a command absent from the text of the earlier variant (I p. 861). As an extension of her body and sign of her momentary ascendancy,[19] Penthesilea's erect helmet plumes are juxtaposed with Achilles' absent helmet, which he replaces later in the scene. Achilles' return to some form of awareness occurs at the conclusion of his treatment, which results not in a return to consciousness, but rather a descent into a gendered form of male blindness: "Kämpft ihr, wie die Verschnittnen, wenn ihr wollt; / Mich einen Mann fühl ich" (I 587-588). Achilles' remark comes just after he replaces his helmet, presumably with its plumage intact. On the one hand, he regains his sense of male self following the re-placement of his male headgear: "*indem er sich den Helm wieder aufsetzt*", which he had removed at the beginning of the scene.[20] On the other, his reference to the "Verschnittnen" ironically addresses his own temporary loss of manhood, as the wounded arm may represent a symbolic, though momentary, castration.

In both versions of this scene, Penthesilea has captured the male gaze of Achilles, who seems unaware of the wound he has sustained in combat, even referring to her as "die Göttliche" in the variant version (I p. 861). The appearance of a bleeding, sweating and disoriented hero, who has just barely escaped with his life from a female pursuer, relativizes Achilles' heroic posturing. The wound, to return to Kowsar's point, must be seen in the context of Achilles' initial teichoscopic appearance. To bandage Achilles' arm is to bind him ("So laß dich [Achilles] auch verbinden" [I 504]), to enclose and restrict his freedom of bodily movement, and, as is the case with the linkages in his armour, to delimit his sphere of action. The dressing complete, he may use his arm, emblematic of a will to action, as he wishes. His replacing his helmet and the restoration of his arm through the bandage renders him whole, by completing the warrior's picture and concealing – yet simultaneously drawing attention to – such an externally visible sign of fragmentation.

The reappearance of this wound in the critical fifteenth scene compounds Kleist's initial emphasis. When Achilles' wounded arm, inscribed with Penthesilea's desire[21] comes to her notice, Achilles unconsciously lends more weight to his wound by attempting to deny its significance. As with his revisions of scene four, Kleist also altered the import and significance of Achilles' injury. In the variant version of the fifteenth scene, Penthesilea notices that he is in-

---

[18] William Reeve: On Feathers, Sex and Related Matters in Kleists Works. In: *Colloquia Germanica* 28.2 (1995). Pp. 127-146, here p. 131.
[19] Ibid. P. 133.
[20] Ibid. P. 136.
[21] Chaouli: Devouring Metaphor. P. 131.

jured, and he replies:

> Geritzt am Arm, du siehst, nichts weiter.
> PENTHESILEA.　　　　　　Was! Mein Spieß!
> ACHILLES *ungeduldig.*
> Er steckt' dir schief am Latz, du hörst. Das Schicksal
> Wenn man mit Weibern kämpft. Was willst du mir? (I p. 872)

In the final version, when she presses the issue, he asks: "Wenn du mich liebst, so sprichst du nicht davon. / Du siehst es heilt schon" (I 1763-64). By gendering the wound, in that Penthesilea's weapon injures his pride (his "ungeduldig" response) and his body, the open wound of the variant scene foreshadows the fate of men who engage in combat or make contact with women who do not recognize limits. This is one of two male fears central to *Penthesilea*, described as: "ein Reflex der alten Angst der Männer vor starken, unkontrollierbaren, verrückten Frauen".[22] However, Kleist's conciliatory revision transforms Achilles' impatience and hostility consistent with generalized male anxieties towards strong women to words of love and healing, thus rendering Achilles more the lover than the soldier. This crucial change in Achilles' role, from warrior to lover, proves to be consistent with the tragic conclusion: "Er [Achilles] aber hat an seinem Leib erfahren müssen, wie gefährlich es sein kann, wenn man einer geliebten Frau nicht als Krieger, sondern ausschließlich als Liebender gegenübertritt".[23]

For Chaouli, this scene brings into play the broader inscription of desire on the body: "we can read it [*Penthesilea*] as a long and increasingly violent writing exercise in which Achilles is writ, is written upon, at steadily decreasing range and with steadily increasing harm", culminating in the use of her teeth, which replace the extension of the arrows and the spear, as writing tools.[24] Ulrich Beil notes that the arrows of Penthesilea represent the arrows of Amor, the hunter's arrows, and the feathered writing instrument of the pen.[25] The textuality of the body, emphasized by Chaouli's understanding of the drama as a monstrous writing exercise, is already articulated in the eleventh scene. Achilles, protected by his Greek allies, but himself unarmed, provokes these words. When an Amazon demands that the arrow ("Pfeil") should hit him, "wo er die Hand jetzt hält" (I 1411), another replies: "Daß er das Herz gespießt ihm,

---

[22] Christa Wolf: Kleists *Penthesilea.* In: *Heinrich von Kleist. "Penthesilea". Ein Trauerspiel.* Wiesbaden [1982]. Pp. 157-167, here p. 165.

[23] Wolf Kittler: *Die Geburt des Partisanen aus dem Geist der Poesie. Heinrich von Kleist und die Strategien der Befreiungskriege.* Freiburg 1987. P. 187.

[24] Chaouli: Devouring Metaphor. P. 139.

[25] Ulrich Beil: Der rasende Gott. Kleists Penthesilea und die Rolle des Anderen in der Mythenrezeption um 1800. In: *Begegnung mit dem "Fremden".* Akte des VIII. Internationalen Germanistenkongresses Tokyo 1990. Ed. by Schichiji and Yoshinori. Vol. 9. Munich 1991. Pp. 293-299, here p. 298.

wie ein Blatt, / Fort mit sich reiß im Flug –" (I 1412-1413). Already wounded on the arm, the heart of the unarmoured Achilles is seen as a target, a sheet of paper to be punctured and torn away by the flight of the arrow/pen, a feathered messenger ("Brautwerber [...] gefiederte" [I 596] in Achilles' words). That the hero as text should be "bound" carries this metaphor further, in the words of the "Meisterin des Bogens" (I 1440): "Die Schenkel will ich ihm zusammen heften" (I 1443), an act that ultimately fixes and immobilizes the moving *Bild* of Achilles. These associations are confirmed by the equivalent usage of "Blatt" for "Bogen" and "Reißen" (to tear, inscribe) for "Ritzen" (to etch) (cf. Chaouli). Already wounded by Penthesilea's spear in their first encounter, later caressed by arrows and iron, the superficial wounding of Achilles concludes with Penthesilea's writing/biting the core of his being, his heart. If Achilles becomes the body inscribed by violence, then the question remains as to how Penthesilea is at first written upon before becoming herself the writer.

When viewed teichoscopically and described by their respective female and male allies, Penthesilea and Achilles are attributed conventionalized female and male characteristics. Achilles is every emerging inch a male warrior, while Penthesilea, preceding her suicide, is described as "sittsam" (I 2677) and "voll Verstand und Würd und Grazie" (I 2680), who sang and danced "reizend" (I 2679).[26] When the Amazons view Achilles, and the Greeks view Penthesilea, the gendered gaze becomes redefined: Penthesilea's silken hair, silver-toned voice and small hands and feet represent "klischeehaft wahrgenommene [...] geschlechts-spezifische Merkmale" which are "Attribute eines Körperwunsch-bildes"[27] and "ein süßes, zärtliches Klischee".[28] Achilles, pursued by Penthe-silea, becomes more feminized as he turns his neck to her, an actor in the "ro-mance of the male heroine".[29] Penthesilea, in contrast, fights like a man and is frequently and predictably compared to an animal or monster.[30] Achilles, in the gaze of his comrades in the third scene, is built up,[31] and is constructed piece by piece; Penthesilea, his pursuer, remains in the eyes of the Greeks a chaotic constellation of "Naturgewalten".[32] That neither Achilles nor Penthesilea rec-ognizes and truly "sees" the other, reflected by the mutual incomprehension of the Greeks and the Amazons, forms the root of the tragedy: "Beide Protagonis-ten [...] bauen ihre Beziehung über konventionelle Leitbilder von Mann und Frau auf und müssen sich gerade deshalb als menschliche individuelle Subjekte

---

[26] Dolf Sternberger: Kampf der Liebendenden. Über Kleists *Penthesilea*. In: *Figuren der Fabel. Essays*. Frankfurt/M. 1950. Pp. 93-105, here p. 102.

[27] Nutz: Lektüre der Sinne. P. 169.

[28] Dolf Sternberger: Kampf der Liebenden. P. 99.

[29] Camille Paglia: *Sexual Personae*. New York 1991. P. 264.

[30] Ingrid Stipa: Kleist's *Penthesilea*. From Misapprehension to Madness. In: *Seminar* 27.1 (1991). Pp. 27-38, here p. 34.

[31] Maximilian Nutz aptly uses the term "aufgebaut". Lektüre der Sinne. P. 170.

[32] Ibid.

verfehlen".[33] Achilles' and Penthesilea's will to subjugate and incorporate the other as lovers and enemies, in a drama of "sadomasochistic oscillation" between submission and domination,[34] causes them to return to the violent origins of the Amazonian society and to reenact its founding ritual. Such an oscillation is already found in the etymological connection between "Geschlecht" and "Schlacht".[35] Yet this war is not, as with *Die Hermannsschlacht*, a war of extermination in which the foreign body is destroyed and expelled; this war centers on the "Vereinigung" of bodies.[36] In addition to their bodies' collisions, what also characterizes their specular fixation is how each creates the other. Achilles is a construct, as is vom Strahl from *Das Käthchen von Heilbronn*, of armour and flesh; Penthesilea is essentialized as a woman, whose bearing armour is viewed as unnatural.

While Achilles is objectified in the gaze of his allies as a faceless constellation of weapons and armour, Penthesilea is likewise missing those facial features also lacking from the teichoscopic description of Achilles (I 356ff):

> Gedankenvoll, auf einen Augenblick,
> Sieht sie in unsre Schar, von Ausdruck leer,
> Als ob in Stein gehaun wir vor ihr stünden;
> Hier diese flache Hand, versichr' ich dich,
> Ist ausdrucksvoller als ihr Angesicht: (I 63-68)

However, Penthesilea's expressionless face transforms before the eyes of those watching her: at the sight of Achilles she, in a moment of gender-specific physiology, blushes: "Und Glut ihr plötzlich, bis zum Hals hinab, / Das Antlitz färbt"(I 78-79). She does so again out of fury or shame, "Die Rüstung wieder bis zum Gurt sich färbend" (I 97-98). Kleist relies on the "Unmittelbarkeit der Gebärde"[37] to enunciate what can be told but not easily shown. Once again, as with his initial presentation of the emerging Achilles, Kleist interrupts this outburst of sensuality at the belt, interrupting the emblematic fusion of bodily sexuality (the glowing skin) with the tools of violence (the reflecting armour). What is important is the emphasis on the "Gurt", "Rüstung" and "Federbüsche", external markers common to both Achilles and Penthesilea. The constellation of characteristics cited above illustrates not only how Kleist distinguishes between bodily representation for male and female figures (Penthesilea blushes, while Achilles sweats and bleeds), but also how in this drama he ex-

---

[33] Sigrid Lange: Kleists *Penthesilea*. In: *Weimarer Beiträge* 37.5 (1991). Pp. 705-723, here p. 719.

[34] Paglia: *Sexual Personae*. P. 261.

[35] Roland Reuss: "Im Geklüfft". Zur Sprache in Kleists *Penthesilea*. In: *Brandenburger Kleist-Blätter* 5 (1992). Pp. 3-27, here p. 5.

[36] Nutz: Lektüre der Sinne. P. 167.

[37] Gerhard Fricke: *Penthesilea*. In: *Das deutsche Drama*. Ed. by Benno von Wiese. Zürich 1964. Pp. 367-389, here p. 369.

plicitly enfolds the identity of Achilles and Penthesilea by means of shared visual signifiers. *Penthesilea*'s metaphors of the written are printed out, expressed ("ausdrücken") in Penthesilea's face: her blood, at their first encounter in which her face was without expression, shoots outward in a blush. One should also note that Penthesilea, as the most "male" of Kleist's female dramatic characters, is the only exception to the generalized gendering of bodily wounding, in that her ability to inflict wounds is balanced by her vulnerability to wounding.

Nearly all critics have noted that *Penthesilea* illustrates the collision of two bodies, "a horror that includes all others in a potent combination of sex and violence".[38] These collisions, played out by alternating roles of "Verfolger und Verfolgtem"[39] and parallel actions, expose their mutual attraction and repulsion, as well as their interchangeability by means of gesture. But the first brutal encounter in the myth of the *Iliad*, as Angress points out, is the desecration of Hector's body,[40] to which Penthesilea refers numerous times in the fifteenth scene. By way of the desecrated body of Hector, Achilles and Penthesilea relate to each other in a way strikingly analogous to the Elector and Homburg's unconscious medium of interaction in *Prinz Friedrich von Homburg*. The blasted and absent body of Froben, literally a stand-in for both "father" and "son" sublimates the mutual aggression between the Elector and Homburg. Correspondingly, Stephens notes how the body of Hector "becomes for both of them the projection of their aggression toward each other"[41] and ultimately the model from which Penthesilea performs "das Namenlose" on Achilles.[42] According to Gallas, what fascinates Penthesilea, aside from his fame and brutal desecration of Hector's corpse, is his armoured torso and marble-like chest; yet at the same time she seeks a vulnerable spot.[43] Their dialogic exchange of Hector's absent body merely speaks of the body; in their combat such violence is made physically manifest.

Their first encounter is a pantomine that encapsulates the tragedy.[44] For example, after falling off her horse in their first narrated encounter, Penthesilea stands "das Haupt entblößt" (I 451) and "Wischt [...], ists Staub ists Blut, sich von der Stirn" (I.453). Immediately thereafter, Achilles *"nimmt den Helm ab"* (I 477ff) and *"wischt sich den Schweiß von der Stirn"* (I 492ff). The parallel gestures of this first combat, which are centered on the head of each protagonist, invoke not only their interchangeability, but also the potential violence of

---

[38] Angress: Kleist's Nation of Amazons. P. 8.

[39] Volker Klotz: *Kurze Kommentare zu Stücken und Gedichten*. Darmstadt 1962 (Hessische Beiträge zur deutschen Literatur). P. 20.

[40] Angress: Kleist's Nation of Amazons. Pp. 6-8.

[41] Anthony Stephens. *Heinrich von Kleist. The Plays and Stories*. Oxford and New York 1994. P. 104.

[42] Angress: Kleist's Nation of Amazons. P. 8.

[43] Gallas: Kleists *Penthesilea* und Lacans vier Diskurse. P. 209.

[44] Fricke: *Penthesilea*. P. 370.

future collisions. Achilles' light arm wound, for example, will be paid back in kind: Odysseus desires to see "die Spur von deinem Fußtritt / Auf ihrer rosen-blütnen Wange" (I 535-536). Penthesilea's face, expressionless as the palm of one's hand, is to be imprinted with the boot of her captor as a sign of presence (since it lacks an imprint) and subjugation. Achilles is not the only character undergoing a process of writing on the body: Penthesilea's lack of facial expression characterizes her first and last encounter with Achilles. Following her killing and consumption of him, her face, belonging to a "Leiche" (the High Priestess' term for Achilles' desecrated body [I 2728]) is described as a "leeres Blatt" (I 2697), marked by the blood of Achilles. Her "körperliche Aus-druckssprache" brings blood to her mouth and hands, except that instead of a blush, this blood belongs to Achilles.[45] Unlike Achilles, whose wound "speaks" as a visual and visible mark of his experience and as an emblem of Penthe-silea's impression on him, Penthesilea remains, however temporarily, exter-nally unmarked.

Internally, however, Penthesilea has been wounded by a vision of herself ("in dem Innersten getroffen" [I 649]) reflected back to her upon gazing at Achilles' armour:

> Ist das die Siegerin, die schreckliche,
> Der Amazonen stolze Königin,
> Die seines Busens erzne Rüstung mir,
> Wenn sich mein Fuß ihm naht, zurückespiegelt? (I 642-645)

Since her deflected gaze cannot penetrate his armour, Penthesilea's desire to reach his most interior space finds fulfilment in her tearing open his unar-moured breast, her consumption of him and consummation with him, and her death.

Penthesilea's fatal wound has already been struck in the fifth scene. Parallel to the "Riß/Biß" and "Küsse/Bisse" (con)fusions, her "Herz" has become forged into "Erz". They have infected each other with desire. In addition to the parallel imagery of the oak tree ("die abgestorbene Eiche steht im Sturm" [I 3041]), Kleist employs this constellation of inner wounding to evoke inner paralysis or momentary suspension, that is the power of a word or sight to im-mobilize or reinforce a character. Penthesilea, for example, feels "Gelähmt" (I 649) after receiving a blow to the breast, which either may come from "Amors Pfeil" (I 1085) or from the fall she suffered in pursuit of Achilles. In the elev-enth scene, Achilles uses the same series of images to describe the Amazons' wounding gaze and to demonstrate their mutual penetrability: "Mit euren Augen trefft ihr sicherer / [...] / Ich fühle mich *im Innersten getroffen*, / Und ein Entwaffneter, in jedem Sinne, / Leg ich zu euren kleinen Füßen mich" (I 1414-1418, my emphasis). In addition to the elements of the body and the forces driving it, their mutual mirror-like capacity to create each other through the

---

[45] Klotz: Kleists extremes Theater. P. 137.

gaze has inspired numerous psychoanalytical interpretations. Achilles is Penthesilea's constructed "Spiegelbild"[46] or her "ins Männliche gespiegelte Verdoppelung".[47] Joachim Pfeiffer also uses a psychoanalytical model: "Die Idolisierung des Liebespartners erscheint [...] als Wiederbelebung archaischer narzißtischer Konfigurationen, als Reaktivierung idealisierter Selbstobjekt-Imagines".[48] This problematic doubling of their selves reflects their mutual fascination, forcefully articulated by the physical and verbal violence of their encounters driven by alternating motives of love and hate.

Such paradoxical impulses are expressed by what Penthesilea desires and what she can obtain, as she wishes to defeat Achilles in single combat without hurting him: "Hier dieses Eisen soll, Gefährtinnen, / Soll mit der sanftesten Umarmung ihn / [...] / An meinen Busen schmerzlos niederziehn" (I 857-860). Understandably, some critics saw the uncomfortable paradox – the tender embrace with iron – as drifting into the rhetorical excess so denounced by Mario Praz as "prententious and ridiculous".[49] They may do so under the assumption that in *Penthesilea* one should expect to find the sentiments of love, even when the two protagonists do not actually speak to each other until the fifteenth scene and continually threaten each other, their enemies and their allies with bodily harm. When seen as exemplifying the relationship between physical power and physical attraction, and between violence and sexuality, Achilles and Penthesilea are not only sexual beings and individuals, but also represent, according to Carrière "Kraftlinien",[50] that is forces such as "zwei Sterne" (I 1080) or "Donnerkeile" (I 1123) whose trajectories inexorably intersect.

In their second encounter, narrated in the seventh scene, the high priestess is shocked at Penthesilea's loss of control to the arrows of Amor (I 1082), since she lacks the "Busen", the "Ziel der giftgefiederten Geschosse" (I 1084-1085). Their lances break, but Penthesilea, "mit zerrißner Brust" (I 1150), is brought back to the Amazonian encampment, while in the thirteenth scene Achilles, previously "in Stahl geschient", throws aside his sword, shield and armour from his breast (I 1159) and follows her. Up to this point, their communication has involved the material collision of metal and iron and the exchange of each other's gaze. Achilles sheds his armour in the hail of arrows from the Amazonian troops and points to his vulnerability:

> Soll ich den seidnen Latz noch niederreißen,
> Daß ihr das Herz mir harmlos schlagen seht? (I 1408-1409)

---

[46] Gallas: Kleists *Penthesilea* und Lacans vier Diskurse. P. 209.

[47] Pickerodt: Penthesilea und Kleist. P. 57.

[48] Joachim Pfeiffer: *Die zerbrochenen Bilder. Gestörte Ordnungen im Werk Heinrich von Kleists*. Würzburg 1989. P. 138.

[49] Mario Praz: *The Romantic Agony*. Trans. by Angus Davidson. 2nd ed. Oxford 1970. P. 10.

[50] Mathieu Carrière: *Für eine Literatur des Krieges, Kleist*. Frankfurt/M. 1990. P. 58.

As an echo of the chinked armour that had failed to protect his arm against Penthesilea's spear, Achilles throws off his armour and in turn opens Penthesilea's armour. In the words of Prothoe, she has been either wounded in body or soul (I 1482-1483), a binary distinction questioned by the drama's characterization and depicted by what Ursula Mahlendorf calls Penthesilea's "wounded self".[51] Without the external trappings of their military roles Penthesilea, no longer "vom Kopf zu Fuß in Erz gerüstet" (I 1881), and Achilles finally speak to one another. The fifteenth scene, in which the drama's time (through Penthesilea's historical narration) and place (through the absence of the battlefield) are suspended, is the apparently "utopische Situation".[52] However, since Penthesilea relates the history of her state's origins, and Achilles neither hears nor understands her history, their failure to validate each other undermines this Utopian dimension. Secondly, this transient idyll owes its existence to a lie, in that the dialogue occurs under the pretense that Achilles is Penthesilea's prisoner.

After drawing attention to his arm wound, the emphasis shifts to the dressing of Achilles, who is no longer to be armoured but to be wreathed with roses. Achilles, described by the first maiden as "leuchtend" and "in Stahl geschient" (I 1037-1038) or by Penthesilea as an "in Erz gepreßte Götterbildung" (I 1264), is transformed under her gaze into a static image, a *Bild*. The retardation of the frenetic movements of the previous scenes takes place in the relative immobility of the protagonists. In this way Penthesilea objectifies Achilles, recognizing him through his armour: "Nicht der prüfende Blick auf seine Gestalt verbürgt die Identität, sondern die Rüstung wird als Beweis akzeptiert".[53] At first an idolized statue of metal built by his male and female percipients, then an unarmoured body covered by roses, Achilles expresses his wish to kiss her but is interrupted by her ritualized dressing of him. The physical contact is replaced by the "Schaulust" of her scopophilic desire: "O sieh, ich bitte dich" (I 1784), a pleasure in seeing that is shared by Achilles, for she appears to him as a "Glanzerscheinung" (I 1809) whose image is locked within him. As no exchange of names (Penthesilea never uses Achilles' name, although she does name herself) or bodily contact takes place, the scene presents an exchange of mental images, of internalized *Bilder*. Names, according to Penthesilea, may disappear and rings may go missing; thus she asks: "Fändst du mein Bild in dir wohl wieder aus? / Kannst dus wohl mit geschloßnen Augen denken?" (I 1821-1822). For Helga Gallas, the postponement of physical intimacy represents the awakening of "Genuß also durch Umgehung des Genusses",[54] a notion expressed by Nutz's terming Penthesilea's pleasure as "Augenlust".[55] Since for Penthesilea

---

[51] Ursula Mahlendorf: Penthesilea's Wounded Self. In: *German Quarterly* 52.2 (1979). Pp. 252-272.

[52] Lange: Kleists *Penthesilea*. P. 711.

[53] Nutz: Lektüre der Sinne. Pp. 174-175.

[54] Gallas: Kleists *Penthesilea* und Lacans vier Diskurse. P. 211.

[55] Nutz: Lektüre der Sinne. P. 176.

"die Gefühle dieser Brust, o Jüngling, / Wie Hände sind sie, und sie streicheln dich" (I 1772-1773), the language of specular or emotional embodiment substitutes for physical presence. The construction of Achilles' body from scene three, teichoscopically presented under the male gaze as an armed and armoured god, becomes a feminized static vision dressed in roses:

> Ich sagte still! Du wirst es schon erfahren.
> – Hier diese leichte Rosenwindung nur
> Um deine Scheitel, deinen Nacken hin –
> Zu deinen Armen, Händen, Füßen nieder –
> Und wieder auf zum Haupt – – so ists geschehen.
> – Was atmest du? (I 1775-1780)

She fixes his position for the ritual of dressing, covering those moving parts of his body which had been previously functionalized as military components. It is not surprising that during this process of turning to stone ("Versteinerung") she asks him what – if at all – he is breathing. As with the bandage which binds him, Penthesilea also wishes to bring him to a standstill, to silence and immobilize him. The idyll is brought to an end by an Amazonian counterattack and the revelation of the deception. Achilles *"reißt sich die Kränze ab"* (1 2264ff) and arms himself with the words and weapons of military discourse: "Mit meinem Wagen rädern will ich sie!" (I 2266), thus transforming the wreath to the wheel. His final challenge demystifies him and reduces him, in the eyes of Penthesilea, to an object of stone, consecrated by her hand: "Ein steinern Bild hat meine Hand bekränzt?" (I 2391). Achilles falls from his status as statue: the warrior of steel, the bearer of roses, of stone, and finally the lover of flesh and blood. The inevitable conclusion of this demystification process is the death of Achilles, and the striking of mutual and reciprocal wounds. One aspect of the recurrent topoi of the hunt (also found in *Die Hermannsschlacht*), is *Penthesilea*'s "constant recourse to the neck"; Reeve points out that the image of Achilles' placing his foot on Penthesilea's neck is mentioned three times,[56] only to have this image ultimately inverted. The Greeks initially view Achilles' strong neck as a sign of his masculinity, which under the gaze of the Amazonian witnesses to his death becomes his Achilles' heel.[57] Penthesilea brings him down with an arrow to the neck, killing her prey in the way that Odysseus had projected Achilles' pursuit and capture of her. Achilles' feminine neck is his Achilles' heel, "phallically penetrated by the Amazon".[58] Penthesilea's shot to the neck aims for the throat, not the heart, forcing Achilles to "learn another form of speech [...] the death rattle of disbelief".[59]

[56] William Reeve: 'Mit dem Hals bezahlt man alls'. A Persistant Kleistian Motif. In: *Seminar* 32.3 (1996). Pp. 240-258, here p. 249.

[57] Ibid. Pp. 256-257.

[58] Paglia: *Sexual Personae*. P. 261.

[59] Carol Jacobs: *Uncontainable Romanticism. Shelley, Brontë, Kleist*. Baltimore and

Correspondingly, Prothoe notices "Eine Wund und das recht tief!" (I 1821) on Penthesilea's neck when removing her scarf. I would argue that Penthesilea's inner wound, struck by her view of Achilles in scene one, extends outwards, for the question remains as to how the wound would be inflicted from under the scarf. Penthesilea's wound of mysterious origin "does preserve the equilibrium between the two main characters, sustaining their at times seeming interchangeability",[60] as it occurs "in spiegelbildlicher Entsprechung".[61]

This penultimate mutual wound on the neck – the final cut being his breast torn from the outside and her self-imposed implosion – produces a mirroring effect at the level of gesture, metaphor, and of body trauma. After their first encounter, for example, it is reported that Penthesilea rests against an oak tree and wipes blood or sweat from her brow. The head is subsequently linked with the wreath, in that Achilles, alluding to his brutalization of Hector's body, wishes to drag her through the streets, "die Stirn bekränzt mit Todeswunden" (I 614). At the drama's conclusion, both have obtained the desired wreath of victory: Penthesilea has "den Lorbeer [...] den dornigen" (I 1818), while Achilles is memorialized through "diese blutgen Rosen! / Ach, dieser Kranz von Wunden um sein Haupt!" (I 2907-2908), foreshadowed by Penthesilea's dressing him in scene fifteen. Victory brings with it sacrifice, a second sacramental meaning of the wreath, supported by Penthesilea's baptism of water (I 2823ff). Moreover, with regard to the oft-discussed interchangeability between the figures of Achilles and Penthesilea, it should not be forgotten that she mourns Achilles' "Kranz von Wunden um sein Haupt" (2906); her bleeding finger with which she wipes away his blood (I 2779-2882) may symbolically invoke his wounded head, and both wounds to their necks occur under the unifying image of the wreath.

Penthesilea is hungry in all her senses: "Sie stürzt sich auf ihn, den sie zuvor mit den Augen verschlungen hat, um es jetzt mit dem Mund zu tun, dem es die Sprache verschlug".[62] She is a consumer through her senses, drinking the air and eating up the distance between them;[63] but Penthesilea is also capable of self-destruction through self-consumption. The variant passages to scene twenty-four (lines 2926 to end) emphasize their mutual identity and schematically projects against Penthesilea her own action against Achilles:

> Eh bög ich hungrig auf mich selbst mich nieder,
> Also, sieh her –! Und öffnete die Brust mir,
> Und tauchte diese Hände so – sieh her!
> Hinunter in den blutgen Riß, und griff
> Das Herz, das junge dampfende, hervor,

London 1989. P. 106.

[60] Reeve: A Persistent Kleistian Motif. P. 255-256.

[61] Pfeiffer: Kleists *Penthesilea*. P. 201.

[62] Klotz: Kleists extremes Theater. P. 138.

[63] Nutz: Lektüre der Sinne. Pp. 170-171.

Um es zu essen, ach, als daß ich nur
Ein Haar auf seiner lieben Scheitel krümmte. (I p. 882)

The listener is not asked merely to hear these words, but to "see" the image ("–
sieh her!") as enacted by the character of Penthesilea, much in the same way
the audience vicariously views Achilles emerging on the horizon in scene three.
These words are tragically ironic when compared to Achilles' conviction that
she would not harm him: "Eh wird ihr Arm, / Im Zweikampf gegen ihren
Busen wüten, / Und rufen: 'Sieg'! wenn er von Herzblut trieft, / Als wider
mich!" (I 2471-2474). She already lacked one breast – and aims for Achilles'
head, but tears at his left side, the site of the heart.[64] If we assume that Penthesilea's act of cannibalism enacts the total incorporation of an other's identity,
then Achilles' metaphor becomes literally true: her breast is his breast, his heart
is her heart.
   What kills Achilles is her final act of penetration: "Sie schlägt, die Rüstung
von ihm reißend, / Den Zahn schlägt sie in seine weiße Brust" (I 2669-2670).
Her constructed image of Achilles can no longer sustain her. Her tearing the
armour off his body, the removal of his reflecting second skin, not only allows
her to enter the temple of his body, but also removes the reflection of her own
image. She bites into his left breast, figuratively rendering him an Amazon and
extinguishing "[d]en Funken des Prometheus" in his breast (I 2923). Most psychoanalytical critics agree on the motivation behind her bodily iconoclasm:
"Indem Penthesilea das ideale Bild des Achill zerstückelt, zerfetzt sie dieses
Bild von sich selbst".[65] Kittler seemingly echoes the words of the wounded
Achilles on the fate of men who fight against women and lose themselves:
"Dem einen Mann, der sich ganz an eine Frau verliert, ist das Schicksal der
Zerstückelung gewiß".[66] Analogous to Amphitryon's fantasy of fragmentation,
"die Desintegration des Ich verbildlicht sich dramaturgisch in der Phantasie von
der Zerstückelung Achills, von dem Zerfall seines Körpers in einzelne Teile".[67]
For Penthesilea, the disintegrated image of Achilles is now of importance, since
her rage is not directed at the person who killed Achilles ("Ich frage nicht, wer
den Lebendigen / Erschlug" [I 2915-2916] or "Ich will nicht wissen, wer aus
seinem Busen / Den Funken des Prometheus stahl" [I 2922-2923]), but at she
who "entstellt" his god-like features (I 2930). Penthesilea's fatal "Versehen",
with its emphasis on the visual, unmakes Achilles:[68]

   – So war es ein Versehen. Küsse, Bisse,
   Das reimt sich, und wer recht von Herzen liebt,
   Kann schon das eine für das andre greifen. (I 2981-2983)

[64] Gallas: Kleists *Penthesilea* und Lacans vier Diskurse. P. 211.
[65] Gallas: Antikenrezeption bei Goethe und Kleist. P. 217.
[66] Kittler: Die Geburt des Partisanen. P. 187.
[67] Pfeiffer: Kleists *Penthesilea*. p. 201.
[68] Paglia: *Sexual Personae*. P. 262.

In her "Küsse/Bisse" rhyme, Penthesilea "wendet [...] das Sprachzeichen des Mundes gegen den Körper selbst",[69] this time as a "Versprechen". The problem of "Versehen" and "Versprechen," in a drama which represents a "Lektüre der Sinne" (in Nutz's phrase), is supplemented by mishearing. Despite his physical and verbal gesture of naming both person (Penthesilea) and function (his "bride") and touching, by which he "Rührt ihre sanfte Wange an, und ruft: / Penthesilea! meine Braut! was tust du?" (I 2663-2664), Penthesilea bites into his chest. Only in the variant is Achilles ascribed the face absent in the drama, with the remainder of his lip bent into a smile: "Sieh, Prothoe, sieh – der Rest von einer Lippe – / Sprich, dünkts dich nicht als ob er lächelte?" (I p. 884). Penthesilea wishes to once more devour Achilles with her gaze, even if the monstrous mouth of the wound – for his mouth is silent and torn – silently speaks to her: "Und wenn mir seine Wunde, / Ein Höllenrachen, gleich entgegen gähnte: / Ich will ihn sehen!" (I 2893-2895). Achilles' "Kastrationswunde"[70] embodies the silence of the emasculated tongue. Moreover, Jacobs points out that *Achilles* means "lipless", for, according to legend, he did not put his lips to the breast of his mother. Thus the pattern of seeing and kissing/biting reverses itself: Achilles the non-eater becomes the eaten. Penthesilea initiates yet again this act of consumption, in that she has already seen and literally eaten of his living body, and wishes to do so again metaphorically, this time articulating the difference between "Küsse/Bisse": "Doch jetzt sag ich dir deutlich, wie ichs meinte: / Dies, du Geliebter, wars, und weiter nichts. / *Sie küßt ihn*" (I 2988ff).

The culmination of Penthesilea's cannibalistic desire eventually and temporarily restores her sense of equilibrium. For Ingrid Stipa, Penthesilea's path to madness is characterized by her regressive movement from the Symbolic order (characterized by the disjunction between sign and signifier) to the Imaginary order (continuous relationship between the two).[71] By Gallas' account, which enumerates her falls, faints, slips of the tongue and of the body, "die Gespaltenheit der Penthesilea" shows itself "im nicht-koordinierten Körper" in danger of collapse.[72] Where Penthesilea falls or fails, the underlying structure of her inner architecture supports her self under the pressure of crisis. While the armour protects their vulnerable bodies and deflects their gaze, the built-in nature of their inner being bears further examination. The armour borne by each protagonist is a synthetic and artificial flesh; likewise is their innermost being also created. Before turning to the drama's concluding fusion of the body and language, or body as language, it is necessary to investigate the structures of the

---

[69] Gerhard Neumann: Hexenküche und Abendmahl. Die Sprache der Liebe im Werk Heinrich von Kleists. In: *Freiburger Universitätsblätter* 91 (1986). Pp. 9-31, here p. 26.

[70] Pfeiffer: Kleists *Penthesilea*. P. 200.

[71] Stipa: Kleists *Penthesilea*. Pp. 33-34.

[72] Gallas: Kleists *Penthesilea* und Lacans vier Diskurse. P. 207.

temple, the forge and the multiply coded "Bogen" which hold Penthesilea the figure and *Penthesilea* the drama together.

The fusion of the inorganic and the organic, the essential and the created is depicted by the collision and collusion of flesh and steel. Although the body encased in armour is one of the dominant motifs of *Penthesilea*, by which flesh fused to metal gives way to flesh incorporating flesh, the play offers a number of metaphorical connections between the body and architecture, namely the metaphorical affiliation of the body to architectonic structures. This link does not surface unexpectedly in a drama centered on the making and unmaking of the body. That Kleist divided the imagery of self-construction and collapse by gender bears further examination, for a line of contrast between Achilles and Penthesilea can be drawn on the basis of their interior architecture. He has the interior depth of a mirror reflecting back the image of the percipient; it is the gaze and the words of Penthesilea (and others) that literally hold his body together. In contrast to Achilles' capacity for surface reflection, Penthesilea's bodily presence and interior space are repeatedly conceived as constructs in crisis that ultimately – and perhaps productively – collapse into the "Ruine ihrer Seele" (I 2789).

However, Achilles' body, constructed piece by piece, becomes a sacred temple, an "unbewußtes Symbol für den Körper des Liebespartners",[73] for Penthesilea is fascinated by his "marmorharten Busen" (2202) and is "voller Bewunderung für die glatte Heldenbrust des Achill, eine marmorharte, erzgepanzerte Brust".[74] Typical gender roles are reversed in the sense that Penthesilea actively and phallically penetrates Achilles:[75]

> Daß eures Tempels Pforten rasselnd auf,
> Des glanzerfüllten, weihrauchduftenden,
> Mir, wie des Paradieses Tore, fliegen! (I 1642-1645)

This fantasy of penetration, abstracted to the temple of Diana as the site of consummation, ascends to the heights of Elysium in the following metaphor used to describe her first blinding view of Achilles:

> [...] – wie wenn zur Nachtzeit
> Der Blitz vor einen Wandrer fällt, die Pforten
> Elysiums, des glanzerfüllten, rasselnd,
> Vor einem Geist sich öffnen und verschließen. (I 2213-2216)

It is through the opening of the portals that Penthesilea desires access to the core of Achilles. Yet these images, in a constant dialectic of opening and closure, illuminate his alternating exposure and invulnerability. But the intruder

---

[73] Pfeiffer: Kleists *Penthesilea*. P. 200.
[74] Gallas: Antikenrezeption bei Goethe und Kleist. P. 214.
[75] Pfeiffer: Kleists *Penthesilea*. P. 200.

does not enter through the portals, but smashes through the walls, through the "Latz" in Achilles' armour. Achilles' broken and opened body becomes itself the open temple, but only in its decay and destruction:

> Doch wer, o Prothoe, bei diesem Raube
> Die offne Pforte ruchlos mied, durch alle
> Schneeweißen Alabasterwände mir
> In diesen Tempel brach [...] (I 2926-2929)

The creation of Achilles as a temple is part of the idolization process that ends in the destruction of Achilles/Penthesilea; such a mode of totalized identification as cannibalistic incorporation is expressed by the reflexive pronoun "mir" and her concept of the robbery of Achilles' body as occuring to her.

The significance of body as temple in *Penthesilea* implies more than a metaphor for destructive sexual intimacy. As competing spatial locations and visions of happiness, the temples of Diana in Themiscyra and the throne in Phtia represent Penthesilea's and Achilles' respective desires to physically overcome the other and to acquire a captive and queen. In the sixteenth scene, the struggle over their destination (Phtia or Themiscyra) concludes with Achilles' nearly comical assertion: "Ich bau' dir solchen Tempel bei mir auf" (I 2292), a casual "fast prahlerisch" remark,[76] as if the struggle were about buildings, rather than dominance of one over the other ("Und wenn der Sel'gen Sitz in Phtia wäre, / Doch, doch, o Freund! nach Themiscyra noch" [I 2288-2289]). Penthesilea wants no architectural copy of a temple, she wants the original, to possess the temple of Achilles' body. His refusal to recognize the sanctity of the literal and actual temple of Diana causes her indirectly to misrecognize and destroy what she visualizes metaphorically as his temple: his body.

The specific and semi-sacred association between Achilles and the temple stands in contrast to the various manifestations of Penthesilea's architectural landscape, which alternate between tropes of collapse and suspension, between animation and stillness. In the first instance, Prothoe urges Penthesilea to retain her sense of physical and psychological equilibrium with an image taken from Kleist's letter of the 16th of November 1800 (II 593), in order to derive a sense of comfort in the face of collapse:

> Steh, stehe fest, wie das Gewölbe steht,
> Weil seiner Blöcke jeder stürzen will!
> Beut deine Scheitel, einem Schlußstein gleich,
> [...]
> Nicht aber wanke in dir selber mehr,
> Solang ein Atem Mörtel und Gestein,
> In dieser jungen Brust, zusammenhält. (I 1349-1351, 1353-1356)

---

[76] Sternberger: Kampf der Liebenden. P. 97.

Here the head is the uppermost stone of the arched structure, the mortar and stone suspended in the breast. Ilse Graham finds this figure "contrived [...] with its incongruent metaphor of breath quickening mortar and stone".[77] Contrived or not, this constructedness of the self – through the blood and breath of the body – is congruent with the thematic fusion of the organic and the inorganic. The "Bogen" metaphor, this time as the arch, illustrates how joint elements can support the whole as a model for human subjectivity.[78] What strikes Carrière about the semiotics of this passage is the location, or dislocation of her self: "Wo ist dieses 'Selbst' der Penthesilea [...]? Dies Zentrum ist der Moment der Spaltung selbst. Es ist das 'Selbst' des katastrophalen Begehrens, ein gespaltenes, deplaziertes, dezentralisiertes Zentrum".[79] The constructed arch metaphor provokes Carrière's account of Penthesilea's self reacting temporally (at the moment of division) and spatially (through displacement and decentering). This architectonic image buttresses an emptiness of desire, in the sense that the arch suspends itself over a spatial absence, creating a gap not unlike the opening and closing doors to Achilles' temple/body.

It is not surprising that Kleist inserts immediately following the "Gewölbe" metaphor the only man-made structure in the drama's stage directions, a bridge, whose appearance literalizes Prothoe's words.[80] Choosing between the heights of the "Felsen" or the depths of the valley as an escape route (I 1358-1359), Penthesilea suddenly stops at a bridge: "*indem sie plötzlich, auf eine Brücke gekommen, stehen bleibt*" (I 1365ff). Once again, the ritual of suspension and projection is repeated, by which she gazes into the river, not only to see herself, but also the reflection of Helios, the sun-god equated with Achilles. Confronted by the insubstantiality of the narcissistic vision which nonetheless collapses her identity with his, she expresses an extreme form of bodily alienation by imploding like an outer shell without a body to support it: like a "Gewand, in unsrer Hand zusammen" (I 1390).

The chain of images continues to present Penthesilea's disembodiment. Prothoe, as part of the ruse to convince her that she was victorious, compares her loss of consciousness with the absence of a host ignoring a guest ("gleich einem jungen Fürsten" [I 1542]) who enters her bosom and is surprised to find the "leibliche Behausung" (I 1544) empty. The pressure from above and outside on the arch, or the refusal of a "Gast" (I 1547), represent forces external to Penthesilea's body, which affect her through their absence. Through the presence of Achilles, however, a force explodes from within as a sexual and biological charge in the third moment of inner architecture:

---

[77] Ilse Graham: *The Word Into Flesh. A Poet's Quest for the Symbol.* Berlin and New York 1977. P. 125.

[78] Chris Cullens and Dorothea von Mücke: Love in Kleist's *Penthesilea* and *Käthchen von Heilbronn.* In: DVjS 63.3 (1989). Pp. 461-493, here p. 477.

[79] Carrière: *Für eine Literatur des Krieges.* P. 76.

[80] Reuss: 'Im Geklüfft'. P. 6.

Hinweg jetzt, o mein Herz, mit diesem Blute,
Das aufgehäuft, wie seiner Ankunft harrend,
In beiden Kammern dieser Brüste liegt.
Ihr Boten, ihr geflügelten, der Lust,
Ihr Säfte meiner Jugend, macht euch auf,
Durch meine Adern fleucht, ihr jauchzenden,
Und laßt es einer roten Fahne gleich,
Von allen Reichen dieser Wangen wehn:
Der junge Nereïdensohn ist mein! (I 1621-1629)

The heart, as with a dwelling, houses chambers. The moment of stasis, in which her blood stood still (Achilles believes that she is dead at the beginning of the thirteenth scene), culminates with a rush of blood summoned forth by Penthesilea. What astonishes in this passage, whose animated vitality is analogous to her death speech, is the bodily self-discipline capable of conjuring a physiological effect, her blush that is metaphorized by a flag waving over a kingdom. This sovereignty over her body is demonstrated by her capacity to reanimate herself through speech, and to talk herself ultimately into death. The physiological effects of Achilles' sight alternate between the recurrent reanimating blush, when conquest and Achilles' proximity seem possible, and physiological collapse, should she suffer defeat.

This passage marks a transformation in the inner architecture of the body, which had up to this point been measured on the stasis of structure and had been expressed through Prothoe. Instead of the rhetorical representations of arches, dwellings and the oak in the mouth of Prothoe, Penthesilea herself produces figures of her own desire which exceed the created and become creative. The arch, suspended over the absence within, shares alternating prominence with the productive figure of the forge. The forge, however, is one element in the constellation of the "Bogen" metaphors (both arch and the bow), and ought to be viewed in relation to the foundation of the Amazonian state. The forge and the bow play a significant role in the fifteenth scene's passage of narrated history, for it acquires sudden relevance when seen opposite the creation of the state and the reshaping of the Amazonian body. This narrative describes how the extermination of one state (the "Stamm der Skythen" [I 1915]) gave birth to another. Following the massacre of the men and the rape of the women by the Ethiopians, the women, including the queen Tanaïs, fashion weapons from jewelry and massacre their oppressors:

Die Betten füllten, die entweihten, sich
Mit blankgeschliffnen Dolchen an, gekeilt,
Aus Schmuckgeräten, bei des Herdes Flamme,
Aus Senkeln, Ringen, Spangen: nur die Hochzeit
Ward, des Äthioperkönigs Vexoris
Mit Tanaïs, der Königin erharrt,
Der Gäste Brust zusamt damit zu küssen. (I 1940-1946)

The events in this passage are described through a series of paradoxes, incongruities, and transformations. Along with Achilles, who notes the paradoxical relationship between a "vernichtend" fate (I 1932) and the granting of life to a state, most commentators – perhaps unconsciously taking Achilles' point of view – have taken such incongruities as symptomatic of an abnormal community. For example, jewelry, as ornamentation, is forged into murder weapons; men are kissed and tickled to death with daggers (I 1951); a wedding night, already a mass rape, is turned into a massacre. This particular jewelry ("Senkeln, Ringen, Spangen") on the one hand adorns the women's body, but seems in its clasping, linking and enclosing functions to constrict its female wearer. The melting of the jewelry at the hearth (a conventional site of female domesticity) sheds and dissolves this female role. The transformation of the jewelry into the murderous weapons of the male aggressor alludes to the extreme transformation of the Amazonian body. Out of such a beginning springs "Ein Staat, ein mündiger [...] [e]in Frauenstaat" (I 1957-1958).

The liberating act of violence does not stop with the liquidation of the enemy. Self-mutilation, with the kissing of the enemy's breast with the daggers as precedent, constitutes the coronation of the queen on the steps of the altar. Jewelry, fitted to the woman's body, becomes the dagger embedded in the man's; the female body, more adaptable than the bow it wishes to bear, must be adapted by way of the same dagger. The bow, now embedded in the female body, emblazons the mark of technology on the body. Tanaïs tears "die rechte Brust sich ab, und taufte / Die Frauen, die den Bogen spannen würden, / Und fiel zusammen, eh sie noch vollendet: / Die Amazonen oder Busenlosen! – / Hierauf ward ihr die Krone aufgesetzt" (I 1986-1990). The sacrificial baptism of blood and the act of self-naming enact the community's establishment. The Amazonian state creates itself "als Welt der Mütter und der namenslosen Körper".[81] The matriarchy is named and defined by the act of identification (rendering the women the same), while the men who participate in the feast of roses are nameless bodies, for to name the body as Penthesilea does, by attaching a signifier to the body of Achilles, is to break the law. The act of self-mutilation not only marks the Amazons as physically different, but also renders them more efficient soldiers. This particular act, however, creates a hybrid gender: in Sigrid Lange's view, "mit einer Brust als 'Sitz der jungen, lieblichen Gefühle' (I 2013) und einer fehlenden, die dem Bogen Platz schafft, sind die Amazonen halb liebende Frau, halb tötender Mann".[82] The bow is not only a prosthesis, but in combination with the body, is also a machine which produces and extends desire ("Agencement"): "Tanaïs verstümmelt, verwandelt ihren Körper, um das neue Agencement Frau-Bogen möglich zu machen", an act which paralyzes her, yet mobilizes the others.[83]

[81] Neumann: Hexenküche und Abendmahl. P. 24.
[82] Lange: Kleists *Penthesilea*. P. 709.
[83] Carrière: *Für eine Literatur des Krieges*. P. 88.

The bow, previously borne by the murdered king, is now appropriated by the high priestess – which she allows to fall:

> Er stürzt', der große, goldene, des Reichs,
> Und klirrte von der Marmorstufe dreimal,
> Mit dem Gedröhn der Glocken, auf, und legte,
> Stumm wie der Tod, zu ihren Füßen sich. – (I 1998-2001)

The descending bow, bequeathed to Penthesilea, foreshadows the apparent end and rebirth of the state, because it forges a link between the bow and the breast, the organic and the inorganic. For the bow returns to play a final consummating role in the death of Achilles:

> [Sie] spannt mit Kraft der Rasenden, sogleich
> Den Bogen an, daß sich die Enden küssen,
> Und hebt den Bogen auf und zielt und schießt,
> Und jagt den Pfeil ihm durch den Hals; er stürzt. (I 2646-2649)

Klotz interprets this overextended metaphor in this way: "wie sich die beiden entgegengesetzten Enden des Bogens berühren, gehen in Penthesilea äußerste Liebe und Vernichtungstrieb ineinander über. Überspannung des Gefühls schafft eine Vereinigung des Unvereinbaren".[84] The bow, stretched so that its ends "kiss", produces a temporary unification of opposites. These opposites may also represent Penthesilea and Achilles, two extremes, who also kiss at the conclusion of the drama's trajectory. Additionally, I would argue that Achilles' bow and Penthesilea's string bind them together as one instrumental force, a force that unites in a kiss in the twenty-third scene. Yet the arrow of Penthesilea's desire kills him. There is also a third possibility: the return of history, whose "Bogen", literally a trajectory or parabola, turns back upon itself to close a circle, and then collapses. After cleaning the arrow that brought Achilles down, Penthesilea "*läßt den Bogen fallen*" (I 2767ff):

> DIE ERSTE AMAZONE.
> Der Bogen stürzt' ihr aus der Hand danieder!
> DIE ZWEITE.
> Seht, wie er taumelt –
> DIE VIERTE.
>   Klirrt, und wankt, und fällt –!
> DIE ZWEITE. Und noch einmal am Boden zuckt –
> DIE DRITTE.   Und stirbt,
> Wie er der Tanaïs geboren ward. (I 2769-2772).

When viewed in the context of the drama's concluding symbolism, the

---

[84] Klotz. *Kurze Kommentare*. Pp. 14-15.

bow's particular positioning becomes relevant. The falling bow, a historical moment that links the first and the last of the Amazonian queens, objectively correlates to the fall of a people, in the same symbolic way that the sovereign's unsteady crown implies instability. Tanaïs had transformed her body by removing one defining characteristic, her breast, and replacing it with another, to make the new combination of woman-bow possible.[85] Penthesilea incorporates Achilles' body, lets the bow fall and creates a new combination: woman-man. Wolf Kittler's discussion of this passage argues that Achilles' death suggests the reincarnation of the spirit of Tanaïs – originally a male figure – which leads to the combination mother-son through the "verschlingende Mutter".[86] There is further evidence to support Kittler's interpretation of this transfer of the name as the return of history. The birth and naming of the Amazonian nation, through Tanaïs' removal of her breast and her defining her people ("taufen") as the "Busenlosen", is mirrored by Achilles' torn breast and Penthesilea's ritual purification through water. After the descent of the bow, Penthesilea returns to the productivity of the forge, which had fired the very beginnings of the Amazonian state.

The forge or hearth, "Feueresse" (I 431) or "Herd" (I 1942), combines the possibilities of domesticity, violence and the self-destructive force of creativity. *Penthesilea* enacts a process of proximity, during which the flames of the hearth, used to forge weapons against the Ethiopians in the pre-history of the Amazon state, finally come to reside in the body of Penthesilea. This spatial transformation can be seen in the consistently more specific associations between the forge and the Amazons. Firstly, the hearth fires had transformed jewelry into weapons. While the collective crash of the Amazon pursuers is seen by the Greeks as chaos personified, "[w]ie in der Feueresse eingeschmelzt" (I 431), this generic grouping gives over to an explicit link to Penthesilea.

The historical digression of the fifteenth scene, with its image of the forge, forms the third term of an organic-inorganic constellation that includes the bow and the breast, a constellation which culminates in the last words of Penthesilea. In a second instance, the forge dematerializes into an affective metaphor, as Penthesilea places a chain of feeling ("eine andere Kette") around Achilles' heart:

> Wie Blumen leicht, und fester doch, als Erz,
> Die dich mir fest verknüpft, ums Herz zu schlagen.
> Doch bis sie zärtlich, Ring um Ring, geprägt,
> In der Gefühle Glut, und ausgeschmiedet. (I 1833-1836)

The "Fesseln" linking Achilles and Penthesilea together are the chains forged by mutual desire, a desire interwoven with the need for domination. For exam-

[85] Carrière: *Für eine Literatur des Krieges*. P. 88.
[86] Kittler: *Die Geburt des Partisanen*. Pp. 187-188.

ple, the symbolic "Fesselkranz" (1608), which Achilles would supposedly place upon himself at Penthesilea's behest, illustrates the paradox of a voluntary submission that must yet be wrested from the other. Achilles is also trapped and framed by Penthesilea's gaze, "In deiner Blicke Fesseln" (I 1613). For the high priestess, who specifically and deliberately trivializes Penthesilea's pursuit in terms of her flapping clothes rather than her military or hunting prowess, these manacles are nothing more than the chains of male oppression:

> Kannst ihn mit flatterndem Gewand ereilen,
> Der dich in Fesseln schlug, und ihm den Riß,
> Da, wo wir sie zersprengten, überreichen. (I 2331-2333)

The high priestess is also aware that only Achilles can fill the empty space created out of Penthesilea's desire; the "Riß" or tear is at once present as an absence, a lack, and cannot be handed over. Since such a break cannot materialize, it can be inflicted on the other: in her laconic "Ich zerriß ihn" (I 2975), Penthesilea speaks of the unspeakable in literal and metaphorical terms. As Chaouli points out, the rhyme pair "Riß" and "Biß", relatively neglected in comparsion to the notoriously misspoken "Küsse/Bisse", "points to a process in which disgusting acts and literary production are fused", since one meaning of "reißen", related to "ritzen", is to write or inscribe letters and signs.[87] There remains yet another reading of this tear or rupture, which represents the linearity of a story which nonetheless has a twist: the word "Riß", which according to *Grimms Deutsches Wörterbuch* contains the meaning of cutting furrows in a field,[88] may encode a reference to Penthesilea's madness. Stipa, citing Foucault on madness, notes that "delirium" also has the same root: "lira" means furrow, while "deliro" means to go out of line, to deviate from the path of reason.[89] The path taken by Penthesilea, her "Riß" that composes her trajectory of pursuit, leads to her slip of the tongue into her "Biß". These terms create the premiss for Penthesilea's conclusion, for she has not changed her course, as suggested by the double meaning of "verrückt", but has remained consistent in her goal: "Ich war nicht so verrückt, als es wohl schien" (I 2999). As final figures on *Penthesilea*'s path from "Riß" to "Biß", the "Bogen" and the productive symbol of the forge mark the beginning and end of the drama's textualized body.

The term "Bogen" includes the meaning of the bow, the arch, and the arc or trajectory, symbolizing the beginning and ending of the drama in a circular movement. This arc represents the core symbol of the drama as a whole. Reuss' close reading of the "Textkörper" of the dramatis personae, with its bowed brackets grouping the Greek and Amazon characters ("{"), investigates the bow's visual and spatial significance. Penthesilea takes a path of pursuit,

---

[87] Chaouli: Devouring Metaphor. P. 139.
[88] Ibid.
[89] Stipa. Kleists *Penthesilea*. p. 37.

following Achilles' bending route ("Bogen"), during which she collides with a rock. Gerhard Neumann, in his account of Kleist's cultural anthropology, finds that the "Straucheln des Körpers" is one of the building blocks for Kleist's view of human fallability (literally: our capacity to fall).[90] It is no coincidence that Juan, of the edited "Vorstufen" of *Die Familie Ghonorez*, has the following fall: "In grader Linie fort durch Strauch und Moor / Und moosigem Gestein mich winde, gleitet / Mein Fuß, mein Haupt zerschlägt sich an dem Felsen" (I 827). Such is the case in *Penthesilea*, when Diomedes compliments Achilles on his prescience in placing "[d]en Feldstein [...], über welchen / Die Königin zusammenstürzen sollte" (I 516-517). In Kleist's world, these obstacles are merely externalized signs of inner imbalance. For Judge Adam of *Der zerbrochne Krug*, everyone has the fall-provoking "leidigen Stein des Anstoßes" (I 6) within him or herself. Penthesilea "fliegt, wie von der Senne abgeschossen" (I 399) and takes a "Sehne", the most direct route towards Achilles, and because of her "Sehn-sucht" she overshoots ("vorbei / Schießt" (I 425-426) her goal and falls;[91] Reuss suggests that Penthesilea's drive in her first pursuit is to "cut off", that is to castrate Achilles in the crossing over of power ("Herrschaft" symbolized by the bow) and gender.[92]

That the formal aspects of architecture and structure are built into the drama itself is further confirmed by the meaning of "Bogen", "Sehne", and "Pfeil" as related mathematical figures. The word "Bogen", according to Adelung's *Grammatisch-kritisches Wörterbuch der Hochdeutschen Mundart* (1793), has the meaning "Ein jeder Theil einer krummen Linie. Daher ist in der Mathematik der Bogen, *arcus*, ein Stück einer Zirkellinie".[93] The geometrical meaning of "Sehne" is outlined as follows: "Nach einer von diesen Bogensehnen entlehnten Figur ist in der Geometrie die Sehne, *Chorda*, eine jede Linie, welche außer dem Mittelpunkt von einem Punkte der Peripherie eines Zirkels zu dem anderen gezogen wird".[94] Grimm states that "bogensehne" is "die einen *bogen* abschneidende gerade linie".[95] Adelung's definition of "Pfeil" complements this constellation: "in der Mathematik wird derjenige Theil von dem halben Durchmesser eines Zirkels, welcher zwischen dem Bogen und seinem *Sinu* liegt, *Sinus versus*, von einigen der Pfeil genannt";[96] architecturally speaking, the "Pfeil" is the rise of an arch or arc. The *Sinu* is the sinew or "Sehne". Grimm's definition of "Bogen" provides further evidence to suggest that Kleist

---

[90] Gerhard Neumann: Das Stocken der Sprache und das Straucheln des Körpers. Umrisse von Kleists kultureller Anthropologie. In: *Heinrich von Kleist. Kriegsfall – Rechtsfall – Sündenfall*. Ed. by Gerhard Neumann. Freiburg 1994. Pp. 13-24.

[91] Chaouli: Devouring Metaphor. P. 133.

[92] Reuss: 'Im Geklüfft'. P. 8.

[93] Johann Christoph Adelung: *Grammatisch-kritisches Wörterbuch der Hochdeutschen Mundart*. Ed. by Helmut Henne. Hildesheim and New York 1970. Vol. 2. P. 1112.

[94] Ibid. Vol. 4. Pp. 26-27.

[95] Jacob and Wilhelm Grimm: *Deutsches Wörterbuch*. Munich 1984. Vol. 16. P. 151.

[96] Adelung. Vol. 3. P. 719.

was thoroughly familiar with these words' connotations: "die krumme linie, im gegensatz zur geraden, der kreis ist eine geschlossene krumme linie, deren beide enden sich wieder berühren",[97] a parallel to the moment in which Penthesilea "spannt mit Kraft der Rasenden, sogleich / Den Bogen an, daß sich die Enden küssen" (I 2646-2647). This geometric allegory may resemble this pattern: Firstly, Penthesilea attempts to cut into Achilles' trajectory, as a "Sehne" cuts into a circle. The circle, however, is none other than a closed arcing line, a "Bogen", which is incised by and connected to the "Sehne"; the arrow/"Pfeil" interrupts in turn the connection between the bow/Achilles and the string/Penthesilea. Penthesilea's "Pfeil"/"Feder" inscribes Achilles' "Bogen"/"Blatt". The reinsertion of this geometric figure, embedded in the topography of the *dramatis personae* (cf. Reuss) and the symbolic structures of the opening scenes, completes the circular nature of the drama's structural logic.

In terms of the play's circularity, Roland Reuss observes how scenes one, two and three offer respectively an expository epic account, a messenger's report, and a teichoscopic narration. The last three scenes, twenty-two, twenty-three and twenty-four, are in relation to the first three "spiegelsymmetrisch", in their teichoscopy, Meroes' report, and Penthesilea's narration.[98] The appearance and disappearance of Achilles' body, whose dominance of the opening scenes is replaced by Penthesilea's predominance in the last scenes, plays out the suicide of Penthesilea, which counterpoints indirect representation/narration, effacing the border between acting and speaking, thereby bringing an end to acting and speaking.[99] The threefold account of Achilles' death, a "Ballung von Teichoskopie, Botenbericht und Selbstdeutung"[100] brings the agent increasingly closer to her actions. In a last act of creativity, which concludes her drive to proximity, Penthesilea forges her own form of writing from within.

In her final monologue, both metal and flesh, language and body melt into a single unity of symbols. The forge activates the body of the queen in her death speech, in a radically interiorized impression of feeling:

> Denn jetzt steig ich in meinen Busen nieder,
> Gleich einem Schacht, und grabe, kalt wie Erz,
> Mir ein vernichtendes Gefühl hervor.
> Dies Erz, dies läutr' ich in der Glut des Jammers
> Hart mir zu Stahl; tränk es mit Gift sodann,
> Heißätzendem, der Reue, durch und durch;
> Trag es der Hoffnung ewgem Amboß zu,
> Und schärf und spitz es mir zu einem Dolch;
> Und diesem Dolch reich ich meine Brust:

---

[97] Grimm. Vol. 2. P. 217.

[98] Reuss: 'Im Geklüfft'. P. 11.

[99] Ibid. P. 11.

[100] Pickerodt: Penthesilea und Kleist. P. 53.

So! So! So! So! Und wieder! – Nun ists gut. (I 3025-3034)

In an effacing movement that extinguishes the difference between the inside and outside, Penthesilea forges an iron dagger from the smithy of her soul and offers it to her breast. She surrenders the dagger and the arrows, the physical implements of death, and substitutes these weapons with the materiality of language. She completes the writing process, which began with her writing on Achilles' body, by writing with and within the body. "Es ist der Moment", suggests Gerhard Neumann, "wo die Frau den Kampf noch einmal aufnimmt: in der Form der tödlichen Sprache der Körper".[101] The physical presence of Achilles must be compensated for the absence of the image: "Sie findet mit dem Mund den Weg ins Innere des Körpers, den ihr Gefühl nicht gefunden hat".[102] Achilles has her "Bild" within himself; when he destroys his "Bild" that exists within her, she must obliterate the living original.[103] Finally, this arch-type, coupled with the illuminating yet consuming image of the forge, invokes the practice of writing: Penthesilea's "Sehn-sucht" (the desire and pursuit of a direct line) not only textualizes Achilles, but embodies writing as a desire, articulated by her own writing within herself with the dagger of language; after pinning Achilles and silencing him with a "Pfeil", she drops and so to speak authorizes the "Bogen", a term which also means a leaf of paper. The author's work is complete; the poisonous pen forged from within is a writing instrument and a weapon with which she writes her death sentence. Perhaps her death meditates on the besmirching and brilliant work of writing, enacted in a drama in which the reader, in the words of Kleist, could find not only the writer's "innerstes Wesen" but also the "ganze Schmutz zugleich und Glanz [s]einer Seele" (II 796).

---

[101] Neumann: Hexenküche und Abendmahl. P. 25.

[102] Nutz: Lektüre der Sinne. P. 181.

[103] Klotz: Kleists extremes Theater. P. 138.

William C. Reeve

Kleist, Büchner, Grillparzer: Three Dramatists' Archetypal Representations of the Body

Indebted to Erich Neumann's Die Große Mutter, this essay explores how Kleist, Büchner, and Grillparzer exploit the archetypal perception of woman as body. As the life-giving womb, the female vessel manifests itself in the flower, chair, fortress or earth over which men claim authority. As the death-inducing tomb, the female body, the vagina dentala, threatens male dominance. The three authors resort to this universal symbolism to suggest censored themes, notably the unconscious and human sexuality.

When one speaks of the body, one almost invariably has the female figure in mind. Since a woman carries a child in her womb, gives birth to it and sustains it through her breast milk, anthropologists and psychologists have argued that she lives on more intimate terms with natural process and accordingly experiences a more immediate relationship with the material foundations of human life. A direct link exists between *mater* and *materia*. In contrast the male has become associated with cerebral, spiritual aspirations and the denial of the corporeal. Therefore, "des Vaters hohes Haupt",[1] the seat of the rational, epitomizes the male principle which seeks to devalue or deny its female, physical origin.

Erich Neumann's *Die Große Mutter* provides an informative and productive model in its depiction of the female archetype of the Great Mother as vessel and its numerous variations and transformations from primordial times to the present. This monumental work will form the basis for my analysis of the female body in the dramas and *Novellen* of Kleist, Büchner, and Grillparzer from the first half of the 19th century. I shall describe in detail the various manifestations of the archetypal female body employed by these playwrights, often to intimate the darker side of the human personality. In fact, all three writers exploit these fundamental images at great length to represent the unconscious as a more reliable measure of human motivation. They thus anticipate the discoveries of Freud and illustrate the theories of Jung and his student, Neumann, in a more consistent manner than any of their literary predecessors.

---

[1] Franz Grillparzer: *Dramen*. Ed. by Helmut Bachmaier. Frankfurt/M. 1987. V. 199. All subsequent references to the plays of Grillparzer will be drawn from this edition. Drama titles, where necessary, and verse numbers will appear directly in the text. All emphases are my own, unless otherwise indicated, and stage directions are italicized in keeping with the editions consulted.

Das Kernsymbol des weiblichen ist *das Gefäß* [Neumann's emphasis]. Von An-
beginn an und bis zu den spätesten Stadien der Entwicklung finden wir dieses
archetypische Symbol als Inbegriff des Weiblichen. Die symbolische Grundglei-
chung Weib = Körper = Gefäß entspricht der vielleicht elementarsten Grunder-
fahrung der Menschheit vom Weiblichen, in der das Weibliche sich selber erlebt,
in der es aber auch vom Männlichen erlebt wird.[2]

According to Neumann we instinctively experience the feminine as
body/vessel because woman carries within herself the child and man enters
into her through sexual intercourse. She thus becomes "das 'Lebensgefäß an
sich', in dem sich das Leben bildet, und das alles Lebendige aus sich heraus
und in die Welt hinein gebiert und entläßt".[3] As a chalice, bowl, or jug, *das
Gefäß* not only contains but also protects and nourishes, hence the tradition
whereby the Greeks are said to have modelled the first bowl after Helen's
breast. This perception of women as predominantly supportive underlies the
works of Kleist (Alkmene, Käthchen, Thusnelda), Büchner (Julie, Lucile),
or Grillparzer (Margarethe, Libussa), but one drama in particular exploits
this archetypal symbol even in its title. *Der zerbrochne Krug* plays extensively upon the figurative value of the jug, a material representation of the
female body formed in clay in keeping with the Genesis prototype. As Frau
Marthe points out to the court: "Wie schön der Krug, gehört zur Sache!"[4],
the physical attractiveness of the jug/woman does have a major bearing on
the plot, more than the speaker realizes, for the names Adam and Eve, re-
calling their mythical namesakes from the Garden of Eden, conjure up the
seductive power of the beautiful female body. According to biblical scholars, the original prohibition against eating the forbidden fruit from the sacred tree (both variants of the female archetype) originated with the ritual
sex practised in Canaanite shrines dedicated to the life goddess as represented by the tree.[5] Eve's youth and beauty have tempted judge Adam and
led to his fall both in the literal and figurative sense. Frequently referred to
as "die Jungfer", Eve has every reason to deplore the breaking of the jug
since folklore has come to regard it as synonymous with a young maiden's
virginity and innocence. There is thus a measured symbolic appropriateness
that it be smashed as the consequence of a thwarted rape and that her reputation be linked to its fate: "Dein guter Name lag in diesem Topfe, / Und vor

---

[2] Erich Neumann: *Die Große Mutter*. Olten und Freiburg/Br. 1977. P. 51.

[3] Ibid. P. 54.

[4] Heinrich von Kleist: *Sämtliche Werke und Briefe*. Ed. by Helmut Sembdner. Munich 1984. V. 679. All subsequent references to the works of Kleist will be drawn
from this edition. For the plays quoted from vol. 1, drama titles and verse numbers
will be used, for prose works from vol. 2, page references.

[5] Cf. Peggy Reeves Sanday: *Female Power and Male Dominance*. Cambridge 1981.
P. 223.

der Welt mit ihm ward er zerstoßen, / Wenn auch vor Gott nicht, und vor mir und dir" (490-92).

This same symbolism plays a key role in Grillparzer's love story, *Des Meeres und der Liebe Wellen*. "*[Leander] den Krug hinhaltend, aus dem er knieend trinkt*", Hero declares at a highpoint towards the end of the second act, "So trink! und jeder Tropfen / Sei *Trost*, und all dies Naß bedeute *Glück*" (818-19). As the nurturer, provider, she willingly offers the basis of life, the female element water, from her jug, the archetypal female body (womb/tomb). This very theatrical staging highlights not only the tragedy's central message but also femaleness to which the male suitor pays homage by kneeling and thus demonstrating his dependence in sexual matters. The purpose of life is to find "Glück"[6] and the greatest human experience most closely approximating the attainment of this supreme happiness is the promise of genital love.[7]

As the bearer of life the female archetype is related to all vegetation born out of the womb-tomb of Mother Earth. Because women have customarily been cast in the role of root or herb gatherers in primitive societies with a primarily plant orientation, they possess an intimate knowledge of natural remedies (cf. Edrita or Libussa). Ancient myths often depict the male sun god's birth out of a flower, a variation of the vessel motif which all three playwrights turn to account. Strahl consistently associates Käthchen with the rose: "Mir, dessen Blick du da liegst, wie die Rose, / Die ihren jungen Kelch dem Licht erschloß" (470-71). The flower (Käthchen) opens its calyx, the husk containing and protecting the seeds, to the light (Wetter vom Strahl), the male principle.[8] The heroine of *Leonce und Lena* portrays herself as a flower after her encounter with her male counterpart: "Aber, liebe Mutter, du weißt man hätte mich eigentlich in eine Scherbe setzen sollen. Ich brauche Thau und Nachtluft wie die Blumen".[9] While watching over her dying father, Libussa has a vision indebted to the identical symbolic significance of the vegetative vessel, here implying an unconscious wish to sur-

---

[6] By examining human behaviour to determine the goal of life, Freud concludes: "[Die Menschen] streben nach dem Glück, sie wollen glücklich werden und so bleiben". *Das Unbehagen in der Kultur. Fragen der Gesellschaft. Ursprünge der Religion*. Studienausgabe. Ed. by Alexander Mitscherlich, Angela Richards, and James Strachey. Vol. 9. Frankfurt/M. 1974. P. 208.

[7] Cf. Freud: *Das Unbehagen*. P. 213: "Eine der Erscheinungsformen der Liebe, die geschlechtliche Liebe, hat uns die stärkste Erfahrung einer überwältigenden Lustempfindung vermittelt und so das Vorbild für unser Glücksstreben gegeben". Woman also embodies man's "Trost" after a hard day's work out in the world away from the hearth which it is the woman's responsibility to protect and advance.

[8] Cf. William C. Reeve: *Kleist's Aristocratic Heritage and "Das Käthchen von Heilbronn"*. Montreal and Kingston 1991. Pp. 114-115.

[9] Georg Büchner: *Sämtliche Werke und Briefe*. Ed. by Werner R. Lehmann. Vol. 1. Hamburg 1967. Pp. 123-124. All subsequent references to the works of Büchner will be drawn from this volume.

render her body to her father: "Da schwebte vor den Augen des Gemüts, / Hatt ichs gehört nun, oder wußt ichs sonst, / Das Bild mir einer Blume, weiß und klein, / Mit siebenspaltgem *Kelch* und schmalen Blättern; / Die gib dem Vater, sprachs, und er genest" (311-15). Since the ideas of fruitful abundance and containment find expression in the image of the cornucopia, it is thus fitting that Homburg in his first monologue acknowledge the abundant blessings of the goddess of Fortuna as a "Füllhorn" (360) seized on the field of battle.

Whereas this relationship between the female body and plant symbolism stresses the positive protective, nurturing function of the vessel, it may also assume an extreme form. As creatures more in tune with nature whose bodies have therefore not forfeited to the same extent as men's the primordial link with human animal origins, women respond more directly to natural urges but may also run the risk of total subjugation to instinctual demands. In this respect the prostitute Marion from *Dantons Tod*, one of the "Priesterinnen mit dem Leib" (p. 23) is a key figure, anticipating Marie from *Woyzeck*.[10] In her monologue describing her *Frühlingserwachen*, her corporeality takes on a life of its own: "Ich gerieth in eine eigne Atmosphäre, sie erstickte mich fast, ich betrachtete meine Glieder" (p. 21). The body as a source of sexual pleasure eventually destroys her individuality, overwhelms any moral prohibition and, in demanding satisfaction of natural needs, contributes significantly to human determinism through the pleasure principle: "Es läuft auf eins hinaus, an was man seine Freude hat, an Leibern, Christusbildern, Blumen oder Kinderspielsachen" (p. 22).

The English expression body tissue traces its etymology to weaving as a metaphor for the fabrication of life in the womb. In pregnancy the child develops as the fabric of the woman's body.[11] Consequently the great goddesses are often weavers who, because they spin and weave the material of existence, become identical with fate: "das Gewebte, welches das Große Weibliche selber verfertigt, ist das Leben und das Schicksal".[12] Many civilizations have thus considered woman and distaff as interchangeable. When Kleist's Jupiter approached Alkmene for the first time, she was lost in thought at her spinning wheel. As a visual announcement of Libussa's resignation to the domestic, supportive lot of wife, the introductory stage directions of the last act dwell upon her servants preparing a cloth and single out *"[im] Vorgrunde rechts ein Stuhl mit einem darangelehnten Spinnrocken"* (II p. 326). In Kleist's "Lustspiel", Jupiter came down to earth and impregnated Alkmene while in Grillparzer's tragedy the subsequent opening dialogue intimates morning sickness (1920-23). Even though soci-

---

[10] Cf. Wolfgang Martens: Zum Menschenbild Georg Büchners. *Woyzeck* und die Marionszene in *Dantons Tod*. In: *Georg Büchner*. Ed. by Wolfgang Martens. Darmstadt 1965. Pp. 373-385.

[11] Neumann. P. 219.

[12] Ibid. P. 216.

ety has come to regard the creation of metaphorical and actual tissues as a diminution in prestige and power: "Du legtest kaum die Spindel aus der Hand. / Ihr seid herabgekommen, gute Mädchen!" (*Libussa* 1929-30), Grillparzer turns to account the other assertive dimension by having Libussa assume the function of seer to foretell the fate of her nation at the end of the act.

One of the main foundations upholding male dominance has been the man's right to claim ownership of the woman's body, a custom which social historians have traced back to the male function as warrior and protector of the "weaker" sex who gives birth and thus assures human survival. In the 18th and 19th centuries husbands had the right, vindicated by the teachings of the Church, to enjoy their wives' bodies even without their consent, an arrangement acknowledged by Alkmene as her conjugal obligation: "Daß du [Amphitryon] dir jede Freiheit hast erlaubt, / Die dem Gemahl mag zustehn über mich" (849-50), and if Julie and Lucile (who have little in common with their historical protypes) are any indication, wives exist solely to dedicate themselves in love to their husbands. With respect to this issue Grillparzer shows greater understanding and a more progressive attitude as he questions this marital duty from the female's perspective. Edrita shudders at the prospect of surrendering herself to the uncivilized, simple-minded Galomir (*Weh dem, der lügt!* 1165-66), while the frigid queen Eleonore from *Die Jüdin von Toledo* only tolerates the idea of sexual intercourse since the Church has sanctified it in the context of the marriage sacrament (1204-07). Libussa, however, both challenges and rejects male control over her body:

> Die Glieder dieses Leibes, die mein eigen,
> Zu Lehen tragen von der Niedrigkeit?
> Der Hand Berührung und des Atems Nähe
> Erdulden, wie die Pflicht folgt einem Recht?
> Mich schaudert. All mein Wesen wird zum: Nein. (1234-38)

This title to possession of the female body adopts numerous metaphorical forms. For example, custom dictates that to sit on something signifies to take ownership of it. "Nicht zufällig ist der Name der größten Muttergöttin der frühen Kulte: 'Isis', der Sitz, der Thron, dessen Symbol sie auf ihrem Haupte trägt; und der König, der die Erde, die Muttergöttin, 'in Besitz nimmt', tut dies, indem er im wahren Sinne des Wortes auf ihrem Schoße sitzt".[13] One of the central visual symbols beyond the jug itself, one that is constantly present in *Der zerbrochne Krug*, is the throne of justice. (*Gerechtigkeit* is also represented allegorically as a female figure.) Walter, the embodiment of a patriarchal judicial system, obliges Adam to take his seat, a "Richtstuhl" raised above all others in the courtroom, to proclaim authority over life and death. With a measure of ironic suitability, Adam, who sought

[13] Neumann. P. 103.

to mount Eve by abusing his power, is finally cast down from the female symbol of that authority through her testimony: "Er dort, der Unverschämte, der dort sitzt, / Er selber wars – / [...] / Geh, schmeiß ihn von dem Tribunal herunter" (1890-91; 1899). Just after Libussa expresses her abhorrence at the thought of yielding control over her own body, she mounts the steps to assume the throne, a dramatic reinforcement of her declaration of corporeal independence. In contrast, once she has accepted Primislaus as her husband, she refuses to sit in his presence, relinquishing the chair/throne to him and therefore indicating that she has voluntarily submitted to her mate. This same theme emerges in *Die Jüdin* where, in the king's absence, *"Die Königin [...] setzt sich auf den Thronsessel"* (1168f). Alphons has forfeited control over his women, both his wife and his mistress. Because the latter rules him through the seductive power of her body and the former through her moral rigidity, he feels suitably admonished in the presence of his throne which he refrains from ascending: "Du hoher Sitz, die andern überragend" (1340).

The mountain presents a variation of the chair symbol, a natural throne that towers over the land, and includes the additional female body symbols of earth and cave. Libussa tellingly rejects the proffered gifts of the miners in favour of "Butterblumen" (612), since the forcible extraction of precious metals from Mother Earth constitutes a metaphorical rape of the feminine vessel. The protecting function typical of the *Gefäß* finds expression in the close relationship between *Berg* and *Burg*:[14] custom regards the female body as a fortress defending its most valuable jewel, virginity. Grillparzer avails himself of this time-honoured symbol in depicting the defensive castle of Libussa's sisters to whose inner confines men are denied access. But perhaps nowhere has this symbol gained greater ironic prominence than through its parodistic variations in Kleist's narrative *Die Marquise von O...* in which the literal storming of a fortress has numerous parallels in the rape and subsequent courtship of the countess by the Russian officer: "Alle kamen darin überein, [...] daß er Damenherzen durch Anlauf, wie Festungen, zu erobern gewohnt scheine" (II p. 114).

Drawing on an early mythological tradition common to many cultures, Grillparzer insinuates another symbolic form of doing violence to the female body. Since the ancient Greeks in their creation myth described Gaia, the earth, as the mother of all things, they interpreted ploughing as a brutal act against the mother and posited a direct relationship between female subservience and exploitation of the soil. *Libussa* consistently associates Primislaus, the man of iron, with his "Pflugschar" and, as ploughing has always symbolized fertilization, his leitmotif announces his sexual potency, the

---

[14] Cf. Neumann. P. 57.

ownership of the phallus that entitles him to rule over his domain, the feminine earth, and eventually Libussa herself.[15]

Neumann also designates the female archetype as "das Große Runde"
(chapter eleven), because it encompasses the totality of nature in its original
unity and is the source of all life. Hence the circle, or more concretely, the
Kette or *Gürtel* takes on a special figurative meaning in many of the works
under discussion. Since a father had complete control over his daughter and
sought to preserve her virginity intact until he relinquishes her to the husband of his choice, the chastity belt represents male authority over the female body. Kleist alludes to this motif at considerable length in *Amphitryon*
where the husband has a crown won at war – victory on the battle field legitimizes possession of the female body[16] and implies virility – transformed
into a belt for his wife, a means of declaring and protecting his property. In
Libussa a father, anxious to keep his harem to himself, has three belts fashioned to secure his continued presence, i.e., authority, over their persons, as
long as the belts remain whole. With Primislaus's intervention in what
amounts to a fantasized rape: "die Gedanken, / Sie haben räuberisch an dir
gesündigt" (1883-84), he breaks the circle: "Des Gürtels reiche Ketten auf-
gesprengt / Und in zwei Stücken ein so schönes Ganze" (55-56) and establishes his own claim. The protective wall surrounding Kattwald's *Burg* in
Weh dem, der lügt! implies the same message. Significantly the key granting
entry or exit hangs above the ruler's bed and it acquires greater symbolic
implications when Edrita steals it from her father and voluntarily hands over
the key to her metaphorical chastity belt to the man she loves, thus obtaining
some say over the disposition of her own body.

Sex has always been an effective weapon to secure advantage over a political enemy, and Kleist fully realized its potential at the time he wrote *Die
Hermannsschlacht*. In *Il principe* Machiavelli had warned how "[h]atred is
aroused most readily by interference with the property and the women of
subordinates".[17] Hence the violation of a young girl by the enemy together
with her violent death at the hands of her outraged father and relatives (who
view her as a piece of property over which they have complete authority)
provides Hermann with the ideal atrocity at the most opportune moment to
unite and incite the country against the Romans. Out of sheer opportunistic
calculation he orders her family members to cut the desecrated body into
fifteen pieces and to distribute them to the corresponding number of Germanic tribes, i.e., he creates by design a political martyr out of a female
body, a manufactured icon for the nation as a whole, to serve his political

---

[15] Cf. William C. Reeve: *Grillparzer's "Libussa": The Tragedy of Separation*.
Montreal and Kingston 1999. Pp. 90-92.

[16] Cf. *Prinz Friedrich von Homburg* 361-363.

[17] Niccolò Machiavelli: *The Ruler*. Trans. by Peter Rodd. London 1954. P. 94.

ends.[18] However, the lengths to which he is prepared to go to destroy the enemy become no more apparent than in his cunning manipulation of his own wife as sex bait to entice the Roman Ventidius into a complacent, unsuspecting frame of mind so that he fails to detect his host's duplicity. Hermann skilfully exploits the body of his wife to lull his adversaries into a false sense of security, for in a struggle for national survival, the end justifies the means.

To this point we have dealt with male possession or dominance over the positive womb, the vessel that protects and sustains and appears as a mouth: "deswegen werden dem weiblichen Genitale 'Lippen' zugeschrieben, und auf Grund dieser positiven Symbolgleichung ist der Mund als 'oberer Schoß' der Geburtsort des Atems und des Wortes, des Logos".[19] It is therefore no accident that a writer's muse, his/her inspiration, has a feminine gender and that seers, prophets, and magicians are often women (cf. Medea and Libussa). But whereas the female body represents the womb of life, it also incarnates the tomb of death and destruction. The female archetype of the womb/tomb dominates Büchner's depiction of women whom he identifies with the grave or coffin, another variation of the vessel motif. For his male characters the desire to escape from an existence, the essence of which is suffering, motivates the longing to return to the womb/tomb in the hope of exchanging a torturing consciousness for peaceful oblivion. Hence Danton, persecuted by an offending conscience, confesses to his wife, "Die Leute sagen im Grab sey Ruhe und Grab und Ruhe seyen eins. Wenn das ist, lieg' ich in deinem Schoß schon unter der Erde. Du süßes Grab, deine Lippen sind Todtenglocken, deine Stimme ist mein Grabgeläute, deine Brust mein Grabhügel und dein Herz mein Sarg" (p. 9). Tormented by an analogous state of mind, Leonce finds Lena's attraction in her close association with *Liebestod*. As he kisses her, he remarks, "Schöne Leiche, du ruhst so lieblich auf dem schwarzen Bahrtuch der Nacht, daß die Natur das Leben haßt und sich in den Tod verliebt" (p. 125). Homburg, another character not at home in reality, finds consolation in the nocturnal garden where the feminine night with her blond hair (an allusion to the moon shining through the trees) embraces him: "So legt ich hier in ihren Schoß mich nieder" (123). Similarly, Grillparzer's Medea has buried close to the sea, a symbolic manifestation of "das Große Runde", the dark deadly powers inherited from her mother, a priestess of Hecate, goddess of the underworld: "Versenkt hab ich sie [instruments of black magic], dir [Jason] zu Lieb versenkt, / Im finstern Schoß der mütterlichen Erde" (1872-73).

While the "Schoß der mütterlichen Erde" promises the sought-after peace of mind for some troubled souls, the Great Mother also has her independent, destructive side, "der verderbliche und tödliche Schoß" that manifests itself

---

[18] Cf. William C. Reeve: *In Pursuit of Power: Heinrich von Kleist's Machiavellian Protagonists*. Toronto 1987. Pp. 64f.

[19] Neumann. P. 165.

"am häufigsten in der archetypischen Form des zähnestarrenden Mundes", the motif of the *"vagina dentala"*.[20] This devouring maw draws life back into her body. The negative transformation of the female body has been attributed to the reluctance of the mother to release her children from her care and the resultant conflict when offspring seek release from an overprotective parent. This may also explain the ensnarling, enticing image of woman, her drive to maintain her influence over the male through her body: hence the beautiful female figure and its charms that arouse desire and lead to death. Men obsessed with women as sexual objects (Marie in *Woyzeck*, Penthesilea/Käthchen, Kunigunde in *König Ottokars Glück und Ende*) provide a theme common to all three dramatists. But perhaps the most explicit treatment of the correspondence between the physical allurement of the feminine body and sexual love occurs in *Die Jüdin*, a tragedy illustrating how a king loses all mastery over his own will despite all protestations to the contrary and succumbs to the temptation of sensuality exuded by a seductive Jewess. The relationship is almost exclusively physical. In the first act Rahel removes her scarf from around her neck in order to show off her breasts to greater advantage and seeks direct contact by pressing her cheek to Alphons's knee. The dramatist himself has supplied a commentary in his diary: "die schöne Jüdin [fällt] zu des Königs Füßen; ihre Arme umfaßen seine Füße, ihr üppiger Busen wogt an seine Kniee gepreßt und – der Schlag ist geschehn. Das Bild dieser schwellenden Formen, dieser wogenden Kugeln [...] verläßt ihn nicht mehr. Ungeheure Gärung in seinem Innern".[21] Her picture, which Alphons carries concealed next to his breast, denotes the power that her body exerts over him and the accompanying chain, emblematic of "das Große Runde", suggests his subjugation to her physical attributes. Commenting upon the force of habit, he inadvertently concedes his *sexuelle Hörigkeit*, his need to satisfy his corporeal needs: "Das Fortgesetzte steigert [Gewohnheit] zum Bedürfnis. / Ists *leiblich* doch auch anders nicht bestellt" (1468-69) and as a visual confirmation of his sexual subservience, after singling out Rahel's attractiveness in the presence of his wife: "Nun ja, die Augen! – Körper, Hals und Wuchs, / Das hat Gott wahrlich meisterhaft gefügt" (1479-80), he replaces chain and picture about his neck. Significantly, only her corpse, "Entstellt, verzerrt, wie sie [Alphons] mißfiel" (1938), can break the hold her sensual beauty has on him, a development theatrically signalled by his reappearance without her picture: "Das böse Bild ist fort von seinem Halse" (1820). In the king's own words, "sie war nicht schön. / [...] / Ein böser Zug um Wange, Kinn und Mund, / Ein lauernd Etwas in dem Feuerblick / Vergiftete, entstellte ihre Schönheit" (1848-51).[22] After Penthesilea has slaughtered Achilles, she outlines the same psy-

---

[20] Ibid. P. 165.

[21] Grillparzer: *Dramen*. Vol. 3. P. 848.

[22] Cf. Dieter Borchmeyer: Franz Grillparzer: *Die Jüdin von Toledo*. In: *Deutsche Dramen*. Ed. by Harro Müller-Michaels. Königstein 1981. Pp. 200-238, here p. 206;

chological process as described in Grillparzer's final play, one triggered by the mutilation of an erotically craved object:

> [...]   wer diesen Jüngling
> Das Ebenbild der Götter, so entstellt,
> Daß Leben und Verwesung sich nicht streiten,
> Wem er gehört, wer ihn so zugerichtet,
> Daß ihn das Mitleid nicht beweint, die Liebe
> Sich, die unsterbliche, gleich einer Metze,
> Im Tod noch untreu, von ihm wenden muß. (2929-35)

In *Die Jüdin* political expediency eliminates the *femme fatale,* but in other instances the voracious mouth with teeth, the devouring monster, can just as easily destroy life, either the defenceless male or the innocent child. Greek mythology issues an unequivocal warning when it groups together the goddesses of love, the hunt, and death. The shocking conclusion of *Penthesilea* has a predecessor in the Acteon myth according to which the latter youth observes the naked body of Artemis while bathing. Offended by this intrusion upon her modesty, the hunt goddess transforms Acteon into a stag which his own dogs pursue and tear to pieces under the eyes of the vengeful goddess. Penthesilea's thwarted passion likewise converts the lightly armed, unsuspecting Achilles into a stag: "Ha! sein Geweih verrät den Hirsch, ruft sie, / [...] / Und jagt den Pfeil ihm durch den Hals" (2645; 2649) and herself into one of the dogs who rip his body to shreds. As the *vagina dentala,* she becomes the death-inducing vessel of the Feminine: "Küsse, Bisse, / Das reimt sich, und wer recht von Herzen liebt, / Kann schon das eine für das andre greifen" (2981-83). Passion, aroused by the physical attraction of two bodies, when thwarted, leads to the sadomasochism of gratifying erotic drives by aggression and consuming the object of one's desire.[23] As noted earlier, eating the forbidden fruit has a long tradition of association with sexual intercourse. In Thusnelda's case from *Die Hermannsschlacht*, the act takes place vicariously: her substitute, a hungry female bear, literally devours the unarmed Ventidius, who, like Achilles, arrives in expectation of a lovers' tryst, while Thusnelda taunts her victim from the sidelines. In this same vein, since the female sea swallows the male

---

Karl Eibl: Ordnung und Ideologie im Spätwerk Grillparzers. Am Beispiel des *argumentum emblematicum* und der *Jüdin von Toledo*. In: DVjS 53 (1979). Pp. 74-95, here p. 90; Dagmar Lorenz: *Grillparzer. Dichter des sozialen Konflikts*. Vienna 1986. P. 110; Ian F. Roe: *An Introduction to the Major Works of Franz Grillparzer, 1791-1872, Austrian Dramatist*. Lewiston 1991. P. 256; George Albert Wells: *The Plays of Grillparzer*. London 1969. P. 141.

[23] Freud, among others, would describe these sexual aberrations at the beginning of the 20th century. See, for example, the first of the *Drei Abhandlungen zur Sexualtheorie*, "Die sexuellen Abirrungen", especially pp. 67f. (Studienausgabe vol. 5).

sun in the west, the rays of the sun correspond to the hair of the masculine deity. "Die Zusammengehörigkeit von Tod, Glatze, Opfer und Kastration ist für die Geweihten der Großen Mutter, von den kahlrasierten Isispriestern bis zur Tonsur der katholischen Mönche, charakteristisch".[24] This image of being consumed by the female body with the implication of castration takes on a special meaning in *Der zerbrochne Krug*: Adam's baldness, which he endeavours unsuccessfully to conceal with a wig, suggests his vulnerability, his sexual dependence on Eve which contributes substantially to his downfall.

Grillparzer's *Medea* presents another variation on the same theme, the terrible mother who eats her young. Once more, however, this occurs out of denied sexual love: Jason's preference for Kreusa over his wife. At one point the latter fantasizes the transformation of her children's tiny hands into animal claws in order to rend the body of her rival into pieces (1637f), but when her own flesh and blood turn against her: "Wenn ich bedenk, daß es mein eigen Blut, / Das Kind, das ich im eignen Schoß getragen" (2034-35), the Terrible Mother, as an act of revenge on her lover, destroys her own offspring, once more in imitation of a mythical protype, Althea, who slew her own son and thus "Die eignes Blut am eignen Blut gerächt" (1828). In a reaction similar to Prothoe's rejection of Penthesilea's atrocity, even Gora, Medea's faithful servant, cannot countenance her mistress's crime: "Die Kinder liegen tot in ihrem Blut, / Erwürgt von der, die sie gebar" (2177-78). Like the Amazon queen, Medea appears as the death-bearing vessel whose mouth spits forth annihilation upon her innocent children and the unsuspecting Kreusa: "Sah wie die Flamme, / Hervor sich wälzend aus dem *Goldgefäß*, / Nach ihr [Kreusa]" (2209-11).

The black fairy tale from *Woyzeck* puts forward this negative view of the female body as inimical to humankind in its most universal, mythological application. Our primitive ancestors, according to Neumann, shared a basic understanding of the cosmos dominated by the Great Mother:

> Die Sonne ist ein Sohn des weiblichen Tageshimmels, so wie der Mond ein Sohn des Nachthimmels ist. Der weibliche Himmel ist das Beständige, Fest-Stehende und Dauernde, die Lichter, Sonne ebenso wie Mond und Sterne, das Auf- und Absteigende, das innerhalb des schwarzweißen Welt-Eis des Großen Weiblichen Wandernde und Vergängliche (214).

Indeed, she swallows them up on a daily basis. When the child visits the celestial bodies, traditionally a source of hope and inspiration, he/she discovers their transient, perishable nature – the moon becomes a piece of rotten wood, the sun a withered sunflower and the stars dead insects transfixed on thorns. After he/she returns to the earth from a heaven dominated by death, "war die Erd ein umgestürzter Hafen" (p. 427). A child would expect

---

[24] Neumann. P. 163.

to receive support and nourishment from the mother, but the open, upper end of the vessel is here turned upside down and thus unable to fulfil its capacity as the nurturing maternal *Gefäß* of the earth. Büchner's nihilistic despair, epitomized by the grandmother's story, chooses to concentrate exclusively upon "das Große Runde" of heaven and earth as hostile and indifferent to the suffering of her children.

In my analysis of the body in the works of Kleist, Büchner and Grillparzer, I have employed Neumann's model of "die Große Mutter" as "Gefäß" to illustrate that, when one speaks of corporeality, almost inevitably the dramatists have the female figure in mind[25] with the emphasis upon sensual beauty and woman's closer affinity to the reproductive process and material existence. Since an archetype portrays a basic pattern of the human mind common to all races and all times, the vessel image, both in its positive, protective, and sustaining functions and in its negative, deadly, and devouring potential, can be readily discovered in the works of any writer in any given period. One has only to turn to Goethe's *Faust* – the speech of the Erdgeist (501-09) or "Gretchen, am Spinnrade" – to ascertain other variations on the same theme. But the authors singled out here do offer a different slant: a greater awareness of the female body in its various archetypal transformations as it relates to the unconscious and to human sexuality, topics that social etiquette and the prevalent moral values abetted by censorship chose not to air publicly. It is no accident that most of the dramas under examination either could not be performed in their original form or were largely ignored or misunderstood until the 20th century.

As a concluding case in point to demonstrate how a writer can take advantage of an archetype to convey a prohibited erotic theme, I shall turn to an acclaimed masterpiece of the *Novelle* genre. *Der arme Spielmann* enjoyed little popularity in the 19th century, but 20th-century critics have praised it as inherently 'modern'.[26] Since Jakob's highly disciplined, prudish upbringing would never permit him to view a woman as sexually desirable, he has discovered in music an admissible sublimation to satisfy his needs. The narrator's description of his improvisation features libidinously flavoured language such as "genuß-reich", or "das [...] wollüstige Schmecken".[27] "Der Alte genoß, indem er spielte" (III p. 156). As a child Jakob hated the violin because he was not allowed to play without a score, i.e., to

---

[25] There are notable exceptions. Sappho is physically attracted to Phaon's beautiful body: "Des Leibes Schönheit ist ein Gut" (264) just as Penthesilea feels drawn to Achilles as "Das Ebenbild der Götter (2930).

[26] Cf. Roy C. Cowan: The History of a Neglected Masterpiece: *Der arme Spielmann*. In: *Grillparzer's* Der arme Spielmann. Ed. by Clifford A. Bernd. Columbia S.C. 1988. Pp. 9-26.

[27] Franz Grillparzer: *Sämtliche Werke*. Ed. by Peter Frank and Karl Pörnbacher. Vol. 3. Munich 1960. P. 155. All subsequent references to *Der arme Spielmann* will be drawn from this edition.

abandon himself to the pleasure principle. Years later a folksong sung by a "Weibsperson" (III p. 162) leads to the rediscovery of his instrument, again conveyed with sensual diction: "Die Luft um mich war wie geschwängert mit Trunkenheit" (III p. 162) and reaching an erotic climax expressed in revealing gestures: "[Ich] küßte die Violine und drückte sie an mein Herz und spielte wieder und fort" (3: p. 162). "All seine zurückgestaute Erotik bricht hier durch und vereinigt ihn mit seinem Instrument, wie er sich nie mit Barbara wird vereinigen können".[28] An archaic abbreviation of the primordial goddess and traceable back as far as 2500 B.C. as an ancient female figure, the violin's shape represents yet another manifestation of the vessel archetype (see Ill. 1 and 2). This body fulfils Jakob's unconscious craving for a means to express vicariously his repressed vitality, one which 19th-century Viennese social convention would deem more acceptable.[29]

---

[28] Heinz Politzer. *Franz Grillparzer oder Das abgründige Biedermeier*. Vienna 1972. P. 381.

[29] Significantly Jakob only once has contact with Barbara's body – he seizes her waist – but solely as the transmitter of his song. When he tries to kiss her, it occurs through a pane of glass, a situation reflecting his impotence in the real world. At the end of the century (1896-97) another Viennese dramatist, Arthur Schnitzler, would be bold enough to deal with the female body and human sexuality in a more explicit manner (*Reigen*).

Illustration 1

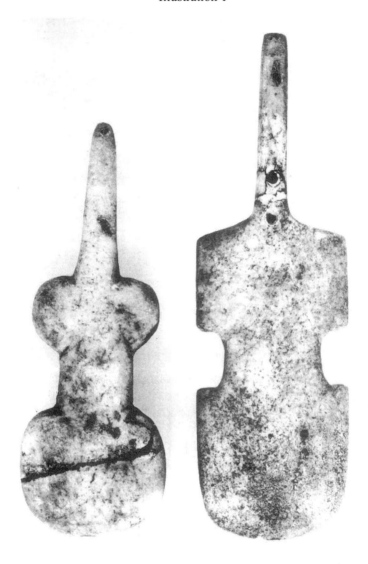

FEMALE FIGURINES
Marble, Cyclades, c. 2500 B.C.

"Female Figurines"
Erich Neumann: *The Great Mother*. ©1995. ©1963 by Bollingen Foundation Inc. Reprinted with the permission of Princeton University Press.

Illustration 2

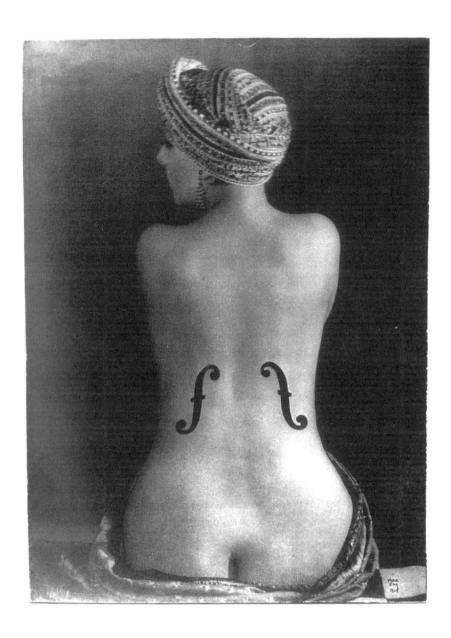

Man Ray: "Le Violon d'Ingres" (1924)
©Estate of Man Ray/ADAGP (Prais / SODRAC (Montreal) 2002.

Jane V. Curran

Bodily Grace and Consciousness: from the Enlightenment to Romanticism

The mechanistic view of the soul as an extension of the body, propounded by de la Mettrie in 1747, finds later variations in Schiller's theory of grace in Anmut und Würde *(1793), in Kleist's* Über das Marionettentheater *(1810) and in Hoffmann's* Der Sandmann *(1815). Schiller binds body and soul in his definition of physical grace; Kleist first removes and then reinstates consciousness as a requisite for grace. Finally, Hoffmann tells of a failed alliance between consciousness and the mechanical.*

The logical methods of inquiry and deduction introduced during the Enlightenment, and the emphasis on empirical evidence as the basis for certain knowledge, inclined the age towards a mechanistic explanation both of the creation of the world and of the origins of the human being. A further consequence was that an increased degree of interest focused on the workings of the world and the mechanics of the human being. One of the more radical philosophical views about the composition of human beings was put forward by the French philosopher Julien Offray de la Mettrie, who pushed beyond Cartesian body-soul dualism in his essay *L'homme machine* of 1747. De la Mettrie argues against the assumption he attributes to Leibniz and Descartes and his followers, that man is composed of two distinct substances. They assert this, he says, as though they had actually seen the two parts and counted them. The title of de la Mettrie's essay alone sums up his own stance very succinctly: we are organised mechanically, he says, like clocks: "Le corps n'est qu'une horloge".[1] Each part is dependent upon the operation of all other parts through a motion evocative of a clock's pendulum; de la Mettrie fittingly describes it as "oscillation". Descartes had already established the comparison between the human body and an automaton but now de la Mettrie extends the metaphor so that it will hold true not only for our physical, but for our spiritual dimension as well. He is guided in this matter by empirical observation alone, and he is persuaded that the senses reveal spiritual as well as material things. He provides several instances which show how physical indisposition affects the spirits and how, on the other hand, physical signs indicate feelings when, for example, the circulation of the blood quickens in response to emotional change. In short, consciousness and sensations are, for de la Mettrie, simply a variation within matter or an extension from it. I shall argue that the problematics of bodily grace in relation to consciousness, as expressed by German writers of the eighteenth and nineteenth

---

[1] Julien Offray de la Mettrie: *Man a Machine* (French-English). La Salle, Illinois 1988. P. 65.

centuries through the vehicle of the mechanical being, have their origins in de la Mettrie's explanation of the relationship between the physical and the spiritual.

From de la Mettrie's position one needs only to take a small step to imagine constructing a mechanically correct physical being whose heartbeat and circulation would call forth a corresponding emotion.[2] The possibility of creating a mechanical body, and the conceivable consequences of such an act, fascinate poets and thinkers alike, in the eighteenth and well into the nineteenth century. For a poetic expression of the new-found freedom from the orthodox concept of God as sole creator, one need look no further than Goethe's poem 'Prometheus'. There the figure of Prometheus celebrates the new understanding of the poet as autonomous self, with productive powers, and capable of creating in his own right. What used to be the preserve of the divine is now firmly grasped by the human; the supernatural is reduced to the level of nature. However, when the focus shifts from the creator to the object created, the mechanistic view is expressed through examples which show the difficulty in determining the boundaries between the mechanical and the real. Goethe's flesh and blood Mignon in *Wilhelm Meisters Lehrjahre* (1795/96) is repeatedly described using phrases suggesting marionettes and wind-up devices. Although human, she is jerky and puppetlike in her movements ("wie Pulcinellpuppen"; "wie es eigentlich nur Holzpuppen aushalten können").[3] In a special dance routine, Mignon accompanies herself on the castanets, whose clacking sound further emphasizes her mechanical execution of the steps, and she moves as "relentlessly as clockwork" (unaufhaltsam, wie ein Uhrwerk"),[4] as the narrator observes. The division within Mignon is symbolised by her ambiguous appearance, her insistence on wearing male clothing. It is also reflected in her inarticulate pattern of speech and her penchant for gnomic utterances. Only in song can she make clear her awareness of the difficulty of communication between the inner and the outer part, as she sings of her fatal inhibitions: "Ich möchte dir mein ganzes Innre zeigen / Allein das Schicksal will es nicht"[5] Although not literally mechanical, Mignon suffers from another form of the fundamental dualism which constitutes the central tension between the body and consciousness in the main works under discussion here: Kleist's essay *Über das Marionettentheater* and E. T. A. Hoffmann's story *Der Sandmann*.

[2] Frank Wittig: *Maschinenmenschen. Zur Geschichte eines literarischen Motivs im Kontext von Philosophie, Naturwissenschaft und Technik.* Würzburg 1997 (Epistemata. Reihe Literaturwissenschaft 212). P. 18.

[3] Johann Wolfgang Goethe: *Werke.* Ed. by Erich Trunz. Vol. VII. Hamburg 1965. P. 326.

[4] Goethe: *Werke.* Vol. VII. P. 116.

[5] Goethe: *Werke.* Vol. VII. P. 356. In a discussion of *Der Sandmann*, Jochen Schmidt lists the two characters Mignon and the Harper as stages on the route from the heyday of the autonomous poetic genius to the realization that this autonomy is a dangerous curse: *Die Geschichte des Genie-Gedankens in der deutschen Literatur, Philosophie und Politik 1750-1945.* Vol. 2. Darmstadt 1985. P. 24.

De la Mettrie implies that a mechanical construction might include the potential production of emotional or spiritual responses, and this suggestion goes hand in hand with the contemporary Promethean optimism which prompted many experiments in, and a degree of obsession with, the artificial construction of a human being. There were some intriguing endeavours, such as the writing android presented by Friedrich von Knauss in Vienna in 1760, Wolfgang von Kempelen's chess-playing automaton (1768), or the lady playing the harmonium constructed by Pierre and Henri-Louis Jaquet-Droz in 1774, but two particularly controversial ones to catch the public's attention were a mechanical flute-player and an anatomically accurate duck – the work of Jacques de Vaucanson in the 1730s.[6] Commentators on these creations included Voltaire and de la Mettrie himself, who both drew an explicit parallel between Vaucanson and Prometheus.

Following in the wake of the mechanical creations, a series of literary examples emerges from the recurring motif of an inanimate, artificial figure taking on, or seeming to take on life. This phenomenon derives from the premise inherited from de la Mettrie that the physiological aspect of a human being shows visible signs or expressions of the inner or psychological disposition and that communication occurs between the outer and the inner. This gives rise to literary examples of physical constructions so skillfully undertaken that it would not be far beyond the realm of the possible to imagine that a being could in fact be produced in which body and soul cohered. Such fabricated literary beings include the magic but soulless golem threatening to impede the course of true love in Achim von Arnim's novella *Isabella von Ägypten* (1812), Frankenstein's artificial monster that runs amok in the novel by Mary Shelley (1818) and Homunculus, the spiritual test-tube baby in Goethe's *Faust II* (1832). More specifically, there arose among German Romantic writers what amounted to a veritable mania for marionettes, puppets and artificial women.[7] Their provenance can be traced back to the deliberations of Descartes, de la Mettrie and others, who tried to capture in words a rational explanation of the relationship between the soul and the body.

The important question for these later, literary approaches to the issue introduced by Descartes and refined by de la Mettrie is how to identify the role of consciousness in relation to the physical movements in an artificial being. For Friedrich Schiller, the presence of reflective consciousness is made clear through bodily grace (*Anmut*) – that quality which differentiates itself from purely nature-given beauty in that it adds to that natural beauty the dimension of subjective consciousness. For Heinrich von Kleist, the task involves the discovery of the source of graceful movement in animate and inanimate beings. And E. T. A.

---

[6] The importance of the duck's contribution to discussions about the meaning of the body in the eighteenth century is examined by Daniel Cottom in his article The Work of Art in the Age of Mechanical Digestion. In: *Representations* 66 (Spring 1999). P. 52-74.

[7] Gerhard Storz: *Klassik und Romantik. Eine stilgeschichtliche Darstellung*. Mannheim 1972. P. 216.

Hoffmann offers an ironic and despairing tale of a young man's failure to make the crucial distinction between mechanical and conscious physical grace.

In his essay *Über das Marionettentheater*, Heinrich von Kleist appears at first to be arguing somewhat provocatively for the superiority of the mechanical creature over the human being. He takes the evident and inimitable grace of the marionette's movements as the starting point of a dialogue between the narrator and a certain Herr C., in which the topic discussed is the relation between reflection and artistic production. Herr C. ultimately suggests that the grace of an inanimate or unreflecting agent can be recreated by taking the journey back to a prelapsarian state, but only through a route forged by consciousness. In E. T. A. Hoffmann's *Der Sandmann*, the mechanical doll Olimpia appears human, and has the poor poet Nathanael in thrall, whereas his fiancée suddenly seems predictable and routine in her habits. Nathanael's inability to identify Olimpia as non-human can be read as Hoffmann's ironic comment on the question of body-soul dualism posed by the Enlightenment.

Kleist argues, in part, for a position which regards the separation from self entailed by reflection as constituting the main hindrance for self conscious beings aiming at attaining natural grace. In doing so he takes up a stance against Idealism. Idealist aesthetics had defined grace as something more than a natural phenomenon. In Schiller's essay *Anmut und Würde*, he develops the view that grace is more than a beauty granted by nature, it can only be the kind of beauty which the subject itself produces. "Anmut ist eine Schönheit, die nicht von der Natur gegeben, sondern von dem Subjekte selbst hervorgebracht wird".[8] Schiller introduces a distinction between grace as present in a body and static, plastic beauty.

Mignon's disjointed nature means that her attempts at physical grace, through dance, too often resemble the mechanical movements of a puppet. Her death is remarkable too, in that the funeral rites and preparation of the body for burial are so elaborate that she is placed in the sarcophagus not simply as a corpse, rather, her body is described as a work of art.[9] In other words, the human being is presented as an artificial construct, like a puppet made of wood. In life, one might say, Mignon was incapable of graceful movements because she never overcame mind and body dualism. In her case, the soul is not an extension of the body, as de la Mettrie believed, and there is no communication between the two; in Schiller's terms, she lacks grace because her physical movements are not an expression of her subjective consciousness.

A much later source of theoretical remarks comparing performances by puppets and by their human equivalents reveals a continued interest in the question in the twentieth century. In his book *On the Art of the Theatre*, the actor and stage director Edward Gordon Craig claims an almost divine status for the pup-

---

[8] *Schillers Werke*. Nationalausgabe. Vol. 21/I: *Philosophische Schriften*. Ed. by Benno von Wiese and Helmut Koopman. Weimar 1963. P. 255.

[9] Helmut Ammerlahn: Puppe-Tänzer-Dämon-Genius-Engel. Naturkind, Poesiekind und Kunstwerdung bei Goethe. In: *German Quarterly* 54 (1981). P. 26.

pet. He maintains it is "a descendant of the stone images of the old temples [...] a rather degenerate form of a god. There is something more than a flash of genius in the marionette", he says, "and there is something in him more than the flashiness of displayed personality".[10] He points out that whereas an actor is always disguised, the puppet is made to order and can coincide exactly with what it represents. Craig may well have had Kleist's essay *Über das Marionettentheater* in mind when arguing for the marionette's superior technique, since there the grace of the inanimate marionette is judged to be superior to what a human dancer can achieve. The puppet's movements are natural, claims Kleist's Herr C., precisely because of a total lack of consciousness; they are only partly constrained by the law of gravity, a natural law. A performance by a human dancer, on the other hand, is always a pose, always affected. Another basis for its elevated status is that a marionette barely needs to do more than sweep across the floor, whereas a ballet dancer is bound to it and can break free only for brief moments and only with great expenditure of effort. Thus, ironically, only the marionette is capable of expressing human nature, because it combines technical perfection with nature in the form of the law of gravity.[11] The "soul" of the marionette and its movements are in a harmonious union. The marionette's effortless grace and tireless execution are compared to the state of mankind before the Fall. In fact, the speaker claims that only a god or a marionette could achieve this grace.

Kleist's essay is composed in the form of a dialogue. The narrator reports that he started the discussion by asking Herr C., an accomplished dancer with the opera, why he is so fascinated by the puppet theatre in the marketplace, given that vastly superior theatre and opera performances are readily available. So this initial inquiry goes straight to the heart of the problem: the comparison of graceful movements in puppets and in human beings. The dialogue form, inherited from Plato, allows one speaker to put forward remarkable theories in response to the other's questions. It also allows the overall argument to move forward dialectically, in a pattern that fittingly reflects those very same swinging movements by the puppets working against the center of gravity which constitute the topic under discussion. There are two more parts to this conversation. Both are anecdotes which illustrate the point that self consciousness and reason place human beings at an aesthetic disadvantage. In the first instance, a young man unconsciously adopts the pose depicted by the ancient and famous Roman marble statue of a boy removing a thorn from his foot. Repeated attempts to recapture the pose consciously are fruitless, and the young man is corrupted, in the end, by his own vanity. In the last part, the story is about Herr C. himself, how he first defeated his host in a fencing match with the greatest of ease and then was persuaded to test his fencing skills further in competition with a

---

[10] Edward Gordon Craig: *On the Art of the Theatre.* London 1911. P. 82.

[11] Rolf-Peter Janz: Die Marionette als Zeugin der Anklage. Zu Kleists Abhandlung *Über das Marionettentheater*. In: *Kleists Dramen. Neue Interpretationen.* Ed. by Walter Hinderer. Stuttgart 1981. P. 33.

trained bear. He relates how effortlessly the bear defeated him. The mismatch arises because the bear's instinctive reactions grant him a considerable advantage over his rational human opponent. The animal's reflexes are automatic, its posture and stance are innate and it can even sense the difference between his human opponent's real attacks and those he is simply feigning.

The episode involving the boy who cannot capture the grace of a statue is apparently a negative comment on Weimar classicism and its aesthetic ideal of mimesis. Here is a clear reference to Winckelmann's elevation of Greek sculpture as a cultural high point which successive generations would do well to emulate. For Kleist, conscious imitation cannot be successful, since it restricts the freedom of nature. The young man is consumed by the determination to recreate that first moment and consequently becomes narcissistically obsessed with himself. The development of obsessive self-consciousness is very clearly demonstrated in the story, since the young man spends hours in front of a mirror, the time-honored symbol of reflective consciousness. The young man loses his balance, both physically and mentally.[12] Gone is the Enlightenment confidence in reason and observation as the forces which will free us from the tyrannies of nature and fate. Kleist reveals rational consciousness itself as a tyrannizing force over subjectivity, usurping the role of fate. To express this in Schiller's aesthetic terms: in Kleist's story of the fencing bear, the naive triumphs over the sentimental. The attempt on the part of reason to subjugate nature is doomed to failure.

In each of the three comparisons, the rational human being is at a disadvantage. The statue wins with static grace and the bear parries and thrusts out of an innate instinct for survival. The marionette, however, is dependent on a force outside itself – the puppeteer – to provide the initial impetus which will allow its superior grace to be demonstrated. The puppet's relation to the puppeteer is analogous to man's relation to God before the fall, as Kleist's character suggests. Only a puppet or a god is capable of such grace, according to Herr C., and one remembers that Gordon Craig also relates the two, by describing the puppet as an effigy of a divine being.

In Kleist's *Über das Marionettentheater*, despite the anecdotal content and dialogic form, the reader finds a strong component of aesthetic theory for which the conversation provides a fictional frame. The Socratic figure in this latter-day Platonic dialogue does not argue simply that rationality places the human player at a disadvantage. His implicit criticism of the classicist aesthetics of Winckelmann and his followers is a step towards the idealist "final chapter" with which he will conclude. The championing of the puppet, with its graceful but unconscious movements is quite possibly a comment on Schiller's position, since it flies in the face of his assertion that beauty without consciousness is not a match for the grace that adheres in beings endowed with subjective conscious-

---

[12] The action-reflection axis is nicely summed up as a loss of balance, attributable to consciousness, in Martin Coles: Heinrich von Kleist: The Quest for Grace and Purity. In: *Theatre History Studies* 6 (1986). Pp. 189-198, here p. 189.

ness. While the upper hand in *Über das Marionettentheater* consistently belongs to the side of instinct or the inanimate, it is also the case that the puppet, because it is identical with its own purpose, is a symbol of the divine. In the puppet's relation to the puppeteer lies the obvious analogy with the relation between man and God.[13] The puppet is affected only very slightly by the law of gravity, which epitomizes the earthly condition, because its movements, once set in motion, are stronger than that law.

Kleist's character Herr C. does ultimately offer a solution to the impasse, and yet even the solution is not free of interpretative difficulties. He suggests a way to bridge the fundamental gap between the inner and outer worlds which the image of the puppeteer first introduced. This final stage, then, is a return to the Garden of Eden, as Kleist has his two characters agree. Inevitably, the reader is led to ask how it is possible for those who, like the youth imitating the statue, are already ruined by the gift of self-reflection, to re-enter the original state of innocence? The second act of partaking of the fruit of the Tree of the Knowledge of Good and Evil is referred to as the last chapter in the history of the world. Some critics see this statement as ambivalent: it could either mean the end of the world or the completion of history.[14] Others ask whether Kleist, perhaps unwittingly, is in fact advocating, under the mask of progress, a route which describes a vicious circle.[15]

In order to approach that final question, it is necessary first to determine what a god and a jointed puppet actually have in common and what leads Kleist to refer to them in the same context. Self-identity is the key to the argument here: a god, by reason of being undifferentiated spirit, and a marionette, for the opposite reason that it completely lacks spirit, both enjoy unmediated self-identity. As Gordon Craig put it, the puppet coincides exactly with the purpose for which it was manufactured. But then how do the other two examples, the stories of the boy with the statue and of the fencing bear fit into the scheme?

The statue, of course, is a work of art – not in itself an example of natural grace – and the boy, in attempting to imitate it, is trying to be as he was the first time, to adopt the same attitude he held in that initial, instinctive pose. He is trying to be identical with himself.

The fencer fights first against his host, whom he easily defeats, and then agrees to take on the bear. His aim is to be evenly matched with his opponent, but this aim is not within his grasp; he cannot reproduce the instinctive reflexes of the animal. An absolutely even match between two opponents would be a symbol of that same sought-after self-identity.

[13] Hermann Reske: *Traum und Wirklichkeit im Werk Heinrich von Kleists*. Stuttgart 1969. P. 51.

[14] Andrea Gnam: Die Rede über den Körper. Zum Körperdiskurs in Kleists Texten *Die Marquise von O…* und *Über das Marionettentheater*. In: *Heinrich von Kleist*. Ed. by Heinz Ludwig Arnold. Munich 1992 (Text und Kritik). P. 172.

[15] Ilse Graham: *Heinrich von Kleist. Word into Flesh: A Poet's Quest for the Symbol*. Berlin 1977. P. 26.

Reason, or the capacity for reflection, prevents both the human dancer from attaining grace and the boy from reproducing the statue's pose. It is this reason also which impedes the instinctive moments in a thinking being and allows the unreflecting bear to triumph over its human fencing partner.

The relation between consciousness, grace and the mechanical is a central theme in Hoffmann's novella *Der Sandmann*. The doll Olimpia is, like the marionettes in Kleist's work, another accomplished dancer. Nathanael has never had a dancing partner who could so flawlessly keep in step with the rhythm, and he cannot imagine why the young men are not lining up to ask her for the next dance. She also plays the piano to perfection and can sing an aria in tones as pure as tinkling glass. At first touch, her hand is as cold as ice, but it gains warmth as he holds it. In reply to his declarations of love, she repeatedly replies, "Ach, ach!" When Nathanael's friend Siegmund, masking his incredulity at Nathanael's obsession with an empty-headed automaton, asks him a few questions, he receives the most remarkable answers. Nathanael admits that Olimpia speaks very little – another characteristic, incidentally, that she shares with Mignon – but claims that her utterances are like hieroglyphs from an inner world of love, they express a knowledge of the spiritual life gained through contemplation of the beyond.[16]

> Sie spricht wenig Worte, das ist wahr, aber diese wenigen Worte erscheinen als echte Hieroglyphe der innern Welt voll Liebe und hoher Erkenntnis des geistigen Lebens in der Anschauung des ewigen Jenseits.[17]

The trouble is that Nathanael already has a fiancée, whose name is Clara.[18] Nathanael loves Clara and finds in her only one fault: she needs constant entertainment, and finds it boring when he reads his (admittedly mediocre) poems out to her. In a moment of exasperation, he curses her as a damned lifeless automaton: "Du lebloses, verdammtes Automat!"[19] This is a cruel but crucial line in the story: for Nathanael, despite the evidence of his fascination with Olimpia and consequent neglect of Clara, the living woman and the lifeless machine have not only changed places, they have become in principle interchangeable. Just as Olimpia needs the physical warmth of his touch to become

---

[16] Hoffmann admired the work of Novalis, and the evaluation of Olimpia's speech is reminiscent of some of the Fragments. To take one example, "Das wird die goldene Zeit seyn, wenn alle Worte – *Figurenworte* – Mythen – und alle Figuren – Sprachfiguren – Hieroglyfen seyn werden – wenn man Figuren sprechen und schreiben – und Worte vollkommen plastisiren, und musiciren lernt": *Novalis Werke*. Ed. by Gerhard Schulz. Munich 1969. P. 437.

[17] E. T. A. Hoffmann: *Fantasie- und Nachtstücke*. Munich 1967. Pp. 356-357.

[18] The name Clara is certainly intended to be significant. See Rudolf Drux: *E. T. A. Hoffmann. Der Sandmann. Erläuterungen und Dokumente*. Stuttgart 1994. P. 5. Drux interprets Clara as the representative of the Enlightenment position.

[19] Hoffmann: *Fantasie- und Nachtstücke*. P. 348.

warm herself, so Clara needs the stimulation of his intellect in order to become animated.

Nathanael first caught sight of Olimpia at a distance; the second viewing was enhanced by the purchase of a telescope from a demonic glass merchant. Eyes and sight are a powerful motif in the story: Nathanael seems unaware for quite some time that Olimpia's eyes stare straight ahead without expression. At the moment of her destruction, when her eyes fall out as the result of a struggle and he has a vision of them lying bloody on the floor, Nathanael finally apprehends the truth: that she is only a lifeless doll. After Nathanael's recovery from the shock, everything returns to normal for a while and relations with Clara are harmonious again. The reversal comes when Clara and Nathanael climb a tower to enjoy the view from above and Nathanael happens to catch Clara in the sight of his telescope. This repetition of the way he once viewed Olimpia unhinges him and triggers an immediate reaction. He calls out a command to Clara, addressing her as a puppet, "'Holzpüppchen, dreh dich'" and attacks her. The failure to distinguish between Clara and Olimpia proves fatal this time. Clara narrowly escapes, rescued by her brother, but Nathanael plunges to his death. In a final vignette, it is reported that Clara had been seen standing in front of an attractive farmhouse, holding hands with a pleasant man, while two lively little boys played beside them.

Earlier on, the narrator, with heavy irony, had described a general movement among couples, based on the view that Nathanael's story could be seen as a didactic tale. The young woman, it is suggested, purposely sings a little offbeat and makes sure to engage in some activity, such as knitting or playing with a lap-dog while being read to, so that the young man can be reassured that he has not fallen in love with a wooden doll. The effect of the irony is particularly poignant, because it was precisely Clara's engagement in the mechanical activity of knitting while Nathanael recited his poems which led to his rejection and condemnation of her. Mechanical actions most emphatically do not offer a reassurance of the presence of spiritual life. It is clear, then, that Hoffman's stance is ironic and cynical. *Der Sandmann* is a complex tale, multi-faceted and laden with motifs and themes. It is partly a parody of a faddish preoccupation with simulacra currently raging among his contemporaries.[20] It is also social satire, since Nathanael's delusions are symptomatic of a whole society where respect for technical accomplishment has taken on grotesque proportions. But the opposite extreme, bourgeois domesticity – based on trusting empiricism untroubled by any doubts about the relation between consciousness and reality – is also unsatisfactory, as Hoffmann makes abundantly clear. His character Clara embodies this principle, and the mocking tone of the final tableau is impossible to overlook. Hoffmann endows his protagonist, Nathanael, with the qualities of the Romantic artist – sensitive, inward-looking – but then appears to turn on

---

[20] Hanne Castein: 'Zerrbilder des Lebens'. E. T. A. Hoffmann's *Der Sandmann* and the Robot Heritage. In: PEGS 67 (1997). Pp. 43-54, here p. 46.

him, and give preference to the more prosaic middle class values represented by Clara.

Not only does this tale caricature the whole concept of La Mettrie's "l'homme machine", it also turns a critical eye on the Romantic cult of the artist as an effusive, rapturous and ultra-sensitive young man. Through the vehicle of Nathanael's madness, Hoffmann's irony addresses the question of the graceful artificial body in its relation to subjective consciousness.[21]

Nathanael is unable to distinguish between Olimpia, who only lives for him,[22] and Clara. Only in his perception do the doll's eyes sparkle with love, and he does not seem to realize that it is the warmth of his own body which imparts a pulse to her artificial hands. Her supposedly spiritual thoughts, an expression of her connection to the spiritual life ("voll [...] hoher Erkenntnis des geistigen Lebens") are a product of his own projection. The distinction between inner and outer worlds collapses into Nathanael's own subjectivity. He can perceive the doll as something living only because he himself gives life to it, both in the physical transfer of warmth and in the endowment of consciousness, courtesy of Nathanael's powers of imagination.

There are many possibilities for analysing Olimpia. She could be the allegory of nature, society, even of language.[23] But since Nathanael animates her, he is on one level her creator, and so she also stands for his life as a poet. In Olimpia's presence, Nathanael is inspired and starts to babble incomprehensibly, "in Worten, die keiner verstand, weder er, noch Olimpia".[24] Clara, by contrast, who is sometimes criticized for being prosaic, is the negation of the poetic. "Clara wurde [...] von vielen [...] prosaisch gescholten."[25] Nathanael is unable to reconcile the life of the imagination with the real world, and the unbearable tension between the two is the cause of his downfall.[26] He does not simply deny the existence of the world outside the self, nor does he undertake a restless motion between the two spheres. He fails unequivocally to distinguish one from the other. As a solution to the problem of overcoming the separation between inner and outer worlds, madness is hardly satisfactory. But then neither is the philistine attitude presented by Clara, whose true aim is uncomplicated

---

[21] Both Romanticism's critique of materialism and Hoffmann's critique of Romanticism are confirmed by Silvio Vietta: Das Automatenmotiv und die Technik der Motivschichtung im Erzählwerk E. T. A. Hoffmanns. In: *Mitteilungen der E. T. A. Hoffmann-Gesellschaft* 26 (1980). Pp. 25-33, here p. 28, 30.

[22] Peter von Matt: *Die Augen der Automaten. E. T. A. Hoffmanns Imaginationslehre als Prinzip seiner Erzählkunst.* Tübingen 1971. P. 85.

[23] Von Matt. P. 85.

[24] Hoffmann. P. 355.

[25] Hoffmann. P. 345.

[26] Jochen Schmidt: Die Krise der romantischen Subjektivität: E. T. A. Hoffmanns Künstlernovelle 'Der Sandmann' in historischer Perspektive. In: *Literaturwissenschaft und Geistesgeschichte. Festschrift für Richard Brinkmann.* Tübingen 1981. P. 370.

bourgeois domesticity.[27] The attempts here to subsume the objective phenomena of life under subjective poetic consciousness, the goal of Romanticism, lead to the ruination of both life and art.[28] Nathanael as a typical sensitive Romantic poet is presented ironically[29] and the realisation that it is the artificial, not the living woman who inspires Nathanael undermines the Romantic cult of woman as muse. So not only is materialism parodied, Romanticism is not allowed to stand unchallenged either. Hoffmann offers perspectives, and cynical observations, but no clear-cut solution.[30]

Reason and reflection inevitably presuppose a separation from self, as was tragically clear in the example of Mignon, in the case of the boy comparing himself to the statue, in the story of the fencer who cannot simply react instinctively and finally in Nathanael's failure to hold onto distinctions. The separation from self, entailed by reflection, is what hinders self conscious beings from attaining natural grace. Idealism defines grace as something more than a natural phenomenon. In Schiller's essay *Anmut und Würde* he stresses the part played by the soul in producing graceful movements: "Wo also Anmut stattfindet, da ist die Seele das bewegende Prinzip, und in ihr ist der Grund von der Schönheit der Bewegung enthalten".[31] Schiller introduces a distinction between grace as present in a body and static, plastic beauty, a distinction of particular relevance to the example of the boy imitating the statue. Just as Kleist shows examples of the loss of grace as the consequence of a separation from self through consciousness, so Schiller sees the presence of true physical grace only when consciousness is an integral part of the body.[32] Is there any reason to be found within Kleist's essay for thinking that in his view of physical grace he ultimately subscribes to and advocates the Schillerian definition of grace?

The form of the essay is worth considering. It is not a dialogue pure and simple, but a reported, or mediated, dialogue. It has been reflected upon, and the narrator intersperses his comments and reactions within the narrative.[33] This alerts us as readers to the fact that we are not compelled to accept the viewpoint of Herr C. Indeed, the anecdotes he chooses in order to elaborate on his theme are not unequivocally supportive of the premise that reflective consciousness

[27] Wolfgang Preisendanz: Eines matt geschliffenen Spiegels dunkler Widerschein. E. T. A. Hoffmanns Erzählkunst. In: *E. T. A. Hoffmann* (Wege der Forschung). Ed. by Helmut Prang. Darmstadt 1976. P. 279.

[28] Schmidt: Die Krise der romantischen Subjektivität. P. 352.

[29] Ulrich Hohoff: *E. T. A Hoffmann. Der Sandmann. Text, Edition, Kommentar.* Berlin 1988. P. 314.

[30] Preisendanz. P. 287.

[31] *Schillers Werke.* Vol. 21/I: *Philosophische Schriften.* P. 255.

[32] "Grace differs from architectonic beauty in that the intelligible is genuinely integrated into the graceful body, is indeed constitutive of the body, which can thus shine with its own light". David Pugh: *Dialectic of Love. Platonism in Schiller's Aesthetics.* Montreal 1996. P. 255.

[33] Helmut J. Schneider: Dekonstruktion des hermeneutischen Körpers. Kleists Aufsatz *Über das Marionettentheater* und der Diskurs der klassischen Ästhetik. In: *Kleist-Jahrbuch* (1988). P. 160.

inhibits physical grace. After all, none of those three examples – the puppet, the statue and the trained bear – is an example of nature in its purest form. The puppet is manufactured, the statue has been chiseled by a sculptor and the bear is tethered, and has been trained to stand on its hind legs. The conscious re-entry into the Garden of Eden and the second bite of the apple do not, then, in the end, constitute a contradiction of the position outlined so far, but rather a successful final stage to the dialectical movement of the work.[34]

Kleist's *Über das Marionettentheater*, then, situates the argument for the absence of consciousness as a defining characteristic of grace within the context of a conversation. The proposed final solution, although more abstract than the exchange has been up to this point nevertheless makes use of an image: the Garden of Eden. Kleist's character sees that the journey back to the Garden of Eden can be undertaken only via reflective consciousness. What Schiller had made clear is that an awareness that the quality of physical grace is present is much more than straightforward admiration for mechanical ingenuity, rather, it requires the recognizable presence of spirit. Correspondingly, doubts about the presence of grace in a mechanical being are not equivalent to the scepticism born of suspicion that a trick is being played on the beholder.

The mechanical being, championed by the Enlightenment, is still undiminished in its fascination for writers of the Romantic period, like Hoffmann and Kleist.

The relationship between body and soul, as introduced by Enlightenment thinkers, and de la Mettrie's view of the soul as an extension of the body could not be made concrete by mechanical creations, because either grace or mental balance would inevitably be forfeited. In Schiller's definition of grace, the theory acquires a firmer footing: for him, the synthesis of body and reflective consciousness is the prerequisite for physical grace. Precisely this synthesis is what Mignon lacks. Physical grace becomes temporarily suspended, disconnected from that requisite consciousness in Kleist's essay before being reintroduced in the final solution. Finally, a new problem-laden dualism asserts itself when E. T. A. Hoffmann depicts the body-soul synthesis as paradoxical and untenable.

---

[34] This feature of the structure is examined in Brian Keith-Smith: Heinrich von Kleist's *Über das Marionettentheater* – Coincidence of Opposites or Dialectical Structure? In: *New German Studies* 12.3 (1984). Pp. 175-199.

Appendix

Wilhelmine von Gersdorf

Die Horatier und Curiatier,
eine dramatische Skizze aus der römischen Geschichte

Herausgegeben von Gaby Pailer

Ruhe beglücke die Seelen der Helden!
Nahmhaft war in Gefahren ihr Muth!
Sie sollen von Wolken getragen
Schweben um mich!
Oßians Fingal.

Erste Szene

Saal im Hause des alten Horatius.
Horatius der Vater, Horatia seine Gattin, Julia Horatia seine Tochter.

HORATIUS: Hört auf Weiber, ich sag's euch! euer weibisches Winseln ändert nicht ein [4] Haarbreit den Schluß der Götter und den Ausspruch der
Mächte! – auch ich vermag's nicht! und wenn ichs vermöchte, wenn ich
alle Gewalt des Jupiters hätte, so wahr ich ein Römer bin, ich ändert's
nicht! –

HORATIA: O ich kenn' euch! – stolz wie der Löwe, und fühllos wie der un-
gezähmte Tiger schreitet ihr unzubändigend eure wilde Bahn daher, sezt
in grausame Härte eure Würde, und macht das Verleugnen der Natur zu
eurer Tugend! – seyd ihr denn nicht Vater? – Vater dreier Söhne, die ich
euch mit Schmerzen gebahr, und mit Mutterliebe erzog? die euer Stolz
sind, und der Stolz euers Vaterlandes? – [5]

HORATIUS: Ha! und wenn sie das nicht wären, würde Suffetius Scharfblik
sie so ruhmvoll auszeichnen? würde auf sie die Wahl des erhabnen Roms
fallen? würde man in die Hände dreier Jünglinge das Wohl Tausender
geben? würde man sie den übermüthigen Albaniern entgegen stellen? und
du kannst murren Weib! Heldenmutter? Ha! wärst du von Geburt eine
Römerin, du murrtest nicht!

HORATIA: Entheret das edle Blut nicht aus dem ich stamme! – auch mein
Volk hat Helden erzeugt; und gab nicht meine eigne Schwester Albanien
ein dreifaches Schild, wie ich euerm Rom? – aber – ach! – ihr Göt=

[6]ter! – wozu bestimmt? – zu grausamen Opfern! O, wir unglüklichen
Mütter! daß wir nicht Jungfrauen blieben, und unser Glük in Männerhän-
de gaben! daß unsre Söhne nicht lieber in der Geburt starben! – Nun sind
sie emporgeschossen, die muthigen Knaben, und Palmbäume worden, die
uns als Greisinnen Schatten geben solten – da will man sie abhauen mit
mörderischer Hand! Man nimmt uns unsre Kinder und stellt sie gegen
einander in Streit, nicht zufrieden, daß sie schon unter den Vertheidigern
ihres Volks zuerst genannt werden! – stellt Brüder gegen Brüder! – deren
Mütter zugleich unter einem Herzen und an einer Brust lagen, die bis jezt
Freunde des Herzens wie des Blutes waren! – Grausam! entsezlich! – die
[7] Natur schaudert, und die Menschlichkeit zittert! –

HORATIUS: Feiges Weib! – Laß sehn wer siegen wird! – Was ist Natur und
Gefühl gegen Ehre und Sieg? winselndes Weibergewäsch! – Auf Atlas
Schultern ruht die Erde, und er trägt sie! Albaniens Wohl ruht auf den
Söhnen deiner Schwester; und, so tapfer sie sind, so muß es sinken, denn
Rom, die Herrscherin der Nationen, übertrug das ihrige unsern Kindern,
und sie – sie werden es tragen! – Ja, Weib! troz deines Winselns, die
Jünglinge müßen streiten, und troz des Muttergeheuls deiner Schwester,
werden die Horatier auf die Leichen der Curiatier treten! – [8]

JULIA HORATIA *(mit äusserstem Schmerz)*: Haltet ein, mein Vater! – oder
wollt ihr auch eure Tochter tödten? oder habt ihrs vergessen, daß ihr mich
mit Curiatius verlobtet? – O warum habt ihr Julia's Liebe gesegnet? warum sie erst so glüklich gemacht, wenn ihr mir solche Martern aufspartet?
– hättet ihr gleich dieses Herz durchbohrt, da es anfieng vor Albanus zu
schlagen!

HORATIUS: Wirfst du mir vor, daß ich weich genung war, euch nachzugeben? – Lag nicht deine Mutter und ihre Schwester mir stets in den Ohren?
erbettelte, ertobte, erseufzte Albanus nicht mein Wort? und du – du! [9]
überschwemmten nicht deine Thränen mein Herz?

JULIA HORATIA: Und nun wollt ihr euer schönstes Werk zerstören, unsre
Glükseligkeit? o, ich weiß sehr gut was es uns allen gekostet hat! schämt
euch nicht, daß ihr Mensch und Vater waret, und sagt – sagt: ist nicht Albanus Curiatius, Julia Horatia werth.

HORATIUS: Werth genung des weichlichen Mädchens mit winselndem Herzen, glatter Larve, glühender Wange, und schlanker Gestalt; aber nicht
werth der Tochter des Horatius, des Weibes aus Römer Blut. Doch – es
sey! – er ist schön und tapfer und stolz wie ein Adler! sein Arm hat im
Gewühl [10] der Schlacht Männer danieder gestürzt, und in Zeiten des
Friedens gute Thaten gethan, wäre nur Curiatius nicht sein Vater, und
hätt' ihn Albanien nur nicht gebohren.

HORATIA: Wenn werdet ihr jene Vorurtheile des Stolzes ablegen, die euch
so fürchterlich machen? – Warum huldigtet ihr einst einer Tochter Albaniens? O, daß je eure Füße die Schwelle meines Vaters betraten? Hätte

doch auch Sequinius zu euch gesagt: Ihr seyd schön und tapfer, Horatius! aber euch hat die Feindin meines Volks erzeugt, geht, und werft eure Wahl auf eine Römerin!

HORATIUS *(zornig)*: Weib! – doch ich hab ihn ja schon gebüßt, den Fehler meines jugendli= [11]chen Auges, das eure stralende Schönheit verblendet hatte; denn – ihm hat Albanus mein Wort zu danken! Auch ihn hat Julia's Reiz entzündet, und ich bin nicht ungerecht genung, ihn eine Thorheit entgelten zu lassen, die auch ich einst begieng! – Kein Römer nimmt sein Wort zurück, und ich hab's bei den Göttern geschworen: daß Julia keines andern werden soll! Aber – nur durch Blut kann er sie kaufen – todt oder Sklav! – Sklav ihrer Brüder, wie Albanien Rom's Fußschemmel!

HORATIA: Die Götter werden eure Grausamkeit ahnden! – Seht ihr welchen Eindruk eure Schwertworte aufs Herz eurer Tochter haben? – Habt ihr denn gar kein Gefühl für eure [12] Kinder? Wollt ihr auch diese Einzige mir rauben, da ihr Geschlecht sie sichert?

JULIA HORATIA: Ich schwöre, mein Vater! diese Abscheulichkeiten überleb' ich nicht, denn mein Herz hat keine Kraft zwischen dem Leben meines Geliebten und meiner Brüder (denn auch die Curiatier sind das!) zu wählen! Drei müssen sterben, sagt ihr, und ich, Vater! ich werde das vierte Schlachtopfer seyn, sag ich euch! – Ihr wißt wie ich meine Brüder liebe, ihr kennt meine Zärtlichkeit für Albanus und mein Gefühl für die Seinigen; die Sieger müssen mir den Tod bringen, sie mögen seyn wer sie wollen!

HORATIUS: Wohlan! so stirb! was verliert das Vaterland durch ein Weib? – [13]

JULIA HORATIA: Nichts! das weiß ich wohl, und eben darum werden die Götter meinen Entschluß rechtfertigen! – Aber ihr? – seyd ihr nicht mein Vater? troz eurer abschrekkenden Kälte, eurer tödtenden Härte mein Vater? – und mein so geliebter Vater? – Euer Blut wallt ja in meinen Adern, bin ich nichts vor euren Augen? – weniger als nichts in eurem Herzen? wollt ihr mich nicht länger zur Tochter? – Wenn ich euch auch nichts gutes zu thun vermochte, womit hab' ich euch wohl je beleidigt? – womit? – sagt's, und ich will eure strafende Hand küssen, und mit heissen Zähren meine Schuld verwaschen! – Oder zürnt ihr mit den Göttern, daß sie euch Kinder gaben, weil ihr uns alle aufopfern wollt? – auch mich, [14] eure arme Julia, eure sonst so geliebte Tochter? Wenn eure Söhne in der Schlacht fallen, wollt ihr da nicht, daß ich euch stüze, daß ich euch des Alters Pfade führe, eure wankenden Schritte leite, und euch einst das Heldenauge zudrükke? – Doch – wenn ihr meinen Untergang beschlossen habt, mein Vater, so murr' ich nicht, so folg ich euch auch noch im Tode mit Freuden! aber nur meine Brüder, nur meinen Albanus erhaltet! – Ihr seyd gerührt, mein Vater? – ihr wendet euch von mir? – o, laßt mich die-

se tröstliche Vaterthräne sehn, die mir den Sieg der Natur verkündet –
(stürzt zu seinen Füßen) Hier lieg ich vor euch, die Erde nezzend mit
meinen Thränen, wie damals, da ich Albanus von euch erflehte! hört
mich, Vater! – hört die [15] Stimme eures Herzens! – rettet eure Kinder!
schlagt dem Staat eure Söhne ab – laßt sie in der Schlacht kämpfen, aber
nicht wider die Brüder ihrer Liebe!

HORATIUS *(gerührt)*: Steh auf, und stürme mir nicht länger aufs Herz! – die
Götter können dir helfen aber ich nicht, und – ich gab mein Wort. Pflicht
und Ehre befiehlt, und die Natur muß schweigen! auch würd' ich eher
drei Löwen bändigen, als deine Brüder, da sie einmal gerufen sind vom
Volk! – Steh auf! ich muß – ich kann dich nur bedauern! *(geht ab)* [16]

Zweite Szene

Julia und Horatia ihre Mutter.

JULIA *(springt trostlos auf)*: So haben die Götter unser Elend beschlossen!

HORATIA: O, du hast Wunder gethan, meine Tochter, mehr als hättest du
einen Löwen im Walde bezähmt, und den kalten Marmor Schweiß abge-
zwängt – deinem Vater eine Thräne entlockt!

JULIA: Blutig fällt sie in mein Herz – diese fruchtlose Thräne! o meine Brüder! – o mein Albanus! keinen von euch werd ich überleben!

HORATIA: Mir das? – Mir! der so glüklichen, nun so elenden Mutter! ist's
[17] nicht genung daß man mir meine Söhne entreißt – daß man sie wider
das Blut meiner Zwillingsschwester stellt, daß man sie aufreiben will,
muß auch meine Julia in ihr Unglük verwikkelt werden? –

JULIA *(an ihrem Herzen)*: Auf daß der Schluß der Götter erfüllt werde! – O
zärtlichste Freundin und Mutter, sonst trozt ich an eurer Brust jedem
Schiksale; aber, diesem zu trozzen vermag ich nicht!

HORATIA: Umsonst sinn' ich nach Trost für dich, für mich! – jeder Gedanke
mehret meine Verzweiflung, und gräbt tiefern Jammer in meine Seele! –
Diesem zornigen Blutgericht zu entgehen, seh ich kein Mittel; Ehre nennt
es die wüthende, stolze Män=[18]nerschaar, und stieg lieber in die
Nächte des Orkus, als daß sie zurükträte! – ha! kann denn der römische
Stolz nur auf der Asche der Horatier und Curiatier empor blühn?

JULIA: Ach Mutter! noch ein Gedanke durchfliegt meine geängstete Brust,
in welcher der grimmigste Schmerz arbeitet; ein kühner, glüklicher Gedanke, ein Lichtstral vom Olymp! – Ihr wißt: daß Suffetius, der die Heere
Albaniens anführet, diese grausame Entscheidung beschloß, daß er sie
unserm Volk vorschlug, und die sechs Jünglinge dazu auszeichnete. Und
– hatten ihn nicht einst Julia's Reize entflammt? wie, wenn ich jezt hin-
gienge und mein Haar in neue Lokken und Flechten schlüge, mir einen

frischen [19] Blumenkranz wände, und ein prächtiges Gewand umwürfe? Wenn ich so geschmückt ins Lager eilte, und zu den Füßen des Mannes, der so oft zu den meinigen jammerte, Aenderung dieses schreklichen Rathschlusses von ihm flehte?

HORATIA: Geh nur, geh! armes Lamm und beginne den Streit mit einem blutdürstigen Wolfe, seine Zähne sind schon gewezt, und du würdest ihm eine neue Beute werden – zu stolz, deine Knie vor diesem Unmenschen zu beugen, ergib dich lieber dem Schiksal! Es ist besser in die Hand der Götter sich werfen, als in die Hände ihrer Geschöpfe! Ach, Tochter! du kennst das Männerherz nicht, wenn du ihm dann, wenn es Ehrgeiz, Zorn und Rache kocht, [20] Gefühl – Gefühl für ein Weib zutraust; und wenn's eine Göttin wäre, kalt würd' er ihre Klage hören, fühllos sie seinem Gözzenbild, der falschen Ehre, aufzuopfern! –

Dritte Szene

Suffetius, der albanische General. Vorige.

SUFFETIUS: Staunt nicht, edle Römerinnen! mich hier zu erblikken; meine Geschäfte, während des Stillestandes der Waffen, brachten mich nach Rom, und wie könnt' ichs verlassen, ohne meinem Freunde Horatius und seinem Hause zu der Auszeichnung der Jünglinge Horatier Glük zu wünschen, die nun unabänderlich von beiden Mächten beschlossen ist! [21]

HORATIA: Ihr kommt unsre Quaalen durch euern Spott zu erhöhn? – Fort, Unmensch aus diesem Heiligthume der Unschuld! und geht in die Wüste, um von wilden Thieren Menschlichkeit zu lernen.

SUFFETIUS: Wie? – winselt ihr auch wie eure albanische Schwester Curiatia, und klagt mich an: ich nähme euch eure Lieblinge? Ich dachte Horatius Römergeist, der sogern die muthigen Söhne uns darstellt, belebe auch sein Weib? Laßt euch rathen, Horatia, und erweicht das Herz der unbärtigen Helden nicht mit euern Zährenbach. Windet doch lieber Kränze für sie, wenn sie anders als Sieger zurükkehren sollten! [22]

HORATIA: Ha! ich bin Mutter, und ihr – ihr seyd ein schadenfrohes Ungeheuer, das sich an unserm Schmerz weidet. Ja, ich kenne euern Haß gegen das Blut des Sequinius, ihr habt das sicherste Mittel gewählt es auszurotten; aber frohlokt nicht zu sehr; dieses unschuldige Blut unsrer Kinder, und das Geheul zweier elender Mütter wird laut wider euch: Rache! Rache! schrein.

SUFFETIUS: Ihr seyd eine ächte Römerin worden! – Kann ich dafür, daß man Menschenblut schonen und sich auf Jünglinge verlassen will? Daß die Götter selbst eure Söhne und die Söhne Flavilliens eurer Schwester, durch das Wunderbare ihrer zu glei=[23]cher Zeit geschehenen Drillingsgeburt, und durch ihre gleiche Erziehung, Muth, Stärke, Schönheit und

Tapferkeit dazu ausgezeichnet haben, Roms oder Albaniens Herrschaft zu entscheiden?

HORATIA: Beschönigt nur immer eure Bosheiten, und nehmt die Götter zum Vorwand, und ihren Willen zum Dekmantel eurer Grausamkeit; dies habt ihr mit den frevelvollsten Sündern gemein, denn jeder Bösewicht macht sich nur gar zu gern diesen götterlästerlichen Mißbrauch der obersten Gewalt zu nuzze! Ich veracht' euch zu sehr, um eurer kleinen, schändlichen Seele ein Wort der Vorbitte zu geben, lieber will ich weinen und mein Elend bejammern! – Heult nicht die Löwin um ein Junges durch den [24] Wald, daß er erbebt, und ihr raubt mir alle meine Kinder und ich soll schweigen?

JULIA: O stolzer Suffetius! dessen Ohr nur Kriegsgeschrei gewohnt ist, vernehmt doch nur ein einzigesmal die Stimme einer Unglüklichen! – hört Julia Horatia, bei euerm vorigen Gefühl für sie, beschwör ich euch! – habt Erbarmen mit unserm Elend, dessen Urheber ihr seyd, daß ihr aber auch noch zu ändern vermögt, wenn ihr wollt. Stellt wenigstens nicht Brüder gegen Brüder – das Blut der Schlachtopfer kommt über euch! *(sie fällt vor ihm nieder)* Seht hier eine Römerin vor euch im Staube! würdigt sie der Erhörung, gebt Brüder und Verlobten ihr wieder, und [25] ihre lezte Zähre wird euch noch segnen als ihren Wohlthäter! –

SUFFETIUS *(sie aufhebend)*: Ha, schöne Bettlerin! hörtest du auch auf Suffetius Flehn, als er so vor dir lag, dein stolzes Herz zu erbitten? – Zogst du nicht den schönen Jüngling in blankem Helm, Curiatius ihm vor? Nun ist auch an mir die Reihe, unerbittlich zu seyn! Alles, was ich aus Erbarmen mit deiner entzückenden Schönheit thun kann ist: den Geliebten dir zu senden, daß ihr euch noch lezzen könnt, eh er den blutigen Reihetanz beginnt! – Jezt geh ich zum Vater Horatius, deine Brüder mit mir zu nehmen in's Lager; lebt wohl Römerinnen! – *(geht ab)* [26]

Vierte Szene

Vorige, hernach die drei Horatier Söhne und Brüder.

HORATIA: Sagt ichs nicht? – O! wenn Orpheus diesem Stein seine göttliche Leier gespielt, Amphion dieser wilden Kreatur gesungen hätte, er wäre Stein und Bestie geblieben!

JULIA: Das Menschengefühl hat die Männerbrust verlassen! Euch und mir bleibt nichts übrig als der Tod! o Mutter! Mutter! daß ich euch nur nicht überlebe – ihr seyd stärker denn ich! – O Curiatius! [27]

(Die drei Horatier in Waffenrüstung treten auf.)

HORATIA: Meine Kinder! ach, meine Kinder!

FULVIUS, DER ÄLTERE: Weint nicht Mutter! – hier sind wir – dankend daß ihr uns gebahrt, weil wir Roms Herrschaft entscheiden sollen! – Seyd ruhig, Horatia! als Sklaven sehet ihr eure Söhne nicht wieder – unsre Losung ist: Sieg oder Tod!

HORATIA: O du! du! – wild und schnaubend wie dein schwarzes Roß! – deines Vaters Liebling und deiner Mutter Geißel! – In dem Feuer, das aus deinen rollenden Augen blizt, sieht mein ahndender Geist die Fakkel des Todes! – [28]

FULVIUS: Laßt's seyn, Mutter! Roms Helden sinken nicht so leicht; aber die Curiatier sollen alle mit bleicher Todtenfakkel über den Lethe geleuchtet werden!

JULIA: Fühlloser! – mir das? – mir! deiner Schwester? – der Verlobten Albanus? – ha! Fluch dir! Fluch der Götter, wenn du ihn tödtest! –

FULVIUS: Ich werde meine Pflicht thun!

LUCIUS, DER MITTLERE: Schweig Tobender! – Grausamkeit ist keine wahre Heldenpflicht!

AURELIUS, DER JÜNGERE: Und diese, die man uns aufbürdet wider unsre Brüder, unsre Freunde zu streiten ist hart, ist unmenschlich! [29] Nie hab ich in fürchterlicher Schlacht gewankt; aber gegen diesen Streit empört sich mein Herz!

LUCIUS: Auch das meinige! Ich und Aurelius haben so eben den Göttern geopfert und von ihnen erfleht: uns eher sinken, als Mörder der Curiatier werden zu lassen!

HORATIA: Dies ist die Sprache meiner Söhne! – kommt an eurer Mutter Herz ihr meine beiden Kinder! – – laßt euch – ach vielleicht zum leztenmal! an ihre Brust drükken! – empfangt ihren besten, schönsten Segen, ihr Erben von Sequinius Tugend! Fulvius! vor deiner Wuth kann ich zittern, aber vor dieser ihr Leben muß ich es! [30]

JULIA: Ihr seyd alle meine Brüder, so heiß von mir geliebt, wie eurer Schwester Liebe es vermag! aber ihr – ihr seyd meinem Herzen nahe! – – Lucius! Aurelius! schont des Mannes meiner Seele, bei den Göttern beschwör ich euch!

LUCIUS UND AURELIUS: Bei den Göttern schwören wir dir, Helden, aber auch Menschen zu seyn!

FULVIUS: Und ich schwör es dir, daß dieser Arm nicht rasten soll, bis keiner von den Curiatiern mehr lebt! – Ich habe nicht Mutter, nicht Schwester, nicht Freunde, ein Vaterland hab ich, das Alles mir ist! Roms Herrschaft will ich gründen, und Albanien [31] in Fesseln werfen! Nur meine Ehre und mein Muth gebieten! Wollen diese Weiber in Waffenrok nicht kämpfen, wollen meine Brüder das Blut der Horatier beschimpfen, wohlan! ich wenigstens will meine Pflicht thun, und das Haus meines Vaters vor

Schande sichern! Ich der junge Römer mit Löwenherz und Tigerstärke! – hab ich deinen albanischen Liebling erwürgt, dann führ ich dich einem Edlen unsers Volks zu, zittre Schwester vor ihm, wenn du mich wiedersiehst! und ihr, Mutter, gehabt Euch wohl! – *(wild ab)*

JULIA: Das mein Bruder! *(sie schaudert)*

HORATIA: Wein' ihm nicht nach, er ists nicht werth! – nicht werth, daß Horatia [32] ihn gebahr! – Aber nicht vor ihn – vor seiner Wuth bangt meinem Herzen!

AURELIUS: Wir müssen nach! Eine schrekliche Pflicht gebeut! Mutter! Schwester! segnet uns! – Lebt wohl! –

LUCIUS: Denkt unsrer! – flehet die Götter für uns! – ach – lebt – lebt wohl! –

HORATIA UND JULIA *(sie inniglich umarmend)*: Kinder! Brüder! Zeus und Mars schirm' und segn' euch!

LUCIUS *(reißt sich los und eilt fort)*: Hört ihr die Stimme unsers Vaters! Es ist Zeit! – fort zum Tode! [33]

AURELIUS *(auch so ihm nach)*: Mutter! Schwester! lebt wohl!

HORATIA: Haltet! haltet, meine Söhne! – Götter, noch einmal laßt mich sie sehn! *(ihnen nach)*

Fünfte Szene

Julia Horatia erst allein, denn Albanus Curiatius.

JULIA *(sinkt kraftlos auf den Fußteppich hin)*: Trennt sich noch nicht meine Seele vom Körper? Wartet sie auf noch entsezlichre Szenen? – *(laut weinend)* O, meine Brüder – Söhne meines Volks! auf den Flügeln des Todes eilt ihr zum Kampf – Götter! mit wem? mit Albanus! – Mein [34] Blut erstarrt, mein Herz wird Eis, und glühet dennoch von Gefühl! – Ha! was sollen diese Kränze, die so bulerisch meine Lokken umwinden? was diese Perlen um mein braunes Haar geschlungen? – *(Sie zerstöhrt ihren Kopfpuz voll wilder Angst.)* Weg! weg! dies gramgedrükte Haupt wird bald zu ewiger Ruhe sich neigen! – Mir gehört nur die Hülle der tiefsten Trauer! – Weg eitler, verhaßter Schmuk, mit Staub und Asche will ich mich bestreuen, und wenn die Götter so unerbittlich sind, wie ihre Geschöpfe, muthig die Bahn der Verzweiflung wallen! –

ALB. CURIATIUS *(tritt ein)*: Wo bist du, Geliebte? – Ins Grab deine Abschiedsküsse zu sammeln, schikt Suffetius mich her, und – [35] ich eilte wie sonst – da ich deiner Liebe Umarmung entgegen flog!

JULIA *(steht auf – wild auf ihn zufliehend)*: Stirb nicht, Albanus! – – oder – laß mich an deiner Seite sterben!

ALBANUS: Edle Julia! in der Hand der Götter steht mein Leben! Ihre Weisheit hat deine und meine Tage gezeichnet! – was zerstöhrst du deine Lokken, daß sie wild wie vom Flug des Sturmwindes gejagt, herab zur Erde rollen? – was wüthest du Sanfte, in dein eignes Herz? – sey standhaft, Tochter des Horatius; vergiß auch im Unglük deine Größe nicht! [36]

JULIA: Meine Größe? – Ha! sie ruhet in meiner Liebe zu dir – und du bist mein Stolz! Dich mir rauben, heißt Alles – Alles mir nehmen, was Welten für mich enthalten können! und die stolzeste unter den römischen Jungfrauen wird – ein kraftloses Mädchen!

ALBANUS: Kann ich deine Empfindung rügen, edle und gefühlvolle Julia, da selbst, bei deiner Liebe Blik in deines Albanus Herzen Muth und Standhaftigkeit sinkt? Nie konnt' ich sie abschwören, die süßen Gefühle der Menschheit, wenn ich deinen sanften Umgang mit dem Getümmel der Heere vertauschte, und in Pallas Heiligthum an deiner Grazienhand mich wagte; aber immer kehrt ich wieder, gern und [37] willig zur blutigen Arbeit fürs Vaterland zurük! Heute, zum erstenmal, schleicht fieberhafter Abscheu durch meine Adern, und die Ehre der man mich würdigt, verstummt vor der stärkern Uebermacht der Liebe und Freundschaft!

JULIA: Ehre? – o! entehre diesen heiligen Namen nicht! – Greuel! Schande! Schmach der Menschheit, Hochverrath der Natur ists, Brüder gegen Brüder zu stellen, daß sie einander aufreiben sollen wie wilde Thiere im Walde! – Auch in Juliens Busen schlägt Hochgefühl und Römersinn, so wahr ich Horatia heiße! aber diese Ehre faßt meine Seele nicht! – Man stelle die Söhne des Horatius in Streit, und mache seine Tochter zu ihrer Waffenträgerin, dann wollen [38] wir stolz seyn auf den Tod für's Vaterland; aber dieser Kampf sey von uns verabscheut.

ALBANUS: Du hast Recht, meine Geliebte! aber wenn lernet der Sterbliche wohl wahre Ehre von falscher unterscheiden? Wenn ist der freieste Mann nicht ein schwacher Sklav seines Wahnes? – O, laß uns Unterwerfung lernen, die den Weisen verherrlicht, theure Horatia! laß uns ohne Murren den Becher des Schiksals lernen, den die Götter uns füllten! – Vielleicht – o Götter! verzeiht diese Zähre, mit der sich mein leztes Gefühl vom Herzen reißt! – vielleicht sieht mein Auge dich nicht wieder! Vielleicht küß ich dich zum leztenmal mit brennenden Lippen! – Ahndung des Todes durchzukt meine Seele! – [39] Aber, sieh Julia, ich murre, ich zittre nicht! Eine eiserne Stirne trag' ich dem Feind der schwachen Natur entgegen; eine Stirn' von keinem Verbrechen gebrandmarkt, und ein Herz – o Wonne! – von dir geliebt! – Dies ists, was mich muthig und glüklich macht – Tugend, und das Andenken an deine Zärtlichkeit; hin, in beßre Welten begleiten mich diese; dich anbetend, entschlummr' ich wie auf Rosen, und dort im Elisium vereinen uns die Götter!

JULIA: Bald – bald! mein Curiatius! – du hast mir deinen Muth mitgetheilt – denn – nur auf Trennung vom Leben kommts an, und was ist die, gegen Trennung von dir? – Es ist Ruhegefühl für mich, daß ich dich nicht überleben werde, daß deine [40] Julia, treu wie eine Römerin, mit dir zugleich in die Gefilde des Friedens wandelt! – Geh! und kümmre dich nicht, mein Entschluß ist fest wie der Grundstein den Romulus legte: Ich sterbe mit dir!

ALBANUS: O du, meiner Seele schönstes Leben! mein Ein und Alles! – Zwar erhebt mich dieser Trost zum Olymp; aber lebe – lebe um die glüklichste unter den Töchtern Roms zu seyn, wie du die schönste und edelste unter ihnen bist! – dein Curiatius geht den Weg seiner Pflicht, aber seinen Sieg zu wünschen, den Sieg über Julias Brüder, dies vermag seine Seele nicht!

JULIA: Komm mit zur Freundin unsrer Liebe, zur zärtlichsten, unglüklichsten [41] Mutter! Horatia weint ihren Kindern nach – komm, daß sie uns segne, ehe denn wir sterben! *(Sie gehn ab.)*

Sechste Szene

Gegend von Rom. – Eine wilde, unangebaute Fläche mit Erd= und Steinhaufen überdekt.

JULIA HORATIA *(allein umherirrend – ihre Haare fliegend – im Gewande der Trauer)*: Endlich fand sie mein irrender Schritt, diese grausenvolle Einöde! wo ich harrend auf die Zurükkunft der Sieger meinen Tod erwarten will! – Wer suchte hier Horatius Tochter? eine edle, römische Jungfrau, einsam und allein vor den Tho=[42]ren wie die ausgestoßenste der Sklavinnen! Julia, noch gestern in Kreis der Gespielinnen bewundert, mit Perlen und Blumen geschmükt – die man die Krone der Mädchen, und das Entzükken der Jünglinge nannte! – Meine Verzweiflung hat keine Schranken mehr, ehrt keine Gesezze! – Ich habe sie übertreten, wie mein Unglük die Grenze meiner Kraft übertrat und bin, entflohen wie das geschrekte, gemarterte Reh, das den tödtlichen Pfeil in der Brust fühlt, mit geflügelter Eil das öde Thal durchrennt, und ihn doch nur tiefer – tiefer hinein stößt! – O, meine Mutter! edle, zärtliche Mutter! auch gegen dich bin ich zur Sünderin worden, auch das Gesez der Kindesliebe hab' ich übertreten! – Ich rang mich aus deinen Armen, riß mich von dei=[43]nem blutenden Herzen! floh unaufhaltsam von dannen, wie der Schwertstreich des Kämpfers! Jezt sizzest du Einsame! Kinderlose! Tochterverlaßne! und jammerst! – deine Klage steigt zu den Göttern, auf Julia ruhet dein ganzes Gefühl! – Ha! auch Julia weinet blutige Zähren über die Leiche ihrer erkalteten Glükseligkeit! Umschwebt von zahllosen Geistern meiner gestorbenen Freude, ruf ich die Vergangenheit auf, die Gegenwart zu richten, und zittre – harrend wie auf den Engel des Todes –

der Zukunft entgegen! *(Sie sinkt nieder, und legt ihr Haupt auf einen Stein.)* Hier will ich ruhn! – wenn anders Ruhe hienieden mich noch beseligen kann! bis sie kommen, und mein Todesurtheil unterzeichnen! Hart ruhet mein Haupt, gewohnt auf den Veil=[44]chenlager der Unschuld zu liegen; aber härtre Steine des Elends drükken mein armes Herz! – Doch – vom Lichtkreise der Unsterblichkeit fällt ein erquikkender Strahl in meine Seele! Ich hoffe Vollendung, und die Gewißheit meiner Hofnung hebt mich mit Adlerflügeln empor! – Götter! – vielleicht ist er schon dahin! – mein Albanus! meines Erdenglükkes ganzer Inhalt! Aber bald – bald werden die Unsterblichen meine Bitte erhören, und mich, erlößt von der Kette des Lebens, wohnen lassen auf einem Stern, mit ihrem Liebling, meinem Geliebten! – – Welches Geschrei! – welch Siegsgetön? – ha! das ist römischer Jubel, dies ist die Stimme meines Volks! – meine Brüder gesiegt! – Götter! ich vermag keine Freude! – Mir ists [45] Leichengesang auf blutbesprüzten Gräbern! – Wehklage des Todes! – Es naht! es naht! wird näher und näher! – rollend wie der mittägliche Donner wälzt es sich über die schauervolle Fläche! – meine Seele erzittert! – kalter Todesschweiß drängt sich aus meinen Adern! ich will die Botschaft vernehmen, und – sterben!

Siebente Szene

Unter lautem Jubelgeschrei erscheinen eine große Menge römischer Bürger und Krieger, in ihrer Mitte Fulvius Horatius mit Siegeskränzen geschmükt, und in blutiger Rüstung. Vier albanische Sklaven tragen ihm die Kleider und Waffen der Ueberwundenen [46] nach, und ein Haufen Volks jauchzt verworren hinter ihm her: "Triumph! Triumph! Rom hat gesiegt! Fulvius Horatius hat überwunden!"

JULIA *(stürzt unter die Vorgänger, die ihr ehrerbietig Plaz machen, und dringt zu ihrem Bruder)*: Ha? jezt ists Zeit für mich, zu zittern, wie du beim Abschied mir drohtest! – mein Bruder! welch Geschrei!

FULVIUS: Wie? du hier? – Eine römische Jungfrau umherirrend vor dem Thore? – Wekte dich der Widerhall meines Siegs, oder jagte Wahnsinn der Liebe dich von dannen, daß du, Kühne! das Gesez übertratest? – [47]

JULIA: Das Unglük kennt keine Gesezze, und das Gefühl keinen Zwang! – Du kommst allein? – Wo sind meine Brüder? – Wo hast du die Söhne meiner Mutter gelassen? – Theilen sie die Lorbeern nicht mir dir? –

FULVIUS: Geh auf jenes Blachfeld, das beide Heere wie Heuschrekken dekken, und frag die blutige Wahlstatt! – nur ich bin überblieben. –

JULIA *(mit wildem Affekt)*: O, meine Brüder! so seyd ihr des Todes Opfer! – und mein Albanus? – mein Verlobter?

FULVIUS: Ich habe gesiegt! – Rom ist gerettet! – ist Herrscherin! – und [48] du fragst nach Brüdern und Verlobten? –

JULIA: Kann ich meine Empfindung verleugnen? die herrschende in meinem Herzen? – ha! wenn auch Er dahin wäre! *(Sie erblikt einen Sklaven, der ein blutiges Oberkleid trägt, und stürzt darauf zu – ausser sich.)* Götter, ich bin verlohren! – Er ist nicht mehr! – dies ist sein Gewand – hier sein kostbares Blut! – Meine Hände haben selbst dieses Kleid gewirkt; mit stolzer Liebe warf ichs einst um seine Schultern! – ich kenn' es wie meinen Augapfel! – und nun wards sein Sterbekleid! – Er ist todt! – Albanus Curiatius ist dahin, und du – du Ungeheuer! hast ihn erwürgt? [49]

FULVIUS: Ich! ja ich! – der Retter deines Volks! – der Vertilger Albaniens! deines Vaters Sohn! und hör' nur hör', daß du dich satt wimmern kannst, auch seine Brüder, unter deren Streichen die unsrigen gefallen waren, sind dahin! – Schon zitterte Rom! da beseelten mich die Götter mit doppelter Stärke. Ich fieng die Curiatier mit List; ich wandte mich zur Flucht, und da ich sie, mich zu verfolgen, nun getrennt sah, stürzt' ich schnell auf den Einzelnen her, wie der Löwe auf den Raub! Ich durchbohrte so, einen nach den andern, und auch deinen Abgott, der, deinen Namen röchelnd, entschlief.

JULIA: Grausamer! Blutdürstiger! Ungeheuer, das die Menschheit entehret! [50] welch eine Wuth beseelte dich, ein Herz zu durchbohren, das vereint mit Juliens schlug? Ein Herz, tausendmal edler als das deinige! – Nenne nicht Pflicht, was du gethan hast, du hast nur deinen unnatürlichen Blutdurst gekühlt! – Nein! ich habe keinen Bruder mehr! die Verwandten meiner Seele entschliefen, und dieser Barbar ist meiner Mutter Sohn nicht!

FULVIUS *(zornig)*: Wie? – Ein Weib? Ein elendes Weib soll meine Thaten wägen? Soll mir meinen Muth brandmarken, und ins Geschrei meines Sieges heulen, während daß mein Volk mich seinen Retter preiset, und Ehrensäulen mir sezzen will? – Sieh! wie mein kühnes, stolzes Haupt von Lorbeerkränzen umwunden hervorragt über alle, wie [51] die Eiche über die Espen? Tullius Hostilius krönte mich damit im Angesicht aller Völker, und im Triumph will ich einziehn in ihre Vaterstadt, die stolz darauf, daß in ihren Mauern ihr Befreier gebohren ward, mir dankbar entgegen jubelt; geh und beschwere mein Ohr nicht mit deinem Geheul, oder zittre vor meiner Rache!

JULIA: Sie ist mir nun verächtlich, da du mir alles genommen hast, was theuer mir war? – O zieh nur immer einher, vom Blute gesättigt, wie der Tiger von der Jagd, mit deinen Siegeskränzen und Jubel! – Juliens Thränen löschen die Fakkel deiner Afterehre, und verwandeln deine Lorbeern in Dornen, die sich einst marternd in dein Felsenherz graben wer=[52]den. Wird man Ehrensäulen dir sezzen, so werden meine Flüche sie niederreissen, und mitten in deiner Vaterstadt wirst du ein Abscheu seyn, so wie deiner Mutter ein Greuel, und deiner Schwester eine Geißel! –

FULVIUS *(wüthend)*: Ha! Rasende! – das dem Sieger? – Ein Weib das dem Helden? – *(er zieht seinen Dolch, und stößt ihn ihr ins Herz)* Da! – röchle deinem Weichling nach! –

JULIA *(taumelt, und sinkt nieder)*: Ich sterbc! – Seegen nun über dir, mein Bruder! – du hast mich glüklich gemacht! – *(Es entsteht ein dumpfes Gemurr unter den Begleitern, man hört rufen: "Welch eine That! wie grausam! – Eine edle Römerin! – die schöne Julia Horatia, [53] seine Schwester! – Man muß es anzeigen!" – und viele aus dem Gefolge verlieren sich und eilen davon.)*

JULIA *(matt und schwach)*: Murret nicht – edle Bürger meines Volks! – mein Tod ist erbeten vom Verhängniße! – Ich eile ihm nach –dem Gemal meiner Seele! – Verzeiht eurem Erretter – wie ich – ihm verzeihe! – Ich fühle keine Schmerzen! – sie wühlen nur im Staube! – O, meine Mutter! – mein Vater! – arme kinderlose Mutter! – troknet – ihre Thränen! – Curiatius! – ach! *(sie stirbt)*

FULVIUS *(schaudert)*: Was hab ich gethan? – Diese That entehrt meinen Sieg! – Ich habe ein schönes, edles Weib getödtet, [54] und es war – meinc Schwester! – Sklav! wirf das Gewand Albanus über den Leichnam, daß kein Vorübergehender schaudre, und ihrem Mörder fluche! – und ihr! – macht, daß wir die Stadt erreichen! – *(geht ab, der Sklav bedekt Juliens Körper mit Albanus Gewand, und das Gefolg geht traurig und ohne Jubel ihm nach).*

Achte Szene

Einige Zeit darauf kommt Horatia die Mutter von einer andern Seite gelaufen, voll wilder Angst, zerstöhrt umher blikkend.

HORATIA: So ist er geschehn der Streich des Todes! – und das Ungeheuer Ehre mit meiner Kinder Blut gesättigt? Wo find ich sie, daß ich ihre heiligen Leichname mit heißen Mutterthränen nezze, und mit Geheul mich [55] zu ihnen hinabstürze in die öde Grube, in welche meine Glückseligkeit versank! – Wer zeigt mir das blutige Leichenfeld, wer die Erschlagnen? – die Erwürgten? Alle – alle meine Söhne! – Alle, alle von dem Blute des Sequinius meines Vaters! Ich ihrer aller tiefgebeugte Mutter! und Julia! Julia! – du noch Einzige, noch Uebrige, noch Gerettete! – mein ganzer Trost! meine einige Wonne! wo weilst du? wo flohst du hin, daß du die Stimme der Freundin nicht beantwortest, die dich gebahr? – *(Sie erblikt das Kleid.)* Ha! was ist das? – Albanus Gewand? von den Händen der Liebe gefertigt, jezt mit seinem Blute beflekt, wer warf das hieher? wer zertrat es am Wege? *(Sie hebt es auf, und – erblikt den Leichnam ih-*

rer Toch=[56]*ter – mit grenzenlosem Schrek und Schauern.)* Götter!
Götter! – meine Julia! meine Tochter! *(Sie fällt mit lautem Schmerz bei
ihr nieder, und schließt sie in ihre Arme.)* Welcher wüthende Tiger hat
mein sanftes Lamm erwürgt? – Welch blutdürstiges Ungeheuer hat sein
Herz zerrissen? – Wer hat ihn mir geraubt, meinen Schaz! mein liebstes
Kleinod? – Ha! und die Sonne leuchtete einer solchen That? und die Fakkel des Tages stürzte nicht in den Abgrund der Finsterniß, da sie diese
Grausamkeit sah? – – O Julia! – Julia! kalt und seellos! – bleich und
starr? – und kein Blik der Liebe mehr für deine Mutter? – ach! der Quell
des Lebens floß aus deinem Herzen, und dieses Herz war fern, das so
willig für dich den tödlichen Streich [57] aufgefangen hätte! – O meine
Tochter! lieblich wie der sanft lächelnde Morgenstern, und holdselig wie
die thauerfrischte Rose! – unter den römischen Jungfrauen die schönste,
und deiner Aeltern Stolz! – was bist du nun? – ach! eine kalte, blutige
Leiche! – hingeworfen am Wege – und zertreten wie die zarte Blume im
Hain! – Alle meine Kinder vernichtet! alle meine Freuden geraubt – und
dein Geist auf himmlischen Flügeln deinem Albanus nach! – Fliehende!
dachtest du nicht im Fliehn an deine arme Mutter? ruftest du sie nicht
dich zu segnen? – und ach! – sie war fern – hörte nicht das sterbende Ge-
lispel deines Mundes! – küßte nicht von der Purpur beraubten Wange die
lezte Perle! – sah nicht deines Hauptes [58] sanftes Neigen! – und das
Erlöschen des Feuerauges, und das Erbleichen der Rosenlippen! und ach!
– konnte nicht deinen wüthigen Mörder erflehn, auch sie mit dir zu er-
würgen! – Wo ist das Ungeheuer, daß es sein verfluchtes Werk vollende!
–

Neunte Szene

Fulvius. Horatius der Vater. Horatia.

FULVIUS *(hinzustürzend – wild)*: Hier ists! – Es war – euer Sohn – Juliens
Bruder! ihr Mörder! – Flucht mir nur, flucht mir, unglückliche Mutter,
ich hab es verdient! – Meine frevelnde Hand durchbohrte sie, als sie mit
den Wehklagen der Liebe mein Siegsgeschrei unterbrach! – [59]

HORATIA *(voll Entsezzen)*: Du – du! – ha, Unmensch! – nicht ihr Bruder! –
nicht mein Sohn! Würger meiner Lieblinge! – Tritt näher, und aus Barm-
herzigkeit würg' auch mich! –

HORATIUS: Armes Weib! arme Mutter! – Recht hast du! *(Auf Juliens Leichnam zeigend – gerührt!)* Da liegt es – das Glück meines Herzens! – die
Krone, der Stolz meines Hauses! – meine jungfräuliche Tochter! auch
noch im Tode schön! – O Vaterland! Vaterland! welche Opfer! –

HORATIA: Zu spät! – zu spät, da ihres Lebens Hauch verduftet ist, wie der
Hauch der Frühlingsblüthe! – Jezt wekken sie eure Klagen nicht! – gieb

sie mir wieder die Schlacht=[60]opfer – deine Kinder, wenn du es kannst! –

HORATIUS: Ist dieser nicht überblieben? – Roms Erretter? – dein Sohn? –

HORATIA: Mein Sohn? – Würde er seine Schwester getödtet haben, wenn er das wäre? – Nein! ich erkenn' ihn nicht mehr – meine ganze Seele empört sich gegen ihn? – ich mag die nicht sein, die ihn gebahr! –

FULVIUS: Schüttet nur aus, Mutter, ihr lüftet mir's Herz! – Hier – hier zwängt michs! hier tobts wie das stürmische Meer! – Ha, Engelsleiche, du bist gerächt! – du hast wahr gesprochen! – Ich bin, wie du gesagt hast: Sieger und Retter! Mörder und Mutterverstoßener! – mit Ehre [61] gekrönt, und mit Schande gebrandmarkt! – das Volk, das ich frei machte, entsezt sich vor mir, und sein dankbarer Jubel wird dumpfes Geschrei nach meinem Blute! –

HORATIUS: Laß es schreien – bin ich nicht dein Vater? – bist du nicht der lezte Zweig meines Stammes, und werden diese Sprößlinge wieder aufleben, wenn ich dich abhauen lasse? – Ein Fremdling hat meine Tochter erschlagen, und ich will sie betrauern; mein Sohn hat Rom errettet, und ich will ihn schüzzen! –

HORATIA: Schüzzet ihn nur, den Elenden; – werdet ihr ihn auch schüzzen können vor den Schlangen seines Gewissens? vor der Rache der Götter? – Nehmt euern Liebling, euern Stolz! [62] das Ungeheuer der Natur! – vergeßt uns alle unter dem Schatten seiner Lorbeern! ich kenn' ihn nicht! – ich habe keine Kinder mehr! nehmt euern Sohn, und laßt mir die Leichen meiner Kinder im Stande der Vernichtung, im Staube selbst mir noch werther, als dieser Unmensch im mörderischen Daseyn! – Eine unglükliche Mutter nimmt nicht Theil an euerm Jubel! – alles was ich begehre ist: daß ich ruhig bleibe bei meinen Todten, und alles was ich bettle, ist: ein Almosen von Erde für ihren Staub! – Auf ihrem Grabe will ich bleiben und o – daß die Götter mein Flehn erhörten! daß sie mich verwandelten in ein Grabmahl meiner Kinder!

Editorische Notiz

Die vorliegende Edition basiert auf dem bisher einzigen Druck des Dramas in der Zeitschrift *Museum für Frauenzimmer von einigen ihrer Mitschwestern.* Zweites Quartal 1790. Weißenfels und Leipzig bei Friedrich Severin, S. 3-62. Hinter dem im Erstdruck abgekürzten Autorinnennamen "Wilhelmine von G..." (Ebd. S. 62) vermutete bereits Carl Wilhelm von Schindel Wilhelmine von Gersdorf, die wohl auch Mitherausgeberin der Zeitschrift war.[1] Nur dieser eine Quartalsband der anonym erschienenen Zeitschrift ist erhalten. Der Veröffentlichung liegt das Exemplar aus der Sächsischen Landesbibliothek – Staats- und Universitätsbibliothek Dresden (Signatur 3.A.857 R.S.) zu Grunde.[2] Handschriften oder weitere Drucke existieren nach gegenwärtigem Erkenntnisstand nicht. Ein Kupferstich auf der dem Titelblatt des Bandes gegenüberliegenden Seite zeigt Julia und Albanus in der fünften Szene und trägt die Bildunterschrift: "Stirb nicht Albanus! –". Er ist signiert "JH. Lips. Del. / fec.", stammt also ebenso wie die Titelvignette der Zeitschrift von dem Schweizer Maler und Kupferstecher Johann Heinrich Lips (1758-1817). Das Drama hat kein Personenverzeichnis. Aufführungen des Dramas sind nicht nachgewiesen.

Um eine philologisch zuverlässige Edition zur Verfügung zu stellen, wurde der Text originalgetreu erfasst, das heißt, Interpunktion, Orthographie und grammatische Formen wurden weder modernisiert noch gemäß dem Sprachstand des ausgehenden 18. Jahrhunderts vereinheitlicht.[3] An drei Stellen wurden indessen Änderungen vorgenommen, die unzweifelhafte Satzfehler betreffen,[4] und zu Beginn der achten Szene wurde der Name Horatia eingefügt. Satztechnisch wurden Szenen- und Regiebemerkungen kursiviert und eine einheitliche Interpunktionspraxis für Szenenüberschriften und Figurenangaben gewählt. Seitenumbrüche des Erstdrucks sind durch Angabe der jeweils neuen Seitenzahl in eckiger Klammer vermerkt.

[1] Carl Wilhelm Otto August von Schindel: *Die deutschen Schriftstellerinnen des neunzehnten Jahrhunderts.* 3 Bde. Leipzig 1823-1825. Bd. 2. Nachdr. Hildesheim, New York 1978. S. 406f. Vgl. zu der Zeitschrift auch Ulrike Weckel: *Zwischen Häuslichkeit und Öffentlichkeit. Die ersten deutschen Frauenzeitschriften im späten 18. Jahrhundert und ihr Publikum.* Tübingen 1998. S. 111-115.

[2] Für die Bereitstellung einer Kopie, die freundliche Auskunft zu den Abbildungen und die Erlaubnis zur Neuedition des Textes sowie zum Abdruck der Kupferstiche danke ich herzlich Herrn Dr. Thomas Haffner von der Handschriftensammlung der Sächsischen Landesbibliothek – Staats- und Universitätsbibliothek Dresden.

[3] Gedankt sei an dieser Stelle Catherine Baird, die sich der Mühe der vergleichenden Korrektur unterzog.

[4] S. 31: "ichd ich" geändert in "ich dich"; S. 53: "demGemal" in "dem Gemal"; S. 54: "Albanius" in "Albanus".

Der Horatier-Stoff geht zurück auf das erste Buch von Titus Livius' *Ab urbe condita* und wurde seit der Antike vielfältig dramatisch gestaltet. Die Drillingssöhne zweier Familien aus Rom und Alba Longa, die sogenannten Horatier und Curiatier, sollen durch einen repräsentativen Waffengang die Entscheidung herbeiführen, welche Stadt künftig herrschen soll. Mit List kann der älteste der römischen Horatier die Schlacht für Rom entscheiden. Als seine Schwester ihm vorwirft, ihren Geliebten, einen der albanischen Helden, getötet zu haben, ersticht er sie. Er wird zunächst für den Mord zum Tode verurteilt, aber auf Fürsprache seines Vaters vom König begnadigt.[5]

Die Autorin Charlotte Eleonore Wilhelmine von Gersdorf[6] wurde am 28. 10. 1768 in Oberbellmannsdorf in der Niederlausitz als Tochter von Christiane Eleonore (geb. von Uechtritz) und Caspar Friedrich von Gersdorf geboren. Sie wurde in Französisch und Geschichte sowie ansatzweise in Latein und Griechisch unterrichtet. Sechzehnjährig begann sie anonym und unter verschiedenen Pseudonymen dichterische Werke zu veröffentlichen. Erst im Alter unterzeichnete sie ihre Werke mit ihrem Namen. Sie heiratete einen Verwandten, Friedrich August Gottlob von Gersdorf. Am 2. November 1847 starb sie in Dresden. Gersdorf hat neben Erzählprosa eine Reihe dramatischer Texte verfasst, unter anderem *Die Familie Walberg, dramatisch bearbeitet von einer jungen Dame in Sachsen*. Prag, Leipzig 1792; und *Die Zwillingsschwestern oder die Verschiedenheit des Glücks. Ein Familiengemälde in drei Aufzügen*. In: *Mnemosyne oder meine Erinnerungen Teil 2. Von der Verfasserin der Familie Wallberg und der Situationen*. Oschatz 1797. Dieser Text liegt auch in einer Neuedition von Karin Wurst vor.[7] Neben Schindel und Wurst verzeichnet in neuerer Zeit Susanne Kord eine Reihe von Dramentiteln.[8] Ein über Autopsie geprüftes Werkverzeichnis des Œuvres Wilhelmine von Gersdorfs stellt jedoch bislang ein Desiderat dar.

[5] S. ausführlicher zum Stoff sowie zu vorgängigen dramatischen Bearbeitungen meinen Beitrag in diesem Band.

[6] Angaben nach Karin Wurst (Hg.): *Frauen und Drama im 18. Jahrhundert*. Köln, Wien 1991. S. 86-89.

[7] In: Ebd. S. 252-291.

[8] Susanne Kord: *Ein Blick hinter die Kulissen. Deutschsprachige Dramatikerinnen im 18. und 19. Jahrhundert*. Stuttgart 1992 (Ergebnisse der Frauenforschung 27). S. 368. Als Erscheinungsdatum des Dramas gibt Kord, wohl versehentlich, das Jahr 1796 an.

Fichte und seine Zeit

Beiträge zum vierten Kongress der Internationalen Johann-Gottlieb-Fichte-Gesellschaft in Berlin vom 03. – 08. Oktober '02

Herausgegeben von Hartmut Traub

Amsterdam/New York, NY 2003. XI, 235 pp.
(Fichte-Studien 21)

ISBN: 90-420-1164-5 € 45,-/US $ 54.-

Inhalt: Vorwort. Rolf AHLERS: Fichte, Jacobi und Reinhold über Spekulation und Leben

Teil I Prinzipen des transzendentalen Idealismus
Heinz EIDAM: Die Identität von Ideal- und Realgrund im Begriff der Wirksamkeit. Fichtes Begründung des kritischen Idealismus und ihr Problemzusammenhang. Katsuaki OKADA: Fichte und Schelling. Robert MARZAŁEK: Das Poetische in der späten Wissenschaftslehre aus dem Blickpunkt von Schellings Philosophie der Mythologie. Hitoshi MINOBE: Die Stellung des Seins bei Fichte, Schelling und Nishida. Yoichi KUBO: Transformation der Deduktion der Kategorien. Fichte in Hegel. Gottlieb FLORSCHÜTZ: Mystik und Aufklärung – Kant, Swedenborg und Fichte.

Teil II Philosophie und Leben
Arkadij V. LUKJANOW: Die Beziehung zwischen Geist und System bei Fichte und Reinhold. Susanna KAHLEFELD: Standpunkt des Lebens und Standpunkt der Philosophie. Jacobis Brief an Fichte aus dem Jahr 1799. Hartmut TRAUB: J.G. Fichte, der König der Juden spekulativer Vernunft – Überlegungen zum spekulativen Anti-Judaismus. Claus DIERKSMEIER: Fichtes kritischer Schüler. Zur Fichtekritik K.C.F. Krauses (1781-1832). Matthias KOßLER: Phantasie und Einbildungskraft. Zur Rolle der Einbildungskraft bei Fichte und Solger. Elvira GAREEVA: Die Bedeutung der Populärphilosophie: J.G. Fichte und A. Schopenhauer.

Zur Diskussion
Klaus HAMMACHER: Hartmut Traub: J.G. Fichte, der König der Juden spekulativer Vernunft – Überlegungen zum spekulativen Anti-Judaismus.

Rezensionen

USA/Canada: One Rockefeller Plaza, Ste. 1420, New York, NY 10020,
Tel. (212) 265-6360, Call toll-free (U.S. only) 1-800-225-3998,
Fax (212) 265-6402
All other countries: Tijnmuiden 7, 1046 AK Amsterdam, The Netherlands.
Tel. ++ 31 (0)20 611 48 21, Fax ++ 31 (0)20 447 29 79
Orders-queries@rodopi.nl   **www.rodopi.nl**
Please note that the exchange rate is subject to fluctuations.

Understanding Evil:
An Interdisciplinary Approach.

Edited by Margaret Sönser Breen

Amsterdam/New York, NY 2003. XIII, 222 pp.
(ATI/PTB 2)

ISBN: 90-420-0935-7   € 45,-/US $ 54.-

Written across the disciplines of law, literature, philosophy, and theology, *Understanding Evil: An Interdisciplinary Approach* represents wide-ranging approaches to and understandings of "evil" and "wickedness."
Consisting of three sections – *"Grappling with Evil"*
"Justice, Responsibility, and War" and *"Blame, Murder, and Retributivism,"* - all the essays are inter-disciplinary and multi-disciplinary in focus. Common themes emerge around the dominant narrative movements of grieving, loss, powerlessness, and retribution that have shaped so many political and cultural issues around the world since the fall of 2001.   At the same time, the interdisciplinary nature of this collection, together with the divergent views of its chapters, reminds one that, in the end, an inquiry into "evil" and "wickedness" is at its best when it promotes intelligence and compassion, creativity and cooperation.
The thirteen essays are originally presented at and then developed in light of dialogues held at the Third Global Conference on Perspectives on Evil and Human Wickedness, held in March 2002 in Prague

USA/Canada: One Rockefeller Plaza, Ste. 1420, New York, NY 10020,
Tel. (212) 265-6360, Call toll-free (U.S. only) 1-800-225-3998,
Fax (212) 265-6402
All other countries: Tijnmuiden 7, 1046 AK Amsterdam, The Netherlands.
Tel. ++ 31 (0)20 611 48 21, Fax ++ 31 (0)20 447 29 79
Orders-queries@rodopi.nl   **www.rodopi.nl**
Please note that the exchange rate is subject to fluctuations

Cultural Expressions of Evil and Wickedness
Wrath, Sex, Crime

Edited by Terrie Waddell

Amsterdam/New York, NY 2003. XVIII, 226 pp.
(At the Interface/Probing the Boundaries 3)

ISBN: 90-420-1015-0   € 50.-/US $ 60.-

Cultural Expressions of Evil and Wickedness: Wrath, Sex, Crime, is a fascinating study of the a-temporal nature of evil in the West. The international academics and researchers who have contributed to this text not only concentrate on political, social and legally sanctioned cruelty from the past and present, but also explore the nature of moral transgression in contemporary art, media and literature. Although many forms and practices of what might be called 'evil' are analysed, all are bound by violence and/or the sexually perverse. As this book demonstrates, the old news media axiom, 'if it bleeds it leads,' also extends to the larger pool of popular culture. This absorbing volume will be of interest to anyone who has ever pondered on the exotic, extraordinary and surreal twists of human wickedness.

USA/Canada: One Rockefeller Plaza, Ste. 1420, New York, NY 10020,
Tel. (212) 265-6360, Call toll-free (U.S. only) 1-800-225-3998,
Fax (212) 265-6402
All other countries: Tijnmuiden 7, 1046 AK Amsterdam, The Netherlands.
Tel. ++ 31 (0)20 611 48 21, Fax ++ 31 (0)20 447 29 79
Orders-queries@rodopi.nl   **www.rodopi.nl**
Please note that the exchange rate is subject to fluctuations.

Zur Wissenschaftslehre

Beiträge zum vierten Kongress der Internationalen Johann-Gottlieb-Fichte-Gesellschaftin Berlin vom 03. – 08. Oktober 2000

Hrsg. von Helmut Girndt

Amsterdam/New York, NY 2003. XIII, 284 pp.
(Fichte-Studien 20)
ISBN: 90-420-1184-X   € 60,-/US$ 71.-

Inhalt: Vorwort. Nachruf auf Jan Garewicz. Wolfgang JANKE: Vielheit des Seins – Einheit des Ich-existiere. Verwahrung und Vertiefung des transzendentalen Gedankens.
Teil I Zur Wissenschaftslehre 1794
Christian HANEWALD: Absolutes Sein und Existenzgewißheit des Ich. Marına A. PUSCHKAREWA: Der Begriff der nicht offenbaren Tätigkeit und Fichtes *Grundlage der gesammten Wissenschaftslehre*. Frank WITZLEBEN: *Wer* weiß? Eine Re-Interpretation der Theorie der Handlung und des Wissens in Fichtes Wissenschaftslehre von 1794. Ernst-Otto ONNASCH: Ich und Vernunft. Ist J.G. Fichte die Begründung seiner *Grundlage der gesammten Wissenschaftslehre* von 1794/95 gelungen?
Zur Diskussion
Wilhelm METZ: Die produktive Reflexion als Prinzip des wirklichen Bewußtseins
Teil II Zur Wissenschaftslehre von 1801 bis 1805
Virginia LÓPEZ-DOMÍNGUEZ: Die Entwicklung der intellektuellen Anschauung bei Fichte bis zur Darstellung der Wissenschaftslehre (1801-1802). Reinhard LOOCK: Das Schweben des absoluten Wissens. Zur Logik der Einbildungskraft in Fichtes Wissenschaftslehre von 1801/02. Diogo FERRER: Die pragmatische Argumentation in Fichtes Wissenschaftslehre 1801/1802. Ulrich SCHLÖSSER: Entzogenes Sein und unbedingte Evidenz in Fichtes Wissenschaftslehre 1804 (2). Urs RICHLI: Genetische Evidenz – was ist das eigentlich? Berlino D'ALFONSO: Strategien zur Widerlegung des Skeptizismus in Fichtes *Wissenschaftslehre 1804, Zweiter Vortrag.* Peter L. OESTERREICH: Fünf Entdeckungen auf dem Wege zu einer neuen Darstellung der Philosophie Fichtes. Manuel JIMÉNEZ-REDONDO: Der Aporetische Begriff der Erscheinung des Absoluten bei Fichtes WL 1805.
Teil III Zur Wissenschaftslehre von 1811 bis 1814
Alessandro BERTINETTO: Die Grundbeziehung von „Leben" und „Sehen" in der ersten Transzendentalen Logik Fichtes. Hiroshi KIMURA: Sehen und Sagen. Das Sehen sieht das Aussagen seines Grundes. Lu DE VOS: Das Absolute und das Spiel der Modalitäten. Johannes BRACHTENDORF: Der erscheinende Gott – Zur Logik des Seins in Fichtes Wissenschaftslehre 1812. Günter ZÖLLER: „On revient toujours...": Die transzendentale Theorie des Wissens beim letzten Fichte. Hartmut TRAUB: Vollendung der Transzendentalphilosophie.

USA/Canada: One Rockefeller Plaza, Ste. 1420, New York, NY 10020,
Tel. (212) 265-6360, Call toll-free (U.S. only) 1-800-225-3998,
Fax (212) 265-6402
All other countries: Tijnmuiden 7, 1046 AK Amsterdam, The Netherlands.
Tel. ++ 31 (0)20 611 48 21, Fax ++ 31 (0)20 447 29 79
Orders-queries@rodopi.nl   www.rodopi.nl
Please note that the exchange rate is subject to fluctuations

Praktische und angewandte Philosophie II

Beiträge zum vierten Kongress der Internationalen Johann-Gottlieb-Fichte-Gesellschaft in Berlin vom 03. – 08. Oktober 2000

Helmut Girndt/Hartmut Traub (Hrsg.)

Amsterdam/New York 2003. VI, 177 pp. (Fichte-Studien 24)

ISBN: 90-420-0855-5 (Bd. 2)   € 36,-/US $ 43.-
ISBN: 90-420-0865-2 (Bde. 1+2)

Inhalt: Thomas Sören HOFFMANN: »… eine besondere Weise, sich selbst zu erblicken«: Zum systematischen Status der Natur nach Fichte. Christian STADLER: Der Transzendentalphilosophische Rechtsbegriff und seine systematische Begründungsleistung. Katja V. TAVER: Fichte und Arnold Gehlen. Fichtes Philosophie des Rechts von 1796 und 1812 im Fokus von Arnold Gehlens philosophischer Anthropologie. Jean-Christophe MERLE: Fichtes Begründung des Strafrechts. Manfred GAWLINA: Verhalten als Synthesis von Recht und Gesinnung. Zur (virtuellen) Auseinandersetzung zwischen Kant, Fichte und Hegel. Carla DE PASCALE: Fichte und die Gesellschaft. Carla AMADIO: Die Logik der politischen Beziehung. Christiana SENIGAGLIA: Die Bestimmung des Bürgers beim späten Fichte. Ferenc L. LENDVAI: Stellung und Spuren einer Sozialethik in Fichtes Philosophie. Teil I: Die Stellung einer Sozialethik in Fichtes Philosophie. Judit HELL: Stellung und Spuren einer Sozialethik in Fichtes Philosophie. Teil II: Die Spuren einer Sozialethik in Fichtes Philosophie. Wladimir Alexejevic ABASCHNIK: Das Konzept des geschlossenen Handelsstaates Fichtes in der Rezeption von Vassilij Nasarovic Karasin. Karl HAHN: Die Relevanz der Eigentumstheorie Fichtes im Zeitalter der Globalisierung unter Berücksichtigung Proudhons und Hegels. Hans HIRSCH: Fichtes Planwirtschaftsmodell als Dokument der Geistesgeschichte und als bleibender Denkanstoß.

USA/Canada: One Rockefeller Plaza, Ste. 1420, New York, NY 10020,
Tel. (212) 265-6360, Call toll-free (U.S. only) 1-800-225-3998,
Fax (212) 265-6402
All other countries: Tijnmuiden 7, 1046 AK Amsterdam, The Netherlands.
Tel. ++ 31 (0)20 611 48 21, Fax ++ 31 (0)20 447 29 79
Orders-queries@rodopi.nl   www.rodopi.nl
Please note that the exchange rate is subject to fluctuations

A JOURNAL OF GERMANIC STUDIES

seminar

Seminar wird seit 1965 im Auftrag des kanadischen Germanistenverbandes (CAUTG) unter Mitarbeit der Germanistenvereinigung von Australien und Neuseeland (German Section, AUMLLA) herausgegeben. Die Zeitschrift bringt Beiträge und Rezensionen zu allen Gebieten der deutschen Literatur und erscheint viermal im Jahr.

Manuskripte in zweifacher Ausfertigung in Englisch, Französisch oder Deutsch, (nach MLA-Style Handbuch 1999, mit alphabetischem Literaturverzeichnis) erbeten an:

RALEIGH WHITINGER   *or*   ALAN CORKHILL
Department of Modern Languages and   Department of German Studies
   Cultural Studies   University of Queensland
University of Alberta   Brisbane Qld 4072
Edmonton, Canada T6G 2E6   Australia

Book Review Editor: JAMES SKIDMORE, University of Waterloo

Bestellungen sind zu richten an:
University of Toronto Press, Journals Department
5201 Dufferin Street, Toronto, Ontario
Canada M3H 5T8
Tel: (416) 667-7810; Fax: (416) 667-7881
Fax toll free in North America: 800-221-9985
e-mail: journals@utpress.utoronto.ca

Der Subskriptionspreis beträgt CAN $35.00 jährlich. Einzelhefte $7.50 ($30.00 pro Jahrgang).

Redefining the Subject: Sites of Play in Canadian Women's Writing.

Charlotte Sturgess

Amsterdam/New York, NY 2003. 158 pp. (Genus 2)

ISBN: 90-420-1175-0   € 32,-/US $38.-

This volume takes up the challenge of Canadian women's writing in its diversity, in order to examine the terms on which subjectivity, in its social, political and literary dimensions, emerges as discourse. Work from writers as diverse as Dionne Brand, Hiromi Goto and Margaret Atwood, among others, are studied both in their specific dimensions and through the collective focus of cultural and textual revision which characterizes Canadian writing in the feminine. Current theorizing on the postcolonial imaginary is brought to bear in the interests of forging or unpacking those links which tie the Self to culture. As such, *Redefining the Subject* sets out to discover the limits of the aesthetic in its encounter with the political: the figures and designs which envisage textual reimaginings as statements of a contemporary Canadian reality.

USA/Canada: One Rockefeller Plaza, Ste. 1420, New York, NY 10020,
Tel. (212) 265-6360, Call toll-free (U.S. only) 1-800-225-3998,
Fax (212) 265-6402
All other countries: Tijnmuiden 7, 1046 AK Amsterdam, The Netherlands.
Tel. ++ 31 (0)20 611 48 21, Fax ++ 31 (0)20 447 29 79
Orders-queries@rodopi.nl   **www.rodopi.nl**
Please note that the exchange rate is subject to fluctuations

Mobilizing Place, Placing Mobility.
The Politics of Representation in a Globalized World.

Edited by Ginette Verstraete and Tim Cresswell.

Amsterdam/New York, NY 2002. 195 pp.
(Thamyris/Intersecting 9)
ISBN: 90-420-1144-0   € 40,-/US $ 48.-

What role does 'place' have in a world marked by increased mobility on a global scale? What strategies are there for representing 'place' in the age of globalization? What is the relationship between 'place' and the varied mobilities of migrancy, tourism, travel and nomadism?

These are some of the questions that run through the ten essays in this collection. The combined effect of these essays is to participate in the contemporary project of subjecting the links between place, mobility, identity, representation and practice to critical interdisciplinary scrutiny. Such notions are not the property of particular disciplines. In the era of globalization, transnationalism and readily acknowledged cultural hybridity these links are more important than ever. They are important because of the taken-for-grantedness of: the universal impact of globalization; the receding importance of place and the centrality of mobile identities. This taken-for-grantedness masks the ways place continues to be important and ways in which mobility is differentiated by race, gender, ethnicity, nationality and many other social markers. This book is a concerted attempt to stop taking for granted these themes of the age. Material discussed in the essays include the creation of cultural routes in Europe, the video's of Fiona Tan, artistic and literary representations of the North African desert, the production of indigenous videos in Mexico, mobile forms of ethnography, the film *Existenz*, Jamaica Kincaid's writing on gardens, the video representation of sex tourism and ways of imagining the global.

USA/Canada: One Rockefeller Plaza, Ste. 1420, New York, NY 10020,
Tel. (212) 265-6360, Call toll-free (U.S. only) 1-800-225-3998,
Fax (212) 265-6402
All other countries: Tijnmuiden 7, 1046 AK Amsterdam, The Netherlands.
Tel. ++ 31 (0)20 611 48 21, Fax ++ 31 (0)20 447 29 79
Orders-queries@rodopi.nl   **www.rodopi.nl**
Please note that the exchange rate is subject to fluctuations

Praktische und angewandte Philosophie I.

Beiträge zum vierten Kongress der Internationalen Johann-Gottlieb-Fichte-Gesellschaft in Berlin vom 03. – 08. Oktober 2000.

Herausgegeben von Helmut Girndt und Hartmut Traub.

Amsterdam/New York 2003. VII, 232 pp.
(Fichte-Studien 23)

ISBN: 90-420-1025-8 (Bd. 1)   € 50,-/US$ 60.-
ISBN: 90-420-0865-2 (Bde. 1+2)

Inhalt: Rainer ADOLPHI: Weltbild und Ich-Verständnis. Die Transformation des >Primats der praktischen Vernunft< beim späteren Fichte. Jacinto RIVERA DE ROSALES: Das Absolute und die Sittenlehre von 1812. Sein und Freiheit. Marek J. SIEMEK: Fichtes und Hegels Konzept der Intersubjektivität. Ewa NOWAK-JUCHACZ: Das Anerkennungsprinzip bei Kant, Fichte und Hegel. Ronald MATHER: On the Concepts of Recognition. Makoto TAKADA: Verwandlung der Individuumslehre bei Fichte. Hans Georg von MANZ: Deduktion und Aufgabe des individuellen Ich in Fichtes Darstellungen der Wissenschaftslehre von 1810/11. Jürgen STAHL: Zur Kultur in der Vermittlungsrolle zwischen empirischem und absolutem Ich. Christoph ASMUTH: Metaphysik und Historie bei J.G. Fichte. Stephan GNÄDINGER: Vorsehung. Ein religionsphilosophisches Grundproblem bei J.G. Fichte. Johannes HEINRICHS: Die Mitte der Zeit als Tiefpunkt einer Parabel. Fichtes Geschichtskonstruktion und Grundzüge der gegenwärtigen Zeitenwende. Marco M. OLIVETTI: Zum Religions- und Offenbarungsverständnis beim jungen Fichte und bei Kant.

USA/Canada: One Rockefeller Plaza, Ste. 1420, New York, NY 10020,
Tel. (212) 265-6360, Call toll-free (U.S. only) 1-800-225-3998,
Fax (212) 265-6402
All other countries: Tijnmuiden 7, 1046 AK Amsterdam, The Netherlands.
Tel. ++ 31 (0)20 611 48 21, Fax ++ 31 (0)20 447 29 79
Orders-queries@rodopi.nl   **www.rodopi.nl**
Please note that the exchange rate is subject to fluctuations

Beyond Boundaries of Biomedicine
Pragmatic Perspectives on Health and Disease

Wim J. van der Steen, Vincent K.Y. Ho, and Ferry J. Karmelk

Amsterdam/New York, NY 2003. XI, 292 pp.
(At the Interface/Probing the Boundaries 4)

ISBN: 90-420-0816-4   Paper € 60,-/US $ 71.-
Pre-publication price (valid until 31 July 2003)   Paper € 42.-/US $ 50.-

Cultural forces shape much of medicine including psychiatry, and medicine shapes much of our culture. Medicine provides us with beneficial treatments of disease, but it also causes harm, increasingly so in the form of overmedication enhanced by the pharmaceutical industry. The book explores boundaries of medicine and psychiatry in a cultural setting by building bridges between unconnected literatures. Boundaries have to be redrawn since effects of the environment, biological, social and political, on health and disease are undervalued. Potential beneficial effects of diet therapies are a recurrent theme throughout the text, with particular emphasis on omega-3 fatty acids. Deficiencies of these acids in common diets may contribute to many chronic diseases and psychiatric disorders. The book uncovers limitations of evidence-based medicine, which fosters a restrictive view of health and disease. Case studies include: the biology of migraine; limitations of biological psychiatry; conventional *versus* alternative medicine; science, religion and near-death experiences.

USA/Canada: One Rockefeller Plaza, Ste. 1420, New York, NY 10020,
Tel. (212) 265-6360, Call toll-free (U.S. only) 1-800-225-3998,
Fax (212) 265-6402
All other countries: Tijnmuiden 7, 1046 AK Amsterdam, The Netherlands.
Tel. ++ 31 (0)20 611 48 21, Fax ++ 31 (0)20 447 29 79
Orders-queries@rodopi.nl   **www.rodopi.nl**
Please note that the exchange rate is subject to fluctuations